DEDICATION

To Betty, Laura, and Vince.

Limits of Liability and Disclaimer of Warranty

Registered Trademarks

PS/2-PC
Assembly Language

Steven Holzner

BRADY

New York

BRADY

Simon & Schuster, Inc.
Gulf + Western Building
One Gulf + Western Plaza
New York, NY 10023

DISTRIBUTED BY PRENTICE HALL TRADE

Manufactured in the United States of America

10   9   8   7   6   5   4   3   2   1

Library of Congress Cataloging-in-Publication Data

Holzner, Steven
    PS/2-PC assembly language
    Includes index.
    1. IBM Personal Computer—Programming. 2. IBM
Personal System/2 (Computer system)—Programming.
3. Assembler language (Computer program language).
I. Title.
QA76.8.I2594H648   1989   005.265   89-879
ISBN 0-13-731878-2

Contents

Introduction

Do I Really Want to Learn Assembly Language?

Welcome to *PS/2-PC Assembly Language.* You may be looking at this book right now and asking yourself: Do I really want to learn assembly language? Do I really have the patience to read this whole book? (It looks awfully thick.) While you can hardly expect the author of a book to give an impartial discussion of its merits ("Oh, well, I guess you'd be better off going to the beach. . ."), I think we can come up with a significant number of reasons for working through it.

The primary reason, of course, is learning how to program your PS/2 or PC. There are many different languages that can do this to a greater or lesser degree: Pascal, BASIC, C, and others. What's so great about assembly language? It turns out that the differences are as many as they are significant.

There are many things that you can create *only* in assembly language: memory-resident programs; fast graphics programs (in fact, fast *anything* programs—there is no programming language that can produce faster code); programs that use the enormous reserve of untapped system resources in DOS and BIOS; programs that undelete deleted files, that pop up windows, and that execute other programs; and fast editors. No serious programmer should be without a knowledge of assembly language.

This is true even if the only thing a programmer uses assembly language for is its speed. Assembly language can be mixed with any other language (and we'll do just that in this book): Lightning code can be written to search for strings of characters, plot graphics, sort records, or restructure disks. Whenever speed is necessary, assembly language can handle it.

But there is another reason as well. Assembly language is the language of your computer's microprocessor, and by learning it, you will learn all there is to know about your computer—and therefore *everything* it can do. You'll learn how the disks work—how they store data or delete files. How the screen is set up and what the best way of working with it is. How sound or color can be produced. How the modem works. By learning to speak the microprocessor's language, you'll be opening the door to a guided tour of the inside of your PS/2 or PC, since all its components speak the same language. And in this book, we're going to take that guided tour; it's the first step from computer neophyte to computer master.

Assembly language is a very popular way of programming the PS/2 or PC (the most popular is still the ubiquitous, system-supplied BASIC; the second is Pascal, followed closely by assembly language). On the one hand, there is much to be said for higher level languages, especially when it comes to working smoothly whoever is running the program, the user. In the same way, however, there is much to be said for making voyages by sea instead of by air. A ship may be slower and go to less places than a plane, but it can also be safer and it may be friendlier. Nonetheless, we will often find that, with a little care, flying is better.

What's Good About This Book

This is a margin note.

This book has been specially designed to make your guided tour a comfortable one. Brady Books is continually refining how they present material to you. Two new methods are the use of comment boxes and margin notes. Margin notes will let you use the text as a reference, leafing through until you find some recalled topic.

> This is a comment box. In these boxes, you'll find (hopefully) pertinent anecdotes, historical notes, and points of interest that will help break the monotony of the text.

You'll also find a stronger emphasis in this book on breaking up the text into bite-sized pieces through the frequent use of headings and subheadings, as well as colored computer code for easy reading, many handy figures, and information you literally can't get anywhere else. In addition, this is the first assembly language text to cover the latest assembler program (Version 5.1). We'll also be using DOS 3.3 and OS/2. Even though DOS 4.0 is due out soon, the only real difference is its inclusion of the Lotus-pioneered Expanded Memory Support (EMS). Since we would not cover this option anyway (it is beyond the scope of this book), DOS 3.3 is the operating system we will primarily use.

But the real philosophy of the book can be expressed in one word: examples.

Examples

Examples are what assembly language books frequently omit. And leaving out the examples is like learning to fly by reading a catalogue of plane parts: it is very difficult to put together. Too often books on programming are just like catalogs: long lists of "classes" of commands and impenetrable discussions of every available option for each instruction—without any coherent means of tying it all together.

But the easiest way to learn is by seeing it work. To readers earnestly making their way through this material, one simple example is worth a thousand descriptions.

Examples can help before you read explanations by whetting your interest. For this reason, we'll frequently start sections with an example that includes a few new lines to help pique your curiosity. And examples help after explanations by bringing it all together. For an author, it's the one sure way of knowing you've answered most of the questions you otherwise might have missed—there's the code, and it works—making it the best way of learning.

Also included in this book are a number of large examples, programs that are useful by themselves. These include SCMP, a smart file comparison program, LOGGER, a memory-resident program that saves whatever goes on the screen to a file on disk, and CRUNCH, a program that compacts files.

The Sequel

Another way that this book is unique is that it already has a sequel. We're not just going to leave you hanging after you're done with this book. The second volume of this set, entitled *Advanced Assembly Language for the IBM PC* (Steven Holzner, Brady Books), is already out. The book you hold in your hands is designed to cover beginning and intermediate level assembly language. It is more complete than any book on the market, and more up to date. But additional material that is not covered in this or other books is covered in the *Advanced* volume. At the highest level, that book contains enough to give you quite a workout: device drivers, fast math bit-by-bit algorithms, macro libraries, the 8087 in depth. But at the lower level, *Advanced Assembly Language for the IBM PC* really the book you should read if you want to program like the pros.

The book you are reading now is specifically tailored to fit in with the second book so that together you'll have what is by far the most complete reference for assembly language on the IBM PS/2 or PC. (And, I hope, the best.)

What Is Needed

In this book, I'll use DOS 3.3, and the Microsoft Macro Assembler Version 5.1. You'll need a version of DOS that is 2.10 or higher, and at least 192K to support the Macro Assembler. Previous versions of the assembler (Microsoft or IBM) are fine, except that they may not support SALUT (a utility to make your code easier to work with), CODEVIEW (the new symbolic debugger), the 8087, or any of the OS/2 material we will discuss. We will not be making heavy use of any of these, so that should not be a difficulty. If you want to use CODEVIEW, you'll need at least 320K. If you want to run the OS/2 programs, you'll need OS/2 and a PS/2 or a PC AT with an 80286 in it, and at least 1.5 MBytes of RAM.

To really use OS/2 fluently, you should have 2 MBytes. This will also allow you to run DOS under OS/2.

You'll also need an editor to type in the programs we develop. Almost any editor will do: If you can print out intelligible English, the macro assembler can read it.

On Your Mark . . .

We are ready for Chapter 1, "What Is Assembly Language?" This book is written in a way that will hopefully keep your interest. I'd appreciate any comments you have to send me, Steven Holzner, care of Brady Books. If I end up boring you, let me know. If what I write is unclear, don't hesistate to bring it to my attention: this book will be revised. (And if I end up pleasing you, please don't hesitate either.) Thanks.

1
What Is Assembly Language?

Introduction
Binary
Switching Bases

Hexadecimal
Registers
Machine versus Assembly
    Language

The MOV Instruction
DEBUG

The Development of Computers

The beginning of computers

Driven by heavy use during World War II, the computer first became a significant tool in the mid 1940s. These machines were often constructed of large, complex frames of wood, to which were attached thousands of vaccuum tubes and mechanical relays. Such computers, or computing machines as they were known, filled entire rooms and generated as much heat as half a dozen ovens. Tubes frequently failed, and relays jammed, so a full-time assistant (frequently a corpsman of low rank) was forever inside the apparatus, fitting new components in.

It is customary for computer books to dismiss these computers as lumbering dinosaurs, but there is no reason to do so. In fact, they were wonderful machines. Their only fault was that they succeeded too well—by demonstrating their great utility, they guaranteed their quick replacement and improvement. That is what made them dinosaurs, not any inherent flaw.

> There is a story that the computer term *bug* came from an actual moth that flew into a giant military computer in 1945 and jammed a relay. The events are true: The moth still exists, taped to a page in a technician's notebook. But whether it gave rise to the term *bug* is unlikely.

In the early days of computing, engineers designed theoretical machines that did fantastic things. Those technicians set the limits on

1

what computers could and could not do; those limits still hold. The pioneers set up complicated mathematical models and wrote important papers. And they laid the groundwork for the present-day machines we know so well.

To us, what a big computer does is obvious: A computer reads in data, works on it, and sends bills in the mail. But in those days, the days even before computers could read paper tape, such ideas were marvels, and many things had to be tacked down.

Computing in the '50s and '60s

In the 1950s and 1960s new scientists built the machines that the earlier ones had designed. The transistor was born at Bell Labs, computers started reading punched cards, and they became connected to screens instead of banks of blinking lights. It was difficult to program in those days: Each instruction had to be punched on a computer card, and stacks of them would be read at a furious rate by the machine. More often than not, there would be a bug of some kind, and some of the stack would have to be typed over—you couldn't just edit the program on a screen as you can now.

The computer scientists of those days could toggle in an operating system on a bank of switches; they didn't need Pascal or BASIC or even assembly language. Great machines were being built; big companies were getting bigger. Mainframe computers—big, centralized machines—were what counted. If you needed a computer, you had better be a big company, because they were expensive.

Artifical Intelligence

Artificial Intelligence became a catchword in the late 1970s, especially around places like MIT and Caltech. Centers such as MIT's Artificial Intelligence lab developed into astonishing showcases of technological miracles: computers that could play chess better than grand masters; computer-driven arms with seven elbows that could pick up secretaries; psychiatrist programs that would psychoanalyze you; computer-generated movies.

By pressing a combination of keys on your keyboard at the MIT lab, you could unlock the outside door. Another combination of keys would summon the elevator to your floor. Graduate students wanted a key that would order a pizza via recorded voice. The computer age had finally arrived.

Microcomputers

The Z80 micro-processor

Meanwhile, high school students and college kids were buying their own chips from chip manufacturers. To actually build a small computer, given the right chips, is no more difficult than building a model ship. But it seemed very much more exciting. Hobbyists would buy circuit boards by the thousands, spending delighted hours over them, wrapping tiny wires around contacts and losing their eyesight. As time went on, this craze developed into a real market, and a number of microprocessors became very popular: the Z80, for one. These hobbyists were the real forefathers of the personal computer market, and cheap chips were their tools.

When it became clear to everyone that there really was a market here, a number of early, tiny microcomputers started appearing. This decentralization of the computer world was a healthy thing, judging from the wealth of innovation that has resulted. Whenever a new machine appeared, dedicated battalions of hobbyists could be counted on to take it home, decipher it, add to it, and then swap it with others.

As time went on, however, the microcomputers became more and more complex, more professional, and more expensive. They found their way into small businesses, and this became the cornerstone of IBM's entry into the market (and the consequent explosion of microcomputers). With their development into complexity, computers may be on their way to becoming mysteries again, and that is a shame, because they are still— at heart—the simple machines that the hobbyists knew and dissected.

Inside Computers

Computers hold an immense number of wires, each of which can either be "live" or not: on or off. If a particular wire has a positive voltage (usually five volts), it is "on," if it holds no voltage, it is "off." These signals are interpreted by the microprocessor itself, as well as by the multitude of components in your computer. To handle all these signals in a convenient way, we can assign a 1 to a wire that is on, and a 0 to a wire that is off.

This is where the transition from electrical device (which works in terms of zero or five volts) to a computer (which works with numbers assigned to these signals, 0 and 1) is made. Each signal now stands for something, a 1 or a 0. This very fact makes the machine a computer, rather than a mere signaling device.

Two digits versus 10 digits

Admittedly, this seems like a poor start if we want to build a computer of any power. How can we manage with only two digits? In fact there is no problem, as you may already know. The numbering system we are used to has 10 digits, 0 . . . 9. This is the decimal system, base 10. There exist, however, numbering systems more congenial to the on-off abilities of computers. In particular, there is the binary numbering system, base 2.

Binary

When we get to 9 in base 10, we have to express the next number with two digits: 10, because we're out of single digits. In binary, base 2, there are only two digits, 0 and 1. This means that when we get to 1 in binary, we have to express the next number the same way: 10, the lowest number with two digits. The difference is that 10 in binary, which most books and assemblers label as 10B (B for Binary), is equal to 2 in decimal.

Decimal	Binary
9	1
+1	+1
10 (decimal)	10 (binary) ←

Here's how we would count in decimal: 1, 2, 3, 4, 5, and so on. In binary, this goes 1, 10B, 11B, 100B, 101B, 110B, 111B, 1000B, and so on. That's what binary numbers look like: 1000B, or 10100101B, or even 101001000101010101B.

Bits

You are almost certainly familiar with the term *bit*; but did you know that it is a condensation of "binary digit"? The bits we hear so much about in our machines are really just an indication of the computer's interpretation of internal signals as binary digits. Since the computer works exclusively in binary, we will make an effort to see what it's all about.

To understand binary, we have to understand how numbers in another base work, and the best way to do that is just by seeing how to convert them back into decimal.

From Binary to Decimal

When the computers of the 1940s wanted to translate their results from binary into decimal, they used a very simple method. This method hinges on seeing that a number like 54 in decimal can be expressed as $5 \times 10 + 4$. A number like 437 can always be broken down like this:

$$437 = 4 \times 100 + 3 \times 10 + 7$$

And this method will enable us to make sense of binary.

Powers of 2

We can express our breakdown of 437 in powers of 10:

$$437 = 4 \times 100 + 3 \times 10 + 7$$
$$= 4 \times 10^2 + 3 \times 10^1 + 7 \times 10^0$$

And binary numbers may also be broken down this way, using increasing powers of 2 (2, 4, 8 . . .) instead of 10 (10, 100, 1000 . . .). The number 1010B can be expressed as:

$$1010B = 1 \times 2^3 + 0 \times 2^2 + 1 \times 2^1 + 0 \times 2^0$$
$$= 1 \times 8 + 0 \times 4 + 1 \times 2 + 0 \times 1$$
$$= 8 + 2 = 10 \text{ (decimal)}$$

We see that we can always break binary numbers down this way, place by place:

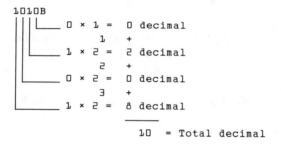

```
1010B
  │││└──── 0 × 1 =  0 decimal
  │││          1       +
  ││└───── 1 × 2 =  2 decimal
  ││           2       +
  │└────── 0 × 2 =  0 decimal
  │            3       +
  └─────── 1 × 2 =  8 decimal
                  ─────────
                  10  = Total decimal
```

Switching bases

And this place-by-place breakdown is the secret of understanding other bases. Breaking up a number this way is very important in assembly language work. The key for switching between bases, and you'll have to do this often in some programs, is that the lowest place in a binary number is the number of 2^0s, or 1s that the number holds; the next place holds the number of 2^1s or 2s, the next holds the number of 2^2s or 4s, the next the number of 8s, and so forth. A daunting binary number such as 1001010B can readily be worked out:

```
The Binary Number →        1    0    0    1    0    1    0B
                           x    x    x    x    x    x    x
What each place stands for → 64   32   16   8    4    2    1
                           │    │    │    │    │    │    │
                           ↓    ↓    ↓    ↓    ↓    ↓    ↓
                           ─────────────────────────────
Can be added to give →     64   +         8    +    2        = 74 decimal
```

To convert from binary to decimal, think of the right-most place as the 1s, the next place as the 2s, the next as the 4s, and so on. With this handle on how binary operates, we can put it to work.

A Very Little Amount of Binary Math

Decimal addition
You're familiar with addition in base 10, such as $5 + 9 = 14$, or $54 + 9 = 63$. It's easy to see how it works: To add 9 to 54, we simply add digits in the corresponding places—here we add the 4 in 54 to the 9:

$$\begin{array}{r} \overset{1}{5}4 \\ +\ 9 \\ \hline 63 \end{array} \quad \text{(A 1 is carried.)}$$

For the 13, put the 3 in the result, carry the 1, add it to the 5 and end up with 63.

Binary addition
Numbers can be added in binary just as in decimal. In fact, any math operation that you can do in decimal, you can do in binary. If you convert a number to binary, store it in a computer, and add another, similarly converted number to it, you'll get a binary result that you can convert back to decimal.

For example, here we're going to add 01B to 10B:

$$\begin{array}{r} 01B \\ +10B \\ \hline 11B \end{array}$$

And we see that $01B + 10B = 11B$. That's what the 1940s computers were doing: binary math, day in, day out (try doing calculations like that fifteen thousand times a second).

Carries in binary
Of course, things get a more complex if there's a carry. For example, let's add 01B to 01B:

$$\begin{array}{r} 01B \\ +01B \\ \end{array}$$

Note that adding the last places together—both are 1s—generates a carry, since there is no single digit for "2." Instead, $1 + 1 = 10B$:

$$\begin{array}{r} \overset{1}{0}1B \\ +01B \\ \hline 10B \end{array} \quad \text{(Note the carry.)}$$

In base 10, the same thing is: $1 + 1 = 2$, but we have to express 2 as 10B in base 2. Adding numbers like this can be expanded to as many places as you like:

$$0\ 1\ 0\ 0\ \overset{1}{1}\ \overset{1}{0}\ \overset{1}{1}\ 1\ 0\ 1\ 0\ \overset{1}{0}\ 1\ B$$
$$+\ 1\ 0\ 1\ 0\ 0\ 1\ 1\ 1\ 0\ 0\ 1\ 0\ 1\ B$$
$$1\ 1\ 1\ 1\ 0\ 0\ 1\ 0\ 0\ 1\ 1\ 1\ 0\ B$$

(note the carries.)

You can do math in binary just as well as in decimal. Everything you can do in decimal, you can also do in binary. If you want to subtract, you would use borrows from higher places if need be, just as you would in decimal math. As long as you keep in mind that $1 + 1 = 10B$, you won't have much trouble with binary numbers.

Length of binary numbers

Binary numbers can get quite long: try adding 0101010001001B to 1011101101001B a thousand times a second. In fact, any number of any size becomes very big in binary very rapidly. The number 1 is just 1B in binary. But 2 is already 10B. Four is 100B. Eight is 1000B. A number like 256 is already equal to 100000000B, but, of course, any simple calculator is expected to handle a number like 256 with ease. Here are a few more binary numbers (this table may be useful later when you have to know which place in a binary number corresponds to a particular power of two):

Table 1.1 Decimal Equivalents of Binary Numbers

Binary	Decimal
1	1
10	2
100	4
1000	8
10000	16
100000	32
1000000	64
10000000	128
100000000	256
1000000000	512
10000000000	1024
100000000000	2048
1000000000000	4096
10000000000000	8192
100000000000000	16384
1000000000000000	32768
10000000000000000	65536

This table indicates how large binary numbers can be before we have even reached a decent size in decimal. As you can see, our binary numbers are quickly becoming unmanageable. How do you tell 1000000000000000 from 10000000000000000 by sight? Scientists working with computers dealt with numbers like this more and more often, until it was decided to group binary digits into more manageable sizes.

Bytes

This is the next step up. A byte is a group of eight binary digits. Different sizes were tried, but the grouping of eight binary digits stuck. Of course you are familiar with the term *byte* (a corruption of *bit*); it's the first thing you mention when you talk of computer capacity. How many bytes on that disk? How many megabytes of memory? (Even so, communications are still done in bits per second. One bit per second is one baud.)

The byte is the real way you keep track of numbers in a computer, not bits. This grouping of eight bits will become more and more familiar to us as we work through the book.

Place values in a byte

Since a byte is eight bits, it is really a binary number of eight digits. The highest digit corresponds to the 128s place (which may sound strange, but it's just like saying "the thousand's place"), and the lowest digit to the 1s place. The place values in a byte will often be of great interest to us, so we'll list them here for the byte 01010101B:

Figure 1.1 The byte 01010101B Broken Down

```
 7    6    5    4    3    2    1    0    ← Bit number
128   64   32   16    8    4    2    1   ← Place Value
 ↓    ↓    ↓    ↓    ↓    ↓    ↓    ↓
 _____
 0    1    0    1    0    1    0    1
```

Bit Numbering

Frequently, we will need this bit-by-bit terminology. We will refer to the left-most bit as the high bit, and the right-most bit as the low bit. Now that we are dealing with multiple-digit numbers, it will become more important to keep track of what bit we are talking about.

When we examine a binary number, say 10110010B, the left-most bit is the high bit, and the right-most bit is the low bit. Only being able to number the top and bottom bits won't help us very much, of course, so the rest of the places are *numbered*, starting from the right and going to the right. For example, look at the binary number 10110010B:

Bit
numbers

Figure 1.2 Bit Numbers in the Byte 10110010B

Bit Number →	7	6	5	4	3	2	1	0
Binary Digit →1	0	1	1	0	0	1	0	

The most convenient way of remembering this system of bit numbering is that the number of each bit (0 to 7) corresponds to its power of 2. The left-most bit, bit 7, tells how many 128s there are in this byte, and 128 = 2^7. Bit number 2 corresponds to the 2^2s place in the byte, Bit number 0 corresponds to the 2^0s, or 1s, place, and so on.

When we are examining a byte, we will refer to bit 3, or bit 5. To find that bit, just count from the right, starting with 0.

> Did you know that four bits together also have a name? They are called (maybe a little too cutely) a *nybble*.

Range of a byte

A byte can range from a value of 00000000, or 0, to a full house: 11111111B, which is (adding up all the places) 255. Note that adding one to a full byte, 11111111B, produces the number 100000000B, or 256 (which is too big for a byte). The biggest a byte can be is 255.

Bytes and
ASCII

We will have many uses for bytes. For example, one ASCII character is stored in exactly one byte of memory. Since they are so frequently used, it became handy to condense them even further. Instead of saying 01010101B all the time, even though it was better than handling numbers like 10101000100111001B, it still could be better. And that's where hexadecimal, base 16, comes in.

Hexadecimal

Binary digits, the lifeblood of a computer, can be grouped together into a single digit in any base that is a power of two. This makes handling them much easier. For example, three binary digits can express exactly the same numbers (0 = 000B to 7 = 111B) as one digit in base 8 (which ranges from 0 to 7).

Why
computers
don't use
decimal

To you this might not seem like such a neat fact, but it made the computer scientists happy. What it meant was that they could group, say, four binary digits together, 0101B, and come up with only one digit in base 16 (16 = 2^4 four binary digits to every hex digit). It's a shame that you can't group three binary digits together to come up with exactly one decimal digit. If you could, we could deal with computers directly in base 10. But three binary digits express only the numbers 0 to 7, not 0 to 9. And four binary digits—which can hold numbers from 0 to 15—are too many for decimal. So we are stuck with base 16, hexadecimal.

Of course, the computers are still binary machines internally, but they can be made to group four of their digits together to form hexadecimal digits, and hexadecimal—hex—is a lot closer to base 10 than base 2 is. This book is going to be filled with hexadecimal.

This should not alarm you. Only very rarely are we going to have to convert a number from hex to base 10. For the most part, the only hex we'll see are addresses, and we'll let either DEBUG or our program handle that. On some rare occasions, we'll need to add or subtract hexadecimal numbers—but that can be done directly with DEBUG's Hex command. Later on, we are going to see a program that will convert hex to decimal for us. In general, hex will prove to be no problem to us, but we will have to know how it works before we can continue.

Hexadecimal Digits

After 9, we run out of digits in the base 10—decimal—system. To supply the lack in other bases, mathematicians have always turned to letters instead: hexadecimal runs from 0 to 9, and then from A to F. That is, A is equal to 10 decimal, B equals 11 decimal, and F is equal to 15 decimal. Sixteen in hex is equal to 10H, where the "H" signifies that we are working in hex.

Table 1.2 Decimal, Hexadecimal, and
Binary Equivalents

Decimal	Hexadecimal	Binary
0	0	0000
1	1	0001
2	2	0010
3	3	0011
4	4	0100
5	5	0101
6	6	0110
7	7	0111
8	8	1000
9	9	1001
10	A	1010
11	B	1011
12	C	1100

Decimal	Hexadecimal	Binary
13	D	1101
14	E	1110
15	F	1111
16	10H	10000B

For us, this means that we will start seeing letters mixed in with our numbers: 643C5FEH is a perfectly fine hex number. The assembler asks that if you are using a hex number that begins with a letter, like FFFFFFH, that you begin it with a 0, like this: 0FFFFFFH, so that it will know that a number was intended, and not a word of some kind.

Grouping Binary Digits Together

Grouping four binary digits into one hex digit works like this: the number 0110100000101111B can be expressed in hex by breaking it up into groups of four digits: 0110 1000 0010 1111, which can be rendered in hex this way:

```
0110      1000      0010      1111
 └─┘       └─┘       └─┘       └─┘
  6         8         2         F
```

And the number 682FH is a much easier package to handle than 0110100000101111B. It will be important later to know how to break hexadecimal numbers up into binary, especially when we work with the mathematical logical operators like OR and AND, both of which will frequently occur.

Binary to Hex

This is a distinct improvement: Now each byte, that is, eight binary digits, can be comfortably grouped into just two hexadecimal digits, like 31H or 5AH. Binary and hexadecimal are the two major numbering systems in use when people deal with computers today. There is a little octal, base 8, but not much.

Even though hex is closer to base 10 than base 2 is, it will take some getting used to. And, of course, in the end, you'll have to print out results in decimal, not hex.

Converting from Hexadecimal to Normal Decimal

How would we convert 682FH into decimal, base 10? The method is the same as the one used for converting binary to decimal and, really, the same used to convert from any base to decimal. This is a technique you'll need if you've been doing some math in the PC or PS/2 and wish to convert your results to something a normal person can read.

As before, we just notice that the left-most place (the F in 682FH) is the 1s place. This digit, like all hex digits, can range from 0 to FH. The next place (the 2 in 682FH) would be the 10s place in a decimal number, but is the 16s place here. The next place is the 16^2, or 256s place, and so forth. We can then dissect and recombine 682FH this way:

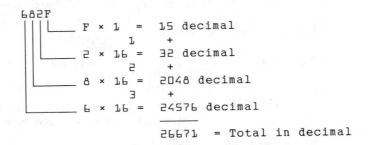

```
682F
│││└────── F × 1   =   15 decimal
││      1      +
││└─────── 2 × 16  =   32 decimal
│      2      +
│└──────── 8 × 16  = 2048 decimal
      3      +
└───────── 6 × 16  = 24576 decimal
                     ──────
                     26671  = Total in decimal
```

By this method, we can see that 682FH = 26671D (where the "D" tells us it's a decimal number). A good idea, if you will be working often with hexadecimal or binary numbers, is to buy one of the cheap programmer's calculators now on the market that convert and can do math in either of those bases.

Bytes in Hex

Since every four successive binary digits can be condensed into one hex digit, we see that a byte, that is, eight bits, will just be two hexadecimal digits. Bytes can run from the all-empty 00000000B to the all-full 11111111B. Hex handles them by breaking them up into 0000 0000B and 1111 1111B, to make 00H and FFH.

```
              Binary  →  Hex
00000000B  →   0000 0000   →   00H   (0 in decimal)
11111111B  →   1111 1111   →   FFH   (255 in decimal)
```

And of course, there is everything in between: the byte 01011010B can be rendered as 0101 1010, or 5AH. 10110011 becomes B3H. What's important to remember is that every time you see two hex digits, they represent a byte.

Words

Similarly, other computer numbers are larger than the byte. The next most common one in use is one you've no doubt heard of: the word. In the PC or PS/2, a word is a 16-bit number, made up of two bytes. A word therefore has four hex digits, two for each byte. We will frequently break words up into their component bytes, just as we may have to break a byte up into its component binary digits.

High and low bytes in a word

A perfectly good word, expressed in hex, might be 5FC3H. Four hexadecimal digits make 16 binary ones, just the number we need. When we want to break this word up into bytes, we will refer to the 5F part as the high byte, and the C3 part as the low byte.

```
5FC3
    |    C3H is the low byte of this word
    |
    |        5FH is the high byte of this word
```

Machine Language

Now that we are in control of the numbering system, we can examine what it is that a computer does more deeply. To the computer, each bit still corresponds to an electronic signal. The machine uses that signal to actually determine what will happen next. Often the five volts or zero volts that the microprocessor sees as one bit in a byte is actually sent out on a line to some outside chip, readying it for action, or making it perform some action at once. The computer is able to take the voltage on the eight wires corresponding to a byte that was just read in and send them out directly. Whether some lines are on or off modifies what the machine will do next.

For example, the byte 01010101B may be read into the microprocessor. By putting this byte in, the programmer may have been telling the computer to perform an action. To complete this example, we'll say that this byte asks the microprocessor to pop a word off the stack. The actual voltages on each of these eight lines determine electronically what happens next. Some "gates" inside the machine are opened, and some shut, directly by these eight voltages. That's how a computer works.

The byte 01010101B was able to make the machine perform some action. The microprocessor decodes the bytes we send in, and performs actions depending on what bytes we send. We call these bytes *machine language*.

Data

Machine language, then, consists of these bytes, comprehensible really only to the processor as the instructions it will use. Often, large numbers of these bytes are involved. In our example, all eight bits of the byte were used to control the action of the microprocessor ("pop a number off the stack," it was told), but more often, only part of the machine-language instruction will be used to tell the computer what to do. The rest of the instruction is data. For example, you can write an instruction to put FFH into a certain memory location. Part of the instruction will be to tell the microprocessor that you want to store a number, part of the instruction will be to tell it the location in memory you want to store the number at, and part of it will be the number itself, FFH.

Although machine-language instructions can be many bytes long, data and the instruction proper never mix across byte boundaries. For example, one machine-language instruction may be all instruction to the microprocessor:

```
01010101
```
Instruction

And some will be a mix of both:

```
10101010   10111010
```
Instruction   Data used by the instruction

or even:

```
01010101   10111010 10010101 001010100
```
Instruction   Data used by the instruction

This data used by the instruction is either memory addresses or actual data, like the FFH we wanted to store in a memory location earlier. The kind of instruction it is determines how much data, in bytes, there will be.

Reading this kind of binary that the microprocessor uses is extremely difficult. Imagine yourself confronted with a page of numbers, all 0s or 1s. Even if such instructions were to be converted to hex, you'd have to look up the meaning of each byte before understanding what was going on (there are tables in the manuals that accompany assemblers listing what binary instructions mean what). But by and large, what means everything to the microprocessor means nothing to us.

Assembly Language

What
assembly
language
does

And this is exactly what assembly language is. It is the direct intermediary between machine language and English. For every machine-language instruction, there is one assembly-language instruction. Rather than using a byte like 10101010B, for instance, an English-language mneumonic is used: MOV AX,5.

This instruction, MOV AX,5, may be terse (all assembly-language instructions we will encounter will be terse; it seems to be a rite of passage for the assembly-language programmer), but it is still an immense improvement on 10101010B, or even 0AAH. What this instruction means is that the byte 10101010B is directing the machine to move (the "MOV" part of MOV AX,5) the value of 5 into one of the 8088's (or 8086's, or 80186's, or 80286's, or 80386's, depending on which machine you have) registers. A *register* is a place for temporarily storing data in the microprocessor. We'll discuss registers very shortly.

What an assembler does is simple: It takes the program you've written in assembly language, and converts it, instruction by instruction, directly into machine language.

The machine language is then run by the microprocessor. Let's see a few examples. These examples are assembly-language instructions that were "assembled" (converted into machine language), and the corresponding machine language for each instruction (all numbers are in hex):

Table 1.3 What An Assembler Does

Assembly Language			Machine Language
MOV	DI,00B0	→	BF B0 00
MOV	COUNTER,00B0	→	C7 06 C3 01 B0 00
MOV	BX,0080	→	BB 80 00
CMP	INDEX,00	→	80 3F 00
JZ	0670	→	74 12
CMP	[SI],0D	→	80 3C 0D

Table 1.3 What An Assembler Does *(continued)*

Assembly Language			*Machine Language*
JZ	0666	→	74 03
MOVSB		→	A4
JMP	065E	→	EB F8

Assembly language is all the official-looking stuff you see on the left. An instruction like MOV COUNTER,00B0 may not look too friendly, but in the end, we'll see that it's clarity itself when compared to something like C7 06 C3 01 B0 00.

> Can you pick out some of the data from the assembly-language instructions as embedded in the machine language? Notice that the high and low bytes of the data seem to have been reversed when moving from the assembly-language part to their machine language counterparts, something that we'll become quite familiar with later. Don't examine this too closely at this stage.

Using Assembly Language

Sometimes assembly language is hard to write, sometimes it's hard to debug; there is no escaping the fact. It would be nice if, with the aid of harmonious symmetries and one or two golden rules, all assembly-language instructions like JZ or MOVSB simply fell out easily, but assembly language isn't like that. It has to follow the design of the microprocessor, and the microprocessor was designed by imperfect people. As we'll see, assembly language for the PC and PS/2 has many idiosyncracies, and many unsymmetrical quirks; but there's no way around it. Regrettable though it is, we can only learn it the way it is, not the way it ought to be.

Assembly language as a tool is at once simple and direct. There is no better way to speak the microprocessor's language, unless you are fluent in binary or hex. Every instruction in assembly language is translated into exactly one instruction in machine language, making the machine do one thing. The microprocessor has a whole instruction set defined—various bytes and groups of bytes will make it do this or that, depending on what you tell it. Every instruction has its assembly-language counterpart—it is the machine's instruction set that determines the instructions available in assembly language.

> Notice how different assembly-language instructions are from a higher-level language's commands: the higher level language's commands are determined by some committee, or by the language's

author. Frequently each instruction will have to be translated into multiple machine-language instructions. Assembly-language instructions are determined by the chip in the heart of your machine.

Registers in Your Microprocessor

Now we are prepared to discuss the insides of your microprocessor on a down-to-earth level. There are many different microprocessors of the 80x86 family in use in IBM PCs and IBM PS/2s. For convenience, we will refer most often to the 8088, unless we make an explicit reference to another chip with an expanded instruction set. Since the 8086–80386 chips all include the 8088's instruction set, it is meant to be clear that we are talking about all of them.

When we wish to deal with instructions particular to only, say, the 80386, we will refer to the chip that way. The 8088 includes almost all the instructions we will cover in this book, and, with the exception of protected mode operating in the later chips, it might be said that the 8088 instruction set includes just about all that is really useful to know when programming for this family; at least so far.

Higher-level language variables

In a higher level language, like BASIC or Pascal, numbers can be stored in variables. Let's say that we wanted to move the contents of the variable INDEX into the variable COUNTER. This is the way we would do it in those two languages:

```
COUNTER = INDEX     (BASIC)
COUNTER := INDEX;   (Pascal)
```

This operation, in either language, takes a number stored in INDEX and moves it into COUNTER. Regrettably, we do not have this option in assembly language (which, of course, means that when translated into machine language, the higher level languages have to perform the above operations in a series of steps).

General purpose registers

The 8088 is built with a number of internal registers, called *general purpose registers*, and we may think of them as predefined variables. Each one of these registers holds exactly one word, 16 bits. There are four general purpose registers, AX, BX, CX, and DX. These registers are always inside the 8088; and it's hard to think of an assembly-language program that could get along without them. They'll hold our data, one word at a time, while we work with it.

Operations that involve moving data around (except for some options with the 8088's extremely useful string moving instructions, which we'll see later) always use these registers in some way. This moving operation will be our introduction to assembly language.

The MOV Instruction

The most fundamental assembly-language instruction is MOV, which moves data between registers and memory. If you have something stored in memory and want to work with it, you can use MOV. MOV is what moves data between any general purpose register (or memory) and other general purpose registers (or memory). Here's how it works:

```
MOV    AX,0FFFFH
```

Here we are putting the number 0FFFFH (= 65535D) into AX. This is the biggest number any register (all are 16 bits) can hold: 0FFFFH. Notice the leading 0, which is added to let the assembler know that we intend 0FFFFH to be taken as a number, and not some English word.

MOVing data between registers

The way MOV works is like this: MOV Destination, Source. The data is moved from the source into the destination. For example, we can take the 0FFFFH in the register AX and move it into the register DX:

```
MOV    DX,AX    (Move the data from AX into DX)
```

Now DX and AX will hold the same value.

Data can also be MOVed into these registers from memory. Let's say we have a memory location with 0 in it: This can be moved into, say, CX, this way:

```
MOV    CX,[Memory Location]
```

or into AX:

```
MOV    AX,[Memory Location]
```

or we can move whatever is in DX into the memory location this way:

```
MOV    [Memory Location],DX
```

However, data *cannot* be moved from memory to memory. Let's take a moment to examine this odd fact.

Moving Data Around

Let's say 5 is in AX. You could move it from AX into CX without prob-lem, because you can always move data from any of the general purpose registers to any other general purpose register.

```
AX        CX
──        ──
 5    →    5              OK.
```

Now let's say that 7 is stored somewhere in memory. As long as we know the address at which that 7 is stored, we can refer to it with no trou-ble. Let's say that it's stored in the word at address 12345H (the particular number, 12345H, is not important right now). We can move the 7 from that location into any general purpose register, AX, BX, CX, or DX (we'll see *how* to use memory locations shortly):

```
[Memory Location 12345H]          AX
──────────────────────────        ──
           7                →       7     OK.
```

On the other hand, we can take the 5 still stored in, say, CX, and move it into the memory word at address 12345H. The previous contents of that word, 7, will be overwritten by the 5:

```
CX              [Memory Location 12345H]
──              ──────────────────────────
 5     →                   5                OK.
```

But now if we had a memory location 54321H, we *could not* move the 5 now in memory location 12345H directly into 12345H:

```
[Memory Location 12345H]          [Memory Location 54321H]
──────────────────────────        ──────────────────────────
          5            −X→                  XXXX          NOT OK
```

This is one of the peculiarities of the 8088. Data cannot go directly from memory location to memory location in one instruction. If we wanted to, we could move data from memory to general purpose register and then to memory again, like this:

```
[Memory Location 12345H]     AX       [Memory Location 54321H]
──────────────────────────   ──       ──────────────────────────
          5            →       5
                               5   →              5
```

In other words, we can move from one memory location to another in two steps. But we can't do it directly. We'll come back to this point many times throughout the book. In the meanwhile, let's put our MOV knowledge to work.

Seeing It Work

There is an excellent program that comes with all DOS versions named DEBUG. It is a shame that this fine utility can only really be used by assembly-language programmers. Ever since DOS came out, people who understood the PC at the assembly language level have been using this little gem to probe through their programs (and probably other people's programs) and the depths of memory.

Ever since DOS 2.0, DEBUG has had the ability to assemble small programs that you write on the spot—a mini-assembler is built right in. We'll use this mini-assembler to convert our instruction MOV AX,5 into machine language, and then run it, watching the value stored in AX change from 0 to 5.

Using DEBUG for the First Time

First, locate a copy of DEBUG.COM on a disk (or one of the disks) that DOS came on. Copy it onto one of your working disks, and start the program. DEBUG will reward you with its terse prompt: a single dash "–". All DEBUG commands (there are 18 of them) are terse—one letter long, to be precise; we'll become more familiar with them later. Keeping DEBUG terse seems to be in keeping with the idea of assembly language as terse and cryptic, which it need not be at all. Here we are in DEBUG:

```
A>DEBUG
```

The DEBUG
R
Command

The command "R" in DEBUG (type "R" and then a carriage return—<cr>) stands for "Registers," and it lets you see the contents of all the 8088's 13 registers. You can pick AX, BX, CX, and DX out readily. (Note: *All* numbers displayed in DEBUG are in hexadecimal, which is standard for assembly-language debuggers. Hex may be more used in assembly-language programming than decimal.)

IIIBradyLine

Insights into tomorrow's technology from the authors and editors of Brady Books.

You rely on Brady's bestselling computer books for up-to-date information about high technology. Now turn to BradyLine for the details behind the titles.

Find out what new trends in technology spark Brady's authors and editors. Read about what they're working on, and predicting, for the future. Get to know the authors through interviews and profiles, and get to know each other through your questions and comments.

BradyLine keeps you ahead of the trends with the stories behind the latest computer developments. Informative previews of forthcoming books and excerpts from new titles keep you apprised of what's going on in the fields that interest you most.

- Peter Norton on operating systems
- Jim Seymour on business productivity
- Jerry Daniels, Mary Jane Mara, Robert Eckhardt, and Cynthia Harriman on Macintosh development, productivity, and connectivity

Get the Spark. Get BradyLine.

Published quarterly, beginning with the Summer 1988 issue. Free exclusively to our customers. Just fill out and mail this card to begin your subscription.

Name _____

Address _____

City _____ State _____ Zip _____

Name of Book Purchased _____

Date of Purchase _____

Where was this book purchased?   *(circle one)*

    Retail Store   Computer Store   Mail Order

FREE

Mail this card for your free subscription to BradyLine

Brady Books
One Gulf+Western Plaza
New York, NY 10023

```
A>DEBUG
-R
AX=0000  BX=0000  CX=0000  DX=0000  SP=FFEE  BP=0000  SI=0000 DI=0000
DS=0EF1  ES=0EF1  SS=0EF1  CS=0EF1  IP=0100     NV UP EI PL NZ NA PO NC
0EF1:0100 9AEC04020F     CALL    0F02:04EC
```

In addition to the registers shown:

```
A>DEBUG
-R
AX=0000  BX=0000  CX=0000  DX=0000  SP=FFEE  BP=0000 SI=0000  DI=0000
DS=0EF1  ES=0EF1  SS=0EF1  CS=0EF1  IP=0100     NV UP EI PL NZ NA PO NC
-------------------------------------------------
0EF1:0100 9AEC04020F     CALL    0F02:04EC
```

The flags

The settings of the internal *flags* of the 8088 are shown (there are eight flags, which will be covered later):

```
A>DEBUG
-R
AX=0000  BX=0000  CX=0000  DX=0000  SP=FFEE  BP=0000  SI=0000 DI=0000
DS=0EF1  ES=0EF1  SS=0EF1  CS=0EF1  IP=0100     NV UP EI PL NZ NA PO NC
0EF1:0100 9AEC04020F     CALL    0F02:04EC
```

DEBUG also tells you the current memory location. For now, it is enough to notice that a memory location is given in a peculiar format—with a colon between two numbers, rather than as just one number. We'll become familiar with this format all too soon. Here, we are at memory location 0EF1:0100:

```
A>DEBUG
-R
AX=0000  BX=0000  CX=0000  DX=0000  SP=FFEE  BP=0000  SI=0000 DI=0000
DS=0EF1  ES=0EF1  SS=0EF1  CS=0EF1  IP=0100     NV UP EI PL NZ NA PO NC
0EF1:0100 9AEC04020F     CALL    0F02:04EC
```

The final part of the DEBUG "R" display indicates just what is to be found at the current memory location. In our case, those are the bytes following the address in the "R" display.

```
A>DEBUG
-R
AX=0000  BX=0000  CX=0000  DX=0000  SP=FFEE  BP=0000  SI=0000 DI=0000
DS=0EF1  ES=0EF1  SS=0EF1  CS=0EF1  IP=0100     NV UP EI PL NZ NA PO NC
0EF1:0100 9AEC04020F     CALL    0F02:04EC
```

DEBUG tries to group bytes together, starting at the current memory location (which only holds one byte) into what would be a valid machine-language instruction. It then provides us with an assembly-language translation of the machine-language instruction that begins at our present location.

When there is in reality no machine-language instruction, as is often the case, the helpful translation for our benefit is meaningless. This is true here: Having just started DEBUG, there is as yet no program to look at. It is just taking left-over bytes in the computer's memory and trying to make sense out of them; in fact they mean nothing.

```
A>DEBUG
-R
AX=0000  BX=0000  CX=0000  DX=0000  SP=FFEE  BP=0000  SI=0000 DI=0000
DS=0EF1  ES=0EF1  SS=0EF1  CS=0EF1  IP=0100     NV UP EI PL NZ NA PO NC
0EF1:0100 9AEC04020F→  CALL     0F02:04EC
```

> You may be curious as to just how the 8088 knows how long the next machine-language instruction will be—one byte, or five? The key is that when it looks at the first byte, it knows at once what type of instruction is indicated, and hence how long it will be. It fetches the remaining bytes from memory to complete the instruction.

Assembling in DEBUG

With all this information surrounding us, let's add a little of our own. We'll use the "A" for "Assemble" command to put our own tiny program in, consisting of only one line: MOV AX,5. The A command needs an address at which to start depositing the machine-language instructions it will generate in memory. Our current address is "0EF1:0100," so we will tell it to assemble the machine language right there, using the shorthand "A100," which means, "Assemble starting at location 100."

```
A>DEBUG
-R
AX=0000  BX=0000  CX=0000  DX=0000  SP=FFEE  BP=0000  SI=0000 DI=0000
DS=0EF1  ES=0EF1  SS=0EF1  CS=0EF1  IP=0100     NV UP EI PL NZ NA PO NC
0EF1:0100 9AEC04020F    CALL     0F02:04EC
-A100                              ← Here is the A100 command.
0EF1:0100                          ← DEBUG's response.
```

Following the A100 command, DEBUG returned with a line "0EF1:0100", showing the current address at which it will deposit assembled code. Here we simply type MOV AX,5 and then a carriage return.

```
A>DEBUG
-R
AX=0000  BX=0000  CX=0000  DX=0000  SP=FFEE  BP=0000  SI=0000 DI=0000
DS=0EF1  ES=0EF1  SS=0EF1  CS=0EF1  IP=0100     NV UP EI PL NZ NA PO NC
0EF1:0100 9AEC04020F    CALL     0F02:04EC
-A100
0EF1:0100 MOV     AX,5             ← Type "MOV AX,5<cr>"
0EF1:0103
```

DEBUG then prompts for the next instruction we wish to give with the address `0EF1:0103`. We don't wish to assemble any more at this time, so we give DEBUG a carriage return. DEBUG interprets the blank line to mean that we are through assembling, and returns to its normal "– " prompt.

```
A>DEBUG
-R
AX=0000  BX=0000  CX=0000  DX=0000  SP=FFEE  BP=0000  SI=0000 DI=0000
DS=0EF1  ES=0EF1  SS=0EF1  CS=0EF1  IP=0100     NV UP EI PL NZ NA PO NC
0EF1:0100 9AEC04020F    CALL    0F02:04EC
-A100
0EF1:0100 MOV       AX,5
0EF1:0103                              ← Type just a <cr> to stop assembling.
                                       ← DEBUG returns
```

And that's all there is to it. We've just assembled our first line of assembly language. To see what occurred, remember that the R command displays the current memory location and instruction. Since we assembled MOV AX,5 at the current memory location, let's give the R command and take a look ("R" functions as the "eyes" of DEBUG):

```
A>DEBUG
-R
AX=0000  BX=0000  CX=0000  DX=0000  SP=FFEE  BP=0000  SI=0000 DI=0000
DS=0EF1  ES=0EF1  SS=0EF1  CS=0EF1  IP=0100     NV UP EI PL NZ NA PO NC
0EF1:0100 9AEC04020F    CALL    0F02:04EC
-A100
0EF1:0100 MOV       AX,5
0EF1:0103
-R                                     ← Let's see what we've done.
AX=0000  BX=0000  CX=0000  DX=0000  SP=FFEE  BP=0000  SI=0000 DI=0000
DS=0EF1  ES=0EF1  SS=0EF1  CS=0EF1  IP=0100     NV UP EI PL NZ NA PO NC
0EF1:0100 B80500        MOV    AX,0005
```

**The DEBUG
T command**

We can see, as part of the normal DEBUG display, our instruction, MOV AX,5 (note the machine-language instruction B8 05 00 corresponding to MOV AX,5 in DEBUG's display). Executing our instruction, now that it's been assembled, is simple with the DEBUG Trace command, abbreviated to "T." Typing "T" once will execute the current instruction, and move us on to the next memory location:

```
A>DEBUG
-R
AX=0000  BX=0000  CX=0000  DX=0000  SP=FFEE  BP=0000  SI=0000 DI=0000
DS=0EF1  ES=0EF1  SS=0EF1  CS=0EF1  IP=0100     NV UP EI PL NZ NA PO NC
0EF1:0100 9AEC04020F    CALL    0F02:04EC
-A100
0EF1:0100 MOV       AX,5
0EF1:0103
-R
AX=0000  BX=0000  CX=0000  DX=0000  SP=FFEE  BP=0000  SI=0000 DI=0000
DS=0EF1  ES=0EF1  SS=0EF1  CS=0EF1  IP=0100     NV UP EI PL NZ NA PO NC
```

```
0EF1:0100 B80500        MOV    AX,0005
-T                      ←   This will execute our MOV instruction.
AX=0005 BX=0000  CX=0000 DX=0000 SP=FFEE BP=0000  SI=0000 DI=0000
DS=0EF1 ES=0EF1  SS=0EF1 CS=0EF1 IP=0103    NV UP EI PL NZ NA PO NC
0EF1:0103 020F          ADD    CL,[BX]
DS:0000=CD
```

After the T command, DEBUG gives its usual display, indicating what the register contents and flags are now. Look in the AX position, the first register displayed. In all the previous displays, AX has held 0, but, after the execution of our MOV instruction, it holds 5. We have changed the contents of the AX register of the computer's microprocessor from 0 to 5 by executing an assembly-language instruction.

All the flags remain unchanged. On the other hand, the memory location *has* changed, from 0EF1:0100 to 0EF1:0103. This is because the machine-language instruction corresponding to MOV AX,5 is three bytes long in memory (B8H 05H 00H). The instruction following it will begin three bytes later; therefore, the 100 has changed to 103. (Note also that DEBUG has tried to unassemble the meaningless, left-over bytes there.)

These kind of addresses, 0EF1:0100 and 0EF1:0103, always given in hex, are the way we will point to memory locations in the PS/2 and PC. The scheme used to point to memory in our computers is a little complex; but of course it is a central part of what we will have to learn. For that reason, it's one of the topics we'll cover in Chapter 2.

▌ Type Q<cr> to exit DEBUG. ▌

2
Our First Programs

A .COM File

In this chapter, we're going to develop our first programs. These programs are going to deal with output—printed characters on the screen. There's nothing like jumping right in, so let's do just that with a little program that will print "A" on your PS/2s or PCs screen.

DEBUG not only allows you to assemble programs, but to write them out to the disk as well. In this, our first real program, we're going to use DEBUG as our assembler. Choose a disk that you won't mind writing on, and start up DEBUG:

```
A>DEBUG
```

First we'll start with the A command, meaning Assemble. As before, we will put our machine language code starting at location 0100H:

```
A>DEBUG
-A100                              ←
0EF1:0100
```

Just type in the following assembly language instructions verbatim, followed by a carriage return after the prompt 0EF1:010A to stop assembling:

```
A>DEBUG
-A100
0EF1:0100 MOV     AX,0200        ←
0EF1:0103 MOV     DX,0041        ←
0EF1:0106 INT     21             ←
0EF1:0108 INT     20             ←
0EF1:010A         ← Just type a <cr> here.
```

25

DEBUG reponds with its prompt, –.

What our progam is doing is loading the registers AX and DX with the MOV instruction. This is the preparation for having the program print out "A."

What happens next is that two INT instructions are given, INT 21H and INT 20H. These instructions will be very important for us. The way we have loaded the registers AX and DX here tells INT 21H to print out an "A" character; at the end we use INT 20H to end the program. (We'll discuss the exact nature of these instructions in our program later.) Remember, all numbers that appear in DEBUG are in hex—although it says INT 21, it means INT 21H. We'll decode the INT instructions after we've finished our program.

Checking Our Program

The DEBUG
Unassemble
Command

Let's check and make sure that our instructions appear properly as machine-language instructions by asking DEBUG to *unassemble* the program we just wrote. The last prompt when we were assembling was the address 0EF1:010A, so that's where the next byte of our program was going to go. That means that our program extends in memory from 0EF1:0100 to 0EF1:0109. To unassemble it, we can use the DEBUG Unassemble, or U, command. We issue the command U100 109, which unassembles the program from 100H to 109H:

```
A>DEBUG
-A100
0EF1:0100 MOV    AX,0200
0EF1:0103 MOV    DX,0041
0EF1:0106 INT    21
0EF1:0108 INT    20
0EF1:010A
-U100 109        ←
0EF1:0100 B80002        MOV    AX,0200    ←   Here is the unassembled program.
0EF1:0103 BA4100        MOV    DX,0041    ←
0EF1:0106 CD21          INT    21         ←
0EF1:0108 CD20          INT    20         ←
```

The DEBUG
Name
Command

DEBUG unassembled the progam for us, showing us the assembly language that matches the generated machine code. These instructions match what we typed in. Since this is what we want, we will write our program out to the disk by naming the program first with the N (for Name) command. Let's call the program PRINTA.COM, following its function. We name it this way:

```
A>DEBUG
-A100
0EF1:0100 MOV    AX,0200
0EF1:0103 MOV    DX,0041
0EF1:0106 INT    21
```

```
0EF1:0108 INT      20
0EF1:010A
-U100 109
0EF1:0100 B80002         MOV    AX,0200
0EF1:0103 BA4100         MOV    DX,0041
0EF1:0106 CD21           INT    21
0EF1:0108 CD20           INT    20
-NPRINTA.COM    ←
```

And now we can write it out (DEBUG will write this file in the current directory). DEBUG needs to be told the number of bytes to write out, and in our case, the program goes from locations 0100H to 0109H. Each memory location holds a byte, so that makes 10 bytes. Of course, DEBUG is expecting hex, so we will give it a value of 0AH.

The DEBUG Write command

The DEBUG W command, Write, has been written to read the number of bytes to write as a file directly out of the CX register. This means that to write our 10-byte program PRINTA.COM, we will have to load the CX register with 0AH and then give the simple, one-letter W command.

To move 0AH into CX, we can use the R (Register) command. If you use the R command without any arguments, DEBUG gives you its standard display, as we've had the chance to see. On the other hand, giving the command RCX indicates to DEBUG that you wish to change the value in CX (this will work with any register of the 13 available). DEBUG gives us the current value in CX (which is 0000) and gives us a colon prompt, :, after which we will type our new value for CX, A (for 0AH), and a carriage return:

```
A>DEBUG
-A100
0EF1:0100 MOV      AX,0200
0EF1:0103 MOV      DX,0041
0EF1:0106 INT      21
0EF1:0108 INT      20
0EF1:010A
-U100 109
0EF1:0100 B80002         MOV    AX,0200
0EF1:0103 BA4100         MOV    DX,0041
0EF1:0106 CD21           INT    21
0EF1:0108 CD20           INT    20
-NPRINTA.COM
-RCX
CX 0000
:A                ← Type A<cr> to set CX to 10D
-
```

Now that we've set the number of bytes to write in CX, we can write PRINTA.COM by giving the W command:

```
A>DEBUG
-A100
0EF1:0100 MOV      AX,0200
0EF1:0103 MOV      DX,0041
0EF1:0106 INT      21
```

```
0EF1:0108 INT      20
0EF1:010A
-U100 109
0EF1:0100 B80002          MOV     AX,0200
0EF1:0103 BA4100          MOV     DX,0041
0EF1:0106 CD21            INT     21
0EF1:0108 CD20            INT     20
-NPRINTA.COM
-RCX
CX 0000
:A
-W                        ← The W command
Writing 000A bytes
-Q
```

DEBUG replies that it is writing 10 bytes to disk. Exit DEBUG and you will find that PRINTA.COM has been written.

Let's run it:

```
>PRINTA
A
A>
```

PRINTA does what it's supposed to do: types out "A" and exits. PRINTA.COM is a unique program perhaps only for its size. How many functioning, executable files do you know for the PS/2 or PC that are only 10 bytes long?

On the other hand, we've cobbled together our first program; now we've got to take a closer look at it. Let's start by looking at the first two lines in the program:

```
A>DEBUG
-A100
0EF1:0100 MOV      AX,0200        ←
0EF1:0103 MOV      DX,0041        ←
0EF1:0106 INT      21
0EF1:0108 INT      20
0EF1:010A
```

What these two instructions are doing is setting things up for the INT 21H instruction that follows. Moving 0200H into AX informs INT 21H that we want to print on the screen, and moving 0041H into DX informs it that the character we want to print is "A."

In fact, all we needed was the 02H in the high byte of AX and the 41H in the low byte of DX to let INT 21H know what we wanted. There is a way of using these bytes as separate registers, and, since it is usually these byte-long registers that are used by the INT instruction, we will cover them before covering INT.

The High and Low Bytes of General Purpose Registers

In the 80x86 microprocessors, there is a way of splitting the general purpose registers—AX, BX, CX, and DX—into their high and low bytes, and using them independently.

Only the general purpose registers can be split up. For example, the top half of AX can be referred to as AH ("H" for high byte) and the bottom byte can be referred to as AL ("L" for low byte). For instance, we could say:

```
MOV     AH,5            or            MOV     AL,3AH
```

in addition to instructions that work with AX as a whole like MOV AX,0FH.

> Notice that the single instruction MOV AX,053AH does the same thing as using both instructions MOV AH,5 and MOV AL,3AH.

The high and low registers that can be used as separate registers are AH, AL, BH, BL, CH, CL, DH, and DL. Very often, when we feed information to DOS or BIOS, as we will, information will have to be passed in some of these one-byte registers.

INT 21H, which we can use to print out our character and do many more things, needs information to be passed to it in the AH and DL registers. Our program, which looked like this:

```
MOV     AX,0200H
MOV     DX,0041H
INT     21H
INT     20H
```

could have been shortened, had we known about high and low registers, to:

```
MOV     AH,02H    ←
MOV     DL,41H    ←
INT     21H
INT     20H
```

This version of PRINTA works just as our old one did. As mentioned, INT instructions often require data in these one-byte-long registers. Now that we are all prepared for the INT instruction that follows, let's look into it.

Interrupts

The INT instruction

Buying a microprocessor chip does not give you a computer (if it did, you could have saved a lot of money). The microprocessor has to be hooked up by someone (IBM, for instance) to the rest of the computer. The computer itself has many important parts that Intel did not design—such as the screen, the disk drives, or the keyboard. What Intel did do is let the computer manufacturers add their own assembly-language programs (at special places in memory) and treat them as if they were assembly-language instructions (like MOV). You can reach these prewritten programs with the INT instruction.

What happens when you give an INT instruction is that some prewritten program is run. For example, one program prints out characters on the screen. To us, using an INT 21H instruction, this makes it practically seem as though there is a new assembly-language instruction just for printing. The programs that are run are parts of DOS or BIOS (depending on which interrupts you select).

These prewritten programs were just written themselves in assembly language. They do all the dirty work of actually handing the disk drive controllers, or the screen controller chips, by having the microprocessor send signals to them. That's not something we should have to do in our programs—every time we want to print on the screen, we don't want to have to check the video controller rescan register and the dozens of other necessary things. With interrupts, all the hard work can be condensed into one instruction.

Intel gave the 8088 the ability to use 256 possible interrupts, from INT 00 to INT FFH. Some of these interrupts are used by DOS, some by BIOS, and some by BASIC.

Here are all the interrupts the PC or PS/2 is capable of, and what part of the operating system they are used by:

Table 2.1 The Interrupts by Groups

Interrupt Number (Hex)	Used By
00–1F	BIOS
18	Starts ROM BASIC
19	BOOTSTRAP (Boots PC)
1A–1F	BIOS
20–3F	DOS
40–5F	BIOS (PC XT and Later)
60–67	Free

Interrupt Number (Hex)	Used By
68–7F	BIOS (PC XT and Later)
80–F0	BASIC
F0–FF	Free

You can see that a group of interrupts, INTs 20H to 3FH, have been set aside for DOS.

The DOS interrupts do many things, from printing on the screen to opening and closing files, from putting keyboard input into a buffer in memory to printing out many characters at once if you so decide. Among the DOS interrupts, numbers 20H to 3FH, there is a giant that we will come to know well, INT 21H.

DOS INT 21H

For some reason, IBM decided to group almost all of DOS' capabilities into INT 21H. If a program wants to work with files on the PS/2 or PC, it calls INT 21H at a low level, for example. These capabilities of DOS are open to us, since we are programming in its home language, assembler. We can use everything DOS has that can be used. For example, here we are typing characters on the screen the same way DOS itself does it, using INT 21H, service 2. INT 21H is divided into numerous services, and the number of services grows with each DOS version.

Using Interrupts

Let's take an example to show how we will work with interrupts: The INT 21H printing service is service number 2. To select an INT 21H service, we have to load its number in the AH register before our INT 21H instruction, as we have done in PRINTA.

```
MOV     AH,02H    ←
MOV     DL,41H
INT     21H
INT     20H
```

In addition, service 2 expects us to supply it with the code—the ASCII code—of the letter it is to type out. If we happen to know that 41H stands for "A" in the ASCII character code, we can use that by loading it where INT 21H expects it, in DL.

```
MOV     AH,02H
MOV     DL,41H   ← 41H means "A" in ASCII
INT     21H
INT     20H
```

Then we can execute the INT 21H instruction, having set ourselves up for it properly:

```
MOV     AH,02H
MOV     DL,41H
INT     21H       ←
INT     20H
```

And "A" appears on the screen.

Table 2.2 presents some possible services that can be used in INT 21H. This list is just to get us started; we will add many more services in later chapters. To use these INT 21H services, just load the registers as shown and execute an INT 21H instruction:

Table 2.2 Some Interrupt 21H Services

Service #	Name	Set These	What Happens
1	Keyboard Input	AH = 1	ASCII code of typed key returned in AL.
2	Character Output	AH = 2 DL = ASCII Code	The character corresponding to the ASCII CODE in DL is put on the screen.
9	String Output	AH = 9 DS:DX = Address of string of characters to print	Prints a string of bytes from memory on the screen (we will use this service in this chapter).

Other INT 21H services create files or subdirectories, delete files, load programs, allocate memory, and many other things.

INT 20H   INT 20H, the last instruction in PRINTA, just lets DOS know that we are done with our program—DOS will exit from the program and we get the A> prompt back. Most of the programs we write will end with INT 20H, the standard ending instruction for assembly-language programs.

> When we work with memory-resident programs, we will end our programs with a different interrupt, often INT 27H, and not INT 20H. This is so the program is added in memory to DOS, and not just flushed out, as INT 20H does.

In many ways, it might be said that the language we work with on the PC or PS/2 is a combination of BIOS and DOS as much as it is straight 80x86 assembly language. With the rich selection of resources that we will find BIOS and DOS offering us, INT will be a prominent instruction for us. And INT is just a condensation of many, BIOS and DOS instructions put there for our convenience so that we do not have to do things like move the disk head into place ourselves, but will be able to simply open files without caring about the details.

> There are also hardware interrupts. You provide software interrupts in your program (with the INT instruction), but when something happens in the machine, such as a key being struck, a "hardware interrupt" causes the microprocessor to suspend what it is doing and attend to it: Here it reads the key in. These hardware interrupts actually interrupt the machine—that's where the name comes from. If you don't want to be bothered, you can "turn hardware interrupts off," so the computer will no longer respond to the keyboard or disk drive events. See the STI and CLI instructions later.

PRINTA.ASM

Let's return to the program we've been working with:

```
MOV     AH,02H
MOV     DL,41H
INT     21H
INT     20H
```

It might work fine in DEBUG, but it would never pass the macro assembler. In what follows, we are going to work on converting this program into one that the macro assembler can assemble, and that the linker can link. We're going to create PRINTA.COM without DEBUG's help here.

Programs that can be assembled have the extention ".ASM" on the disk, so we'll refer to this program as PRINTA.ASM. When the time comes, you'll be able to type it in with your word processor.

To be able to set up a program like PRINTA.COM ourselves, we're going to have to know more than we do about the way memory is set up in the PC or PS/2. In particular, we're going to have to learn that a program is cut up into at least two different parts: a section for the code, called the code segment, and a section for the data, called the data segment. We will use such segments in PRINTA.ASM.

The idea of segments comes from the way memory is used in the PC or PS/2: If you have a code segment and a data segment in your program, they are put into separate parts of memory. Learning to use memory (in particular, "segments"), and then defining segments in a program is the first step towards building PRINTA.ASM.

Memory in the PS/2 and PC

The 8088's View of Memory

One-byte
micro-
processors

Without memory, our machine would be useless. We could only execute the instruction currently held in the CPU; beyond that, nothing. Using memory is a big consideration in assembly-language programming because of the segmented way it is addressed. Before writing real assembly-language programs, we've got to understand what's going on. We won't be able to write .ASM files until we understand segments, and we won't be able to understand them until we understand memory usage. So let's begin by examining the use of memory.

Early microprocessors were able to address only limited amounts of memory. Since early chips only worked with one byte at a time, they could only handle numbers from 0 to 255. This meant that they could only specify the *address* of 256 memory locations. That is, a microprocessor that could only handle bytes could only address as many memory locations as it could indicate with that byte. Since a byte only runs from 0 to 255, that's not a whole lot ($1/4$K).

One-word
micro-
processors

The generation of 16-bit machines did considerably better. In a 16-bit word, you can hold numbers running from 0 to 0FFFFH, or 0 to 65535. That is, since the microprocessor could handle 65,536 (i.e., 0 to 65535) different numbers, it could specify which of 65,536 different memory locations to use (65,536 = 64K = 10000H) Beyond that, the microprocessor could no longer indicate, with the 16-bit registers that it used, any additional addresses.

Although 64K was at one time a good deal of memory, it is terribly restricting today. These days, machines with 3 MBytes—three megabytes—of memory are not uncommon (in the same way, the demand on disk space has forced their capacity to jump tremendously over the past few years). When Intel came out with the 8088, they knew that 64K was an inadequate amount of memory for a serious computer.

On the other hand, using two words—32 bits—to address memory seemed a monstrously large amount to them. Using 32 bits allows you to point to four gigabytes (that is, four *billion* bytes) of memory, and that seemed uncomfortably large and unecessary. So they compromised. Instead of a 16 bit address to memory, they used 20.

The 8088's
20-bit
addresses

That's the way the 8088 sees memory—as locations that it can reference with a 20-bit address. A 20-bit number in the world of computers may seem odd—we're used to powers of 2: 4, 8, 16, 32, and so on. The explanation is at once ingenious and exasperating, as we'll see. What they did was introduce the concept of memory segments.

Segments are going to prove central to almost everything we do from now on. Using memory is fundamental to our machine; it views memory as made up of pieces called *segments*. Let's dig into the way segments are used in the PC or PS/2 (and, along the way, we'll understand the use of four more registers).

> Most computers larger than microcomputers have two types of memory: regular memory, which takes about 120 nanoseconds (120 billionths of a second) to retrieve data from memory, and cache memory, superfast memory—25 to 50 nanoseconds—which stores the most recently used sections of memory. The chances are highest that the CPU will require something from memory close to the last location it needed, and cache memory, holding the most recent chunk of memory, can supply it much faster. In this way, computers can save a good deal of time.

Segmentation

You may recall that in DEBUG, at the end of the last chapter, we saw addresses as they're used in the PS/2 and PC for the first time. The address we saw looked like this: 0EF1:0100.

The address 0EF1:0100 is made up of two hex numbers, each 16 bits long. This is usual for PC or PS/2 addresses—two words are involved. The 0EF1H in 0EF1:0100 is known as the *segment address* of that particular memory location. The 0100H is known as the *offset address*.

The way Intel's chip designers get 20 bits out of these two 16-bit numbers, the segment address and the offset address, is to take the segment address—0EF1H—*shift* it to the right one hex place, and then add it to the offset address, 0100H. The resulting address is 20 bits long. It works like this:

```
    0EF1   ← Note: Segment address shifted one place over
+   0100   ← And added to the Offset address
    ----
    0F010  ← Gives this five hex digit result.
```

Adding the two together then gives a result with five hex digits. Since each hex digit can be represented with four binary digits, this is indeed 20 bits, since 20 = 5 (hex digits) × 4 (bits per hex digit).

The resulting 20-bit number can hold addresses ranging from 00000H to FFFFFH, or 0 to $2^{20} - 1 = 1048575$. Counting 0, the 8088 can thus hold the addresses of 1,048,576 memory locations. This is one megabyte, 1024K (i.e., 1024K = 1024 * 1024 bytes/K = 1,048,576).

Figure 2.1 Converting from Segmented to Real Addresses

```
        Segmented Address              Real Address
        _____           _____

    ┌       F000:FFFF   │ 1 Byte │    FFFFFH  ←  The top of memory
    │                   │        │               (FFFFFH = 1 MByte ( 1)
    │       F000:FFFE   │ 1 Byte │    FFFFEH
    │                   │        │
    │       F000:FFFD   │ 1 Byte │    FFFFDH
    │                   │        │
    │       F000:FFFC   │ 1 Byte │    FFFFCH
    │                   └────────┘
    │                       :
    │                   ┌────────┐
    │       C000:AAAA   │ 1 Byte │    CAAAAH
    │                   │        │
    │       C000:AAA9   │ 1 Byte │    CAAA9H
    │                   │        │
One Megabyte  C000:AAA8 │ 1 Byte │    CAAA8H
    │                   │        │
    │       C000:AAA7   │ 1 Byte │    CAAA7H
    │                   └────────┘
    │                       :
    │                   ┌────────┐
    │       0000:0003   │ 1 Byte │    00003H
    │                   │        │
    │       0000:0002   │ 1 Byte │    00002H
    │                   │        │
    │       0000:0001   │ 1 Byte │    00001H
    │                   │        │
    ▼       0000:0000   │ 1 Byte │    00000H   ←The bottom of memory
                        └────────┘
```

Moving the segment address over by one place before adding it to the offset address can be thought of as multiplying it by 16, since each place represents a factor of 16 in a hex number.

Segments in Memory

A segment is the memory space that can be addressed with one particular segment address. For example, the segment that starts at the bottom of memory, segment 0000, can extend from 0000:0000 to 0000:FFFF (keeping the segment address, 0000, unchanged). This is segment 0000. Using the 20-bit address properly, this segment extends from 00000 to 0FFFFH. A segment can go from xxxx:0000 to xxxx:FFFF—64K. Once you choose a segment address, such as 0000, you have a 64K workspace you can use without having to change the segment address again.

Over-
lapping
segments

On the other hand, even though segments can describe such a large area, they can overlap easily. The next possible segment is segment 0001. This segment extends from 0001:0000 to 0001:FFFF. Converting these numbers to 20-bit addresses gives 00010 to 1000F. (Remember, to create the 20-bit address, shift the segment address left by one place and add to the offset address.)

In other words, segment 0001 starts just 16 bytes after segment 0000 (00000H compared to 00010H, or 0 compared to 16). And Segment 0002 starts just 16 bytes after Segment 0001. You might visualize them as overlapping sheets of clear acetate. What is important to know is that choosing a segment gives you a 64K work space, but that 64K workspace overlaps with many other segments, too.

Figure 2.2 Overlapping Segments

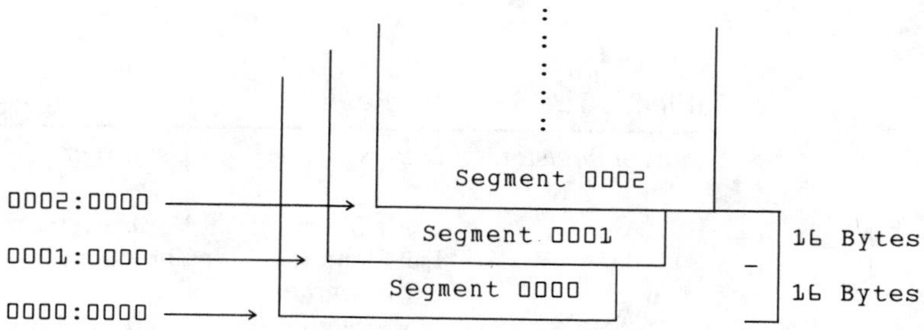

Paragraphs

The 16-byte boundaries in memory that segments can start on have become so important that they are given a special name: paragraphs. Thus, 0000:0000 starts the first paragraph in memory, 0001:0000 starts the second, and so on. Each paragraph is 16 bytes long.

Using Segments

Although you'll read long complicated explanations in other books, the way you use segments is to define a workspace that is 64K long in which to put your program code or data. You choose a segment for this purpose and then, for most purposes, forget it. Choosing a segment in memory carves out a section that you've defined as your work area. Understanding this gives us a handle on the PC's or PS/2's memory.

The segment address can be thought of as the name of a hotel, where, say, a convention is being held. The offset address can be thought of as a room number in that hotel. Putting the two together, an address can be thought of as Hotel:Room. Usually, you spend time at a convention going from room to room, and don't keep choosing hotels. In the same way, a segment should be thought of as a memory workspace up to 64K bytes long.

Segment Registers

To let you set the segment that you want to choose as your work area, the 8088 provides four *segment registers*. You set these segment registers typically at the beginning of a program, or let them be set automatically for you, and then get on with your work. Keep in mind, however, that they only define a 64K area. If you want something outside that area, you'll have to worry about segments again.

The CS, DS, ES, SS registers

The four segment registers are CS, DS, ES, and SS. They stand for this: Code Segment, Data Segment, Extra Segment, and Stack Segment.

Table 2.3 The Segment Registers

Segment Register	Means	Used With
CS	Code Segment	Your program's instructions
DS	Data Segment	The data you want to work on
ES	Extra Segment	Auxilary data segment register
SS	Stack Segment	Set by DOS; holds the "stack"

Let's take them in turn—we'll see them in just about every program from now on.

Code Segment

The code segment is where the instructions for your program will be stored. Instructions will be machine-language instructions, such as the bytes we saw meaning MOV AX,5, and so on. Anything that the 8088 can directly read in and execute will be stored here.

When your program is loaded (by DOS) to run, the code segment is chosen for it by the program loader. You will not have to set this segment register, CS, for the things we are going to do in this book. If, however, a program wants to know where it was placed in memory (i.e., what the segment address of the code is), it can read the value in CS at any time.

Figure 2.3 The Code Segment

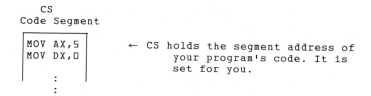

Data Segment

The DS register holds the value of the data segment. Anything that you want to store as data, and not have the computer execute (cell entries in a spreadsheet, for example, or text in a word processor), can be stored here.

The DS register is one that programs often set themselves. When you write a program, you will be able to specify what parts of it will be the data segment, and what parts the code segment. You'll put all your instructions in the code segment. In the data segment part, you'll be able to define your data with special instructions to the assembler, as we'll see. Then, when the program is run, CS will be set to what you have called the code segment part, and DS will be set to what you have called the data segment part (the segments of the program itself might be right next to each other in memory—it depends on how DOS loads the program).

Using DS

Again, we will usually set DS, the data segment register, if ever, at the beginning of the program and then leave it alone. If, however, we want to read bytes from far-away places in memory—to see what's in the screen buffer, or how the keyboard is working, for example—we'll have to set DS before we can address them. Using DS as the high word of our addresses, we can reach and read (or write) any byte in memory.

Let's say that our program is running, with our code in the segment 2000H, and data in the segment at 3000H:

Figure 2.4A Data in Segment 3000H

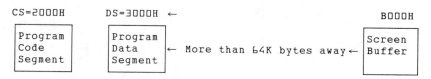

Now let's say that we want to change data in the video buffer (i.e., the letters that appear on the screen), which is at segment B000H for a monochrome monitor. We'd have to change the data segment that we're using, in DS, to B000H:

Figure 2.4B Changing the Data Segments

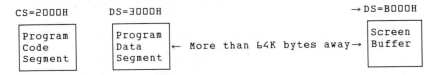

```
CS=2000H        DS=3000H                            → DS=B000H
┌─────────┐     ┌─────────┐                         ┌─────────┐
│Program  │     │Program  │                         │Screen   │
│Code     │     │Data     │ ← More than 64K bytes away→ │Buffer   │
│Segment  │     │Segment  │                         │         │
└─────────┘     └─────────┘                         └─────────┘
```

And then we could reference any data there with our instructions.

Whenever we read from memory using labels like VALUE, or write to it, the 8088 checks the value of DS for the segment part of the address. Instructions that reference memory locations (like the MOV we used earlier) automatically mean that DS will be used as the segment address. Soon we will learn how to name memory locations, and then we will see how this works first-hand. For now, just keep in mind that when we want to specifically read from memory, we'll almost always use DS.

But sometimes we'll use ES.

Extra Segment

The Extra Segment can be used as another data segment. For example, the 8088 has a number of fast string instructions that can move strings of bytes from one location in memory to another extremely quickly. If the location we are sending bytes to is far away, we cannot point to both source and destination with the same segment register, DS. Instead, we can use ES, and will later on, as a second "DS" for that far destination.

The string instructions in the 8088 require that you use ES as well as DS, as we will see when we get to them (but do not worry about ES until then: we'll have no use for it until that time).

Figure 2.5 Using the Extra Segment

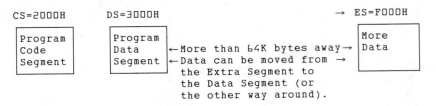

```
CS=2000H        DS=3000H                            → ES=F000H
┌─────────┐     ┌─────────┐                         ┌─────────┐
│Program  │     │Program  │ ←More than 64K bytes away→ │More     │
│Code     │     │Data     │ ←Data can be moved from  → │Data     │
│Segment  │     │Segment  │   the Extra Segment to    │         │
└─────────┘     └─────────┘   the Data Segment (or    └─────────┘
                              the other way around).
```

Stack Segment

The stack is something really internal to the machine, and we will not worry about it right now. It is used in the following way: It is possible, through the "Call" instruction, to execute code far away in memory. When you are done there, you would like to return to the point you were after you "Called" that far routine. DOS stores the address you were at before the "Call" on the stack, an area of memory put aside for this purpose. Since DOS maintains it, we will pay little attention to the stack until later.

Segment Registers in Use: .COM Files

Do not feel that you have to memorize these definitions; the first programs we write will be .COM files, and the default for .COM files is to set all four segment registers to the same value, the Code Segment. We will do this expressly so that we do not have to worry too much about the segment registers just at the time when we are being introduced to our first programs, although we will have to know about them.

Everything that goes on in a .COM file will be limited to one 64K workspace. And when the program is loaded, DOS sets that segment address for us. That means in practice that we will not have to be careful about how the segment registers are set, until we want to do some slightly more fancy things later.

Figure 2.6 One Segment for A .COM File.

```
.COM File (One Segment)
 CS (= DS = ES = SS)
```

```
All the code,
data, and the
stack fit into
one segment in
a .COM file
       :
       :
```

.COM files   A .COM file is the simplest working program you can write on the PC or PS/2 (although the .COM format is no longer supported if you run OS/2), so they provide a good place for us to start. Our first program will be a .COM file. After we write it, we will add data to it, using our knowledge of how memory works.

A .COM file is, quite literally, just machine-language instructions, ready to be executed. In the other format available, .EXE files, there are all kinds of things that have been added on by the linker or macro assembler—a whole header that we will talk about later. We know a little about how memory works, and a little about writing an assembly program. Now we have to pull all that together into the framework of .ASM files that can be made into .COM files.

Our First .ASM Program

Now that we know about segments, we turn to the job of using them with the assembler.

When you write an .ASM file that will be turned into a .COM file, you have to specify where you want the code to be placed in the code segment, what the name of the code segment will be, whether you will have a separate data segment, and similar things. You set up your segments with Pseudo-Ops.

Pseudo-Ops

In addition to our simple assembly-language instructions, we are going to have to add a number of directions for the assembler. This will be a large part of learning to program in assembly language. These directions—read only by the macro assembler—are called Pseudo-Ops. The Pseudo-Ops do not generate any code. What they do is give directions to the assembler (and only that).

You can set up either code or data segments when you are writing a program, and you use Pseudo-Ops to do it. If you are setting up a code segment, your program instructions themselves will go there. If you are setting up a data segment, you are predefining some variables or constants that your program will later use—or you are just setting aside some blank space that the program will use.

The SEGMENT and ENDS Pseudo-Ops

The assembler needs to know which segment is which. That is, it has no way of knowing how the segment registers, CS, DS, and so on, will be set when the program is run. You might have expected that it would take care of all this, but that is not the case. Since you can switch segments with ease just by moving a new value (a 16-bit word) into a segment register, and since the macro assembler has no idea of how exactly your program will run, we have to tell it what the various segment registers will be holding, at all times.

In practice, this means that everything we put into our .ASM files will be enclosed inside a segment definition, giving a name to the segment (since we don't have the segment register's actual value, which will be set only when the program runs). Then we can tell the assembler to assume, for example, that CS will hold the value for what we have named CODE_SEG, and so on. We can add SEGMENT definitions to PRINTA immediately:

```
CODE_SEG        SEGMENT                  ←

MOV     AH,2
MOV     DL,41H
INT     21H
INT     20H

CODE_SEG        ENDS                     ←
```

When we define a segment name, we use the SEGMENT Pseudo-Op. At the end of the segment defition, you must use the ENDS Pseduo-Op, as we have here, to let the assembler know that we are done defining the segment.

The ASSUME Pseudo-Op

Enclosing all our code inside CODE_SEG this way means that we can refer to the value that *will* be in CS easily. We tell the assembler to *assume* that CS will be set to CODE_SEG this way, with the ASSUME Pseudo-Op:

```
CODE_SEG        SEGMENT

        ASSUME  CS:CODE_SEG,DS:CODE_SEG,ES:CODE_SEG      ←
        MOV     AH,2
        MOV     DL,41H
        INT     21H
        INT     20H

CODE_SEG        ENDS
```

Notice here that we used the Pseudo-Op (that is, it is only a direction to the assembler—it generates no machine-language code) ASSUME CS:CODE_SEG,DS:CODE_SEG,ES:CODE_SEG. Here we are telling the assembler that CS, DS, ES, and SS will all be using the same segment, the one we will call CODE_SEG. Since we are building a .COM file, this is exactly right. There is only *one* segment in a .COM file, which is used to store data as well as code. This is why .COM files are so easy—we won't have to worry about the segment registers unduly.

Whenever your program changes the value of a segment register, you should immediately precede it in the program with an ASSUME so the assembler knows the new value of the segment register. We will, of course, have many examples of this.

Labeling

We can label our data byte by byte, or word by word, if we wish to. Similarly, we can label an instruction in our program itself so that we can jump from the current instruction to the labeled one, which may be some distance away, if we wish to.

Because of the way the 8088 was designed, when MOV AH,2 is translated into machine language, it will be three bytes. We can label that instruction START, and the last instruction (INT 20H), EXIT.

```
CODE_SEG          SEGMENT

          ASSUME  CS:CODE_SEG,DS:CODE_SEG,ES:CODE_SEG
START:    MOV     AH,2      ←
MOV       DL,41H
INT       21H
EXIT:     INT     20H       ←

CODE_SEG          ENDS
```

As you can see, a label is just a name followed by a colon. If, during our program, we wanted to leave quickly, we could just go to the label EXIT, and the INT 20H instruction would be executed, causing us to finish and quit. If we did decide to go there, the assembler would have to know the address of the EXIT instruction. It finds this by counting the number of machine-language bytes it has produced from the beginning of the code segment (what we have labeled START).

Labels   The assembler translates all these labels into offsets—that is, 16-bit words holding the distance in bytes of the label from the beginning of the appropriate segment—when it assembles the code. If we are dealing with a data label, the label is translated into the offset from the beginning of what we have called the data segment (the segment address of the data segment will be in DS at run time). If we are dealing with a label we have given to an instruction, the assembler uses the offset from the beginning of the code segment (which will be stored in CS at run time). The offsets of the labels are actually stored in the machine-language program; the labels themselves aren't.

Labels will come in very handy when we write programs: Anything that gets more English into the program can help. Define a label that points to an instruction by putting the label, followed by a colon, before that instruction. Now we can refer to it by name: this will become very useful soon.

> You may make labels as long as you wish. However, only the first 31 characters count—that's all the assembler reads.

Positioning Our Code in the Code Segment

When .EXE files are loaded, they are put right at the very beginning of the code segment they have been given, at CS:0000. Their first instruction can start right there. .COM files, on the other hand, are given a little boost in life by DOS. They are supplied with a header that is loaded in before they are; the header is put at CS:0000, not at the first instruction of the .COM file. This header is 100H—256 decimal—bytes long. The header thus runs from CS:0000 to CS:00FF, and the .COM file, now loaded into memory, starts exactly at CS:0100.

Figure 2.7 File Headers.

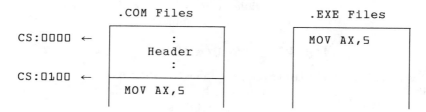

What this means is that we are going to have to start the code at offset 0100H in the code segment. Now we know why we started assembling at 0100H in our DEBUG example (using A100): In a .COM file, machine-language instructions must start at offset 0100H inside the program. If we were writing an .EXE file here, we could have issued an A0000 command.

The ORG Pseudo-Op

Since we are building a .COM file, the code does not begin at CS:0000 (where it does now in our program's definition), but at CS:0100. In DEBUG we were able to start assembling at 100H; we do a similar thing here with the ORG—for Origin—Pseudo-Op:

```
CODE_SEG        SEGMENT

        ASSUME  CS:CODE_SEG,DS:CODE_SEG,ES:CODE_SEG
        ORG     100H        ←
START:  MOV     AH,2
        MOV     DL,41H
        INT     21H
EXIT:   INT     20H

CODE_SEG        ENDS
END     START
```

This tells the assembler that the offset of START (the line right *after* the ORG Pseudo-Op) from the beginning of the code segment is not really zero, but 0100H. ORG will set the offset of the next line of code in an .ASM file. It is a Pseudo-Op, purely for the assembler's use. What happens in practice is that the assembler now treats the instruction MOV AH,2 as though it will be placed at CS:0100, and not at CS:0000 (and everything to follow gets treated as though it were placed after this instruction).

This is indeed where the code will be when the .COM file is loaded, since it will follow the header already there. Again, the reason the assembler needs to know this is because it has to calculate the offsets of all labels in the .ASM file. Telling it that we start at CS:0100 and not CS:0000 is therefore necessary. The reason DEBUG is so much simpler is that we cannot use labels in DEBUG—if we had wanted to refer to data or some instruction while assembling in DEBUG, we would have had to calculate the correct offset address ourselves.

The END Pseudo-Op

The Entry
Point

The last required action is to let the assembler know where we wanted to start the program. It does not know that we are making a .COM file, so it does not know that DOS is supposed to enter at 100H. We could have been making an .EXE file, for example.

Here we will set the location to start the program—called the entry point—with the final Pseudo-Op for this program, called END. Every .ASM file needs to end with END so the assembler knows when to stop. At the same time, you can set the "entry point" by giving its location to END. In our case, we want the entry point, where the program will start, to be at 0100H in the code segment. Looking at our program, we see that we have labeled that instruction already, and called it START. So, our final Pseudo-Op will be the (somewhat oxymoronic) END START—

```
CODE_SEG        SEGMENT

        ASSUME  CS:CODE_SEG,DS:CODE_SEG,ES:CODE_SEG
        ORG     100H
START:  MOV     AH,2
```

```
            MOV     DL,41H
            INT     21H
    EXIT:   INT     20H

    CODE_SEG        ENDS
            END     START
```

The Instruction Pointer

When the .COM file is loaded into memory for the first time, we know that the value chosen by DOS for the code segment will be placed into CS. But there is also a special register that will hold the offset address in the code segment of the instruction about to be executed. This register is called IP, the Instruction Pointer.

When the program is loaded, and CS is set, IP is loaded with 0100H (for a .COM file). The next instruction about to be executed is always at CS:IP; here that will be CS:0100. When .COM files begin, IP is automatically given a value of 0100H. In .EXE files, however, the offset address of the first instruction to execute can be anywhere in the code segment, so IP is loaded from a value stored in the .EXE file's header.

Use this Shell

Our example is now a working .ASM file. In a minute, we will type it in and assemble it.

One important thing to know is that programming is often reusing and modifying your old programs, and we can start that practice right now. When you start a new .ASM file, don't approach it with all the theoretical considerations we have been discussing. Just use the .ASM file we have been developing as a shell—complete with all Pseudo-Ops in place—and replace our assembly language instructions (the MOV and INT parts) with your own program. Use what we have developed as a shell, and it will make programming easier.

Using MASM and LINK

MASM in Action

Here's where we put it all to work. If you have a word processor or editor, use it to type our program into a file that you name PRINTA.ASM. As mentioned, assembly-language source code files—where the assembly-language instructions are kept—end with ".ASM." Use your editor to produce PRINTA.ASM. The assembler is an inflexible software package—spelling errors will count.

We are ready to use the macro assembler. The assembler we will be using is Microsoft's MASM Version 5.1 (the most recent at the time of this writing). Type this command at the A> prompt:

```
A>MASM PRINTA;
```

And the macro assembler will do this:

```
A>MASM PRINTA;
Microsoft (R) Macro Assembler Version 5.10
Copyright (C) Microsoft Corp 1981, 1988.  All rights reserved.

  50144 + 31277 Bytes symbol space free

      0 Warning Errors
      0 Severe  Errors
```

> If you are having difficulty getting PRINTA to assemble properly, go back into your editor and check the version in the book. Even one mispelling can sometimes make the difference.

If everything goes correctly, MASM will produce the raw assembled code in a file called PRINTA.OBJ. Check your directory to make sure that you see PRINTA.OBJ.

LINK in Action

This is not yet a .COM file. The next step is stripping off some information left by MASM in the .OBJ file by the linker, LINK. This is a step we will always have to go through. Although what LINK is really useful for is combining .OBJ files into big executable files, even single .OBJ files have to go through LINK on their way to becoming .COM files. We'll take full advantage of the linker's abilty to do this later.

The LINK no-stack warning

The linker checks all segments, among other things. Since this is going to be a .COM file, there is only one segment. In particular, it is our CODE_SEG. Programs that are not .COM files need all segments to be explicitly spelled out—and LINK is going to give us a warning here that we have no STACK segment.

This is fine—it is exactly the normal warning you receive when you are producing .COM files. Still, LINK tells you this as a warning; but you'd think that after all these years of producing .COM files this customary message would be something a little less threatening. Here's how to use LINK:

▌   LINK is provided with the macro assembler, on the same disk.   ▌

```
A>LINK PRINTA;
```

And the linking program comes back with this:

```
A>LINK PRINTA;
Microsoft (R) Overlay Linker  Version 3.64
Copyright (C) Microsoft Corp 1983-1988.  All rights reserved.

LINK : warning L4021: no stack segment
```

The warning is there, and we are now almost ready: LINK has taken the .OBJ file named PRINTA.OBJ and produced an .EXE file, PRINTA.EXE. However, we did not set this up as an .EXE file (that will take some doing, and is the subject of a later chapter). We set our program up to be a .COM file. For the final step, stripping off the header that LINK left in the .EXE file, we run a program called EXE2BIN.

EXE2BIN in Action

This is the last program that we need to run, and it converts the linker .EXE output to .COM format:

```
EXE2BIN PRINTA PRINTA.COM
```

▌   EXE2BIN doesn't type anything on the screen, as LINK or MASM ▌
    do.

And finally, our .COM file is there, ready to go. Try running it to confirm that it prints out the "A." The size of PRINTA.COM on disk is only a puny 8 bytes, shorter even than the version we made with DEBUG, because we switched from using the full registers to using the high and low registers. This saved one byte in each of the two MOV instructions (MOV AX,0200H became MOV AH,02 and MOV DX,0041H became MOV DL,41H).

Give PRINTA a try—you will see that it prints out "A," just as our DEBUG version did. Now we've got a working .ASM file:

```
CODE_SEG        SEGMENT

        ASSUME  CS:CODE_SEG,DS:CODE_SEG,ES:CODE_SEG
        ORG     100H
START:  MOV     AH,2
```

```
          MOV      DL,41H
          INT      21H
EXIT:     INT      20H

CODE_SEG           ENDS
          END      START
```

On the other hand, this is really only half the story. As it stands, PRINT.ASM is a fine, working program, but it is not a very representative .COM file. In almost all .COM files, some data will be stored.

Storing Data

What do we mean by data? Every variable used in a program is data, like the variable VALUE, which we might set to 5. We might want to read in a file from the disk and store it in the data area, treating it as data. Or we might have program messages like "Serious Error: Please Get An Adult." in the data area, ready to be typed out when needed. Everything that our program uses that is not code is data.

Let's look at an example. Here we will show how you can use variables in assembly language, just like higher level languages. We will use the DB, or Define Byte Pseudo-Op.

The DB Pseudo-Op

We know all about the instruction

```
MOV     AX,5
```

This will move the value 5 into the AX register (in BASIC this is equivalent to the statement AX = 5). On the other hand, we can give a name, say, VALUE, to a byte in the data segment. If we had stored 5 in VALUE, then we could load it into AX like this:

```
MOV     AX,VALUE
```

Introducing DB

The way that we define bytes like VALUE in the data segment is with special instructions in the part of your program that you have set aside as the data segment. To define a byte named VALUE, use DB, or Define Byte, in a data segment definition like this:

```
VALUE DB 5
```

If they were separate, the code and data segments might look something like Figure 2.8

Figure 2.8 Separate Code and Data Seqments

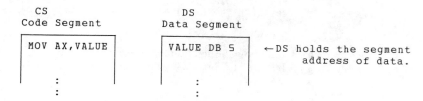

```
CS                          DS
Code Segment                Data Segment

MOV AX,VALUE                VALUE DB 5       ←DS holds the segment
                                               address of data.
       :                          :
       :                          :
```

Now we are free to store data in VALUE as well:

```
MOV VALUE,AX
```

This is how to use memory in the PC or PS/2: Set up storage for it in the part of your program that you will label the data segment (or the common segment in a .COM file), and give names of variables to all the bytes you set aside (with DB or, as we will see, similar Pseudo-Ops). Then, you can use these names just like variables in a higher level language.

Adding Data to PRINTA.ASM

Let's say that we want to put this to work and add some data to PRINTA.ASM. About the only data we have is the character we're going to print out, "A," so let's store that in memory:

```
CODE_SEG        SEGMENT

        ASSUME  CS:CODE_SEG,DS:CODE_SEG,ES:CODE_SEG
        ORG     100H
        Our_Character   DB "A"   ←
START:  MOV     AH,2
        MOV     DL,41H
        INT     21H
EXIT:   INT     20H

CODE_SEG        ENDS
        END     START
```

DB tells the assembler that the data that follows is to be put in just as bytes, and not interpreted: It is data. We have set aside a location, one byte, that we've called Our_Character, and initialized it by putting the character "A" in it. The assembler will translate the "A" for us into the ASCII code that the machine needs: 41H. (We could have alternatively said "Our_Character DB 41H"—it is the same thing exactly to the assembler.) Here are some DB examples:

```
Flag    DB 0
  Char_Z DB ""Z''
  Numbers DB 1,2,3,4,5,0   ← 6 bytes are put aside.
  Prompt  DB "How long has it been since you called "
          DB "your mother?"
```

> Notice how the definition of Prompt takes two lines, and how there is a DB for each line. We will cover strings like this later in this same chapter.

When we refer to the names Flag, Char_Z, Numbers, or Prompt, we are actually referring to the first byte in what follows DB. For example, if we were now to say:

```
MOV     AH,Numbers
```

the 1, that is, the first number after DB, would be loaded into AH. We will see how we can get the other numbers later, when we talk about arrays or indexed addressing.

In PRINTA.ASM, here is how we load our character into DL, just before printing it out:

```
CODE_SEG        SEGMENT
        ASSUME  CS:CODE_SEG,DS:CODE_SEG,ES:CODE_SEG
        ORG     100H
        Our_Character   DB "A"
START:  MOV     AH,2
        MOV     DL,Our_Character  ←
        INT     21H
EXIT:   INT     20H

CODE_SEG        ENDS
        END     START
```

That is how we define and use variables in assembly language. We've been able to label and use a memory location now.

On the other hand, we've left ourselves with a problem. The label START is supposed to be at 100H in the code segment, and now that we've added one byte of memory space just before it, it will be at the wrong location (specifically, 101H). To solve this problem, we do the thing that .COM files that use data do, even though it is inelegant. We set aside a data area at the beginning of the program, and add a *jump* command, so that when things start up at 100H, the first thing the microprocessor will do is jump *over* the data area and to the first instruction. It looks like this:

```
CODE_SEG          SEGMENT

        ASSUME    CS:CODE_SEG,DS:CODE_SEG,ES:CODE_SEG
        ORG       100H
START:  JMP       PRINTA    ←
        Our_Character   DB "A"
PRINTA: MOV       AH,2
        MOV       DL,Our_Character
        INT       21H
        EXIT:     INT       20H

CODE_SEG          ENDS
        END       START
```

Do you see what's happening? We've moved the label START to point to an instruction that is indeed at 100H, but that command says "JMP PRINTA," which means the microprocessor will jump to the label PRINTA and then continue. We've safely jumped over the data.

The JMP command

JMP is a new assembly-language command for us. It is like a GOTO in BASIC. All that happens is that the computer jumps to wherever you tell it, and starts executing there.

> Later we will see "conditional" jumps. They are the assembly-language version of IF . . . THEN . . . ELSE statements. There are many different types of conditional jumps in assembly language, JZ means Jump if Zero, JNZ means Jump if NOT Zero, JCXZ means Jump if CX is Zero, and so on.

To use JMP, just provide it with a label to jump to, as we have done here (JMP PRINTA). That's all there is to it.

The .COM File Shell with Data

In general, this is how a .COM file shell looks:

```
CODE_SEG          SEGMENT

        ASSUME    CS:CODE_SEG,DS:CODE_SEG,ES:CODE_SEG
        ORG       100H
START:  JMP       PROG
_____
                  :
        This the data area. Use DB here.
_____
PROG:             :
```

```
                    And this is where the program goes.
                    ────────────────────────────────────
        EXIT:    INT    20H

        CODE_SEG        ENDS
                 END    START
```

There is an area set aside for data (using DB) and a part for the program (use this shell for your own programs). Now we've updated PRINTA.ASM to include data, and a data area.

Strings in Memory

We still have not resolved how to store character strings in memory or, for that matter, how to store whole 16-bit words (DB only stores byte by byte). A character string, as in Pascal or BASIC, is just a number of letters, one after the other, that makes sense to us but not to the computer. We want to keep them together: The computer only sees a number of bytes with no apparent relation.

Strings in assembly language are just stored as bytes, one after the other. Each ASCII value for any character the PC or PS/2 is capable of printing out has a one-byte ASCII value associated with it. As we saw, 41H is the ASCII value for "A." Strings are stored like PROMPT before:

```
Prompt   DB "How long has it been since you called"
         DB "your mother?"
```

In our final .COM file, this would appear as a number of bytes in the data area, one for each letter. The assembler lets you store strings this way—using the quotation marks as shorthand (otherwise, you'd have to use DB for each letter).

INT 21H Service 9—Print a String

The string printing service, service 9, of INT 21H prints out strings. Since there is no strong "typing" as in Pascal, service 9 has no way of knowing when it has come to the end of the string it was supposed to print out. To terminate the string for this service, a "$" is added as the last character. This is a message to service 9 to stop printing. Here's how it would look if we changed our program to PRINTAAA:

```
CODE_SEG          SEGMENT

        ASSUME  CS:CODE_SEG,DS:CODE_SEG,ES:CODE_SEG
        ORG     100H
START:  JMP     PRINTA
        Our_Characters  DB 'AAA$'  ←
PRINTA: MOV     AH,2
        MOV     DL,Our_Character
        INT     21H
EXIT:   INT     20H

CODE_SEG          ENDS
        END     START
```

Notice the "$" character as the last byte in the string. Now we have to tell service 9 where to find the string it should print, and change the call from service 2 to service 9. It turns out that what service 9 requires is the address at which the string to print begins in memory, and it requires this address to be in DS:DX. If the address is 0EF1:0105, for example, we'd have to load 0EF1H into DS, and 0105H into DX.

Since we are dealing with a .COM file here, the value of DS never changes (to make it change, our program would MOV a new value into it, which it doesn't do), so DS is all set for service 9: When the program runs, DS will be pointing at the data segment—which is the ONLY segment. To get the offset address of Our_Characters, we use what is called the *OFFSET* Pseudo-Op like this:

```
CODE_SEG          SEGMENT

        ASSUME  CS:CODE_SEG,DS:CODE_SEG,ES:CODE_SEG
        ORG     100H
START:  JMP     PRINTA
        Our_Characters  DB 'AAA$'
PRINTA: MOV     AH,9
        MOV     DX, OFFSET Our_Characters           ←
        INT     21H
EXIT:   INT     20H

CODE_SEG          ENDS
        END     START
```

The OFFSET Pseudo-Op

The OFFSET Pseudo-Op gives you something's offset value from the beginning of the data segment. For example, our line:

```
MOV     DX, OFFSET Our_Characters
```

will load the offset of Our_Characters into DX. OFFSET is a handy Pseudo-Op that we'll use often, since many interrupt services require that we pass them the address of data (such as the address of the string of data to print here).

That's all there is to it; we now have a new working .ASM file that prints out "AAA" instead of just "A." We've improved on our program's data storage even more.

Using Comments

The final thing in this chapter is the use of comments. Comments can be added in assembly language by preceding them with a semicolon, ";", like this for PRINTAAA:

> Comments play an important role in debugging. If you can, be liberal with comments; it always seems to help, especially if anyone else is going to read your programs.

```
CODE_SEG        SEGMENT             ;This will be the code segment.

        ASSUME  CS:CODE_SEG,DS:CODE_SEG,ES:CODE_SEG
        ORG     100H                ;Set up for a .COM file.
START:  JMP     PRINTA              ;JMP over data area.
        Our_Characters  DB "AAA$"        ;We will print out this string.
PRINTA: MOV     AH,9                ;Request INT 21H service 9.
        MOV     DX, OFFSET Our_Characters    ;Point to our string.
        INT     21H                 ;And print it out here.
EXIT:   INT     20H                 ;End the program.

CODE_SEG        ENDS                ;End the code segment.
        END     START               ;Set entry point to label START.
```

Just by reading down the side of the program, you can see what was intended by each line. Even though you don't think you'll need them, it's very wise to include comments in your programs (see, for example, the sample programs in the end of this book, which would be all but incomprehensible without comments).

3

Getting Some Keyboard Input

Adding Input to Our Output

After our work in the previous chapter, we've become familiar with the form used in .COM files, and how to use software interrupts.

This opens new vistas for us: We can explore the available interrupts without having to develop much more in the way of programming skills. With the .COM file shell, we've put ourselves at the threshold of unlocking the system secrets of the PS/2 and PC.

In this chapter, we'll examine the services and interrupts most commonly used to read what's been typed—how to accept typed input, how to accept input into a buffer in memory, and so on.

Here we will begin to flesh out our picture of what DOS and BIOS have to offer us. In the following chapters, we'll become familiar with the major groups of services that the system—DOS and BIOS—provides for our use. Those groups revolve around the major tasks that the PS/2 or PC can undertake: working with files, doing graphics, unravelling the screen's complexities and others.

Accepting Input with INT 21H Service 1

The most basic of the DOS services is service number 1, which waits for keyboard input. This is the primary input service. You request service 1 from INT 21H by filling AH with 1, and executing an INT 21H instruction. When a key is typed, it is returned in the AL register or, rather, its ASCII code is returned in the AL register:

DOS Service	Name	Set These	What Happens
1	Input	AH = 1	AL returns the struck key's ASCII code

Let's develop an example that uses service 1 so that we see it in action.

The Program CAP.COM

This small example program will accept a letter that you type, capitalize it, and type it back. For the first time, we will get our assembly-language program to accept input. Let's start with the .COM file shell:

```
CODE_SEG        SEGMENT
        ASSUME  CS:CODE_SEG,DS:CODE_SEG,ES:CODE_SEG,SS:CODE_SEG

        ORG 100H
START:  JMP CAP
        ;Data Area
CAP:
        ;Program will go here.

EXIT:   INT     20H

CODE_SEG        ENDS
        END START
```

And add the instructions that will let us accept input:

```
CODE_SEG        SEGMENT

        ORG 100H
START:  JMP CAP
        ;Data Area
CAP:    MOV     AH,1    ;Request keyboard input  ←
        INT     21H     ;From INT 21H            ←

EXIT:   INT     20H

CODE_SEG        ENDS
        END START
```

What is returned after the INT 21H instruction is the ASCII code of the typed character, in AL. We mentioned that there is an ASCII code assigned to each of the characters that the PS/2 or PC is capable of printing. This code is given to the various typing or printing services to make the character appear. When we get the ASCII code of the type key, our job is to capitalize the letter and type it back.

There is an easy way to capitalize such a letter. You will find tables of all the printable characters in a number of IBM or Microsoft manuals—for example, in the back of the BASIC manual. If you examine one of these tables, you will find that the ASCII codes for the small letters, (e.g. "a") have higher values than the ASCII codes for the capital letters (e.g., "A"). The ASCII codes for "A" to "Z" run from 65 to 90; for "a" to "z" from 97 to 122. Also, they are all in a row: After A comes B and C and so forth; after a comes b and c and so on.

Table 3.1 ASCII Codes for Small and Capital Letters

Capital letters	Code	Small letters	Code
A	65	a	97
B	66	b	98
C	67	c	99
D	68	d	100
E	69	e	101
F	70	f	102
. . .		. . . .	
W	87	w	119
X	88	x	120
Y	89	y	121
Z	90	z	122

To capitalize a letter, then, we just have to *subtract* a certain number from its ASCII code to move the code from its place in the a . . . z part of the table to its corresponding place in the A . . . Z part.

Table 3.2. Capitalizing

Capital letters	Code	Small letters	Code
A	65←subtract 32—a		97
B	66←subtract 32—b		98
C	67←subtract 32—c		99
D	68	d	100
E	69	e	101
F	70	f	102
. . .		. . .	
W	87	w	119
X	88	x	120
Y	89	y	121
Z	90	z	122

The number we have to subtract is just equal to ASCII("a") — ASCII("A"), which is $97 - 65 = 32$. This is the distance between the two parts of the table. Here's how we capitalize the ASCII value in AL, introducing the new 8088 instruction, SUB, for subtract:

```
CODE_SEG       SEGMENT
       ASSUME  CS:CODE_SEG,DS:CODE_SEG,ES:CODE_SEG,SS:CODE_SEG

       ORG 100H
START: JMP CAP
       ;Data Area
CAP:   MOV    AH,1    ;Request keyboard input
INT    21H     ;From INT 21H
→      SUB    AL,"a"-"A"      ;Capitalize the typed key


EXIT:  INT    20H

CODE_SEG       ENDS
       END START
```

The SUB Instruction

SUB subtracts this way:

```
→      SUB    AL,5
```

Here, 5 is subtracted from the contents of AL; AL is changed. Similarly, you could say:

```
SUB    AX,DX
```

which subtracts DX from AX. AX is changed, DX is not. Besides the SUB, (subtraction) instruction, there is ADD, the built-in add instruction. We will use ADD and SUB in more depth later in Chapter 9, Fast Math.

Since the assembler lets us use expressions like "a" or "A," we can actually use a line like this:

```
SUB    AL,"a"-"A"
```

which makes what we are doing much clearer than if we simply said:

```
SUB    AL,32
```

Using +
and − with
MASM

This is a standard programmer's trick: If you see the expression "a" − "A" in any assembly language program, you can be sure that this is what is happening. Similarly, expressions like "a" + "A" are allowed.

Since the assembler understands + and − like this, it's often a good idea to use them to make your code clearer. For example, let's say that you want to read data from a file in 1K chunks, and that each chunk is prefaced by a header of 256 bytes. When you get ready to read, a line like this:

```
MOV    DX, 256 + 1024
```

can make it a lot clearer that you are going to be interested in using a header and one data chunk than a line like:

```
MOV    DX,1280
```

The Pseudo-Ops + and − are referred to as assembler operators; we'll see more of these operators in future chapters.

Printing Out Our Capital Letter

Now, all that is left to us is to type the newly capitalized letter on the screen. We can do that simply with service 2, as we've already seen. Service 2, which types a character, expects to find the ASCII code of the character it's supposed to type in DL. So we have to move the ASCII code from AL to DL with MOV DL,AL first:

```
CODE_SEG           SEGMENT
        ASSUME  CS:CODE_SEG,DS:CODE_SEG,ES:CODE_SEG,SS:CODE_SEG

        ORG 100H
START:  JMP CAP

        ;Data Area
CAP:    MOV    AH,1     ;Request keyboard input
INT     21H      ;From INT 21H
SUB     AL,"a"-"A"  ;Capitalize the typed key
MOV     DL,AL    ;Set up for service 2.    ←

EXIT:   INT     20H

CODE_SEG           ENDS
        END START
```

And then we are free to use INT 21H service 2:

```
CODE_SEG           SEGMENT
        ASSUME  CS:CODE_SEG,DS:CODE_SEG,ES:CODE_SEG,SS:CODE_SEG

        ORG 100H
START:  JMP CAP
        ;Data Area
CAP:    MOV    AH,1        ;Request keyboard input
        INT    21H         ;From INT 21H
        SUB    AL,"a"-"A"          ;Capitalize the typed key
```

```
            MOV     DL,AL     ;Set up for service 2.
            MOV     AH,2      ;Request character output ←
            INT     21H       ;Type out character.      ←
   EXIT:    INT     20H

   CODE_SEG         ENDS
            END START
```

CAP.ASM is complete. We read in a typed key with INT 21H service 1, capitalize it ourselves, and then type it out with INT 21H service 2. Type it in, assemble and produce CAP.COM, and run it (putting yourself in lowercase on the PC first).

> To make CAP.COM, type the assembly-language program into a file you name CAP.ASM, then do this: MASM CAP;<cr>LINK CAP<cr>EXE2BIN CAP CAP.COM<cr>.

Here is what we see:

```
A>cap
```

And the program just sits there, waiting for your key. As soon as you strike a key, say "s," it echoes your typed "s" and prints out a capital "S" as well before exiting:

```
A>cap
sS
A>
```

Character Echoing

The first "s" is generated by service 1 of INT 21H: It echoes what you type on the screen. The second "S" in our output was put there by our program, after it capitalized "s." CAP.COM is a success.

INT 21H Keyboard Input Services 6, 7, and 8

Not all character input services echo the typed character; there is more than one way of reading a single character. Besides INT 21H service 1, there are also services 6, 7, and 8. They all return the key that was struck in AL. Of them, only service 1 echoes the typed character on the screen. Some of them will quit when a Control-Break is typed, some will not. Service 6 will not wait until a key is struck.

Here is a list of just how DOS single-character input services work:

Table 3.3 The INT 21H Single-Character Input Services

INT 21H Service	Will Wait	^Break Seen	Will Echo
1	X	X	X
6			
7	X		
8	X	X	

If we had wanted to rewrite CAP so that the "s" wasn't echoed on the screen, we could have used service 8, for example, instead of service 1:

```
CODE_SEG        SEGMENT
        ASSUME  CS:CODE_SEG,DS:CODE_SEG,ES:CODE_SEG,SS:CODE_SEG

        ORG 100H
START:  JMP CAP
        ;Data Area
CAP:    MOV     AH,8       ;Request keyboard input ←
        INT     21H        ;From INT 21H
        CMP     AL,"a";Compare the incoming ASCII code to "a".
        JB      EXIT    ;If the letter is not lower case, exit.
        CMP     AL,"z";Compare the incoming ASCII code to "z".
        JA      EXIT    ;If the letter is not lower case, exit.
        SUB     AL,"a"-"A"     ;Capitalize the typed key
        MOV     DL,AL   ;Set up for service 2.
        MOV     AH,2    ;Request character output
        INT     21H        ;Type out character.
EXIT:   INT     20H

CODE_SEG        ENDS
        END START
```

The new CAP.COM will wait silently for your typed-in key, capitalize it, and print only that on the screen:

```
A>cap
S
A>
```

Although it is gratifying to get the result we expected, there are any number of problems with this program. Perhaps the most serious one is: What happens if you type in a character other than a lowercase letter? Try it with any character—you'll get funny results. Odd characters will be printed, not what you might expect at all.

This problem may be forestalled if we check the incoming ASCII code to make sure that it really is a lowercase letter. In other words, we have to check to make sure that the ASCII code is between the values of "a" and "z." And this type of checking brings us to a topic we could not go on without—conditional jumps.

Conditional Jumps

What we want to do, to keep CAP.ASM working, is to check that the incoming ASCII code is between "a" and "z." If it is not, let's exit without explanation (hardly a user-friendly program).

This should be divided into two steps. The ASCII code will come back from service 1 in AL. The first step is to check: Is AL greater than or equal to "a"? If not, we will exit. Then we check: Is AL less than or equal to "z"? If not, we exit again. If both tests pass, we capitalize the letter, type it, and exit.

Figure 3.1 Capitalizing Flowchart

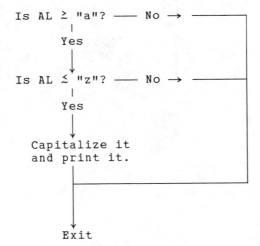

```
Is AL ≥ "a"? ——— No →
              |
             Yes
              |
              ↓
Is AL ≤ "z"? ——— No →
              |
             Yes
              |
              ↓
       Capitalize it
       and print it.



              ↓
            Exit
```

The CMP Instruction

Checking a value like this against some known comparison value is done with the assembly-language instruction Compare, CMP. To check the results of the comparison, we use a *conditional jump* immediately after the CMP instruction. Here, our code to check that AL is above or equal to "a" is the following (JB means "jump if below"):

```
CODE_SEG          SEGMENT
          ASSUME  CS:CODE_SEG,DS:CODE_SEG,ES:CODE_SEG,SS:CODE_SEG

ORG 100H
START:   JMP CAP
         ;Data Area
CAP:     MOV     AH,1      ;Request keyboard input
         INT     21H       ;From INT 21H
→        CMP     AL,"a"    ;Compare the incoming ASCII code to "a".
→        JB      EXIT      ;If the letter is not lower case, exit.

         SUB     AL,"a"-"A"    ;Capitalize the typed key
         MOV     DL,AL     ;Set up for service 2.
         MOV     AH,2      ;Request character output
         INT     21H       ;Type out character.
EXIT:    INT     20H

CODE_SEG          ENDS
          END START
```

What's happened is that we compared DL to the ASCII value for "a":

```
CMP     AL,"a"  ;Compare the incoming ASCII code to "a".
```

And then immediately followed this with a JB—Jump if Below—instruction:

```
CMP     AL,"a"  ;Compare the incoming ASCII code to "a".
JB      EXIT      ;If the letter is not lower case, exit.
```

If the comparison showed that the AL (the first item in the CMP instruction) was below "a" in numerical value, we will jump, with JB (jump if below) to the exit (the line labeled EXIT) and leave without capitalizing the ASCII code.

Now we know that the ASCII code in AL is above or equal to the ASCII code for "a." On the other hand, we must check to see that the ASCII code is below or equal to "z." This is done with an instruction whose name you could probably guess: JA, or Jump if Above.

```
CODE_SEG          SEGMENT
          ASSUME  CS:CODE_SEG,DS:CODE_SEG,ES:CODE_SEG,SS:CODE_SEG

ORG 100H
START:   JMP CAP
         ;Data Area
CAP:     MOV     AH,1      ;Request keyboard input
         INT     21H       ;From INT 21H
         CMP     AL,"a";Compare the incoming ASCII code to "a".
         JB      EXIT      ;If the letter is not lower case, exit.
→        CMP     AL,"z"    ;Compare the incoming ASCII code to "z".
→        JA      EXIT      ;If the letter is not lower case, exit.
         SUB     AL,"a"-"A"    ;Capitalize the typed key
         MOV     DL,AL     ;Set up for service 2.
```

```
              MOV    AH,2      ;Request character output
              INT    21H       ;Type out character.
      EXIT:   INT    20H

      CODE_SEG        ENDS
              END START
```

That completes the program CAP.ASM. It will check to make sure that what is typed is a small letter before capitalizing it.

Give the new, error-checking CAP.ASM a try. Many other things could be added to this program, of course, such as a prompt asking you for a character to capitalize, or an explanation for why we are exiting without capitalizing an illegal ASCII value, but the point is made. We can accept input with our programs, and work with that input.

In developing CAP, we've come across a new type of instruction, called conditional jumps. With conditional jumps, we can check on certain conditions before continuing—and, depending on what we find, we can jump to some label somewhere else in the program if we want to.

More Conditional Jumps

So far, we have seen the two new instructions, JA and JB. These follow a CMP—Compare—instruction and, depending on the result, the jump is made or not. There are many conditional jumps. In fact, there are even variations of JA and JB. In addition to these two, there are JNA (Jump if Not Above) JNB (Jump if Not Below), JNAE (Jump if Not Above or Equal) and JNBE (Jump if Not Below or Equal). All of these are used after a CMP instruction.

Probably the two most common conditional jumps are JE, Jump if Equal, and JNE, Jump if Not Equal. We will be using these soon. Two more conditional jumps are JZ (Jump if Zero) and JNZ (Jump if Not Zero).

Flags   A conditional jump works in two stages. First, the 8088's *flags* are set by the CMP instruction. Flags are new to us, although we saw them briefly in the last chapter. What's important about flags for us is that each conditional jump reads and acts on particular flags. For example, JZ, Jump if Zero, checks the zero flag. This is the second stage of a conditional jump—the jump itself. The JA instruction uses a number of the internal flags to decide what to do after a comparison has been made:

```
      CMP    AX,5    ←  Sets Flags
      JA     OVER    ←  Reads Flags
```

Here are a number of conditional jumps:

Table 3.4 Conditional Jumps

Conditional Jump	Means
JA	Jump if Above
JB	Jump if Below
JAE	Jump if Above or Equal
JBE	Jump if Below or Equal
JNA	Jump if Not Above
JNB	Jump if Not Below
JNAE	Jump if Not Above or Equal
JNBE	Jump if Not Below or Equal
JE	Jump if Equal
JNE	Jump if Not Equal
JZ	Jump if result was Zero
JNZ	Jump if result was Not Zero

These conditional jumps will pepper our programs from now on.

The FINDx Program

We see how to accept single-character input with INT 21H service 1, but there is a way to accept many typed characters at once. This is called *buffered input*.

Buffered Input

Buffers in memory

Buffered input is offered by INT 21H service 0AH. A *buffer* is just a number of bytes set aside in memory and referred to by name as a single group. To create such a buffer, we will set aside some bytes with DB, the Define Byte Pseudo-Op.

Our sample program here has the following task: If we type in up to nine characters, our program, called FINDx, must tell us the location of the character "x" in what we've typed. To actually find "x," we're going to use the 8088's string instructions, and so introduce ourselves to them.

We start off with our .COM file shell, naming our program FINDx:

```
CODE_SEG        SEGMENT
        ASSUME  CS:CODE_SEG,DS:CODE_SEG,ES:CODE_SEG,SS:CODE_SEG

        ORG 100H
START:  JMP FINDX            ←
        ;Data Area
```

```
FINDX:                    ←
        ;Program will go here.

EXIT:   INT    20H

CODE_SEG        ENDS
        END START
```

INT 21H service 0AH takes as input a number of items. As usual, we set AH to select the service we want (0AH). Then we must load DS:DX with the address of a buffer that we have prepared for this service.

Table 3.5 INT 21H Service 0AH

DOS Service	Name	Set These	What Happens
0AH	Buffered Input	AH = 0AH DS:DX = address of buffer	Buffer gets filled.

The preparation of our buffer must go like this: Besides setting aside the bytes with DB, we must set the first byte of our buffer to the number of bytes we can accept for service 0AH (how many typed characters we can read as a maximum):

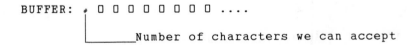

```
BUFFER:  0 0 0 0 0 0 0 0 ....
         |
         |_____Number of characters we can accept
```

Since we do not want to tangle with conversions from hex to decimal, let's restrict ourselves to just nine characters in FINDx. The position of "x" in these nine can easily be typed out with a single digit. Therefore, we will set this first byte to 9. If the user of this program types more than nine bytes, the PS/2 or PC will beep, and refuse to accept anything but a carriage return. DOS itself often uses this service when accepting input; the beep you hear is from this service.

In the second byte of the buffer, service 0AH will return the number of characters actually typed; the typed characters will be returned starting in the third byte. This means that we have to set aside 11 bytes—the first one tells service 0AH how many typed keys we are willing to accept, the second byte is where the service will tell us how many actually were typed, and finally comes the nine-byte buffer itself.

```
                ←   9 Bytes   →
BUFFER:  9  #  0 0 0 0 0 0 0 0 0
            |_____Service 0AH will return the # of characters
            |_____Number of characters we can accept
```

DB allows us to initalize the bytes, and we can take advantage of this fact to set the first byte to 9 immediately in FINDx.ASM:

```
CODE_SEG        SEGMENT
        ASSUME  CS:CODE_SEG,DS:CODE_SEG,ES:CODE_SEG,SS:CODE_SEG

        ORG 100H
START:  JMP FINDX
        THE_BUFFER      DB 9, 10 DUP(0)  ←
FINDX:
        ;Program will go here.

EXIT:   INT     20H

CODE_SEG        ENDS
        END START
```

The DUP Pseudo-Op

The remaining nine bytes have been set to zero with the "DUP" Pseudo-Op. DUP stands for duplicate (assembly language never spells anything out), and the line:

```
THE_BUFFER      DB 9, 10 DUP(0)
```

will be understood by the assembler as:

```
THE_BUFFER      DB 9, 0, 0, 0, 0, 0, 0, 0, 0, 0, 0  ← 10 zeroes.
```

DUP comes in *very* handy when you are setting aside large amounts of space—such as space to read files into, as we will do in the following chapter.

Now we add the request for service 0AH to the program:

```
CODE_SEG        SEGMENT
        ASSUME  CS:CODE_SEG,DS:CODE_SEG,ES:CODE_SEG,SS:CODE_SEG

        ORG 100H
START:  JMP FINDX
        THE_BUFFER      DB 9, 10 DUP(0)
FINDX:  MOV     AH,0AH                  ←
        MOV     DX,OFFSET THE_BUFFER    ←
        INT     21H                     ←

EXIT:   INT     20H

CODE_SEG        ENDS
        END START
```

Note again the use of the OFFSET Pseudo-Op. We have to put the address of the buffer into DS:DX. Since we will never change DS, it is all set. MOV DX,OFFSET THE_BUFFER lets us do the rest.

So far, we are ready to accept input, in buffered form. When the program is run, it will wait for you to type characters. When you finish and type a carriage return, it will fill the buffer.

> The program we are developing, FINDx, can already be run, although you will see nothing happen. If you debug FINDx with DEBUG, you can actually examine memory, however, and you will see the bytes typed were put into the buffer directly.

Now that our data is in our buffer, we have to initiate the search part of the program—that part where FINDx finds "x." To do this, we will use the microprocessor's string instructions. These instructions are important, and we'll have to spend a little time on them before we will be able to use them in FINDx.

The String Instructions

What a programmer wants to regard as a string of bytes in memory is just unconnected bytes to the microprocessor. Originally, working with such strings was a weak point in assembly language with the Intel chips, until the string instructions were added. These instructions are as follows:

SCASB   Scan Byte String at ES:DI for byte in AL
CMPSB   Compare Byte String at ES:DI to one at DS:SI
MOVSB   Move Byte String byte by byte from DS:SI to ES:DI
STOSB   Store Byte in AL to string at ES:DI

> Starting with the 80286, two more string instructions were added, INS and OUTS, input string from a port, and output string to a port. A port is how I/O devices are connected to the PS/2 or PC: port 60H is where data comes in from the keyboard, for example.

The one we will use for FINDx is SCASB, scan byte string. This instruction will scan a string in memory for an element that you specify.

Each of the string instructions listed above has two forms. Like all the rest, SCASB can be used as either SCASB or SCASW. Simply by adding the final letter—B for byte or W for word—you can let the string instructions know what type of string is meant:

SCASW   Scan Word String at ES:DI for word in AX
CMPSW   Compare Word String at ES:DI to one at DS:SI
MOVSW   Move Word String word by word from DS:SI to ES:DI
STOSW   Store Word in AX to string at ES:DI

> In this book, we are going to work exclusively with byte, not word, strings.

In FINDx, we want to find only "x," one ASCII byte, so we will use SCASB, Scan String Byte. SCASB will scan the string (THE_BUFFER) for a match to the byte that is in AL. For that reason, we will put "x" into AL to get ready for the scan:

```
CODE_SEG          SEGMENT
          ASSUME  CS:CODE_SEG,DS:CODE_SEG,ES:CODE_SEG,SS:CODE_SEG

          ORG 100H
START:    JMP FINDX
          THE_BUFFER      DB 9, 10 DUP(0)
FINDX:    MOV     AH,0AH
          MOV     DX,OFFSET THE_BUFFER
          INT     21H
          MOV     AL,"x"                        ←

EXIT:     INT     20H

CODE_SEG          ENDS
          END START
```

The question is now: How does SCASB know what string we will be searching? The answer comes from the use of a new pair of registers.

The DI and SI Registers

The SCASB instruction *assumes* that the address of the string to be scanned is already loaded into a new register, DI. To be exact, the address of the string that SCASB will work with must be stored in ES:DI.

> In the 80386, string instructions can be used with *double words*; the instruction there for SCAS can be SCASD.

DI is one of the two registers specially put aside for string operations. String manipulation is so important that both these registers are primarily meant to be used for them. The other register is SI—DI stands for Destination Index, and SI stands for Source Index. The use of these registers will become clear in examining the workings of MOVSB, move string byte.

The MOVSB Instruction

Every time you execute the instruction MOVSB, one byte is taken from the location DS:SI and copied to ES:DI. DS:SI is the *source* address, and ES:DI is the *destination* address. Also, like all string instructions, MOVSB automatically increments the registers it uses, SI and DI:

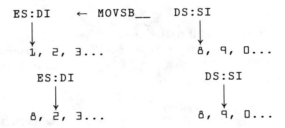

> SI and DI can automatically be set to *decrement* instead of increment, by setting the direction flag. Just use the instruction STD, Set Direction Flag, to do this. To clear the flag, use CLD, Clear Direction Flag. We will not use the direction flag ourselves; when programs are loaded, string commands are set to increment as a default, and we will stick with that.

To scan our string, we are going to have to set the address ES:DI to point to the beginning of the character string in THE_BUFFER. This is not the first byte in THE_BUFFER—the first byte holds the number of characters that we will accept, and the second byte will hold the number of characters actually typed upon return from service 0AH.

Let's give a label to both the byte that holds the number of bytes actually typed, and the position where the characters actually start by restructuring our THE_BUFFER DB... definition this way:

```
CODE_SEG        SEGMENT
        ASSUME  CS:CODE_SEG,DS:CODE_SEG,ES:CODE_SEG,SS:CODE_SEG

        ORG 100H
START:  JMP FINDX
        THE_BUFFER      DB 9                    ←
        BYTES_TYPED     DB 0                    ←
        CHARACTERS      DB 9 DUP(0)             ←
FINDX:  MOV     AH,0AH
        MOV     DX,OFFSET THE_BUFFER
        INT     21H
        MOV     AL,"x"

EXIT:   INT     20H

CODE_SEG        ENDS
        END START
```

This buffer is the same as before, but we have added names for two more bytes, BYTES_TYPED and CHARACTERS. Using these labels, we can now set up ES:DI to point at the actual characters typed in, which starts at the label CHARACTERS. This instruction is MOV DI,OFFSET CHARACTERS (recall that, with only one segment in a .COM file, ES = DS):

```
CODE_SEG        SEGMENT
        ASSUME  CS:CODE_SEG,DS:CODE_SEG,ES:CODE_SEG,SS:CODE_SEG

        ORG 100H
START:  JMP FINDX
        THE_BUFFER      DB 9                    ←
        BYTES_TYPED     DB 0                    ←
        CHARACTERS      DB 9 DUP(0)             ←
FINDX:  MOV     AH,0AH
        MOV     DX,OFFSET THE_BUFFER
        INT     21H
        MOV     AL,"x"
        MOV     DI,OFFSET CHARACTERS            ←

EXIT:   INT     20H

CODE_SEG        ENDS
        END START
```

Now we want to scan CHARACTERS for "x." However, the string instructions by themselves don't automatically scan or move the whole string. MOVSB by itself would only move one byte—we would have to keep repeating MOVSB to scan the whole string. SCASB by itself would only scan one byte—the one pointed to by ES:DI—and compare it to the byte we have stored in AL.

Therefore, we cannot simply put SCASB into our program FINDx:

```
CODE_SEG        SEGMENT
        ASSUME  CS:CODE_SEG,DS:CODE_SEG,ES:CODE_SEG,SS:CODE_SEG

        ORG 100H
START:  JMP FINDX
        THE_BUFFER      DB 9
        BYTES_TYPED     DB 0
        CHARACTERS      DB 9 DUP(0)
FINDX:  MOV     AH,0AH
        MOV     DX,OFFSET THE_BUFFER
        INT     21H
        MOV     AL,"x"
        MOV     DI,OFFSET CHARACTERS
        SCASCB                  ←-X-

EXIT:   INT     20H

CODE_SEG        ENDS
        END START
```

This would only scan *one* byte of CHARACTERS for a match to the character in AL. Instead, to work with the whole string, the string Pseudo-Op REP is needed.

The REP Pseudo-Op

There are three forms of REP: REP itself, REPE (Repeat While Equal), and REPNE (Repeat While NOT Equal). REP just stands for Repeat; it will repeat a string operation a number of times. This number is set by the value in the CX register. For example,

```
      MOV     CX,5
REP   MOVSB
```

> Note that REP or REPE or REPNE are in the part of the line where labels usually go (like START:). This is normal for these REP instructions.

will copy five bytes, in order, from DS:SI to ES:DI. If the bytes at those locations looked like this to begin with:

```
DS:SI                         ES:DI
↓                             ↓
0, 1, 2, 3, 4, 5, 6...        9, 9, 9, 9, 9, 9...
```

they will look this way after REP MOVSB (where CX was 5 to start):

```
              DS:SI                         ES:DI
              ↓                             ↓
0, 1, 2, 3, 4, 5, 6...        0, 1, 2, 3, 4, 9...
```

REPE means Repeat While Equal. In other words, the string operation will be continued until the two items being compared are found to be equal—or until the value in CX becomes 0 as it is decremented each time the string instruction is executed.

The one we want is REPNE—repeat the scanning operation while the byte in the string is *not* equal to the byte in AL ("x"). This way we will keep scanning until we find the byte that *is* equal to "x," and then stop.

We want to load ES:DI with the address of the string to be scanned, put the letter we want SCASB to use in AL ("x"), and set CX to the number of bytes in the string (remember that we are writing a program for the assembler here—numbers are in decimal as a default; it is in DEBUG that they are in hex as a default).

CX must hold the number of bytes to scan. This is just the number of bytes typed in, which will be stored in BYTES_TYPED (the label now attached to the second byte of THE_BUFFER). But this is a little awkward. All we have is one byte to fill a 16-bit register with. Later, we will overcome such problems with type overrides, but for now, let's just load the byte BYTES_TYPED into the lower part of CX, the register CL. To make sure that CX holds the correct value, we also make CH zero (if it had held some nonzero value, REPNE would have interpreted the whole value in CX as huge):

```
CODE_SEG        SEGMENT
        ASSUME  CS:CODE_SEG,DS:CODE_SEG,ES:CODE_SEG,SS:CODE_SEG

        ORG 100H
START:  JMP FINDX
        THE_BUFFER      DB 9
        BYTES_TYPED     DB 0
        CHARACTERS      DB 9 DUP(0)
FINDX:  MOV     AH,0AH
        MOV     DX,OFFSET THE_BUFFER
        INT     21H
        MOV     AL,"x"
        MOV     DI,OFFSET CHARACTERS
        MOV     CH,0                        ←
        MOV     CL,BYTES_TYPED              ←

EXIT:   INT     20H

CODE_SEG        ENDS
        END START
```

Now we are all set. We have loaded AL with the byte that we want to scan for. We have loaded the correct address of the string into ES:DI. And we have set up CX to make REPNE repeat over the typed-in characters:

```
MOV     AL,"x"                      ←
MOV     DI,OFFSET CHARACTERS        ←
MOV     CH,0                        ←
MOV     CL,BYTES_TYPED              ←
```

So we are ready for REPNE SCASB:

```
CODE_SEG        SEGMENT
        ASSUME  CS:CODE_SEG,DS:CODE_SEG,ES:CODE_SEG,SS:CODE_SEG

        ORG 100H
START:  JMP FINDX
        THE_BUFFER      DB 9
        BYTES_TYPED     DB 0
        CHARACTERS      DB 9 DUP(0)
FINDX:  MOV     AH,0AH
        MOV     DX,OFFSET THE_BUFFER
        INT     21H
        MOV     AL,"x"
        MOV     DI,OFFSET CHARACTERS
```

```
            MOV      CH,0
            MOV      CL,BYTES_TYPED
REPNE    SCASB                                  ←

EXIT:    INT      20H

CODE_SEG           ENDS
         END START
```

After REPE SCASB is finished, we know one of two things will be true: It will have found a letter that was "x" (it will repeat while NOT equal), or it will have run out of bytes to scan in the string.

It is easy to check if it reached the end of the string: We just examine CX. If it is zero, REPNE SCASB stopped because it ran out of bytes to examine. On the other hand, if CX is not zero, then REPNE SCASB must have quit because it found a matching byte in the string.

If CX is not zero, then we've found "x". We know where "x" is in the string because the address ES:DI, always updated each time SCASB is performed, will be pointing to the byte *after* the one in which the matching byte was found.

The JCXZ Instruction

We can easily check what happened: Was "x" found? Did we run out of bytes to scrutinize? There is a convenient conditional jump instruction for just this purpose, JCXZ: Jump if CX is Zero. If CX is zero, "x" was not found: We just exit, without printing a location for "x." In other words, we add this instruction to the code:

```
CODE_SEG         SEGMENT
         ASSUME   CS:CODE_SEG,DS:CODE_SEG,ES:CODE_SEG,SS:CODE_SEG

         ORG 100H
START:   JMP FINDX
         THE_BUFFER      DB 9
         BYTES_TYPED     DB 0
         CHARACTERS      DB 9 DUP(0)
FINDX:   MOV      AH,0AH
         MOV      DX,OFFSET THE_BUFFER
         INT      21H
         MOV      AL,"x"
         MOV      DI,OFFSET CHARACTERS
         MOV      CH,0
         MOV      CL,BYTES_TYPED
REPNE    SCASB
         JCXZ     EXIT       ←

EXIT:    INT      20H

CODE_SEG         ENDS
         END START
```

The INC and DEC Instructions

Now we have to plan the part of the code that prints out the location of "x" in the typed string, since we have already eliminated the case where "x" was not found. As mentioned, DI will hold the offset address of the byte *after* the match. So, we first decrement DI by one, with a handy instruction, DEC. DEC is one of a pair of assembly-language instructions; the other being, predictably, INC, for increment. DEC DI will decrease DI by 1, just as INC BX will increment BX by 1. Here we use DEC to point DI back at "x."

Now all we have is the offset address of "x" in DI, but what we need is the place number of "x" in the typed string, the string that follows characters. To get this number, all we need do is *subtract* the offset value of the label CHARACTERS from the current value in DI. This will leave us with the number of bytes the "x" is after CHARACTERS:

```
CODE_SEG          SEGMENT
        ASSUME    CS:CODE_SEG,DS:CODE_SEG,ES:CODE_SEG,SS:CODE_SEG

        ORG 100H
START:  JMP FINDX
        THE_BUFFER      DB 9
        BYTES_TYPED     DB 0
        CHARACTERS      DB 9 DUP(0)
FINDX:  MOV       AH,0AH
        MOV       DX,OFFSET THE_BUFFER
        INT       21H
        MOV       AL,"x"
        MOV       DI,OFFSET CHARACTERS
        MOV       CH,0
        MOV       CL,BYTES_TYPED
REPNE   SCASB
        JCXZ      EXIT
        DEC       DI                        ←
        SUB       DI,OFFSET CHARACTERS      ←

EXIT:   INT       20H

CODE_SEG          ENDS
        END START
```

| More math, such as ADD and SUB, will be covered later, along with the multiply and divide instructions, MUL and DIV.

The value left in DI is the number of bytes past CHARACTERS that "x" occurs. If this value is zero, then the "x" was the first byte typed, and we should print out "1." If the value in DI is 1, then "x" occured one byte after the first one in CHARACTERS—that is, as the second typed byte—and we should print out "2."

There is a simple way of doing this. Take a look at the ASCII table: You will see that all the digits, "1," "2," "3," and so on are one right after the other.

Table 3.5 ASCII Codes for the single digits

Digit	Code
0	48
1	49
2	50
3	51
4	52
5	53
6	54
7	55
8	56
9	57

Thus, if we add the ASCII code for "1" to the value in DI, we will have the ASCII code corresponding to the place number of "x" (remember that if DI is zero, we should print "1"; if DI is 1, we should print "2," and so on). This is a standard way of converting single digit numbers in assembly language to ASCII codes that can be printed out, and it all relies on the fact that the ASCII codes for the digits are in order.

Therefore, to print out the place number, we simply have to add "1" to DI, move it to DL, and use INT 21H service 2 to print it out:

```
CODE_SEG        SEGMENT
        ASSUME  CS:CODE_SEG,DS:CODE_SEG,ES:CODE_SEG,SS:CODE_SEG

        ORG 100H
START:  JMP FINDX
        THE_BUFFER      DB 9
        BYTES_TYPED     DB 0
        CHARACTERS      DB 9 DUP(0)
FINDX:  MOV     AH,0AH
        MOV     DX,OFFSET THE_BUFFER
        INT     21H
        MOV     AL,"x"
        MOV     DI,OFFSET CHARACTERS
        MOV     CH,0
        MOV     CL,BYTES_TYPED
REPNE   SCASB
        JCXZ    EXIT
        DEC     DI
        SUB     DI,OFFSET CHARACTERS
        ADD     DI,"1"      ←
        MOV     DX,DI       ←
```

```
            MOV     AH,2      ←
            INT     21H       ←
EXIT:       INT     20H

CODE_SEG            ENDS
        END START
```

One More Thing

If you've been industrious and typed FINDx in, you've probably discovered that there is a problem, a bug, in it. What happens if the last character we type is "x"? In other words, if you give FINDx this as input:

```
A>FINDx
abcdefgx
```

you will see that FINDx does not find the "x." Why is this?

It is because REPNE decrements CX before the SCASB part is done. This means that even though the last character matched, CX will be left at 0—because it was the *last* character that matched. If seven characters had been typed, CX would have been 7. If the first character had been the "x," then CX would have been left at 6 when REPNE SCASB was done. In the same way, CX is left at 0 when the last character is the "x":

```
             String = "xbcdefg"
CX = 7   →   REPNE SCASB  →  CX = 6


             String = "abcdefx"
CX = 7   →   REPNE SCASB  →  CX = 0
```

This means that, even though the last character did match, we would interpret it as though we had run out of characters to check, since CX was left at 0.

This may indeed sound like a tedious point, but it is exactly the kind of programming problem that leads to errors. For this reason, it is standard to precede the JCXZ instruction with a JE instruction after any string search. SCASB sets the flags just as CMP does, so we can use JE to determine whether the last comparison showed the two items being compared (the "x" in AL and the last byte that was typed in) as equal. If they were, then we do not want to exit:

```
CODE_SEG        SEGMENT
        ASSUME  CS:CODE_SEG,DS:CODE_SEG,ES:CODE_SEG,SS:CODE_SEG

        ORG 100H
START:  JMP FINDX
        THE_BUFFER      DB 9
        BYTES_TYPED     DB 0
```

```
            CHARACTERS      DB 9 DUP(0)
FINDX:  MOV     AH,0AH
        MOV     DX,OFFSET THE_BUFFER
        INT     21H
        MOV     AL,"x"
        MOV     DI,OFFSET CHARACTERS
        MOV     CH,0
        MOV     CL,BYTES_TYPED
REPNE   SCASB
        JE      NO_EXIT  ←
        JCXZ    EXIT
NO_EXIT:DEC     DI           ←
        SUB     DI,OFFSET CHARACTERS
        ADD     DI,"1"
        MOV     DX,DI
        MOV     AH,2
        INT     21H
EXIT:   INT     20H

CODE_SEG        ENDS
        END START
```

If the last byte matched, JE will produce a jump (jump if equal). If it did not, then there will be no jump. We will go on to check CX with JCXZ. If CX is not 0, we can be sure that there was an "x" in the typed string, and that we got it. We type out its place number. Type in FINDx.ASM and give it a try!

> JCXZ is the *only* conditional jump that doesn't check the flags. You need not worry about the condition of the flags before executing it. In general, however, put conditional jump instructions right after comparison instructions and you'll be all set. If you're ever in doubt about what instructions do what to the flags, all the information is in the macro assembler reference volume.

Words in Memory—The DW Pseudo-Op

String instructions can work with either byte strings or word strings in memory—but the idea of word strings is new to us. We will be able to store words in memory in a manner similar to that used to store bytes, except that instead of DB, we will use DW.

The use of DW is similar to DB, but you have to use word-length items. Here are two examples:

```
ALL_FULL   DW 0FFFFH

  NUMBERS   DW 1234H, 5678H, 9ABCDH
```

When the assembler sees the definition of ALL_FULL, it will set aside one word (two bytes) for it. We may work with ALL_FULL this way:

```
MOV     AX,ALL_FULL

MOV     ALL_FULL,DX
```

But we may *not* do the following:

```
MOV     AL,ALL_FULL
```

Because ALL_FULL was defined with DW, Define Word, and AL is only an eight-bit register. The assembler always needs to match the types it works with in an instruction: It will not simply place a value that was defined as byte-length (or that comes in a byte-length register) into one that was defined as word-length (or a word-length register).

High- and Low-Byte Order

There is another peculiarity that we need to be aware of. When we store a byte, like 5, in memory, then naturally one byte simply becomes 5. We can do this in DEBUG, assembling a DB 5 Pseudo-Op:

```
-A100
0EF1:0100 DB      5
0EF1:0101
```

By dumping, we can see the 5 in memory at location CS:0100:

```
-D100        |
             ↓
0EF1:0100   05 EC 04 02 0F 8B E5 5D-CB 00 00 00 00 00 00 00   .......].........
0EF1:0110   00 00 2E F6 06 00 00 01-74 0E BA DA 03 EC A8 08   ........t.......
0EF1:0120   74 FB BA D8 03 B0 21 EE-C3 2E F6 06 00 00 01 74   t.....!........t
0EF1:0130   06 BA D8 03 B0 29 EE C3-8C D8 8E C0 8B 3E 4C F6   .....).......>L.
0EF1:0140   8B 0E 96 F6 B0 0A FC C3-E8 ED FF 8B 1E 48 F6 2B   .............H.+
0EF1:0150   1E 58 F6 74 0D FD 4F 4F-F2 AE 83 EB 50 75 F9 47   .X.t..OO....Pu.G
0EF1:0160   47 FC C3 E8 E2 FF 89 3E-4C F6 CB E8 CA FF 2B CF   G......>L.....+.
0EF1:0170   F2 AE E3 03 EB 16 90 B8-00 00 CB E8 BA FF 3B 3E   ..............;>
```

However, things are not so straightforward with DW. Here we can use DW 0102H, for example:

```
-A100
0EF1:0100 DW      0102
0EF1:0102
```

And also dump it:

```
-D100        |    |
             ↓    ↓
OEF1:0100  02 01 04 02 0F 8B E5 5D-CB 00 00 00 00 00 00 00   .......].........
OEF1:0110  00 00 2E F6 06 00 00 01-74 OE BA DA 03 EC A8 08   ........t........:
OEF1:0120  74 FB BA D8 03 B0 21 EE-C3 2E F6 06 00 00 01 74   t.....!........t
OEF1:0130  06 BA D8 03 B0 29 EE C3-8C D8 8E C0 8B 3E 4C F6   .....).......>L.
OEF1:0140  8B OE 96 F6 B0 0A FC C3-E8 ED FF 8B 1E 48 F6 2B   .............H.+
OEF1:0150  1E 58 F6 74 OD FD 4F 4F-F2 AE 83 EB 50 75 F9 47   .X.t..OO....Pu.G
OEF1:0160  47 FC C3 E8 E2 FF 89 3E-4C F6 CB E8 CA FF 2B CF   G......>L.....+.
OEF1:0170  F2 AE E3 03 EB 16 90 B8-00 00 CB E8 BA FF 3B 3E   ..............;>
```

You might have expected to see 01 02 in memory, not 02 01. This is because the 8088 *reverses* the order of the bytes in a word that it stores in memory. One common way of remembering this is to remember that the high byte (01) is stored at a higher memory location. This will not affect the way you store or read words, however. If you defined:

```
WORD_VARIABLE   DW      0
```

and then accessed that word like this:

```
MOV     WORD_VARIABLE,0102H     ← Storing
```

or this:

```
MOV     AX,WORD_VARIABLE     ← Reading
```

then AX would be left with 0102H, as you'd expect. How the bytes of a word are stored is important only if you examine the individual bytes of a stored word in memory.

The DD Pseudo-Op

There is even a way of storing two words at once—what is called a *doubleword*. We will work with doublewords also in the book, and examine them later. You can use it like this:

```
BIG_NUMBER      DD 01020304H
```

The way this number is stored is even worse—the high word (0102H) is stored at the higher location in memory, the low one at the lower location—*and* both bytes in either word are switched also. Thus, BIG_NUMBER would appear in memory as:

```
04 03 02 01
```

This is one more eccentricity of our microprocessor, one that assembly language programmers know well.

The PSP: A DOS Resource

Perhaps you recall that the reason .COM files are made to begin at 0100H in the code segment is that DOS prepares a 100H byte-long header in memory before the .COM file is loaded in. This header, called the *Program Segment Prefix* (or PSP), is there for the programmer's convenience.

Figure 3-2 A.COM File

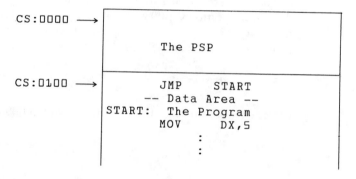

We won't cover the PSP here (it is fully covered in the sequel to this book, *Advanced Assembly Language for the IBM PC*).

File Control Blocks

Most of what the PSP has to do is provide the program easy access to what are called File Control Blocks, which was the way DOS handled files under DOS 1.0 and 1.1. Ever since then, file handles have been used instead, and we will use file handles also. What this means is that we will have little real need for the PSP except for this one time.

If you've ever wondered what happens to the characters you type after a file name like "FILE.TXT" here:

```
A>EDIT FILE.TXT
```

here's the answer: They go into the PSP, ready to be read by the program. Every program, from huge editors to the small file-handling programs we'll write in the next chapter can read what was typed after their names in the PSP. And, since the way the characters are stored there are very much like the way we've set up our buffer THE_BUFFER in FINDx, we can easily convert FINDx to use this information. This way, you'll be able to type:

```
A>FINDx abcxdef
```

instead of

```
A>FINDx
   abcxdef
```

This new method of handling keyboard input can add an element of professionalism to your programs, and make them look snappier.

The characters typed after the program's name can be found in the PSP starting at location CS:0080H. This first byte holds the number of characters that were typed—including the space that separated them from the program's name. In other words, for this command:

```
A>FINDx abcxdef
```

FINDx would find the string in the PSP at CS:0080:

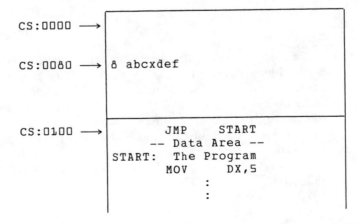

The area at CS:0080H would look like this:

```
CS:80H  81H  82H  83H  84H  85H  86H  87H  88H  89H
   8    " "  "a"  "b"  "c"  "x"  "d"  "e"  "f"  0DH
```

where "a" means the ASCII code for a and so on. The first byte contains the number of bytes typed, eight including the leading space, and at the end is the byte 0DH, which is ASCII for a carriage return. This buffer always ends with the 0DH carriage return byte, which is not included in the byte count. Since this information is very similar to what we have in THE_BUFFER, we can easily change FINDx to use this buffer instead of the one we have set aside (THE_BUFFER). Using this default buffer will allow us to accept input without using INT 21H service 0AH.

Using the PSP Command-Line Buffer

We know the actual offset address at which the byte count will be— 0080H. We also know the offset address where the typed characters will start. This address is not 81H, since the leading space is there, but rather 82H. Since we know the actual offset values, we no longer have to type things like MOV DI, OFFSET CHARACTERS.

Instead, we can simply change this line:

```
FINDX:    MOV      AH,0AH
          MOV      DX,OFFSET THE_BUFFER
          INT      21H
          MOV      AL,"x"
          MOV      DI,OFFSET CHARACTERS    ←
             :
REPNE     SCASB
          JE       NO_EXIT
          JCXZ     EXIT
NO_EXIT:DEC        DI
          SUB      DI,OFFSET CHARACTERS
          ADD      DI,"1"
          MOV      DX,DI
          MOV      AH,2
          INT      21H
EXIT:     INT      20H
```

To this:

```
FINDX:    MOV      AH,0AH
          MOV      DX,OFFSET THE_BUFFER
          INT      21H
          MOV      AL,"x"
          MOV      DI,82H    ←
             :
REPNE     SCASB
          JE       NO_EXIT
          JCXZ     EXIT
NO_EXIT:DEC        DI
          SUB      DI,OFFSET CHARACTERS
          ADD      DI,"1"
          MOV      DX,DI
          MOV      AH,2
          INT      21H
EXIT:     INT      20H
```

This instruction will point ES:DI at the location of the first character in the string in the PSP.

The EQU Pseudo-Op

In fact, however, this does not make very easy-to-read code. Someone reading our program might not know what was intended here. Instead, let's define a constant with the name CHARACTERS_ADDR to hold the address of our characters. We can use a new Pseudo-Op, named EQU, to define this constant and use it in our program:

```
         CHARACTERS_ADDR EQU 82H            ←
FINDX:   MOV     AH,0AH
         MOV     DX,OFFSET THE_BUFFER
         INT     21H
         MOV     AL,"x"
         MOV     DI,CHARACTERS_ADDR         ←
         :
REPNE    SCASB
         JE      NO_EXIT
         JCXZ    EXIT
NO_EXIT: DEC     DI
         SUB     DI,OFFSET CHARACTERS
         ADD     DI,"1"
         MOV     DX,DI
         MOV     AH,2
         INT     21H
EXIT:    INT     20H
```

The Pseudo-Op EQU is only valuable in making assembly-language programs easier to understand and modify. If you define a number of constants in the beginning of your program, like this:

```
CHARACTERS_ADDR EQU 82H H
```

then you can refer to CHARACTERS_ADDR throughout your program. Later, if you want to modify the value of CHARACTERS_ADDR before you reassemble your program, you need only change the constant definitions, the EQU instructions, to change CHARACTERS_ADDR throughout your program, rather than hunting down every place you used 82H. Using EQU is a good programming habit.

Next, we have to set up CX in preparation for REPNE SCASB. We used to be able to get the number of bytes typed directly from the byte in THE_BUFFER that we labeled BYTES_TYPED:

```
FINDX:   MOV     AH,0AH
         MOV     DX,OFFSET THE_BUFFER
         INT     21H
         MOV     AL,"x"
```

```
            MOV      DI,CHARACTERS_ADDR
            MOV      CH,0                       ←
            MOV      CL,BYTES_TYPED             ←
   REPNE    SCASB
```

Referencing bytes by address or value

Now, however, the number of bytes typed will be at address CS:0080, not in THE_BUFFER. This is new. Before, we always used labels to refer to memory locations, because we didn't know their real offsets. Here, however, we know the actual offset (80H), so we can use that instead.

Referencing memory specifically by address and not label will be a new experience for us. To do it, we will use something called *indirect addressing*.

Indirect Addressing

The question is: If we know the address of a byte in memory, but have no label for the byte itself, how can we load the value of the byte into a register? The solution turns out to be easy: If you know a memory location's address, just enclose it in brackets, and the assembler will use the value at that memory location, not the address of the memory location.

For example, if we use EQU to define:

```
BYTES_TYPED_ADDR EQU 80H
```

we could say:

```
   MOV      CL,BYTES_TYPED_ADDR
```

And that would move 80H into CL. On the other hand, we could get the *value* of the byte at CS:80H moved into CL instead by saying:

```
   MOV      CL,[BYTES_TYPED_ADDR]
```

and this does the trick. BYTES_TYPED_ADDR is treated as an address, not an an immediate value. This means that we can get the byte count from CS:0080 this way:

```
CHARACTERS_ADDR EQU 82H
BYTES_TYPED_ADDR EQU 80H                    ←
FINDX:   MOV      AL,"x"
         MOV      DI,CHARACTERS_ADDR
         MOV      CH,0
         MOV      CL,[BYTES_TYPED_ADDR]      ←
   REPNE    SCASB
```

Even so, this count includes the leading space, which we will not scan for "x" as part of our string. So, we decrement CX before starting off with REPNE SCASB:

```
CHARACTERS_ADDR EQU 82H
BYTES_TYPED_ADDR EQU 80H
FINDX:  MOV     AL,"x"
        MOV     DI,CHARACTERS_ADDR
        MOV     CH,0
        MOV     CL,[BYTES_TYPED_ADDR]
        DEC     CL          ← So we don't count leading space in the byte count.
REPNE   SCASB
```

Now that we know how, here is FINDx.ASM, modified to read characters from the .COM file header. Note that SUB DI, OFFSET CHARACTERS has become SUB DI,CHARACTERS_ADDR. Assemble it and run it just like the old version, but type:

```
A>FINDx abcxdef
```

instead of:

```
A>FINDx
  abcxdef
```

```
CHARACTERS_ADDR EQU 82H
BYTES_TYPED_ADDR EQU 80H
CODE_SEG        SEGMENT
        ASSUME  CS:CODE_SEG,DS:CODE_SEG,ES:CODE_SEG,SS:CODE_SEG
        ORG 100H
START:  JMP FINDX
        ;Note: No THE_BUFFER
FINDX:  MOV     DI,CHARACTERS_ADDR
        MOV     CH,0
        MOV     CL,[BYTES_TYPED_ADDR]
        DEC     CL
        MOV     AL,"x"
REPNE   SCASB
        JE      NO_EXIT
        JCXZ    EXIT
NO_EXIT:DEC     DI
        SUB     DI,CHARACTERS_ADDR      ←
        ADD     DI,"1"
        MOV     DX,DI
        MOV     AH,2
        INT     21H
EXIT:   INT     20H

CODE_SEG        ENDS
        END START
```

More on Indirect Addressing

There is another way to use indirect addressing: We didn't have to use the instruction MOV CL,[BYTES_TYPED_ADDR]. The BX register has a particular genius in being used this way. If we load BX with 80H, then the instruction:

```
MOV     CL,[BX]
```

does the same thing as:

```
MOV     CL,[BYTES_TYPED_ADDR]
```

Using addresses like this is called indirect addressing because we are not giving a label attached to something, but rather its address. This way of referring to things is enormously popular in the PS/2 and PC.

Indexed addressing

Indirect addressing will be particularly handy when we have to read from areas that have been formatted in some way: To pick up successive bytes, all we have to do is successively increment BX. We can store indexed data this way: Say we are storing salaries by employee number. To retrieve a salary value, we'll just load BX with the employee number. We don't have to know what memory location (i.e., what employees we'll be interested in) we'll want when we assemble the program; that can depend on the user when he types an employee number in.

Another example is the case when you don't know beforehand what memory location you'll want to use (it may depend on user input); here you can load BX with the correct address when you know it.

Using SI and DI in indirect addressing

The BX register is not the only register that can be used this way: So can SI and DI. With DI, however, the segment register ES is assumed to hold the segment address (that is, MOV AX,[DI] is equal to MOV AX,ES:[DI]). Through the use of indirect addressing, we'll find that our programs can move around in memory at will: All we have to do is fill a register like BX and we can get a byte like this: MOV AX,[BX].

MOV AL,[BX] will fill AL with the byte at location DS:BX, and MOV AX,[BX] will fill AX with the word that starts at the same location. The macro assembler decides whether you want a byte or a word from memory from the type of register (byte or word?) or memory location (defined with DB or DW?) that you are moving data into or from.

The FINDCAT Program

First we read in single characters, and next a whole buffer of characters. Then we searched the buffer for a single character. The next logical step is to search the buffer for a number of characters.

Our final example program dealing with input from the user is FIND-CAT. In the same way that FINDx found "x" in a string of typed characters, so FINDCAT will find "CAT"—three bytes—in a similar string. The FINDCAT program is a long one, and points out the difficulties of routinely using string manipulations in assembly language.

Breaking programs into procedures

Procedures are fundamental to programs of any size, and FINDCAT will introduce us to the use of procedures in assembly language. They can break tasks up into manageable chunks, so the beleaguered programmer doesn't have to handle everything at once. This idea will become clear in FINDCAT, and expose us to two new Pseudo-Ops, PROC and ENDP.

FINDCAT will also introduce us to the LOOP instruction, an 8088 instruction that makes up the counterpart of loops in higher level languages, and give us practice with string instructions.

Let's start off by using part of the program FINDx—the part that reads in buffered input for us with service 0AH:

```
CODE_SEG        SEGMENT
        ASSUME  CS:CODE_SEG,DS:CODE_SEG,ES:CODE_SEG,SS:CODE_SEG

        ORG 100H
START:  JMP FINDCAT                                    ←
        THE_BUFFER      DB 9
        BYTES_TYPED     DB 0
        CHARACTERS      DB 9 DUP(0)
FINDCAT:MOV     AH,0AH                                 ←
        MOV     DX,OFFSET THE_BUFFER
        INT     21H

EXIT:   INT     20H

CODE_SEG        ENDS
        END START
```

After the characters have been read in, we have to consider how to find "CAT" in the string that starts at CHARACTERS:

```
CHARACTERS:There is a CAT over there
```

We will develop FINDCAT incrementally, adding instructions stage by stage, and mimic the actual programming process as much as possible.

First let's consider the problem with a sort of pseudo programming language. We want to read in the typed string. Then, we want to check if the string "CAT" starts at the first character of the read-in string. If it does not, then we go to the next character and see if "CAT" starts there. We keep going until we find "CAT" at a particular place in the typed-in string, and that place—the position of "CAT"—is just what we want to report. Here's how we might set it up:

```
         GET INPUT INTO THE_BUFFER
         SET PLACE_NUMBER TO 1
    ┌──→CHECK IF "CAT" STARTS AT THIS PLACE_NUMBER
    │  ┌─IF ANSWER WAS YES, PRINT PLACE_NUMBER AND EXIT
    │  │ INCREMENT PLACE_NUMBER _ No "CAT" yet, check next PLACE_NUMBER
    │  └─CHECK AGAIN IF WE ARE NOT AT THE END OF INPUT
    │   ┌─REACHED END OF INPUT AND NO "CAT" FOUND, JUST EXIT
    │ ┌─→PRINT PLACE_NUMBER
    └─┼─→EXIT
```

The first part is already accomplished, getting the input into THE_BUFFER. We will call our place number in the typed-in string PLACE_NUMBER. We can steadily increment PLACE_NUMBER, checking each time if "CAT" starts at the current place number.

PLACE_NUMBER can be initialized to 1, starting us off in the input string at the first place, like this:

```
CODE_SEG        SEGMENT
        ASSUME  CS:CODE_SEG,DS:CODE_SEG,ES:CODE_SEG,SS:CODE_SEG

        ORG 100H
START:  JMP FINDCAT
        PLACE_NUMBER    DW 1     ←
        THE_BUFFER      DB 9
        BYTES_TYPED     DB 0
        CHARACTERS      DB 9 DUP(0)
FINDCAT:MOV     AH,0AH
        MOV     DX,OFFSET THE_BUFFER
        INT     21H

EXIT:   INT     20H

CODE_SEG        ENDS
        END START
```

Now what we're going to have to do is set up a loop. Here we will "loop" over each place number, from 1 to the end of the input string in THE_BUFFER, checking for the string "CAT":

```
CHARACTERS:There is a CAT over there
           Loop>
```

In reality, we only have to check up to the end of the input string minus two, since "CAT" needs at least three letters to be spelled. The loop is this part of our pseudo-code:

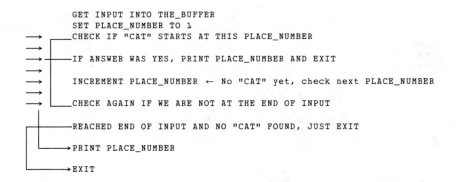

```
               GET INPUT INTO THE_BUFFER
               SET PLACE_NUMBER TO 1
   ───→        CHECK IF "CAT" STARTS AT THIS PLACE_NUMBER
   ───→
   ───→        IF ANSWER WAS YES, PRINT PLACE_NUMBER AND EXIT
   ───→
   ───→           INCREMENT PLACE_NUMBER  ← No "CAT" yet, check next PLACE_NUMBER
   ───→
   ───→        CHECK AGAIN IF WE ARE NOT AT THE END OF INPUT

               REACHED END OF INPUT AND NO "CAT" FOUND, JUST EXIT

           ──→ PRINT PLACE_NUMBER

           ──→ EXIT
```

The LOOP Instruction

LOOP is an assembly-language instruction that allows you to repeat a set of instructions a certain number of times. You use it like this: If you want to execute a loop named CATLOOP five times, load 5 into the loop index register, which is CX, and then proceed like this:

```
          MOV      CX,5
CATLOOP:
          MOV      AX,0
          INC      PLACE_NUMBER
          LOOP     CATLOOP
```

LOOP uses the CX register as a counter—notice that we loaded CX with 5 before entering our loop here. Each time through the loop, CX is decremented. When it reaches 0, the LOOP instruction at the end does not cause you to jump back to the label at the beginning of the loop (as LOOP CATLOOP causes us to jump to the label CATLOOP), but just continues on to the next instruction after the loop. If you want to loop 317 times, fill CX with 317 before entering your loop.

> Notice that if you change the value of CX inside the body of the loop, you will change the number of times the loop is executed! Be careful about this: The LOOP instruction decrements CX each time it is encountered, and if CX does not end up 0, LOOP TOP will send you back to the label TOP. ("TOP" is just a sample label. Any instruction label could be used.)

Here's the idea: The first time through the loop we will check whether "CAT" starts at the first place in the input string.

```
                    Check for "CAT" starting here.
                        ↓
Input String:       "There is a CAT over there."
                    Loop →
```

If we don't find it there, the next time through the loop, we will look for "CAT" starting at the next place number:

```
                    Check for "CAT" starting here.
                        ↓
Input String:       "There is a CAT over there."
                    Loop →
```

And so forth down the string. The number of bytes in this input string will be returned by service 0AH in the byte we have labeled BYTES_TYPED. As mentioned, "CAT" needs three characters, so we only have to loop over the number of typed characters minus two. In other words, we will loop BYTES_TYPED − 2 times to search the whole input string for "CAT." After setting CX to hold the number of times we want to loop (BYTES_TYPED − 2), we enter the loop CATLOOP:

```
CODE_SEG         SEGMENT
         ASSUME  CS:CODE_SEG,DS:CODE_SEG,ES:CODE_SEG,SS:CODE_SEG

         ORG 100H
START:   JMP FINDCAT
         PLACE_NUMBER    DW 1
         THE_BUFFER      DB 9
         BYTES_TYPED     DB 0
         CHARACTERS      DB 9 DUP(0)
FINDCAT:MOV     AH,0AH
        MOV     DX,OFFSET THE_BUFFER
        INT     21H
        MOV     CH,0               ←
        MOV     CL,BYTES_TYPED     ←
        SUB     CX,2               ←
CATLOOP:
.......
:       ;Search for "CAT" at current PLACE_NUMBER here.
:
:       INC     PLACE_NUMBER
:......LOOP     CATLOOP

EXIT:   INT     20H

CODE_SEG         ENDS
         END START
```

Inside the loop, we search for "CAT" at the current place number. If it wasn't found, we increment the place number and loop again to see if

"CAT" starts at the next place number in the string. In code it looks like this:

```
        MOV     CH,0
        MOV     CL,BYTES_TYPED
        SUB     CX,2
CATLOOP:
        ......
→       ;Search for "CAT" at current PLACE_NUMBER here.
→       INC     PLACE_NUMBER
→.....LOOP      CATLOOP
```

All we have to do now is add the code to search for "CAT" at the current PLACE_NUMBER, and put that into the body of our loop.

This is where procedures can make things easier. We'll set up a procedure called SEEKCAT that does just that: It checks for the three letters "CAT" starting at the current PLACE_NUMBER in the input string. Here's how our loop will look:

```
        MOV     CH,0
        MOV     CL,BYTES_TYPED
        SUB     CX,2
CATLOOP:
        ......
:       CALL    SEEKCAT           ←
:
:       INC     PLACE_NUMBER
:.....LOOP      CATLOOP
```

Simple. In other words, we first use SEEKCAT at PLACE_NUMBER = 1:

```
                SEEKCAT will check for "CAT" starting here.
                |
                ↓
Input String:   "There is a CAT over there."
                Loop→
```

And then if "CAT" was not found, we increment PLACE_NUMBER and use SEEKCAT (which checks for "CAT" at the current PLACE_NUMBER) the next time through the loop, PLACE_NUMBER = 2, and so forth all through CATLOOP.

Results from SEEKCAT

How will we know what SEEKCAT found? SEEKCAT will return information to us in a way that will let us use a JE instruction right after it. The JE will be taken if "CAT" was found. If the jump is made, we've found "CAT." We jump to a label named PRINT_PLACE_NUMBER, where we do just that:

```
              MOV       CH,0
              MOV       CL,BYTES_TYPED
              SUB       CX,2
      CATLOOP:
      .......CALL       SEEKCAT
      :      JE         PRINT_PLACE_NUMBER  ←
      :      INC        PLACE_NUMBER
      :......LOOP       CATLOOP
      PRINT_PLACE_NUMBER:                    ←
              ;Print PLACE_NUMBER            ←

      EXIT:   INT       20H
```

Note also that if the JE jump is *not* taken, we will increment PLACE_NUMBER and check once more for "CAT" by calling SEEK-CAT. In this way, we keep looping over the places in the input string, calling SEEKCAT for each place until we've run out of places to check.

Our CATLOOP is done. Take a moment to look through it. By compartmentalizing our task, we've made it much easier. All that's left is to write the "procedure" SEEKCAT.

The PROC and ENDP Pseudo-Ops and the CALL Instruction

Now we are going to add the procedure SEEKCAT to our program:

```
CODE_SEG         SEGMENT
         ASSUME  CS:CODE_SEG,DS:CODE_SEG,ES:CODE_SEG,SS:CODE_SEG

         ORG 100H
START:   JMP FINDCAT
         PLACE_NUMBER    DW 1
         THE_BUFFER      DB 9
         BYTES_TYPED     DB 0
         CHARACTERS      DB 9 DUP(0)
FINDCAT:MOV       AH,0AH
        MOV       DX,OFFSET THE_BUFFER
        INT       21H
        MOV       CH,0
        MOV       CL,BYTES_TYPED
        SUB       CX,2
CATLOOP:
        CALL      SEEKCAT
        JE        PRINT_PLACE_NUMBER
        INC       PLACE_NUMBER
        LOOP      CATLOOP

PRINT_PLACE_NUMBER:
        ;Print PLACE_NUMBER

EXIT:   INT       20H
```

```
SEEKCAT PROC NEAR               ←
        ;Body of SEEKCAT will go here
SEEKCAT ENDP                    ←
CODE_SEG        ENDS
        END START
```

NEAR and FAR

The PROC Pseudo-Op lets the assembler know that you want to define a procedure. You have to let it know in advance if the procedure will be called from within its code segment, or can be called from far away. In the first case, you type PROG PROC NEAR; in the latter case, type PROG PROC FAR. In the .COM files we'll be working in, with only one segment, it will always be NEAR. We won't work with FAR until we deal with .EXE files in a later chapter.

At the end of the procedure, use a line like PROG ENDP so that the assembler knows that the procedure is over:

```
SEEKCAT PROC NEAR           ←
        ;Body of SEEKCAT will go here
SEEKCAT ENDP                ←
```

Now when the command CALL SEEKCAT is executed, the first instruction in the body of SEEKCAT will be executed. We have added our first procedure to a program.

Now that we have added a small procedure to the program, we should enclose the rest of it in a procedure as well. Until now, we've only had one section of code, and that's all it held. Now that we are dividing one section of the code into a procedure, MASM will demand that everything go into its own procedure so that it can understand the code. Let's call the main procedure, which calls SEEKCAT, PROG:

```
CODE_SEG        SEGMENT
        ASSUME  CS:CODE_SEG,DS:CODE_SEG,ES:CODE_SEG,SS:CODE_SEG

        ORG 100H
START:  JMP PROG            ←
        PLACE_NUMBER    DW 1
        THE_BUFFER      DB 9
        BYTES_TYPED     DB 0
        CHARACTERS      DB 9 DUP(0)
PROG    PROC NEAR          ←            ................
        MOV     AH,0AH                               :
        MOV     DX,OFFSET THE_BUFFER                 :
        INT     21H                                  :
        MOV     CH,0                                 :
        MOV     CL,BYTES_TYPED                       :
        SUB     CX,2                                 : Procedure PROG
CATLOOP:                                             :
        CALL    SEEKCAT                              :
        JE      PRINT_PLACE_NUMBER                   :
        INC     PLACE_NUMBER                         :
        LOOP    CATLOOP                              :
```

```
PRINT_PLACE_NUMBER:                         :
        ;Print PLACE_NUMBER                  :
                                             :
EXIT:   INT     20H                          :
PROG    ENDP              ←       .................:
                                  .............
SEEKCAT PROC NEAR
        ;Body of SEEKCAT will go here        : Procedure SEEKCAT
SEEKCAT ENDP                      .............:
                                  
CODE_SEG        ENDS
END START
```

This looks more like a normal .COM file. Even when there are not multiple procedures, it is normal to enclose all the code in a .COM file in a procedure by using PROC at the top and ENDP at the bottom. Technically, this is not necessary if there is only one procedure, and we've been leaving PROC and ENDP out for simplicity's sake.

If there were two procedures, say PROG and SEEKCAT, and SEEK-CAT was called by PROG, then whenever the instruction CALL SEEK-CAT was executed in PROG, the commands in SEEKCAT would be executed. SEEKCAT could handle a particular chore that needs to be done over and over again, and there could be multiple calls to SEEKCAT in PROG. This is how the .COM file shell would look:

```
CODE_SEG        SEGMENT
        ASSUME  CS:CODE_SEG,DS:CODE_SEG,ES:CODE_SEG,SS:CODE_SEG

        ORG 100H

START:  JMP PROG

        ;Data goes Here.

PROG....PROC NEAR.......................
   :       :                            :
   :    ┌─CALL     SEEKCAT              :
   :    │ MOV      AX,5  ←──────────┐   : Procedure PROG
   :    │   :                       │   :
EXIT:   │ INT      20H              │   :
PROG.   │..ENDP..................│..:
        ↓                          │
SEEKCAT.PROC NEAR...............│......
   :       ;The body of SEEKCAT│goes here.  : Procedure SEEKCAT
   :       RET──────────────────┘   :
SEEKCAT.ENDP........................:

CODE_SEG        ENDS
        END START
```

The RET Instruction

When the instruction CALL SEEKCAT is reached in the procedure PROG, the microprocessor jumps to the first line of SEEKCAT. At the end of SEEKCAT, there is a special instruction just for subprocedures, called RET (for return). When the end of SEEKCAT is reached, the RET instruction is executed. The microprocessor then immediately returns to the line in PROG right after the CALL SEEKCAT instruction. In other words, CALL SEEKCAT sends you to SEEKCAT. At the end of SEEK-CAT, the RET instruction sends you back, to the line in the calling procedure immediately following CALL SEEKCAT.

Figure 3.3 Calling and Returning

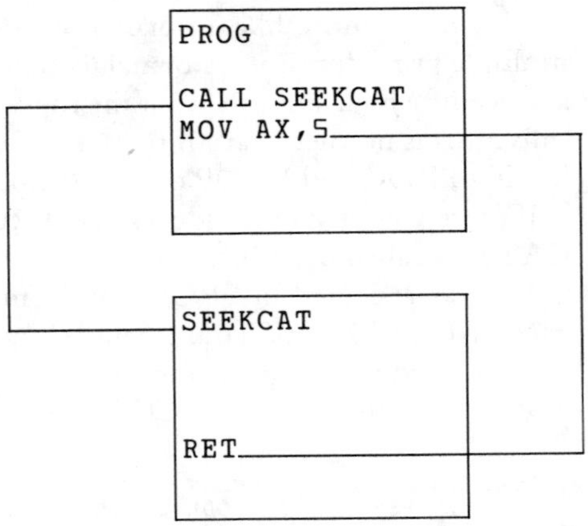

```
PROG
CALL SEEKCAT
MOV AX,5
```

```
SEEKCAT

RET
```

Let's construct SEEKCAT now. Its only task will be to inform the main program if "CAT" begins at the current PLACE_NUMBER. We know that SEEKCAT must end with RET to return us to the main calling procedure:

```
SEEKCAT PROC NEAR
        :
        RET                     ←
SEEKCAT ENDP
```

The CMPSB instruction

The procedure SEEKCAT will have access to the same variables (i.e., it can reference the same data labels) as the main procedure—in particular, it will need to know what place we are at in the typed-in string, and it can find that in the variable PLACE_NUMBER.

Using String Instructions in SEEKCAT

What we want to do is check whether "CAT" starts at PLACE_NUMBER in the typed-in string. There is a string instruction that is especially made to compare strings, called CMPSB, and we can use it since we will be comparing two strings here—"CAT" and the typed-in string. CMPSB works like CMP, except that it compares the bytes at DS:[SI] and ES:[DI] automatically, then increments both SI and DI by 1.

Again, REPE (repeat while equal) can be used to execute CMPSB more than once. Using REPE CMPSB, we will keep comparing bytes as long as they match. In other words, if "C" is found, then we'll move on to check if the next character is "A." If it matches, then we'll keep checking, looking for "T." Depending on how REPE CMPSB ended, we will be able to tell whether or not all three letters of "CAT" were found.

Since REPE CMPSB is used to compare two strings, we need to set up a reference string with "CAT" in it that SEEKCAT can use. Let's put a string named CAT_STRING into the data area:

```
CODE_SEG        SEGMENT
        ASSUME  CS:CODE_SEG,DS:CODE_SEG,ES:CODE_SEG,SS:CODE_SEG

        ORG 100H
START:  JMP PROG
        PLACE_NUMBER    DW 1
        CAT_STRING      DB "CAT"    ←
        THE_BUFFER      DB 9
        BYTES_TYPED     DB 0
        CHARACTERS      DB 9 DUP(0)
PROG    PROC NEAR
        :
PROG    ENDP

SEEKCAT PROC NEAR
        :
        RET
SEEKCAT ENDP
```

Now we can set up DS:[SI] with the address of CAT_STRING and ES:[DI] with the address we are at in the input string so that we may compare them.

Pointing to the Input String

To find the offset address of our position in the input string (it will go into DI for REPE CMPSB), we have to add our place number in that string to the address of the beginning of the string. In other words, we will have to add PLACE_NUMBER to the offset address of our label CHARAC-TERS, and then subtract one (since PLACE_NUMBER starts at 1, not 0) to position us correctly. CAT_STRING will be pointed to with DS:SI, and the input string with ES:DI:

```
SEEKCAT PROC NEAR
        MOV     SI,OFFSET CAT_STRING    ←
        MOV     DI,OFFSET CHARACTERS    ←
        ADD     DI,PLACE_NUMBER         ←
        DEC     DI                      ←
        RET
SEEKCAT ENDP
```

If DS:SI and ES:DI were set up like this in SEEKCAT:

```
DS:SI           ES:DI
↓               ↓
CAT             There is a CAT over there
```

then REPE CMPSB would quit after the first comparison; REPE means repeat while equal. On the other hand, later in CATLOOP, let's say that DS:SI and ES:DI were set up this way:

```
DS:SI                   ES:DI
↓                       ↓
CAT             There is a CAT over there
```

In this case, REPE would execute CMPSB three times, and all three times the comparison would be successful. After REPE CMPSB, the flags will be set according to the *last* comparison it made. If the last comparison REPE CMPSB made showed two equal bytes, then the reason REPE CMPSB quit is because it ran out of bytes to compare, not because it found a mismatch. In this case, all bytes matched, and "CAT" has been found.

In this case, a JE jump like this one:

```
REPE    CMPSB
        JE      PRINT
```

will be made. On the other hand, the JE we want to make is JE PRINT_PLACE_NUMBER, which is the instruction back in PROG that follows CALL SEEKCAT. Can we return to PROG and have the jump safely executed there?

Yes we can. The RET at the end of SEEKCAT that immediately follows REPE CMPSB will not change the flags. This means that immediately after the call in PROG, you must check the flags with a conditional jump instruction. When we return to PROG, we can put our line containing JE PRINT_PLACE_NUMBER right after the instruction CALL SEEKCAT. If the last comparison in REPE CMPSB indicated a match, all three bytes matched, "CAT" was found, and the JE will be taken to PRINT_PLACE_NUMBER.

All we do now is convert the value in PLACE_NUMBER to an ASCII value in DL and hand it to service 2 of INT 21H. (Since PLACE_NUMBER is a word long, we could not say MOV DL,PLACE_NUMBER, but have to say instead MOV DX,PLACE_NUMBER. Since we are only interested in the lower byte, which will go into DL anyway, there is no problem.)

```
CODE_SEG        SEGMENT
        ASSUME  CS:CODE_SEG,DS:CODE_SEG,ES:CODE_SEG,SS:CODE_SEG
        ORG 100H
START:  JMP FINDCAT
        PLACE_NUMBER    DW 1
        :
FINDCAT:MOV     AH,0AH
        :
CATLOOP:
        CALL    SEEKCAT
.....JE         PRINT_PLACE_NUMBER  ←
:       INC     PLACE_NUMBER
:       LOOP    CATLOOP
:
PRINT_PLACE_NUMBER:
        MOV     DX,PLACE_NUMBER  ←
        ADD     DL,"0"           ←
        MOV     AH,2             ←
        INT     21H              ←
EXIT:   INT     20H

SEEKCAT PROC NEAR
        MOV     SI,OFFSET CAT_STRING
        MOV     DI,OFFSET CHARACTERS
        ADD     DI,PLACE_NUMBER
        DEC     DI
        MOV     CX,3
REPE    CMPSB
        RET     ;Return information in flags: was last comparison
                successful?
SEEKCAT ENDP

CODE_SEG        ENDS
        END START
```

If "CAT" was not found, we do not jump to PRINT_PLACE_NUMBER. Instead, we increment PLACE_-NUMBER and loop back to the top of CATLOOP, where we call SEEKCAT. In this case, we keep looping down the input string until we find "CAT" or run out of bytes to check.

Now we've put together SEEKCAT and made CATLOOP complete. As CATLOOP increments over the places in the typed-in string, SEEK-CAT checks for "CAT" at each PLACE_NUMBER. If "CAT" is found, we jump out of CATLOOP to PRINT_PLACE_NUMBER. Everything should work; but it does not.

One Last Problem

Is that possible after all our work? Very much so—and this example points out a common problem with using subprocedures. The CX register is used in the LOOP CATLOOP as the loop index:

```
          MOV     CH,0            ←
          MOV     CL,BYTES_TYPED  ←
          SUB     CX,2            ←
CATLOOP:
         ┌─CALL    SEEKCAT
         │ JE      PRINT_PLACE_NUMBER
         │ INC     PLACE_NUMBER
         └─LOOP    CATLOOP

PRINT_PLACE_NUMBER:
          MOV     DX,PLACE_NUMBER
          ADD     DL,"0"
          MOV     AH,2
          INT     21H
EXIT:     INT     20H
```

But CX is also used by the procedure called in CATLOOP, which is SEEKCAT:

```
SEEKCAT PROC NEAR
          MOV     SI,OFFSET CAT_STRING
          MOV     DI,OFFSET CHARACTERS
          ADD     DI,PLACE_NUMBER
          DEC     DI
          MOV     CX,3            ←
REPE      CMPSB                   ←
          RET
SEEKCAT ENDP
```

The REPE prefix here uses CX to hold the number of times to repeat. When we return to CATLOOP, we will have destroyed the loop index counter, CX.

Saving and restoring registers

This is a good example of what often happens when you call another procedure. Frequently, registers that your procedure uses should not be changed when you return to the main procedure; if they are, something may be set awry. Here, SEEKCAT should not change the loop index CX, even though we will use CX inside SEEKCAT for REPE. The solution is to store CX when we enter SEEKCAT and to restore it when we exit. This is done with the assembly-language instructions PUSH CX and POP CX.

PUSH and POP

PUSH CX (or PUSH any register) places the value of CX on the internal stack. POP CX restores the original value in CX again:

```
SEEKCAT PROC NEAR
        PUSH    CX              ←
        MOV     SI,OFFSET CAT_STRING
        MOV     DI,OFFSET CHARACTERS
        ADD     DI,PLACE_NUMBER
        DEC     DI
        MOV     CX,3      ←
REPE    CMPSB             ←
        POP     CX        ←
        RET
SEEKCAT ENDP
```

This is a very frequent occurance in subprocedures: At the beginning push all the registers you are going to use, and just before leaving, pop them again.

> The 80286 and the 80386 have the commands PUSHA and POPA, single instructions that push all registers and pop all registers. Both are very useful.

At Last

Here's how the whole thing looks put together, with SEEKCAT in place (along with its PUSH CX and POP CX):

```
CODE_SEG        SEGMENT
        ASSUME  CS:CODE_SEG,DS:CODE_SEG,ES:CODE_SEG,SS:CODE_SEG

        ORG 100H
START:  JMP FINDCAT
        PLACE_NUMBER    DW 1
        CAT_STRING      DB "CAT"
        THE_BUFFER      DB 9
        BYTES_TYPED     DB 0
        CHARACTERS      DB 9 DUP(0)
FINDCAT:MOV     AH,0AH
        MOV     DX,OFFSET THE_BUFFER
        INT     21H
        MOV     CH,0
        MOV     CL,BYTES_TYPED
        SUB     CX,2
CATLOOP:
        CALL    SEEKCAT
        JE      PRINT_PLACE_NUMBER
        INC     PLACE_NUMBER
        LOOP    CATLOOP

PRINT_PLACE_NUMBER:
        MOV     DX,PLACE_NUMBER
```

```
                ADD     DL,"0"
                MOV     AH,2
                INT     21H
        EXIT:   INT     20H

        SEEKCAT PROC NEAR
                PUSH    CX              ←
                MOV     SI,OFFSET CAT_STRING
                MOV     DI,OFFSET CHARACTERS
                ADD     DI,PLACE_NUMBER
                DEC     DI
                MOV     CX,3
        REPE    CMPSB
                POP     CX              ←
                RET     ;Return information in flags: was last comparison
                        successful?
        SEEKCAT ENDP

        CODE_SEG        ENDS
                END START
```

Goodbye to Input

FINDCAT is done, and, with it, the chapter on input. We've been storing our input, so far, in memory; but of course, the computer also has a
long-term memory as well, and that is on disk. The way you save data on
disks is in files, and that is the subject of the next chapter. As we'll see,
DOS is an expert in filehandling, and it's where our operating system will
get a chance to shine.

4
Working with Files

So far, we've covered the basics of input and output for assembly language programs, and developed the assembly-language instruction set needed to accomplish those tasks. We've made great progress; in developing our example programs so far, we've seen a large number of instructions and Pseudo-Ops:

Table 4.1 Instructions and Pseudo-Ops Thus Far

8088 Instructions	*Pseudo-Ops*
MOV, JMP, PUSH, POP, DEC, INC, INT, ADD, SUB, CALL, RET, LOOP, CMP, JA, JB, JE, JCXZ, SCASB, MOVSB, CMPSB, REP.	SEGMENT, ASSUME, PROC, ENDP, DB, DW, DD, ENDS, END, OFFSET, ORG, EQU +,.

We understand addressing, have been introduced to indirect addressing, and know how to use INT 21H services 1, 2, 6, 7, 8, 9, and 0AH, as well as INT 20H. All our new expertise will be put to good use right here, in the current chapter. Now we're going to work with some real data in the PS/2 or PC—as we dig into file handling.

The real goal of computing is to produce something useful that can be seen outside the program. Output on the screen is one such method: But without files, computers would be hopelessly lost. Files represent the long-term storage of the PS/2 or PC, and they're still there when you turn your machine off. They can be printed out. They can be arranged to hold data, they can hold letters to the editor, they can be programs. And

DOS is equal to the challenge, with its rich set of file-handling services, again in INT 21H.

> The services of INT 21H represent most of the resources that the assembly-language programmer uses in DOS. Besides INT 20H (end program), and the interrupts that make files memory resident, the only other really useful DOS interrupts are the disk-reading and writing ones, INT 25H and INT 26H. Meanwhile, the number of services that INT 21H provides just keeps growing. In DOS 3.3, we are up to service 68H.

File Control Blocks

Before DOS 2.0, DOS used to work with files through what were called *File Control Blocks*, or FCBs. FCBs held information about files: their names, the drive they were on, and, although it was in the "reserved" system part, their sizes. However, FCBs restricted file names to 11 characters, (eight characters of filename plus three of extension, like BASE-BALL.BAT) and this proved to be their fatal flaw.

Beginning with DOS 2.0, IBM introduced directories, and suddenly file names had to include pathnames as well. And there is just no way to fit C:\PROGRAMS\ASSEMBLER\MASM.EXE into 11 characters, so *file handles* were introduced.

File Handles

A file handle is a 16-bit word that stands, to DOS, for a file. When you want to use a file, you give DOS a file name, and DOS returns a file handle in a register (usually AX). Whenever you want to do something with that file—rename it, open it, read from it—the INT 21H service will need that 16-bit file handle in some register (usually BX)

Typical file-copying sequence
. A typical sequence for copying a file runs like this: Set up the filename as a string in memory, and make the last byte a 0 (*not* as ASCII "0," but a byte whose value is zero). This is referred to as an ASCIIZ string (ASCII Zero), and tells the INT 21H service that the filename is ended now:

```
FILE_36 DB "C:\Novel\Chapter.89",0
```

Open the file and get a file handle for it (execute an INT 21H service 3DH). Create a new file (service 3CH). Read from the first file (service 3FH), write to the new file (service 40H), and then close them both (service 3EH). Compared to other languages, this is pretty easy.

We are going to work with file handles only in this book, for four reasons: First, FCBs have been out of date for five years; second, handles are much easier to use; third, the list of things you can do with file handles keeps growing—but not with FCBs; and fourth, no one uses FCBs anymore. If you want to learn about FCBs, you will find them covered in the sequel to this book, *Advanced Assembly Language for the IBM PC*.

The DOS File-Handle Services

There are so many INT 21H file-handle services that one can get lost. To avoid that, we will list all the usual file-handle services DOS offers here instead of letting them them get strung over the whole chapter. Table 4.1 collects the services we will use into one convienient place that you can refer back to easily. Looking over it now will indicate what file services are available in DOS:

Table 4.2 File-Handle Services

File-Handle Service	Number	You Set	It Returns
Create Subdirectory	39H	DS:DX to ASCIIZ string	If CY = 1, AX has error
Delete Subdirectory	3AH	DS:DX to ASCIIZ string	If CY = 1, AX has error
Change Directory	3BH	DS:DX to ASCIIZ string	If CY = 1, AX has error
Create File	3CH	DS:DX to ASCIIZ string CX = attribute	If CY = 1, AX has error If CY = 0, AX = File Handle
Open File	3DH	DS:DX to ASCIIZ AL = mode	If CY = 1, AX has error If CY = 0, AX = File Handle
Close File	3EH	BX = File Handle	If CY = 1, AX has error
Read from File	3FH	BX = Handle CX = #Bytes wanted DS:DX = Buffer	If CY = 1, AX has error If CY = 0, AX = #Bytes Read
Write to File	40H	BX = Handle CX = #Bytes wanted DS:DX = Buffer	If CY = 1, AX has error If CY = 0, AX = #Bytes actually written
Delete a File	41H	DS:DX to ASCIIZ string	If CY = 1 AX has error

Table 4.2 File-Handle Services *(continued)*

File-Handle Service	Number	You Set	It Returns

Move Read/Write Pointer	42H	CX:DX = #Bytes to move
		BX = File Handle
		AL = "method"
			If CY = 1, AX has error
			If CY = 0 DX:AX = new location in file.

Find First Matching File (use with wildcards)	4EH	DS:DX to ASCIIZ
		CX = Attribute
			If CY = 1, AX has error
			If CY = 0 then DTA has
			  21 bytes reserved
			  1 byte: file's attrib.
			  1 word: file's time
			  1 word: file's date
			  1 Dword: file's size
			  13 bytes: ASCIIZ name

Find Next Matching File	4FH	DTA as set by service 4EH	Same as for 4EH
Rename File	56H	DS:DX to ASCIIZ ES:DI to new name (also ASCIIZ)	If CY = 1, AX has error

As you can see, there are plenty of services, including some that create temporary files, get or set file's times or dates, and so on. Let's begin to unpack some of this information right now, as we develop a small example program, RUBOUT, whose only purpose is to delete a specified file.

The Program RUBOUT

About the simplest program we could write that works with files is one that deletes them, using service 41H. This service doesn't even require a handle to delete the file: All that is needed is an ASCII character string, followed by a zero byte—an ASCIIZ string— holding the file's pathname and filename.

We have already written programs that can read typed input into a buffer, and we'll use that knowledge in RUBOUT to read the file's name that we are to delete. Here's the program shell, taken from FINDx.ASM:

```
CODE_SEG        SEGMENT
        ASSUME  CS:CODE_SEG,DS:CODE_SEG,ES:CODE_SEG,SS:CODE_SEG


        ORG 100H
START:  JMP RUBOU
        THE_BUFFER      DB 50              ←
        BYTES_TYPED     DB 0
        CHARACTERS      DB 50 DUP(0)       ←
RUBOUT  PROC NEAR                      ←
        MOV     AH,0AH
        MOV     DX,OFFSET THE_BUFFER
        INT     21H
        :
```

```
        :
EXIT:   INT     20H
RUBOUT  ENDP                              ←

CODE_SEG        ENDS
        END START
```

Here we have made the buffer 50 characters long to accept both path and filenames, and made the code into a procedure named RUBOUT. What the program does so far is fill THE_BUFFER. What it will fill it with is the ASCII string we type to RUBOUT, which will be the name of the file we want deleted.

> There are easier ways of deleting files than writing RUBOUT, but it is worth noticing that DOS itself—in the DEL command—uses these same services to delete files too.

When the ASCII string is typed in, the last character put into the buffer will be 0DH, which is ASCII for a carriage return. On the other hand, we want our ASCII string to end with zero, to make it ASCIIZ. To do this, we must replace the 0DH with 00H. This is not so hard.

We do not know in advance the location of the byte we have to make zero: It will be at the end of the ASCII string. This is where indirect addressing comes in handy. We will simply put the offset of the begining of the string (the offset of the label CHARACTERS) into the BX register, add the number of bytes actually typed to BX, and then make the 0DH into 00H with an instruction MOV [BX],0. (Remember that service 0AH does not count the final 0DH in the total count of characters that were typed.)

BX is a word-long register. To add BYTES_TYPED (a byte, defined with DB) to it, we will have to be careful. Here is how we do it: We first fill BH with zero, followed by MOV BL,BYTES_TYPED. Now the value of BYTES_TYPED is in BX. Then we can ADD BX, OFFSET CHARACTERS:

```
RUBOUT  PROC NEAR
        MOV     AH,0AH
        MOV     DX,OFFSET THE_BUFFER
        INT     21H
        MOV     BH,0                      ←
        MOV     BL,BYTES_TYPED            ←
        ADD     BX,OFFSET CHARACTERS      ←
        :
```

BX is all set with the address of the 0DH byte that we want to make into zero. Here's the line that we'd like to add:

```
RUBOUT  PROC NEAR
        MOV     AH,0AH
        INT     21H
        MOV     BH,0
        MOV     BL,BYTES_TYPED
        ADD     BX,OFFSET CHARACTERS
        MOV     [BX],0              ←
        :
```

And it seems to make sense—we are moving the zero into the byte whose offset address (from the beginning of DS) is held in BX. BX is set properly to point to the 0DH byte. But there is a problem.

Type mismatching

The problem is that MASM doesn't know whether you are pointing to a word starting at location DS:BX, or just one byte. The same instruction, MOV [BX],0, might conceivably be written by programmers to mean either of those two different things. If we had said MOV AL,0, of course, there would be no problem, since MASM knows that AL is one byte long. But how long is [BX]? All it has here is an address. The macro assembler won't let you assemble until this—an unknown type error— is fixed.

The PTR Pseudo-Op

The cure is to give [BX] a size, and that is done with the PTR Pseudo-Op. PTR stands for pointer. It tells MASM what type—byte or word—we mean in ambiguous cases like this. This is a proper instruction:

```
MOV     BYTE PTR[BX],0  H
```

And we'll add it to RUBOUT to get rid of the 0DH character:

> PTR has other uses too. It can be used, as we will later, to override defined types (like DB or DW).

```
CODE_SEG        SEGMENT
        ASSUME  CS:CODE_SEG,DS:CODE_SEG,ES:CODE_SEG,SS:CODE_SEG

        ORG 100H
START:  JMP RUBOUT
        THE_BUFFER      DB 50
        BYTES_TYPED     DB 0
        CHARACTERS      DB 50 DUP(0)
RUBOUT  PROC NEAR
        MOV     AH,0AH
        MOV     DX,OFFSET THE_BUFFER
        INT     21H
        MOV     BH,0
        MOV     BL,BYTES_TYPED
        ADD     BX,OFFSET CHARACTERS
        MOV     BYTE PTR[BX],0          ←
        :
```

```
           :
EXIT:   INT     20H
RUBOUT  ENDP

CODE_SEG        ENDS
        END START
```

To delete a file, we check the entry in our DOS file services table earlier:

File-Handle Service	Number	You Set	It Returns
Delete a File	41H	DS:DX to ASCIIZ string	If CY = 1, AX has error

All we have to do is direct DS:DX to CHARACTERS, where the ASCIIZ string will start, and execute INT 21H, service 41H to delete the file whose name is at CHARACTERS:

```
CODE_SEG        SEGMENT
        ASSUME  CS:CODE_SEG,DS:CODE_SEG,ES:CODE_SEG,SS:CODE_SEG

        ORG 100H
START:  JMP RUBOUT
        THE_BUFFER      DB 50
        BYTES_TYPED     DB 0
        CHARACTERS      DB 50 DUP(0)
RUBOUT  PROC NEAR
        MOV     AH,0AH
        MOV     DX,OFFSET THE_BUFFER
        INT     21H
        MOV     BH,0
        MOV     BL,BYTES_TYPED
        ADD     BX,OFFSET CHARACTERS
        MOV     BYTE PTR[BX],0
        MOV     DX,OFFSET CHARACTERS     ←
        MOV     AH,41H                   ←
        INT     21H                      ←
EXIT:   INT     20H
RUBOUT  ENDP

CODE_SEG        ENDS
        END START
```

RUBOUT.ASM is ready to be assembled and run. You will find that it works as written, but that, while running, it is irritatingly mysterious. When you type RUBOUT at the DOS prompt, the program just silently waits for you to type a filename for it to delete. This is less than user friendly.

User prompts

We can easily add a prompt to RUBOUT, so that when run, it will prompt: "File to delete?". This is done with service 9 of INT 21H, the string printing service. We simply define a string to print (called PROMPT here), and type it out in the beginning:

```
CODE_SEG           SEGMENT
          ASSUME   CS:CODE_SEG,DS:CODE_SEG,ES:CODE_SEG,SS:CODE_SEG

          ORG 100H
START:    JMP RUBOUT
          THE_BUFFER        DB 50
          BYTES_TYPED       DB 0
          CHARACTERS        DB 50 DUP(0)
          PROMPT            DB "File to delete? $"    ←
RUBOUT    PROC NEAR
          MOV      DX,OFFSET PROMPT          ←
          MOV      AH,9                      ←
          INT      21H                       ←
          MOV      AH,0AH
          MOV      DX,OFFSET THE_BUFFER
          INT      21H
          MOV      BH,0
          MOV      BL,BYTES_TYPED
          ADD      BX,OFFSET CHARACTERS
          MOV      BYTE PTR[BX],0
          MOV      DX,OFFSET CHARACTERS
          MOV      AH,41H
          INT      21H
EXIT:     INT      20H
RUBOUT    ENDP

CODE_SEG           ENDS
          END START
```

> Don't forget the "**$**" to terminate strings printed out by service 9. Many system programs use service 9 to print out their messages. If you debug COMMAND.COM (type DEBUG COMMAND.COM<cr>), and repeatedly type D<cr>, which is DEBUG's command to dump memory, you will see all the errors COMMAND.COM can give you, followed by "$" ("Terminate Batch Job (Y/N) $" etc.).

This simple addition makes RUBOUT much clearer to use.

Error Checking

When we are dealing with files, we encounter something that we have not seen before: the possibility of some error in carrying out an instruction. What if the name of the file is mispelled? What if it can't be found on the specified disk or in the specified subdirectory? RUBOUT should let the user know.

Error checking is a major part of programming when using files. For that reason, we will build (rudimentary) error checking into our example

RUBOUT. If you check the table at the beginning of this chapter, you will see the line "If CY = 1, AX has error" in the entry for service 41H (delete file):

File-Handle Service	Number	You Set	It Returns
Delete a File	41H	DS:DX to ASCIIZ string	If CY = 1, AX has error

The CY stands for one of the internal flags—the carry flag. Setting the carry flag is DOS' normal way of indicating that there has been an error of some kind.

The carry flag is normally set when a math operation produced a carry while combining two numbers—and we'll use it in Chapter 9, Fast Math. Here, however, if the carry flag is set, then an error code will be returned in the AX register.

Error Codes

There are 88 different error codes in DOS 3.3, too many to cover here. However, here are the more common ones (they are returned in AX):

Table 4.3 Error Codes

Error Code	Means
1	Invalid function number
2	File not found
3	Path was not found
4	Too many files open at once
5	Access denied for this operation
6	File Handle used is invalid
7	Memory Control Blocks destroyed
8	Insufficient memory
15	Invalid drive was specified
16	Cannot delete current directory
19	Cannot write on a write-protected diskette
21	Drive not ready
23	Disk data error
25	Disk seek error
27	Sector not found
28	Printer needs paper
29	Write fault
30	Read fault
61	Print queue is full

All these codes, and more information, may be found in a volume that IBM sells called the *DOS Technical Reference Manual* which also contains all the INT 21H services, and can be quite useful.

> There is now a service 59H, get extended error, which we will not cover because it is huge (it would take the entire chapter). This service returns information on the error that has occurred, where it is, and even suggests what you should do. This advanced service can be found in the *DOS Technical Reference*.

We are not going to get very complex in RUBOUT. We are just going to assume that if there was no error, the file was deleted, and if there was an error, that it was not. We will want, therefore, to check the carry flag; this is done with the JC and JNC conditional jumps.

JC and JNC

If the carry flag is 1, it is set. If it is set, the instruction JC OVER_THERE will cause the program to jump to the label OVER_THERE. Conversely, JNC will cause a jump if the carry flag is *not* set. We will do the following: Immediately after service 41H was requested, we will put a JNC instruction that will cause the message "File deleted" to be printed out. If the JNC is not taken, we will print out a message "File NOT deleted," and jump to the exit. Here's how it looks:

```
CODE_SEG        SEGMENT
        ASSUME  CS:CODE_SEG,DS:CODE_SEG,ES:CODE_SEG,SS:CODE_SEG

        ORG 100H
START:  JMP RUBOUT
        THE_BUFFER      DB 50
        BYTES_TYPED     DB 0
        CHARACTERS      DB 50 DUP(0)
        PROMPT          DB "File to delete? $"
        OK_MESSAGE      DB "File deleted $"          ←
        NOT_OK_MESSAGE  DB "File NOT deleted $"      ←
RUBOUT  PROC NEAR
        MOV     DX,OFFSET PROMPT
        MOV     AH,9
        INT     21H
        MOV     AH,0AH
        MOV     DX,OFFSET THE_BUFFER
        INT     21H
        MOV     BH,0
        MOV     BL,BYTES_TYPED
        ADD     BX,OFFSET CHARACTERS
        MOV     BYTE PTR[BX],0
        MOV     DX,OFFSET CHARACTERS
        MOV     AH,41H
        INT     21H
        JNC     ALL_OK                               ←
        MOV     DX,OFFSET NOT_OK_MESSAGE             ←
        JMP     PRINT                                ←
```

```
ALL_OK:  MOV      DX,OFFSET OK_MESSAGE              ←
PRINT:   MOV      AH,9                              ←
         INT      21H
EXIT:    INT      20H                               ←
RUBOUT   ENDP

CODE_SEG          ENDS
END START
```

Notice our use of JNC right after the return from INT 21H. That's it for RUBOUT, which has taught us about deleting files, ASCIIZ, the PTR Pseudo-Op, and error handling.

To do anything more than delete files, you need to work with file handles, and our next example does that often enough.

The Program BACK.ASM

Using file handles to work with files has made a difficult task into a (if not pleasant, at least) mercifully short business. To do the things we're going to do in BASIC, or practically any higher level language, would be impossible. This is the clean approach of assembly language—there are no layers buffering you from the data. If you want 12 bytes here in memory, just put them there. If you want to read in 279 bytes from a file and not worry about records or readlns or anything, assembly language is for you. If you feel a need to read error messages when you try to read in a non-ASCII file, you should probably look elsewhere.

Using BACK.ASM

BACK.ASM will demonstrate the fluid way that assembly language can work with data. All we'll do in BACK.ASM is make a backup copy of a file you specify, changing the file's extension to ".BAK". For example, if you type: BACK<cr>NOVEL.ONE, then BACK will copy NOVEL.ONE into a new file named NOVEL.BAK.

BACK is just a demonstration program. Since we are going to have to fit all data and code into the same segment, CODE_SEG, we will restrict BACK.COM to work with only files of less than 60K, for example. It is not difficult to modify BACK.ASM so that it will read files larger than 60K in installments, and write them out the same way, letting the program handle files of any size. We'll point out where this can be done. Also, we'll write such a program under OS/2 later, so you can see how it works.

In addition (to thoroughly destroy any utility the program may have had), we are going to limit BACK to accepting file names with eight-letter names and three-letter extensions—no pathnames. This is to avoid having to do fancy string manipulations when we copy the name over and substitute ".BAK" for the extension. Again, this can be changed with a little work, but these details of string handling would detract from the main points of file handling.

The Stack in .COM Files

The stack in memory

Here is a point that will be important when you deal with large amounts of data, as file copying programs can. The stack—which DOS uses to store addresses to return to when CALLs are made, or that we use with PUSH and POP—shares the same segment as our program. In fact, you may have wondered where it was. It is at the top of the segment.

Stack segment register and stack pointers

The final two registers in the 8088 set deal with the stack, and we will not cover them until we deal with OS/2, except to mention their names: SP and BP.

The current location in the stack is always pointed to by SS:SP, and BP is an auxiliary stack pointer. When the program begins, SP is set to the end of the segment (as you can see in DEBUG R commands we used earlier). It is vital that the program not write over the stack; if it does, it will crash. This means that you should not allow anything to come closer to the end of the segment than about 256 words, or you stand a chance of overwriting the stack.

Figure 4.1 A .COM File

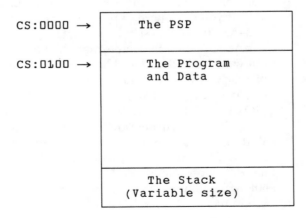

We will examine the stack later, but one thing you should know is that it has a variable size—the more it is used, the bigger it gets. The stack "grows downward"—every time you push a word, SP is *decremented*.

In .COM files, the stack starts off as just the single word at the top of the segment and grows downward word by word as you push values.

> If a .COM file is made memory resident, on the other hand, the stack that it uses from then on is DOS' own internal one, and there is no similar need to worry.

BACK.ASM in Outline

We'll start out by taking what we need from RUBOUT. Here the program BACK will ask for a file to back up, accept a name, and make an ASCIIZ string out of it:

```
CODE_SEG        SEGMENT
        ASSUME  CS:CODE_SEG,DS:CODE_SEG,ES:CODE_SEG,SS:CODE_SEG

        ORG 100H
START:  JMP BACK
        THE_BUFFER      DB 13
        BYTES_TYPED     DB 0
        FILE_ONE        DB 12 DUP(0)
        MAKE_ME_ZERO    DB 0
        FILE_TWO        DB 8 DUP(0), ".BAK",0
        PROMPT          DB "Filename to back up: $"
BACK    PROC NEAR
        MOV     DX,OFFSET PROMPT                ←
        MOV     AH,9                            ←
        INT     21H                             ←
        MOV     AH,0AH                          ←
        MOV     DX,OFFSET THE_BUFFER            ←
        INT     21H                             ←
        :
        :
EXIT:   INT     20H
BACK    ENDP

CODE_SEG        ENDS
        END START
```

Note that we've changed the label CHARACTERS to FILE_ONE, since that will be where the first file's name will appear. Also, we've added FILE_TWO, with the extension ".BAK" already. We've set THE_BUFFER to accept 13 characters—eight bytes of filename, the ".", the three byte extension, and one last byte for the trailing 0DH that is ALWAYS returned as the last byte in the buffer by service 0AH (keep in mind that BACK, as written, will *only* work with 12-character filenames—so we can always count on the thirteenth byte being 0DH). To make it easy to write over this byte, we give it a label, MAKE_ME_ZERO:

```
THE_BUFFER      DB 13
BYTES_TYPED     DB 0
FILE_ONE        DB 12 DUP(0)
MAKE_ME_ZERO    DB 0
FILE_TWO        DB 8 DUP(0), ".BAK",0
PROMPT          DB "Filename to back up: $"
```

If we didn't restrict the file's name to exactly 12 characters, we could use indirect addressing to find the end of buffer character—0DH—and set it to zero, as we did in RUBOUT. Even if service 0AH did not tell us how many characters were typed, we could find the 0DH by steadily incrementing the value of BX along the buffer and checking the value of [BX].

First, we set MAKE_ME_ZERO to zero, making the read-in filename an ASCIIZ string, this way:

```
        ORG 100H
START:  JMP BACK
        THE_BUFFER      DB 13
        BYTES_TYPED     DB 0
        FILE_ONE        DB 12 DUP(0)
        MAKE_ME_ZERO    DB 0
        FILE_TWO        DB 8 DUP(0), ".BAK",0
        PROMPT          DB "Filename to back up: $"
BACK    PROC NEAR
        MOV     DX,OFFSET PROMPT
        MOV     AH,9
        INT     21H
        MOV     AH,0AH
        MOV     DX,OFFSET THE_BUFFER
        INT     21H
        MOV     MAKE_ME_ZERO,0  ←
                :
```

If the file's name was BASEBALL.BAT, then THE_BUFFER would have looked like this before we made MAKE_ME_ZERO zero:

```
                                              MAKE_ME_ZERO─────────┐
                                                                   ↓
THE_BUFFER 13 12 "B" "A" "S" "E" "B" "A" "L" "L" "." "B" "A" "T" 0DH
```

and this afterwards:

```
                                              MAKE_ME_ZERO─────────┐
                                                                   ↓
THE_BUFFER 13 12 "B" "A" "S" "E" "B" "A" "L" "L" "." "B" "A" "T" 0
```

The Second File Name

The MOVSB instruction

Now we need to duplicate the file name with the extension .BAK. Since we've insisted on eight-letter names and three-letter extensions, all we have to do is move eight letters from FILE_ONE to FILE_TWO using MOVSB. MOVSB means move string byte, and it is one of the string commands that we've already had a brief introduction to.

MOVSB and MOVSW give the names source index to SI and destination index to DI. MOVSB assumes that bytes come from DS:SI and that they go to ES:DI, all the while incrementing SI and DI. To use MOVSB, we can set DS:SI to FILE_ONE and ES:DI to FILE_TWO:

```
            ORG 100H
   START:   JMP BACK
            THE_BUFFER      DB 13
            BYTES_TYPED     DB 0
            FILE_ONE        DB 12 DUP(0)
            MAKE_ME_ZERO    DB 0
            FILE_TWO        DB 8 DUP(0), ".BAK",0
            PROMPT          DB "Filename to back up: $"
   BACK     PROC NEAR
            MOV     DX,OFFSET PROMPT
            MOV     AH,9
            INT     21H
            MOV     AH,0AH
            MOV     DX,OFFSET THE_BUFFER
            INT     21H
            MOV     MAKE_ME_ZERO,0
            MOV     SI,OFFSET FILE_ONE      ←
            MOV     DI,OFFSET FILE_TWO      ←
            :
            :
   EXIT:    INT     20H
   BACK     ENDP
```

And then just move the eight bytes of the name by using the REP prefix for MOVSB. To use REP, we have to fill CX with 8. This is how we do it:

```
            ORG 100H
   START:   JMP BACK
            THE_BUFFER      DB 13
            BYTES_TYPED     DB 0
            FILE_ONE        DB 12 DUP(0)
            MAKE_ME_ZERO    DB 0
            FILE_TWO        DB 8 DUP(0), ".BAK",0
            PROMPT          DB "Filename to back up: $"
   BACK     PROC NEAR
            MOV     DX,OFFSET PROMPT
            MOV     AH,9
            INT     21H
            MOV     AH,0AH
            MOV     DX,OFFSET THE_BUFFER
            INT     21H
            MOV     MAKE_ME_ZERO,0
            MOV     CX,8                    ←
            MOV     SI,OFFSET FILE_ONE
            MOV     DI,OFFSET FILE_TWO
   REP      MOVSB                           ←
            :
            :
   EXIT:    INT     20H
   BACK     ENDP
```

The ASCIIZ name of the original file is in FILE_ONE. And now the ASCIIZ name of the new, back-up file is in FILE_TWO. We will want to copy from file one to file two. To start, let's open file one.

File access
modes

There are three ways to open a file: for reading only, for writing only, and for reading and writing. Each of these can be selected with the "access mode" passed in AL to the open file service, service 3DH. Here's what that information looked like in the table at the beginning of this chapter:

File-Handle Service	Number	You Set	It Returns
Open File	3DH	DS:DX to ASCIIZ AL = mode	If CY = 1, AX has error If CY = 0, AX = File Handle

The access mode, passed in AL, is 0 for reading only, 1 for writing only, and 2 for both.

Access Mode for Opening Files	Means
0	Open file for read only.
1	Open file for write only.
2	Open file for both read and write.

We will set AL to 0. Here's how we open file one:

```
          ORG 100H
START:    JMP BACK
          THE_BUFFER      DB 13
          BYTES_TYPED     DB 0
          FILE_ONE        DB 12 DUP(0)
          MAKE_ME_ZERO    DB 0
          FILE_TWO        DB 8 DUP(0), ".BAK",0
          HANDLE_1        DW 0   ←
          HANDLE_2        DW 0   ←
          PROMPT          DB "Filename to back up: $"
BACK      PROC NEAR
          MOV    DX,OFFSET PROMPT
          MOV    AH,9
          INT    21H
          MOV    AH,0AH
          MOV    DX,OFFSET THE_BUFFER
          INT    21H
          MOV    MAKE_ME_ZERO,0
          MOV    CX,8
          MOV    SI,OFFSET FILE_ONE
          MOV    DI,OFFSET FILE_TWO
REP       MOVSB
          MOV    DX,OFFSET FILE_ONE      ←        ;Open first file
          MOV    AX,3D00H                ←
          INT    21H                     ←
          MOV    HANDLE_1,AX             ←
                 :
                 :
EXIT:     INT    20H
BACK      ENDP
```

Notice that we have combined loading AH with 3DH and AL with 0 into one instruction, MOV AX,3D00H. The *file handle* for file one is returned by service 3DH in AX. We will store the handle (the way we will reference file one from now on) in HANDLE_1.

> The top three bits of AL, bits 7,6,5, can also be set in service 3DH, in DOS Versions after 2.10, to indicate a network sharing mode. These modes set bits 7,6,5 this way for various "modes': 000 = compatible with all, 001 = deny read/write, 010 = deny write, 011 = deny read, 100 = deny none. Sharing modes will become important in OS/2.

After opening the first file, we'll have to create the new, backup version of the file. To do this, we'll use INT 21H service 3CH. Here is service 3CH from the table of file handling services at the beginning of the chapter:

File-Handle Service	Number	You Set	It Returns
Create File	3CH	DS:DX to ASCIIZ string CX = attribute	If CY = 1, AX has error If CY = 0, AX = File Handle

When you create a file you can set its attribute. Here are a list of possible attributes you can set:

Table 4.4 Possible File Attributes

File Attribute	Means
0	Plain old file
1	Read-only
2	Hidden file (hidden from directory searches)
4	A system file (like IBMDOS.COM)
8	Used for the volume label of a disk
10H	This file name is the name of a subdirectory

To select the attribute, you must load it into CX for service 3CH. We will select an attribute of 0. Service 3CH then returns a file handle for file two in AX, and we will store that in HANDLE_2:

```
CODE_SEG      SEGMENT
        ASSUME  CS:CODE_SEG,DS:CODE_SEG,ES:CODE_SEG,SS:CODE_SEG

        ORG 100H
START:  JMP BACK
        THE_BUFFER      DB 13
        BYTES_TYPED     DB 0
```

```
                 FILE_ONE        DB 12 DUP(0)
                 MAKE_ME_ZERO    DB 0
                 FILE_TWO        DB 8 DUP(0), ".BAK",0
                 HANDLE_1        DW 0 ←
                 HANDLE_2        DW 0 ←
                 PROMPT          DB "Filename to back up: $"
        BACK     PROC NEAR
                 MOV     DX,OFFSET PROMPT
                 MOV     AH,9
                 INT     21H
                 MOV     AH,0AH
                 MOV     DX,OFFSET THE_BUFFER
                 INT     21H
                 MOV     MAKE_ME_ZERO,0
                 MOV     CX,8
                 MOV     SI,OFFSET FILE_ONE
                 MOV     DI,OFFSET FILE_TWO
        REP      MOVSB
                 MOV     DX,OFFSET FILE_ONE            ;Open first file
                 MOV     AX,3D00H
                 INT     21H
                 MOV     HANDLE_1,AX
                 MOV     DX,OFFSET FILE_TWO       ←
                 MOV     AH,3CH                  ←    ;Create backup file.
                 MOV     CX,0                    ←
                 INT     21H                     ←
                 MOV     HANDLE_2,AX             ←
                   :
                   :
        EXIT:    INT     20H
        BACK     ENDP

        CODE_SEG        ENDS
                END START
```

Now file one is ready to be read from, and file two ready to be written to.

Figure 4.2 After BASEBALL.BAK Is Open.

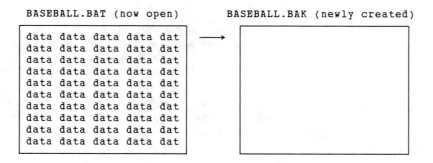

BASEBALL.BAT (now open)   BASEBALL.BAK (newly created)

Storing data   We will have to read the data from the first file into a data area in memory before writing it out to the second file. We can prepare a data area simply by adding a label DATA at the end of the program, but still inside the code segment. This point, immediately after the program, is where data will be read in:

```
               ORG 100H
    START:     JMP BACK
               :
    BACK       PROC NEAR
               :
               MOV      DX,OFFSET FILE_ONE        ;Open first file
               MOV      AX,3D00H
               INT      21H
               MOV      HANDLE_1,AX
               MOV      DX,OFFSET FILE_TWO
               MOV      AH,3CH                    ;Create backup file.
               MOV      CX,0
               INT      21H
               MOV      HANDLE_2,AX
               :
               :
    EXIT:      INT      20H
    BACK       ENDP
    DATA:                               ←

    CODE_SEG        ENDS
               END START
```

Using a label outside our procedure is fine. All this means is that all our data will go immediately after the program in memory. Notice that it was not necessary to reserve space in DATA with DB. This is because, after our program code is finished, we have the rest of the segment (excluding the stack at the high end) to work with. On the other hand, unless we deliberately set aside space in the normal .COM file data area with DB or DW, no space would be reserved. By using the DATA label at the end of our program, we avoid having to set up a 60K data buffer with DB, which would make our program BACK.COM larger than 60K.

Reading from Files

We have to read the data from file one into the data area at the end of the program.

**INT 21H
service 3FH**

Service 3FH reads from an open file. We do not know the file's length, so we do not know how many bytes to read in. However, all we have to do is to ask for the maximum possible, 60K, and service 3FH will read in as many as it can. It reports the *actual number* of bytes read in AX, and that is all we need—we will tell the writing service, service 40H, to write that many to the second file. This is common practice when working with files in assembly language—it does not generate an error.

▌ This is where we could modify BACK.ASM to work with files ▌
▌ greater than 60K. If service 3FH reports that a full 60K bytes were ▌

| read in, as requested, then you should write those bytes, and go back to check if there were more, using service 3FH again. |

This is how to use service 3FH, from our file-handle services table:

File-Handle Service	Number	You Set	It Returns
Read from File	3FH	BX = Handle CX = #Bytes wanted DS:DX = Buffer	If CY = 1, AX has error If CY = 0, AX = #Bytes Read

Service 3FH needs this input—point DS:DX to the buffer used for data (our label DATA), load BX with the file handle (HANDLE_1), and CX with the number of bytes to read (60K). Here we read the data in from file one:

```
            ORG   100H
START:      JMP BACK
            THE_BUFFER      DB 13
            BYTES_TYPED     DB 0
            FILE_ONE        DB 12 DUP(0)
            MAKE_ME_ZERO    DB 0
            FILE_TWO        DB 8 DUP(0), ".BAK",0
            HANDLE_1        DW 0
            HANDLE_2        DW 0
            PROMPT          DB "Filename to back up: $"
BACK        PROC NEAR
            MOV     DX,OFFSET PROMPT
            MOV     AH,9
            INT     21H
            MOV     AH,0AH
            MOV     DX,OFFSET THE_BUFFER
            INT     21H
            MOV     MAKE_ME_ZERO,0
            MOV     CX,8
            MOV     SI,OFFSET FILE_ONE
            MOV     DI,OFFSET FILE_TWO
REP         MOVSB
            MOV     DX,OFFSET FILE_ONE          ;Open first file
            MOV     AX,3D00H
            INT     21H
            MOV     HANDLE_1,AX
            MOV     DX,OFFSET FILE_TWO
            MOV     AH,3CH                     ;Create backup file.
            MOV     CX,0
            INT     21H
            MOV     HANDLE_2,AX
            MOV     AH,3FH            ←
            MOV     CX,60*1024       ←
            MOV     DX,OFFSET DATA   ←
            MOV     BX,HANDLE_1      ←
            INT     21H              ←
            :
            :
EXIT:       INT     20H
BACK        ENDP
DATA:
```

The *
Pseudo-Op

You may have noticed the use of a new Pseudo-Op here, "*", a math operator. This operator makes the assembler multiply for us; in particular, 60 times 1024. This is particularly handy, because, reading the code, it's clear that we want 60K here, and it wouldn't be so clear if we had typed in 61440 instead. Another handy assembler operator is "/", used for division (512/2 returns 256). The use of these special operators can make code clearer, and easier to write, as we already saw with "+" and "—".

Writing the Data to File Two

Next we write the data out to file two, the back-up file, with service 40H. Here's how to use it from our file-handle service table:

File-Handle Service	Number	You Set	It Returns
Write to File	40H	BX = Handle CX = #Bytes DS:DX = Buffer	If CY = 1, AX has error If CY = 0, AX = #Bytes actually written

This service requires that DS:DX point to the data as well (our label DATA), that CX must hold the number of bytes to write (returned from the read operation in AX), and that BX must hold the file handle (HANDLE_2). The only trick here is loading CX for service 40H with the number of bytes actually read, returned in AX by service 3FH. All we'll have to do is transfer the value in AX to CX, and then write the bytes in DATA out:

```
            ORG 100H
START:      JMP BACK
            THE_BUFFER      DB 13
            BYTES_TYPED     DB 0
            FILE_ONE        DB 12 DUP(0)
            MAKE_ME_ZERO    DB 0
            FILE_TWO        DB 8 DUP(0), ".BAK",0
            HANDLE_1        DW 0
            HANDLE_2        DW 0
            PROMPT          DB "Filename to back up: $"
BACK        PROC NEAR
            MOV     DX,OFFSET PROMPT
            MOV     AH,9
            INT     21H
            MOV     AH,0AH
            MOV     DX,OFFSET THE_BUFFER
            INT     21H
            MOV     MAKE_ME_ZERO,0
            MOV     CX,8
            MOV     SI,OFFSET FILE_ONE
            MOV     DI,OFFSET FILE_TWO
```

```
REP      MOVSB
         MOV      DX,OFFSET FILE_ONE         ;Open first file
         MOV      AX,3D00H
         INT      21H
         MOV      HANDLE_1,AX
         MOV      DX,OFFSET FILE_TWO
         MOV      AH,3CH                     ;Create backup file.
         MOV      CX,0
         INT      21H
         MOV      HANDLE_2,AX
         MOV      AH,3FH
         MOV      CX,60*1024
         MOV      DX,OFFSET DATA
         MOV      BX,HANDLE_1
         INT      21H
→        MOV      CX,AX                      ;Set number of bytes to write to
                                             ;number actually read.
→        MOV      AH,40H
→        MOV      BX,HANDLE_2
→        INT      21H1
         :
         :

EXIT:    INT      20H
BACK     ENDP
DATA:
```

After this step, we've copied file one to file two on the disk:

Figure 4.3 BASEBALL.BAK After Being Filled.

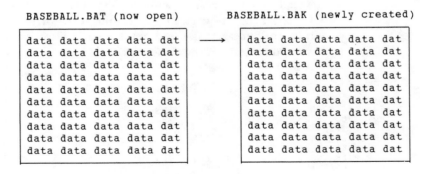

Now that it's done, all that remains is to close the two files. That is done with service 3EH. From our table:

File-Handle Service	Number	You Set	It Returns
Close File	3EH	BX = File Handle	If CY = 1, AX has error

All this service needs is the file's handle in BX (we'll give it both HAN-DLE_1 and HANDLE_2). Here it is:

```
CODE_SEG         SEGMENT
        ASSUME   CS:CODE_SEG,DS:CODE_SEG,ES:CODE_SEG, SS:CODE_SEG]

        ORG 100H
START:  JMP BACK
        THE_BUFFER       DB 13
        BYTES_TYPED      DB 0
        FILE_ONE         DB 12 DUP(0)
        MAKE_ME_ZERO     DB 0
        FILE_TWO         DB 8 DUP(0), ".BAK",0
        HANDLE_1         DW 0
        HANDLE_2         DW 0
        PROMPT           DB "Filename to back up: $"
BACK    PROC NEAR
        MOV      DX,OFFSET PROMPT
        MOV      AH,9
        INT      21H
        MOV      AH,0AH
        MOV      DX,OFFSET THE_BUFFER
        INT      21H
        MOV      MAKE_ME_ZERO,0
        MOV      CX,8
        MOV      SI,OFFSET FILE_ONE
        MOV      DI,OFFSET FILE_TWO
REP     MOVSB
        MOV      DX,OFFSET FILE_ONE        ;Open first file
        MOV      AX,3D00H
        INT      21H
        MOV      HANDLE_1,AX
        MOV      DX,OFFSET FILE_TWO
        MOV      AH,3CH                    ;Create backup file.
        MOV      CX,0
        INT      21H
        MOV      HANDLE_2,AX
        MOV      AH,3FH
        MOV      CX,60*1024
        MOV      DX,OFFSET DATA
        MOV      BX,HANDLE_1
        INT      21H
        MOV      CX,AX                     ;Set number of bytes to write to
                                          ;number actually read.
        MOV      AH,40H
        MOV      BX,HANDLE_2
        INT      21H
        MOV      AH,3EH             ←
        MOV      BX,HANDLE_1        ←
        INT      21H               ←
        MOV      BX,HANDLE_2        ←
        INT      21H               ←
EXIT:   INT      20H
BACK    ENDP
DATA:

CODE_SEG         ENDS
        END START
```

And that's it! Assemble it and give it a try, but make sure to give it the name of a file with an eight-letter name and a three-letter extension, like BASEBALL.BAT. BACK.COM will produce and fill BASE-

BALL.BAK (up to 60K, of course). Our program is capable of copying files. It's not so difficult in assembly language, and it works at high speed, too.

Inside Files

In this chapter, we have seen how to delete files simply by storing their names in memory, pointing to them, and using service 41H of INT 21H. There's not much work needed in just deleting files, however.

Next we saw how to work with the entire file—all the data at once—by copying the file whole and producing a back-up copy. This is also pretty easy to do, compared to higher level languages, which often insist on making distinctions between binary or ASCII files, have rigidly enforced records, and add end–of–file markers or any number of things. All we had to do was open the file we wanted to back up, create a new file, copy from file one into file two, and then close them both.

File records

On the other hand, we did very little with the data actually in the file itself. BACK.COM can swallow whole files at once, and write them back elsewhere on the disk, but it knows nothing about what's in them. This is where all the protocol one usually finds in higher level languages was designed to work—with formatting your file into what are known as records.

Records

A record works like this: suppose you wanted to store all your friends' telephone numbers—a pretty simple example. Each *record* might then be simply, say, 16 bytes that you set aside for the person's name, and another 16 bytes that you set aside for their telephone number. For example this might be a record,

    ←   *16-Bytes*   →

    . . . .   ← The person's name will go here.
    . . . .   ← The telephone number will go here.

In the old days, using FCBs, one did have to define record sizes and block lengths and so on before formatting a file. Using file handles, where you simply select the number of bytes to be read in, is much easier.

You could define such a record with DB in memory, like this:

```
NAME     DB 16 DUP(0)
NUMBER   DB 16 DUP(0)
```

This means that each record is 32 bytes long, and begins at label NAME. If you had a name of a good friend to store, say "Albert Einstein," and a number, say "299-7980," you could put those bytes— or rather, their ASCII equivalents—into NAME and NUMBER, leaving the left-over bytes at the end untouched.

Record fields

Both NAME and NUMBER are referred to as *fields*. This record has two fields, NAME and NUMBER. You could set up in advance, in this particular case, like this:

```
NAME     DB "Albert Einstein", 0
NUMBER   DB "299-7980", 8 DUP(0)
```

> The formal way of setting up records in assembly language is by setting up what is referred to as a data structure, with the Pseudo-Op STRUC. But that's a topic for *Advanced Assembly Language on the IBM PC*.

Notice that in each case, we carefully added zeroes at the end of the field to make sure that the field length in memory stayed the same. This way, every record will be the same length in the file when we write it out, and it is critical that they should be so. A fundamental property about records that you want to retrieve from anywhere in a file is that they have the same length to make finding them easier. Each of our records are 32 bytes long. Here is how Albert Einstein's would look:

```
Albert Einstein.      ← The person's name will go here.
299-7980........      ← The telephone number will go here.
```

> Making sure records have the same length makes it easy to choose a record at random from anywhere in a file. This is called random access—the only type of file formatting we'll deal with here. The other method allows you to have variable-length records, but constrains you to put end-of-record markers into the file to show the boundaries between records. This end-of-record marker is often a carriage return in higher level languages. This is called *sequential access*, since you have to read from the beginning of the file to know the number of the record you are at.

To write this record out to a file, open or create the file, point at NAME, and tell service 40H to write 32 bytes. That's how a record is written in assembly language—as long as you know the record length, you'll always know where you are, or where a given record number is in a file, because the INT 21H services let you specify the number of bytes you want and choose the record length.

You can then make another record with another name and number, say Enrico Fermi, whose number is 271-8281. This is how the record would look:

```
←——16-Bytes——→
Enrico Fermi....
271-8281........
```

The dots indicate a zero byte. You can add this information your data file, which we can call NUMBERS.DAT. To add Enrico Fermi, just write out the 32 bytes of this record. Since we've already written out Albert Einstein, Enrico Fermi will be placed right after him:

```
The data file

┌────────────────────┐
│Albert Einstein.    │  ← First record
│299-7980........    │
│Enrico Fermi....    │  ← Second record
│271-8281........    │
│            :       │  ← Third record, etc.
│            :       │
└────────────────────┘
```

You can continue in like manner, until NUMBERS.DAT is as full as you want it, depending on how many friends you have. NUMBERS.DAT will always be a multiple of 32 bytes in length. After NUMBERS.DAT is fully stocked, however, there might come a day when you realize that you've forgotten Enrico Fermi's telephone number, and want to look it up. How would you do that?

Retrieving Data from Files

There's not much point in writing beautiful data files unless you can use them. And using them isn't as hard as you might think. Here we want to read in a record—the second record of NUMBERS.DAT, that is, Enrico Fermi's name and telephone number.

Reading in
all records
at once

You might expect that we can simply open NUMBERS.DAT and request to read 64 bytes in, which encompasses both the first two records, and, of course, we can. But this method demands that we read in two records; it is clear this might use up a lot of memory if we want record 32,001.

Reading
records
one after
another

Another method might be to read in the first record, 32 bytes, and then to read in the second record in the same location in memory, so that it will overwrite the first record. Then we'd have record two at no additional memory expense. Of course, if we want record 32,001, we'll have to wait a long time to reach it. Fortunately, there is a better way.

Using the Read/Write Pointer

This better way is quite simple. You can set the location in the file that you want to start reading bytes from; that location is called the *read/write pointer*. In other words, this is how NUMBERS.DAT looks now:

```
            NUMBERS.DAT
            _____

Albert Einstein.
299-7980........    ____
                    ____| Record 1
Enrico Fermi....
271-8281........    ____
                    ____| Record 2
Wolfgang Pauli..
314-1592........    ____
                    ____| Record 3
                :
                :
    ←——16-Bytes——→
```

And to read the second record, we could simply position the Read/Write pointer 32 bytes into the file, that is, at the beginning of record two:

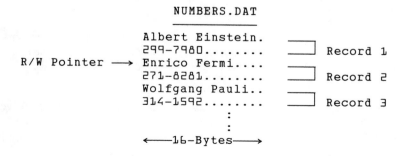

```
                        NUMBERS.DAT
                        _____

                   Albert Einstein.
                   299-7980........    ____
                                       ____| Record 1
R/W Pointer  ——→   Enrico Fermi....
                   271-8281........    ____
                                       ____| Record 2
                   Wolfgang Pauli..
                   314-1592........    ____
                                       ____| Record 3
                            :
                            :
                   ←——16-Bytes——→
```

And then read in that record—ask for 32 bytes to be read in. It's simple.

You read from a file or write to it at the Read/Write pointer. By setting this pointer yourself, you can position yourself in any file.

**INT 21H
service 42H**

To position the Read/Write pointer, use service 42H, Move Read/Write Pointer. Here's the entry for service 42H in Table 4.2:

File-Handle Service	Number	You Set	It Returns

Move Read/Write Pointer	42H	CX:DX = #Bytes to move
		BX = File Handle
		AL = "method"
			If CY = 1, AX has error
			If CY = 0 DX:AX = new location in file.

To use this service, just set CX:DX to the number of bytes that you want to move. The reason two words are specified for this distance is that you may want to move more than 64K bytes, and 64K − 1 is the largest number that a word can hold. If the number is larger than that, you'll need more than 16 bits to hold it.

For example, 68K in hex is 11000H; if you wanted to move the Read/Write pointer that many bytes, you'd set the low word—in DX—to 1000H, and the high word—in CX—to 0001H. Together, CX and DX as CX:DX would make 0001:1000 = 00011000H. Don't make the mistake of treating CX:DX as an address; INT 21H services always request segment addresses to be stored in segment registers, and CX is not a segment register. Although it's unfortunate that the same format is used, CX:DX is meant to indicate a single number, whose high word is CX and whose low word is DX.

Besides setting up the number of bytes to move, BX must hold the file's handle so service 42H knows which file you mean to use.

> As its name implies, you can either read or write at the Read/Write pointer's location—it sets the location at which the next read or write operation will take place in the file.

**File
pointer's
method**

In addition, you have to tell service 42H *how* to move the Read/Write pointer. This is called the *method*, and can range from 0 to 2. The method is passed to service 42H in AL; here are the possible methods:

Table 4.5 Methods for INT 21H Service 42H

Method (in AL)	Means
0	Set R/W pointer to CX:DX bytes from the beginning of the file.
1	Mov R/W pointer CX:DX bytes from where we are now.
2	Set R/W pointer to CX:DX bytes from end of file.

Note: New location of R/W pointer returned in DX:AX. If CY = 1, error code will be in AX.

Read/Write
pointer
method 0

Read/Write
pointer
method 1

Read/Write
pointer
method 2

The standard method is to move the Read/Write pointer the specified number of bytes from the beginning of the file. This is method 0.

Method 1 moves the Read/Write pointer CX:DX from the Read/Write pointer's current position. For example, if the Read/Write pointer is at byte 32,000 in a file, and you specify method 1, and a distance of one byte, you will end up positioned at 32,001.

Method 2 moves the Read/Write pointer to the end of the file, plus the value stored in CX:DX (that is, past the end of the file). This method is almost always used only for determining the length of the file.

Start at the beginning of the file, use method 2 to place the Read/Write pointer at the end of the file, and set CX:DX to 0000:0000. In other words, we are asking that the Read/Write pointer be placed at the end of the file. When service 42H returns, it always sets the new location of the pointer in DX:AX (DX is the high word, AX the low word), and, in this case, DX:AX will simply hold the length of the file, from beginning to end, in bytes.

Using the Read/Write Pointer

This means that we can get any record we want. If we know each record is 32 bytes long, and we want the second record, we can use service 42H, method 0, to position the pointer 32 bytes from the beginning of the file, after the first record, and then read in the second record. If we wanted record 32,001, we would position the pointer at byte 32,000*32, and read the record there in.

Let's put this knowledge to work, and see how it operates in practice, with a new example program. We can even use the file we have been talking about, NUMBERS.DAT. The program, which will look up phone numbers, will be called PHONE.COM.

PHONE.ASM

It would be a long, strenuous exercise to write the program that creates NUMBERS.DAT, and then a second program, PHONE.ASM, to read it in. So we'll cheat a little. We will create NUMBERS.DAT using DEBUG, and not an assembly-language program, since the real point here is data retrieval—we've already written to files. PHONE.ASM will get us started working with the Read/Write pointer.

Making the Data File NUMBERS.DAT

First let's make NUMBERS.DAT. We want to make it just as a program would write it—with 32 bytes, that is, ASCII characters, for each record. Instead of padding the record fields with zero's to fill them out, however, let's use the character "$". This will be a shortcut for us in PHONE.ASM, since we can then just use the string printing service, INT 21H service 9, to print out both name and phone number—service 9 stops printing when it reaches a "$", the end of the NAME or NUMBER field.

Start up DEBUG:

```
A>DEBUG
-
```

The DEBUG Fill Command

We can use the DEBUG *Fill* command, F, to fill memory with "$" characters. Let's give NUMBERS.DAT three records, each 32 bytes long, for a total of 3 × 32 = 96 bytes. In other words, our file, NUMBERS.DAT, will be 96 bytes long. DEBUG starts us off at location CS:0100, so we want to fill the 96 bytes (60H) from CS:0100 to CS:015F with "$"s. This is the way to do it:

```
A>DEBUG
-F 100 15F "$"
```

Let's check to make sure, with the D, or *Dump*, command. D will dump memory locations for you, letting you know what's there:

```
A>DEBUG
-F 100 15F "$"
-D100            ←
0EF1:0100  24 24 24 24 24 24 24 24-24 24 24 24 24 24 24 24   $$$$$$$$$$$$$$$$
0EF1:0110  24 24 24 24 24 24 24 24-24 24 24 24 24 24 24 24   $$$$$$$$$$$$$$$$
0EF1:0120  24 24 24 24 24 24 24 24-24 24 24 24 24 24 24 24   $$$$$$$$$$$$$$$$
```

```
0EF1:0130  24 24 24 24 24 24 24 24-24 24 24 24 24 24 24 24   $$$$$$$$$$$$$$$$
0EF1:0140  24 24 24 24 24 24 24 24-24 24 24 24 24 24 24 24   $$$$$$$$$$$$$$$$
0EF1:0150  24 24 24 24 24 24 24 24-24 24 24 24 24 24 24 24   $$$$$$$$$$$$$$$$
0EF1:0160  24 FC C3 E8 E2 FF 89 3E-4C F6 CB E8 CA FF 2B CF   .......>L.....+.
0EF1:0170  F2 AE E3 03 EB 16 90 B8-00 00 CB E8 BA FF 3B 3E   ..............;>
```

It looks like we're all set. Now we have to enter our names and numbers. There will be two lines of "$"s (each line is 16 characters in the DEBUG dump—just the size of our fields) for each record, and since there are six lines of "$"s, we will be able to put in three records.

DEBUG is a poor editor

Unfortunately, DEBUG makes a particularly bad editor. We have to enter our data with the deposit byte, DB, Pseudo-Op, just as if we were writing a program. Each field will be easy to locate since it is just 16, that is, 10H, bytes apart. We have to assemble (the A command) at the beginning of each field, and use DB to put the string in. Here's how it looks for the NUMBERS.DAT we've developed, as we (tediously) fill each of the six fields:

> You might try this with your word processor, but the reason DEBUG was selected for this exercise is that word processors usually insert unwanted carriage returns.

```
-A100  ←
0EF1:0100 DB "Albert Einstein"
0EF1:010F
-A110  ←
0EF1:0110 DB "299-7980"
0EF1:0118
-A120  ←
0EF1:0120 DB "Enrico Fermi"
0EF1:012C
-A130  ←
0EF1:0130 DB "271-8281"
0EF1:0138
-A140  ←
0EF1:0140 DB "Wolfgang Pauli"
0EF1:014E
-A150  ←
0EF1:0150 db "314-1592"
0EF1:0158
```

Now that memory should be set up correctly, let's dump it again and check:

```
-D100                    ←
0EF1:0100  41 6C 62 65 72 74 20 45-69 6E 73 74 65 69 6E 24   Albert Einstein$
0EF1:0110  32 39 39 2D 37 39 38 30-24 24 24 24 24 24 24 24   299-7980$$$$$$$$
0EF1:0120  45 6E 72 69 63 6F 20 46-65 72 6D 69 24 24 24 24   Enrico Fermi$$$$
0EF1:0130  32 37 31 2D 38 32 38 31-24 24 24 24 24 24 24 24   271-8281$$$$$$$$
0EF1:0140  57 6F 6C 66 67 61 6E 67-20 50 61 75 6C 69 24 24   Wolfgang Pauli$$
0EF1:0150  33 31 34 2D 31 35 39 32-24 24 24 24 24 24 24 24   314-1592$$$$$$$$
0EF1:0160  24 FC C3 E8 E2 FF 89 3E-4C F6 CB E8 CA FF 2B CF   .......>L.....+.
0EF1:0170  F2 AE E3 03 EB 16 90 B8-00 00 CB E8 BA FF 3B 3E   ..............;>
```

Everything is there, ready to be written out. This is exactly the way NUMBERS.DAT would look if it had been written out by a program. We can write NUMBERS.DAT with DEBUG's W command, first filling CX with the number of bytes to fill—60H—and then naming the file with the N command, as we've seen when we used DEBUG as an assembler:

```
-NNUMBERS.DAT
-RCX
CX 0000
:60
-W
Writing 0060 bytes
-Q
```

Our data file, NUMBERS.DAT, is all set. Now that we've got the data, we've got to read it in.

Writing PHONE.ASM

We're ready for the program itself. PHONE will not be so hard to write, because we already know what file we'll be reading in, NUMBERS.DAT. Let's make an ASCIIZ string containing NUMBERS.DAT and open the file here in the beginning of PHONE.ASM, storing the file handle in FILEHANDLE:

```
CODE_SEG        SEGMENT
        ASSUME  CS:CODE_SEG,DS:CODE_SEG,ES:CODE_SEG,SS:CODE_SEG

        ORG 100H
START:  JMP PHONE
        FILENAME        DB "NUMBERS.DAT",0       ←
        FILEHANDLE      DW 0                     ←
PHONE   PROC NEAR
        MOV     DX,OFFSET FILENAME       ←
        MOV     AL,0    ;Read Only       ←
        MOV     AH,3DH                   ←
        INT     21H                      ←
        MOV     FILEHANDLE,AX            ←
        :
        :
EXIT:   INT     20H
PHONE   ENDP

CODE_SEG        ENDS
        END START
```

Notice that we set the "access mode," in AL, to 0 (read only) so that we can only read NUMBERS.DAT. If your program wants to write data as well as read it, use access mode 2 (read and write). We open the file and store the handle, returned in AX, for future use.

In preparation for reading in records, let's set up the two fields that we will need, and that we might as well call PERSON_NAME and NUMBER, as we did before:

```
CODE_SEG           SEGMENT
          ASSUME   CS:CODE_SEG,DS:CODE_SEG,ES:CODE_SEG,SS:CODE_SEG

          ORG 100H
START:    JMP PHONE
          FILENAME            DB "NUMBERS.DAT",0
          FILEHANDLE          DW 0
          PERSON_NAME         DB 16 DUP(0)          ←
          NUMBER              DB 16 DUP(0)          ←
PHONE     PROC NEAR
          MOV      DX,OFFSET FILENAME
          MOV      AL,0     ;Read Only
          MOV      AH,3DH
          INT      21H
          MOV      FILEHANDLE,AX
          :
          :
EXIT:     INT      20H
PHONE     ENDP

CODE_SEG           ENDS
          END START
```

Next we'll have to find out what to do from the user: Which record—1, 2, or 3—should we read in? Or should we quit? Let's type out a prompt that lists the available options:

```
CODE_SEG           SEGMENT
          ASSUME   CS:CODE_SEG,DS:CODE_SEG,ES:CODE_SEG,SS:CODE_SEG

          ORG 100H
START:    JMP PHONE
          FILENAME            DB "NUMBERS.DAT",0
          FILEHANDLE          DW 0
          PERSON_NAME         DB 16 DUP(0)
          NUMBER              DB 16 DUP(0)
          PROMPT              DB "Get phone number (1-3) or Quit (Q): $"  ←
PHONE     PROC NEAR
          MOV      DX,OFFSET FILENAME
          MOV      AL,0     ;Read Only
          MOV      AH,3DH
          INT      21H
          MOV      FILEHANDLE,AX
ASK:      MOV      DX,OFFSET PROMPT           ←
          MOV      AH,9                       ←
          INT      21H                        ←
          MOV      AH,1                       ←
          INT      21H                        ←
          :
          :
EXIT:     INT      20H
PHONE     ENDP

CODE_SEG           ENDS
          END START
```

Here we also use service 1 to get a one-letter response. If that response is "Q," as indicated in the prompt, we should quit. Before we do, however, we must close the files.

Service 1 delivers the typed key's ASCII code in AL. To check whether or not this is "Q," we use CMP. If our response turned out indeed to be "Q," then we have to close the file (service 3EH) and exit, like this:

```
CODE_SEG        SEGMENT
        ASSUME  CS:CODE_SEG,DS:CODE_SEG,ES:CODE_SEG,SS:CODE_SEG

        ORG 100H
START:  JMP PHONE
        FILENAME        DB  "NUMBERS.DAT",0
        FILEHANDLE      DW  0
        PERSON_NAME     DB  16 DUP(0)
        NUMBER          DB  16 DUP(0)
        PROMPT          DB  "Get phone number (1-3) or Quit (Q): $"
PHONE   PROC NEAR
        MOV     DX,OFFSET FILENAME
        MOV     AL,0    ;Read Only
        MOV     AH,3DH
        INT     21H
        MOV     FILEHANDLE,AX
ASK:    MOV     DX,OFFSET PROMPT
        MOV     AH,9
        INT     21H
        MOV     AH,1
        INT     21H
        CMP     AL,"Q"                  ←
        JE      QUIT                    ←
        :
        :
QUIT:   MOV     BX,FILEHANDLE   ←       ;Close the files.
        MOV     AH,3EH          ←
        INT     21H             ←
EXIT:   INT     20H
PHONE   ENDP

CODE_SEG        ENDS
        END START
```

If the response was not "Q," then we'll assume it was a number, 1 to 3. To convert the ASCII code now in AL to a record number, we only have to subtract "0" from AL. This converts the ASCII digit to hex.

After getting the record number, we have to set the Read/Write pointer. To read in the first record, we want the Read/Write pointer at offset 0; for the second record, at offset 32, and for the third, at 64. In other words, the location of the pointer will be (record number − 1) x 32 bytes from the beginning of the file. Here's how we get the record number and calculate the number of bytes to move the pointer:

```
CODE_SEG        SEGMENT
        ASSUME  CS:CODE_SEG,DS:CODE_SEG,ES:CODE_SEG,SS:CODE_SEG

        ORG 100H
```

```
         START:    JMP PHONE
                   FILENAME         DB  ""NUMBERS.DAT",0
                   FILEHANDLE       DW  0
                   PERSON_NAME      DB  16 DUP(0)
                   NUMBER           DB  16 DUP(0)
                   PROMPT           DB  "Get phone number (1-3) or Quit (Q): $"
         PHONE:    PROC NEAR
                   MOV       DX,OFFSET FILENAME
                   MOV       AL,0    ;Read Only
                   MOV       AH,3DH
                   INT       21H
                   MOV       FILEHANDLE,AX
         ASK:      MOV       DX,OFFSET PROMPT
                   MOV       AH,9
                   INT       21H
                   MOV       AH,1
                   INT       21H
                   CMP       AL,"Q"
                   JE        QUIT
                   SUB       AL,"0"    ←
                   MOV       CL,5      ←
                   DEC       AL        ←
                   SHL       AL,CL     ←
                      :
                      :
         QUIT:     MOV       BX,FILEHANDLE              ;Close the files.
                   MOV       AH,3EH
                   INT       21H
         EXIT:     INT       20H
         PHONE     ENDP

         CODE_SEG            ENDS
                   END START
```

Multiplying by factors of 2

    Here we were lucky enough to be able to use the SHL command, which is an easy way to multiply by factors of two in the PS/2 and PC.

SHL and SHR

These two instructions *shift* operands left or right by a specified number of binary spaces. SHL shifts left and SHR shifts right. For example, taking this binary number:

    00000001B

Shifting it left by one place would yield:

    00000010B

Using SHL to multiply by 2

    This is just the same as multiplying by two. Conversely, shifting right by one place would convert

    00000010B

back to

```
000000001B
```

Shifting to the right has the same effect as dividing by two. This is the easy way to multiply in our computer—as long as you can do it in multiples of two. You can shift eight-bit registers, 16-bit registers, and memory locations too. To shift AL left by one bit, for example, do this:

```
SHL     AL,1    H
```

You'd think that shifting it left by two bits would be SHL AL,2. Unfortunately not, at least in the 8088 and 8086. In these two processors, you can only shift left or right by one, or a value held in CL; these are the only two valid ways of shifting AL left:

```
SHL     AL,1    or    SHL     AL,CL
```

where CL has previously been filled with some value (the same format holds for SHR). On the 80186-80386 processors, there is no problem: you don't have to use CL:

```
SHL     AL,5
```

is OK (here we'll stick to what the 8088 can handle, as usual, for compatibility with those readers who don't have a later processor).

> The 80386 also supports the use of double words—32 bits—and can shift them with one instruction, SHLD or SHRD.

When CL equals 5, the SHL AL,CL instruction will have the effect of multiplying AL by 32, just the length of a record.

We've taken the number in AL from ASCII character to record number by subtracting "0," then adjusted it and multiplied it so that it now holds the offset into the file at which we want to start reading. Now we can set the Read/Write pointer.

Setting the Read/Write Pointer

To set the Read/Write pointer in PHONE, we must move the number of bytes to move (in AL) into CX:DX. We will only be using the lowest byte of this combination—DL (since our maximum distance to move will be 64 bytes). To set up CX:DX, we set CX and DH to 0, and then transfer our value from AL (the byte position of the Read/Write pointer) to DL.

After the byte offset is ready, we will load the file handle (in FILE-HANDLE) into BX. Service 42H also demands a method—the position from which to set the pointer; we are using method 0. This method will set the pointer CX:DX bytes from the beginning of the file. This is how we set the pointer at the asked-for record:

```
CODE_SEG        SEGMENT
        ASSUME  CS:CODE_SEG,DS:CODE_SEG,ES:CODE_SEG,SS:CODE_SEG

        ORG 100H
START:  JMP PHONE
        FILENAME        DB "NUMBERS.DAT",0
        FILEHANDLE      DW 0
        PERSON_NAME     DB 16 DUP(0)
        NUMBER          DB 16 DUP(0)
        PROMPT          DB "Get phone number (1-3) or Quit (Q): $"
PHONE   PROC NEAR
        MOV     DX,OFFSET FILENAME
        MOV     AL,0    ;Read Only
        MOV     AH,3DH
        INT     21H
        MOV     FILEHANDLE,AX
ASK:    MOV     DX,OFFSET PROMPT
        MOV     AH,9
        INT     21H
        MOV     AH,1
        INT     21H
        CMP     AL,"Q"
        JE      QUIT
        SUB     AL,"0"
        MOV     CL,5
        DEC     AL
        SHL     AL,CL
→       MOV     CX,0
→       MOV     DH,0
→       MOV     DL,AL
→       MOV     AH,42H
→       MOV     AL,0    ;Set the method.
→       MOV     BX,FILEHANDLE
→       INT     21H
        :
        :
QUIT:   MOV     BX,FILEHANDLE           ;Close the files.
        MOV     AH,3EH
        INT     21H
EXIT:   INT     20H
PHONE   ENDP

CODE_SEG        ENDS
        END START
```

Now we just read in the data, the 32-byte record, into our prepared record area, which starts at the label PERSON_NAME:

```
CODE_SEG        SEGMENT
        ASSUME  CS:CODE_SEG,DS:CODE_SEG,ES:CODE_SEG,SS:CODE_SEG

        ORG 100H
START:  JMP PHONE
        FILENAME        DB "NUMBERS.DAT",0
```

```
          FILEHANDLE      DW 0
          PERSON_NAME     DB 16 DUP(0)
          NUMBER          DB 16 DUP(0)
          PROMPT          DB "Get phone number (1-3) or Quit (Q): $"
PHONE     PROC NEAR
          MOV     DX,OFFSET FILENAME
          MOV     AL,0      ;Read Only
          MOV     AH,3DH
          INT     21H
          MOV     FILEHANDLE,AX
ASK:      MOV     DX,OFFSET PROMPT
          MOV     AH,9
          INT     21H
          MOV     AH,1
          INT     21H
          CMP     AL,"Q"
          JE      QUIT
          SUB     AL,"0"
          MOV     CL,5
          DEC     AL
          SHL     AL,CL
          MOV     CX,0
          MOV     DH,0
          MOV     DL,AL
          MOV     AH,42H
          MOV     AL,0      ;Set the method.
          MOV     BX,FILEHANDLE
          INT     21H
   →      MOV     DX,OFFSET PERSON_NAME
   →      MOV     BX,FILEHANDLE
   →      MOV     CX,32
   →      MOV     AH,3FH
   →      INT     21H
          :
          :
QUIT:     MOV     BX,FILEHANDLE            ;Close the files.
          MOV     AH,3EH
          INT     21H
EXIT:     INT     20H
PHONE     ENDP

CODE_SEG        ENDS
          END START
```

Now the record is in memory. The person's name is in the field we have labeled PERSON_NAME, and the phone number is in the field we have named NUMBER. In Enrico Fermi's case, the second record, this is how things look:

```
PERSON_NAME     "Enrico Fermi$$$$"
NUMBER          "271-8281$$$$$$$$"
```

We can print out both the name and number using service 9, the string printing service of INT 21H, simply by pointing DS:DX at the correct field to print. After we print out the correct field, let's jump back to the top of the program to see if there's another record we should print out (jumping back to the place where we print out the prompt, the label ASK). Here is the final program:

```
CODE_SEG         SEGMENT
         ASSUME  CS:CODE_SEG,DS:CODE_SEG,ES:CODE_SEG,SS:CODE_SEG

                 ORG 100H
START:   JMP PHONE
         FILENAME        DB "NUMBERS.DAT",0
         FILEHANDLE      DW 0
         PERSON_NAME     DB 16 DUP(0)
         NUMBER          DB 16 DUP(0)
         PROMPT          DB "Get phone number (1-3) or Quit (Q): $"
PHONE    PROC NEAR
         MOV     DX,OFFSET FILENAME
         MOV     AL,0      ;Read Only
         MOV     AH,3DH
         INT     21H
         MOV     FILEHANDLE,AX
ASK:     MOV     DX,OFFSET PROMPT
         MOV     AH,9
         INT     21H
         MOV     AH,1
         INT     21H
         CMP     AL,"Q"
         JE      QUIT
         SUB     AL,"0"
         MOV     CL,5
         DEC     AL
         SHL     AL,CL
         MOV     CX,0
         MOV     DH,0
         MOV     DL,AL
         MOV     AH,42H
         MOV     AL,0      ;Set the method.
         MOV     BX,FILEHANDLE
         INT     21H
         MOV     DX,OFFSET PERSON_NAME
         MOV     BX,FILEHANDLE
         MOV     CX,32
         MOV     AH,3FH
         INT     21H
→        MOV     AH,9
→        MOV     DX,OFFSET PERSON_NAME
→        INT     21H
→        MOV     DX,OFFSET NUMBER
→        INT     21H
→        JMP     ASK
QUIT:    MOV     BX,FILEHANDLE              ;Close the files.
         MOV     AH,3EH
         INT     21H
EXIT:    INT     20H
PHONE    ENDP

CODE_SEG         ENDS
         END START
```

Carriage returns and linefeeds

PHONE.COM as it stands is not very user friendly. There is no error checking, a serious oversight when working with files, and the prompt is pretty terse. Even worse, it prints things out one after the other, without even putting in carriage returns. This is easily fixed by printing out a carriage return linefeed pair (ASCII 13 and 10 respectively), when necessary, with INT 21H service 2.

```
CR_LF    DB 13,10
```

Even so, PHONE gets the point across. You can store data in an efficient manner, ensuring that it is easily accessible, in the PS/2 and PC just by using files. As you see, retrieving any record that you have stored is not so difficult using the Read/Write pointer. We've gained a good deal of mastery in working with files.

5
Screen Handling and Fast Graphics

CGA
MDA
EGA
EGA Palettes
BIOS INT 10H
Screen Buffers

Character Attributes
Video Modes
Palettes
Line Drawing
VGA
rgbRGB Settings

The VGA
DAC Registers
256 Colors
Animation
Shape Tables

The CGA   Screen displays on the PC machines have become steadily better over time—a popular improvement. The original Color Graphics Adapter (CGA) could only display four colors at a time, with a poor resolution of 320×200 (320 vertical colums, 200 horizontal rows), and it flickered badly. The individual pixels on the screen were so large that they were better called squares than dots.

The MDA   The other option, the Monochrome Display Adapter (MDA) didn't flicker, had good resolution, but it also didn't do graphics: All it uses are alphanumeric characters. With the introduction of other competing machines, it became clear that graphics was an up and coming issue in hardware, and IBM eventually followed the lead.

The EGA   In 1984 the Enhanced Graphics Adapter (EGA) was introduced, which has since become the standard for PC displays. The EGA can select 16 colors to display at once from a selection of 64, doesn't flicker, and has pretty good resolution: 640×350 (almost as good as the monochrome display, which has 720×350). In addition, the EGA could display anything that the CGA (Color Graphics Adapter) or MDA (Monochrome Graphics Adapter) could—it even used the same character set as the monochrome screen. The improvement can be readily seen in the difference in memory size allocated to the CGA—16K—versus the EGA—(up to) 256K.

The VGA   Then, in April 1987, along with the introduction of the PS/2, the VGA was born. The Video Graphics Adapter is built with IBM chips (or rather, chip), and can do everything the EGA could do (in turn, the EGA can do everything that the CGA and MDA could do) and more. Specifically, of course, is the tremendous expansion in the number of colors that can be displayed. In a particular (low-resolution) mode, the VGA can display 256 colors at once, chosen from among 256K possibilities. This immense number is slightly qualified by the poor resolution in this mode: only 320 × 200. Other VGA graphics modes allow higher resolution display (such as 640 × 480), but with a correspondingly lower number of available colors.

Graphics and color on the PC and PS/2 had clearly become an important issue.

Exploring Screen Handling and Fast Graphics

BIOS INT 10H

This chapter, on screen handling and graphics, will largely be an exploration of BIOS INT 10H (remember, BIOS was assigned the low interrupt numbers), because, for most purposes, it *is* screen handling and graphics on the PS/2 and PC. Even the services of INT 21H that print on the screen (only alphanumerics) call BIOS to do it. BIOS is the software in ROM (augmented now by what is read in from disk), and is the lowest level of support in your PC—even below DOS.

Our primary goal in this chapter is to explore what assembly language can do well on the screen. Even so, we'll examine the most pertinent of the other services of INT 10H as well—there are 20 total—but not all of them (we'll skip lightpen support, for example).

This is our first introduction to BIOS: but the INT instruction works just as it did before: Load a service number into AH, load any other required registers, and execute the INT instruction.

INT 10H does not preserve AX, SI, or DI

One thing you should know before we even begin unraveling the huge INT 10H is that you can't count on it to preserve the AX, SI, and DI registers. When we use it, we'll have to protect those ourselves. DOS would return those registers without problem, but this is the lowest level of our machine—BIOS.

> The term *pixel* is a condensation of "picture element," and refers to each dot on the screen. A pixel can be made to display many different colors, depending on the monitor.

The BIOS Screen-Handling Services

We'll begin by scrutinizing the screen-handling services. What we'll do here is look at how BIOS can put characters on the screen—it can do many things that DOS cannot. For example, here is where we will learn about colored characters, the video or screen buffer, character attributes, and how to move the cursor around or scroll the screen. When we've finished with the screen-handling services, we'll turn to graphics.

We'll begin with the first screen-handling services available. What could be more fundamental to screen handling than moving the cursor around? And that's what services 2 and 3 do.

Services 2 and 3—Set and Get Cursor Position

Service 2, Set Cursor—Set these things:

```
AH =2
DH,DL = Row, Column of new position (0,0 is upper left of screen)
BH = Page Number (usually 0)
```

Service 3, Get Cursor—Set these things:

```
AH =3
BH = Page Number (usually 0)
Returns:
DH, DL = Row, Column of current cursor position
```

We'll use service 2 in our program CHECKER.COM very soon. This service gives you the chance to position the cursor where you want it on the screen. The cursor position is always given as coordinates: (Row, Column). To set this position, just put the row and column numbers in DH, DL respectively. The upper left of the screen is (0,0), and values increase from there:

```
(0,0) Columns increase  →
Rows
Increase


  ↓
```

Service 3 allows you to get the current cursor position. This is useful if you are writing, say, a popup program (see Chapter 6, Popup Programs), and want to use an INT 10H service to write a notepad on the screen. With service 3, you can get the original cursor position (before you popped up) so that you can restore it later, after writing your notepad.

Page Numbers

You also have to load the *page number* into BH to use these services. The page number takes a little more explaining. The video memory can be divided up, in some video modes, into *pages*. Although we will not deal with pages here, we can at least examine the concept.

Some video modes require more memory than others. If there is unused memory in some particular video mode, IBM lets you use it as extra pages of screen display.

The CGA, when it is doing pixel-by-pixel graphics, requires 16K instead of the 4K it uses for its alphanumeric mode (as we'll see shortly). This memory is always available on the CGA card, and since it is enough to make up four full screens of text, IBM allows you to use pages in the graphics monitor when dealing with text. This is how pages were born.

Normally, all pages are copies of each other, and page 0 is displayed. With BIOS, though, it is possible to skip around and selectively write to particular pages. The default page is 0; that's the one we will always use here (the use of pages is not common).

To use the cursor services, set the page number in BH to 0. If you want to set the cursor position, you can pass new coordinates to service 2 in (DH,DL). If you want to get the current position, service 3 will return it to you in the same way. We'll have a chance to set the cursor for ourselves later.

There is more to screen handling than just using the cursor; besides working with the cursor, we can scroll the screen up or down (in OS/2, you can even scroll it *sideways*). This is done with services 6 and 7.

Services 6 and 7—Scroll Active Page Up and Down

Set these things:

```
AH = 6 → Scroll Up.
   = 7 → Scroll Down.
AL = Number of lines to scroll (blank lines will be inserted). AL = 0
     means blank the whole active window.
(CH,CL) = Row, Column of upper-left corner of scroll window.
(DH,DL) = Row, Column of lower-right corner of scroll window.
BH = Attribute to be used on blank line.
```

This is how scrolling is done in the PS/2 and PC. You can even scroll some small section of the screen independently, and it makes a startling effect. Here you set the scroll area's boundaries with (CH,CL)—row, column of upper-left corner of scroll window, and (DH,DL)—row, column of lower-right corner of scroll window. To scroll this window up, use INT 10H service 6; to scroll down, use service 7.

We could go from this:

```
It was a dark
and stormy
night. Heath-
cliffe jumped
```

to this, by scrolling up:

```
and stormy
night. Heath-
cliffe jumped
```

Blank lines are inserted into the window, and they are ready for you to type into:

```
and stormy
night. Heath-
cliffe jumped
```

→

You can select the color of the new line yourself; this is our first introduction to color. To select the color in alphanumeric modes, you choose what is called the *attribute*.

Attributes

The attribute is a one-byte-long value that determines how the character you will be printing is printed. For example, you can select green characters on a blue background, or yellow characters on a red background.

When you set the attribute of the new line, every position in it is given the same attribute byte (even though there is no character there yet). This will determine what the characters that you print there will look like. That is, if you print new characters there, they will use the attribute already set for that line (it is also possible to set attributes character by character when printing, if you want to do it that way).

An attribute byte looks like this:

Figure 5.1 Attribute Byte

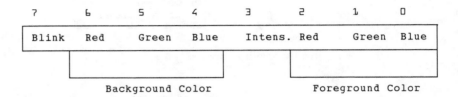

Note: Set bit to 1 to turn on that particular color.

One attribute byte is reserved for each position on the screen. By setting the attribute byte for a character, you can select the mix of red, green, and blue for both the foreground color (the color of the character) and the background color (the color of the rest of the screen). Also, you can set bit 3 for high-intensity display, and bit 7 to make the character blink. A red foreground on a green background has an attribute byte of 00100100B, or 24H.

Figure 5.2 Red Foreground on Green Background

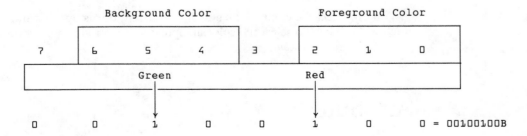

You can mix the colors by adding the respective bit values together. Here are the bit values to add in forming your attribute byte:

Table 5.1 Attribute Byte Bit Values

Bit Value	Color Generated	
1	Blue	Foreground
2	Green	Foreground
4	Red	Foreground
8	High Intensity	
16	Blue	Background
32	Green	Background
64	Red	Background
128	Blinking	

For example, to get a normal setting of white on black, you would turn all the foreground colors (the letter itself) on this way: 1 + 2 + 4 = 7. All the background colors are off, so they are set to 0. This value of 7 is the normal start-up screen attribute value. If you wanted to make that high intensity, you would add 8 to give 15 = 0FH. If you wanted blinking reverse video in white, set all the background colors on, and add 128 to make it blink: 16 + 32 + 64 + 128 = 240 = 0F0H.

On monochrome screens you can't use the individual colors, but you can use the normal screen (7), high intensity (0FH), blinking normal (87H), blinking reverse video (F0H), and underlined, which graphics monitors don't have. To turn on underlining, use a blue foreground (making an attribute of 1). You can also have intense underlining (attribute of 9).

We will use the attribute byte character by character when we print out colored characters in service 9.

The Screen Buffer and Attribute Bytes

A character's ASCII and attribute bytes are stored in the screen buffer. This buffer, therefore, carries two bytes per character in alphanumeric modes. The bytes go like this: character, attribute, character, attribute, and so on. The first character in the buffer goes on the top left of the screen.

There are 25 lines (numbered 0–24) × 80 columns (numbered 0–79) = 2000 positions on the screen, so the screen buffer requires 4,000 bytes of memory (about 4K) to display a single alphanumeric page. In monochrome monitors, this memory starts at B000:0000, and in graphics monitors at B800:0000. For the EGA and VGA modes, this memory starts at A000:0000. In graphics mode, things work similarly, but with pixels, not bits. In the CGA 320×200 mode, there are 320 × 200 = 64,000 pixels. In that mode, the CGA allows four colors, so each pixel needs two bits in memory; this means that the total CGA memory requirement will be 64,000 pixels × 2 bits/pixel ÷ 8 bits/byte = 16,000 bytes. This is rounded up to 16K.

Say that we wanted to write directly to a monochrome adapter's (MDA) memory. We could use the DEBUG edit command like this:

```
A>DEBUG
-EB000:0000
B000:0000  20.  ←
```

DEBUG will let us edit the byte at B000:0000, the first byte in the monochrome video buffer (use B800:0000 for a CGA). It tells us that this byte is currently a 20H = 32 = ASCII space character. We can type our own value, which will appear directly after the "cp"—let's use ASCII 41H (= 65 = ASCII "A"):

```
A>DEBUG
-EB000:0000
B000:0000  20.41    ← Type 41
```

Follow this with a space, and DEBUG will skip on to the next byte, and the "A" will appear on the screen:

```
A>DEBUG
-EB000:0000
B000:0000  20.41    07.
-Q
```

This is the attribute byte of the first screen position. Let's change it from normal video (attribute 7) to blinking reverse video (attribute F0H), followed by a space bar, then a <cr> to quit editing:

```
A>DEBUG
-EB000:0000
B000:0000  20.41    07.F0    20.  ← type a <cr>
-Q
```

This enters a flashing "A" on the screen, writing directly to the monochrome video buffer.

Figure 5.3 From Video Buffer to Screen

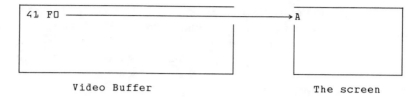

Video Buffer   The screen

For each screen location, both an ASCII code and an attribute byte are stored. Writing directly to the buffer to change these values is the way professional word processors often work.

We can write characters with attributes that we select to, as we'll do now.

Service 9—Write Attribute/Character at Cursor Position

Set these things:

```
AH = 9
AL = ASCII code of character to write
BH = Page Number (usually 0)
BL = Character's attribute
CX = Number of times to write character (restricted to one line on screen)
```

This is how to type out colored characters on the screen—you can even type out multiple copies of the same character if you set CX to a value greater than one.

> When you are typing multiple copies of the same character, however, this service will not type more than one line—it doesn't add carriage return linefeeds.

No cursor advancement

However, the cursor is not automatically moved to the next space after this call is done—it remains pointing at the just-typed character! If you want to use this service to type both characters and attributes, you will have to take care of the cursor yourself, which we'll do immediately in an example.

> To type out with cursor advancement, use service 0EH, "teletype write." However, service 0EH will not type attributes.

An Example: CHECKER.ASM H

Let's dig into an example named CHECKER.ASM. This will bring home the screen-handling services we've been seeing. What CHECKER does is prints out all of the 255 ASCII characters that the PC or PS/2 is capable of. Each one will have an attribute matching its ASCII code (0–255). This way we'll get a look at everything that the PC or PS/2 can type, and in color.

Start with the normal .COM file shell:

```
CODE_SEG          SEGMENT
ASSUME   CS:CODE_SEG, DS:CODE_SEG
         ORG     100H
ENTRY:
                  :
                  :
         INT     20H
CODE_SEG          ENDS
         END     ENTRY
```

We will use LOOP to loop over all characters and attributes. This means that we must set the loop index, CX, to 255. Also, INT 10H service 9, which prints out characters and attributes, requires the ASCII code in AL and the attribute in BL, as we just saw. Let's initialize them both to 0:

```
CODE_SEG          SEGMENT
ASSUME   CS:CODE_SEG, DS:CODE_SEG
         ORG     100H
ENTRY:   MOV     CX,255   ←      ;Loop over all 255 combinations
         MOV     AL,0     ←      ;Start with character 0
         MOV     BL,0     ←      ;And attribute 0
         :
         :
         INT     20H
CODE_SEG          ENDS
         END     ENTRY
```

Since this is a BIOS character-printing service, we'll have to set the cursor ourselves. That is done with INT 10H service 2, which expects the new cursor row to be in DH, and its column to be in DL. Let's start off at, say, row 4 and column 0 (4,0). We need to set DH and DL, and then we can enter our character printing loop:

```
CODE_SEG          SEGMENT
ASSUME   CS:CODE_SEG, DS:CODE_SEG
         ORG     100H
ENTRY:   MOV     CX,255          ;Loop over all 255 combinations
         MOV     AL,0            ;Start with character 0
         MOV     BL,0            ;And attribute 0
         MOV     DL,0     ←      ;Start at column 0
         MOV     DH,4     ←      ;And row 4
```

```
        COLOR_LOOP:                      ←
             ......PUSH     AX           ←
             :      MOV     AH,2         ←        ;Set cursor
             :      INT     10H          ←
             :      POP     AX           ←
             :      :
             :.....LOOP     COLOR_LOOP   ←        ;Keep going
                    INT     20H
        CODE_SEG            ENDS
                    END     ENTRY
```

We also want to set the cursor position inside our loop, since each time through the loop we will have to change it. Notice that, since we can't count on AX being returned from INT 10H safely, we have enclosed our call to INT 10H with PUSH AX and POP AX:

```
        CODE_SEG           SEGMENT
        ASSUME  CS:CODE_SEG, DS:CODE_SEG
                ORG        100H
        ENTRY:  MOV        CX,255           ;Loop over all 255 combinations
                MOV        AL,0             ;Start with character 0
                MOV        BL,0             ;And attribute 0
                MOV        DL,0             ;Start at column 0
                MOV        DH,4             ;And row 4
        COLOR_LOOP:
             ......PUSH     AX           ←
             :      MOV     AH,2                  ;Set cursor
             :      INT     10H
             :      POP     AX           ←
             :      :
             :.....LOOP     COLOR_LOOP   ←        ;Keep going
                    INT     20H
        CODE_SEG            ENDS
                    END     ENTRY
```

Now we're ready to print out the character, having set our position on the screen. We can use service 9:

```
→ AH = 9
  AL = ASCII code of character to write
  BH = Page Number (usually 0)
  BL = Character's attribute
  CX = Number of times to write character (restricted to one line on screen)
```

We've already loaded AL (ASCII code) and BL (attribute), so we just execute INT 10H, service 9. As you can see, service 9 also requests a character count, which will be 1 for us, in CX. Since we are also using CX as a loop index, we will push it as well as AX before executing INT 10H, and restore it afterward:

```
        CODE_SEG           SEGMENT
        ASSUME  CS:CODE_SEG, DS:CODE_SEG
                ORG        100H
        ENTRY:  MOV        CX,255           ;Loop over all 255 combinations
                MOV        AL,0             ;Start with character 0
```

```
            MOV     BL,0              ;And attribute 0
            MOV     DL,0              ;Start at column 0
            MOV     DH,4              ;And row 4
COLOR_LOOP:
.....PUSH     AX
:     MOV     AH,2              ;Set cursor
:     INT     10H
:     POP     AX
:     MOV     AH,9              ;Now type character/attribute
:     PUSH    AX        ←
:     PUSH    CX        ←
:     MOV     CX,1      ←
:     INT     10H       ←
:     POP     CX        ←
:     POP     AX        ←
:     :
:.....LOOP    COLOR_LOOP        ;Keep going
            INT     20H
CODE_SEG    ENDS
            END     ENTRY
```

We've printed out our first character and attribute. Now we have to increment both the ASCII code (in AL) and the attribute (in BL) to prepare for printing again:

```
CODE_SEG        SEGMENT
ASSUME  CS:CODE_SEG, DS:CODE_SEG
        ORG     100H
ENTRY:  MOV     CX,255            ;Loop over all 255 combinations
        MOV     AL,0              ;Start with character 0
        MOV     BL,0              ;And attribute 0
        MOV     DL,0              ;Start at column 0
        MOV     DH,4              ;And row 4
COLOR_LOOP:
.....PUSH     AX
:     MOV     AH,2              ;Set cursor
:     INT     10H
:     POP     AX
:     MOV     AH,9              ;Now type character/attribute
:     PUSH    AX
:     PUSH    CX
:     MOV     CX,1
:     INT     10H
:     POP     CX
:     POP     AX
:     INC     AL        ←       ;Select next character
:     INC     BL        ←       ;And next attribute
:     :
:.....LOOP    COLOR_LOOP        ;Keep going
            INT     20H
CODE_SEG    ENDS
            END     ENTRY
```

Also, of course, we have to prepare DH and DL with the new row and column number to set the cursor to. We just increment the column number. If we are at the end of the screen (compare DL to 79), then we reset the column number to zero (MOV DL,0), and increment the row, moving us down to the next line (INC DH):

```
CODE_SEG         SEGMENT
ASSUME  CS:CODE_SEG, DS:CODE_SEG
        ORG     100H
ENTRY:  MOV     CX,255                  ;Loop over all 255 combinations
        MOV     AL,0                    ;Start with character 0
        MOV     BL,0                    ;And attribute 0
        MOV     DL,0                    ;Start at column 0
        MOV     DH,4                    ;And row 4
COLOR_LOOP:
        PUSH    AX
        MOV     AH,2                    ;Set cursor
        INT     10H
        POP     AX
        MOV     AH,9                    ;Now type character/attribute
        PUSH    AX
        PUSH    CX
        MOV     CX,1
        INT     10H
        POP     CX
        POP     AX
        INC     AL                      ;Select next character
        INC     BL                      ;And next attribute
        INC     DL            ←         ;Find new cursor column
        CMP     DL,79         ←         ;Might have to go to next row
        JB      OK_CURSOR ←
        MOV     DL,0          ←
        INC     DH            ←         ;Go to next row
OK_CURSOR:                    ←
        LOOP    COLOR_LOOP              ;Keep going
        INT     20H
CODE_SEG         ENDS
        END     ENTRY
```

That completes the loop and, with it, CHECKER.ASM. When you run it, you'll notice that halfway through the display, the blinking bit (bit 7 in the attribute byte) gets set, so the second half of the display blinks.

What if we wanted to print on the screen, but didn't want to have to set the attribute as well? For example, when we scroll a line with the scrolling services, we can set the attribute of the whole line. We might want to preserve those attributes when we print in that new line.

In that case, we could use INT 10H, service 0AH. Service 0AH is useful when you're printing on the screen and don't want to disturb the colors already there (which is often). Since it's so useful, let's take a look at this service:

Service 0AH—Write Character Alone at Current Cursor Position

Set these things:

```
AH = 0AH
AL = ASCII code of character to write
BH = Page Number (usually 0)
CX = Number of times to write character (restricted to one line on screen)
```

This is the same as service 9, except that it does not change the attribute as it writes. In other words, if the character it is overwriting is red on blue, the new character will be red on blue, too.

Also, just as service 9 does, this service leaves the cursor pointing at the just-typed character.

We'll get a chance to use this service in Chapter 6, Popup Programs. If you'd like, you can supplant service 9 in CHECKER.ASM with this one. There is one remaining character-handling service before we head into graphics, 0EH, the "teletype write" service. This is the BIOS printing service that *does* handle the cursor correctly.

Service 0EH—Teletype Write

Set these things:

```
AH = 0EH
AL = Character to write
```

This service types characters more in the way you'd expect. Services 9 and 0AH type characters, but do not advance the cursor past the last character typed, and put symbols on the screen for screen control characters like the linefeed or carriage return.

Service 0EH both advances the cursor and treats carriage returns and linefeeds as commands, not characters to print. However, this service will not print out attributes. You'll either have to handle the cursor yourself when you print out, or forego attributes and use 0EH.

That's all the options: printing with attributes, printing without attributes, and printing with cursor advancement. That's also the end of our screen-handling (alphanumeric) work in INT 10H. Let's turn from screen handling to handling graphics instead.

Graphics

Write Dot

Despite the rich number of colors now available to us, the actual BIOS programming support for drawing graphics is terrible. The graphics support in BIOS only allows you to write one dot (that is, one pixel). This support is minimal, compared to Macintosh, which has built in "Toolbox" routines (like QuickDraw) that can draw circles, lines, boxes, fill shapes, and so on—and quickly.

Later on in this chapter we'll develop a program that will draw boxes on the screen, and that's at least a small improvement. There is a line-drawing program in Advanced Assembly Language for the IBM PC, and even though it doesn't use any fancy method (e.g., Bresenham's algorithm), it still takes up pages. The program is so long because of the awkwardness of using integer arithmetic for floating-point calculations—if it used the coprocessor (also covered in the advanced book), it could have been shorter.

Before we start to draw boxes, we'll have to learn how to select what mode (that is, resolution and color options) the screen is running in, and how to specify what color the dot on the screen will be. We can select graphics modes or alphanumeric modes. All that is done in INT 10H, service 0.

INT 10H Service 0—Set Video Mode

Set these things:

```
AH = 0
AL = New Video Mode
```

This is a big one. Here we will see all the modes possible on all the PS/2 and PC machines—how many colors they support and how many lines they use on the screen. Whenever you want to do graphics, you'll first have to set the mode to the desired resolution. After that has been done, it stays that way until it is set some other way. Setting the mode is a thing done usually quite early in graphics programs.

To set the video mode for your particular screen (CGA, MDA, EGA, or VGA), put 0 in AH, and the new mode in AL. Here are *all* the possible modes:

Table 5.2 Video Modes

Mode (in AL)	Display Lines	Number of Colors	Adapters	Maximum Pages
0	40×25	B&W text	CGA, EGA, VGA	8
1	40×25	Color text	CGA, EGA, VGA	8
2	80×25	B&W text	CGA, EGA, VGA	4 (CGA) 8 (EGA, VGA)
3	80×25	Color text	CGA, EGA, VGA	4 (CGA) 8 (EGA, VGA)
4	320×200	4	CGA, EGA, VGA	1
5	320×200	B&W	CGA, EGA, VGA	1
6	640×200	2 (on or off)	CGA, EGA, VGA	1
7	80×25	Monochrome	MDA, EGA, VGA	1 (MDA) 8 (EGA, VGA)
8	160×200	16	PCjr	1
9	320×200	16	PCjr	1
AH	640×200	1	PCjr	1
BH	Reserved for future use.			

Table 5.2 Video Modes *(continued)*

Mode (in AL)	Display Lines	Number of Colors	Adapters	Maximum Pages
CH	Reserved for future use.			
DH	320 × 200	16	EGA, VGA	8
EH	640 × 200	16	EGA, VGA	4
FH	640 × 350	monochrome	EGA, VGA	2
10H	640 × 350	16	EGA, VGA	2
11H	640 × 480	2	VGA	1
12H	640 × 480	16	VGA	1
13H	320 × 200	256	VGA	1

Some of these modes are alphanumeric—that is, they are text modes that don't support graphics (modes 0 to 3, and 7). You can still use text as usual in graphics modes, however.

▌ In graphics modes, the cursor will not appear on the screen. ▌

You can see how the modes are partitioned by adapter—modes 0 to 6 are used on the CGA (and EGA and VGA, since they're compatible), mode 7 is the monochrome display adapter, MDA (and EGA and VGA again since they can mimic the MDA), modes 8 to 0AH are the PCjr, modes 0DH to 10H are the EGA and VGA (here the VGA is emulating the EGA for compatibility), and modes 11H to 13H are just for the VGA (mode 13H is the 256 color one).

Table 5.3 Video Modes and Their Supporting Adapters

Mode	Adapter			
0		CGA	EGA	VGA
1		↓	↓	↓
2				
3				
4				
5				
6				
7	MDA	↓		
DH				
EH				
FH				
10H			↓	
11H				
12H				
13H				↓

Black and White Versus Color

The CGA can work with monitors that have all colors (color monitors) or black and white ones (B&W—often black and green on monitors without color). Its text modes are set up accordingly: Modes 0 and 1 are the same, except that Mode 0 is B&W, and Mode 1 displays in color, modes 2 and 3 are B&W and color, respectively.

Next come the CGA graphics modes: Mode 4 is color, and mode 5 is B&W, as indicated in Table 5.2. In addition, in mode 6, pixels can only be on or off—even though two colors are listed. One is black, the other white.

To set the screen the way you want it, just select from the listed modes, and use INT 10H, service 0. That's it. Now that we've set up the screen, let's see if we can't select some colors to use.

Service 0BH—Set CGA Color Palette (Colors in CGA 320 × 200 Mode Only)

Set these things:

```
AH = 0BH
BH = Palette Color ID (0 or 1, see below)
BL = Color(s) to set with that Palette Color ID (see below)
BH = 0
        BL = Background Color (0_31) From now on, this will
             be color value 0 to be used in Write and
             Read Dot. What colors 0_15 actually mean
             (blue, red, etc.) is discussed below. * In
             alphanumeric modes, this background color
             will determine the screen border color
             (0_31; 16_31 means high intensity.)
BH = 1
        BL = Palette to be used
             BL = 0 Selects Green/Red/Yellow Palette.
                  Color value 1 in Write and Read Dot
                  will be green, color value 2 will be
                  red, 3 will be yellow.
             BL = 1 Selects this palette and color
                  values: cyan (color value will be
                  1)/magenta (2)/ white (3).
```

This is another big service. Here you set the four colors the CGA can draw (and the EGA and VGA when operating in the CGA modes) in its 320 × 200 resolution mode. The additional colors that the EGA or VGA can use are set by service 10H—this is only for the CGA compatibility screen modes.

There are actually three modes of resolution in the CGA—low, medium, and high. The number of pixels up and down (in the Y direction) is always the same—200. The number across (the X direction) varies from 160 (low-resolution) through 320 (medium-resolution) to 640 (high-resolution).

You can only display the maximum number of colors available, 16, in low-resolution mode. However, there is *no* support in the PC's or PS/2's software, BIOS or DOS, for low-resolution. The graphics video controller can be put in low resolution mode, though, so if you want to take the time, you can provide support yourself. As it is, we will concentrate here only on medium- and high-resolution graphics.

Palettes

In medium-resolution graphics on the CGA (320×200) you can display four colors at any pixel, and in high-resolution (640×200) only two—black and white (on and off). Here are the CGA's graphics modes:

Table 5.4 CGA Graphic Modes

Mode (in AL)	Display Lines	Number of Colors	Adapters	Maximum Pages
0	40×25	B&W text	CGA, EGA, VGA	8
1	40×25	Color text	CGA, EGA, VGA	8
2	80×25	B&W text	CGA, EGA, VGA	4 (CGA) 8 (EGA, VGA)
3	80×25	Color text	CGA, EGA, VGA	4 (CGA) 8 (EGA, VGA)
4	320×200	4	CGA, EGA, VGA	1
5	320×200	B&W	CGA, EGA, VGA	1
6	640×200	2 (on or off)	CGA, EGA, VGA	1

Even the four colors of medium resolution are an illusion, because you are free to pick only one of the four; the other three (colors 1,2, and 3) can only be chosen by picking one of two *palettes*.

CGA palette colors

There are two CGA palettes: green, red, yellow; and cyan, magenta, white. When you turn a pixel on with the Write Dot service, you specify which color value—0, 1, 2, or 3—to make it. The palette colors make up color values 1, 2, and 3 in order (the background color will make up color value 0).

Let's see this more clearly. To select which palette to use, use service 0BH. From our table for this service:

Set these things:

```
AH = 0BH
BH = Palette Color ID (0 or 1, see below)
BL = Color(s) to set with that Palette Color ID (see below)
```

```
BH = 0
        BL = Background Color (0-31) From now on, this will be
             color value 0 to be used in Write and Read Dot.
             What colors 0-15 actually mean (blue, red, etc)
             is discussed below. * In alphanumeric modes,
             this background color will determine the screen
             border color (0-31; 16-31 means high intensity.)

BH = 1
        BL = Palette to be used
             BL = 0 Selects Green/Red/Yellow Palette. Color
                    value 1 in Write and Read Dot will be
                    green, color value 2 will be red, 3 will
                    be yellow.
             BL = 1 Selects this palette and color values:
                    cyan (color value will be 1)/magenta (2)/
                    white (3).
```

Set BH to 1, to indicate that you want to select a three-color palette. Then set BL to either 0 or 1, depending on which palette you want. (Palette 0 = green, red, yellow; palette 1 = cyan, magenta, white).

After you've selected the palette, you've selected colors 1 to 3 of the colors that will be used by the CGA. Whenever you write a dot on the screen, you can pass a color value that is 0 to 3 (when in 320×200 CGA resolution mode). For example, if you select palette 1, you can write cyan, magenta, or white dots on the screen. The Write Dot service that we will cover requires a color value for the dot. If you pass it color value 1 with this CGA palette, you will draw a cyan dot.

The CGA Background Color

Color values 1 to 3 come from the palette, and color value 0 is the background color, which you can choose out of 16 choices:

Figure 5.4 CGA Possible Color Values

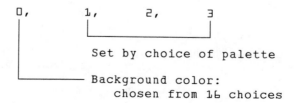

To choose the color that will become color value 0, let's look at our table for this service again:

Set these things:

```
AH = 0BH
BH = Palette Color ID (0 or 1, see below)
BL = Color(s) to set with that Palette Color ID (see below)

BH = 0
        BL = Background Color (0-31) From now on, this will
             be color value 0 to be used in Write and
             Read Dot. What colors 0-15 actually mean
             (blue, red, etc.) is discussed below. * In
             alphanumeric modes, this background color
             will determine the screen border color (0-
             31; 16-31 means high intensity.)

BH = 1
        BL = Palette to be used
             BL = 0 Selects Green/Red/Yellow Palette.
                    Color value 1 in Write and Read Dot
                    will be green, color value 2 will be
                    red, 3 will be yellow.
             BL = 1 Selects this palette and color
                    values: cyan (color value will be
                    1)/magenta (2)/ white (3).
```

First, set BH to 0, to inform this service that you want to select the CGA background color. Then put the background color number that you want in BL, and execute service 0BH.

CGA colors to choose from

There are 32 possible colors to choose from—16 colors and 16 more high-intensity versions of the same colors. Here are the colors available to fill BL with (add 16 to make the color high intensity):

Table 5.5 Colors Available (CGA)

Color Number	Color
0	Black (off)
1	Blue
2	Green
3	Cyan (green + blue)
4	Red
5	Magenta (red + blue)
6	Brown
7	White
8	Black
9	Light blue
10	Light green
11	Light cyan
12	Light red

Color Number	Color
13	Light magenta
14	Yellow
15	Light white

(These are also the default first 16 color numbers for the EGA and VGA.)

In setting the background color, note that the *whole* background will no longer be black, but will become the color you've selected.

This is how you select the color values 0 to 3 that you will pass to the Write Dot service later to draw on the screen: Select one of two palettes to choose color values 1 to 3, and select the background color to choose color value 0. When you want to specify a color to be used, this color value (0 to 3 in the CGA) is what you will pass.

High-Resolution CGA Mode

In high-resolution CGA mode, 640x200 pixels (mode 6), you cannot choose four colors, but only two: on or off, 0 or 1. With the amount of memory available to it, the CGA can only save one bit per pixel in this higher resolution mode (i.e., 320×200 versus 640×200). Since there are 200 lines down (on graphics monitors, characters are eight scan lines high, and 8×25 lines = 200) and 640 lines across, there are $640 \times 200 = 128,000$ bits needed. This makes 16,000 bytes, rounded up in the CGA's video buffer to 16K.

In medium-resolution, 320×200, we can specify one of four colors for each pixel, so we need two bits to hold the possible values for each pixel. Since there are only half as many pixels (320 across versus 640 across), we still use the same size video buffer, 16K.

Now we've set the screen mode and selected our colors. It's time to draw on the screen.

Service 0CH—Write Dot

Set these things:

```
AH = OCH
DX = Row Number (0-199, 0-349, 0-479)
CX = Column Number (0-319 or 0-639)
AX = Color Value
BH = Page number (0 based) for multipaged graphics modes
```

Here it is! Graphics on the PS/2 and PC, right here. To set a pixel anywhere on any screen (if you've set the mode, service 0, correctly), use Write Dot. Set DX = Row Number (0 to 199, 0 to 349, 0 to 479), and CX = Column Number (0 to 319 or 0 to 639). (0,0) is at the top left of the screen.

```
(0,0) Columns increase ──→
Rows
Increase

    │
    ↓
```

The big issue in the write dot service is in the innocuous line AX = Color Value, because the color value has three different interpretations under the three different graphics standards: CGA, EGA, and VGA.

The color value can range from 0 to 3 on CGA (but only 0 to 1 in high CGA resolution, 640 × 200), 0 to 15 on EGA, and 0 to 255 on VGA (but only in VGA mode 13H—otherwise it's 0 to 15). In CGA modes, these color values are set with service 0BH; in EGA and VGA modes with service 10H. Once the color values are set, you can draw anywhere on the screen with this service—that's what it's designed for.

Let's put Write Dot to use at once. Here is where we can draw boxes on the screen—our first graphics work.

Putting Graphics to Use

Graphics
and integer
math

We will take all the graphics knowledge we've acquired and put it to use here. Any graphics tools we design will help augment the PS/2 and PC BIOS services. Unfortunately, these kinds of tools are not usually easy to write—not because of some graphics complexities usually, but because of the difficulty of doing integer math when you really need floating point math.

Even drawing a line becomes a real struggle when you have to try to preserve accuracy in the slope as you go from pixel to pixel. You might be able to imagine how difficult it is to write a program that can draw circles or ellipses (where squares and square roots can be involved).

We don't need to draw ellipses to get started, though; we can introduce ourselves to using graphics by drawing rectangular boxes. Provided with the coordinates of the box's upper-left corner and the coordinates of the lower-right corner, we can use Write Dot to get the job done effectively. Let's give it a try.

Our program will be called BOX.ASM. Even though the two corner coordinates are already written into the data area, you can change the program easily to ask for user input, or pass the coordinates in registers when calling BOX from a larger program (make the procedure BOX part of your .ASM file, in the code segment, and call it).

BOX.ASM

Our aim in BOX is to draw rectangles on the screen. First we take a standard .COM file shell:

```
CODE_SEG        SEGMENT
        ASSUME  CS:CODE_SEG, DS:CODE_SEG, ES:CODE_SEG, SS:CODE_SEG
        ORG     100H
START:  JMP     BOX
        :
BOX     PROC    NEAR
        :
        INT     20H
BOX     ENDP

CODE_SEG        ENDS
        END     START
```

Add the things we know we'll need: space for the corner coordinates of the box, and the color value that will be used. For this demonstration program, let's choose CGA video mode 6 (640×200 high resolution CGA graphics—two color), just to make sure that this program can be used by almost everyone. In this mode, any non-zero color value turns the pixel on—so we'll set the color value to 15. To make your rectangle colored, just set the color value you want and choose a mode that your machine can support to display it in (instead of 6).

We should also set some values for the corner coordinates: The CGA screen is 0 to 199 and 0 to 319, so let's set these values for our first box:

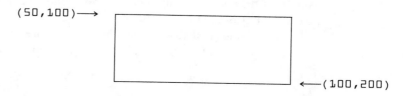

Here's what our new data area looks like:

```
CODE_SEG        SEGMENT
        ASSUME  CS:CODE_SEG, DS:CODE_SEG, ES:CODE_SEG, SS:CODE_SEG
        ORG     100H
START:  JMP     BOX
        TOPROW  DW      50        ←
        TOPCOL  DW      100       ←
        BOTROW  DW      100       ←
        BOTCOL  DW      200       ←
        COLOR   DB      15        ←
BOX     PROC    NEAR
        :
        INT     20H
BOX     ENDP

CODE_SEG        ENDS
        END     START
```

First, we set the video mode, using (what else?) INT 10H:

```
CODE_SEG        SEGMENT
        ASSUME  CS:CODE_SEG, DS:CODE_SEG, ES:CODE_SEG, SS:CODE_SEG
        ORG     100H
START:  JMP     BOX
        TOPROW  DW      50
        TOPCOL  DW      100
        BOTROW  DW      100
        BOTCOL  DW      200
        COLOR   DB      15
BOX     PROC    NEAR
→       MOV     AH,0
→       MOV     AL,6
→       INT     10H
        :
        INT     20H
BOX     ENDP

CODE_SEG        ENDS
        END     START
```

This is where you can set the mode to whatever you want on your own machine, if desired. If you're curious to see what a particular color looks like on your monitor, you can use that color as COLOR in BOX (and use a screen mode other than 6, which only displays white or black).

Three loops in BOX

Here is how to proceed: We will draw the box from the top to bottom, using LOOP. First, we will draw the top of the box, then the sides, and finally the bottom. This will take three loops.

To make things easier, let's add a little procedure to actually write the dot on the screen. Here, in WRITEDOT, we will set everything up for the Write Dot service, and then write the dot. To use WRITEDOT, we will need some way of passing the dot's coordinates. Let's use the SI and DI registers, since they are not doing anything just now:

```
CODE_SEG        SEGMENT
        ASSUME  CS:CODE_SEG, DS:CODE_SEG, ES:CODE_SEG, SS:CODE_SEG
        ORG     100H
START:  JMP     BOX
        TOPROW  DW      50
        TOPCOL  DW      100
        BOTROW  DW      100
        BOTCOL  DW      200
        COLOR   DB      15
BOX     PROC    NEAR
        MOV     AH,0
        MOV     AL,6
        INT     10H
        :
        INT     20H
BOX     ENDP

WRITEDOT        PROC
→       PUSH    AX
→       PUSH    CX
→       PUSH    DX
→       MOV     DX,SI
→       MOV     CX,DI
→       MOV     AL,COLOR
→       MOV     AH,0CH
→       INT     10H
→       POP     DX
→       POP     CX
→       POP     AX
→       RET
WRITEDOT        ENDP

CODE_SEG        ENDS
        END     START
```

Note in particular the use of PUSHes and POPs in WRITEDOT to save the registers that WRITEDOT uses. If BOX called WRITEDOT, and WRITEDOT changed all the registers that BOX was counting on, it would be a serious problem. Notice also the use of RET at the end of WRITEDOT, which returns us to BOX after the call is completed. To use WRITEDOT, we'll load the row number into SI and the column number into DI.

Now let's add the first loop, the one that draws the top of the box. Here we will want to write dots starting with (TOPROW,TOPCOL) at the left and ending with (TOPROW,BOTCOL) on the right. In other words, here is our box with all four corners:

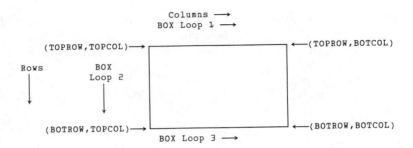

In this first loop, we'll have to increment the column number from TOPCOL to BOTCOL; in other words, we want to loop BOTCOL-TOPCOL times, drawing a dot each time. To do this, we'll put BOTCOL-TOPCOL in CX, which LOOP uses to determine the number of times to loop. Here it is:

```
CODE_SEG            SEGMENT
         ASSUME     CS:CODE_SEG, DS:CODE_SEG, ES:CODE_SEG, SS:CODE_SEG
         ORG        100H
START:   JMP        BOX
         TOPROW     DW     50
         TOPCOL     DW     100
         BOTROW     DW     100
         BOTCOL     DW     200
         COLOR      DB     15
BOX      PROC       NEAR
         MOV        AH,0
         MOV        AL,6
         INT        10H
         MOV        CX,BOTCOL     ←    ;Draw the top of the box
         SUB        CX,TOPCOL     ←    ;Find number of columns to loop over
         MOV        SI,TOPROW     ←    ;SI holds row number of current pixel
         MOV        DI,TOPCOL     ←    ;DI holds column number of current pixel
TOPLOOP:CALL        WRITEDOT      ←    ;Loop over the columns
         INC        DI            ←
         LOOP       TOPLOOP       ←
         :
         INT        20H
BOX      ENDP

WRITEDOT            PROC
         PUSH       AX
         PUSH       CX
         PUSH       DX
         MOV        DX,SI
         MOV        CX,DI
         MOV        AL,COLOR
         MOV        AH,0CH
         INT        10H
         POP        DX
         POP        CX
         POP        AX
         RET
WRITEDOT            ENDP

CODE_SEG            ENDS
         END        START
```

Next we have to loop through Loop 2, drawing the sides:

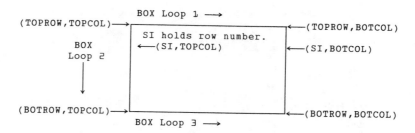

Here we move downward in rows, starting at row TOPROW and ending at row BOTROW. In other words, we want to loop BOTROW-TOPROW times (remember, (0,0) is at top left on the screen, so BOTROW is bigger than TOPROW). Now we will put BOTROW-TOPROW into CX.

In each row we want to write a dot on the left side and on the right side. As we loop through Loop 2, the row number that is stored in SI will be steadily incremented. By looking at the diagram, we see that we have to draw the dot for the left side at (SI,TOPCOL), and the dot for the right side at (SI,BOTCOL). Here's what that is in code:

```
CODE_SEG      SEGMENT
      ASSUME  CS:CODE_SEG, DS:CODE_SEG, ES:CODE_SEG, SS:CODE_SEG
      ORG     100H
START:  JMP   BOX
      TOPROW  DW    50
      TOPCOL  DW    100
      BOTROW  DW    100
      BOTCOL  DW    200
      COLOR   DB    15
BOX     PROC  NEAR
        MOV   AH,0
        MOV   AL,6
        INT   10H
        MOV   CX,BOTCOL           ;Draw the top of the box
        SUB   CX,TOPCOL           ;Find number of columns to loop over
        MOV   SI,TOPROW           ;SI holds row number of current pixel
        MOV   DI,TOPCOL           ;DI holds column number of current pixel
TOPLOOP:CALL  WRITEDOT            ;Loop over the columns
        INC   DI
        LOOP  TOPLOOP
        MOV   CX,BOTROW
        SUB   CX,TOPROW
        MOV   SI,TOPROW
SIDELOOP:
        MOV   DI,TOPCOL         ←
        CALL  WRITEDOT          ←
        MOV   DI,BOTCOL         ←
        CALL  WRITEDOT          ←
        INC   SI               ←
        LOOP  SIDELOOP          ←
        :
        INT   20H
BOX     ENDP

WRITEDOT      PROC
        PUSH  AX
        PUSH  CX
```

```
                PUSH      DX
                MOV       DX,SI
                MOV       CX,DI
                MOV       AL,COLOR
                MOV       AH,OCH
                INT       10H
                POP       DX
                POP       CX
                POP       AX
                RET
WRITEDOT        ENDP

CODE_SEG        ENDS
        END     START
```

The last step is to write the bottom of the box, Loop 3. This is similar to writing the top, except that instead of going from (TOPROW,TOPCOL) to (TOPROW,BOTCOL), we'll be going from (BOTROW,TOPCOL) to (BOTROW,BOTCOL). This means that we want to draw BOTCOL-TOPCOL pixels, each in a different column (so we'll increment DI, which holds the column number).

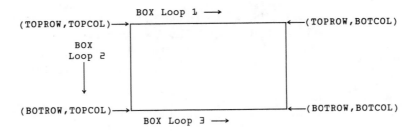

Here that is:

```
CODE_SEG        SEGMENT
        ASSUME  CS:CODE_SEG, DS:CODE_SEG, ES:CODE_SEG, SS:CODE_SEG
        ORG     100H
START:  JMP     BOX
        TOPROW  DW      50
        TOPCOL  DW      100
        BOTROW  DW      100
        BOTCOL  DW      200
        COLOR   DB      15
BOX     PROC    NEAR
        MOV     AH,0
        MOV     AL,6
        INT     10H
        MOV     CX,BOTCOL       ;Draw the top of the box
        SUB     CX,TOPCOL       ;Find number of columns to loop over
        MOV     SI,TOPROW       ;SI holds row number of current pixel
        MOV     DI,TOPCOL       ;DI holds column number of current pixel
TOPLOOP:CALL    WRITEDOT        ;Loop over the columns
        INC     DI
        LOOP    TOPLOOP
        MOV     CX,BOTROW
        SUB     CX,TOPROW
```

```
            MOV       SI,TOPROW
      SIDELOOP:
            MOV       DI,TOPCOL
            CALL      WRITEDOT
            MOV       DI,BOTCOL
            CALL      WRITEDOT
            INC       SI
            LOOP      SIDELOOP
            MOV       CX,BOTCOL        ←
            SUB       CX,TOPCOL        ←
            MOV       SI,BOTROW        ←
            MOV       DI,TOPCOL        ←
      BOTLOOP:CALL    WRITEDOT         ←
            INC       DI               ←
            LOOP      BOTLOOP          ←
            INT       20H
      BOX   ENDP


      WRITEDOT        PROC
            PUSH      AX
            PUSH      CX
            PUSH      DX
            MOV       DX,SI
            MOV       CX,DI
            MOV       AL,COLOR
            MOV       AH,0CH
            INT       10H
            POP       DX
            POP       CX
            POP       AX
            RET
      WRITEDOT        ENDP

      CODE_SEG        ENDS
            END       START
```

Drawing slanted lines

BOX.COM is complete—give it a try. It may be rudimentary, but at least it does a little graphics on the screen. From this example, we can see that graphics can take some work. It can be more difficult if you want to draw slanted lines.

The 45-degree case is easy—all you do is increment the row and column number each time:

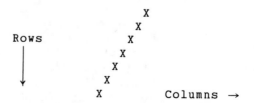

However, what if you wanted to draw a line at some different angle—not quite straight up and down, but like this:

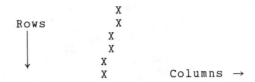

Here you can see that a simple loop would not work. Even though each pixel has a different row number, some pixels have the same column number as others—you could not just loop over column numbers. As you go to different angles, this problem has to be faced.

Of course, drawing figures from scratch is not always the best thing to do. Sometimes you might want to predefine certain shapes that can be placed instantly on the screen. This can be done with what are called *shape tables*. And, with shape tables, you can do some animation, which we'll do at the end of this chapter.

Beyond CGA

There are other adapters beyond the CGA (often way beyond). We will want to be able to handle the EGA and VGA as well. The Write Dot service will work as before, but we can handle more colors now. To do that, we have to learn how to set the 16 colors the EGA can handle—and the up to 256 colors of the VGA. To select these colors, the new BIOSes use service 10H of INT 10H, just as the CGA used service 0BH to set its palette. You can modify BOX fairly easily to work in any of these colors after you select them.

The EGA uses a palette just like the CGA does, but a bigger one. In the EGA palette, registers go from 0 to 15, not 0 to 3, and you can select each color independently from 64 choices. Let's start off our investigation of higher resolution monitors by understanding how the EGA works.

The EGA

EGA intensities

The EGA has two levels of intensity for each of the three primary colors (red, green, and blue). They are low intensity (we will refer to those levels as r, g, b) and medium intensity (R, G, B). When they are both on at some pixel location, the result is high intensity (like r + R). When they are both off, the result is nothing. Thus, there are four levels of *combined* intensity for each of the three colors. In the case of pure red, the levels are: off = 0, low = r, medium = R, and high = r + R.

The rgbRGB settings

Using both low and medium intensity at the same time, we can fill six bits—rgbRGB—to create a color. With these six bits, we can specify values from 0 to 63—and this is where the 64 choices of the EGA come from. You can set the 16 palette colors (color values 0 to 15) from among these 64 possibilities in any 16-color mode.

The default colors in 16-color mode

When the PS/2 or PC is turned on, default EGA color values are set in the EGA palette, and they may be good enough for most purposes. The color values (given to the Write Dot service), colors, and rgbRGB settings for the default colors are these:

Table 5.6 Default Palette Colors (0–15) on EGA

Color Value	Color	rgbRGB
0	Black	000000
1	Blue	000001
2	Green	000010
3	Cyan	000011
4	Red	000100
5	Magenta	000101
6	Brown	010100
7	White	000111
8	Dark gray	111000
9	Light blue	111001
10	Light green	111010
11	Light cyan	111011
12	Light red	111100
13	Light magenta	111101
14	Yellow	111110
15	Intense white	111111

This means that if you select a color value of 3 and pass that on to the Write Dot service in a 16-color EGA or VGA mode, a cyan dot will appear (unless you change the defaults).

Designer Colors in the EGA

You can make up your own colors for the EGA by selecting which of the six bits you want in each palette register. Palette registers go from 0 to 15—one for each color value. To specify a color to use for a particular color value, you can fill the palette registers with the appropriate rgbRGB number (0 to 63).

Say you load a value of 000011B = 3 (cyan) into palette register 5. From then on, when you ask for color value 5 in 16 color modes, rgbRGB will be set to 000011B, or 3, and you'll get cyan. Let's jump in and see how to set one of the EGA palette registers ourselves.

The Service 10H Functions

All the EGA and VGA services use INT 10H, service 10H to set colors. The way you distinguish between EGA and VGA services is through the setting of AL. In this first service, where we will set an EGA palette register, AL is 0. This is also referred to as INT 10H, service 10H, *function 0*.

Service 10H Function 0—Set Individual EGA Palette Register (Set 1 of 16 colors for 16-color mode)

Set these things:

```
AH = 10H
AL = 0
BL = EGA Palette register to set (0-15)
BH = rgbRGB value to set it to (0-63)
```

Here's where you set any of the 16 color values in the EGA palette. You can assign a particular rgbRGB setting to any of the EGA palette registers:

10H	→	AH
0	→	AL
Color value to change (0-15)	→	BL
rgbRGB value to change it to (0-63)	→	BH

To do that, select an rgbRGB setting in six bits, and put it into BH. Select a palette register (which is the same as the color value, the number that Write Dot will see) from 0 to 15, and put it into BL, then use this function. (Congratulations! you've just installed a color for use by your program.)

For example, color value 5 is magenta under the default settings. Let's change that to cyan, rgbRGB = 000011B = 3. In other words, we want to change palette register 5 to use an rgbRGB setting of 3:

$$
\begin{array}{rcl}
\text{10H} & \rightarrow & \text{AH} \\
\text{0} & \rightarrow & \text{AL} \\
\text{Palette register 5} & \rightarrow & \text{BL} \\
\text{New rgbRGB setting 3} & \rightarrow & \text{BH}
\end{array}
$$

In code it looks like this:

```
→      MOV     AH,10H      ;Use INT 10H service 10H
→      MOV     AL,0        ;Function 0
→      MOV     BL,5        ;Change palette register 5
→      MOV     BH,3        ;To rgbRGB = 3, cyan
→      INT     10H
```

It's simple. From now on, when you pass color value 5 to Write Dot, you'll get cyan instead of magenta. That's it for the EGA palette. (Note: Every time the mode is reset, the palette colors return to the default setting.)

If you're using a VGA

The EGA palette can set the colors used in 16-color modes whether you're using an EGA or a VGA. By setting this palette, you can select from 64 choices. If you're really using a VGA, however, you might want to select these 16 colors from among its 256K choices instead. Or you might want to use its 256-color mode (mode 13H). Let's take some time to scrutinize these possibilities.

The VGA

The Digital to Analog Converter (DAC)

The VGA is different from other displays in that it is an *analog* display. Internally, this means that the VGA has what is called a Digital to Analog Converter, or DAC, to help in selecting color.

DAC registers

The DAC has 256 registers, and they can act like the palette registers we've just seen. This is quite an enhancement over the 16-palette registers—here color values can go from 0 to 255. In each of the 256 DAC registers there is an 18-bit number, so DAC registers can hold numbers ranging up to 256K. In other words, if you use the DAC registers to set colors, you have a choice of up to 256K colors to work with.

From CGA to EGA to VGA

In CGA modes, you select the background color and choose from one of two palettes for a total of four colors. Color values range from 0 to 3.

Color Value

Background color (0–15) $\longrightarrow$ 0
$\longrightarrow$ 1
Choosing 1 of 2 palettes sets all these $\longrightarrow$ 2
$\longrightarrow$ 3

In EGA modes, you can select up to 16 colors using the EGA palette. These numbers, 0 to 15, become the color values you can pass to Write Dot. Each color can be selected individually as a six-bit rgbRGB setting; to set color value 2 we'd load palette register 2:

Color Value

0
1
rgbRGB $\longrightarrow$ 2
3
:

In any VGA 16-color mode, you can also set the colors using the EGA palette registers, just as with the EGA. When you set a palette register, you are setting that color value (0 to 15) from a six-bit selection (rgbRGB), giving you 64 possibilities.

On the other hand, in 16-color modes, the VGA is really using the first 16 DAC registers (since it's a VGA, it always uses the DAC registers). These first 16 DAC registers correspond to the 16 available color values. If you set a color in an EGA palette register while using a VGA, your rgbRGB setting will be translated into an 18-bit setting for the corresponding DAC register. Setting color value 2 looks like this:

Color Value

0
1
rgbRGB $\longrightarrow$ 18-bit DAC setting $\longrightarrow$ 2
3
:

This means that you can set the 16 colors of a VGA *either* by changing the EGA palette, where you can select from among 64 rgbRGB possibilities, or by changing a DAC register directly, where you can use 18-bit numbers—giving you a choice of 256K colors.

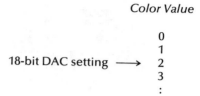

Color Value

0
1
18-bit DAC setting ⟶ 2
3
:

> The default for the VGA is using the first 16 DAC registers as the first 16 color values; you can select which set of DAC registers to use by selecting *color pages*, which we will not do here.

For example, if you want to change color value 5 from its default of magenta in the VGA, you could do it by setting palette register 5 to another of the 64 possible colors (we've used cyan before). Your rgbRGB setting would then be translated into an 18-bit number for DAC register 5.

Or you could set this DAC register directly, by putting a new 18-bit number in DAC register 5. With 18 bits to work with, you can specify 256K colors this way. To be able to change a DAC value like that, we've got to be able to decode the 18-bit DAC numbers, which we'll do next.

Using the DAC Registers

The way 18 bits are used in a DAC register is as follows: The first six bits give the intensity of the red in this color, the next six the intensity of the green, and the last six the intensity of the blue. This means that you can always design new DAC colors for yourself.

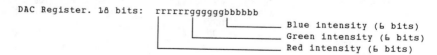

```
DAC Register. 18 bits:  rrrrrrggggggbbbbbb
                                │      │        └──── Blue intensity (6 bits)
                                │      └───────────── Green intensity (6 bits)
                                └──────────────────── Red intensity (6 bits)
```

Let's see how to set one of these DAC registers ourselves. We will use service 10H, with AL = 10H. (That makes this INT 10H, service 10H, function 10H.)

Service 10H Function 10H—Set DAC Register (Set 1 of 255 VGA Colors)

Set these things:

```
AH = 10H
AL = 10H
BX = Register to set (0-255)
CH = Green intensity
CL = Blue Intensity
DH = Red Intensity
```

Here's where we select 1 of the 16 or 256 colors (depending on the screen mode) that the VGA can display from 256K possible choices. Decide on the relative intensities of the green, blue, and red you want in your color, convert them into six-bit arguments, and place them in their respective registers:

```
CH  ←  Green intensity
CL  ←  Blue intensity
DH  ←  Red intensity
```

Then execute this service, and you've set a color for use by the VGA.

Default VGA settings

The default setting of the first 16 DAC registers gives the same colors as the default colors of the EGA (although they use 18 bits and the EGA palette uses six, the DAC values are set to closely match the EGA colors).

But we can change that. Let's work through our earlier example and say that we wanted to change DAC register 5 from its default setting (magenta) to an intense green (green value = 00111110B). Here's how we would do that:

```
→    MOV    AH,10H            ;Select service 10H
→    MOV    AL,10H            ;Select subservice 10H
→    MOV    BX,5              ;Select DAC register to change
→    MOV    CH,00111110B      ;Select new green value
→    MOV    CL,0              ;Set new red and blue values to 0
→    MOV    DH,0
→    INT    10H
```

Now, DAC register 5 has become green. When we pass a color value of 5 to the Write Dot service in a VGA mode, green will appear. Besides 16-color modes, the VGA can handle 256-color modes. Let's look at what makes them different.

VGA 16-Color Modes

As we've seen in 16-color modes on the VGA, you can select colors in two ways. The first is simply by loading one of the possible EGA colors—rgbRGB (0 to 63)—into the register of the EGA palette. What this really does is set the corresponding DAC register to that color. In other words, your rgbRGB setting gets translated into an 18-bit DAC register value, and it's stored in the corresponding DAC register.

The second way is by changing one of the first 16 DAC register contents directly:

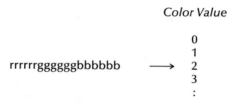

In 16-color modes in the VGA, the first 16 DAC register numbers and the color values are all the same things.

It's worth noting that if you set colors the first way, you can choose from only 64 choices, while if you change one of the DAC registers (which are what really hold the color settings anyway), you can select from 256K choices.

VGA-Only 256-Color Mode

In 256-color VGA mode, you can make up colors by selecting red, green, and blue values (six bits each) and putting your values into any of the DAC registers. As usual, the DAC register number is the color value (now 0 to 255) you will pass to Write Dot. Only the first 64 DAC registers are initalized with default values. In fact, you may even want to stick to the first 16 default color values, which are the same as the EGA ones.

What Monitor Is in Use

With the vast number of services available through BIOS INT 10H, it's often hard to know which ones you can use—will your program have to use a CGA, MDA, EGA, or VGA?

For this reason, an identification service was developed that reports on what advanced video equipment equipment is in use. This is service 1AH of INT 10H.

Service 1AH—Determine Video Equipment

Set these things:

```
AH = 1AH
AL = 0
        Returns:
        AL = 1AH  →  This function is supported.
                     If supported, BL = Display Code (see below).
```

Table 5.7 Display Codes and Results

Display Codes	Results In
0	No Display
1	MDA
2	CGA
4	EGA with standard color
5	EGA with monochrome display
6	PGA (professional Graphics Adapter)
7	VGA with analog monochrome display
8	VGA with analog color display

This service is used to determine what video monitor a PS/2 has attached to it. This is how IBM suggests that you determine what monitor will be in use.

First, execute an INT 10H Service 1AH with AL = 0 (i.e., service 1AH, function 0). If, when the function returns AL = 1AH, then this equipment determination service is supported. The *Display Code* will be in BL.

```
After INT 10H, Service 1AH, Function 0 is AL = 1AH?
         |                               |
        No                              Yes
         |                               |
         ?                              Display code in BL
```

You can determine the type of display from Table 5.7, Display Codes, above.

If AL does not return 1AH, then this service is not supported. In that case, the display options remaining are: EGA, CGA, and MDA.

Checking for an EGA

There is a special way to check for an EGA. Execute INT 10H, service 12H, with BL set to 10H. If, on return, BL is *not* equal to 10H, then an EGA is present. This is the "return EGA information" function of service 12H:

```
After INT 10H, Service 1AH, Function 0 is AL = 1AH?
         |                            |
        No                           Yes
         |                            |
         |                   Display code in BL (see above)
After INT 10H, Service 12H
with BL = 10H, does BL still
equal 10H?                 |
         |                 |
        No                Yes
         |                 |
EGA is present             ?
```

If BL *does* equal 10H, then there is no EGA. The only two choices you have left are CGA and MDA modes. Let's say that BL equals 10H—that is, an EGA is not present. There is one last step to determine which monitor is present. You have to use the Read Mode service, INT 10H service 0FH (video modes 0 to 6 will be CGA, and video mode 7 will be MDA).

Service 0FH Read Current Video State

Set these things:

```
AH = 0FH

       Returns:

AL = Current Mode (see service 00 for a description of modes)
AH = number of character columns on the screen
BH = current active page (0 based)
```

If this service returns a mode (in AL) or 0 to 6, you're working with a CGA (if you've already made sure that there's no EGA or VGA). If it returns a mode of 7, with a monochrome display adapter, the MDA:

```
After INT 10H, Service 1AH, Function 0 is AL = 1AH?
    |                                  |
    No                                 Yes
    |                                  |
    |                                  Display code in BL (see above)
After INT 10H, Service 12H
with BL = 10H, does BL still
equal 10H?                   |
    |                        |
    No                       Yes
    |                        |
EGA is present      Check the video mode
                    with INT 10H, service
                    0FH. Is the mode in AL
                    equal to ??  |
                        |        |
                        Yes      No
                        |        |
                        MDA      CGA
```

It's a lot of work to make out what display is being used.

Writing Graphics Images Directly in Memory

Most professional programs do not use the BIOS Write Dot routine, since it is quite slow, but instead they write directly to memory (which is at least three times as fast). However, writing to memory is different in all the IBM monitors; and that fact is encouragement to use the BIOS routines only (the monitor may be different, but Write Dot will take care of that). We will stick to the BIOS routines.

CGA video buffer in 2 colors

Even so, let's get an idea of what writing directly to the screen in graphics modes is like. In the CGA, for example, there is a 16K buffer. In high-resolution CGA mode (640x200), dots can either be on or off—that's it. Each dot is stored as one bit in a certain area of memory named the video or screen buffer.

The CGA buffer starts at B800:0000—the even lines on the screen (lines 0, 2, 4, 6 . . . 198) are stored in the first half of the CGA's video buffer, and the odd lines (1, 3, 5 . . . 199) are stored in the second half of the video buffer. This is to accommodate the CGA controller chip (made by Motorola), which first scans the even lines on the screen and then the odd ones.

Here's how to turn a pixel on the screen on: First, find whether it's in an even or odd line, and use the correct half of the video buffer. Then, find the correct bit in the buffer, and make the bit 1 (1 = on, 0 = off). It's a good amount of work—for just one pixel.

The CGA
buffer in 4
colors

In four-color mode (320x200), each pixel takes two bits to store in the video buffer, since four colors (i.e., color values 0 to 3) can be specified with two bits. The first, upper-left, pixel is stored in the first two bits of the video buffer, the next pixel in the next two bits, and so on until the end of the line.

The next screen line (1) is odd, so those bits will appear in the second half of the buffer. Even though there are twice as many bits to specify for each pixel, there are half as many screen lines (200 versus 400), so the video buffer is the same length (16K). To turn a pixel on here, you'll have to first find the appropriate two bits in memory, and then set them to the color value you want (0 to 3).

VGA
graphics
video
buffer

Probably the easiest of the EGA or VGA modes to directly work with in memory is, almost paradoxically, the 256 VGA color mode (320 × 200). This is because an entire byte is set aside for each pixel in order to hold 256 colors that can be displayed. The video buffer starts at A000:0000; to set the color of the pixels, you can work byte by byte. You can find more about this and other aspects of the EGA and VGA in Sutty and Blair's book: *Programmer's Guide to the EGA/VGA* (Brady 1988).

However, you should remember that working directly with the video buffer is *very* machine- and model-dependent. Unless you have a commitment to upgrade for each new machine, it is better to use BIOS.

In *Advanced Assembly Language on the IBM PC*, you can see more about how to directly use graphics in the video memory buffer.

Let's do a little graphics ourselves.

Animation

Shape
tables

Many programs create shape tables to store various shapes that can be quickly drawn on the screen. If several shape-table entries of the same figure are slightly modified, animation can take place.

That's what we're going to do here, at least in a crude way. We'll define a shape table with three entries and, when run, the whole program will put a little figure on the screen that will walk across it. This program may not be art, but it does illustrate animation.

We're going to use WRITEDOT again here to do the actual work of drawing pixels. Also, our shape tables will be pretty crude, just 8 × 8 pixels (about one centimeter high on the screen). In a shape table, you can turn a pixel on (by putting a 1 in the appropriate place in the shape table or off (by putting a zero there).

Let's have a procedure that puts all the pixels in a shape table onto the screen. We will call it DRAWSHAPE. Here's our .COM file shell for DRAWSHAPE (which draws one shape table) with a shape table already all set up:

```
CODE_SEG        SEGMENT
        ASSUME  CS:CODE_SEG, DS:CODE_SEG, ES:CODE_SEG, SS:CODE_SEG
        ORG     100H
START:  JMP     DRAWSHAPE
        SHAPE_1 DB  0,0,1,1,1,0,0,0
                DB  0,0,1,1,1,0,0,0
                DB  0,0,0,1,0,0,0,0
                DB  0,0,1,1,1,0,0,0
                DB  0,1,0,1,0,1,0,0
                DB  0,0,1,0,1,0,0,0
                DB  0,1,0,0,0,1,0,0
                DB  1,0,0,0,0,0,1,0
        ROW     DW      50          ←
        COL     DW      50          ←
        SHAPE_ADDR      DW      0           ←
DRAWSHAPE       PROC NEAR
        :
        INT     20H
DRAWSHAPE       ENDP
WRITEDOT        PROC
        PUSH    AX
        PUSH    CX
        :
        POP     CX
        POP     AX
        RET
WRITEDOT        ENDP

CODE_SEG        ENDS
        END     START
```

You probably can't see it, but SHAPE_1 holds the figure of a little man; 1s mean the bit will be turned on, and 0s means the bit will be off. The words ROW and COLUMN will hold the location at which the shape table is to appear on the screen:

```
ROW     DW      50      ←
COL     DW      50      ←
SHAPE_ADDR      DW      0
```

Our procedure DRAWSHAPE can only draw one shape table. To be able to animate these drawings later, we will have to be able to call DRAWSHAPE many times with different shape tables. To do so, we will have to pass it the address at which the shape table that it is to draw starts. Before calling DRAWSHAPE, we will simply load the offset address of the shape table that it is to draw into SHAPE_ADDR. DRAWSHAPE

will be written to take it from there. To use SHAPE_ADDR, let's include
it in the data area:

```
ROW       DW      50
COL       DW      50
SHAPE_ADDR        DW      0    ←
```

This variable will tell DRAWSHAPE where to look for the bits it is to
draw.

DRAWSHAPE's Loop Within a Loop

We will have to have a loop within a loop in DRAWSHAPE. The outer
loop will loop over the eight rows of our drawing on the screen, and the
inner loop will loop over the eight columns in each row:

```
Out_Loop.....              ←Loops over rows
:
: In_Loop..                ←Loops over columns
: :   CALL WRITEDOT
: :...Inc  Column
:
:.....Inc  Row
```

This means that we will first do all the pixels in a row:

```
┌─────────────────────────┐
│        X   X   X         │
│        X   X   X         │
│            X             │
│    X    →                │
│                          │
│                          │
└─────────────────────────┘
```

until the row is finished, and then go on to the next row:

```
┌─────────────────────────┐
│        X   X   X         │
│        X   X   X         │
│            X             │
│        X   X   X         │
│    X    →                │
│                          │
└─────────────────────────┘
```

until the whole figure is done:

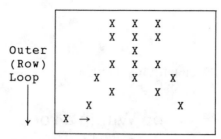

Again, we'll use SI and DI to hold row and column since we have to pass them to WRITEDOT. Here's the outer loop in DRAWSHAPE—this is the loop that will loop over the eight rows, incrementing SI each time:

```
CODE_SEG          SEGMENT
        ASSUME    CS:CODE_SEG, DS:CODE_SEG, ES:CODE_SEG, SS:CODE_SEG
        ORG       100H
START:  JMP       DRAWSHAPE
        SHAPE_1 DB 0,0,1,1,1,0,0,0
                DB 0,0,1,1,1,0,0,0
                DB 0,0,0,1,0,0,0,0
                DB 0,0,1,1,1,0,0,0
                DB 0,1,0,1,0,1,0,0
                DB 0,0,1,0,1,0,0,0
                DB 0,1,0,0,1,0,0,0
                DB 1,0,0,0,0,0,1,0
        ROW       DW       50
        COL       DW       50
        SHAPE_ADDR      DW       0
DRAWSHAPE         PROC NEAR
        MOV       SI,ROW            ←
        MOV       DI,COL            ←
        MOV       CX,8              ←
ROWLOOP:                            ←
........
   :
   :      ;Draw the row here.
   :
   :      INC       SI              ← INC SI means INC row number
   :......LOOP      ROWLOOP         ←
   :
   :      INT       20H
DRAWSHAPE         ENDP

WRITEDOT          PROC
        PUSH      AX
        PUSH      CX
        :
        POP       CX
```

```
          POP      AX
          RET
WRITEDOT           ENDP

CODE_SEG           ENDS
          END      START
```

In the inner loop, we will actually draw the pixels. To do this, we have to get 1s or 0s from the shape table, which starts at the address that will be set up for us, SHAPE_ADDR. We will load SHAPE_ADDR into BX, so that we can pull entries from the shape table with indirect addressing (i.e., [BX]). By simply incrementing BX, we can march through the table, all 64 entries, easily. Here's where we set up BX:

```
CODE_SEG           SEGMENT
          ASSUME   CS:CODE_SEG, DS:CODE_SEG, ES:CODE_SEG, SS:CODE_SEG
          ORG      100H
START:    JMP      DRAWSHAPE
          SHAPE_1 DB 0,0,1,1,1,0,0,0
                  DB 0,0,1,1,1,0,0,0
                  DB 0,0,0,1,0,0,0,0
                  DB 0,0,1,1,1,0,0,0
                  DB 0,1,0,1,0,1,0,0
                  DB 0,0,1,0,1,0,0,0
                  DB 0,1,0,0,0,1,0,0
                  DB 1,0,0,0,0,0,1,0
          ROW      DW       50
          COL      DW       50
          SHAPE_ADDR    DW       0
DRAWSHAPE          PROC NEAR
          MOV      SI,ROW
          MOV      CX,8
          MOV      BX,SHAPE_ADDR    ←
ROWLOOP:
........
:
:         ;Draw the row here.
:
:         INC      SI
:......LOOP        ROWLOOP
          INT      20H
DRAWSHAPE          ENDP

WRITEDOT           PROC
          PUSH     AX
          PUSH     CX
          :
          POP      CX
          POP      AX
          RET
WRITEDOT           ENDP

CODE_SEG           ENDS
          END      START
```

And now here's the inner loop, which loops over the eight columns in each row:

```
CODE_SEG          SEGMENT
        ASSUME    CS:CODE_SEG, DS:CODE_SEG, ES:CODE_SEG,
SS:CODE_SEG
        ORG       100H
START:  JMP       DRAWSHAPE
        SHAPE_1 DB 0,0,1,1,1,0,0,0
                DB 0,0,1,1,1,0,0,0
                DB 0,0,0,1,0,0,0,0
                DB 0,0,1,1,1,0,0,0
                DB 0,1,0,1,0,1,0,0
                DB 0,0,1,0,1,0,0,0
                DB 0,1,0,0,0,1,0,0
                DB 1,0,0,0,0,0,1,0
        ROW       DW        50
        COL       DW        50
        SHAPE_ADDR      DW          0
DRAWSHAPE         PROC NEAR
        MOV       SI,ROW
        MOV       CX,8
        MOV       BX,SHAPE_ADDR
ROWLOOP:
   .......MOV     DI,COL
   :      PUSH    CX                  ←
   :      MOV     CX,8                ←
COLLOOP:
   : .....MOV     AL,[BX]             ←
   : :    INC     BX                  ←
   : :    CALL    WRITEDOT            ←
   : :    INC     DI                  ←
   : :....LOOP    COLLOOP             ←
   :      POP     CX                  ←
   :      INC     SI
   :......LOOP    ROWLOOP
          INT     20H
DRAWSHAPE         ENDP

WRITEDOT          PROC
        PUSH      AX
        PUSH      CX
        :
        POP       CX
        POP       AX
        RET
WRITEDOT          ENDP

CODE_SEG          ENDS
        END       START
```

With the addition of this inner loop, DRAWSHAPE is complete. Let's decipher what's going on in these two loops to make sure we understand them.

DRAWSHAPE's Two Loops

Here are our two loops:

```
ROWLOOP:
   .......MOV     DI,COL
   :      PUSH    CX
   :      MOV     CX,8
COLLOOP:
```

```
:  .....MOV       AL,[BX]
: :     INC       BX
: :     CALL      WRITEDOT
: :     INC       DI
: :....LOOP       COLLOOP
:       POP       CX
:       INC       SI
:......LOOP       ROWLOOP
```

The outer loop is a loop over the eight rows. The inner loop is a loop over the eight columns in each row. Every time we finish the inner loop that goes across one row, we have to reset our column index back to the first column of the figure, with MOV DI,COL. Also, since we use LOOP for both the inner and outer loops, we have to PUSH CX (the LOOP index) when we enter the inner loop and POP it when we leave. To set this index up for the eight columns that the inner loop will loop over, we load CX with 8:

```
ROWLOOP:
.......MOV       DI,COL
:      PUSH      CX                        ←
:      MOV       CX,8                      ←
COLLOOP:
:
:
:
```

Now we enter the inner loop. Here, we want to get 1s or 0s from the shape table. We have already loaded SHAPE_ADDR into BX, so it's only necessary to get an entry from [BX] and then increment BX to move to the next shape table element for next time.

We can call WRITEDOT to actually write the pixel now that we have the correct (row,column) values (= (SI,DI)). The inner loop loops over the columns, incrementing DI each time. The outer loop increments SI when we have drawn the whole row.

After writing the dot, we increment DI (the column number) here in the inner loop to move to the next location in this row with INC DI:

```
ROWLOOP:
.......MOV       DI,COL
:      PUSH      CX
:      MOV       CX,8
COLLOOP:
: .....MOV       AL,[BX]                   ←
: :    INC       BX                        ←
: :    CALL      WRITEDOT                  ←
: :    INC       DI                        ←
: :....LOOP      COLLOOP                   ←
:
:
:
```

After finishing the inner loop, we've done one row, so in the outer loop, we increment the row number, held in SI:

```
ROWLOOP:
.......MOV      DI,COL
:       PUSH    CX
:       MOV     CX,8
COLLOOP:
: .....MOV      AL,[BX]
: :     INC     BX
: :     CALL    WRITEDOT
: :     INC     DI
: :....LOOP     COLLOOP
:       POP     CX              ←
:       INC     SI              ←
:......LOOP     ROWLOOP         ←
```

This finishes the two loops. We've taken the shortcut of feeding the 0 or 1 in the shape table directly to WRITEDOT as the color value to put on the screen. Since any non-zero value lights the pixel in high-resolution CGA mode, this is fine: The 1s in SHAPE_1 will turn on, the 0s in SHAPE_1 will stay off.

ANIMATE.ASM

Now DRAWSHAPE is done. We will have to call it many times to draw the successive shapes on the screen. Let's add another routine to do the animation, called ANIMATE. DRAWSHAPE is now a subprogram, so we will have to change the INT 20H at the end of DRAWSHAPE to a RET. The INT 20H will appear at the end of ANIMATE:

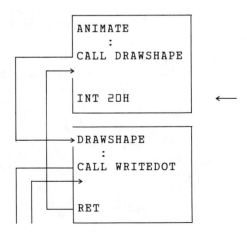

```
ANIMATE
   :
CALL DRAWSHAPE


INT 20H              ←


DRAWSHAPE
   :
CALL WRITEDOT


RET
```

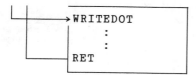

In ANIMATE, we will steadily increment the column at which the shape table will be drawn, moving it across the screen. This means we'll have to loop and call DRAWSHAPE. Every time we loop, we'll draw three figures to make it appear as though the figure is moving its arms and legs vigorously (thus calling DRAWSHAPE three times every time we loop). Then we'll increment the column at which the next figure will appear and call DRAWSHAPE three more times.

To switch between shape tables, all we need to do is load a new shape table's offset into SHAPE_ADDR, set ROW and COL for the new shape table's position on the screen, and call DRAWSHAPE. Here's what ANI-MATE.ASM, the final program looks like, with all shape tables in place:

Listing 5.1 ANIMATE.ASM

```
CODE_SEG          SEGMENT
        ASSUME    CS:CODE_SEG, DS:CODE_SEG, ES:CODE_SEG, SS:CODE_SEG
        ORG       100H
START:  JMP       ANIMATE
        SHAPE_1 DB 0,0,1,1,1,0,0,0
                DB 0,0,1,1,1,0,0,0
                DB 0,0,0,1,0,0,0,0
                DB 0,0,1,1,1,0,0,0
                DB 0,1,0,1,0,1,0,0
                DB 0,0,1,0,1,0,0,0
                DB 0,1,0,0,0,1,0,0
                DB 1,0,0,0,0,0,1,0
        SHAPE_2 DB 0,0,1,1,1,0,0,0
                DB 0,0,1,1,1,0,0,0
                DB 0,0,0,1,0,0,0,0
                DB 0,1,1,1,1,1,0,0
                DB 0,0,0,1,0,0,0,0
                DB 0,0,0,1,1,0,0,0
                DB 0,0,0,1,1,0,0,0
                DB 0,0,0,1,1,0,0,0
        SHAPE_3 DB 0,0,0,0,0,0,0,0
                DB 0,0,0,0,0,0,0,0
                DB 0,0,0,0,0,0,0,0
                DB 0,0,0,0,0,0,0,0
                DB 0,0,0,0,0,0,0,0
                DB 0,0,0,0,0,0,0,0
                DB 0,0,0,0,0,0,0,0
                DB 0,0,0,0,0,0,0,0
        ROW     DW        50
        COL     DW        50
        SHAPE_ADDR      DW        0

ANIMATE         PROC      NEAR
```

Listing 5.1 ANIMATE.ASM *(continued)*

```
    →       MOV       CX,200                           ;Number of sets of 3 to draw
    →       MOV       AH,0                             ;Set up video mode.
    →       MOV       AL,6
    →       INT       10H
MAINLOOP:
    →       MOV       SHAPE_ADDR,OFFSET SHAPE_1  ;Draw a set of 3shapes
    →       CALL      DRAWSHAPE
    →       MOV       SHAPE_ADDR,OFFSET SHAPE_3
    →       CALL      DRAWSHAPE
    →       ADD       COL,2                            ;Move figure to the right
    →       MOV       SHAPE_ADDR,OFFSET SHAPE_2
    →       CALL      DRAWSHAPE
    →       MOV       SHAPE_ADDR,OFFSET SHAPE_3
    →       CALL      DRAWSHAPE
    →       ADD       COL,2
    →       LOOP      MAINLOOP
    →       INT       20H
ANIMATE         ENDP


DRAWSHAPE       PROC NEAR
    →       PUSH      CX                               ;Push CX added to preserve CX
            MOV       SI,ROW
            MOV       CX,8
            MOV       BX,SHAPE_ADDR
ROWLOOP:
            MOV       DI,COL
            PUSH      CX
            MOV       CX,8
COLLOOP:
            MOV       AL,[BX]
            INC       BX
            CALL      WRITEDOT
            INC       DI
            LOOP      COLLOOP
            POP       CX
            INC       SI
            LOOP      ROWLOOP
    →       POP       CX
    →       RET                                        ;INT 20H becomes RET
DRAWSHAPE       ENDP


WRITEDOT        PROC
            PUSH      AX
            PUSH      CX
            PUSH      DX
            MOV       DX,SI
            MOV       CX,DI
            MOV       AH,0CH
            INT       10H
            POP       DX
            POP       CX
            POP       AX
            RET
WRITEDOT        ENDP


CODE_SEG        ENDS
        END       START
```

Give ANIMATE.ASM a try—it draws a little 10-second movie of a tiny figure walking across the screen. As mentioned, it may not be art; but it is fun.

On that note, we end our graphics work. Graphics on the PC and PS/2 has improved many fold over the years. It may not be particularly easy to use, but the results can be worth it.

6
Popup Programs

Popups
Memory-Resident Code
Interrupt Vector Table
LEA
IRET
PUSHF

POPF
Indirect Calls
LABEL Pseudo-Op
Re-Entrant BIOS
Intercepting the Keyboard

Keyboard Buffer
Scan Codes
BIOS Data Area
AND
OR

One of the main reasons assembly language is popular is its ability to run behind the scenes, so to speak, and support popup, memory-resident programs. They have become so prevalent that they can hardly be left out of a book on assembly-language programming, and it is not difficult to write them.

Popup examples

Popular examples of memory-resident programs include calculators that can "pop up" onto the screen even when you're running another program, screen clocks that are always there, notepads, utilities that can dial phone numbers, report on the printer, catch disk errors, let you run DOS commands, and so forth.

Memory-resident programs are just that: They stay in memory, even when you start to run other programs. Usually, the program loader in COMMAND.COM loads programs in right after the space used by DOS runs your program, and then exits, marking that space as free once again. With a memory-resident program, that final step does not occur. Instead, the space that is marked as DOS's is increased, until the code you've written is protected from being written over by the next program to be run. In this way, it becomes part of DOS. Only .COM files, with their compact format, can be made memory resident.

> What memory-resident programs can appear to do—let two programs run at once, for example, when you pop up a calculator—OS/2 does for real. With a popup, you have to explicitly select it to run it. Under OS/2, the machine itself can automatically give time to many different programs.

Writing Memory-Resident Code

Even though it may sound difficult, making programs memory resident is really simple. The real problem to be solved is this: Even if you add a section of code to DOS, it will do nothing by itself until called. Just making it memory-resident doesn't mean it will run—it will lie fallow until you can enter it again. For example, we could add the commands:

```
MOV     AX,5
    MOV     DX,32001
    INC     DI
```

to the end of DOS rather easily with either of the two DOS interrupts (INT 27H or INT 31H) designed to make code memory resident. This would work simply by setting a few registers and ending the program with one of those interrupts, not with INT 20H as we have usually done. Now that those instructions are there, however, they are just bytes in memory—there is no reason they will run until CS:IP is set to them. In the same way, the code in DOS and BIOS doesn't all run at once everywhere—it waits until called.

> In the language of OS/2, we say DOS only has one *thread*. OS/2 can have multiple threads, which means many programs can be active at once.

There is really only one way to run memory-resident code like this, and that is with software or hardware interrupts. Software interrupts we know about—they are just the INT instruction. Hardware interrupts are not generated by a program, but instead they occur when something happens in the PS/2's or PC's peripherals. For example, if you touch a key on the keyboard, interrupt 9 is generated. The disk can generate other hardware interrupts if some operation takes place there, as can an internal clock inside the PS/2 and PC. (The clock interrupt is in fact made 18.2 times a second, unless you turn it off.)

Hardware interrupts

A hardware interrupt causes the PS/2 or PC to temporarily stop—interrupt—the program it is running and attend instead to the hardware interrupt. Hardware interrupts can be "turned off" (except for some serious, low-level ones) by programs with the CLI instruction, Clear Interrupt flag. This internal flag is there simply to indicate whether hardware interrupts will be recognized or ignored by the microprocessor. If your program executes a CLI instruction, no typed keys will be recognized or recorded, for example. You can reset this flag with STI, Set Interrupt flag, which allows hardware interrupts to be recognized again.

> We'll see examples of CLI and STI in use later, when we don't want to be interrupted.

Typically, memory-resident programs are summoned with a "hot key"—a key that, when pressed, pops the calculator or whatever onto your screen. This is because they make use of the keyboard interrupt. Hardware interrupts are much like software interrupts in that every time they occur, some program can be run. In this case, the program that will be run is our memory-resident one. For memory-resident code in popup programs, we use hardware, not software, interrupts. This is because the software interrupts would have to be executed by the program then running, while you could interrupt that program with a hot-key hardware interrupt at any time; that is what we are aiming for.

Interrupt routine addresses

Hardware and software interrupts do share one thing, however, and that is the way the microprocessor finds the address of the program to run when they occur. If your program executes an INT 10H instruction, for example, the microprocessor searches for the program that is to be run to handle it in the same way that it does if you pressed a key on the keyboard and generated an INT 9.

Since it is our intention to get our program to run when a hardware interrupt is generated, we'll have to understand what this process is.

Interrupts

As mentioned near the beginning of the book, Intel added interrupts to its microprocessors so that the microprocessor's instruction set could be expanded. They wanted to let the builders of computers add their own code so that operations such as opening a file would seem to be only another simple instruction (using, in this case, INT 21H). In our microprocessor, we can have up to 256 of these interrupts.

Interrupt vector table

What actually occurs when an interrupt (hardware or software) is executed is this: The microprocessor loads the address of the program for that interrupt from a specially designed table in low memory, called the *interrupt vector table*. This table is so important, and is such a large part of what the microprocessor does, that it is given the very first position in memory, starting at 0000:0000.

> Although it is a slight misnomer, the interrupt vector table is named after the idea of vectors in physics, where a vector can point in a cer-

tain direction. An interrupt vector points to the routine in memory that is to be run if that interrupt occurs.

The Interrupt Vector Table

The idea behind this important-sounding name, the Interrupt Vector Table, is easy to understand. For each interrupt, two words are stored: the segment address, and the offset address of the program that is to be run when that interrupt occurs.

The first two words in memory correspond to interrupt 0, the next two correspond to interrupt 1, and so on.

Figure 6.1 The Interrupt Vector Table

```
                            :
                            :
          0000:000E    CS        Address of Interrupt 3
          0000:000C    IP

          0000:000A    CS        Address of Interrupt 2
          0000:0008    IP

          0000:0006    CS        Address of Interrupt 1
          0000:0004    IP

          0000:0002    CS        Address of Interrupt 0
Bottom of memory →  0000:0000    IP
```

Remember, as you look at the addresses corresponding to the interrupts, that the addresses are in bytes, and both the segment address and the offset address take up one word. Therefore, the addresses of these words go: 0000:0000, 0000:0002, 0000:0004, and so forth.

To find the address of the interrupt handling routine, the microprocessor turns to the interrupt vector table. It multiplies the interrupt number by four (actually, it shifts it left twice), and produces the address at which the interrupt's vector (that is, the full address of the interrupt's routine) is stored. Each interrupt vector takes up four bytes.

Stack use in interrupts

Then the microprocessor pushes three words onto the stack to preserve them for later use: the current value of all the flags (these are stored as bits in one 16-bit word), the current value of IP, and the current value of CS. Then, it heads off to handle the interrupt. After the interrupt is done, the microprocessor can pop these values from the stack, restoring them, and continue with the program that was in progress when the interrupt occurred (even down to the flags). This is done for either software or hardware interrupts.

At the end of the interrupt routine, you might expect a RET instruction. In fact, that is quite close. However, since three words were pushed onto the stack—the full return address and the settings of the flags—there is a special 8088 instruction to handle returns from interrupts, IRET.

IRET

If you write a procedure for an interrupt, it must end with IRET, not RET. IRET pops all three words off the stack, restores them, and the interrupted program can continue.

> In the RET we have been using, used between NEAR procedures (that is, in the same segment), only the offset address (one word) of the return address is pushed onto the stack. In FAR returns, two words are pushed, the return address' CS and IP values. With interrupts, three words: CS, IP, and the flags.

For example, in a notepad program, let's say you type a key. An INT 9 is generated, and code will have been added that checks every INT 9 to see if the hot key has been pressed. If not, a normal INT 9, ending with IRET, is executed (the microprocessor finds the address from 4 x 9 = 36 = 24H, or 0000:0024). If the hot key has been pressed, the notepad becomes active. It may have its own program, also ending with IRET, that will handle typed-in keys from then on.

Intercepting Interrupt Vectors

A clever program will set itself up in memory by changing the interrupt vector stored for a particular interrupt so that when that interrupt occurs, the microprocessor will come to the program, not to the interrupt routine. This is how memory-resident programs get run.

For example, our notepad program would change the address stored at 0000:0024, the INT 9 vector, to point to itself instead. It might store the original address of INT 9 to let it handle what the notepad doesn't want.

Here's the way the interrupt vector might start out in the interrupt vector table:

```
              :
              :
             CS
             IP
          _____
             CS
             IP
```

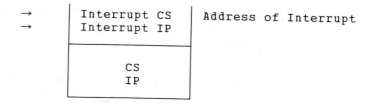

```
  →       Interrupt CS        Address of Interrupt
  →       Interrupt IP

                  CS
                  IP


                  :
```

And our program might be at some high point in memory, at a specific
value of CS:IP:

```
CS:IP of Program  →    JMP      PROG

                           Data Area

                       PROG     PROC     NEAR
                                MOV      AX,5
                                MOV      DX,32001
                                CMP      AX,DX
                                JE       GO
                                         :
                                         :
                                         :
```

What we want to do is supplant the routine that services the interrupt
with our own program, PROG. In other words, we want the two words
in the interrupt vector table called Interrupt CS and Interrupt IP to be
changed to the corresponding values of our program's beginning location, Program CS and Program IP:

```
                       :
                       CS
                       IP

                       CS
                       IP

  →      Program CS          Address of Interrupt
  →      Program IP
```

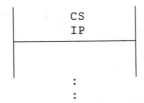

Usually, a program that intercepts an interrupt doesn't handle all the functions of that interrupt, but occasionally passes on those things it doesn't want to do to the old interrupt routine. For this reason, Interrupt CS and Interrupt IP are stored in the data area of the program:

```
CS:IP of Program  →   JMP      PROG
These will be filled  →   OLD_INT_CS      DW 0
                  →   OLD_INT_IP      DW 0

                      PROG     PROC     NEAR
                               MOV      AX,5
                               MOV      DX,32001
                               CMP      AX,DX
                               JE       GO
                                :
                                :
                                :
```

That's all there is to it; when that interrupt occurs, control will come to us, not to the old interrupt routine. Our program PROG was loaded by COMMAND.COM into the beginning of available memory—when we make it memory resident, PROG will stay where it is (that is, Program CS and Program IP will not change), and the address at which programs get loaded will be moved to the end of PROG.

Reaching the interrupt vector table

At this point we have to investigate how to fill the interrupt vector of a selected interrupt with the addresses CS and IP of our own program. The interrupt vectors are at the very bottom of memory; that is, outside our segment. How do we reach them?

> After memory-resident programs are installed, how do you un-install them when memory becomes too full? There are a number of programs that you can run before installing memory-resident programs, and they (also memory-resident) will un-install added-on programs for you by resetting the top of available memory and resetting interrupt vectors. Or you could design your program to un-install itself.

The Get and Set Interrupt Vector Services of INT 21H

The DOS INT 21H comes to our aid here. There is a service to get an interrupt's current vector, service 35H. And there is also one to set the interrupt's vector to a new address, service 25H.

Since we will usually want to use the old interrupt routine for some things (for example, we will let the keyboard routine read the keyboard port and interpret the key that was typed for us), we want to retain its address before setting the vector to point to us. We can do that by storing the original interrupt vector in the data area of our own program. There we will set up two memory words in our program's data area, beginning at our label OLD_INTERRUPT like this:

```
CODE_SEG        SEGMENT
        ASSUME  CS:CODE_SEG
        ORG     100H                ;ORG = 100H to make this into a .COM file
FIRST:  JMP     LOAD_PROG           ;First time through jump to initialize routine
        :
→       OLD_INTERRUPT   DW 2 DUP(0)
        :
PROG    PROC    NEAR                ;The keyboard interrupt will now come here.
```

Now we can copy the old interrupt vector into these two words at OLD_INTERRUPT in our program's data area. To get this old vector, we use INT 21H, service 35H, Get Vector:

```
INT 21H Service 35H Get Vector
-------------------------------
Input: AH= 35H
       AL = Interrupt Number
Output:ES:BX = Interrupt's Vector
```

Getting the Old Vector

To get the old interrupt vector, we'll put service 35H to work. Let's say that we want to intercept the keyboard interrupt, interrupt 9. In that case, we could set a constant named INTERRUPT_NUMBER to 9:

```
INTERRUPT_NUMBER        EQU     9
```

And then get the old interrupt vector like this:

```
        INTERRUPT_NUMBER        EQU 9
        :
        :
  →     MOV     AH,35H               ;Get old vector into ES:BX
  →     MOV     AL,INTERRUPT_NUMBER  ;See EQU at beginning
  →     INT     21H
        :
```

It's simple. Later, if we want to change the interrupt we're intercepting, all we have to do is change the value of INTER-
RUPT_NUMBER. Service 35H returns the interrupt's vector in ES:BX;
we want to store this address in the space we have set aside in the data
area—the two words named OLD_INTERRUPT:

```
CODE_SEG     SEGMENT
      ASSUME CS:CODE_SEG
      ORG    100H            ;ORG = 100H to make this into a .COM file
FIRST: JMP    LOAD PROG       ;First time through jump to initialize routine
      :
  →   OLD_INTERRUPT   DW 2 DUP(0)
      :
PROG   PROC   NEAR            ;The keyboard interrupt will now come here.
```

Later, we are going to treat these two words as a single, double-word
quantity. If you recall, the 8088 stores doublewords with the low word
first, so the offset address of the old interrupt's vector (in BX) goes into
the first word of our storage place:

```
        INTERRUPT_NUMBER        EQU 9
        :
        :
        MOV     AH,35H               ;Get old vector into ES:BX
        MOV     AL,INTERRUPT_NUMBER  ;See EQU at beginning
        INT     21H
  →     MOV     OLD_INTERRUPT,BX     ;Store old interrupt vector
        :
```

And the segment address (in ES) goes into the second word. That can
be done with a line like this:

```
        INTERRUPT_NUMBER        EQU 9
        :
        :
        MOV     AH,35H               ;Get old vector into ES:BX
        MOV     AL,INTERRUPT_NUMBER  ;See EQU at beginning
        INT     21H
        MOV     OLD_INTERRUPT,BX     ;Store old interrupt vector
  →     MOV     OLD_INTERUPT[2],ES
        :
```

**Indexed
addressing**

This is a new way of using indirect addressing, called *indexed addressing*.
OLD_INTERRUPT[2] refers to the location two bytes (that is, one
word) after the label OLD_INTERRUPT.

This method can prove quite useful. You can also index an array using BX, like this: ARRAY[BX]. Just set BX to the location of the byte in ARRAY, and you're set.

Arrays

For example, you might have an array set up like this:

```
ARRAY   DB 50 DUP(0)
```

You could use it like this:

```
        ARRAY   DB 50 DUP(0)
                :
                :
→       MOV     AX,ARRAY[2]
```

Here we have defined an area of 50 bytes called ARRAY (there is nothing special about the name; we could have called it ARRAY_15, or anything). To move the first byte of ARRAY into AX, we would say MOV AX,ARRAY[0], to move the second byte into AX we would say MOV AX,ARRAY[1], and so on.

> Note: MOV AX,ARRAY and MOV AX,ARRAY[0] are identical to the assembler.

Two-dimensional arrays

Two-dimensional arrays are possible as well, like this: (This really indicates the item at ARRAY[BX + SI]. See the macro assembler manual for more details.)

```
MOV     DX,ARRAY[BX][SI]
```

In our case, we want to point to the word after OLD_INTERRUPT, so we simply use OLD_INTERRUPT[2]; we use 2 since indirect addressing is indexed in bytes, and a word is two bytes:

```
        INTERRUPT_NUMBER    EQU 9
        :
        :
        MOV     AH,35H                  ;Get old vector into ES:BX
        MOV     AL,INTERRUPT_NUMBER     ;See EQU at beginning
        INT     21H
        MOV     OLD_INTERRUPT,BX        ;Store old interrupt vector
→       MOV     OLD_INTERRUPT[2],ES
        :
```

Resetting the Interrupt Vector

It's time to move ourselves into the interrupt vector table. We want to be able to change the vector to point to us, not the old interrupt routine. That is, we want to load our program's IP and Program CS into the interrupt's vector.

To do this, we can use INT 21H, service 25H, Set Vector:

```
INT 21H Service 25H Set Vector
------------------------------
Input: AH= 25H
       AL = Interrupt number
       DS:DX = New interrupt handler address
Output:(None)
```

What we've done so far is store the old interrupt vector:

```
      INTERRUPT_NUMBER      EQU 9
      :
      :
      MOV     AH,35H                ;Get old vector into ES:BX
      MOV     AL,INTERRUPT_NUMBER   ;See EQU at beginning
      INT     21H
→     MOV     OLD_INTERRUPT,BX      ;Store old interrupt vector
→     MOV     OLD_INTERUPT[2],ES
      :
```

And now we can add some lines to reset the interrupt vector to us. We have to give service 25H the new address, the address of our program, in DS:DX. Since we haven't changed DS in our .COM file, we can leave that alone, but we do have to get the offset of our program—let's call it PROG—into DX. We can do that with a new instruction, LEA:

```
      INTERRUPT_NUMBER      EQU 9
      :
      :
      MOV     AH,35H                ;Get old vector into ES:BX
      MOV     AL,INTERRUPT_NUMBER   ;See EQU at beginning
      INT     21H
      MOV     OLD_INTERRUPT,BX      ;Store old interrupt vector
      MOV     OLD_INTERUPT[2],ES

→     MOV     AH,25H                ;Set new interrupt vector
→     LEA     DX,PROG
→     INT     21H
      :
```

The LEA Instruction H

LEA means Load Effective Address. An instruction like LEA DX,PROG is just like MOV DX,OFFSET PROG, except that LEA will only load offset addresses into registers—if you had a memory location named APPLES, you couldn't say LEA APPLES,PROG. We'll see LEA later in Chapter 7, Linking Files Together.

At this point, we have changed the interrupt's interrupt vector so that it points to our program. Every time that interrupt is executed, we will get control. We have reset the interrupt vector in the interrupt vector table:

```
        :                                   :
   ┌─────────────┐                    ┌─────────────┐
   │    CS       │                    │    CS       │
   │    IP       │                    │    IP       │
   ├─────────────┤                    ├─────────────┤
   │    CS       │                    │    CS       │
   │    IP       │                    │    IP       │
   ├─────────────┤                    ├─────────────┤
   │ Interrupt CS│      →             │ Program CS  │
   │ Interrupt IP│      →             │ Program IP  │
   ├─────────────┤                    ├─────────────┤
   │    CS       │                    │    CS       │
   │    IP       │                    │    IP       │
   └─────────────┘                    └─────────────┘
        :                                   :
```

We were able to do this very easily with the INT 21H services 25H and 35H—but there is another way as well. We could have worked directly in the interrupt vector table itself. In fact, before these services were available, this is how programs made themselves memory resident.

Working with a second segment in a .COM file is new to us. Since we will need that information later, let's take a look at that idea now.

Our Second Segment and the AT Pseudo-Op

**The AT
Pseudo-Op**

To reach the interrupt vectors directly, we could define a new segment, named INTERRUPTS. While using our segment CODE_SEG, we did not specify its address (that is, the program's segment address), because we could not—that is set when the program is run, and not before. However, we know that INTERRUPTS has to be the segment that starts at 0000:0000, so we can define it with the new Pseudo-Op *AT*, this way:

```
INTERRUPTS      SEGMENT AT OH   ←
INTERRUPTS      ENDS            ←

CODE_SEG        SEGMENT
        ASSUME  CS:CODE_SEG
        ORG     100H            ;ORG = 100H to make this into a .COM file
FIRST:  JMP     LOAD_PROG       ;First time through jump to initialize routine
        :
```

That's all there is to it: From now on, if we want to reach memory in the INTERRUPTS segment (starting at 0000:0000), we can just set a segment register to point to INTERRUPTS.

Now we have to find a way to point at the old interrupt vector inside segment INTERRUPTS. Let's use INT 9, the keyboard interrupt, as an example.

We can use ORG to set our location inside INTERRUPTS (ORG just tells the assembler the offset to use inside the current segment), and DW to name the first word of the interrupt's address. Since we don't know what value will be in this location, and do not wish to fill it ourselves, we will use DW ?, which means, leave this location alone.

Here is how we will be able to point to the interrupt's vector (this is for INT 9), using the name THE_INTERRUPT to point to the first word of the vector (which holds the INT 9 routine's IP address):

```
INTERRUPTS      SEGMENT AT OH
        ORG     9H*4                    ← For INT Z, use ORG Zx4 here.
THE_INTERRUPT   DW ?                    ←
INTERRUPTS      ENDS

CODE_SEG        SEGMENT
        ASSUME  CS:CODE_SEG
        ORG     100H            ;ORG = 100H to make this into a .COM file
FIRST:  JMP     LOAD_PROG       ;First time through jump to initialize routine
        :
```

Now that we can point to the word that holds IP, we can point to the word that holds CS as well, using indirect addressing. We can call this word THE_INTERRUPT[2]. However, before using these labels in our program, we have to set the DS (data segment) register point to INTERRUPTS.

Resetting the DS Register to INTERRUPTS

Segment registers have one peculiarity: You cannot do anything as rational as loading an immediate number into them, like what we want to do here, MOV DS,0. Instead, they have to be loaded from a general purpose register, like this: MOV AX,0 MOV DS,AX. So we would do it that way when we set up DS to point at INTERRUPTS:

```
→    ASSUME   DS:INTERRUPTS      ;The data segment will be the Interrupt area
→    MOV      AX,INTERRUPTS      ← Note: Do not use OFFSET here!
→    MOV      DS,AX
```

Our data segment is now INTERRUPTS. In other words, the labels we will refer to as we usually do (MOV DX,APPLES) will come from INTERRUPTS. Don't forget to use an ASSUME Pseudo-Op whenever you change a segment register so that the assembler knows what's going on.

> One of the biggest sources of program error is setting segment registers to some segment, and not setting them back when they're needed. Addresses for your data labels will be calculated from the current value of DS, and if what the assembler thinks DS will be (from ASSUMES) is not what it actually is when the program runs, there will be problems as the wrong data locations are accessed.

If we wanted to, we'd be free to change interrupt vectors directly now. We can refer to the low word of the interrupt's vector as THE_INTERRUPT (as in MOV THE_INTERRUPT,DX) and the high word as THE_INTERRUPT[2].

You'll often see something like this in old memory-resident programs. This ability to address any location in memory by enclosing it in a defined segment is one we will need soon to access the keyboard buffer when we write our hot-key popup shell.

Making Code Memory Resident

Our code is now able to reset the interrupt so that it will come to us instead of the old interrupt-handling routine. But how do we make sure that our program will stay in memory? There are two ways to do this: DOS INT 27H and INT 21H service 31H. To use INT 27H, simply set DS:DX to the last address you want to keep in memory, and execute INT 27H; that's it.

INT 21H
service 31H

INT 21H service 31H can give a "return code," which can be examined by the ERRORLEVEL batch command, or with another INT 21H service (4DH). Since we are not going to use return codes in this book, we will be using INT 27H. Nevertheless, to use INT 21H service 31H, set the number of paragraphs that you want to keep in memory (a paragraph is 16 bytes) into DX. Move the number you want to use as the return code into AL, set AH to 31H, and execute INT 21H.

The Booster part of the program

Here's how we will use INT 27H. As most programs that install themselves in memory do, we will set up a small initialization part of the program at the very end of the code. This part is only to install the program in memory, and it will be jettisoned when the program is installed. For this reason, it is occasionally called the *booster*. Our program is called PROG; let's call our booster LOAD_PROG. LOAD_PROG will come after PROG in the .ASM file.

When we first run the .COM file that will attach itself in memory, we start at ORG 100H. At this location, we have been used to seeing the instruction JMP PROG. In this case, that will change to JMP LOAD_PROG. What LOAD_PROG will do, the first time that the .COM file is run, is to reset the appropriate interrupt vectors so that they point to PROG. We do not want to run PROG when we run the .COM file (so we didn't say JMP PROG at ORG 100H); we only want PROG to run when the interrupts it is intercepting are executed.

Instead, this first time, LOAD_PROG is run. After resetting the correct interrupt vectors to PROG, LOAD_PROG will point DS:DX at the very beginning of itself, LOAD_PROG, and execute an INT 27H. This means that INT 27H will retain in memory all our program up to the point where LOAD_PROG starts. The next program that is loaded will therefore preserve PROG but write over LOAD_PROG. Here's how it looks (PROG will become memory resident, and LOAD_PROG will be jettisoned after the INT 27H):

```
            CODE_SEG SEGMENT
                    ORG 100H
    →       START:JMP LOAD_PROG              ← Program that will
                    Data Area                 be made memory resident
            PROG PROC NEAR


                    Program Area

            PROG ENDP

            LOAD_PROG PROC NEAR
             Interrupt Vectors
             Reset to PROG here.             ← The Booster that is
            MOV DX,OFFSET LOAD_PROG           jettisoned
            INT 27H
            LOAD_PROG ENDP
            CODE_SEG ENDS
            END START
```

We have already written the part of our "booster" that resets the interrupt vector. All we have to add is the part that secures PROG in memory. That looks like this:

```
        :
        :
        :
PROG    ENDP

LOAD_PROG       PROC  NEAR            ;This procedure intializes everything

        MOV     AH,35H                ;Get old vector into ES:BX
        MOV     AL,INTERRUPT_NUMBER   ;See EQU at beginning
        INT     21H
        MOV     OLD_KEY_INT,BX        ;Store old interrupt vector
        MOV     OLD_KEY_INT[2],ES

        MOV     AH,25H                ;Set new interrupt vector
        LEA     DX,PROG
        INT     21H

EXIT2:  MOV     DX,OFFSET LOAD_PROG   ←
        INT     27H                   ←
LOAD_PROG       ENDP

        CODE_SEG        ENDS
```

Now we are installed safely in memory. This is the entire LOAD_PROG procedure—the whole booster used in our program. Soon we will bring all this together into a .COM file shell that can be made memory resident, but first we have to make sure that PROG can handle interrupts.

Writing a Program that Can Handle Interrupts

We've finished designing the booster part of our program. Now we come to more familiar territory: the program itself, which simply handles whatever it is we want to do when the interrupt is executed. Let's look at that part in some detail.

In outline, the program, which we'll call PROG for this example, will fit in like this:

```
CODE_SEG SEGMENT
        ORG 100H
START:JMP LOAD_PROG
        Data Area           ← Program that will
PROG PROC NEAR                be made memory resident
```

```
                  Program Area

PROG ENDP
```
```
LOAD_PROG PROC NEAR
  Interrupt Vectors               ← The Booster that is
  Reset to PROG here.               jettisoned
MOV DX,OFFSET LOAD_PROG
INT 27H
LOAD_PROG ENDP
CODE_SEG ENDS
END START
```

And after the booster has installed the program, all we'll be left with is this:

```
CODE_SEG SEGMENT
         ORG 100H
START:JMP LOAD_PROG
         Data Area                 ← Program that will
PROG PROC NEAR                       be made memory resident

                 Program Area

PROG ENDP
```

This program has the normal data area and code areas that we're used to. In essence, it will be like any other program we've written, with one or two changes.

Those changes are these: We will usually include a call to the original interrupt routine to let it handle some things (like reading keys from the keyboard port—and then we'll read the key from memory).

Also, we'll be extra careful at the beginning and end of the program, saving and then restoring all registers. The reason we save and then restore all registers is common sense: Imagine that you had just pressed a hot key for your popup calculator program. When you're done, you press it again, and the program you had been running takes up where it left off.

You can see how things would be if all the registers had been changed—it's like changing all the variables in mid-program, which will most likely cause our program to crash. To avoid this, we'll push all registers and pop them before exiting. Here is PROG:

> We do not have to push the flags—although we could have, since they have already been pushed when the interrupt was first executed. Note also that all these pushes can be condensed into a single PUSHA in the 286 and 386, and all the pops into POPA.

```
CODE SEG       SEGMENT
        ASSUME CS:CODE_SEG
        ORG    100H            ;ORG = 100H to make this into a .COM file
FIRST:  JMP    LOAD_PROG       ;First time through jump to initialize routine
        :
        Data Area
        :
PROG    PROC   NEAR            ;The keyboard interrupt will now come here.
        ASSUME CS:CODE_SEG
→       PUSH   AX              ;Save the used registers for good form
→       PUSH   BX
→       PUSH   CX
→       PUSH   DX
→       PUSH   DI
→       PUSH   SI
→       PUSH   DS
→       PUSH   ES

        ;Prog goes here.

EXIT:→  POP    ES              ;Having done Pushes, here are the Pops
→       POP    DS
→       POP    SI
→       POP    DI
→       POP    DX
→       POP    CX
→       POP    BX
→       POP    AX
→       IRET                   ;An interrupt needs an IRET
PROG    ENDP
```

IRET, PUSHF, and POPF

Also, we have ended our program PROG with IRET, the proper end for an interrupt routine. At the end of every executed INT instruction, there is an IRET or something equivalent. IRET is a normal FAR return (that is, both CS and IP are retrieved from the stack) with the flags added on. You can push all the microprocessor's flags with the instruction PUSHF and pop them again, restoring all flags, with POPF.

It is important to realize that we can no longer rely on DS and ES being set to CODE_SEG: If we interrupt another program, then the segment registers will naturally be set to the ones it was using at the time we took over control. This means that we will often fill those registers from the CS value, giving us more the enviroment we are used to, using only one segment. (That is, we can simply use MOV AX,CS, then MOV DS,AX—but don't forget an ASSUME DS:CODE_SEG as well.) CS will be set to CODE_SEG, since that is the value that we put into the interrupt vector, and CS:IP are set from those values.

Calling the Old Interrupt

Usually, we will want the old interrupt to do things for us. As mentioned, the keyboard interrupt reads keys that were struck directly from the keyboard, port 60H on the I/O bus. This information would be practically meaningless to us—the keyboard interrupt does a lot of processing to convert that key into an ASCII code (it has to look the bytes it receives up in an internal table, for example), work that we don't want to duplicate.

However, when the key is interpreted, it is placed in memory in the *keyboard buffer*, a section of memory that we will discuss later in this chapter. It is a simple matter to read the keyboard buffer to see what was typed, and whether or not the key was our hot key. For this reason, we'll want to call the keyboard interrupt to read the struck key and interpret it for us. Before we return to the program that was interrupted by the keystroke, we will be able to examine the key that was struck in the keyboard buffer.

That's why you often want to call the old interrupt routine—you can let it do its work and, before you return to the interrupted program, examine what happened.

Even if we do not want to use the old interrupt routine for anything, it is often a good thing to call it anyway, in case another memory-resident program has already been installed that intercepts this interrupt. Unless we called the interrupt, this earlier memory-resident program would never get run.

Let's see how the call will work. We've already stored the old interrupt routine's address in the data area of PROG (LOAD_PROG did that). Now all we have to do is call it.

Indirect Calls and the DD and LABEL Pseudo-Ops

There is a simple way to call such addresses. Up until now, we've had to name our procedures and call them by name, like this:

```
ORG     100H
FIRST:  JMP PROG_A
          :
     Data Area
          :
PROG_A  PROC NEAR
          :
```

```
   →            CALL     PROG_B
                :
     PROG_A  ENDP

     PROG_B  PROC NEAR
                :
                RET
     PROG_B  ENDP
```

On the other hand, we could have said this:

```
     ORG      100H
     FIRST:   JMP PROG_A
   → PROG_B_ADDR        DW 0
     PROG_A  PROC NEAR
                :
   →            MOV      PROG_B_ADDR,OFFSET PROG_B
   →            CALL     PROG_B_ADDR
                :
     PROG_A  ENDP

     PROG_B  PROC NEAR
                :
                RET
     PROG_B  ENDP
```

**Indirect
CALLs**

All that we've done is to store the offset address of the label PROG_B in a memory word, PROG_B_ADDR. Then, the microprocessor allows us to execute an instruction like this: CALL PROG_B_ADDR, which is the same thing as CALL PROG_B. This is helpful to us here, since we do not know in advance where the old interrupt routine will be in memory, and therefore cannot give it a name like PROG_B.

**The DD
Pseudo-Op**

In our case, however, we cannot assume that only the offset address is needed—the old interrupt routine is almost certainly not in our current segment. Instead, we will have to use both words of the address—offset and segment addresses. We have already stored these in locations we named OLD_INTERRUPT and OLD_INTERRUPT[2]; but we cannot call either one of them, since they are just a word long—the assembler knows how many words to use in determining the called address from the declaration DW. Doublewords, which we've seen briefly before, can also be declared, and they use the DD Pseudo-Op.

If we can just store the old interrupt's address in OLD_INTERRUPT_ADDR, declared like this:

```
OLD_INTERRUPT_ADDR       DD       ?        ;Location of old interrupt
```

we'll be fine, and can CALL OLD_INTERRUPT_ADDR to execute the old interrupt routine.

In addition to DB, DW, and DD, there is DQ (Define Quadword) and DT (Define Ten bytes).

On the other hand, we'll have problems with the part of LOAD_PROG that loads these addresses, because the assembler will find itself trying to load single words into something that was defined with DD, not DW, and it will refuse to do it. Remember, this is how we filled THE_INTERRUPT in LOAD_PROG, storage for the old interrupt's address (and what we now want to call OLD_INTERRUPT_ADDR, defined with DD):

```
LOAD_PROG        PROC    NEAR     ;This procedure intializes everything

        MOV     AH,35H          ;Get old vector into ES:BX
        MOV     AL,INTERRUPT_NUMBER     ;See EQU at beginning
        INT     21H

→       MOV     THE_INTERRUPT,BX        ;Store old interrupt vector
→       MOV     THE_INTERRUPT[2],ES

        MOV     AH,25H          ;Set new interrupt vector
        LEA     DX,PROG
        INT     21H

EXIT2:  MOV     DX,OFFSET LOAD_PROG     ;Set up everything but LOAD_PROG to
        INT     27H                     ;stay and attach itself to DOS
LOAD_PROG        ENDP
```

The LABEL Pseudo-Op

In other words, we now want to refer to the same memory location two different ways—as if it were a word, and as if it were a doubleword. This can be solved using the Pseudo-Op LABEL, which is built into the macro assembler for exactly this type of case.

The LABEL Pseudo-Op

We will define OLD_INTERRUPT_ADDR with DD this way in the data area of our program:

```
CODE_SEG        SEGMENT
        ASSUME  CS:CODE_SEG
        ORG     100H            ;ORG = 100H to make this into a .COM file
FIRST:  JMP     LOAD_PROG       ;First time through jump to initialize routine
→       OLD_INTERRUPT_ADDR      DD      ?       ;Location of old interrupt

PROG    PROC    NEAR            ;The interrupt will now come here.
        ASSUME  CS:CODE_SEG
        PUSH    AX              ;Save the used registers for good form
        PUSH    BX
        PUSH    CX
        PUSH    DX
        PUSH    DI
        PUSH    SI
```

```
        PUSH    DS
        PUSH    ES
        PUSHF                       ;First, call old interrupt
        CALL    OLD_INTERRUPT_ADDR

        ;Prog goes here.

EXIT:   POP     ES              ;Having done Pushes, here are the Pops
        POP     DS
        POP     SI
        POP     DI
        POP     DX
        POP     CX
        POP     BX
        POP     AX
        IRET                        ;An interrupt needs an IRET

PROG    ENDP
```

so that we can CALL OLD_INTERRUPT_ADDR. And then we will LABEL the first word as OLD_INTERRUPT like this:

```
CODE_SEG        SEGMENT
        ASSUME  CS:CODE_SEG
        ORG     100H            ;ORG = 100H to make this into a .COM file
FIRST:  JMP     LOAD_PROG       ;First time through jump to initialize routine
→       OLD_INTERRUPT   LABEL   WORD
        OLD_INTERRUPT_ADDR      DD      ?       ;Location of old interrupt

PROG    PROC    NEAR            ;The interrupt will now come here.
        ASSUME  CS:CODE_SEG
        PUSH    AX              ;Save the used registers for good form
        PUSH    BX
        PUSH    CX
        PUSH    DX
        PUSH    DI
        PUSH    SI
        PUSH    DS
        PUSH    ES
        PUSHF                   ;First, call old interrupt
        CALL    OLD_INTERRUPT_ADDR

        ;Prog goes here.

EXIT:   POP     ES              ;Having done Pushes, here are the Pops
        POP     DS
        POP     SI
        POP     DI
        POP     DX
        POP     CX
        POP     BX
        POP     AX
        IRET                    ;An interrupt needs an IRET
PROG    ENDP
```

LABEL gives the current location a name, just like DD or DW does, except that it does not reserve any space for the name in memory. LABEL is most useful when you have to refer to a particular memory location in two ways, as if, for example, it was defined with DW *and* DD. LOAD_PROG is satisfied, since it will be able to load individual words into OLD_INTERRUPT, and PROG itself is satisfied, because it will be able to CALL OLD_INTERRUPT_ADDR as a doubleword.

Using PUSHF

Waiting at the end of the old interrupt routine that we are about to call, however, is not a normal return, but an IRET, and IRET pops the flags off the stack (this is the final word it pops before returning to the calling program). To take care of this, we will not simply call OLD_INTERRUPT_ADDR this way:

```
CALL    OLD_INTERRUPT_ADDR
```

but instead will add the flags to the stack first with PUSHF:

```
PUSHF                       ;First, call old interrupt
  CALL    OLD_INTERRUPT_ADDR
```

And now we are all set to call the old interrupt without trouble.

Use This Shell

Here is how our entire memory-resident .COM file shell looks:

```
INTERRUPT_NUMBER        EQU     9  ← Put the INT number here

CODE_SEG       SEGMENT
        ASSUME CS:CODE_SEG
        ORG    100H                ;ORG = 100H to make this into a .COM
                                    file
FIRST:  JMP    LOAD_PROG           ;First time through jump to
                                    initialize routine
        OLD_INTERRUPT   LABEL   WORD

        OLD_INTERRUPT_ADDR      DD      ?       ;Location of old interrupt

PROG    PROC   NEAR                 ;The interrupt will now come here.
        ASSUME CS:CODE_SEG
        PUSH   AX                   ;Save the used registers for good
form
        PUSH   BX
        PUSH   CX
        PUSH   DX
        PUSH   DI
        PUSH   SI
        PUSH   DS
```

```
        PUSH    ES
        PUSHF                           ;First, call old interrupt
        CALL    OLD_INTERRUPT_ADDR

        ;Prog goes here.

EXIT:   POP     ES                      ;Having done Pushes, here are the
Pops
        POP     DS
        POP     SI
        POP     DI
        POP     DX
        POP     CX
        POP     BX
        POP     AX
        IRET                            ;An interrupt needs an IRET
PROG    ENDP

LOAD_PROG       PROC    NEAR            ;This procedure intializes everything

        MOV     AH,35H                  ;Get old vector into ES:BX
        MOV     AL,INTERRUPT_NUMBER     ;See EQU at beginning
        INT     21H

        MOV     OLD_INTERRUPT,BX        ;Store old interrupt vector
        MOV     OLD_INTERRUPT[2],ES

        MOV     AH,25H                  ;Set new interrupt vector
        LEA     DX,PROG
        INT     21H

EXIT2:  MOV     DX,OFFSET LOAD_PROG     ;Set up everything but LOAD_PROG to
        INT     27H                     ;stay and attach itself to DOS
LOAD_PROG       ENDP

        CODE_SEG        ENDS

        END     FIRST                   ;END "FIRST" so 8088 will go to
                                        FIRST first.
```

Now that it's built, we can simply use this shell, and not have to build it from scratch each time. As it stands, this shell is a little barren; we will add some code to it specifically so that it can intercept the keyboard interrupt (the most widely intercepted interrupt) and report the character that was typed in DX a little later. Before we do that, we will develop an example, using the shell as it stands.

Some Things You Can't Do

It would be great if you could do anything from a memory-resident program; however, you cannot. You cannot, for example, use any DOS interrupts (including DOS INT 21H)! You can use the BIOS interrupts without problem. The reason is that the DOS interrupts are comparatively fragile. If your main program is executing something in INT 21H, and you take over with a memory-resident program and try to run the same code, you'll destroy the memory variables that were already set for the first program. When you finish and go back to the first program, everything will be a shambles. BIOS doesn't have this failing. For that reason, we are going to use INT 10H to print on the screen while memory resident, not INT 21H.

> In computer language, DOS is not *re-entrant* (OS/2 is re-entrant). The DOS interrupts actually *can* be used, if you add a tremendous amount of programming, but we're not going to do that here.

Some Things You Can Do

One thing we can do is write an example program right now. After having developed all the technology of memory-resident programs, let's put it into practice.

The timer interrupt, INT 8

You may recall that there is no cursor on the screen in graphics modes, so we'll make a program that will add one. It will be very simple indeed. There is a hardware interrupt that is very useful to memory-resident programs called the *timer interrupt*, INT 8. This interrupt is made 18.2 times a second all the time—your PC or PS/2 is stopping work 18.2 times a second to check on the timer (unless you turn off hardware interrupts).

We'll intercept that interrupt and use it, 18.2 times a second, to print out an underscore, "_", as a cursor at the current cursor position with INT 10H service 0AH (recall that although INT services 9 and 0AH write out characters, they do not advance the cursor).

> It's a good thing we turned off hardware interrupts before redirecting the timer interrupt. Imagine if a timer interrupt occured just after we had set CS of the timer interrupt's vector, but not yet IP.

Our program PROG will be very simple. All we really have to do is make sure we set INTERRUPT_NUMBER to 8 and then print out "_". Here's the program:

```
INTERRUPT_NUMBER        EQU     8     ←

CODE_SEG        SEGMENT
        ASSUME CS:CODE_SEG
        ORG     100H                    ;ORG = 100H to make this into a .COM file
FIRST:  JMP     LOAD_PROG               ;First time through jump to initialize
                                         routine
        OLD_INTERRUPT LABEL WORD
        OLD_INTERRUPT_ADDR  DD   ? ;Location of old interrupt

PROG    PROC    NEAR                    ;The interrupt will now come here.
        PUSH    AX                      ;Save the used registers for good form
```

```
              PUSH    BX
              PUSH    CX
              PUSH    DX
              PUSH    DI
              PUSH    SI
              PUSH    DS
              PUSH    ES
              PUSHF
              CALL    OLD_INTERRUPT_ADDR     ;First, call old interrupt
    →         MOV     AH,0AH
    →         MOV     CX,1
    →         MOV     BH,0
    →         MOV     AL,"_"
    →         INT     10H
              POP     ES                     ;Having done Pushes, here are the Pops
              POP     DS
              POP     SI
              POP     DI
              POP     DX
              POP     CX
              POP     BX
              POP     AX
              IRET                           ;An interrupt needs an IRET
PROG          ENDP

LOAD_PROG     PROC    NEAR                   ;This procedure intializes everything

              MOV     AH,35H                 ;Get old vector into ES:BX
              MOV     AL,INTERRUPT_NUMBER    ;See EQU at beginning
              INT     21H
              MOV     OLD_INTERRUPT,BX       ;Store old interrupt vector
              MOV     OLD_INTERRUPT[2],ES

              MOV     AH,25H                 ;Set new interrupt vector
              LEA     DX,PROG
              INT     21H

EXIT:  MOV    DX,OFFSET LOAD_PROG            ;Set up everything but LOAD_PROG to
       INT    27H                            ;stay and attach itself to DOS
LOAD_PROG     ENDP

       CODE_SEG        ENDS
       END    FIRST                          ;END ""FIRST'' so 8088 will to go FIRST
                                             ;first.
```

The body of PROG just types out this cursor, "_". We select graphics page 0 (the usual page) with MOV BH,0; set the count of characters to write to 1 with MOV CX,1; select service 0AH with MOV AH,0AH, and type a "_"—MOV AL,"_".

```
       MOV     AH,0AH
       MOV     CX,1
       MOV     BH,0
       MOV     AL,"_"
       INT     10H
```

This is our first memory-resident program. To use it, just type it in or read it from the diskette that accompanies this book, assemble link, and run it through EXE2BIN. Then put yourself in a graphics mode on the screen, as we discussed in the previous chapter (note there is no cursor), and run CURSOR.COM.

A cursor will appear; just the unblinking, somewhat sullen-looking underscore. But it will stay wherever the cursor is. Unfortunately, sometimes the cursor is moved around on the screen discontinuously—that is, no character is typed to overwrite the "_" before the cursor moves on. Most of the time this is not the case, but sometimes you will see little underscores in odd places on the page.

> You can easily make the cursor blink by counting how often the timer interrupt has been called, and typing either a "_" or a blank space " ". You can also fix the problem of left-behind cursors (when the cursor is moved discontinuously), if you really want to, but you will have to intercept INT 10H also, and check when the move cursor service, service 2, is called.

Intercepting the Keyboard Interrupt

This is the big one, the interrupt that most popup programs really use: the keyboard interrupt. As mentioned before, whenever a key is struck, an INT 9 is generated. The PS/2 or PC stops work to go off to the keyboard interrupt routine (whose vector is at 4 x 9 = 36 = 24H; 0000:0024); this routine reads in the key codes, and places the key's ASCII code into the keyboard buffer, along with its scan code.

The Keyboard Buffer and Scan Codes

For each of the 83 keys on the basic PC keyboard or the 101 keys on the PS/2 keyboard, there is a code called a *scan code*, which the microprocessor in the keyboard sends to the PC when a key is typed. All the scan codes are listed in many PC and PS/2 manuals. If you want to find the ASCII and scan codes for any key, this BASIC program:

```
10      FOR I=1 TO 10:KEY I,"":NEXT I
20      DEF SEG = &H40
30      FKEY$=INKEY$:IF FKEY$="" GOTO 30
40      TAIL=PEEK(26):TAIL=TAIL-2:IF TAIL < 30 THEN TAIL = 60
50      CODE1=PEEK(TAIL):CODE2=PEEK(TAIL+1)
60      PRINT HEX$(CODE1) SPC(1) HEX$(CODE2) SPC(2);:GOTO 20:END
```

will read any typed key's scan and ASCII code directly from the keyboard buffer and print them out in hex; ASCII code followed by scan code. The

"A" key has an ASCII code of 41H and a scan code of 1EH. The "S" key, right next to it, has an ASCII code of 53H and a scan code of 1FH.

Scan and ASCII codes in the keyboard buffer

Both the typed character's scan code and its ASCII code are stored in the keyboard buffer (two bytes total).

The keyboard buffer itself is a set of 16 words in memory in the BIOS data area. These bytes are set up to be what is called a circular buffer. Since the reading and writing operations from and to this buffer are independent, circular buffering allows you to put in and take out keys easily. At any given time, one of these 16 words, called the *head*, is the position that the next character will be read from.

Circular buffers

Another, the *tail*, is the position that the next character can be written to. When keys are typed in, the tail advances. When you read one, the head advances. When either comes to the end of their 16-word range, they wrap around to the beginning again. A good model for this circular buffer is a ring of 16 words, with the head forever chasing the tail. Two more bytes in the BIOS data area hold the current addresses of the head and the tail.

When everything is read, the head catches up with the tail; the two are at the same address, and the buffer is empty. Conversely, if the tail wraps around and comes up from behind the head, the buffer is full.

The BIOS Data Area

The keyboard buffer is in the BIOS data area in memory, segment 40H. There is an immense amount of information in the BIOS Data Area:

Table 6.1 BIOS Data Areas

Address(es)	Contents
40:0000 - 40:0006	Addresses of RS 232 adapters 1–4
40:0008 - 40:000E	Addresses of printer adapters 1–4
40:0010	Equipment Flag (returned by Int 11H)
40:0012	Manufacturer's test mark
40:0013	Motherboard memory (in Kbytes)
40:0015	I/O channel memory
40:0017	The Keyboard Flags (see below)
40:0019	Numbers input with Alt key
40:001A	Location of Keyboard Buffer Head
40:001C	Location of Keyboard Buffer Tail
40:001E - 40:003D	Keyboard Buffer
40:003E	Status of Diskette Seek
40:003F	Status of Diskette Motor
40:0040	Timeout of Diskette Motor
40:0041	Status of Diskette

Table 6.1 BIOS Data Areas *(continued)*

Address(es)	Contents
40:0042 - 40:004D	Status Bytes of Diskette Controller (the NEC)
40:0049	Display Mode (see the section on Clock)
40:004A	Number of columns (40 or 80)
40:004C	Length of Video Regen. Buffer
40:004E	Starting Address in Regen. Buffer
40:0050 - 40:005E	Positions of cursors on screen pages 1–8
40:0060	Mode of the Cursor
40:0062	Active Page Number
40:0063	Address of current display adapter

While we are here, we should examine the two bytes that begin at 40:0017 because they are often useful to assembly–language programmers (it is the byte at 40:17 that INT 16H Service 2 returns in AL). Table 6.2 is a breakdown of 40:17 and 40:18 bit by bit, starting with bit 0.

Table 6.2

Bit	State	Byte at 40:0017	Byte at 40:0018
0	Right Shift	1 → Key is pressed	
1	Left Shift	1 → Key is pressed	
2	Cntrl Shift	1 → Key is pressed	
3		1 →Alt Shift Pressed	1 →~Num Lock On
4	Scroll-Lock	1 → On	1 → Key is pressed
5	Num-Lock	1 → On	1 → Key is pressed
6	Caps-Lock	1 → On	1 → Key is pressed
7	Insert	1 → On	1 → Key is pressed

Any program that can get into these bytes can change the keyboard state of the PC, since the scan codes that come in from the keyboard are interpreted with the aid of this byte. We can write, in DEBUG, a small program named TURNCAPS.COM that simply turns on the CapsLock state of the PC by ORing 40H, or 01000000B, with the status byte at 40:17. Using DEBUG we can write TURNCAPS.COM:

```
A> DEBUG
    NTURNCAPS.COM
    A100
    MOV AX,40
    MOV DS,AX
    MOV BX,17
    OR BYTE PTR [BX],40
    INT 20
```

```
          <CR>
          RCX
          D
          W
          Q
```

Examining the Keyboard Buffer

It is the keyboard buffer that we will be interested in with our example
program. With DEBUG, we should be able to take a direct look at the
keyboard buffer at 40:1E. In particular, we can examine it with the Dump
command. Let's fill the buffer with As and then examine it. To avoid
having to type D0040:001E, which would fill the buffer up, let's do a
Dump of 128 bytes before 40:1E so we only have to type D <cr> since
Dump takes up just where it stopped. Here's how it looks:

```
-D0:39E         ← 128 Bytes before the keyboard buffer
0000:030E  00 00                                             ..
0000:03A0  00 00 00 00 00 00 00 00-00 00 00 00 00 00 00 00   ................
0000:03B0  00 00 00 00 00 00 00 00-00 00 00 00 00 00 00 00   ................
0000:03C0  00 00 00 00 E5 FE 00 F0-E5 FE E5 FE 00 F0 FF FF   ....e~.pe~e~.p...
0000:03D0  5D EF FF FF 40 00 3A EF-00 F0 06 00 00 00 01 00   ]o..a.:o.p......
0000:03E0  40 00 6F EC 00 00 43 E6-80 00 02 00 00 00 01 00   @.ol..Cf........
0000:03F0  00 7C 21 E7 00 F0 46 F2-04 00 CF E5 00 F0 97 F2   .!!g.pFr..Oe.p.r
0000:0400  00 00 00 00 00 00 00 00-BC 03 00 00 00 00 00 00   ........<.......
0000:0410  BD 40 00 00 01 C0 00 40-00 00 38 00 38 00         =a...a.a..8.8.
-AAAAAAAAAAAAAAAA           ← Fill the buffer with "A"
  ~ Error                  ← Which DEBUG naturally thinks is an error.
-D                         ← And now examine it.
0000:041E        41 1E                                       A.
0000:0420  41 1E 41 1E 41 1E 41 1E-41 1E 41 1E 41 1E 41 1E   A.A.A.A.A.A.A.A.
0000:0430  41 1E 41 1E 41 1E 41 1E-0D 1C 44 20 0D 1C 03 80   A.A.A...D ....
0000:0440  3A 00 04 00 00 0D 01 03-02 07 50 00 00 40 00 00   %.........P..a..
0000:0450  00 18 00 00 00 00 00 00-00 00 00 00 00 00 00 00   ................
0000:0460  07 06 00 B4 03 29 30 E6-0A 00 00 00 98 4D 11 00   ...4.)0f.....M..
0000:0470  00 00 FF FF 00 00 00 00-14 14 14 14 01 01 01 01   ................
0000:0480  1E 00 3E 00 00 00 00 00-10 00 00 00 00 00 00 00   ..>.............
0000:0490  00 00 00 00 00 00 00 00-10 00 00 00 00 00 00      ..............
-Q
```

If you look at the ASCII part of the display you'll see our typed
As. Each A is stored as a 41H (its ASCII code) and a 1E (its scan code).
At the end of the last A, the carriage return we typed (i.e.,
AAAAAAAAAAAAAAAA<cr>) is stored as 0D (= ASCII 13) 1C (its
scan code). Finally, you can see our D<cr> command. This last <cr>
leaves us at the top of the buffer. The next key typed would be wrapped
around, and stored at the beginning at 40:1E.

We can set up labels for all the parts of the keyboard buffer by defining
a segment with the AT Pseudo-Op, just as we did for INTERRUPTS.
Here's our ROM_BIOS_DATA segment:

Using AT
to check
ROM_
BIOS_DATA

```
ROM_BIOS_DATA    SEGMENT AT 40H        ;BIOS statuses held here, also keyboard
                                        buffer
        ORG     1AH
        HEAD DW     ?                   ;Unread chars go from Head to Tail
        TAIL DW     ?
        BUFFER      DW  16 DUP (?) ;The buffer itself
        BUFFER_END  DW ?

ROM_BIOS_DATA    ENDS
```

Reading from the Keyboard Buffer

When an INT 9 is generated, our memory-resident program takes over. Its first action is to call the old keyboard interrupt, which places the scan and ASCII codes of the struck key into the keyboard buffer.

The actual details of reading the struck key from the keyboard buffer are not important for us to cover here—they will add no new knowledge, and simply take up much time. Let's just go over them in outline.

To read a key from the keyboard buffer, we'll have to set DS to the ROM_BIOS_DATA segment, and check where the tail is in the keyboard buffer (the location where the next key will be placed). The key just before that in the keyboard buffer is the new one. We'll read it from the buffer and place its scan code in DH, and its ASCII code in DL. Your program can then take over and see if it's the hot key expected. If not, you should just exit—that is, jump to the label EXIT.

Removing Keys from the Keyboard Buffer

If the key is the one you were expecting, your program might want to spring into action and start intercepting all keys as input. This means that your program will have to remove keys from the keyboard buffer as soon as they are typed (and place them into a notepad, for example).

To remove a key from the keyboard buffer, all you need to do is move the tail of the buffer to overwrite the key. At the point your program takes over (made clear in the keyboard-intercepting .COM file shell to follow), BX will hold the offset address of the current key in the buffer. To remove this key, just use the instruction MOV TAIL,BX.

```
At the point your program takes over:
        [Check scan code (in DH) and ASCII code (in DL)]
            [Is it a key you want to accept as input?]
                |                           |
               Yes                          No
                |                           |
                ↓                           ↓
```

```
[Remove this key          [JMP to EXIT, leaving this
 from the keyboard         key to be used by other
 buffer with MOV TAIL,BX]  programs.]
[Do work]
[JMP to EXIT]
```

For example, if your program wanted to remove all typed ^Ns (so they never appeared on the screen or got read by any program), it would check for the correct scan code in DH (31H) and the correct ASCII code in DL (0EH). If it found what it was looking for, it would remove the key. If not, it wouldn't interfere. To do this, all you would need are these instructions in the .COM file shell where you take over:

```
CMP    DX,310EH    ;Is this a ^N?
JNE    EXIT        ;No, just exit
MOV    TAIL,BX     ;Yes, remove it
JMP    EXIT        ;And leave
```

We'll develop an example after introducing our key–intercepting .COM file shell to make this clear.

The Key-Intercepting .COM File Shell

Here is the keyboard-intercepting .COM file shell, complete with instructions on what to do when your program takes over, and how to accept a typed key as input by removing it from the keyboard buffer:

Listing 6.1 Keyboard-Intercepting .COM File Shell

```
INTERRUPT_NUMBER        EQU     9

ROM_BIOS_DATA   SEGMENT AT 40H             ;BIOS statuses held here, also keyboard buffer

        ORG     1AH
        HEAD DW     ?                       ;Unread chars go from Head to Tail
        TAIL DW     ?
        BUFFER      DW     16 DUP (?)        ;The buffer itself
        BUFFER_END  LABEL  WORD

ROM_BIOS_DATA   ENDS

CODE_SEG        SEGMENT
        ASSUME  CS:CODE_SEG
        ORG     100H                        ;ORG = 100H to make this into a .COM file
FIRST:  JMP     LOAD_PROG                   ;First time through jump to initialize routine

        OLD_KEY_INT     LABEL   WORD
        OLD_KEYBOARD_INT        DD    ?     ;Location of old kbd interrupt

PROG    PROC    NEAR                        ;The keyboard interrupt will now come here.
        ASSUME  CS:CODE_SEG
        PUSH    AX                          ;Save the used registers for good form
        PUSH    BX
        PUSH    CX
        PUSH    DX
        PUSH    DI
        PUSH    SI
```

Listing 6.1 Keyboard-Intercepting .COM File Shell *(continued)*

```
          PUSH    DS
          PUSH    ES
          PUSHF                               ;First, call old keyboard interrupt
          CALL    OLD_KEYBOARD_INT
  →       ASSUME  DS:ROM_BIOS_DATA            ;Examine the char just put in
          MOV     BX,ROM_BIOS_DATA
  →       MOV     DS,BX

  →       MOV     BX,TAIL                     ;Point to current tail
  →       CMP     BX,HEAD                     ;If at head, kbd int has deleted char
  →       JE      IN                          ;So leave
  →       SUB     BX,2                        ;Point to just read in character
  →       CMP     BX,OFFSET BUFFER            ;Did we undershoot buffer?
  →       JAE     NO_WRAP                     ;Nope
  →       MOV     BX,OFFSET BUFFER_END        ;Yes -- move to buffer top
  →       SUB     BX,2                        ;Point to just read in character
NO_WRAP:MOV     DX,[BX]      ←               ;Char in DX now
```

NOTE: Your program takes over here (keep in mind that DS is still at ROM_BIOS_DATA segment). The just-struck key's scan code is in DH and its ASCII code in DL at this point. If you want to remove this key from the keyboard buffer (i.e. accept it as input), use the instruction MOV TAIL,BX here. Otherwise, you may exit by jumping to the label EXIT.

```
          ;MOV    TAIL,BX                     ; ←Optional removal of key from buffer.
          :
    [Your code here.]
          :
EXIT:    POP     ES                          ;Having done Pushes, here are the Pops
          POP     DS
          POP     SI
          POP     DI
          POP     DX
          POP     CX
          POP     BX
          POP     AX
          IRET                                ;An interrupt needs an IRET
PROG     ENDP

LOAD_PROG        PROC    NEAR                ;This procedure intializes everything

          MOV     AH,35H                      ;Get old vector into ES:BX
          MOV     AL,INTERRUPT_NUMBER         ;See EQU at beginning
          INT     21H

          MOV     OLD_KEY_INT,BX              ;Store old interrupt vector
          MOV     OLD_KEY_INT[2],ES

          MOV     AH,25H                      ;Set new interrupt vector
          LEA     DX,PROG
          INT     21H

          MOV     DX,OFFSET LOAD_PROG         ;Set up everything but LOAD_PROG to
          INT     27H                         ;stay and attach itself to DOS
LOAD_PROG        ENDP

          CODE_SEG        ENDS

          END     FIRST                       ;END "FIRST" so 8088 will go to FIRST first.
```

Let's put together an example!

SWITCH.ASM: A Memory-Resident Hot Key Program

Here we'll put our keyboard interceptor to work and see how everything fits together. We'll write a program named SWITCH.ASM that lets you switch between two screens, the MDA and CGA, if you have both installed. The hot key will be Alt-S. In other words, when you are using one screen and type Alt-S, you will switch to the other screen, no matter what program is running.

To switch screens, it is not enough to simply switch video modes. If you are using the same screen, switching video modes is fine, but it will not automatically change the monitor you are using if your current monitor does not support the mode you select.

Using the BIOS equipment flag

You also must change one of the words in the BIOS data area, the equipment word (also called, inaccurately, the equipment flag). In this case, you load this word from 40:0010 (see Table 6.1, above) into some register—for example, CX. The instruction AND CX,11101111B will reset the appropriate bit to switch to the graphics screen. OR CX,00010000B will set you up for monochrome (then, of course, you must return the contents of CX to 40:0010).

Introduction to AND and OR

The two 8088 instructions AND and OR are very useful for working with individual bits in a word. Both AND and OR will be covered in Chapter 9, Fast Math. Here we can say that OR is just like the logical Or used in mathematics: If we use OR on two bits, the result will always be 1 unless both bits were 0. Conversely, AND is just like logical And; using AND on two bits will always yield 0 unless both bits were 1. OR and AND are frequently used to change individual bits in a word or byte because of these properties—AND can turn bits off, and OR can make sure they are on. Both these instructions will be covered in Chapter 9.

Using Alt-S as a hot key

Checking a particular bit in the equipment word, we can tell whether or not a monochrome screen or a CGA screen is in use, and then toggle to the other option. The hot key here is Alt-S, which means the scan code we are looking for is 1FH and the ASCII code is 0. DX will hold 1F00 if Alt-S has been typed when our program takes over from the keyboard-intercepting shell, and we will spring into action. (You can find the scan and ASCII codes of the keys you want to use as hot keys in your program by using the BASIC program earlier, or checking the IBM manuals.)

If Alt-S *has* been typed, we remove it from the keyboard buffer. In that way, the Alt-S will not be left over after we've finished changing screens.

To erase the key, we'll use MOV TAIL,BX. Here is the part of the program that both detects whether or not the hot key was typed, and if it was, erases it from the buffer (and, if it was not, exits):

```
                MOV     BX,TAIL                 ;Point to current tail
                CMP     BX,HEAD                 ;If at head, kbd int has deleted char
                JE      OUT                     ;So leave
                SUB     BX,2                    ;Point to just read in character
                CMP     BX,OFFSET BUFFER        ;Did we undershoot buffer?
                JAE     NO_WRAP                 ;Nope
                MOV     BX,OFFSET BUFFER_END    ;Yes_move to buffer top
                SUB     BX,2                    ;Point to just read in character
NO_WRAP:        MOV     DX,[BX]                 ;Char in DX now
   →            CMP     DX,1F00H                ;Is the char an ALT-S?
   →            JNE     EXIT                    ;No
   →            MOV     TAIL,BX                 ;Yes_delete it from buffer
```

Here is the whole program SWITCH, which just switches us back and forth between monochrome and CGA:

Listing 6.2 SWITCH.ASM

```
        ;Uses ALT-S to toggle between screens (Graphics  →   Monochrome)
INTERRUPT_NUMBER        EQU     9

ROM_BIOS_DATA   SEGMENT AT 40H          ;BIOS statuses held here, also
                                         keyboard buffer

        ORG     1AH
        HEAD DW     ?                    ;Unread chars go from Head to Tail
        TAIL DW     ?
        BUFFER      DW      16 DUP (?)  ←;The buffer itself
        BUFFER_END  LABEL   WORD

ROM_BIOS_DATA   ENDS

CODE_SEG        SEGMENT
        ASSUME  CS:CODE_SEG
        ORG     100H                    ;ORG = 100H to make this into a .COM
                                         file
FIRST:  JMP     LOAD_PROG               ;First time through jump to initialize
                                         routine

        OLD_KEY_INT     LABEL   WORD
        OLD_KEYBOARD_INT        DD      ? ;Location of old kbd interrupt

PROG    PROC    NEAR                    ;The keyboard interrupt will now come
                                         here.

        ASSUME  CS:CODE_SEG
        PUSH    AX                      ;Save the used registers for good form
        PUSH    BX
        PUSH    CX
        PUSH    DX
        PUSH    DI
        PUSH    SI
        PUSH    DS
        PUSH    ES
        PUSHF                           ;First, call old keyboard interrupt
        CALL    OLD_KEYBOARD_INT
```

Listing 6.2 SWITCH.ASM *(continued)*

```
              ASSUME   DS:ROM_BIOS_DATA        ;Examine the char just put in
              MOV      BX,ROM_BIOS_DATA
              MOV      DS,BX

              MOV      BX,TAIL                 ;Point to current tail
              CMP      BX,HEAD                 ;If at head, kbd int has deleted char
              JE       EXIT                    ;So leave
              SUB      BX,2                    ;Point to just read in character
              CMP      BX,OFFSET BUFFER        ;Did we undershoot buffer?
              JAE      NO_WRAP                 ;Nope
              MOV      BX,OFFSET BUFFER_END    ;Yes -- move to buffer top
              SUB      BX,2                    ;Point to just read in character
NO_WRAP:MOV      DX,[BX]                 ;Char in DX now
              CMP      DX,1F00H                ;Is the char an ALT-S?
              JNE      EXIT                    ;No
              MOV      TAIL,BX                 ;Yes -- delete it from buffer

              MOV      BX,10H                  ;Get equipment flag
              MOV      AX,[BX]
              MOV      CX,AX                   ;Put a copy in CX
              AND      AX,00010000B            ;Is CGA in use?
              CMP      AX,0
              JE       TO_MONOCHROME           ;Yes
TO_GRAPHICS:                                   ;No, switch to CGA
              AND      CX,11101111B            ;Set up equipment byte
              MOV      [BX],CX                 ;And reinstall it
              MOV      AX,0002                 ;Set up a CGA screen mode
              INT      10H
              JMP      EXIT                    ;And leave
TO_MONOCHROME:                                 ;Turn on monochrome here
              OR       CX,00010000B            ;Set up equipment byte
              MOV      [BX],CX                 ;And reinstall it
              MOV      AX,0007                 ;Set up monochrome video mode
              INT      10H

EXIT:     POP      ES                      ;Having done Pushes, here are the Pops
              POP      DS
              POP      SI
              POP      DI
              POP      DX
              POP      CX
              POP      BX
              POP      AX
              IRET                             ;An interrupt needs an IRET
PROG      ENDP

LOAD_PROG         PROC    NEAR            ;This procedure intializes everything

              MOV      AH,35H                  ;Get old vector into ES:BX
              MOV      AL,INTERRUPT_NUMBER     ;See EQU at beginning
              INT      21H
              MOV      OLD_KEY_INT,BX          ;Store old interrupt vector
              MOV      OLD_KEY_INT[2],ES

              MOV      AH,25H                  ;Set new interrupt vector
              LEA      DX,PROG
              INT      21H

              MOV      DX,OFFSET LOAD_PROG     ;Set up everything but LOAD_PROG to
              INT      27H                     ;stay and attach itself to DOS
LOAD_PROG         ENDP
              CODE_SEG        ENDS
                      END     FIRST
```

There's not much to this program: We just check to see if the CGA is in use. If it is, turn on monochrome instead by setting the equipment byte and changing to the monochrome video mode. If the CGA was not in use, we turn it on by setting up the equipment byte and changing to a CGA video mode. Of course, we restore all registers to the way they were before returning to the program then running (including segment registers).

Writing a notepad

If we had wanted instead to write a popup notepad, we would have simply used BIOS INT 10H, service 9 or 0AH, to write out our notepad on the screen. Then, while the pad was active, we would have removed typed keys from the keyboard buffer (MOV BX,TAIL) and put them into the notepad area of memory. When the hot key was typed again, we would have just stopped intercepting typed characters, and take our notepad off the screen.

That is the end of our discussion of memory-resident programs. Their uses vary from programs that will: take snaphots of the screen; log screen output; remember what's gone on the screen many screen-fuls ago (and let you scroll through it); pop up utilities of all descriptions; put in disk "caches" to make your disk go faster; and all kinds of things. And now, you too know how to write them. It may have originally looked difficult because of the bewildering number of details, but now that we've developed a working .COM file shell, most of the details are solved.

7

Linking Files Together

JMP SHORT
Nested Procedures
External Data
EXTRN Pseudo-Op

PUBLIC Pseudo-Op
LINK
PUBLIC Segments
External Procedures

Groups
Libraries
The Library Manager LIB
Library Modules

**Larger
source files**
All the programs we've written so far have been small, demonstration programs, because large, unwieldy programs make terrible examples. However, hardly any real–life assembly-language programs are only one-half page in length. The majority of real applications written in assembly language are long, ranging up to hundreds of pages. This is possible even on a microcomputer because of the compact code generated. For example, the program for a popup calculator can easily run 35 pages or more, but 35 pages of .ASM files will probably assemble into about 6K of .COM file (or less if you leave out help screens). You can imagine what would be required to write a 64K communications program in assembly language.

To make this job easier, or at least tractable, you can break the parts up into many different files. Each of these .ASM files can be fully debugged; then, when you encounter a bug, you might only have to debug the newest .ASM file instead of facing 100 pages of everything all at once. Typically, any project in assembly language is broken up into separate files this way, and *linked* to other files before the .COM or .EXE file is created.

Also, high-level languages can be compiled into .OBJ format, and you can link assembly-language written code in, from another .OBJ file produced by the assembler (as we'll do later). This process can then merge high-level languages and assembly language, although it has to be done with real care.

Libraries
Large-scale applications in any language are almost always broken up into separate files and worked on individually, then linked together. Completely separate teams may develop whole libraries of programs inside .OBJ files that other teams can link into their programs later.

When this happens, *libraries* are made. When you link a .OBJ file together with another one, everything inside the .OBJ files are included in the resulting .EXE file (which might then be converted to .COM format). On the other hand, when you put a number of .OBJ files together to form a library (with the new LIB command in DOS), then you can take just the subprograms you need from the library file—not everything—with LINK. This can be enormously useful, and simplifies tasks a great deal.

To start working in this world, we'll need to know how to link files and run them. We'll do that in this chapter. Even though the technique is meant for large-scale files, we'll keep ours as small as possible so that the point can be clearly made, and not obscured by details.

All we'll use is a simple example, one that has both a little bit of data and a little bit of code. We will just use INT 21H service 9 (the string printer) to print out the message: "No Worries." That's all we'll actually *do*, but the ways of doing it are practically endless, and we'll use this example as a way of demonstrating them. The philosophy of this book is learning through examples, and here we'll learn a little more about what is legal in assembly language.

Some of these ways will take us into the territory of macros in the next chapter. You may have wondered why the assembler is called the Macro Assembler; we'll answer that question in that chapter. Even though macros can get wonderfully complex, we are going to limit them to modest size, again so that the point doesn't get lost.

> More about macros can be found in the second book of this set, *Advanced Assembly Language on the IBM PC*, if you are interested. This subject can become extraordinarily difficult very quickly; you can define macro libraries, and even write your own programming language. But here we are just going to give an introduction to the subject.

No Worries

Just to make sure we are on solid ground, the first few methods of printing out "No Worries." will be familiar to us. We already know some methods of doing this: The first is simply to put together a .ASM file that will do it, without even a procedure. That might look like this:

```
CODE_SEG           SEGMENT
        ASSUME     CS:CODE_SEG,DS:CODE_SEG,ES:CODE_SEG,SS:CODE_SEG
        ORG        100H
ENTER:  MOV        DX,OFFSET ALL_OK          ←
        MOV        AH,9                      ←
        INT        21H                       ←
        INT        20H                       ←
ALL_OK  DB "No Worries.$"
CODE_SEG           ENDS
        END        ENTER
```

This is just raw code, nothing but the basics. There is no PROC, there is no data area; but this program works. DOS will give control to the program at the location ENTER, since the end of the program terminates with the assembler command END ENTER, and ENTER is a label that does correspond, as it must, to the the location at 100H (ORG 100H) inside the code. The code will be run, from first to last. Notice that the actual data is at the end of the program, which isn't a problem since the microprocessor stops executing when it reaches the INT 20H instruction.

```
CODE_SEG           SEGMENT
        ASSUME     CS:CODE_SEG,DS:CODE_SEG,ES:CODE_SEG,SS:CODE_SEG
        ORG        100H
ENTER:  MOV        DX,OFFSET ALL_OK
        MOV        AH,9
        INT        21H
        INT        20H
ALL_OK  DB "No Worries.$"                    ← Data
CODE_SEG           ENDS
        END        ENTER
```

Remember, to the 8088, everything in the program is just bytes in memory. If it happens to be at CS:IP, the 8088 (or 8086, or 80186, or 80286, or 80386 of course) will try to read it in and execute it. Only we know where there is data and where there is code in this example, and we have to keep the microprocessor in the right area.

We could assemble this program, which we'll call ALLOK1.ASM, link it, and EXE2BIN it, making ALLOK1.COM. If we were to DEBUG ALLOK1.COM, we'd first see the code, which we could disassemble like this:

```
A>DEBUG ALLOK1.COM
-U
0F06:0100 BA0901        MOV     DX,0109
0F06:0103 B409          MOV     AH,09
0F06:0105 CD21          INT     21
0F06:0107 CD20          INT     20
0F06:0109 4E            DEC     SI
0F06:010A 6F            DB      6F
0F06:010B 20576F        AND     [BX+6F],DL
0F06:010E 7272          JB      0182
0F06:0110 69            DB      69
```

```
OF06:0111 65        DB    65
OF06:0112 732E      JNB   0142
OF06:0114 2440      AND   AL,40
OF06:0116 50        PUSH  AX
OF06:0117 B8D30F    MOV   AX,0FD3
OF06:011A 50        PUSH  AX
OF06:011B 8D4680    LEA   AX,[BP-80]
OF06:011E 50        PUSH  AX
OF06:011F FF163601  CALL  [0136]
```

The instructions after INT 20H are meaningless: they just come from our data, as we can see if we dump memory, starting with CS:100:

```
-D100
OF06:0100  BA 09 01 B4 09 CD 21 CD-20 4E 6F 20 57 6F 72 72  ......!. No Worr
OF06:0110  69 65 73 2E 24 40 50 B8-D3 0F 50 8D 46 80 50 FF  ies.$@P...P.F.P.
OF06:0120  16 36 01 83 C4 08 80 3E-38 41 00 75 06 80 7E 80  .6.....>8A.u..~.
OF06:0130  00 75 15 8B 1E 46 43 D1-E3 D1 E3 2B C0 89 87 BE  .u...FC....+....
OF06:0140  3D 89 87 BC 3D E9 64 FF-8D 46 80 50 8D 86 FC FE  =...=.d..F.P....
OF06:0150  50 E8 B2 32 83 C4 04 B8-FF FF 50 B8 05 00 50 8D  P..2......P...P.
OF06:0160  86 FC FE 50 E8 A5 82 83-C4 06 8B 1E 46 43 D1 E3  ...P........FC..
OF06:0170  D1 E3 A1 0E 3C 8B 16 10-3C 89 87 BC 3D 89 97 BE  ....<...<...=...
-Q
```

There is our message, "No Worries.$" (the final "$" is added to terminate the string for INT 21H service 9).

Using the Normal .COM File Data Area

Although this works, it's often easier to define a data area in the beginning of the .ASM file, in typical .COM format style. In order to do this, we have to add a line that will make the microprocessor jump over the data, and start the code at the right place, as we've done before:

```
CODE_SEG        SEGMENT
        ASSUME  CS:CODE_SEG,DS:CODE_SEG,ES:CODE_SEG,SS:CODE_SEG
        ORG     100H
ENTER:  JMP     PRINT                               ←
ALL_OK  DB      "No Worries.$"
PRINT:  MOV     DX,OFFSET ALL_OK                    ←
        MOV     AH,9
        INT     21H
        INT     20H
CODE_SEG        ENDS
        END     ENTER
```

Still we have no PROC here, which is fine since there is only one procedure anyway. All that happens is that the entry point is set to the label ENTER, and when there, control jumps to the label PRINT. This leaves us space for an untouched data area following the ENTER: line, which is where we put the definition of ALL_OK. Later, we move the offset address of ALL_OK into DX and execute INT 21H as normal. This type of .COM file is one that we're familiar with.

> Note that PROC is really nothing more than another way of defining a label that can be jumped to, and nothing fancy.

Putting Data Anywhere

However, there is no real reason that the data area has to go at the beginning of the file (although it is usually more convenient there, and it makes sense to define data items before you use them). As long as we jump over the data, which the microprocessor would simply try to interpret as instructions, we are ok. Here we put ALL_OK in an odd place:

```
CODE_SEG        SEGMENT
        ASSUME  CS:CODE_SEG,DS:CODE_SEG,ES:CODE_SEG,SS:CODE_SEG
        ORG     100H
ENTER:  MOV     DX,OFFSET ALL_OK
        MOV     AH,9
        JMP     INT21H              ←
ALL_OK  DB "No Worries.$"
INT21H: INT     21H
        INT     20H
CODE_SEG        ENDS
        END     ENTER
```

This method can have utility if you want to define something like ALL_OK just before using it and then don't want to use it later on (although you could define data this way, it'd be hard to find by eye in the program). You can break up your data area and scatter it all around, although there is usually no reason for that.

The JMP SHORT Instruction

With such a short jump, it is worth mentioning that the JMP instruction is assembled into a long number of bytes, because every time you use it, it will store the entire address it is supposed to jump to—segment and offset (although conditional jumps only store the offset address). JMP SHORT is the form that should be used for shorter JMPs; it only stores the offset of the target address. Here it would look like this:

```
CODE_SEG        SEGMENT
        ASSUME  CS:CODE_SEG,DS:CODE_SEG,ES:CODE_SEG,SS:CODE_SEG
        ORG     100H
ENTER:  MOV     DX,OFFSET ALL_OK
        MOV     AH,9
        JMP     SHORT INT21H            ←
```

```
ALL_OK   DB   "No Worries.$"
INT21H:  INT      21H
         INT      20H
CODE_SEG          ENDS
         END      ENTER
```

Consistent use of JMP SHORT can save quite a few bytes, if that is a consideration.

Using PROC

Of course, the code can be encapsulated inside a procedure, as we have been doing. This means that we have to use the PROC and ENDP Pseudo-Ops. The beginning of the procedure is marked with PROC, and the end with ENDP. Even if you only have one procedure in an .ASM file, it is usually a good idea to use PROC and ENDP for clarity. Here, they replace the simple label PRINT:

```
CODE_SEG          SEGMENT
         ASSUME   CS:CODE_SEG,DS:CODE_SEG,ES:CODE_SEG,SS:CODE_SEG
         ORG      100H
ENTER:   JMP      PRINT
         ALL_OK   DB "No Worries.$"
PRINT    PROC     NEAR                                          ←
         MOV      DX,OFFSET ALL_OK
         MOV      AH,9
         INT      21H
         INT      20H
PRINT    ENDP                                                   ←
CODE_SEG          ENDS
         END      ENTER
```

The assembler will watch if you've gotten your procedures tangled up, and give you what is called a "block nesting error." In other words, as we'll see in a moment, procedures can be *nested*, one within the other. In any event, our procedure here is just the simple PRINT:

```
PRINT    PROC     NEAR
         MOV      DX,OFFSET ALL_OK
         MOV      AH,9
         INT      21H
         INT      20H
PRINT    ENDP
```

Calling Subprograms

If we had more to do, then we might want to call a subprogram, like WRITEDOT. As soon as you have more than one procedure in a program, you must use PROC and ENDP. We've seen how this works as well:

```
PRINT     PROC      NEAR
.....┌──CALL      SUB_PRINT
:    │
:....│  INT       20H
PRINT│  ENDP
     │
     │
     ↓
SUB_PRINT          PROC NEAR
....
:
:...     RET
SUB_PRINT          ENDP
```

Both procedures are in the same file here, and one calls the other. The procedure SUB_PRINT can use data from the main data area without problem: Anything in the current file has easy access to the data area. Here's how it looks in code:

```
CODE_SEG           SEGMENT
        ASSUME     CS:CODE_SEG,DS:CODE_SEG,ES:CODE_SEG,SS:CODE_SEG
        ORG        100H
ENTER:  JMP        PRINT
        ALL_OK     DB "No Worries.$"
PRINT   PROC       NEAR
        CALL       SUB_PRINT
        INT        20H
PRINT   ENDP
SUB_PRINT          PROC NEAR
        MOV        DX,OFFSET ALL_OK
        MOV        AH,9
        INT        21H
        RET
SUB_PRINT          ENDP
CODE_SEG           ENDS
        END        ENTER
```

Control enters at the location ENTER in the beginning of the file, before either procedure starts. We then jump to PRINT, the first procedure. The only things that PRINT does in this example are to call SUB_PRINT, and to exit with INT 20H. SUB_PRINT is where the printing is done, so we put the actual instructions that type out the "No Worries." message there. At the end of SUB_PRINT is RET, so control returns to PRINT, where it finds INT 20H and exits.

This type of program is common for small and even some medium-sized applications. There is a main procedure that calls the others. This way of doing things can really make everything much easier. For example, consider the main procedure MAIN:

```
MAIN     PROC    NEAR
         CALL    GET_THE_FILENAME
         CALL    OPEN_THE_FILE
         CALL    GET_NEW_DATA
         CALL    WRITE_NEW_DATA
         CALL    CLOSE_THE_FILE
         INT     20H
MAIN     ENDP
```

How much simpler this is to understand than a mass of code! By breaking the problem into manageable chunks, half the trouble is solved. Making a very simple main procedure is a common programming practice, and can make debugging much easier. The main procedure is often nothing more than a "dispatcher" that calls the needed procedures to do what is required.

Nesting Procedures

There is no reason why you cannot define a procedure inside a procedure, although it is more rare. For example, we could take SUB_PRINT and put it right inside PRINT, like this:

```
CODE_SEG           SEGMENT
          ASSUME   CS:CODE_SEG,DS:CODE_SEG,ES:CODE_SEG,SS:CODE_SEG
          ORG      100H
ENTER:    JMP      PRINT
          ALL_OK   DB "No Worries.$"
PRINT     PROC     NEAR
........CALL       SUB_PRINT
:         INT      20H
:
SUB_PRINT          PROC NEAR               ←
: ......MOV         DX,OFFSET ALL_OK        ←
: :      MOV         AH,9                   ←
: :      INT         21H                    ←
: :.....RET                                 ←
SUB_PRINT          ENDP                     ←
:........
PRINT     ENDP

CODE_SEG           ENDS
          END      ENTER
```

If we were to assemble this program and debug it, we would simply find the 8088 instructions, without all the Pseudo-Ops, which are meant only for the assembler. First we jump over the data area with the DEBUG Trace command, T, which executes one instruction, and then we unassemble the program:

```
-R
AX=0000  BX=0000  CX=001C  DX=0000  SP=FFFE  BP=0000  SI=0000 DI=0000
DS=0F06  ES=0F06  SS=0F06  CS=0F06  IP=0100     NV UP EI PL NZ NA PO NC
0F06:0100 EB0D              JMP     010F
-T
```

```
AX=0000  BX=0000  CX=001C  DX=0000  SP=FFFE  BP=0000  SI=0000 DI=0000
DS=0F06  ES=0F06  SS=0F06  CS=0F06  IP=010F   NV UP EI PL NZ NA PO NC
0F06:010F E80200           CALL    0114
-U
0F06:010F E80200           CALL    0114
0F06:0112 CD20             INT     20
0F06:0114 BA0301           MOV     DX,0103
0F06:0117 B409             MOV     AH,09
0F06:0119 CD21             INT     21
           :
           :
-Q
```

The CALL SUB_PRINT has been made into CALL 0114, but the meaning is clear. We call the set of instructions at the end of the program, they type out the message, and then return to the top, where INT 20H is executed.

> Note that the nested procedure example produces the same .COM file as the previous, unnested, example in this case.

Putting Data into a Subprocedure

The next step will be to make our printing subroutine, SUB_PRINT, more self-contained by putting the definition of ALL_OK into it. Until now, the data SUB_PRINT uses was at the beginning of the file; now it will be inside SUB_PRINT itself.

This simple change, which might seem obvious, will give us a good deal of difficulty when we try to move the procedure SUB_PRINT to another file.

> If the data is in another file, its offset will be calculated from the beginning of that file. If that file is linked in after another file to make the final code segment, the offset will be wrong. We'll work through problems such as this one soon.

Local data

It is a good idea to take purely local data out of the main data area and move it into the procedure that alone uses it. In most high-level languages, there is a distinction between global variables (available to all procedures) and local variables (available only to the local procedure). Assembly language does not have such a distinction but, nonetheless, it is a good idea to keep the main data area as uncluttered as you can. Since the ALL_OK message is only used by SUB_PRINT in this example, we can move it into the definition of SUB_PRINT like this:

```
CODE_SEG        SEGMENT
        ASSUME  CS:CODE_SEG,DS:CODE_SEG,ES:CODE_SEG,SS:CODE_SEG
        ORG     100H
ENTER:
PRINT   PROC    NEAR
        CALL    SUB_PRINT
        INT     20H
PRINT   ENDP
SUB_PRINT       PROC NEAR
        JMP     GO
        ALL_OK  DB "No Worries.$"              ←
GO:     MOV     DX,OFFSET ALL_OK
        MOV     AH,9
        INT     21H
        RET
SUB_PRINT       ENDP
CODE_SEG        ENDS
        END     ENTER
```

Putting purely local data into the procedure that uses it makes sense, and, if you have a lot of procedures, might be a good idea. If we spent the whole book developing one example program, we'd use this technique, since it can save us from a main data area that is five pages long. As it is, of course, none of our programs are long enough to demand it.

Linking

Code in One File, Data in the Other

Now we'll start working with two files. Let's suppose that all the program code itself is in one file, and the data (ALL_OK) is in another. This would look something like this:

PROG1A.ASM   ← This is the first file.

```
        :
MOV     DX,OFFSET ALL_OK
MOV     AH,9
INT     21H
INT     20H
        :
```

PROG1B.ASM   ← This is the second file.

```
        :
ALL_OK  DB "No Worries.$"
        :
```

Our job now is to reconcile this split between code and data. What will happen to the assembler when it reaches the line MOV DX,OFFSET ALL_OK in FILE1A.ASM? The message ALL_OK is defined in another file, FILE1B.ASM, and the assembler won't be able to find it.

There is a standard way of telling the assembler that we don't have what it needs now, but we will soon, and that is with the EXTRN (for external) Pseudo-Op.

Using EXTRN

EXTRN lets the assembler know that it won't find the definition of ALL_OK in the present file. Instead, it instructs the assembler to put aside some space for ALL_OK whenever it is encountered. This space, which will be filled in later by the linker, will hold ALL_OK's address.

For this reason, the assembler has to know more: Will two words (segment and offset) be required for ALL_OK's address? Two words will be required if ALL_OK will be more than 64K away in the final executable file. Or will only one word (the offset address) be required? In .COM files, where there is only one segment, the answer will always be one word, but with .EXE files, there can be multiple segments.

> Note that *every* time you want to use a label that is not defined in the current file you'll have to use EXTRN for that label.

To let the assembler know something about the address of the label that is EXTRN, we use a line like this: EXTRN ALL_OK:NEAR. This tells the assembler that only one word will be required for ALL_OK's address. The other option is EXTRN ALL_OK:FAR, which reserves places for both segment and offset addresses.

> Saving space for both ALL_OK's segment and offset addresses with FAR will work here, but it is overkill—all we need is the offset address.

The EXTRN definition must be right at the top of the file, before the assembler has the chance to run across what it would consider undefined labels (like ALL_OK unless we told it that ALL_OK is external). Here is what FILE1A, the first file that holds just the code, will look like:

```
CODE_SEG        SEGMENT PUBLIC
        EXTRN   ALL_OK:NEAR        ←
        ASSUME  CS:CODE_SEG,DS:CODE_SEG,ES:CODE_SEG,SS:CODE_SEG
        ORG     100H
ENTER:
```

```
                    MOV       DX,OFFSET ALL_OK
                    MOV       AH,9
                    INT       21H
                    INT       20H
         CODE_SEG   ENDS
                    END       ENTER
```

Note the EXTRN right at the top. In the other file, we will have to match this EXTRN Pseudo-Op with something similar, PUBLIC. This Pseudo-Op tells the assembler that the public label, ALL_OK, will be required by another program.

The PUBLIC Pseudo-Op

Converting labels into hex addresses

Usually when the assembler is done assembling a file, it has translated all the labels from English to hexadecimal addresses. This is what a label is, really; just a name for a particular address in a file. Of course, working with labels is much handier than calling a point like PRINT_NOW: by a number, 023AH. The assembler's job, however, is to make this conversion, and there's no reason for it to keep the labels around that we used to make it more understandable to us.

The problem is that our file FILE1A will need to know the location of what was once called ALL_OK in FILE1B. Unless we do something special, that information will be lost in the generation of machine-language code. That something special is the Pseudo-Op PUBLIC.

PUBLIC, as its name hints, indicates that something—in particular, a label—in the current file will be used by another file later on, when the two files are linked together. If we put the line PUBLIC ALL_OK at the beginning of FILE1B.ASM, where the message ALL_OK is stored, then the assembler will keep the name around until link time, when it will match what we need in FILE1A.

For every EXTRN in one file, there must be a matching PUBLIC in another file. If you do not supply enough PUBLICs for all the EXTRNs, you will get a message from the linker about "unresolved externals."

Using ORG when linking

But that is not the only thing we need to make sure of in FILE1B. When the two files are linked together, we will say LINK FILE1A + FILE1B; this means that the contents of FILE1B will be put right after the contents of FILE1A in the .EXE file that is generated (and then later converted to a .COM file). Usually, we have said ORG 100H in the beginning of our .ASM files, but that can only be true for one part of the whole program; we can't have ORG 100H in FILE1A *and* FILE1B. Only one set of instructions can start there, not both.

For that reason, we leave the ORG 100H out of FILE1B. It is not important where the data ALL_OK goes, as long as its address is properly known when the linking is done. On the other hand, it is very important that the code start at 100H, because control is transferred to a .COM file at that point. We will therefore make sure there is an ORG 100H in FILE1A.

PROG1A.ASM   ← This is the first file.

```
       EXTRN:  ALL_OK
   →   ORG     100H
               :
       MOV     DX,OFFSET ALL_OK
       MOV     AH,9
       INT     21H
       INT     20H
               :
```

PROG1B.ASM   ← This is the second file.

```
       PUBLIC  ALL_OK
       ALL_OK  DB "No Worries.$"
               :
```

No multiple-entry points

For the same reason, we say END at the end of FILE1B, but not END ENTER, or use some other way of setting the enter address, because the entering address is not in this file. This is important to remember: When you link, one of the files has to be the main one, and it will define the entry point for the whole program. The others will not specify this entry point. In practice this won't be too hard to remember, since what you will be linking in will be subprocedures, and there will be only one main program. Anyway, the linker will be sure to tell you if multiple-entry points have been defined, and you'll know what the problem is.

PROG1A.ASM   ← This is the first file.

```
       EXTRN:  ALL_OK
       ORG     100H
   →   ENTER:
       MOV     DX,OFFSET ALL_OK
       MOV     AH,9
       INT     21H
       INT     20H
               :
   →   END     ENTER
```

```
PROG1B.ASM                              ← This is the second file.

 PUBLIC   ALL_OK
 ALL_OK   DB "No Worries.$"
                :
→ END
```

The data in FILE1B will be put after the code in FILE1A when we link. Then the total number of bytes will be made into a .COM file. We'll take a look at the result with DEBUG. Here's what FILE1A.ASM and FILE1B.ASM look like (note that FILE1B.ASM is complete with PUB-LIC ALL_OK, and only END at the end):

```
-----     FILE1A.ASM    --------

CODE_SEG        SEGMENT PUBLIC
        EXTRN   ALL_OK:NEAR       ←
        ASSUME  CS:CODE_SEG,DS:CODE_SEG,ES:CODE_SEG,SS:CODE_SEG
        ORG     100H
ENTER:
        MOV     DX,OFFSET ALL_OK
        MOV     AH,9
        INT     21H
        INT     20H
CODE_SEG        ENDS
        END     ENTER

-----     FILE1B.ASM    --------

CODE_SEG        SEGMENT PUBLIC
        PUBLIC  ALL_OK            ←
        ASSUME  CS:CODE_SEG,DS:CODE_SEG,ES:CODE_SEG,SS:CODE_SEG
        ALL_OK  DB "No Worries.$"

CODE_SEG        ENDS
        END
```

We can assemble FILE1A.ASM and FILE1B.ASM, like this:

```
C>MASM FILE1A;

Microsoft (R) Macro Assembler Version 5.10
Copyright (C) Microsoft Corp 1981, 1988.  All rights reserved.

  50106 + 31315 Bytes symbol space free

    0 Warning Errors
    0 Severe  Errors

C>MASM FILE1B;

Microsoft (R) Macro Assembler Version 5.10
Copyright (C) Microsoft Corp 1981, 1988.  All rights reserved.

  50260 + 31161 Bytes symbol space free

    0 Warning Errors
    0 Severe  Errors
```

The way to actually link these two together is give LINK a command like this: LINK FILE1A + FILE1B;. Here it is:

```
C>LINK FILE1A+FILE1B;

Microsoft (R) Overlay Linker  Version 3.64
Copyright (C) Microsoft Corp 1983-1988.  All rights reserved.

LINK : warning L4021: no stack segment
```

This generates an .EXE file named FILE1A.EXE. If you end your command to the linker with a semicolon " ; ", it will create an .EXE file using the first filename. This is the default way of doing it; you could also, if you wanted to produce an .EXE file named, say, PROG1.EXE, link this way:

```
C>LINK
Microsoft (R) Overlay Linker  Version 3.64
Copyright (C) Microsoft Corp 1983-1988.  All rights reserved.

Object Modules [.OBJ]: FILE1A+FILE1B     ← Type this response.
Run File [FILE1A.EXE]: PROG1             ← And this one.
List File [NUL.MAP]:
Libraries [.LIB]:

LINK : warning L4021: no stack segment
```

If we use FILE1A.EXE, we can finally EXE2BIN it, and then we can run our program:

```
C>EXE2BIN FILE1A FILE1B.COM

C>FILE1A
No Worries.
```

It worked.

Debugging FILEA.COM

Let's take a look at FILE1A.COM with DEBUG. We will be able to see where the data from FILE1B went into the final .COM file. It should be right behind the code from FILE1A. First, we unassemble to find the code:

```
C>DEBUG FILE1A.COM
-U
0F06:0100 BA1001          MOV     DX,0110
0F06:0103 B409            MOV     AH,09
0F06:0105 CD21            INT     21
0F06:0107 CD20            INT     20
         :
         :
```

And then dump memory to look at the data:

```
-D100
0F06:0100  BA 10 01 B4 09 CD 21 CD-20 00 00 00 00 00 00 00   ......!. ........
0F06:0110  4E 6F 20 57 6F 72 72 69-65 73 2E 24 46 43 D1 E3   No Worries.$FC..
0F06:0120  D1 E3 A1 0E 3C 8B 16 10-3C 89 87 BC 3D 89 97 BE   ....<...<...=...
0F06:0130  3D FF 36 46 43 E8 0C 22-83 C4 02 8B 1E 46 43 D1   =.6FC..".....FC.
0F06:0140  E3 D1 E3 8B 87 BC 3D 8B-97 BE 3D 89 86 7C FF 89   ......=...=..|..
0F06:0150  96 7E FF 05 0C 00 52 50-E8 7D 6A 83 C4 04 50 E8   .~....RP.}j...P.
0F06:0160  6C FB 83 C4 02 0A C0 75-03 E9 F6 FE C6 06 D9 37   l......u......?
0F06:0170  FF 8B 1E 46 43 D1 E3 8B-87 A0 3C A3 60 3E 8B 1E   ...FC.....<.>..
-Q
```

You can see from the unassembly that the program ends at CS:108, and you can see that the data starts at CS:0110 ("No Worries.$"). So that much is quite correct—the data does indeed follow the code, which is correct, since FILE1B was linked after FILE1A. On the other hand, it does not follow the data directly; there are a number of zeroes stuck in after the code and before the data starts:

```
            |   |   |   |   |   |   |
            ↓   ↓   ↓   ↓   ↓   ↓   ↓
-D100
0F06:0100  BA 10 01 B4 09 CD 21 CD-20 00 00 00 00 00 00 00   ......!. ........
0F06:0110  4E 6F 20 57 6F 72 72 69-65 73 2E 24 46 43 D1 E3   No Worries.$FC..
0F06:0120  D1 E3 A1 0E 3C 8B 16 10-3C 89 87 BC 3D 89 97 BE   ....<...<...=...
0F06:0130  3D FF 36 46 43 E8 0C 22-83 C4 02 8B 1E 46 43 D1   =.6FC..".....FC.
0F06:0140  E3 D1 E3 8B 87 BC 3D 8B-97 BE 3D 89 86 7C FF 89   ......=...=..|..
0F06:0150  96 7E FF 05 0C 00 52 50-E8 7D 6A 83 C4 04 50 E8   .~....RP.}j...P.
0F06:0160  6C FB 83 C4 02 0A C0 75-03 E9 F6 FE C6 06 D9 37   l......u......?
0F06:0170  FF 8B 1E 46 43 D1 E3 8B-87 A0 3C A3 60 3E 8B 1E   ...FC.....<.>..
-Q
```

Why are they there, and are they just wasting space?

LINK's Paragraph Default

The answer is that, yes, they are just wasting space. When the linker put the data "No Worries.$" at the end of the program, it knew that it had to fill the address of that data in the previous part of the program, since it resolved an external reference (to ALL_OK) that way. It fixed up the instruction MOV DX,OFFSET ALL_OK exactly as it should have. This is what the linker does; it actually fills in addresses of items that have been missing until now. On the other hand, the linker starts linked files out on successive *paragraphs*—16 byte boundaries—as its default.

This is what happened to us. FILE1B was loaded in to start on the next paragraph boundary, as the DEBUG display clearly shows (the DEBUG memory dump lists 16 bytes on every line, and "No Worries.$" starts at the beginning of the second line). To take care of this problem, we let the linker know that it's OK to start the linked file at the next byte boundary, not paragraph, with the BYTE Pseudo-Op in conjunction with SEG-MENT. We go from this:

```
------      FILE1A.ASM   ------

CODE_SEG        SEGMENT PUBLIC
        EXTRN   ALL_OK:NEAR
        ASSUME  CS:CODE_SEG,DS:CODE_SEG,ES:CODE_SEG,SS:CODE_SEG
        ORG     100H
ENTER:
        MOV     DX,OFFSET ALL_OK
        MOV     AH,9
        INT     21H
        INT     20H
CODE_SEG        ENDS
        END     ENTER
```

To this:

```
FILE1B.ASM                  ↓
CODE_SEG        SEGMENT BYTE PUBLIC
        PUBLIC  ALL_OK
        ASSUME  CS:CODE_SEG,DS:CODE_SEG,ES:CODE_SEG,SS:CODE_SEG

        ALL_OK  DB "No Worries.$"
CODE_SEG        ENDS
        END
```

This will make sure that there is no distance in bytes between the end of the first file and the beginning of the second one.

Here's a DEBUG examination of the new file (which we can call FILE2A.COM), which doesn't waste any space between code and data:

```
C>DEBUG FILE2A.COM
-U100 107
0F06:0100 BA0901         MOV     DX,0109
0F06:0103 B409           MOV     AH,09
0F06:0105 CD21           INT     21
0F06:0107 CD20           INT     20                                       |
-D100                                                                     ↓
0F06:0100  BA 09 01 B4 09 CD 21 CD-20 4E 6F 20 57 6F 72 72   ......!. No Worr
0F06:0110  69 65 73 2E 24 A5 82 83-C4 06 8B 1E 46 43 D1 E3   ies.$.......FC..
0F06:0120  D1 E3 A1 0E 3C 8B 16 10-3C 89 87 BC 3D 89 97 BE   ....<...<...=...
0F06:0130  3D FF 36 46 43 E8 0C 22-83 C4 02 8B 1E 46 43 D1   =.6FC..".....FC.
0F06:0140  E3 D1 E3 8B 87 BC 3D 8B-97 BE 3D 89 86 7C FF 89   ......=...=..|..
0F06:0150  96 7E FF 05 0C 00 52 50-E8 7D 6A 83 C4 04 50 E8   .~....RP.}j...P.
0F06:0160  6C FB 83 C4 02 0A C0 75-03 E9 F6 FE C6 06 D9 37   l......u.......?
0F06:0170  FF 8B 1E 46 43 D1 E3 8B-87 A0 3C A3 60 3E 8B 1E   ...FC.....<.>..
-Q
```

Using PUBLIC with SEGMENT

You may have noticed that the segments are also declared PUBLIC. This is to let the assembler know that there is more of CODE_SEG than is in this file alone, the same kind of information that PUBLIC ALL_OK indicates.

```
                           ↓
CODE_SEG        SEGMENT BYTE PUBLIC
        PUBLIC  ALL_OK
        ASSUME  CS:CODE_SEG,DS:CODE_SEG,ES:CODE_SEG,SS:CODE_SEG
        ALL_OK  DB "No Worries.$"

CODE_SEG        ENDS
        END
```

What it tells the linker is that the current file has a part of CODE_SEG, and that it should be linked right after previously linked sections of CODE_SEG. The linker puts CODE_SEG sections from different files together this way. Since we will only be linking files with one segment, this is immaterial for us, but when you get complicated and deal with many segments of different names, you can group the material in the same segments together this way.

Here PUBLIC works just as it does for labels—it tells the assembler to keep the name of the segment around for later use in linking. Then, when the linker takes over, it will match each successive piece of the various segments together.

How the Linker Links

Let's work through what the linker does, especially with EXTRN and PUBLIC. When you assemble .ASM files, .OBJ files are created. These are the files that the linker works on. Inside these .OBJ files are the machine-language instructions that the program will use, along with some header information. If you link two such files in the same segment—but different files—together, the one linked first will go first in the created .EXE file, and the one linked second will go second. Since we've been using .COM file format (i.e., ORG 100H), this .EXE file can then be turned into a .COM file and run.

Using labels in different files

If you have some labels that are referenced (like MOV DX,OFFSET ALL_OK) in the first file, but the label definition is actually in the second file (ALL_OK DB "No Worries.$"), then the assembler will inform the linker, via the .OBJ file header, that some addresses in the first file are incomplete. These addresses are calculated at link time, by the linker, and filled in where they are needed. Files with declared EXTRNs get addresses put in the proper place as soon as the linker knows what the correct address of whatever was EXTRN will be. In this way, files can be *linked* together.

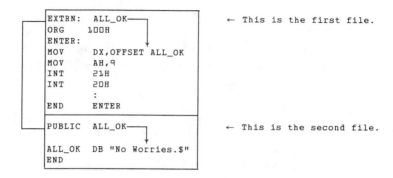

```
EXTRN:  ALL_OK
ORG     100H
ENTER:
MOV     DX,OFFSET ALL_OK
MOV     AH,9
INT     21H
INT     20H
        :
END     ENTER
```
← This is the first file.

```
PUBLIC  ALL_OK
ALL_OK  DB "No Worries.$"
END
```
← This is the second file.

Using Data in the First File

What we've done so far is to define ALL_OK in the second file, and reference it—that is, use it—in the first file. This means that ALL_OK is declared as EXTRN in the first file. When this file is linked, it will be followed by the second file, which has ALL_OK declared as PUBLIC. After the two files are linked, the linker can count the number of bytes from the beginning of the whole program to the label ALL_OK, and go back to the early reference to it, filling in the address, which it now knows.

Note that we did not try to use ALL_OK with code in the second file. There was no instruction in the second file, for example, that said MOV DX,OFFSET ALL_OK.

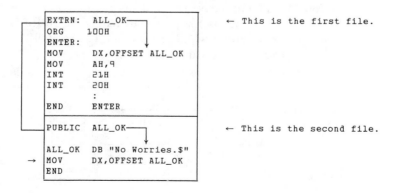

```
EXTRN:  ALL_OK
ORG     100H
ENTER:
MOV     DX,OFFSET ALL_OK
MOV     AH,9
INT     21H
INT     20H
        :
END     ENTER
```
← This is the first file.

```
PUBLIC  ALL_OK
ALL_OK  DB "No Worries.$"
MOV     DX,OFFSET ALL_OK
END
```
← This is the second file.

Using Data From the Second File

If there had been such code in the second file, we would have had trouble, since the assembler would have calculated the address of ALL_OK immediately (because ALL_OK is in the same file), something like this:

```
MOV      DX,OFFSET ALL_OK   →   MOV      DX,0004H
```

When the two files are linked, one after the other, the instruction MOV DX,0004 will be wrong since ALL_OK is now linked after the second file.

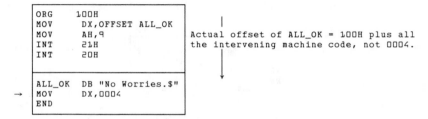

```
ORG      100H
MOV      DX,OFFSET ALL_OK
MOV      AH,9
INT      21H
INT      20H


ALL_OK   DB "No Worries.$"
→  MOV      DX,0004
END
```

Actual offset of ALL_OK = 100H plus all the intervening machine code, not 0004.

Putting MOV DX,OFFSET ALL_OK in the first file is fine, because ALL_OK isn't there—the linker will have to calculate the final address at link time, when the whole file is together. But when we want to have data and use it in the second file where despite what the assembler thinks) the final offset of that data isn't known, we will have to be careful.

Linking Procedures Together

External
procedures

The next step up from having pure data in file 2 is to have a procedure there. In the previous example, we put data into file 2; now we have to explore the other option and put code there instead. Note that there will not be both data *and* program code in file 2 until we make special preparations, because of the offset problems just mentioned. In this example, all we have is a rather useless procedure named SUBPROG in file 2 that calls the real procedure, PRINT, back in file 1. This will, however, introduce us to the idea of external procedures.

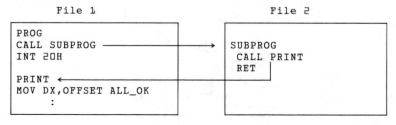

In file 1, although SUBPROG is called, it is not defined, so it is declared EXTRN. To match this, SUBPROG is declared PUBLIC in file 2.

Similarly, in file 2, although PRINT is called, it is not defined, so it is declared EXTRN. PRINT is declared PUBLIC in file 1.

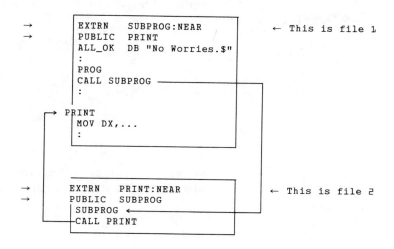

And here are the two files in code:

```
--------- File 1 ----------

CODE_SEG           SEGMENT PUBLIC
         EXTRN     SUBPROG:NEAR      ←
         PUBLIC    PRINT             ←
         ASSUME    CS:CODE_SEG,DS:CODE_SEG,ES:CODE_SEG,SS:CODE_SEG
         ORG       100H
ENTRY:   JMP       PROG
         ALL_OK    DB "No Worries.$"
PROG     PROC      NEAR
         CALL      SUBPROG
         INT       20H
PROG     ENDP
PRINT    PROC NEAR
         MOV       DX,OFFSET ALL_OK
         MOV       AH,9
         INT       21H
         RET
PRINT    ENDP
CODE_SEG           ENDS
         END       ENTRY

--------- File 2 ----------

CODE_SEG           SEGMENT BYTE PUBLIC
         ASSUME    CS:CODE_SEG,DS:CODE_SEG,ES:CODE_SEG,SS:CODE_SEG
         EXTRN     PRINT:NEAR        ←
         PUBLIC    SUBPROG           ←
```

```
SUBPROG PROC    NEAR
        CALL    PRINT
        RET
SUBPROG ENDP
CODE_SEG        ENDS
        END
```

That was simple enough. When linked, the whole program will look just like this in the final .COM file:

```
ENTRY:  JMP     PROG
        ALL_OK  DB "No Worries.$"
PROG:   CALL    SUBPROG
        INT     20H
PRINT:  MOV     DX,OFFSET ALL_OK
        MOV     AH,9
        INT     21H
        RET
SUBPROG:CALL    PRINT
        RET
```

Again, there was no problem with the address of ALL_OK, since it was in the first file, and its final offset will be the same as was calculated in first file.

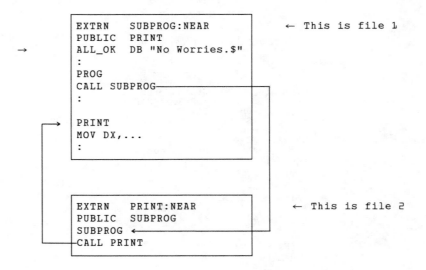

```
EXTRN   SUBPROG:NEAR          ← This is file 1
PUBLIC  PRINT
ALL_OK  DB "No Worries.$"
:
PROG
CALL SUBPROG
:

PRINT
MOV DX,...
:
```

```
EXTRN   PRINT:NEAR            ← This is file 2
PUBLIC  SUBPROG
SUBPROG ←
CALL PRINT
```

Using data
in file 1
from file 2

For that same reason, we can even reference ALL_OK in the second file. The thing we cannot do yet is have ALL_OK in the second file and reference it also, because the assembler would immediately put in an off-set address for it. If ALL_OK is in file 1, and we reference it in file 2, there is no problem. Here is how that might look if we used a procedure named SUB_PRINT in file 2:

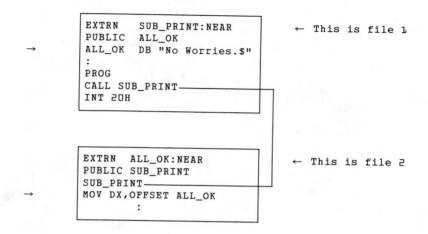

Here is the matching code:

```
---------- File 1 ----------

CODE_SEG          SEGMENT PUBLIC
→         EXTRN   SUB_PRINT:NEAR
→         PUBLIC  ALL_OK
          ASSUME  CS:CODE_SEG,DS:CODE_SEG,ES:CODE_SEG,SS:CODE_SEG
          ORG     100H
ENTER:    JMP     SHORT PRINT
→         ALL_OK  DB "No Worries.$"
PRINT:    CALL    SUB_PRINT          ←
          INT     20H
CODE_SEG          ENDS
          END     ENTER

---------- File 2 ----------

CODE_SEG          SEGMENT PUBLIC
→         EXTRN   ALL_OK:NEAR
→         PUBLIC  SUB_PRINT
          ASSUME  CS:CODE_SEG,DS:CODE_SEG,ES:CODE_SEG,SS:CODE_SEG

SUB_PRINT         PROC NEAR
          MOV     DX,OFFSET ALL_OK          ←
          MOV     AH,9
          INT     21H
          RET
SUB_PRINT         ENDP

CODE_SEG          ENDS
          END
```

Since the assembler does not know ALL_OK's address in file 2, it will not put anything in for it yet, but will reserve space for it. The problem comes when we want to put something like this in the second file:

```
-------- File 2 ----------
CODE_SEG          SEGMENT PUBLIC
        PUBLIC    SUB_PRINT
        ASSUME    CS:CODE_SEG,DS:CODE_SEG,ES:CODE_SEG,SS:CODE_SEG
                  ALL_OK DB "No Worries.$"'          ←
SUB_PRINT         PROC NEAR
        MOV       DX,OFFSET ALL_OK                   ←
        MOV       AH,9
        INT       21H
        RET
SUB_PRINT         ENDP

CODE_SEG          ENDS
        END
```

After all, what could be more normal than having the data in the same file that uses it? But, as mentioned, when the assembler comes to the line MOV DX,OFFSET ALL_OK, it sees that ALL_OK has already been defined earlier in the file, and, assuming there is no problem, puts an off-set address in for it.

In this case, ALL_OK is exactly at the beginning of the file, so its offset address is 0. Thus the line MOV DX,OFFSET ALL_OK will be assembled into MOV DX,0. When the two files are linked, however, ALL_OK's offset address will be something past the end of the first file, and since the first file starts at 100H (ORG 100H is used in file 1), we know that an offset address of 0 cannot possibly be correct.

You might be tempted to do something like this, where we declare ALL_OK as EXTRN in its own file, so that the assembler would not cal-culate an offset address for it:

```
CODE_SEG          SEGMENT PUBLIC
        EXTRN     ALL_OK:NEAR           ←
        PUBLIC    SUB_PRINT
        ASSUME    CS:CODE_SEG,DS:CODE_SEG,ES:CODE_SEG,SS:CODE_SEG
                  ALL_OK DB "No Worries.$"         ←
SUB_PRINT         PROC NEAR
        MOV       DX,OFFSET ALL_OK
        MOV       AH,9
        INT       21H
        RET
SUB_PRINT         ENDP

CODE_SEG          ENDS
        END
```

But the assembler counts that as an error. The only real way to make sure that you can have data wherever you want it and use it too is with *groups*. These are just like segments, but they can span several files.

Groups

Groups are basic in assembly-language programming for the simple reason that if you want to spread your programs over several files, using groups is the only safe way to make sure that the offsets will be calculated properly.

Groups were constructed to fill precisely the need we have now: to tell the assembler that the offset addresses we are calculating right now should be calculated from the beginning of what will be the final file, not from the beginning of the present file. As it is now, the second of these two files:

```
CODE_SEG        SEGMENT
ASSUME CS:CODE_SEG,DS:CODE_SEG
ORG     100H
PROG    PROC NEAR
CALL    PRINT
INT     20H
PROG    ENDP
CODE_SEG        ENDS
```

```
CODE_SEG        SEGMENT
ASSUME CS:CODE_SEG,DS:CODE_SEG

ALL_OK DB "No Worries$"

PRINT   PROC NEAR
MOV     DX,OFFSET ALL_OK
MOV     AH,9
INT     21H
RET
PRINT   ENDP
CODE_SEG        ENDS
```

will be assembled to produce:

```
CODE_SEG          SEGMENT
ASSUME CS:CODE_SEG,DS:CODE_SEG

ALL_OK DB "No Worries$"

PRINT  PROC NEAR
MOV    DX,0
MOV    AH,9
INT    21H
RET
PRINT  ENDP
CODE_SEG          ENDS
```

On the other hand, we could use groups this way:

```
CODE_GROUP        GROUP CODE_SEG
CODE_SEG          SEGMENT
ASSUME CS:CODE_GROUP,DS:CODE_GROUP
       ORG  100H
PROG   PROC NEAR
       CALL PRINT
       INT  20H
PROG   ENDP
CODE_SEG          ENDS
```

```
CODE_GROUP        GROUP CODE_SEG
CODE_SEG          SEGMENT
ASSUME CS:CODE_GROUP,DS:CODE_GROUP

ALL_OK DB "No Worries$"

PRINT  PROC NEAR
MOV    DX,OFFSET ALL_OK
MOV    AH,9
INT    21H
RET
PRINT  ENDP
CODE_SEG          ENDS
```

And the offsets would be done correctly—the offset of ALL_OK would not be put into the code until the final file was all in one piece. The only differences here are relatively minor: We added a line at the top of each file saying CODE_GROUP GROUP CODE_SEG. This just defines for the assembler a new entity, named CODE_GROUP.

Setting segment registers to groups

The benefit of CODE_GROUP is that you can set segment registers to it, just as you can with segments defined with SEGMENT, but groups can span across files. We take advantage of that with the second change:

```
ASSUME  CS:CODE_SEG,DS:CODE_SEG
```

becomes:

```
ASSUME  CS:CODE_GROUP,DS:CODE_GROUP
```

No longer will the assembler assume that it knows where CS:0000 is, the position where offsets are calculated from. Since groups can include many files, the assembler will wait and not calculate *any* offsets before link time.

The change was easy to make, and, once you get used to it, automatic. Just add a line like: CODE_GROUP GROUP CODE_SEG at the top of the files you are writing, and then use ASSUMEs to tell the assembler that CODE_GROUP will be used. Groups act by letting the assembler know that files will be grouped together; the present file is only part of the whole.

Use GROUP as the 1st line

In practical terms, this means that when you split a program into various files, the first line of each file should be a GROUP definition. From then on, you can write in each file safely, as though it were part of one file, and not separate from the others.

> The most important thing about splitting files up is simply to use GROUPs from then on. That's what they were designed for.

Here are our two files, file 1 and file 2, with groups:

```
---------  File 1 ----------

CODE_GROUP        GROUP CODE_SEG                       ←
        EXTRN     PRINT:NEAR
CODE_SEG          SEGMENT
        ASSUME    CS:CODE_GROUP, DS:CODE_GROUP         ←
        ORG       100H
PROG    PROC      NEAR
        CALL      PRINT
        INT       20H
PROG    ENDP

CODE_SEG          ENDS

        END       PROG
```

```
---------- File 1 ----------
CODE_GROUP      GROUP    CODE_SEG                       ←
CODE_SEG        SEGMENT
        ASSUME  CS:CODE_GROUP, DS:CODE_GROUP   ←
        PUBLIC  PRINT
        ALL_OK  DB "No Worries.$"

PRINT   PROC    NEAR
        LEA     DX,ALL_OK
        MOV     AH,9
        INT     21H
        RET
PRINT   ENDP

CODE_SEG        ENDS
        END
```

Now, you may proceed in complete safety. As you can see, we are able to both have data in file 2 and use it now without problem. You can think of groups as sort of super-segments. All you need to do to work with multiple files now is to switch from the single-file type:

```
CODE_SEG        SEGMENT
        ASSUME  CS:CODE_SEG, DS:CODE_SEG
                :
                :
```

To the multiple-file type:

```
CODE_GROUP      GROUP    CODE_SEG
CODE_SEG        SEGMENT
    ASSUME  CS:CODE_GROUP, DS:CODE_GROUP
                :
                :
```

And make sure you use EXTRN and PUBLIC when needed. Including groups like this in your code makes the programming process easier, very close to the one we're already familiar with for single-file programs. As soon as you start working with multiple-file programs, you should automatically start thinking in terms of offsets from a group, not a segment. The segments will be put together into the group when everything is linked. We'll need the idea of groups when we come to write assembly-language code to link into higher level languages later.

LEA Instead of OFFSET

There is one more thing that must be corrected. The assembler Pseudo-Op OFFSET is designed to return a number immediately: MOV DX,OFFSET ALL_OK. It is still converted by the assembler at assembly time.

LEA only loads in registers

We do not want that to happen, so we no longer use OFFSET. Instead, we use the microprocessor instruction LEA, Load Effective Address. We've seen LEA before. In fact, it could have been used instead of OFFSET in any one of our programs until now. The only drawback of LEA instead of OFFSET is that LEA will only load a label's offset into a register, not a memory location. For example, although you could say MOV ALL_OK_ADDR,OFFSET ALL_OK if ALL_OK_ADDR was a memory word declared with DW, you could *not* say LEA ALL_OK_ADDR, ALL_OK.

LEA was designed for instructions like LEA DX,ALL_OK, and that's what we'll use it for. If we leave file 2 with OFFSET, the assembler will interpret it as requesting the offset from the beginning of the current file:

```
---------- File 2 ----------
CODE_GROUP      GROUP    CODE_SEG
CODE_SEG        SEGMENT
        ASSUME  CS:CODE_GROUP, DS:CODE_GROUP
        PUBLIC  PRINT
        ALL_OK  DB "No Worries.$"

PRINT   PROC    NEAR
        MOV     DX,OFFSET ALL_OK        ← This becomes LEA DX,ALLOK.
        MOV     AH,9
        INT     21H
        RET
PRINT   ENDP

CODE_SEG        ENDS
        END
```

If we had used file 2 with OFFSET, and then debugged it, we would have seen that MOV DX,OFFSET ALL_OK had been assembled into MOV DX,0:

```
A>DEBUG FILE3A.COM
-R                              ← Find out where we are.
AX=0000  BX=0000  CX=0024  DX=0000  SP=FFFE  BP=0000  SI=0000 DI=0000
DS=0F06  ES=0F06  SS=0F06  CS=0F06  IP=0100   NV UP EI PL NZ NA PO NC
0F06:0100 E81900          CALL    011C
-T                              ← Trace through the call to PRINT.
AX=0000  BX=0000  CX=0024  DX=0000  SP=FFFC  BP=0000  SI=0000 DI=0000
DS=0F06  ES=0F06  SS=0F06  CS=0F06  IP=011C   NV UP EI PL NZ NA PO NC
0F06:011C BA0000          MOV     DX,0000
-U11C 123
```

```
0F06:011C BA0000         MOV    DX,0000      ← This is PRINT.
0F06:011F B409           MOV    AH,09
0F06:0121 CD21           INT    21
0F06:0123 C3             RET
-Q
```

If we use LEA instead, like this:

```
---------- File 2 ----------
CODE_GROUP      GROUP    CODE_SEG
CODE_SEG        SEGMENT
        ASSUME  CS:CODE_GROUP, DS:CODE_GROUP
        PUBLIC  PRINT
        ALL_OK  DB "No Worries.$"

PRINT   PROC     NEAR
        LEA      DX,ALL_OK    ←
        MOV      AH,9
        INT      21H
        RET
PRINT   ENDP

CODE_SEG        ENDS
        END
```

Then there is no problem:

```
C>FILE4A

No Worries.
```

Using
OFFSET

Keep in mind that if you need to find the offset from the beginning of the current file, OFFSET is available for use, as it was designed. However, if you want to use addresses from what will be the beginning of the whole file, as you'll almost always want to do, use LEA instead.

We've now successfully broken our code up into two files, with the help of GROUP and LEA. Each file can be worked on, edited, and debugged independently, without worrying about how they will fit together. Although this is how the use of GROUP is recommended, it can do more: It can group together segments with different names. Although we'll never use this capability in this book, let's take a look at how it works. This will be our last subject on groups.

Grouping Different Segments Together

GROUPs can act as a super-SEGMENT, putting together a number of different segments to form one final file. For example, let's assume that we are using CODE_SEG in file 1 and CSEG in file 2:

```
CODE_SEG
   :
   :



```

```
CSEG
   :
   :



```

And we want to merge the code in the final file this way:

```
CODE_SEG
   :
   :


CSEG
   :
   :



```

Then all we have to do is to define CODE_SEG as part of CODE_GROUP in file 1 and CSEG as part of CODE_GROUP in file 2, like this:

```
CODE_GROUP GROUP CODE_SEG
CODE_SEG
   :
   :


```

```
CODE_GROUP GROUP CSEG
CSEG
    :
    :
```

When the two files are linked together (LINK FILE1 + FILE2;) the code from CSEG will immediately follow the code from CODE_SEG. Here's how it would look with our example program:

```
--------- File 1 ----------
CODE_GROUP          GROUP CODE_SEG
        EXTRN       PRINT:NEAR
CODE_SEG            SEGMENT
        ASSUME      CS:CODE_GROUP, DS:CODE_GROUP
        ORG         100H

PROG    PROC        NEAR
        CALL        PRINT
        INT         20H
PROG    ENDP

CODE_SEG            ENDS

        END         PROG


--------- File 2 ----------

CODE_GROUP          GROUP    CSEG
CSEG                SEGMENT                              ←
        ASSUME      CS:CODE_GROUP, DS:CODE_GROUP    ←
        PUBLIC      PRINT
        ALL_OK      DB "No Worries.$"

PRINT   PROC        NEAR
        LEA         DX,ALL_OK
        MOV         AH,9
        INT         21H
        RET
PRINT   ENDP

CSEG    ENDS                                             ←
        END
```

In this way, you can group segments with different names together if you want to. If you are interested in this, the linker has a whole set of rules on how segments with different names are loaded, and you should check the linker documentation.

Libraries

This part of the chapter has to do with *libraries*, also used in linking, but somewhat advanced. For this reason, the rest of the material in this chapter can be skipped or regarded as optional if you won't be dealing frequently with large, multifile programs.

Programming in scientific installations

On the other hand, if you will be working with many files, then there comes a point where the use of libraries is almost necessary. In large scientific installations, for example, many different people write procedures for different tasks. One, for example, might write a procedure that unpacks data from the condensed format in which it is typically stored. Another might write a procedure that analyzes part of the data collected by the apparatus that that person was responsible for.

The individual scientist who is writing a program doesn't want to either unpack the data or do the low-level analysis, typically. Instead, he wants to work on his own project, which takes the data as semi-analyzed, and performs some of his own calculations on it. Rather than knowing that register 1003772 had a value of 17 in it, he'd like to know that a charged particle track passed through a certain particle detector at a particular time. What he does, then, is to CALL the other procedures to do the preliminary work for him, even though these procedures may in themselves be very complex.

In order to call those procedures, he simply links his own program to a library of procedures that was created at his lab. This library contains all the procedures that he wants to call, and even the procedures that the called procedures call. The scientist doesn't want to link in *all* the procedures that are available—there could be thousands—but just the ones needed for his program.

This is the idea of a library. When we link .OBJ files, the whole thing becomes part of the code (stripped of the .OBJ file header). When we link in a library, the linker looks for "unresolved externals"—that is, things that have been declared EXTRN but not yet found in an .OBJ file—and takes only those it needs. Although the library could contain a thousand commonly used procedures, only the ones that the linker needs to complete your file will be taken from it.

The Library Manager LIB

We can create such libraries with the program LIB.EXE. This program comes on the utility disk accompanying the macro assembler.

If we take the two files that introduced GROUPs to us, for example:

```
---------- File 1 ----------
CODE_GROUP       GROUP CODE_SEG
        EXTRN    PRINT:NEAR
CODE_SEG         SEGMENT
        ASSUME   CS:CODE_GROUP, DS:CODE_GROUP
        ORG      100H

PROG    PROC     NEAR
        CALL     PRINT
        INT      20H
PROG    ENDP

CODE_SEG         ENDS

        END      PROG
---------- File 2 ----------
CODE_GROUP       GROUP     CODE_SEG
CODE_SEG         SEGMENT
        ASSUME   CS:CODE_GROUP, DS:CODE_GROUP
        PUBLIC   PRINT
        ALL_OK   DB "No Worries.$"

PRINT   PROC     NEAR
        LEA      DX,ALL_OK
        MOV      AH,9
        INT      21H
        RET
PRINT   ENDP

CODE_SEG         ENDS
        END
```

We can start by making a library out of the second file. Let's call this library PRINT.LIB. Whenever we want to use the procedure PRINT from now on, all we have to do is tell the linker that we want it to search PRINT.LIB. LINK will then find PRINT in this library and link it in.

❚ Library files always have the extension .LIB ❚

Here's how to take FILE2.ASM (which contains the procedure PRINT) and make it into a library PRINT.LIB:

```
C>MASM FILE2;
Microsoft (R) Macro Assembler Version 5.10
Copyright (C) Microsoft Corp 1981, 1988.  All rights reserved.


    50192 + 31229 Bytes symbol space free

        0 Warning Errors
        0 Severe  Errors
C>LIB PRINT.LIB+FILE2.OBJ;
Microsoft (R) Library Manager  Version 3.10
Copyright (C) Microsoft Corp 1983-1988.  All rights reserved.
```

This LIB command—LIB PRINT.LIB + FILE2.OBJ;—creates a library file named PRINT.LIB, which contains only file 2's object code. We could have have said: LIB PRINT + FILE2. The .LIB extension is assumed for the first file and .OBJ for the second and any following ones (like LIB PRINT + FILE2 + FILE3).

If PRINT.LIB already existed, this command would not create it, but would add FILE2.OBJ to it. We'll see this when we add a new routine to PRINT.LIB. Now that we have PRINT.LIB, let's use it. First, assemble FILE1.ASM, and then link it, including PRINT.LIB:

```
C>LINK
Microsoft (R) Overlay Linker  Version 3.64
Copyright (C) Microsoft Corp 1983-1988.  All rights reserved.

Object Modules [.OBJ]:FILE1   ← Type this.
Run File [TA.EXE]:
List File [NUL.MAP]:
Libraries [.LIB]:PRINT        ← And this.

LINK : warning L4021: no stack segment
```

Now we can use EXE2BIN on the created file, FILE1.EXE, and run it:

```
C>EXE2BIN FILE1 FILE1.COM

C>FILE1A
No Worries.
C>
```

Adding a Second Module

Modules

So far, there has been no advantage to using the library file PRINT.LIB; we could just as well have linked in FILE1.OBJ entirely. On the other hand, we can now add a second procedure to PRINT.LIB. Everything that comes from an .OBJ file and goes into a library is referred to as a *module*. So far, all we have is the FILE2 module. But we could write another

.ASM file, identical to FILE2.ASM except for the message, and call this file 3:

```
---------  File 3  --------
CODE_GROUP      GROUP     CODE_SEG
CODE_SEG        SEGMENT
        ASSUME  CS:CODE_GROUP, DS:CODE_GROUP
        PUBLIC  PRINT2
        ALL_NOT_OK      DB "Well, some worries.$"      ←

PRINT2  PROC    NEAR
        LEA     DX,ALL_NOT_OK                          ←
        MOV     AH,9
        INT     21H
        RET
PRINT2  ENDP

CODE_SEG        ENDS
        END
```

Here we define the procedure PRINT2, which prints out "Well, some worries." We can assemble this file and add it to the already-existing library file PRINT.LIB this way:

```
C>MASM FILE3;
Microsoft (R) Macro Assembler Version 5.10
Copyright (C) Microsoft Corp 1981, 1988.  All rights reserved.

  50192 + 31229 Bytes symbol space free


        0 Warning Errors
        0 Severe  Errors


C>LIB PRINT.LIB+FILE3.OBJ;       ← This adds PRINT2 to PRINT.LIB
Microsoft (R) Library Manager  Version 3.10
Copyright (C) Microsoft Corp 1983-1988.  All rights reserved.
```

This time, PRINT.LIB is not created since it already exists, but FILE3.OBJ is added to it. Now the PRINT library holds both PRINT ("No Worries.") and PRINT2 ("Well, some worries.").

We can still link FILE1.OBJ with PRINT.LIB this way:

```
C>LINK
Microsoft (R) Overlay Linker  Version 3.64
Copyright (C) Microsoft Corp 1983-1988.  All rights reserved.

Object Modules [.OBJ]:FILE1  ← Type this.
Run File [TA.EXE]:
List File [NUL.MAP]:
Libraries [.LIB]:PRINT        ← And this again.

LINK : warning L4021: no stack segment
```

And it will *only* take PRINT from PRINT.LIB, since there is no call to PRINT2. Theoretically, there could be hundreds of procedures in PRINT.LIB, and we'd only take the one(s) we needed.

> Note the consistent use of GROUPS, even inside .OBJ files being put into libraries. Library files only make linking together what you want easy—they do not alter the code in any way, which means we still need groups.

Of course, we can add a call to PRINT2 (in addition to PRINT) in our main file, FILE1, like this:

```
CODE_GROUP       GROUP CODE_SEG
        EXTRN    PRINT:NEAR,PRINT2:NEAR   ←
CODE_SEG         SEGMENT
        ASSUME   CS:CODE_GROUP, DS:CODE_GROUP
        ORG      100H

PROG    PROC     NEAR
        CALL     PRINT
        CALL     PRINT2   ←
        INT      20H
PROG    ENDP

CODE_SEG         ENDS

        END      PROG
```

As long as we add PRINT2 to our declaration of what labels will be external:

```
CODE_GROUP       GROUP CODE_SEG
        EXTRN    PRINT:NEAR,PRINT2:NEAR   ←
CODE_SEG         SEGMENT
        ASSUME   CS:CODE_GROUP, DS:CODE_GROUP
        ORG      100H

PROG    PROC     NEAR
        CALL     PRINT
        CALL     PRINT2   ←
```

FILE1 can then be assembled, linked, and run:

```
C>MASM FILE1;
Microsoft (R) Macro Assembler Version 5.10
Copyright (C) Microsoft Corp 1981, 1988.  All rights reserved.

  50202 + 31219 Bytes symbol space free


      0 Warning Errors
      0 Severe  Errors

C>LINK
```

```
Microsoft (R) Overlay Linker  Version 3.64
Copyright (C) Microsoft Corp 1983-1988.  All rights reserved.

Object Modules [.OBJ]:FILE1   ←
Run File [TA.EXE]:
List File [NUL.MAP]:
Libraries [.LIB]:PRINT        ←

LINK : warning L4021: no stack segment

C>EXE2BIN FILE1 FILE1.COM

C>FILE1
No Worries.Well, some worries.
```

As you can see, both calls are made; that is, both PRINT and PRINT2 have been found in the library PRINT.LIB. (We didn't provide a space in our strings between messages, so they come out right next to each other.)

> Notice that LINK only asks for the names of library files after you've given it a full list of .OBJ files to include. If a version of PRINT was in one of them, it would not be taken from the file PRINT.LIB, since the EXTRN had already been satisfied.

Deleting Modules

If there came a time when you wanted to delete a module from a library file like PRINT.LIB, you would use the "−" sign instead of "+". This is done easily enough; let's delete PRINT2 from PRINT.LIB:

```
C>LIB PRINT-FILE3;
Microsoft (R) Library Manager  Version 3.10
Copyright (C) Microsoft Corp 1983-1988.  All rights reserved.
```

PRINT.LIB now won't include PRINT2 any more. When you subtract modules this way, you have to supply the name of the original .OBJ file (FILE3.OBJ), not the name of the procedure you want to subtract (PRINT2). You cannot subtract individual procedures—only whole .OBJ modules.

Extracting Modules

There is also a provision for "extracting" modules, and not just deleting them from a library. This is useful if you want to reorganize your libraries. For example, you could *extract* FILE3.OBJ from PRINT.LIB, and then add it to another library file, BADNEWS.LIB.

Extraction is done with the "*" symbol. For example, this is how we could move PRINT2 (that is, FILE3.OBJ) from PRINT.LIB and install it into BADNEWS.LIB:

```
C>LIB PRINT*FILE3;
Microsoft (R) Library Manager  Version 3.10
Copyright (C) Microsoft Corp 1983-1988.  All rights reserved.

C>LIB BADNEWS+FILE3;
Microsoft (R) Library Manager  Version 3.10
Copyright (C) Microsoft Corp 1983-1988.  All rights reserved.
```

Once again, you have to extract the entire .OBJ file—not just individual procedures. Once you become used to it, using and mananging libraries may become an everyday task for you.

Linking to Something That Isn't There

Let's see what would happen if we were to link FILE1 with PRINT.LIB after now that we've extracted PRINT2 from PRINT.LIB:

```
C>LINK
Microsoft (R) Overlay Linker  Version 3.64
Copyright (C) Microsoft Corp 1983-1988.  All rights reserved.

Object Modules [.OBJ]:FILE1
Run File [TA.EXE]:
List File [NUL.MAP]:
Libraries [.LIB]:PRINT

LINK : warning L4021: no stack segment

LINK : error L2029: Unresolved externals:

PRINT2 in file(s):
 FILE1.OBJ(FILE1.ASM)

There was 1 error detected
```

As you can see, LINK is unable to satisfy the call to PRINT2, and gives us an error message calling PRINT2 an "Unresolved external."

Replacing Modules

Frequently, newer versions of some modules may be produced. You may debug some code, or there may be changes in what the program is supposed to do. To handle these changes, you could subtract the module and then add a new one. For example, if the .OBJ module put into a library was ALERT.OBJ, and you wanted to change it to a new version, which is now ready on the disk, you could do this:

```
C>LIB PRINT-ALERT;
Microsoft (R) Library Manager  Version 3.10
Copyright (C) Microsoft Corp 1983-1988.  All rights reserved.

C>LIB PRINT+ALERT;
Microsoft (R) Library Manager  Version 3.10
Copyright (C) Microsoft Corp 1983-1988.  All rights reserved.
```

Or, if you wish, the library manager lets you do both operations at once, with the combined operation "–+," which stands for replace. If there is an .OBJ file on the disk, then "–+" will delete the current module in the specified library and add the new one from the disk file. For example, to update ALERT in PRINT.LIB in one step, just type:

```
C>LIB PRINT-+ALERT; Microsoft (R) Library Manager  Version 3.10
Copyright (C) Microsoft Corp 1983-1988.  All rights reserved.
```

> Keep in mind that if a procedure in one of your .LIB files calls a procedure in some other .LIB file, link the one with the call first. LINK won't know that it is supposed to include a particular procedure until that procedure is called. If it has already searched the correct library before you make the call, it won't be able to find the called procedure when you finally do call it.

Libraries can be very useful at helping you to manage your programs. They can help when programs become very large. On the other hand, you should keep your library up to date. If the library contains old versions of particular modules, they will be linked in.

**IBM
Libraries**

IBM supplies some libraries itself for various use, and to be used with various compilers. One of these libraries provides conversion routines that may be called to convert numbers from and to the format the Intel math coprocessors (8087, 80287, etc) use. Now that you know how, you can even add your own procedures to those libraries.

8
.EXE Files and Macros

DOS supports two kinds of files that you can just run: .COM files and .EXE files. The .COM file form we know by now; even with the restriction that you have to start it at 100H instead of just anywhere, it's pretty easy to use. We never had to worry about segment registers or stacks or NEAR and FAR that much: We simply wrote our code and that was that. There was no code in a .COM file that the programmer didn't put there—we were responsible for everything there. Also, of course, .COM files can be made memory resident, due to their compact format.

On the other hand, there are times when you need something bigger than compact format. Sometimes you just can't squeeze everything into 64K or less. Or perhaps you want the freedom of defining segments wherever you want them. In cases like these, you can use the .EXE file format. In addition, OS/2 supports *only* .EXE files—it does not support .COM files. For this reason, we will have to be familiar with .EXE format before we can unlock OS/2 later.

> There seems to be a fair list of things that the standard version of OS/2 does not support, including .COM files, graphics of any kind—not even Write Dot (you are expected to write a "graphics device" handler and work with the screen directly), and interrupts.

The second half of this chapter has to do with macros, those labor-saving devices that can save you time and effort both when programming and when assembling. A macro in its simplest form is just a set of assembly-language instructions surrounded by the Pseudo-Ops MACRO and ENDM. In its most complex form, it can totally restructure the way you program. Whenever the assembler sees the name of a defined macro in the program it is assembling, it expands that macro into all the instructions that the macro stands for. This can cover a large amount of territory, and do surprising things, as we'll see.

The .EXE Difference

The big change, really, between .COM files and .EXE files is that we'll have to become very aware of the segment registers, and how they're set. We didn't need to worry about them so much in .COM files, where there was only one segment, but now, with multiple segments, we will.

With .COM files, the one segment was usually divided up this way:

```
ENTER: JMP      PROG
          :
      Data Goes Here
          :
PROG   PROC NEAR
          :
      Program Goes Here
          :
PROG   ENDP

          :
          :

      Stack Goes Here.
```

with the stack at the very end of the 64K segment, put there by DOS. If CS was set to 1111H, then the .COM file had free use of 1111:0000 to 1111:FFFF, although the first 100H bytes were taken up by the program segment prefix, or PSP.

Entry points
in .EXE files

In an .EXE file, the segments can go where you want them, as can the entry point (no longer restricted to 100H):

```
DATA_SEG        SEGMENT
     :
    Data Goes Here
     :
DATA_SEG        ENDS

CODE_SEG        SEGMENT
     :
    Program Code Goes Here
     :
CODE_SEG        ENDS

STACK           SEGMENT
     :
    The Stack Goes Here.
     :
STACK           ENDS
```

This now means that we are responsible for defining the stack—DOS no longer does it automatically.

The Stack

The stack is where return addresses are stored while calls or interrupts are being executed, or where variables are stored (PUSH AX) to be restored later (POP AX). OS/2 makes even more heavy use of the stack. Instead of passing values to the system services by loading the registers and then using an INT instruction, all values are loaded onto the stack by pushing them, and then the system services are *called*, not reached with interrupts. There is an OS/2 call to correspond to almost every BIOS and DOS service, and some extra ones besides.

OS/2 uses the stack to pass values rather than the registers to make OS/2 more easily reachable by high-level languages, which can easily push values on a stack and call an address (that's the usual way they call their own subroutines), but which have a hard time loading registers directly and executing an INT instruction.

The Stack Pointer SP

The stack is just a number of memory words (always words, not bytes—you cannot push a byte, only a word) set aside for this purpose. The stack segment register is SS, and the "stack pointer" is SP; SS:SP points to the current word in the stack. When you push a word onto the stack, the word is stored in memory at SS:SP, and then the stack pointer SP is *decremented* by two. It makes sense to move in units of two, since addresses are in bytes, and each stack location is two bytes, one word. But decrementing the stack pointer takes people by surprise. This means that the stack "grows" towards lower memory.

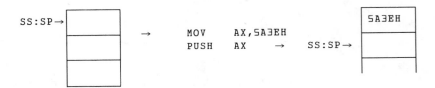

When you pop a word off the stack, the last word into the stack is the first one that is popped—this is referred to as Last In, First Off (LIFO). For example, if you have a "stack" of books, the first one you take off the top of the pile is the last one you put on it; you will "pop" the very first book put onto the stack (the bottom one) only after all the others have been removed.

```
                1234H                      SS:SP→ 1234H
SS:SP→ 3201H  →     POP    AX                     
                   (AX now holds 3201H)  →        
```

In a .COM file, the stack segment register, SS, holds the common segment, of course; and SP starts off pointing at the very last word in that segment, FFFEH (the very last byte is CS:FFFFH, the very last *word* is CS:FFFE). In .EXE files, you define your own stack segment, like this:

```
DATA_SEG        SEGMENT
      :
      Data Goes Here
      :
DATA_SEG        ENDS

CODE_SEG        SEGMENT
      :
      Program Code Goes Here
      :
CODE_SEG        ENDS

→   STACK           SEGMENT   STACK
→       DB          30 DUP("STACK ")
→   STACK           ENDS
```

and SP starts off pointing to the very last word in the segment you've defined. Usually it's a good idea to use a stack at least 100 words long (more in OS/2).

We have to tell the assembler that we intend this segment to be used as the stack; that is done by defining it as a stack type with the STACK Pseudo-Op:

```
STACK     SEGMENT  STACK   ←
```

When the .EXE file gets loaded into memory, SS will hold the segment address of the beginning of the stack, and SP will point to the last defined word. Next we set aside space for the stack, filling it with the characters "STACK " over and over again.

```
STACK     SEGMENT  STACK

→         DB    30 DUP("STACK ")
```

This is a debugging aid. Can you tell where the stack starts in this DEBUG dump of a .EXE file?

```
-D
0F16:0000  1E 33 C0 50 B8 16 0F 8E-D8 CB 00 00 00 00 00 00   .3.P............
0F16:0010  53 54 41 43 4B 20 53 54-41 43 4B 20 53 54 41 43   STACK STACK STAC
0F16:0020  4B 20 53 54 41 43 4B 20-53 54 41 43 4B 20 53 54   K STACK STACK ST
0F16:0030  41 43 4B 20 53 54 41 43-4B 20 53 54 41 43 4B 20   ACK STACK STACK
```

```
0F16:0040   53 54 41 43 4B 20 53 54-41 43 4B 20 53 54 41 43   STACK STACK STAC
0F16:0050   4B 20 53 54 41 43 4B 20-53 54 41 43 4B 20 53 54   K STACK STACK ST
0F16:0060   41 43 4B 20 53 54 41 43-4B 20 53 54 41 43 4B 20   ACK STACK STACK
0F16:0070   53 54 41 43 4B 20 53 54-41 43 4B 20 53 54 41 43   STACK STACK STAC
-Q
```

To make sure that SS:0000 points to the bottom of the stack, don't use the BYTE Pseudo-Op when defining a stack, just use "STACK SEGMENT STACK" as shown. Let the assembler place this segment at the default paragraph boundary. This will make life easier when debugging.

Finally, we end the stack segment with a normal ENDS:

```
STACK     SEGMENT STACK

          DB     30 DUP("STACK ")

STACK     ENDS  ←
```

We are now responsible for the stack that the program will use, so we'll have to include a stack segment in *every* .EXE file we produce (but only one stack segment—don't define multiple stacks if you're going to link files together to make your .EXE file).

The Data Segment

We can also have (but it's not mandatory) a data segment separate from the code segment:

```
→   DATA_SEG     SEGMENT
→                :
→         Data Goes Here
→                :
→   DATA_SEG     ENDS

    CODE_SEG     SEGMENT
                 :
          Program Code Goes Here
                 :
    CODE_SEG     ENDS

    STACK        SEGMENT STACK
         DB      30 DUP("STACK ")
    STACK        ENDS
```

In order to use this data segment, we have to set DS ourselves—that's become our responsibility too. This can be done easily, like this:

```
MOV     AX,DATA_SEG
MOV     DS,AX
ASSUME  DS:DATA_SEG
```

but we should not forget to do it whenever we are writing .EXE files. We'll include these lines in our .EXE file shell, developed in a moment. This will set up DS for us so that whenever we use a label that refers to data, the assembler will know where we mean.

The .EXE File Header

Before we develop an .EXE file shell that can be used, we will have to know how .EXE files are loaded into memory—the very first instructions in every DOS .EXE file are necessary because of this loading process.

Loading .EXE files in

Here's how that process works: At the A> prompt, you type the name of an .EXE file that you want to run. DOS (actually the resident part of COMMAND.COM) reads what you have to say, checks whether your command is an internal DOS one, finds it isn't, and then locates the .EXE file on the disk.

A PSP (Program Segment Prefix) for the .EXE file is set up at the lowest available memory location, just as it is for a .COM file. On the other hand, the PSP is not so visible in .EXE file format; in .COM files, the first 100H bytes are set aside for the PSP since everything must fit inside the common segment, but this is not the case for an .EXE file.

Default settings of ES, DS, and CS

Only ES and DS are set to the same segment as the program segment prefix. The PSP starts at DS:0000 (or ES:0000, which is the same thing). CS, on the other hand, is set to the code segment—the first instruction will be at CS:0000. SS will be set to the location of the stack in the file when it's loaded.

So far, the program segment prefix has been set up in memory. Next, DOS reads in the beginning of the .EXE—the part that is called the .EXE file header. There is no comparable thing in .COM files to the .EXE file header, and, since we are going to encounter it again in OS/2, let's give it some attention.

> The .EXE file header under OS/2 includes a DOS .EXE file header and a special OS/2 one. By using a special utility, you can write programs that will run under either DOS or OS/2 (which operating system is in use is determined by the .EXE file header). Also, the

> Microsoft assembler 5.1 includes EXEHDR.EXE, a utility to display the contents of an OS/2 .EXE file header.

As you know, .EXE files can differ from .COM files in that .EXE files can use multiple segments. In .COM files, all addresses used are in offset form—that is, one word only, indicating a distance from the beginning of the segment. We could use two word addresses only under special circumstances—when we knew what the segment address was already, as when we set up a "SEGMENT AT XXXX." In other words, segment addresses never appear in the code of a .COM file unless they are already known and can be assembled in.

For .EXE files, addresses must be able to hold both segment and offset values, since we can reach multiple segments. This means that in a typical .EXE file, a great number of the instructions must hold both segment and offset values. For example, a JMP instruction that is to jump more than 64K must have both segment and offset addresses to jump to.

However, until the program is loaded in to run, the segment value will not be known. In other words, we have defined segments like CODE_SEG and so on, and we know the offsets of addresses from that point, but the actual value of CODE_SEG will not be known until you load your program in. (This is not a problem in one-segment .COM files, where everything is measured from the beginning of the common segment.)

> The segment at which the .EXE file will be loaded in will vary with the size of the operating system that fits into memory before it, and the number and size of the memory-resident programs you may have.

Using the .EXE File Header

This means that many locations in the .EXE file cannot be filled in until the program is loaded. The .EXE file header was created for this purpose. It holds the position of *every* such location in the .EXE file. When the file is loaded in to run, the .EXE file header tells DOS which locations must be filled with the segment address. (This process is called *relocation*, but the term need not concern us here.)

This .EXE file header is why .EXE files are larger than corresponding .COM files.

DOS reads in the beginning of the header. Since there can be many or few locations to update, the header is of variable size. Bytes 8 and 9 in the header give the header's length in paragraphs, that is, in 16-byte chunks, rounded up. A 17-byte header would have a 2 here (17/16 = 1 with a remainder of 1, which rounds up to 2). The rest of the header is read in with this information.

Bytes 2 to 5 hold the size of the .EXE file itself. When DOS subtracts the size of the header, which it already knows, what is left is that size of the actual program itself, called the load module.

Other information found in the header includes the location of the stack in the load module, so that SS:SP may be set, and the location of the first instruction in the load module, from which DOS will calculate CS:IP when it gives control to the program. For reference only, Table 8.1 shows what an .EXE file header looks like.

Table 8.1 .EXE File Header

Word Starts	Explanation
00	Always 4D 5A. Marks this file as a .EXE file.
02	Remainder after dividing load module's size by 512.
04	Size of file in 512-byte pages.
06	Number of relocation table items.
08	Size of header in paragraphs (16 bytes).
0A	Minimum number of paragraphs required after loaded program.
0C	Maximum number of paragraphs required after loaded program.
0E	Offset of Stack in load module in paragraphs
10	SP register loaded with this word.
12	Negative sum (ignore overflow) of all words in file (checksum).
14	IP register loaded with this word.
16	Offset of code segment in load module in paragraphs.
18	Offset of first relocation item.
1A	Overlay number. If no overlays used, this number is 0.

Following the header is the table that holds the positions of the locations that need to be fixed up with the segment address. For each location, there is a two-word address in this table that gives the location's distance from the beginning of the load module. DOS loads in the load module, and sets these locations correctly.

After that, CS:IP is set to the entry point, which you can set to anywhere in the program. The way you set it is just the same as we have in .COM files: with the END Pseudo-Op. For example, END START sets the entry point to the label START, and you can put START wherever you want it. ES and DS are set to the segment address of the PSP. SS:SP is set to the location of the stack, and the program is ready to run.

> Once again, if you are linking files together, there can only be one entry point. Only set it once, in the *main* file. Finish your other .ASM files with a simple "END."

An .EXE File Shell

Everything we've discussed so far is necessary to understand the environment that we'll be working in inside an .EXE file. Now we've come to the point where we can introduce our .EXE file shell. Let's start with what we know so far:

```
        DATA_SEG        SEGMENT
            :                       ;Put data here.
        DATA_SEG        ENDS
        CODE_SEG        SEGMENT
            :                       ;Put code here
        PROG_NAME       ENDP
        CODE_SEG        ENDS

STACK       SEGMENT STACK
    DB        30 DUP("STACK ")
STACK       ENDS
        END     PROG_NAME
```

While CS is set to CODE_SEG, we have to be careful to let the assembler know that SS will be set to the stack segment, STACK. By declaring our stack of type "STACK," we've indicated that SS should point there when the file is loaded. Now we have to tell the assembler the same thing. Notice that there is no ASSUME for DS—we have not set a value for it yet.

```
        DATA_SEG        SEGMENT
                                    ;Put data here.
        DATA_SEG        ENDS
        CODE_SEG        SEGMENT
  →             ASSUME  CS:CODE_SEG,SS:STACK

        CODE_SEG        ENDS

STACK       SEGMENT STACK
    DB        30 DUP("STACK ")
STACK       ENDS
        END     PROG_NAME
```

Next comes the actual program itself, which we have called PROG_NAME. Note that it is declared as FAR:

```
        DATA_SEG        SEGMENT
                                    ;Put data here.
        DATA_SEG        ENDS

        CODE_SEG        SEGMENT
            ASSUME  CS:CODE_SEG,SS:STACK
```

```
→       PROG_NAME        PROC    FAR
                 :
                RET
→       PROG_NAME        ENDP
        CODE_SEG         ENDS

STACK      SEGMENT STACK
     DB      30 DUP("STACK ")
STACK   ENDS
        END     PROG_NAME
```

NEAR and FAR

Until now, we have only dealt with the NEAR Pseudo-Op, but, now
that we've got multisegment abilities, we have to think about FAR.
There are two types of return instructions RET. When we define a procedure NEAR:

```
PROG    PROC NEAR       ←
        MOV     AX,5
        MOV     DX,32001
        RET
PROG    ENDP
```

it means that this procedure will only be called from within the same segment. Only one word—the offset address—will be put onto the stack
when this procedure is called, so at the end of the procedure, only one
word has to be popped. The assembler puts in this type of RET instruction, a short return, because the procedure has been declared NEAR. In
other words, the RET at the end will be made to match the way the procedure is defined, NEAR or FAR.

If we declare something FAR:

```
PROG    PROC FAR        ←
        MOV     AX,5
        MOV     DX,32001
        RET
PROG    ENDP
```

then the RET is made into a FAR return, which will pop off two words,
both segment and offset addresses. This kind of procedure can be called
across segments if needed.

Return Addresses when Calling

How about the other side: How does the assembler know to push one or
two words when something is called? How does it know that this CALL
will be to a FAR item or to a NEAR item? The type of CALL, after all,
has to match the type of return that will be waiting at the end of the called
procedure.

Again, the assembler can simply look to see how the procedure was declared—with NEAR or FAR, and set up the type of machine-language CALL instruction accordingly. If the item being called isn't in the present file, as you may remember, we have to tell EXTRN whether it will be a NEAR or FAR item, so the assembler can set up the CALL accordingly.

The main procedure in a .EXE file is always FAR:

```
        DATA_SEG        SEGMENT
                                ;Put data here.
        DATA_SEG        ENDS

        CODE_SEG        SEGMENT
                ASSUME  CS:CODE_SEG,SS:STACK
→       PROG_NAME       PROC    FAR

→               RET
        PROG_NAME       ENDP
        CODE_SEG        ENDS

STACK     SEGMENT STACK
      DB      30 DUP("STACK ")
STACK     ENDS
      END       PROG_NAME
```

This means that the RET at the end will be a FAR RET; that is standard in .EXE files. When this FAR RET is reached, two words will be popped off the stack; what will they be? It turns out that they will be the address of the very first byte in the PSP.

Ending an .EXE file

When the FAR return at the end of the program is encountered, the location we will return to is this very first byte in the PSP. The reason is that the first two bytes in the PSP are CDH 20H, the machine-language instruction for INT 20H, our normal way of ending a program. .EXE files are ended by returning to this first byte of the PSP, not by explicitly including an INT 20H instruction.

```
    ┌──→ CDH 20H

                   PSP


         CODE_SEG
         PROG PROC FAR
             :

    └─  RET
         PROG ENDP
```

It is usual to jump to this CDH 20H instruction instead of placing an INT 20H at the end of the .EXE file program, because CS should be set to the segment holding the PSP when an INT 20H is executed (as required by DOS), and, by setting CS:IP to the first location in the PSP, we make sure CS is set correctly. Otherwise, in an .EXE file, CS could be set anywhere when the program ends.

> CDH 20H are the first two bytes in any PSP, even the one used for .COM files

Priming the Stack

We are going to have to push this return address onto the stack ourselves. This is done at the beginning of every DOS .EXE file (not in OS/2 ones, however). The two words to push form the address of the very first byte of the program segment prefix. This address is DS:0000 (recall that DS is set to the segment of the PSP upon entering an .EXE file).

When a far call is executed, first a segment address is pushed onto the stack, then an offset address. Since we want to set up a return from a far call, we push DS first:

```
              DATA_SEG        SEGMENT
                                     ;Put data here.
              DATA_SEG        ENDS

              CODE_SEG        SEGMENT
                      ASSUME  CS:CODE_SEG,SS:STACK
              PROG_NAME       PROC    FAR
   →               PUSH    DS
                     :                       ;Prog starts here.
                     :
                   RET
              PROG_NAME       ENDP
              CODE_SEG        ENDS

STACK     SEGMENT  STACK
     DB       30 DUP("STACK ")
STACK     ENDS
          END     PROG_NAME
```

Note that DS is pushed immediately upon entering the program, before we set it to our own data segment. This is to make sure that we push the PSP's segment address, and not the segment address of the data segment.

Next we have to push a word of zeroes. To do that, we make the contents of AX zero and push AX. When the far return is reached, DS:0000 will be popped off, and we will go to the correct location.

The XOR Instruction

AX may be set to zero with MOV AX,0, but you often see the instruction XOR AX,AX instead. This instruction is commonly found in the beginning of .EXE files, so let's introduce XOR here (and discuss it further in our Chapter 9, Fast Math).

XOR is the Exclusive Or instruction, and it is occasionally used by professional programmers because it is faster than a MOV. XOR works this way: It takes two words and matches them up bit by bit. If a zero meets a zero, the result is zero. If a one meets a zero, the result is one. If a one meets a one, the result is zero:

```
XOR | 0  1
----+--------
 0  | 0  1
 1  | 1  0
```

When you XOR a number with itself, all ones are sure to meet ones and all zeroes sure to meet zeros, so the result is zero. XOR AX,AX is sure to make the contents of AX zero:

```
              DATA_SEG      SEGMENT
                                      ;Put data here.
              DATA_SEG      ENDS
              CODE_SEG      SEGMENT
                    ASSUME  CS:CODE_SEG,SS:STACK
              PROG_NAME     PROC    FAR
                    PUSH    DS
     →              XOR     AX,AX
     →              PUSH    AX
                    :                         ;Prog starts here.
                    :
                    RET
              PROG_NAME     ENDP
              CODE_SEG      ENDS

      STACK     SEGMENT  STACK
            DB      30 DUP("STACK ")
      STACK     ENDS
              END     PROG_NAME
```

Now that the stack is set up for the far return to the beginning of the PSP, we can change the value in DS. We will want to set DS to our own data segment. That is accomplished in the usual way, including an ASSUME Pseudo-Op to let the assembler know what's going on:

```
          DATA_SEG          SEGMENT
                                      ;Put data here.
          DATA_SEG          ENDS

          CODE_SEG          SEGMENT
                  ASSUME    CS:CODE_SEG,SS:STACK
          PROG_NAME         PROC      FAR
                  PUSH      DS
                  XOR       AX,AX
                  PUSH      AX
→                 MOV       AX,DATA_SEG
→                 MOV       DS,AX
→                 ASSUME    DS:DATA_SEG
                  :                             ;Your Program starts here.
                  :
                  RET
          PROG_NAME         ENDP
          CODE_SEG          ENDS

STACK        SEGMENT  STACK
     DB       30 DUP("STACK ")
STACK        ENDS
          END       PROG_NAME
```

And the whole thing is all set up, ready to run. Note that these first instructions will be the same in almost any .EXE file, so they are included in our .EXE file shell.

Putting .EXE Files to Work

We can easily convert our "No Worries." program to .EXE file format. We just put the data (ALL_OK DB "No Worries.$") into the data segment and the code that prints out the string (using INT 21H service 9) into the program area, like this:

```
          DATA_SEG          SEGMENT
          ALL_OK  DB "No Worries.$"        ←
          DATA_SEG          ENDS

          CODE_SEG          SEGMENT
                  ASSUME    CS:CODE_SEG,SS:STACK
          PROG_NAME         PROC      FAR
                  PUSH      DS
                  XOR       AX,AX
                  PUSH      AX
                  MOV       AX,DATA_SEG
                  MOV       DS,AX
                  ASSUME    DS:DATA_SEG
→                 LEA       DX,ALL_OK           ;Prog starts here.
→                 MOV       AH,9
→                 INT       21H
                  RET
          PROG_NAME         ENDP
          CODE_SEG          ENDS

STACK        SEGMENT  STACK
     DB       30 DUP("STACK ")
STACK        ENDS
          END       PROG_NAME
```

The whole program is about double the length of a similar program set up to use .COM format. We can assemble the program, link it, and run it (no EXE2BIN required!):

```
C>MASM ALLOK;
Microsoft (R) Macro Assembler Version 5.10
Copyright (C) Microsoft Corp 1981, 1988.  All rights reserved.

  50152 + 31269 Bytes symbol space free

       0 Warning Errors
       0 Severe  Errors

C>LINK ALLOK;
Microsoft (R) Overlay Linker  Version 3.64
Copyright (C) Microsoft Corp 1983988.  All rights reserved.

C>ALLOK
No Worries.
C>
```

Now we're going to do something surprising, something that could not be done in a .COM file. We are going to make sure that ALL_OK is more than 64K away from the instruction LEA DX,ALL_OK, and still have the program work. This can be done very easily, with the insertion of just one line:

```
        DATA_SEG        SEGMENT
        ALL_OK  DB "No Worries.$"
        FILLER  DB 65524 DUP(0)  ←
        DATA_SEG        ENDS

        CODE_SEG        SEGMENT
                ASSUME  CS:CODE_SEG,SS:STACK
        PROG_NAME       PROC    FAR
                PUSH    DS
                XOR     AX,AX
                PUSH    AX
                MOV     AX,DATA_SEG
                MOV     DS,AX
                ASSUME  DS:DATA_SEG
                LEA     DX,ALL_OK       ;Prog starts here.
                MOV     AH,9
                INT     21H
                RET
        PROG_NAME       ENDP
        CODE_SEG        ENDS

  STACK     SEGMENT STACK
      DB       30 DUP("STACK ")
  STACK     ENDS
        END     PROG_NAME
```

FILLER represents 65,524 bytes of zeroes. This fills up the data segment (there are 12 characters in "No Worries.$", and 12 + 65524 = 65,536, the maximum number of bytes in a segment).

You can assemble and link the new program ALLOK.ASM—it just makes a large .EXE file. When run, however, it gives the same result as before:

```
C>ALLOK
No Worries.
C>
```

Linking Multiple Files to Form .EXE Files

Just like writing .COM files, multiple files can be linked together to form .EXE files. Here, however, because of the multiple segments allowed, you have to be careful how things combine. What you should do is instruct the assembler to keep the segment's name around so that it may be combined with other parts of the same segment from different files. This is done with the PUBLIC Pseudo-Op. We can break our example ALLOK.ASM up into two files with PUBLIC, like this:

```
-------- File 1 -----------
        DATA_SEG        SEGMENT
        ALL_OK  DB "No Worries.$"


        DATA_SEG            ENDS
        CODE_SEG            SEGMENT PUBLIC        ←
                ASSUME  CS:CODE_SEG,SS:STACK
                EXTRN   SUB_PROG:NEAR
                PUBLIC  PRINT
        PROG_NAME       PROC    FAR
                PUSH    DS
                XOR     AX,AX
                PUSH    AX
                MOV     AX,DATA_SEG
                MOV     DS,AX
                ASSUME  DS:DATA_SEG
                CALL    SUB_PROG
                RET
        PROG_NAME       ENDP

        PRINT   PROC    NEAR
                LEA     DX,ALL_OK           ;Prog starts here.
                MOV     AH,9
                INT     21H
                RET
        PRINT   ENDP
        CODE_SEG            ENDS

STACK       SEGMENT STACK
     DB     30 DUP("STACK ")
STACK       ENDS

        END     PROG_NAME
-------- File 2 -----------
        CODE_SEG            SEGMENT PUBLIC    ←
                ASSUME  CS:CODE_SEG
```

```
                         EXTRN    PRINT:NEAR
                         PUBLIC   SUB_PROG
             SUB_PROG              PROC      NEAR
                         CALL     PRINT
                         RET
             SUB_PROG              ENDP
             CODE_SEG              ENDS

             END
```

Note the use of EXTRN and PUBLIC for the labels used, not just for CODE_SEG.

Using GROUPs in .EXE Files

Of course, the same thing can be done with groups, and, to make sure data offsets are calculated correctly, that is the recommended method:

```
--------- File 1 -----------
         CODE_GROUP     GROUP    CODE_SEG        ←

         DATA_SEG       SEGMENT
         ALL_OK  DB "No Worries.$"
         DATA_SEG       ENDS


         CODE_SEG       SEGMENT
                ASSUME  CS:CODE_GROUP,SS:STACK   ←
                EXTRN   SUB_PROG:NEAR
                PUBLIC  PRINT
         PROG_NAME      PROC      FAR
                PUSH    DS
                XOR     AX,AX
                PUSH    AX
                MOV     AX,DATA_SEG
                MOV     DS,AX
                ASSUME  DS:DATA_SEG
                CALL    SUB_PROG
                RET
         PROG_NAME      ENDP

         PRINT   PROC    NEAR
                LEA     DX,ALL_OK        ;Prog starts here.
                MOV     AH,9
                INT     21H
                RET
         PRINT   ENDP
         CODE_SEG               ENDS

    STACK     SEGMENT STACK
         DB       30 DUP("STACK ")
    STACK     ENDS

         END     PROG_NAME
---------- File 2 ---------
         CODE_GROUP     GROUP    CODE_SEG        ←
         CODE_SEG       SEGMENT
                ASSUME  CS:CODE_GROUP            ←
                EXTRN   PRINT:NEAR
```

```
               PUBLIC   SUB_PROG
     SUB_PROG           PROC     NEAR
               CALL     PRINT
               RET
     SUB_PROG           ENDP
     CODE_SEG           ENDS

     END
```

These files can just be assembled, linked together, and run as an .EXE file. The rules in the previous chapter on linking apply to .EXE files as well as to .COM files.

That's the end of .EXE file format for us until we reach our OS/2 section. Until then, we will have no reason to write programs so large that they require .EXE format. .COM files have advantages for us; for example, they can be made memory resident, they do not include hard-to-decipher headers, and they only contain the code that we put there.

DOS Running Priority

If there are two files on your disk—TESTING.EXE and TEST-ING.COM—you may have wondered how DOS knows which one to run when you type TESTING. DOS always chooses the .COM file first, which is logical since any .COM files that were recently created also recently passed through the .EXE file stage, and the (unrunnable) .EXE files may still be around. The order in which files are chosen to run is: .COM, .EXE, and .BAT.

Introduction to Macros

Now we'll turn away from linking, and onto the subject of macros. Macros are simply collections of assembly-language and Pseudo-Op instructions that are placed in an .ASM file. When a macro that you've defined is reached by the macro assembler, it is "expanded" into the full set of assembly-language and Pseudo-Op instructions that it contains.

These can become powerful constructions. For example, you could write your own personal (high-level) computer language with macros. Every time that the assembler came to one of your instructions like OpenTheFile (NOVEL.TXT), it would expand OpenTheFile into the correct assembly-language instructions for doing just that.

Macro use in switching machines

Macros are popular with professional programmers for a number of reasons. For example, suppose that you, a professional programmer, want to write code that can easily be made to run on several machines, but that relies heavily on the nature of the individual video controller chip used. Instead of including explicit instructions in your .ASM file to set up the video controller, you could write a macro, SetUpTheVideoController. This macro would then appear throughout your .ASM file. When you changed machines, all you'd have to do is change the contents of this macro.

Use of macros at assembly time

Macros can also help at assembly time. For example, one common way of dealing quickly with data records in memory is to skip quickly over them by incrementing the DS register. Every time you increment DS, you point to the next 16 bytes, which allows you to easily manage records of the same size. What this means, though, is that you might want the records in memory to start at paragraph boundaries, and macros can let you do so. They can know the current byte position inside your partially assembled file, and fill out the area ahead of you with 0s to make sure you are positioned properly.

Our First Macro

Even though macros seem exotic to many people, they are not. On one hand, there is a reason that the program is named the *macro* assembler. On the other hand, macros are not tools typically used by beginners.

Macros can be short, and all they need are two Pseudo-Ops, MACRO and ENDM. A macro is really just some lines of code, like this one:

```
PRINT   MACRO
        MOV     AH,9
        LEA     DX,ALL_OK
        INT     21H
        ENDM
```

From now on, when you use PRINT in your program, like this:

```
CODE_SEG SEGMENT
        ASSUME CS:CODE_SEG,DS:CODE_SEG
        ORG     100H
ENTRY:
        PRINT           ←
        INT     20H
CODE_SEG ENDS
        END     ENTRY
```

the macro assembler will expand PRINT into these three lines:

```
        MOV     AH,9
        LEA     DX,ALL_OK
        INT     21H
```

and your program will appear like this:

```
CODE_SEG SEGMENT
         ASSUME CS:CODE_SEG,DS:CODE_SEG
         ORG    100H
ENTRY:
  →      MOV    AH,9
  →      LEA    DX,ALL_OK
  →      INT    21H
         INT    20H
CODE_SEG ENDS
         END    ENTRY
```

Defining Macros

In order to do this, the macro must be defined at the beginning of the program. Here's how it might be defined if we wanted to print out the "No Worries." message:

```
PRINT    MACRO                      ←
         MOV    AH,9                ←
         LEA    DX,ALL_OK           ←
         INT    21H                 ←
         ENDM                       ←

CODE_SEG         SEGMENT
         ASSUME  CS:CODE_SEG,DS:CODE_SEG
         ORG     100H
ENTRY:   JMP     PROG
ALL_OK           DB "No Worries.$"
PROG:
         PRINT                      ←
         INT     20H
CODE_SEG         ENDS
         END     ENTRY
```

Listing (.LST) files

There is an easy way to check whether or not the assembler did what we wanted faithfully, and that is to ask it to produce a listing, or .LST file. Let's call our just-written program PROG.ASM, and assemble it.

This time, however, we will respond to the prompts, asking it to produce PROG.LST. In the prompts that it types, the macro assembler gives the default filenames in square brackets. For example, after the command MASM PROG, the default .OBJ filename will be PROG.OBJ. The default .LST name is NUL.LST, which is the assembler's shorthand way of saying that it won't produce one.

> NUL means the "null" device: Sending output there means that that output won't be saved. NUL can be used like the other devices under DOS: COM, PRN, etc.

We can tell MASM to produce PROG.LST, as follows:

```
C>MASM PROG
Microsoft (R) Macro Assembler Version 5.10
Copyright (C) Microsoft Corp 1981, 1988.  All rights reserved.

Object filename [PROG.OBJ]
Source Listing [NUL.LST] PROG.LST        ←
Cross-reference [NUL.CRF]

   48082 + 48697 Bytes symbol space free

        0 Warning Errors
        0 Severe  Errors
```

This produces the file PROG.LST, which really contains more information in it than we want. Let's take a look at the whole thing:

Listing 8.1 PROG.ASM

```
Microsoft (R) Macro Assembler Version 5.10

                                                               Page 1-1


              PRINT    MACRO
                       MOV      AH,9
                       LEA      DX,ALL_OK
                       INT      21H
                       ENDM
0000                   CODE_SEG        SEGMENT
                       ASSUME CS:CODE_SEG,DS:CODE_SEG
0100                           ORG      100H
0100  EB 0D 90          ENTRY:  JMP    PROG
0103  4E 6F 20 57 6F 72          ALL_OK  DB "No Worries.$"
      72 69 65 73 2E 24
010F             PROG:
                       PRINT
010F  B4 09                     1          MOV    AH,9
0111  8D 16 0103 R              1          LEA    DX,ALL_OK
0115  CD 21                     1          INT    21H
0117  CD 20                     INT    20H
0119                   CODE_SEG        ENDS
                       END      ENTRY
Microsoft (R) Macro Assembler Version 5.10

                                                               Symbols-1


Macros:

        N a m e        Lines
PRINT . . . . . . . . . . . .        3

Segments and Groups:
               N a m e               Length    Align   Combine Class
CODE_SEG . . . . . . . . . . . .     0119      PARA    NONE

Symbols:
               N a m e               Type    Value    Attr

ALL_OK . . . . . . . . . . . .       L BYTE   0103    CODE_SEG
```

Listing 8.1 PROG.ASM (continued)

```
ENTRY  . . . . . . . . . . . . .     L NEAR    0100    CODE_SEG
PROG . . . . . . . . . . . . . .     L NEAR    010F    CODE_SEG

@CPU . . . . . . . . . . . . . .     TEXT   0101h
@FILENAME  . . . . . . . . . . .     TEXT   PROG
@VERSION . . . . . . . . . . . .     TEXT   510


    17 Source  Lines
    20 Total   Lines
    10 Symbols


 48082 + 48697 Bytes symbol space free


     0 Warning Errors
     0 Severe  Errors
```

As you can see, it is lengthy, even for a short .ASM file. The second page gives us information primarily about the symbols that were used, and the segments that were defined which we aren't interested in here. This information is good if something has gone wrong with assembling a file and you need to know what the assembler thinks it is doing.

The full "source listing" is on the first page, and it includes a fully expanded set of instructions. You can see that the macro PRINT was expanded correctly. The digit "1" appears before each line that was expanded, so you know that it came from a macro, and was not present in the original .ASM file:

```
        PRINT   MACRO
                MOV     AH,9
                LEA     DX,ALL_OK
                INT     21H
                ENDM

0000            CODE_SEG        SEGMENT
                ASSUME CS:CODE_SEG,DS:CODE_SEG
0100            ORG     100H
0100  EB 0D 90      ENTRY:  JMP     PROG
0103  4E 6F 20 57 6F 72          ALL_OK   DB    "No Worries.$"
      72 69 65 73 2E 24
010F            PROG:
                PRINT
010F  B4 09         1           MOV     AH,9        ←
0111  8D 16 0103 R  1           LEA     DX,ALL_OK   ←
0115  CD 21         1           INT     21H         ←
0117  CD 20             INT     20H
0119            CODE_SEG        ENDS
                END     ENTRY
                  :
                  :
```

Macros Versus Subroutines

So far, macros seem of somewhat limited utility. After all, we could probably just put all the instructions we wanted to expand from a macro into a subroutine—that would even save space, right? Instead of putting the full code in each time the macro is used, we would just use CALL PRINT.

Letting a
macro
redefine
itself

It turns out that macros can handle this too. We can design a macro that works this way: The first time it is used, it defines a procedure named PRINT, and then calls it. The second and all following times that it is used, it will just expand to CALL PRINT, the subroutine that has already been defined.

Let's call this macro MESSAGE. When it expands the first time, MESSAGE will define the procedure PRINT (which prints out "No Worries."), and then call it. The procedure PRINT will appear right there in the middle of the code of the surrounding program, but there is no problem with that, as long as we jump over it. However, MESSAGE will also contain these lines at its end:

```
MESSAGE MACRO    ←
CALL    PRINT    ←
ENDM             ←
```

When the assembler reads these lines, it will *redefine* the macro MESSAGE. Every time that MESSAGE is used from then on, it will simply expand into CALL PRINT. That's because we have redefined MESSAGE into the new, miniversion above, which contains just CALL PRINT.

In this way, macros can redefine themselves. You could even keep going, redefining a macro every time it is used. The most common use of this ability, however, is to do just what we are about to do: Define and call a subroutine the first time, and then call that subroutine every time thereafter.

Writing the MESSAGE Macro

MESSAGE will expand the first time with the full definition of the procedure PRINT, right there in the program, so we have to put a JMP at the top of MESSAGE so that control will jump over the procedure definition. Since we want to CALL PRINT this first time too (after all, the purpose of using MESSAGE is to type out the message), the instruction jumped to is CALL PRINT. After that, there is the new definition of

MESSAGE, which only the assembler will read. Here's how MESSAGE looks. As usual, we enclose it with MACRO and ENDM:

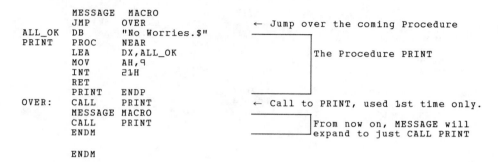

```
         MESSAGE  MACRO
         JMP      OVER              ← Jump over the coming Procedure
ALL_OK   DB       "No Worries.$"
PRINT    PROC     NEAR
         LEA      DX,ALL_OK              The Procedure PRINT
         MOV      AH,9
         INT      21H
         RET
PRINT    ENDP
OVER:    CALL     PRINT             ← Call to PRINT, used 1st time only.
         MESSAGE  MACRO
         CALL     PRINT                  From now on, MESSAGE will
         ENDM                            expand to just CALL PRINT

         ENDM
```

And here's how it's used (after defining it at the beginning of the program):

```
CODE_SEG SEGMENT
         ASSUME   CS:CODE_SEG,DS:CODE_SEG
         ORG      100H
ENTRY:   MESSAGE                                      ←
         MESSAGE                                      ←
         INT      20H
CODE_SEG          ENDS
         END      ENTRY
```

Let's see what the assembler makes of this. We can assemble this new PROG.ASM and take a look at the listing file. In PROG.LST, the first thing is the definition of MESSAGE. This is followed by the actual program. The first time MESSAGE is used, the whole thing appears, including the part where MESSAGE is redefined. The second time MESSAGE is used, just CALL PRINT appears:

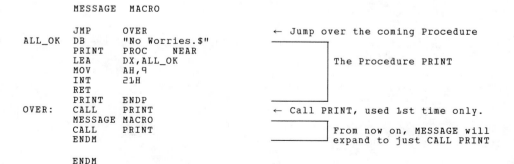

```
MESSAGE  MACRO

         JMP      OVER              ← Jump over the coming Procedure
ALL_OK   DB       "No Worries.$"
PRINT    PROC     NEAR
         LEA      DX,ALL_OK              The Procedure PRINT
         MOV      AH,9
         INT      21H
         RET
PRINT    ENDP
OVER:    CALL     PRINT             ← Call PRINT, used 1st time only.
         MESSAGE  MACRO
         CALL     PRINT                  From now on, MESSAGE will
         ENDM                            expand to just CALL PRINT

         ENDM
```

```
0000        CODE_SEG SEGMENT
                ASSUME   CS:CODE_SEG,DS:CODE_SEG
0100            ORG      100H
0100    ENTRY:  MESSAGE              ← Expand the macro MESSAGE for the 1st time.
0100    EB 16 90            1            JMP      OVER  ← The whole macro
0103    4E 6F 20 57 6F 72   1 ALL_OK  DB       "No Worries.$"
010F                        1            PRINT    PROC    NEAR
010F    8D 16 0103 R        1            LEA      DX,ALL_OK
0113    B4 09               1            MOV      AH,9
0115    CD 21               1            INT      21H
0117    C3                  1            RET
0118                        1            PRINT    ENDP
0118    E8 010F R           1 OVER:    CALL     PRINT
                MESSAGE     ← Expand the macro MESSAGE again.
011B    E8 010F R           1            CALL     PRINT← This time only CALL!
011E    CD 20               INT      20H
0120    CODE_SEG            ENDS
            END     ENTRY
```

MESSAGE did its stuff. The first time it was used, it expanded to its full version (excluding the part where it was redefined to just CALL PRINT, which only MASM sees).

```
0000        CODE_SEG SEGMENT
                ASSUME  CS:CODE_SEG,DS:CODE_SEG
0100            ORG      100H
0100    ENTRY:  MESSAGE              ← Expand the macro MESSAGE for the 1st time.
0100    EB 16 90            1            JMP      OVER  ← The whole macro ←
0103    4E 6F 20 57 6F 72   1 ALL_OK  DB       "No Worries.$"
010F                        1            PRINT    PROC    NEAR
010F    8D 16 0103 R        1            LEA      DX,ALL_OK
0113    B4 09               1            MOV      AH,9
0115    CD 21               1            INT      21H
0117    C3                  1            RET
0118                        1            PRINT    ENDP
0118    E8 010F R           1 OVER:    CALL     PRINT
```

The second time it was used, only CALL PRINT appears:

```
0000        CODE_SEG SEGMENT
                ASSUME   CS:CODE_SEG,DS:CODE_SEG
0100            ORG      100H
0100    ENTRY:  MESSAGE              ← Expand the macro MESSAGE for the 1st time.
0100    EB 16 90            1            JMP      OVER  ← The whole macro
0103    4E 6F 20 57 6F 72   1 ALL_OK  DB       "No Worries.$"
010F                        1            PRINT    PROC    NEAR
010F    8D 16 0103 R        1            LEA      DX,ALL_OK
0113    B4 09               1            MOV      AH,9
0115    CD 21               1            INT      21H
0117    C3                  1            RET
0118                        1            PRINT    ENDP
0118    E8 010F R           1 OVER:    CALL     PRINT
                MESSAGE     ← Expand the macro MESSAGE again.
011B    E8 010F R           1            CALL     PRINT
```

This kind of thing is useful—you don't have to worry whether or not you've included an error-message procedure before using it, for example. You can see that it's not necessary to have a macro expand to the same full length every time; code need not be wasted.

On the other hand, these macros only work one way, and that's just the beginning of macros. Even elementary macros usually can have some internal branching in them.

> An entire book could be written on the subject of macros and how to use them. For more advanced macro topics, like the IRPC Pseudo-Op and macro libraries, see *Advanced Assembly Language on the IBM PC*.

IF, ENDIF, and $

As mentioned, macros can assist you when your program is being assembled. They are often able to get information not available to you—for example, at what position a certain label will be in the .OBJ file.

There is a special, one-character symbol for the current offset location (in bytes) from the beginning of the segment, and that is "$". Whenever you use "$", it will be replaced with the current value of the offset.

Earlier we mentioned a macro that will set you on a paragraph boundary. Here it is:

```
PARAGRAPH  MACRO
    ....IF $ MOD 16
    :   ORG $+16-($ MOD 16)
    :...ENDIF
        ENDM
```

This example will take a little explaining, introducing as it does not only "$", but also IF, ENDIF, and MOD.

Using IF

When we use IF like this,

```
        IF $ MOD 16
           [Body of IF]
        ENDIF
```

the assembler will evaluate the commands [Body of IF] if the expression $ MOD 16 is *not* zero. In other words, the body of the IF statement is evaluated (at assembly time) if the argument to IF is non-zero. Note that this branching takes place at assembly time.

The expression, $ MOD 16, can be translated into (in the code segment): IP MOD 16 (where that is IP as in CS:IP.) The MOD Pseudo-Op

The MOD
Operator

is just another of the assembler's math operators, like "+", "−", or "*" (we will take a look at the available operators in a minute). This one, MOD, returns the remainder after a division.

For instance, 17 MOD 16 is 1. 32 MOD 16 is 0. In our PARAGRAPH macro, if the current offset (that is, "$") is some multiple of 16, then $ MOD 16 will be zero, and the instructions in the body of the IF statement will not be executed. In other words, if we are on a paragraph boundary, the macro does nothing.

```
IF $ MOD 16    ← If $ MOD 16 = 0
    [Body of IF]    ← Then [Body of IF] is not done by MASM
ENDIF
```

Using ORG   On the other hand, if $ MOD 16 is NOT zero, the body of the IF statement IS executed.

```
IF $ MOD 16    ← If $ MOD 16 is NOT 0
    [Body of IF]    ← Then [Body of IF] IS done by MASM
ENDIF
```

That body is an ORG statement that looks like this:

```
PARAGRAPH  MACRO
    ....IF $ MOD 16
 →     ORG $+16-($ MOD 16)
    :...ENDIF
       ENDM
```

This is only an ORG pseudo-Op. We want to set the ORG to the next paragraph beginning, that is, at the next multiple of 16. That will be at the current location, "$", plus the number of bytes left in the current paragraph.

We are $ MOD 16 bytes into the current paragraph, so the number of bytes left in the paragraph is 16 − ($ MOD 16). If we add this to "$", we will be at the beginning of the next paragraph:

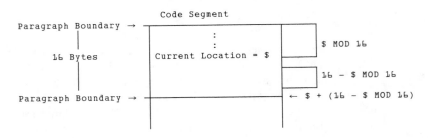

We can see that the Pseudo-Op ORG $ + 16 − ($ MOD 16) places us at the head of the next paragraph at any time. In this way, we can gain a little control over where we are in the final code.

When the IF argument ($ MOD 16) is non-zero, MASM executes the body of the IF statement. In our case, that was an ORG Pseudo-Op that placed us at the next paragraph boundary. If the argument to IF ($ MOD 16) had been zero, MASM would never have seen the ORG Pseudo-Op.

Assembler Math Pseudo-Ops

A number of math Pseudo-Ops are available to you inside the assembler. We already saw how they could be useful with our multiplication 60*1024 when we wanted to read in a 60K chunk of a file. A number like 61440 simply does not look like 60K, while an expression like 60*1024 does. Math Pseudo-Ops can make the code much clearer this way.

They also have real utility, as we just saw in our PARAGRAPH macro. Table 8.2 presents a list of the available math Pseudo-Ops.

Table 8.2 Math Pseudo-Ops

Operation	Example
Multiplication	TEST EQU 5*1024
Integer Division	MOV AX,5/2 will assemble into MOV AX,2. The assembler manual says nothing about division, but MASM does perform it.
Addition	MOV BX,1010110B + 10001101B
Subtraction	WREAD EQU 1200-983
Modulo	MOV BP,23 MOD 7
Shift Left, Shift Right	MOV CX,16 SHL 3
AND	MOV DI, 0FF00H AND 11001100B
OR	ADD AX,0F0F0H OR 0AAAAH
XOR	SUB AX,0F0F0H XOR 0AAAAH
NOT	MOV DX,NOT 0BBBBH

> The AND, OR, XOR, and NOT operations will be discussed more in Chapter 9, Fast Math.

These can all be used in your .ASM files and macros. There are other IFs, too—variations on the straight IF version that we've seen. Let's take a look at some of them.

Other IFs

The use of IF allows you to select what code goes into the final program—some code will be selected if the IF condition is true, for example, and some other code if the condition is false.

The conditions you can select include whether or not a symbol has been defined as EXTRN, or whether or not some expression is zero (such as $ MOD 16). Table 8.3 is a list of some of the IFs you can use.

Table 8.3 IFs

Type of IF	Condition
IF X	True if X is NOT 0.
IFE X	True if X is 0.
IFDEF SYM	True if SYM has been defined.
IFNDEF SYM	True if SYM is undefined.
IFB <XXX>	True if XXX is blank—see below.
IFNB <XXX>	True if XXX is not blank—see below.
IFIDN <XXX>,<YYY>	True if string XXX is the same as string YYY.
IFDIF <XXX>,<YYY>	True if string XXX is different from string YYY.
ENDIF	EVERY IF must end with an ENDIF.
ELSE	An option to make IFs into Either-Or blocks.

The simplest type of IF works like the one we've already seen:

```
PARAGRAPH  MACRO
        ─IF $ MOD 16
        │ ORG $+16-($ MOD 16)
        └ENDIF
         ENDM
```

If the expression $ MOD 16 is zero, then the following line(s) are executed. Notice the use of ENDIF at the end—ENDIF must follow *all* IF statements.

Passing values to macros

As you can see, there are many types of IFs. These are extremely useful when using macros. Let's look at an example. It's possible to pass values to macros. For example, here is a simple case:

```
DEFINE_VALUE MACRO  A_VALUE
        VALUE   DB   A_VALUE
ENDM
```

Whenever we want to define VALUE, we can use the DEFINE_VALUE macro. If we said DEFINE_VALUE 5, then 5 would take the place of

A_VALUE (which we used in the first line of the macro definition:
DEFINE_VALUE MACRO A_VALUE) throughout the macro. Here's
DEFINE_VALUE in use:

```
            DEFINE_VALUE MACRO   A_VALUE
                         VALUE   DB  A_VALUE
            ENDM

CODE_SEG SEGMENT
         ASSUME CS:CODE_SEG,DS:CODE_SEG
         ORG    100H
ENTRY:   JMP    PROG
         DEFINE_VALUE 5   ←
PROG     PROC   NEAR
```

The assembler produces this:

```
CODE_SEG SEGMENT
         ASSUME CS:CODE_SEG,DS:CODE_SEG
         ORG    100H
ENTRY:   JMP    PROG
         VALUE  DB 5     ←
PROG     PROC   NEAR
```

Another example is MOV_DX:

```
        MOV_DX MACRO A_NUMBER
               MOV   DX,A_NUMBER
        ENDM
```

We can use MOV_DX in a program, as long as we define it first:

```
        MOV_DX MACRO A_NUMBER
               MOV   DX,A_NUMBER
        ENDM

CODE_SEG SEGMENT
         ASSUME CS:CODE_SEG,DS:CODE_SEG
         ORG    100H
ENTRY:   JMP    PROG
         VALUE  DB 5
PROG     PROC   NEAR
         MOV_DX 32001   ←
         :
```

This is assembled to yield this:

```
CODE_SEG SEGMENT
         ASSUME CS:CODE_SEG,DS:CODE_SEG
         ORG    100H
ENTRY:   JMP    PROG
         VALUE  DB 5
PROG     PROC   NEAR
         MOV    DX,32001  ←
         :
```

Now, using an IF, we can check to see whether any parameter was filled. In other words, we can check if just MOV_DX was used or MOV_DX 5 was used.

The ERRORMESSAGE Macro

Let's assume that you have a set of programs, and most of the time you have an error message that you want to use that simply says: "An error has occurred." Sometimes, however, you don't want to use this default, but want to use a really strong message: "Look Out! BIG Error!" Here's a macro that you could use:

```
ERRORMESSAGE MACRO LEVEL
IFNB <LEVEL>
ERROR_MSG DB "Look out! BIG Error!$"
ELSE
ERROR_MSG DB "An error occurred.$"
ENDIF
ENDM
```

This makes use of IFNB, If Not Blank. The parameter that we fill here is called LEVEL. If we specify no value for level (the default) then the line in the program where ERRORMESSAGE was used will be assembled into:

```
ERROR_MSG DB "An error occurred.$"
```

On the other hand, if you wanted to use error message 2 for ERROR_MSG in this case, you could put ERRORMESSAGE 2 in your program. Since LEVEL is no longer "blank," the other error message would be put in:

```
ERROR_MSG DB "Look out! BIG Error!$"
```

> Note that LEVEL was filled with 2, but any value at all would have made it nonblank.

This is because of the IFNB ELSE ENDIF structure used:

```
          ERRORMESSAGE MACRO LEVEL
→         IFNB <LEVEL>
                        ERROR_MSG DB "Look out! BIG Error!$"
→         ELSE
                        ERROR_MSG DB "An error occurred.$"
→         ENDIF
          ENDM
```

The ELSE Pseudo-Op

Notice the ELSE in ERRORMESSAGE. A common way of using IF Pseudo-Ops is with ELSE. Here it is in general (we always have to end IFs with ENDIF, don't forget):

```
IF[NB, etc] <Condition>
    [Do This]
ELSE
    [Else Do This]
ENDIF
```

This allows some things to happen, depending on what the parameter was, for instance. Here is ERRORMESSAGE at work:

```
→       ERRORMESSAGE MACRO LEVEL
→       IFNB <LEVEL>
→       ERROR_MSG DB "Look out! BIG Error!$"
→       ELSE
→       ERROR_MSG DB "An error occurred.$"
→       ENDIF
→       ENDM

CODE_SEG SEGMENT
        ASSUME  CS:CODE_SEG,DS:CODE_SEG
        ORG     100H
ENTER:  JMP     SHORT TEST
        ERRORMESSAGE                    ← Macro default being used.
TEST:   INT     20H
CODE_SEG        ENDS
        END     ENTER
```

This will become:

```
CODE_SEG SEGMENT
        ASSUME  CS:CODE_SEG,DS:CODE_SEG
        ORG     100H
ENTER:  JMP     SHORT TEST
        ERROR_MSG DB "An error occurred.$"        ←
TEST:   INT     20H
CODE_SEG        ENDS
        END     ENTER
```

In another file, the error might be more critical, and you could use ERRORMESSAGE 2:

```
        ERRORMESSAGE MACRO LEVEL
        IFNB <LEVEL>
        ERROR_MSG DB "Look out! BIG Error!$"
        ELSE
        ERROR_MSG DB "An error occurred.$"
        ENDIF
        ENDM

CODE_SEG SEGMENT
        ASSUME  CS:CODE_SEG,DS:CODE_SEG
```

```
          ORG     100H
ENTER:    JMP     SHORT TEST
          ERRORMESSAGE 2              ← Macro being used.
TEST:     INT     20H
CODE_SEG          ENDS
          END     ENTER
```

And this will be assembled as though you had written:

```
CODE_SEG SEGMENT
          ASSUME  CS:CODE_SEG,DS:CODE_SEG
          ORG     100H
ENTER:    JMP     SHORT TEST
          ERROR_MSG DB "Look out! BIG Error!$"      ←
TEST:     INT     20H
CODE_SEG          ENDS
          END     ENTER
```

Multiply-defined labels in macros

Using ERRORMESSAGE is fine, but you can only use it *once* in a file. If you use it more than once (can you guess?) you would be defining the label ERROR_MSG more than once, and the macro assembler does not allow multiple labels with the same name. This is a problem; the solution is another Pseudo-Op named LOCAL.

The LOCAL Pseudo-Op in Macros

What LOCAL does is define a unique label that will only be used by the instructions in the macro. Whenever you use LOCAL, it *must* be the line immediately following the macro definition. In the following example, we are defining ALL_OK as LOCAL in the macro PRINTOUT. This means that whenever PRINTOUT is invoked, it will use a unique name for ALL_OK, so we will not be redefining the label.

LOCAL is almost always used when the macro needs internal labels, but not when these labels are to be referenced externally (such as ERROR_MSG or VALUE above). In PRINTOUT, we will want to make use of these instructions:

```
          JMP     SHORT OVER
          ALL_OK  DB MESSAGE,"$"
OVER:     MOV     AH,9
          LEA     DX,ALL_OK
          INT     21H
```

MESSAGE will be defined when the macro is used, like PRINTOUT "Help!" Our macro PRINTOUT sets aside space for the message to print out, ALL_OK, and jumps over it, using another label, OVER.

```
        JMP     SHORT OVER
        ALL_OK  DB MESSAGE,"$"    ←
OVER:   MOV     AH,9              ←
        LEA     DX,ALL_OK
        INT     21H
```

If we used PRINTOUT more than once, ALL_OK and OVER would
be multiply-defined, so we define them as local:

```
PRINTOUT MACRO  MESSAGE
        LOCAL   ALL_OK,OVER       ←
        JMP     SHORT OVER
        ALL_OK  DB MESSAGE,"$"
OVER:   MOV     AH,9
        LEA     DX,ALL_OK
        INT     21H
        ENDM

CODE_SEG        SEGMENT
        ASSUME CS:CODE_SEG,DS:CODE_SEG
        ORG     100H
ENTRY:  PRINTOUT "No Worries."    ←
        INT     20H
CODE_SEG ENDS
        END     ENTRY
```

PRINTOUT can now be used more than once:

```
PRINTOUT MACRO  MESSAGE
        LOCAL   ALL_OK,OVER
        JMP     SHORT OVER
        ALL_OK  DB MESSAGE,"$"
OVER:   MOV     AH,9
        LEA     DX,ALL_OK
        INT     21H
        ENDM

CODE_SEG        SEGMENT
        ASSUME CS:CODE_SEG,DS:CODE_SEG
        ORG     100H
ENTRY:  PRINTOUT "No Worries."              ←
        PRINTOUT "Really, No Worries."      ←
        INT     20H
CODE_SEG ENDS
        END     ENTRY
```

Let's take a look at the listing file for this program:

```
PRINTOUT MACRO  MESSAGE
        LOCAL   ALL_OK,OVER
        JMP     SHORT OVER
        ALL_OK  DB MESSAGE,"$"
OVER:   MOV     AH,9
        LEA     DX,ALL_OK
        INT     21H
        ENDM

0000    CODE_SEG        SEGMENT
        ASSUME CS:CODE_SEG,DS:CODE_SEG
```

```
0100                    ORG    100H
0100            ENTRY:  PRINTOUT "No Worries."
0100   EB 0C                        1        JMP     SHORT ??0001
0102   4E 6F 20 57 6F 72            1        ??0000: DB "No Worries.","$"
010E   B4 09                        1 ??0001: MOV     AH,9
0110   8D 16 0102 R                 1        LEA     DX,??0000
0114   CD 21                        1        INT     21H
0116            PRINTOUT "Really, No Worries."
0116   EB 14                        1        JMP     SHORT ??0003
0118   52 65 61 6C 6C 79            1        ??0002: DB "Really, No Worries.","$"
012C   B4 09                        1 ??0003: MOV     AH,9
012E   8D 16 0118 R                 1        LEA     DX,??0002
0132   CD 21                        1        INT     21H
0134   CD 20                 INT    20H
0136            CODE_SEG ENDS
                END    ENTRY
```

As you can see, PRINTOUT was expanded twice. The first time, the
labels ??0000 and ??0001 were used, and the second time, the labels ??0002
and ??0003. In this way, MASM assigns a unique name for labels defined
as LOCAL; you're free to use labels that are internal to a macro easily.

Using the = Pseudo-Op

What if we had wanted to use our old macro MOV_DX, but didn't have
a value ready for A_NUMBER, like MOV_DX 32001? What if the value
we wanted to use depended on our position in the program? For example,
we may have wanted to move 1 into DX first, then move 2 into it, and so
forth.

We can do that using a counter called, say, VALUE. VALUE will take
on different values at different points in the program. We start off in the
beginning of the program by setting VALUE to 1, with VALUE = 1.
This is just like VALUE EQU 1, except that constants set with EQU
cannot be changed; if you set a parameter with "=", it can be changed.

```
        MOV_DX MACRO A_NUMBER
                MOV    DX,A_NUMBER
        ENDM

        VALUE = 1                        ←
CODE_SEG SEGMENT
        ASSUME CS:CODE_SEG,DS:CODE_SEG
        ORG    100H
        :
        :
```

VALUE (an arbitrary name) is something that only the assembler sees:
VALUE = 1 will not become code. The line VALUE = 1, where
VALUE is used for the first time, defines it for MASM. Now we can use
it with our MOV_DX macro, changing the value of VALUE along the
way (with VALUE = VALUE + 1 or something similar):

```
         MOV_DX MACRO A_NUMBER
                MOV    DX,A_NUMBER
         ENDM

         VALUE = 1                        ←

CODE_SEG SEGMENT
         ASSUME CS:CODE_SEG,DS:CODE_SEG
         ORG    100H
ENTRY:   JMP    PROG
         APPLES DB 5
PROG     PROC   NEAR
         MOV_DX VALUE                     ←
         :
         VALUE = VALUE + 1                ←
         MOV_DX VALUE                     ←
         :
```

This, when assembled, becomes:

```
CODE_SEG SEGMENT
         ASSUME CS:CODE_SEG,DS:CODE_SEG
         ORG    100H
ENTRY:   JMP    PROG
         APPLES DB 5
PROG     PROC   NEAR
         MOV    DX,1                      ←
         :
         MOV    DX,2                      ←
         :
```

What we have seen is that you can pass not only immediate parameters
to a macro, like this:

```
         MOV_DX 32001    ← MOV_DX is our macro
```

but that you can also pass parameters whose values won't be set until
assembly time:

```
         VALUE = 1
         MOV_DX VALUE
         VALUE = VALUE + 1
         MOV_DX VALUE
```

This gives macros an added dimension of flexibility.

@CPU and Other Predefined Macros

In recent Microsoft assembler packages, there are a number of predefined
macros. One of these is @Version (macro assembler 5.1 and later versions), which returns a three-character string with the version number.
That is, @Version is replaced by the character string when your program
is assembled. In Version 5.1, this string is "510", and you can check it to

make sure that you are using a recent MASM. Another predefined macro is @FileName, which returns a character string with the file's name.

> @FileName returns just the filename without the extension. Thus, when assembling PROG.ASM, @FileName would be equal to "PROG."

A very useful predefined macro is @CPU. This macro returns information about which CPU is being used, and whether or not math coprocessors are present.

The CPU macro returns information in the bits of a word (16 bits). These bits will be set if the following chips are installed:

Table 8.4 Bits Set by the @ CPU Macro

Bit Number	Means
0	8086 or 8088 Installed
1	80186
2	80286
3	80386
7	286 or 386 Protected Mode Running
8	8087
10	80287
11	80387

One thing to note is that since an 80286 has the capabilites of an 8086 and an 80186, all three bits, 0, 1, and 2, will be set. Any chip sets the bits for the chips whose instruction set it can handle. Let's write an example using @CPU.

Using @CPU

PUSHA and POPA

The 80186, 286, and 386 all contain the instructions PUSHA and POPA, which push and pop all registers (except the flag and segment registers). Let's write a macro that checks to see whether we can use PUSHA and POPA or have to include all the pushes and pops explicitly.

To check the word returned by @CPU, we only have to AND it with some value. The value returned for an 80186 microprocessor would be 0000000000000011B, or 3. To make sure at least an 80186 is present, we are interested only in bit 1, not bit 0 (which is set for 8088s and 8086s as well). The 286 and 386 microprocessors will have bit 1 set also—the only microprocessors that won't will be the 8088 and 8086 chips. Therefore, if the quantity

```
                    (@CPU AND 00000010B)
```

(where we are just using the lower byte since we are not interested in the
math coprocessors) is zero, then we *cannot* use PUSHA and POPA. Here,
then, are our macros, using IF:

> Remember, the instructions following IF are used if the condition
> (@CPU AND 00000010B) is *not* zero.

```
PUSHA_MACRO       MACRO
          IF (@CPU AND 00000010B)
                    PUSHA
          ELSE
                    PUSH      AX
                    PUSH      CX
                    PUSH      DX
                    PUSH      BX
                    PUSH      SP
                    PUSH      BP
                    PUSH      SI
                    PUSH      DI
          ENDIF
          ENDM

POPA_MACRO        MACRO
          IF (@CPU AND 00000010B)
                    POPA
          ELSE
                    POP       DI
                    POP       SI
                    POP       BP
                    POP       SP
                    POP       BX
                    POP       DX
                    POP       CX
                    POP       AX
          ENDIF
          ENDM
```

We can put them to work right away, in our earlier program that used
PRINT:

```
PRINT     MACRO
          MOV       AH,9
          LEA       DX,ALL_OK
          INT       21H
          ENDM

PUSHA_MACRO       MACRO
          IF (@CPU AND 00000010B)
                    PUSHA
          ELSE
                    PUSH      AX
                    PUSH      CX
                    PUSH      DX
                    PUSH      BX
                    PUSH      SP
                    PUSH      BP
                    PUSH      SI
```

```
                        PUSH    DI
           ENDIF
           ENDM

POPA_MACRO      MACRO
           IF (@CPU AND 00000010B)
                        POPA
           ELSE
                        POP     DI
                        POP     SI
                        POP     BP
                        POP     SP
                        POP     BX
                        POP     DX
                        POP     CX
                        POP     AX
           ENDIF
           ENDM

CODE_SEG        SEGMENT
           ASSUME CS:CODE_SEG,DS:CODE_SEG
           ORG     100H
ENTRY:     JMP     PROG
           ALL_OK   DB "No Worries.$"
PROG:
           PUSHA_MACRO      ←
           PRINT
           POPA_MACRO       ←
           INT     20H
CODE_SEG        ENDS
           END     ENTRY
```

The PURGE Pseudo-Op

The last of the macro Pseudo-Ops that we'll cover is PURGE. PURGE is very simple—it eliminates a specified macro. For example, we could have said PURGE MOV_DX above, and removed the definition of MOV_DX from memory, allowing that space to be used for another macro definition. If you merely want to change the definition of a particular macro, however, you need not PURGE it first. Just redefining the macro will overwrite its definition.

That's it for macros. Their real power is only exploited in large programs, or in programs that need to be transported between machines. Still, this introduction has hopefully given you an indication of their use.

9

Fast Math

Computers were made to do at least one thing well—work with numbers. A large part of the 8088 instruction set is set up exclusively to handle numbers. We will see some of these instructions in this chapter, like IMUL, IADD, ADC, SHR, NOT, NEG, SBB, ROR, and others. In fact, we will discover that there is a whole new way of looking at numbers in the PS/2 or PC—as signed numbers, where we will use conditional jumps like JG and JL, rather than JA and JB. Our picture of what our computer can do in handling numbers will be made complete in this chapter. Let's begin by covering just how signed numbers can be used in the PS/2 and PC.

Signed Numbers

The 8088 instructions only work with integer arithmetic—no floating point calculations. The math coprocessors, like the 8087, are designed to work with huge floating point numbers.

> If you have a Microsoft high-level language, you can use some 8087 emulation routines, even if you do not have an 8087. See the "/E" option for assembling programs. After assembling, you can link with the high-level language's modules, and the 8087 emulation code will be linked in. Of course, emulating the real thing is slower than actually using it.

Up to this point, all the numbers we've been using have been unsigned whole numbers. A number could range from 0000H to FFFFH and that was it. *Unsigned* means, positive, and positive numbers are only half the story. Temperatures run negative as well as positive, as do budgets or voltages or any number of categories. To keep track of these, any modern computer has to be able to use signed numbers.

The Sign Bit

The highest bit—the left-most bit—in a byte or word is used as the sign bit. What makes a number a signed number is whether or not you pay attention to this bit. In unsigned bytes or words, this bit was always there, certainly—but it was only the highest bit, and had no other significance. To make a number signed you just have to treat it as signed—which means starting to pay attention to the sign bit. To let us treat this bit specially, there are a whole new set of instructions that we will examine here; for example, conditional jumps like JA change to their signed equivalent JG (jump if greater). What's important to realize is that the byte or word looks the same as before—it is the significance that we give to the highest bit that determines whether we are treating it as signed or not. A 1 in the highest bit will mean that the number, if thought of as signed, is negative.

Figure 9.1 Use of the High Bit

```
      ┌──── Highest Order Bit (Treating this byte as unsigned)
      │
      ↓
┌───────┬───────┬───────┬───────┬───────┬───────┐
│   1   │   1   │   0   │  0  1 │ 1  1  │   0   │
│       │       │       │    a  │    a  │       │
└───────┴───────┴───────┴───────┴───────┴───────┘

      ┌──── Sign Bit (Treating this byte as signed)  →  Negative number
      │
      ↓
┌───────┬───────┬───────┬───────┬───────┬───────┐
│   1   │   1   │   0   │  0  1 │ 1  1  │   0   │
│       │       │       │    a  │    a  │       │
└───────┴───────┴───────┴───────┴───────┴───────┘
```

How Signed Numbers Work

The whole scheme of signed numbers in the 8088 comes from the simple fact that $1 + (-1) = 0$. We realize that if we want to do any calculation with negative numbers in the PS/2 or PC, the number we choose to be , when added to 1, has to give 0. Yet this seems impossible. Can you think of an eight-bit number that, when added to 1, will give a result of 0? It seems as though the result must always be 1 or greater.

In fact, if we limit ourselves to the eight bits of the byte, there is an answer. If we add 255 (= 11111111B) and 1:

Ignoring the carry flag

it yields 100000000B, that is, the 8-bit register is left holding 00000000, or 0, and there is a carry, since the 1 is in the 2^8 place (256), more than the register's capacity to hold. This carry means that the *carry flag* will be set. If we ignore this carry, and only look at the eight bits that fit into the byte, we are left with 00000000B; in other words, FFH + 1 = 0.

This is what happens when we are working with negative numbers; we will ignore the carry flag. The only way it is used is if we explicitly check it (with, for example, JC), and with signed calculations, we ignore the way it is set. Therefore, to us, 11111111B + 1 = 0, when dealing with signed numbers.

About Negative Numbers

It might seem very odd that a number like FFFFH is equal to −1, even if we understand the reasoning. The positive numbers in a byte can range from 00000000B to 01111111B (=127), and there seems to be no problem with that: We can have positive numbers all the way up to the point where the sign bit is set.

The fewer 1s, the more negative

But the negative numbers reach from 11111111B = −1 to 10000000B = −128. This seems very odd. On the one hand, we can see that it is true, since 10000000B (−128) + 01111111B (127) = 11111111B (−1), but understanding that the more ones you have in a negative number, the *less* negative it is (−1 is less negative than −128) is difficult.

Let's take a look at a few of these numbers with DEBUG, which provides a way of working in Hex with its Hex, or H, command. We will see that as the numbers get more negative, they seem to decrease in magnitude.

Using DEBUG's Hex Command

The Hex command is given two numbers, like this: H 0 1. DEBUG both adds and subtracts 0 and 1, and gives you both results. For H 0 1, here is what you would see:

```
C>DEBUG
-HO 1
  0001  FFFF
-
```

DEBUG returns both 0 + 1 and 0 − 1:

```
          C>DEBUG
          -HO 1
0+1 = 1 →  0001  FFFF  ← 0-1 = -1 = FFFFH
          -
```

We can see that 0 + 1 = 1, and that 0 − 1 = FFFF. Let's take a look at some others:

```
-HO 1              [Subtract 0 - 1]
0001  FFFF         [-1 = FFFF]
-HO 2
0002  FFFE         [-2 = FFFE]
-HO 3
0003  FFFD         [-3 = FFFD]
-HO 4
0004  FFFC         [-4 = FFFC]
-HO 5
0005  FFFB         [-5 = FFFB]
-HO 80             [-80H = -128 = FF80]
0080  FF80
-HO FFFF           [-(-1) = 1]
FFFF  0001
```

This is how negative numbers work: It seems that their magnitude is decreasing the more and more negative you get. For example, −1 = FFFFH, but −2 = FFFEH, and −3 = FFFDH. This way of thinking takes a little practice.

> Note that the most negative number you can have for a byte is 80H = −128. Similarly, 8000H is the most negative number you can have in a word, −32768.

Finding a Two's Complement

As a practical matter, how are these negative numbers found? For instance, if we wanted to know what *09 was, how could we find it?*

To find −109, we would start with 109 and find what is called its *two's complement.* Two's complement math is the math used in computers for dealing with negative numbers. We already know one two's complement: The two's complement of 1 is FFFFH.

The two's comple-ment of 5

We can find any two's complement easily. We begin by noting that if you take a number like 5, which is 00000101B in binary, then flip all its bits, 11111010B (= FAH), and add the two together, you get all 1s:

```
  00000101  ← 5
+ 11111010  ← 5 with bits flipped [ FAH ]
  11111111    = FF
```

That is, 5 + FAH = 11111111B. This is close to what we want— adding 1 to this sum gives us 0 with a carry. If we ignore the carry, we can see that 5 + FAH + 1 = 0. In other words, adding 5 to (FAH + 1) gives 0 with the (ignored) carry:

```
+ (FAH + 1)
        0
```

We know that 5 plus −5 equals zero:

```
        5
+     − 5
        0
```

And this means that −5 must equal (FAH + 1), which is FBH. This is how negative numbers are found. The rule is simple: To find any two's complement (and thus to change the number's sign), just flip the bits and add 1. Thus we see that −1 = Flip(1) + 1 = 11111110B + 1 = 11111111B = FFH (in byte form).

The NOT and NEG Instructions

To flip the bits in a word or byte, you can use the NOT instruction. For example, if AX was equal to 00000000, then NOT AX would make AX equal to 11111111. If BX was equal to 01010101, then NOT BX would make it 10101010.

If you NOT a word or byte, and then add 1 to the result, you will have that word or byte's two's complement.

There is a special 8088 instruction that does just this: NEG. NEG is the same as NOT, except that it adds 1 at the end to make a two's complement of the number. If AX held 1, then NEG AX would give it 1111111111111111 or FFFF.

> Note that NEG flips signs; it does not always make signs negative. For example, NEG −1 = 1.

Ranges

The number of positive numbers you can hold in a word or byte is one less than the number of negative numbers, since 00000000—0—is treated as part of the positive range.

An unsigned byte can hold numbers from 0 to 255. A signed byte can hold numbers from −128 (10000000B = 80H) to 127 (01111111 = 7FH). For words, the unsigned range goes from 0 to 65535. If we treat the word as signed, the range is from −32768 (= 8000H) to 32767 (= 7FFFF).

New Jumps, Not New Numbers

When we decide to use signed numbers, the registers in our machine do not change—they are still the same. The way we know that we are using signed numbers is by paying special attention to the sign bit, and ignoring the carry flag.

Besides this, how we make comparisons will have to change. The way we used to compare two numbers, say FFH (= 11111111B) and 7FH (=01111111B) was with conditional jumps like JA or JB. For example:

```
MOV     AX,11111111B    [FF]
CMP     AX,01111111B    [7F]
JA      AX_BIG
```

If this jump is made, then we'd say that the value in AX, 11111111B, is bigger than the value it's being compared to, 01111111B. That is completely true if we are using unsigned numbers—FFH is bigger than 7FH. On the other hand, if we want to use signed numbers, we use a new set of conditional jumps that pay attention to the sign. Here, we use JG, or jump if greater:

```
       MOV     AX,11111111B    [ -1  ]
       CMP     AX,01111111B    [ 127 ]
  →    JG      AX_BIG
```

The JG instruction sees that 127 is greater than -1. The jump to AX_BIG is NOT made. In this way, we will be able to work with negative as well as positive numbers.

For all the comparison jumps, there is both an unsigned and a signed version, as shown in Table 9.1. "Above" becomes "Greater" and "Below" becomes "Less."

Table 9.1 Corresponding Jumps for Unsigned And Signed Numbers

Unsigned		Signed	
JA	Jump if Above	JG	Jump if Greater
JNA	Jump if Not Above	JNG	Jump if Not Greater
JB	Jump if Below	JL	Jump if Less
JNB	Jump if Not Below	JNL	Jump if Not Less
JAE	Jump if Above or Equal	JGE	Jump if Greater or Equal
JNAE	Jump if Not Above or Equal	JNGE	Jump if Not Greater or Equal
JBE	Jump if Below or Equal	JGE	Jump if Greater or Equal
JNBE	Jump if Not Below or Equal	JNLE	Jump if Not Less or Equal

> Note the "N" jumps, like JNA and JNB—the "N" means "not." JNA means Jump if Not Above (an unsigned comparison) and JNB means Jump if Not Below (also an unsigned comparison).

Now we've got a pretty good idea how negative numbers work in the PC and PS/2. Here's an example: Let's say we want a program to take the number stored at the memory location NUMBER and put its absolute value at ABS_VAL. We start with a normal .COM file shell:

```
CODE_SEG        SEGMENT
        ASSUME  CS:CODE_SEG,DS:CODE_SEG
        ORG     100H
ENTRY:  JMP     PROG
        NUMBER  DW  -1
        ABS_VAL DW  ?
PROG    PROC    NEAR
        INT     20H
PROG    ENDP
CODE_SEG        ENDS
        END     ENTRY
```

(As you can see, we can use DW with negative as well as positive numbers.) Our first step is to load NUMBER into AX. Then we test it: If it is less than zero, we use NEG. Otherwise, we just store it at ABS_VAL:

```
CODE_SEG         SEGMENT
        ASSUME   CS:CODE_SEG,DS:CODE_SEG
        ORG      100H
ENTRY:  JMP      PROG
        NUMBER   DW -10
        ABS_VAL  DW ?
PROG    PROC     NEAR
        MOV      AX,NUMBER         ←
        CMP      AX,0              ←
        JG       LOAD_ABS_VAL      ←
        NEG      AX                ←
LOAD_ABS_VAL:                      ←
        MOV      ABS_VAL,AX        ←
        INT      20H
PROG    ENDP
CODE_SEG         ENDS
        END      ENTRY
```

This little program will leave 10 in ABS_VAL. We can see that in cases like these, we have to use the signed conditional jump, JG, and not the unsigned version, JA (remember that JA treats a number like FFFFH as bigger than a number like 0003H).

The Overflow Flag

There is still a problem with this scheme. Having so cavalierly done away with the carry flag, we've left ourselves without a means of checking on possible overflows. For instance, if we were to add −1 and −128:

$$\begin{array}{r} 11111111 \\ + \underline{10000000} \\ 101111111 \end{array}$$

the result is 129. Now, −129 is more negative than the most negative number can be and still be in one byte (−128). The byte is left holding 01111111B, which looks like a positive number, not −129 at all. There is a special new flag, which is set when a number's sign is inadvertently changed; that is, when the result of some math operation gave a result that could not be held in the byte or word's two's complement capacity.

This is the *overflow flag*. When we were concerned about the possible size of a result, we could use the carry flag:

```
        ADD      AX,BX
   →    JC       TOO_BIG
```

If adding AX and BX gave an unsigned number greater than FFFFH, the carry flag would be set, and, checking it, we could make the appropriate corrections.

When dealing with signed numbers, the overflow flag is used in the same way, with JO (Jump if Overflow) and JNO (Jump if No Overflow):

```
        ADD     AX,BX
  →     JO      SIGN_CHANGED
```

If we are worried that the result of a calculation exceeded the size that was legal, we can check with the overflow flag this way.

That completes our introduction to negative numbers in the PS/2 and PC, although we'll have more to say about them later in this chapter. But before then, we'll take a look at the built-in MUL and DIV instructions.

The MUL Instruction

The MUL instruction is the 8088's whole number multiplication instruction. You can either multiply two bytes with it, or two words.

If you multiply two bytes together, each can hold values up to almost 2^8 (really $2^8 - 1$). This means that their product can reach up to $(2^8 - 1) \times (2^8 - 1) = 2^{16} - 2 \times 2^8 + 1$, so we'll need a full word (16 bits), in which to hold the result. Therefore, if we multiply two bytes together, we'll need a word for the answer. Similarly, if we multiply two words together, we'll need two words in which to hold the result.

> The 80386 can even multiply larger numbers here, since its registers can be used as 32-bit registers.

The way MUL does this is to *assume* that the AX register is used in some way when you want to use MUL. When you multiply two bytes together, using the instruction:

```
MUL     BL
```

the microprocessor multiplies AL × BL, and puts the result into AX (using the whole word). When you multiply this way:

```
MUL     BX
```

the microprocessor multiplies AX × BX and puts the result into DX:AX. DX holds the high word of the result, and AX the low word. Let's give this a try in DEBUG.

We can load AL with 2 and BL with 4, and put the instruction MUL BL in with the assembly command:

```
-RAX
AX 0000
:2
-RBX
BX 0000
:4
-A100
0EF1:0100 MUL      BL
0EF1:0102
-R
AX=0002  BX=0004  CX=0000  DX=0000  SP=FFEE  BP=0000  SI=0000  DI=0000
DS=0EF1  ES=0EF1  SS=0EF1  CS=0EF1  IP=0100    NV UP EI PL NZ NA PO NC
0EF1:0100 F6E3            MUL  BL              ←
```

> Even though we only wanted to load AL and BL in DEBUG, we had to load AX and BX, since the Register command does not work with 8-bit registers.

Now we are all ready to go. If we type T, the Trace instruction, we will execute the instruction at CS:IP, which is MUL BL. 2 is in AL and 4 is in BL—the result should be 8. Here goes:

```
-R
AX=0002  BX=0004  CX=0000  DX=0000  SP=FFEE  BP=0000  SI=0000 DI=0000
DS=0EF1  ES=0EF1  SS=0EF1  CS=0EF1  IP=0100    NV UP EI PL NZ NA PO NC
0EF1:0100 F6E3            MUL  BL
-T                        ← Execute the Trace instruction
      ↓
AX=0008  BX=0004  CX=0000  DX=0000  SP=FFEE  BP=0000  SI=0000 DI=0000
DS=0EF1  ES=0EF1  SS=0EF1  CS=0EF1  IP=0102    NV UP EI PL ZR NA PE NC
0EF1:0102 0402            ADD  AL,02
```

And the result is indeed 8. Let's try this with something more challenging. Let's try to multiply FFFFH by 100H. The result will be bigger than a word, but smaller than two words, so we will need a word multiplication. First we load the registers, FFFFH in AX and 100H in BX:

```
-RAX
AX FF00
:FFFF
-
-RBX
BX 0100
:100
```

Then we reset the program counter IP back to 100H, and assemble MUL BX there:

```
-RIP
IP 0102
:100
-A100
0EF1:0100 MUL        BX
0EF1:0102
-R
AX=FFFF  BX=0100   CX=0000  DX=0000   SP=FFEE   BP=0000   SI=0000 DI=0000
DS=0EF1  ES=0EF1   SS=0EF1  CS=0EF1   IP=0100    NV UP EI PL ZR NA PE NC
0EF1:0100 F7E3              MUL   BX
```

Again, we are ready to multiply FFFFH by 100H. We trace through the instruction and get the result in DX:AX, like this:

```
-R
AX=FFFF  BX=0100   CX=0000  DX=0000   SP=FFEE   BP=0000   SI=0000 DI=0000
DS=0EF1  ES=0EF1   SS=0EF1  CS=0EF1   IP=0100    NV UP EI PL ZR NA PE NC
0EF1:0100 F7E3              MUL   BX
-T


AX=FF00  BX=0100   CX=0000  DX=00FF   SP=FFEE   BP=0000   SI=0000 DI=0000
DS=0EF1  ES=0EF1   SS=0EF1  CS=0EF1   IP=0102    OV UP EI PL NZ NA PE CY
0EF1:0102 0402              ADD   AL,02
```

The answer we get is DX:AX, or FFFF00H, which is exactly correct, FFFFH × 100H = FFFF00H.

Multiplication can be done this way on the PS/2 or PC, but it is a slow process—not recommended for graphics programs, for example. On the other hand, multiplication was not available on Intel chips before the 8088 at all, so it is a marked improvement.

The DIV Instruction

To match MUL, there is DIV. This instruction does what you would expect—it divides (unsigned numbers). However, you have to keep in mind that this is not floating point arithmetic: The answer we will get is not something like 1.212331127, but will rather come in the form of a quotient and a remainder.

Again, the use of AX is assumed. If you execute an instruction like this:

```
DIV     BL
```

then the number in AX is divided by BL. The quotient is returned in AL and the remainder into AH. For example, let's divide 17 by 3. In whole number arithemetic, 17/3 goes like this:

DIV
assumes
the use of
DX:AX or
AX

$$\begin{array}{r} 5 \leftarrow \text{Quotient} \\ 3\overline{)17} \\ \underline{15} \\ 2 \leftarrow \text{Remainder} \end{array}$$

In other words, 17/3 is equal to 5, with a remainder of 2. If we had put 17 into AX, and 3 into BL, we will set 5 in AL and 2 in AH.

If we had used a 16-bit register in our DIV instruction:

```
DIV     BX
```

then the register pair DX:AX would be divided by BX. The quotient goes into AX and the remainder into DX:

```
DIV     BX → (DX:AX)/BX → Quotient in AX, Remainder in DX.
DIV     BL → AX/BL → Quotient in AL, Remainder in AH.
```

Let's give this a try in DEBUG too. We'll take the number FFFF05H and divide it by 100H. First, we load DX with the high part of this number, FFH (that is, 00FFH goes into DX), then the low part, FF05H, goes into AX. Then we can load BX with 100H, and finally, assemble our DIV BX at CS:100:

```
-RDX                ← Load DX
DX 0000
:00FF
-RAX                ← Load AX
AX 0000
:FF05
-RBX                ← Load BX
BX 0000
:100
-A100               ← Put in DIV BX
0EF1:0100 DIV BX
0EF1:0102
-R
AX=FF05  BX=0100  CX=0000  DX=00FF  SP=FFEE  BP=0000  SI=0000 DI=0000
DS=0EF1  ES=0EF1  SS=0EF1  CS=0EF1  IP=0100     NV UP EI PL NZ NA PO NC
0EF1:0100 F7F3          DIV   BX
```

We're all set. DX:AX together contain FFFF05H, and BX contains 100H. All we have to do is trace through this instruction and we'll find the result in AX and the remainder in DX:

```
-R
AX=FF05  BX=0100  CX=0000  DX=00FF  SP=FFEE  BP=0000  SI=0000 DI=0000
DS=0EF1  ES=0EF1  SS=0EF1  CS=0EF1  IP=0100     NV UP EI PL NZ NA PO NC
0EF1:0100 F7F3          DIV   BX
-T                  ← Trace through DIV BX
```

```
   Result                     Remainder
      |                           |
      ↓                           ↓
AX=FFFF  BX=0100  CX=0000  DX=0005  SP=FFEE  BP=0000  SI=0000 DI=0000
DS=0EF1  ES=0EF1  SS=0EF1  CS=0EF1  IP=0102   NV UP EI PL NZ NA PE NC
0EF1:0102 0402              ADD   AL,02
-Q
```

AX holds the result FFFFH, and DX holds the remainder, 00005. That is, FFFF05H/100H = FFFFH with a remainder of 5.

Let's put this new knowledge to work at once with an example program.

Converting Hex to ASCII

This is a program that introductory-assembly language books should always have in them. It converts a number from a register to an ASCII string, ready to be printed out.

If you're not feeling very adept at hexadecimal yet, this program could help you when you have to convert your results into output. Just call it as a subroutine—it will take the number in AX and convert it into an ASCII string at the location ASCII_STRING. Here, we will make it a stand alone .COM file, but, of course, you could include it as a procedure in your own programs.

We start with the usual .COM file shell:

```
CODE_SEG            SEGMENT
          ASSUME    CS:CODE_SEG,DS:CODE_SEG
          ORG       100H
ENTRY:    JMP       CONVERT
          ASCII_STRING   DB 7 DUP("$")    ←
CONVERT PROC        NEAR
          :
          INT       20H
CONVERT ENDP
CODE_SEG            ENDS
          END       ENTRY
```

The ASCII string that we are going to use will be terminated with "$", so we can be smart and set up ASCII_STRING with more "$"s than we'll need, insuring us of at least a 1 at the end of the string after we put all our characters in place.

> Note that if you use CONVERT more than once in a program, you should reset ASCII_STRING to all "$"s.

Let's store our current location in the character string, ASCII_STRING, in SI. This means that, to write an ASCII digit, we'll just have to write it to [SI]. To begin, we load SI with the offset address of the beginning of ASCII_STRING:

```
CODE_SEG         SEGMENT
        ASSUME   CS:CODE_SEG,DS:CODE_SEG
        ORG      100H
ENTRY:  JMP      CONVERT
        ASCII_STRING   DB 7 DUP("$")
CONVERT PROC     NEAR          LEA     SI,ASCII_STRING          ←
        :
        INT      20H
CONVERT ENDP
CODE_SEG         ENDS
        END      ENTRY
```

The number will be passed in AX. All we have to do is convert it into ASCII. The first thing we'll do is check to see if it's a positive number.

If not, we can store a minus sign "–" in the beginning of ASCII_STRING. Since it will be easier for us to work with DIV using positive numbers, we will change the number's sign to positive with NEG after storing the "–" in ASCII string:

```
CODE_SEG         SEGMENT
        ASSUME   CS:CODE_SEG,DS:CODE_SEG
        ORG      100H
ENTRY:  JMP      CONVERT
        ASCII_STRING   DB 7 DUP("$")
CONVERT PROC     NEAR
        LEA      SI,ASCII_STRING
        CMP      AX,0                      ←
        JGE      POSITIVE                  ←
        NEG      AX                        ←
        MOV      BYTE PTR [SI],"-"         ←
        INC      SI                        ←
POSITIVE:
        :
        INT      20H
CONVERT ENDP

CODE_SEG         ENDS

        END      ENTRY
```

Recall that if nothing tells the assembler what the size of the operands are going to be, as in an instruction like: MOV [SI],"–", then we have to let it know explicitly, with a BYTE PTR Pseudo-Op, like this:

```
MOV      BYTE PTR [SI],"-"
```

Now that the sign has been taken care of (we do not load a " + " sign if the number is positive), we have to consider how to change this number in AX into base 10.

Converting Between Bases

If we had a number like 503, in decimal already, we could just divide it by 10 and check the remainder: 503/10 = 50 with a remainder of 3. This remainder, 3, is the right-most digit in the number—this is where remainders come in handy.

If we kept going, 50/10 = 5 with a remainder of 0, and 5/10 = 0 with a remainder of 5, we see that, each time we divide by 10, the remainder gives us successive digits (in backwards order: 3, 0, 5).

This will work if we divide hex numbers, too. If we take the hex number 10H (= 16 decimal), and divide it by 10 (decimal), then the result would be 1 with a remainder of 6. That is, if we had 10H in the AX register, and divided it by 10D (10D = 10 decimal), then we would get a result of 1 and a remainder of 6. In this way, we can keep dividing numbers by 10, and storing the remainders, until there is nothing left. Each time we divide by 10D, we peel off another decimal digit.

Here, we will load BX with 10 to prepare for the division. We are going to take the number in DX:AX, and divide it by one word, BX, which will always hold 10.

```
CODE_SEG        SEGMENT
        ASSUME  CS:CODE_SEG,DS:CODE_SEG
        ORG     100H
ENTRY:  JMP     CONVERT
ASCII_STRING    DB 7 DUP("$")
CONVERT PROC    NEAR
        LEA     SI,ASCII_STRING
        CMP     AX,0
        JGE     POSITIVE
        NEG     AX
        MOV     BYTE PTR [SI],"-"
        INC     SI
POSITIVE:
        MOV     BX,10       ←
        :
        INT     20H
CONVERT ENDP

CODE_SEG        ENDS

        END     ENTRY
```

Using a word register, BX, with DIV means that we will be dividing DX:AX by BX. In fact, all we really want to do is divide AX by 10, not DX:AX, so why are we using a word division? As we will see later, it will be easier for us if the remainder of the division is put into a word register, as it will be if we divide DX:AX by BX (remainder goes into DX). We will want the remainder in a 16-bit register later. Although it could be done either way, dividing DX:AX by BX will result in a quicker, more efficient central loop, so we'll do it that way. Since we only want to divide the number in AX by BX, we will make sure that DX is always 0 before the division.

We will need the loop next. In this loop, we will keep dividing the number in AX by 10 until there is nothing left. Inside this loop, we will keep track of the number of times we have looped in CX—this will be the number of digits.

```
CODE_SEG        SEGMENT
        ASSUME  CS:CODE_SEG,DS:CODE_SEG
        ORG     100H
ENTRY:  JMP     CONVERT
        ASCII_STRING    DB 7 DUP("$")
CONVERT PROC    NEAR
        LEA     SI,ASCII_STRING
        CMP     AX,0
        JGE     POSITIVE
        NEG     AX
        MOV     BYTE PTR [SI],"-"
        INC     SI
POSITIVE:
        MOV     BX,10
        MOV     CX,0                            ←
THELOOP:                                        ←
        MOV     DX,0                 ← Set up DX:AX
        [Divide by 10.]                         ←
        [Store the remainder.]                  ←
        [Increment CX = Number of digits.]      ←
        [Check whether the result is zero yet.] ←
        JNE     THELOOP                         ←
        INT     20H
CONVERT ENDP

CODE_SEG        ENDS

        END     ENTRY
```

Here is what our loop looks like in pseudo-programming language:

```
THELOOP:
        MOV     DX,0    ← Set up DX for the division DX:AX/BX
        [Divide AX by 10.]
        [Store the remainder.]
        [Increment CX = Number of digits.]
        [Check whether the result is zero yet.]
        JNE     THELOOP
```

Dividing by 10 is easy—all we have to do is say DIV BX (since BX will always hold 10). This will leave the result in AX and the remainder in DX. We want to save the remainder, and keep the result for the next time, when we divide by 10 again.

Notice that as we divide successively by 10, we will be shaving decimal digits off in reverse order. 503 will come apart like this: 3, 0, 5. There is a perfect way of storing these numbers and then retrieving them in the reverse order that we want—the stack. This is the usual thing to do when converting numbers to base 10. As base 10 digits are peeled off, we could push them onto the stack (3, 0, 5). Later, when we pop them, they'll be in the right order (5, 0, 3). This means that storing the remainder is easy—we just have to push the register it's in, DX (this is why it's more convenient to have the remainder returned in a 16-bit register):

```
CODE_SEG        SEGMENT
        ASSUME  CS:CODE_SEG,DS:CODE_SEG
        ORG     100H
ENTRY:  JMP     CONVERT
        ASCII_STRING    DB 7 DUP("$")
CONVERT PROC    NEAR
        LEA     SI,ASCII_STRING
        CMP     AX,0
        JGE     POSITIVE
        NEG     AX
        MOV     BYTE PTR [SI],"-"
        INC     SI
POSITIVE:
        MOV     BX,10
        MOV     CX,0
THELOOP:
        MOV     DX,0
        DIV     BX          <-
        PUSH    DX          <-
        INC     CX          <-
        [Check whether the result is zero yet.]
        JNE     THELOOP
        INT     20H
CONVERT ENDP
CODE_SEG        ENDS
        END     ENTRY
```

Now we have to prepare for the next time we divide DX:AX by 10. At the top of the loop, we set DX to zero, so DX:AX will really be 0000:AX, as it should be. AX holds the result of the last division, as it should—because this is the result that we want to divide by 10 again the next time around.

Before we do that, however, we have to check and see whether or not AX—the result—is zero. If it is, there are no more digits to get; if there are no more digits to get, then we want to finish with this loop. We can check this with the last two lines in the loop:

```
CODE_SEG        SEGMENT
        ASSUME  CS:CODE_SEG,DS:CODE_SEG
        ORG     100H
ENTRY:  JMP     CONVERT
        ASCII_STRING    DB 7 DUP("$")
CONVERT PROC    NEAR
```

```
                LEA     SI,ASCII_STRING
                CMP     AX,0
                JGE     POSITIVE
                NEG     AX
                MOV     BYTE PTR [SI],"-"
                INC     SI
        POSITIVE:
                MOV     BX,10
                MOV     CX,0
       _THELOOP:
      |         MOV     DX,0
      |         DIV     BX
      |         PUSH    DX
      |         INC     CX
      |         CMP     AX,0      ←
      |__JNE    THELOOP   ←
                :
                INT     20H
        CONVERT ENDP
        CODE_SEG        ENDS
                END     ENTRY
```

If AX is not zero, we will keep looping until it is, and all the digits have been peeled off onto the stack.

Getting the Digits Off the Stack

After the loop is done, we have to start thinking about getting the digits off the stack and into ASCII_STRING. We kept track of how many digits there were, in CX. That means that we can simply pop CX times—using CX as a loop index—and put the digit popped each time into ASCII_STRING. Our location in ASCII_STRING is [SI], which we will have to increment each time we put a character into it. Here's how the POP loop looks:

```
        CODE_SEG        SEGMENT
                ASSUME  CS:CODE_SEG,DS:CODE_SEG
                ORG     100H
        ENTRY:  JMP     CONVERT
                ASCII_STRING    DB 7 DUP("$")
        CONVERT PROC    NEAR
                LEA     SI,ASCII_STRING
                CMP     AX,0
                JGE     POSITIVE
                NEG     AX
                MOV     BYTE PTR [SI],"-"
                INC     SI
        POSITIVE:
                MOV     BX,10
                MOV     CX,0
       _THELOOP:
      |         MOV     DX,0
      |         DIV     BX
      |         PUSH    DX
      |         INC     CX
      |         CMP     AX,0
      |__JNE    THELOOP
    →   POPLOOP:POP     AX
                :
```

```
              :
→             LOOP      POPLOOP
              INT       20H
      CONVERT ENDP
      CODE_SEG          ENDS
              END       ENTRY
```

Every time we pop a value into AX, the digit we want will be in AL.
To make it an ASCII value, we will have to add "0" to it. Then we can
store it in ASCII_STRING, at location [SI], increment SI for the next
digit, and loop again to pop the next digit:

```
      CODE_SEG          SEGMENT
              ASSUME    CS:CODE_SEG,DS:CODE_SEG
              ORG       100H
      ENTRY:  JMP       CONVERT
              ASCII_STRING   DB 7 DUP("$")
      CONVERT PROC      NEAR
              LEA       SI,ASCII_STRING
              CMP       AX,0
              JGE       POSITIVE
              NEG       AX
              MOV       BYTE PTR [SI],"-"
              INC       SI
      POSITIVE:
              MOV       BX,10
              MOV       CX,0
      THELOOP:
              MOV       DX,0
              DIV       BX
              PUSH      DX
              INC       CX
              CMP       AX,0
              JNE       THELOOP
      POPLOOP:POP       AX
              ADD       AL,"0"          ←
              MOV       [SI],AL         ←
              INC       SI              ←
              LOOP      POPLOOP
              INT       20H
      CONVERT ENDP
      CODE_SEG          ENDS
              END       ENTRY
```

That's all there is to the program CONVERT. Give it a try, or use it in
your own programs—just pass a number in AX, and the corresponding
base 10 number will appear in ASCII in ASCII_STRING.

A little program like this has many uses, since it converts from
machine arithmetic to human arithmetic. For example, if you are
debugging, and want to know the contents of one of the registers, you
can have CONVERT make up an ASCII string, and have it printed out
at run time.

Signed Multiplication—IMUL

The 8088 also has the ability to do multiplication and division that will keep track of the correct sign. These two commands are IMUL and IDIV.

> For accuracy, you might sometimes want to use all bits in a word, even the sign bit. In that case, you should use unsigned numbers, but keep track of the sign yourself, adjusting it correctly at the end of the calculation.

IMUL is the integer multiply instruction. Fundamentally, it is just like MUL, but it works with signed numbers. If you say:

```
IMUL    CL
```

then the microprocessor will multiply AL x CL (including signs) and put the result in (the full 16 bits of) AX. If you say:

```
IMUL    CX
```

then the microprocessor will multiply AX × CX (including signs, of course), and put the result into DX:AX. Let's give this a try by multiplying 5 by −1. We already know that −5 = FBH, so we expect that as an answer. In byte multiplication, you end with a full word answer, so we expect a result of FFFBH.

In DEBUG, we load the registers (let's use BL) assemble an IMUL BL, and then trace through it:

```
A>DEBUG
-RAX                    ← Load AL with 5
AX 0000
:5
-RBX                    ← Load BL with
BX 0000
:FF
-A100
0EF1:0100 IMUL    BL    ← Get our IMUL instruction ready
0EF1:0102
-R
AX=0005  BX=00FF  CX=0000  DX=0000  SP=FFEE  BP=0000  SI=0000 DI=0000
DS=0EF1  ES=0EF1  SS=0EF1  CS=0EF1  IP=0100   NV UP EI PL NZ NA PO NC
0EF1:0100 F6EB            IMUL    BL
-
```

And we're all ready to trace through IMUL and multiply 5 by −1. Here's the result:

```
-R
AX=0005  BX=00FF  CX=0000  DX=0000  SP=FFEE  BP=0000  SI=0000 DI=0000
DS=0EF1  ES=0EF1  SS=0EF1  CS=0EF1  IP=0100     NV UP EI PL NZ NA PO NC
0EF1:0100 F6EB           IMUL    BL
-T                           ← Trace through IMUL


AX=FFFB  BX=00FF  CX=0000  DX=0000  SP=FFEE  BP=0000  SI=0000 DI=0000
DS=0EF1  ES=0EF1  SS=0EF1  CS=0EF1  IP=0102     NV UP EI PL ZR AC PE NC
0EF1:0102 0402           ADD     AL,02
-Q
```

The result, as expected, is FFFBH, the word representation of -5.

> Note that the byte representation of −5 is FBH, the word representation is FFFBH, and the doubleword representation is FFFF:FFFBH.

Just to see what happens, let's multiply the two bytes FFH (−1) by FFH (−1). We expect an answer of 1 to show up in AX:

```
A>DEBUG
-RAX                 ← Load AL with −1
AX 0000
:FF
-RBX                 ← Load BL with −1
BX 0000
:FF
-A100
0EF1:0100 IMUL    BL    ← Get ready to IMUL them.
0EF1:0102
-R
AX=00FF  BX=00FF  CX=0000  DX=0000  SP=FFEE  BP=0000  SI=0000 DI=0000
DS=0EF1  ES=0EF1  SS=0EF1  CS=0EF1  IP=0100     NV UP EI PL NZ NA PO NC
0EF1:0100 F6EB           IMUL    BL                ← All set. Let's Trace.
-T


AX=0001  BX=00FF  CX=0000  DX=0000  SP=FFEE  BP=0000  SI=0000 DI=0000
DS=0EF1  ES=0EF1  SS=0EF1  CS=0EF1  IP=0102     NV UP EI PL ZR NA PE NC
0EF1:0102 0402           ADD     AL,02
-Q
```

And we find that IMUL handled the sign correctly, $-1 \times -1 = 1$.

The IDIV Instruction

IDIV is the corresponding signed division instruction. Again, you use it just like DIV, but the signs are kept track of automatically.

If you say:

```
IDIV    CL
```

then AX/CL is calculated and the result goes into AL and the remainder into AH. If you say:

```
IDIV    CX
```

then, as before, DX:AX/CX is calculated; the result goes into AX and the remainder into DX.

▌ What's wrong with an instruction like IDIV DX? ▌

Using IMUL and IDIV can be important if you want to keep track of signs. Keep in mind that, once you choose, you must stick with using IMUL and IDIV throughout your program—FFFFH looks like −1 to IMUL and IDIV, but it looks like a big number to MUL and DIV. If you mix these instructions, you'll get mixed results.

Using the Carry Flag

ADC—Add with Carry

One word isn't really very long. At best, values up to 65,535 can be stored. Can you imagine a calculator that could only work with numbers up to 65,535? That's only four places of accuracy. If you wanted to enter a number like 90,017, you'd be beyond the calculator's range.

That is just what happens in the 8088. If you are restricted to one-word numbers, then your accuracy is very poor (unless you have a math coprocessor inside your machine). In an effort to help rectify this, INTEL added some instructions that let you chain a number of addition or subtraction instructions together by keeping track of the carry bit. ADC is the instruction for adding when the carry bit is involved—ADC means Add with Carry.

ADC is an add instruction you use after ADD. If you wanted to use double word numbers (and couldn't take advantage of the 80386's 32-bit registers) like DX:AX and BX:CX, you can still add them together using ADD followed by ADC. What we want is this:

```
  DX:AX
+ BX:CX
```

And this can be broken down into adding AX and CX first—this might produce a carry—and then adding the possible carry with DX and BX.

In assembly language, this is the way you'd do it:

```
ADD     AX,CX
ADC     BX,CX     ←
```

First we add AX and CX in the usual way. If there was a carry, then the carry flag was set. The ADC BX,CX instruction adds the carry flag (1 = set, 0 = not set) in with the two registers, BX and CX.

> Keep in mind that carries in the binary addition of two numbers can only be 0s or 1s—you cannot have a carry of 3, for example. Thus the carry flag is adequate to hold the carry bit.

In this way, the carry from the first addition is correctly treated. Keep in mind that the second addition (ADC BX,CX) could have produced a carry as well, and, to be sure, you should check for it.

Here's an example that preserves 48-bit accuracy. If we have a program with six memory word locations—A1–A3 and B1–B3, and we want to add them like this:

```
  B3:B2:B1
+ A3:A2:A1
```

Our program might look something like this:

```
CODE_SEG        SEGMENT
        ASSUME  CS:CODE_SEG,DS:CODE_SEG
        ORG     100H
ENTRY:  JMP     PROG
        A3      DW      ?           ← Define A1 - A3
        A2      DW      ?
        A1      DW      ?
        B3      DW      ?           ← Define B1 - B3
        B2      DW      ?
        B1      DW      ?
        CARRY   DW      0           ← Possible carry from whole addition
PROG    PROC    NEAR
        MOV     AX,A1               ← Put A1, A2, A3 into AX, BX, CX
        MOV     BX,A2
        MOV     CX,A3
        MOV     DX,0                ← Clear DX
        ADD     AX,B1               ← First ADD
        ADC     BX,B2               ← Then ADC
        ADC     CX,B3
        ADC     CARRY,DX            ← Put carry into CARRY.
        INT     20H
PROG    ENDP
CODE_SEG        ENDS
        END     ENTRY
```

What happens here is that first we load the memory words A1–A3 into the registers AX, BX, and CX for easy handling. This is because we cannot ADD A1 to B1 directly—you cannot use two memory locations in the same instruction. We have to add a memory location to a register instead. Then we simply use ADD followed by ADC:

```
ADD     AX,B1          ← First ADD
ADC     BX,B2          ← Then ADC
ADC     CX,B3
```

At the very end, we include this line, having previously set DX to 0:

```
ADC     CARRY,DX       ← Put carry into CARRY.
```

All this does is keep track of the possible carry from the whole addition A3:A2:A1 + B3:B2:B1. If there is a carry, CARRY will end up being 1. If there was no carry, CARRY will be 0.

The carry from the whole calculation could be treated as an error, if you wanted to. If we wanted to add the number held in DX:AX to the number held in BX:CX, and if both were unsigned (or could be made so by finding their two's complements), we might use these instructions:

```
ADD     AX,CX          [Add DX:AX + BX:CX]
ADC     DX,BX
JC      ERROR
```

We first add the lower 16 bits of both numbers, held respectively in AX and CX. The result is stored in AX. If this answer is too large to hold in 16 bits, there will be a carry and the carry flag will be set. To include that carry in the subsequent addition of the top 16 bits, we use ADC:

```
       ADD     AX,CX          [Add DX:AX + BX:CX]
 →     ADC     DX,BX
       JC      ERROR
```

ADC includes the carry, if there was one, in this addition. The final result is stored in DX:AX. In this calculation we are not prepared for answers longer than 32 bits (although that can be handled with an additional ADC to as many stages as you desire), so if there was a carry after the second addition, we jump to a location marked Error.

The SBB Instruction

There is a counterpart for subtraction, SBB. SBB means Subtract with Borrow. After subtracting the two operands, it subtracts the carry flag from the result.

If we subtract a big number from a small one, we have to borrow from higher order places. Intel's designers included the SBB command for expressly this use:

```
    SUB     AX,CX       [Sub DX:AX - BX:CX]
→   SBB     DX,BX
    JC      ERROR
```

Here we are figuring out what DX:AX − BX:CX is:

$$DX:AX$$
$$-\ \underline{BX:CX}$$

First we subtract CX from AX (with SUB AX,CX). If this left the carry flag set, a "borrow" from a higher place was required. This is taken into account when we use SBB for the second instruction (with SBB DX,BX). The result will be left in DX:AX.

Again, if there is a net carry, we consider it an error and jump to ERROR, although you could handle it another way if you wished.

Big Time Multiplying

What if we did not want to limit ourselves to multiplication results that were only two words long? What if what we were doing required more accuracy? We've just seen how to extend addition and subtraction calculations to arbitrary lengths (by the use of ADD, followed by successive ADCs, or SUB followed by SBBs). Can we do the same for MUL and DIV?

The MUL instruction insists that you start out with the AX register. If you say MUL BX, then the 8088 multiplies AX by BX and leaves the 32-bit result in DX:AX. If we wanted to multiply AX:DX by BX:CX, we must be prepared for a 64-bit result, using up all our registers.

More common when we deal with multiplication of larger numbers is the use of memory locations. We could, for instance, multiply the number Y1:Y0, held in 16-bit words we've named Y1 and Y0, by the number Z1:Z0, locations Z1 and Z0. We would have to be prepared to store our result in four memory words as the number, say, A:B:C:D.

In other words, this is what we want to do:

$$\begin{array}{r} Y1 \;:\; Y0 \\ \times \; \underline{Z1 \;:\; Z0} \\ Z0 \times Y0 \\ + \; Z0 \times Y1 \\ + \; Z1 \times Y0 \\ + \; \underline{Z1 \times Y1} \end{array}$$

$$2^{32}\, Z1 \times Y1 \;+\; 2^{16}\, Z0 \times Y1 \;+\; 2^{16}\, Z1 \times Y0 \;+\; Z0 \times Y0$$

We supply Y1:Y0 and Z1:Z0—what we want to get out is A:B:C:D, and this number is equal to the final line above:

$$A:B:C:D = 2^{32}\, Z1 \times Y1 + 2^{16}\, Z0 \times Y1 + 2^{16}\, Z1 \times Y0 + Z0 \times Y0$$

Let's write a program to do this, giving us four-word multiplication accuracy. We're not going to go through this program step by step—it would be too tedious. All we are doing is mirroring the normal multiplication process anyway. Here's the program. To use it, load Z1:Z0 and Y1:Y0 in the data area. The result will be left in A:B:C:D;

```
CODE_SEG        SEGMENT
        ASSUME  CS:CODE_SEG,DS:CODE_SEG
        ORG     100H
ENTRY:  JMP     MULTI
        Y0      DW      0
        Y1      DW      0
        Z0      DW      0
        Z1      DW      0
        A       DW      0
        B       DW      0
        C       DW      0
        D       DW      0
MULTI:  MOV     B,0                     ;Multiplies Y1:Y0 by Z1:Z0 to get A:B:C:D
        MOV     A,0
        MOV     AX,Z0
        MUL     Y0
        MOV     D,AX
        MOV     C,DX
        MOV     AX,Z0
        MUL     Y1
        ADD     C,AX
        ADC     B,DX
        ADC     A,0
        MOV     AX,Z1
        MUL     Y0
        ADD     C,AX
        ADC     B,DX
        ADC     A,0
        MOV     AX,Z1
        MUL     Y1
        ADD     B,AX
        ADC     A,DX
        INT     20H
CODE_SEG        ENDS
        END     ENTRY
```

By breaking up the result into partial results, we were able to multiply Y1:Y0 by Z1:Z0 to get A:B:C:D. This result is 64 bits long—not bad as far as accuracy is concerned (although the math coprocessor's registers are 80 bits long).

Big Time Division

Unfortunately, we are not so lucky when it comes to division. While we can break up multiplication into what you saw—partial products—there is no similar way to handle division.

Instead, there are fast, bit-by-bit algorithms that can do large divisions for you. They mimic the process of long division in some clever time- and space-saving ways. Such an algorithm may be found in *Advanced Assembly Language for the IBM PC*, where it is examined in excruciating detail. Other than that, you'll have to stick to the DIV commands.

Bit Manipulations

It is frequently important in assembly language to work with individual bits in a word or byte. As we have seen, the operating system stores information in the bits of specific bytes in its data areas.

There are a number of assembly-language instructions that we can use here. The first are our old friends, SHL and SHR.

> The 80386 has a series of *bit test* instructions, BT, BTC, BTR, and BTS. These can be very useful when needed.

SHR and SHL

These two, SHR and SHL, shift quantities to the right and left, respectively. You can shift a number of times to the right or left; on the 8088 and 8086, if the number of places to shift is greater than one, place it into CL (then use SHR AX,CL). Otherwise, you can say SHR BX,1 or SHL CX,1. On the 80186–80386, you can use an immediate number; you do not need to use CL.

With SHR and SHL, the bit that is "opened" up is set to 0. For example, if we shift AL to the right one:

```
AL:     10101010
          :
     Shift to the right by 1 using SHR
          :
        01010101
          →
```

Use of the carry flag while shifting

In addition, the bit that was shifted "out" by SHR or SHL—here a 0 was shifted off the right hand side—goes into the carry flag. You can test what this bit was with JC or JNC. In fact, this is a common way of checking bit values.

```
Shifting Right      AL: 10101010
─────────────               :
                        SHR AL,1
                            :
                        01010101  →  0  →  Carry Flag
                            →
Shifting Left       AL: 10101010
─────────────               :
                        SHL AL,1
                            :
Carry Flag     ←  1  ←  01010100
                            ←
```

Using SHL for multiplication

SHL may be used for multiplication, as well. Every time you shift one place to the left, it is the same as mutliplying by two. For example, you could multiply AX by 5 (5 = 2 × 2 + 1) this way:

```
MOV     BX,AX     ← Make a copy of AX
SHL     AX,1      ← Multiply it by 2
SHL     AX,1      ← And 2 again to make 4
ADD     AX,BX     ← Add the copy in BX to make 5
```

Since SHL and ADD combinations are *much* faster than ordinary MUL instructions, use them whenever you can. Graphics routines, where time is crucial, usually try to break up math this way.

Using SHR to divide

In the same way, SHR can be used as a crude version of DIV, since shifting to the right once is equivalent to dividing by 2. The "remainder" of this division will be put into the carry flag.

SAR and SAL

These two instructions, SAR and SAL, stand for Arithmetic Shift Right and Arithmetic Shift Left. You can use these on signed numbers.

If you shift a number like 01010101B to the left by 1 with SAL, the sign bit will change (since the new number is 10101010B). On the other hand, SAL will set the overflow flag in this case, and you can check it to see if the sign did change. (For some reason, the overflow flag is only set correctly if you shift to the left once—more than that means that the overflow flag will be undefined.)

The SAR instruction preserves the sign of the operand it is shifting to the right. Let's look at the number 10101010B. This can be regarded as a negative number; SAR would have preserved its sign, whereas SHR would not (remember that SHR always sets the newly opened bit to 0). SAR will place a 1 in the top bit to preserve the sign bit in this case:

```
AL:      10101010
              :
    Shift to the right by 1 using SHR
              :
          11010101
             →
```

Again, the bit that is pushed off either end will go into the carry flag.

```
Arithmetic Shifting Right     AL: 10101010
_____            :
                               SAR AL,1
                                       :
                               11010101 → 0 → Carry Flag
                                  →
Arithmetic Shifting Left      AL: 10101010
_____             :
                               SAL AL,1
                                       :
                Carry Flag ← 1 ← 01010100
                                  ←
```

The Rotate Instructions: RCL, RCR, ROL, and ROR

Here are four more instructions that work on a bit-by-bit level on either bytes or words. These instructions *rotate* words or bytes.

For example, let's examine ROL, rotate left. When ROL is used, the top-most bit, that is, the left-most bit, is taken out, and all the other bits are shifted to the left by 1. Then the original left-most bit goes into the right-most location. It looks like this if we ROL AX,1:

```
AX:      0001000100010001  ←  Start like this

AX:       001000100010001  ←  Take left-most bit.
          └──────┐
                 0

          →
AX:   ←  001000100010001   ←  Shift everything left 1
         └──────┐
                0

AX:      001000100010001   ←  Move original left-most
         └─────────────┐        bit into bottom place
               └─0──────┘
                 →
AX:      0010001000100010  ←  Yielding this
```

We can see that 0001000100010001B rotated once to the left becomes 0010001000100010B. Let's do this exact example in DEBUG. We start off with AX = 0001000100010001B = 1111H (since there are four binary digits per hex digit), and we'll ROL a few times by assembling ROL AX,1 starting at 100H:

```
C>DEBUG
-A100
0EF1:0100 ROL        AX,1              ← Set up our ROLs
0EF1:0102 ROL        AX,1
0EF1:0104 ROL        AX,1
0EF1:0106 ROL        AX,1
0EF1:0108
-RAX                                   ← Set up AX to 1111H
AX 0000
:1111
-R
AX=1111  BX=0000  CX=0000  DX=0000  SP=FFEE  BP=0000  SI=0000 DI=0000
DS=0EF1  ES=0EF1  SS=0EF1  CS=0EF1  IP=0100    NV UP EI PL NZ NA PO NC
0EF1:0100 D1C0          ROL    AX,1    ← Ready to rotate
-T
```

We can trace through the first ROL AX,1. As we saw, this changed 0001000100010001B to 0010001000100010B. Here's what happens:

```
-R
AX=1111  BX=0000  CX=0000  DX=0000  SP=FFEE  BP=0000  SI=0000 DI=0000
DS=0EF1  ES=0EF1  SS=0EF1  CS=0EF1  IP=0100    NV UP EI PL NZ NA PONC
0EF1:0100 D1C0          ROL    AX,1    ← Ready to rotate.
-T                      ← Rotate AX to the left once.
  ↓
AX=2222  BX=0000  CX=0000  DX=0000  SP=FFEE  BP=0000  SI=0000 DI=0000
DS=0EF1  ES=0EF1  SS=0EF1  CS=0EF1  IP=0102    NV UP EI PL NZ NA PO NC
0EF1:0102 D1C0          ROL    AX,1
```

The result is 2222H, as it should be; 0010001000100010B = 2222H. We can rotate again to get 4444H, then 8888H; then a final rotation (the fourth) will move the original 1s back into place, one hex digit higher. Here it is:

```
-R ↓
AX=1111  BX=0000  CX=0000  DX=0000  SP=FFEE  BP=0000  SI=0000 DI=0000
DS=0EF1  ES=0EF1  SS=0EF1  CS=0EF1  IP=0100     NV UP EI PL NZ NA PO NC
0EF1:0100 D1C0           ROL     AX,1        ← Ready to rotate.
-T ↓                        ← Rotate AX to the left once.

AX=2222  BX=0000  CX=0000  DX=0000  SP=FFEE  BP=0000  SI=0000 DI=0000
DS=0EF1  ES=0EF1  SS=0EF1  CS=0EF1  IP=0102     NV UP EI PL NZ NA PO NC
0EF1:0102 D1C0           ROL     AX,1
-T ↓

AX=4444  BX=0000  CX=0000  DX=0000  SP=FFEE  BP=0000  SI=0000 DI=0000
DS=0EF1  ES=0EF1  SS=0EF1  CS=0EF1  IP=0104     NV UP EI PL NZ NA PO NC
0EF1:0104 D1C0           ROL     AX,1
-T ↓

AX=8888  BX=0000  CX=0000  DX=0000  SP=FFEE  BP=0000  SI=0000 DI=0000
DS=0EF1  ES=0EF1  SS=0EF1  CS=0EF1  IP=0106     OV UP EI PL NZ NA PO NC
0EF1:0106 D1C0           ROL     AX,1
-T ↓

AX=1111  BX=0000  CX=0000  DX=0000  SP=FFEE  BP=0000  SI=0000 DI=0000
DS=0EF1  ES=0EF1  SS=0EF1  CS=0EF1  IP=0108     OV UP EI PL NZ NA PO CY
0EF1:0108 CB            RETF
-Q
```

That's how ROL works. ROR works the same way, except that bits are rotated to the right instead. For example, if we rotate 1111H to the right once, we'll end up with 8888H.

```
AX:     0001000100010001  ← Start like this

AX:     0001000100001000  ← Take right-most bit
           → 1_____|

AX:     0001000100001000→ Shift everything right 1
              1_____|

AX:     0001000100001000  ← Move original right-most
        |_____          bit into the top place
             |
        |____1_____|
           ←
AX:     1000100010001000  ← Yielding this.
```

Rotating Through the Carry

RCL and RCR are somewhat different. They include the carry flag in their rotations: The bit that is rotated "out" becomes the new carry flag, and the carry flag is rotated in to take its place. In other words, these instructions rotate *through* the carry flag.

Let's look at RCL. If we have 1111H in AX, and 1 in the carry flag (CY), then here's what will happen when we use RCL AX,1:

```
AX:       0001000100010001  ←  Start like this
                CY          ←  CY = 1


AX:   ←   001000100010001   ←  Now RCL
          :
          :              1
          :..0   CY......:
          →           →
AX:       0010001000100011  ←  Yielding this
                CY          ←  CY = 0
```

In this case, we would get 2223H, since the carry flag was rotated in to make the last digit 3, not 2 (and CY became 0).

If you think of the carry flag as the 9 bit of a byte, or the seventeenth bit of a word, then RCL and RCR rotate these nine-bit bytes or 17-bit words. If you want to examine the carry bit, or want to move a bit into the carry bit, this is good way to do it.

RCR also rotates through the carry flag, but to the right. If we have 0 in the carry flag (CY) and 1111H in AX, this is what RCR AX,1 look like:

```
AX:       0001000100010001  ←  Start like this
                CY          ←  CY = 0


AX:       000100010001000  →  Now RCR
                         :
          0              :
          :....CY   1....:
          ←        ←
AX:       0000100010001000  ←  Yielding this
                CY          ←  CY = 1
```

In this case, RCR AX,1 yields 0888H (and CY = 1). Again, with ROL, ROR, RCL, and RCR, you have to specify the number of times to rotate in CL—if that number is greater than 1—on the 8088 and 8086. With the 80186 –80386, you can give immediate values.

Logical Instructions

There is a last class of math instructions in the PS/2 or PC, the logical instructions: AND, OR, and XOR. We are going to include TEST in this group because, as we shall see, it operates much like AND.

AND and OR

We have already seen AND and OR in action, at least briefly. Their chief use in assembly-language programs is setting (i.e. setting equal to 1), resetting (setting equal to 0) bits in a byte, or testing the value of a certain bit.

AND does a bit-by-bit comparison of the two operands. When the bits meet, here is how AND calculates the result:

```
AND │ 0   1
────┼──────
  0 │ 0   0
  1 │ 0   1
```

Using masks

As you can see, both bit 1 *and* bit 2 have to be 1 before the result will be 1. This is a useful property is making up what are called *masks*.

Suppose that we were interested in bit 1 (that is, the 2s place—the right-most bit is bit 0) of a byte, which we have in AL.

```
                    │
                    ↓
AL  =   01010111
```

If we wanted to isolate that bit, and check whether it was set, we could AND AL with a "mask," which was set to this value in binary: 00000010B. In other words, only bit 1 of this mask is set. When we AND AL,00000010B, then all the other bits in AL will meet 0s, and their results will be zero. If the second bit in AL was set, the result of AND AL,00000010B will be 00000010B, or two. If the bit was *not* set, the result will be 00000000B, or zero.

Masks are a frequently used tool to isolate individual bits.

On the other hand, masks can also be used with OR to set bits. OR works like this on a bit-by-bit level:

```
OR  │ 0   1
────┼──────
  0 │ 0   1
  1 │ 1   1
```

In other words, if either bit 0 *or* bit 1 is one, the result of ORing them will be one. In this case, if we had the same mask, 00000010B, we could OR AL,00000010B. All the bits besides bit 1 will meet zeroes. If a zero is ORed with a zero, the result is zero. If a one is ORed with zero, the result is one. That is, all the other bits will have their identities preserved. ORing a byte with 00000000 will not change the byte.

But bit 1's place in the mask is already one. This means that—no matter what bit 1 was before—when it is ORed with one, it will become one. No matter what the bit was before, ORing it with one will set it to one. The bit will be set. When used with OR, masks are tools to set bits in a word or byte.

XOR

XOR, or Exclusive OR does this on a bit-by-bit level:

```
XOR | 0  1
----+------
 0  | 0  1
 1  | 1  0
```

When XORed, two ones will become zero. Also, two zeroes XORed together become zero. Any two of the same thing XORed together will become zero—that means that anything XORed with itself will become zero. We saw this in the beginning of our .EXE file shell when we set AX to zero with the instruction:

```
XOR     AX,AX
```

▌   Notice that XOR is identical to OR except when two ones meet.   ▐

TEST

The TEST instruction is just like AND, except that it does not change either operand being ANDed. All it does is set up the flags so that an appropriate jump may be made. For example,

```
TEST    AL,00000010B
```

will AND AL with 00000010B—as far as the flags are concerned. It won't actually change the value in AL. If bit 1 (the second bit from the right) was zero, TEST AL,00000010B will give a result of zero. We can check this result with a conditional jump that we have seen before—JZ. The JZ conditional jump is taken if some mathematical operation just resulted in a value of zero. For example, if 0 is in AL, the instructions:

```
TEST    AL,00000010B
JZ      AL_BIT_1_IS_ZERO
```

will cause us to jump to the label AL_BIT_1_IS_ZERO. Using TEST, you can check an individual bit in a word or byte. All you have to do is to set the mask correctly—put a one in the bit place(s) you want to test, and a zero in all other places. If the bit was set, the result will not be zero; if the bit was not set, the result will be zero. Following TEST by JZ is not an uncommon sight in assembly-language code, and most often it means that a bit or set of bits is being tested to see if they are set.

Introduction to the Math Coprocessors

The rest of this chapter has to do with the math coprocessors that can be installed into a PS/2 or PC, and, as such, may be regarded as optional. Many people, however, have the idea that working with the 8087 or 80287 is difficult, but it is not. In fact, the macro assembler provides support for the math coprocessors—it will assemble instructions meant for them.

The 8087 is stack oriented

The 8087 is a stack-oriented chip. Instead of the normal registers we are used to, operands are put onto the 8087's stack. There are eight stack registers, and each one is 80 bits—10 bytes—long. This is much more than the PS/2 or PC has in the microprocessor; 80 bits can give you an accuracy of 16 decimal digits.

> It is worth noting that the accuracy of the 8087 is considerably greater than that of most mainframe computers.

It is easy knowing what assembly-language instructions are meant for the 8087—they all begin with F. For example, there is FADD, FSUB, and so forth. None of the microproccessors (8088- 80386) begin with F. Let's take a very quick look at the 8087 and get to know it a little better.

A Short 8087 Program

If you want to use 8087 instructions in your .ASM file, you have to include the .8087 Pseudo-Op:

```
.8087              ←
        CODE_SEG         SEGMENT
        ASSUME  CS:CODE_SEG,DS:CODE_SEG
        ORG     100H
                  :
```

This Pseudo-Op informs the assembler that 8087 code will be included in the program (DEBUG, by the way, can also disassemble 8087 instructions).

8087 wait states

Since the coprocessor is a separate chip, some coordination must go on. For example, the microprocessor must know if the coprocessor is done with a certain calculation before reading the result in. This is done with the WAIT instruction, which the assembler includes automatically (meaning that we don't have to worry about it). The 8088 will wait until the 8087 is done processing before proceeding.

Let's examine one of the simplest of examples: adding two integers. We will just add 3 and 1, to get a result of 4. Here's the code, in a program that is ready to run:

```
CODE_SEG SEGMENT
.8087
        ASSUME   CS:CODE_SEG,DS:CODE_SEG
        ORG      100H
ENTRY:  JMP      PROG
        OPERAND1 DW     3
        OPERAND2 DW     1
        RESULT   DW     0
PROG:   FILD     OPERAND1
        FIADD    OPERAND2
        FISTP    RESULT
        INT      20H
CODE_SEG ENDS
        END      ENTRY
```

This looks like a normal .COM file program until we get to these instructions:

```
PROG:   FILD     OPERAND1
        FIADD    OPERAND2
        FISTP    RESULT
```

As you can see, these 8087 instructions begin with F. The very first one:

```
PROG:    FILD     OPERAND1              ←
         FIADD    OPERAND2
         FISTP    RESULT
```

is an instruction telling the 8087 to load the number at OPERAND1 onto the top of its internal stack. FILD means "Integer Load"; FLD means floating point load. Here the operands will only be one-word integers, the simplest of the 8087 formats (there are six of them). The next instruction:

```
PROG:    FILD     OPERAND1
         FIADD    OPERAND2              ←
         FISTP    RESULT
```

which is FIADD OPERAND2, is the instruction used for integer addition. Now that we have loaded OPERAND1 into the 8087's stack, we can add OPERAND2 to it simply with FIADD OPERAND2. This is what we want—the result will now be on top of the 8087's stack. To take a look at it, we store it in memory in the location RESULT with the instruction FISTP RESULT:

```
PROG:    FILD     OPERAND1
         FIADD    OPERAND2
         FISTP    RESULT                ←
```

This command is an integer store—as opposed to FST, the floating point store—and pop command. The number on the top of the stack is stored and then the stack is popped, leaving it free for further operations.

Since the 8087 is a stack-oriented chip, you have to pop the stack regularly. If you do not, then the stack will become full, halting execution. You cannot simply overwrite old values as you can in the AX-DX registers—when you load a value it goes onto the top of the stack and the other values are pushed down one.

Here is our data area:

```
OPERAND1 DW     3
OPERAND2 DW     1
RESULT   DW     0              ←
```

When the program is finished running, RESULT will have been filled by our last 8087 instruction, the integer store instruction FISTP. In this case, RESULT will hold 4.

Floating point work can be very complex in the 8087; the format in which floating point numbers are stored is difficult to work with. Here, however, some conversion libraries are available that you can link with your assembler programs, and they will help (one such library is IBMU-TIL.LIB, available with the IBM macro assembler).

The math coprocessor chips can represent enormous power for your programs—if they might be of help to you, don't avoid using them because they seem too mysterious. It takes a little work to learn how to operate them, but the result often well justifies the investment.

10

Linking to BASIC, FORTRAN, C, and Pascal

Linking assembly-language routines into your high-level programs is often a good idea where speed or system resources (that otherwise might not be available) are concerned. Not all languages let you link assembly-language routines in with your program (for example, Turbo BASIC does not), but most do. And when you can link in assembly-language routines to high-level language programs, you can add some zest to their lives.

Interface standards

As surprising as it may seem in the frenetic world of microcomputing, there are certain conventions that are set for such interfaces that almost all high-level languages conform to. This means that what we develop here for, say, Pascal, can be used with almost any Pascal package around, because of the *Pascal calling convention*. This is a convention that sets the order in which parameters passed in a call are pushed onto the stack. There are calling conventions for BASIC, FORTRAN, Pascal, and C.

For this reason, even though the examples we develop here will be written in Microsoft languages, they can be just as well called from most other developer's languages (for instance, Borland's Turbo series).

Besides linking to high-level languages, we are going to also include a section in this chapter on DEBUG. While DEBUG is not a complicated program, it does take some exposure to it before one can become fluent with it. Since its use is so widespread, it merits a more formal look here before we leave DOS and continue on to OS/2 in the last two chapters (DEBUG won't work under OS/2).

Calling Conventions

High-level languages pass parameters to subroutines and functions on the stack. To interact with high-level languages, we are going to have to pick these parameters off the stack. If we had a function defined in Pascal named SUMMER, which just sums two numbers—SUMMER(3,2) would return 5, for example—then Pascal will place the parameters, 3 and 2, onto the stack before calling the address it has for SUMMER.

However, different languages do this differently. A calling convention indicates how a higher level language passes parameters to routines that it calls. It specifies these things: the order parameters are pushed in, how they are pushed (as addresses or immediate values), and how to reset the stack when we're done. If we are going to successfully link to the high-level language, we are going to have to mimic what it might expect from its own library of routines.

Some languages push parameters in the order you see them, and some in reverse order; some languages (like FORTRAN) don't push the values 3 and 2 at all but, rather, their addresses. Also, at the end of the call, when we are about to return, we will have to make sure that the stack is reset in the proper way. This *usually* (BASIC, FORTRAN, and Pascal) means that after returning to the high-level language, the stack should be just the way it was before the parameters were pushed for the call. In other words, we will have to pop the pushed parameters off before we return.

The C language, however, takes care of this for us, so when linking to C programs, we will just end with a RET, and not worry about popping the pushed parameters. This information all comes together in Table 10.1, the calling convention table (as you can see, no calling convention matches any other).

Table 10.1 Calling Conventions

Language	Parameters Pushed	Parameters Passed	Return Type
BASIC	In order	As offset addresses	RET #
FORTRAN	In order	As FAR addresses	RET #
C	In REVERSE order	As values	RET
Pascal	In order	As values	RET #

Notes: Pushing parameters in order means that SUMMER(3,2) would go like this: PUSH 3, PUSH 2, CALL SUMMER.
Parameters are passed as immediate values or as addresses.
Where RET # is used, # = the total size in bytes of all pushed parameters.

Similarly, Table 10.2 indicates how parameter passing works—
whether parameters are passed by address or by their actual value.

Table 10.2 Parameter Passing

Language	Near References	Far References	By Value
BASIC	Everything		
FORTRAN		Everything	
C	Near Arrays	Far Arrays	Everything else
Pascal	VAR, CONST	VARS, CONSTS	Everything else

Our Pascal Example

Our strategy when called will be the same one that library routines normally use—instead of actually popping parameters off the stack, we will
make a copy of the stack pointer, SP, in the BP register. BP can be used as
a base pointer, which means using indirect addressing like this: MOV
AX,SS:[BP], while SP cannot.

In fact, not only can we have instructions like this:

```
MOV     AX,SS:[BP]
```

but we can also have instructions like this:

```
MOV     AX,SS:[BP+8]
```

where we can use the (unchanged) BP pointer as a base, and simply pick
off words from the stack at will by adding immediate values to BP. This
method will work with *any* form of indirect addressing, [BX] included.
Using BP this way will make it easy to retrieve parameters from the stack
without a confusing number of pops and pushes.

For example, let's return to our Pascal function SUMMER. If we had
this line in a Pascal program:

```
program add1(input, output);
function summer(a,b:integer):integer; extern;
var
        a:integer;
        b:integer;
begin
        a := 3;
        b := 2;
        writeln("3 + 2 = ",summer(a,b));
end.
```

then Pascal would print out the character string "3 + 2 = ", followed by the value of the function call, SUMMER(3,2). To reach SUMMER, Pascal will first push the parameters on the stack and then call SUMMER, like this:

```
PUSH    3
PUSH    2
CALL    SUMMER
```

When we arrive at our procedure SUMMER, this is what the stack would look like (we are assuming Pascal integer format for parameters 3 and 2, which means that they are each stored as one word):

```
┌──────────┐
│    3     │    ← SP+6
├──────────┤
│    2     │    ← SP+4
├──────────┤
│ Return   │    ← SP+2
│ Address  │    ← SP
└──────────┘
```

Keep in mind that the stack "grows" downwards in memory. That is, SP is decremented *by two* every time you push something onto the stack. This means that 3 is pushed first:

```
┌──────────┐
│    3     │    ← SP
└──────────┘
```

Then 2:

```
┌──────────┐
│    3     │    ← SP+2
├──────────┤
│    2     │    ← SP
└──────────┘
```

and then the call is made. Whenever a CALL is executed, the return address is pushed onto the stack: a one-word (offset) address is pushed if the call is NEAR, and a two-word (four-byte) address if the call is FAR.

As we will see, we will always be receiving FAR calls, except for C programs that have been declared to be of a certain size beforehand (see the .MODEL Pseudo-Op below). A FAR return address will take up two words; when we arrive at SUMMER, this is what we will see:

```
┌──────────┐
│    3     │   ← SP+6
├──────────┤
│    2     │   ← SP+4
├──────────┤
│ Return   │   ← SP+2
│ Address  │   ← SP
└──────────┘
```

Using BP

In all our procedures, however, we will first make a back-up copy of BP by pushing it onto the stack, and then loading it with the current value of SP. That is, the first two lines of SUMMER will look like this:

```
SUMMER  PROC    FAR
        PUSH    BP          ←
        MOV     BP,SP       ←
```

Doing this is standard. It provides us with a copy of SP in BP, which can now be used to pick parameters off the stack. On the other hand, it also means that the stack that we will have to deal with will really look like this:

```
┌──────────┐
│    3     │   ← BP+8
├──────────┤
│    2     │   ← BP+6
├──────────┤
│ Return   │   ← BP+4
│ Address  │   ← BP+2
├──────────┤
│ Old BP   │   ← BP
└──────────┘
```

Now if we wanted to, we could just pick the parameters off the stack. In our procedure SUMMER, we could place the first parameter (3) into AX and the second parameter (2) into BX like this:

```
SUMMER  PROC    FAR
        PUSH    BP
        MOV     BP,SP
        MOV     AX,[BP+8]       ←
        MOV     BX,[BP+6]       ←
```

It's easy enough; the only real trouble is keeping track of the number to add to BP. The examples we'll develop later for each language will make that clear. On the other hand, the high-level language usually assumes that some of the registers passed to you with the call will be preserved. At a minimum, you should preserve DI, SI, SS, and DS. Here is what SUMMER may look like with those pushes added:

```
SUMMER  PROC    FAR
        PUSH    BP
        MOV     BP,SP

        PUSH    SI        ←
        PUSH    DI        ←
        PUSH    DS        ←
        PUSH    SS        ←

        MOV     AX,[BP+8]
        MOV     BX,[BP+6]
        :
```

And in the end, before leaving the program, we'll want to restore the saved registers:

```
SUMMER  PROC    FAR
        PUSH    BP
        MOV     BP,SP

        PUSH    SI
        PUSH    DI
        PUSH    DS
        PUSH    SS

        MOV     AX,[BP+8]
        MOV     BX,[BP+6]
        :

        POP     SS        ←
        POP     DS        ←
        POP     DI        ←
        POP     SI        ←
```

Notice that even though we used the stack here (to save registers with), we did not change the numbers added to BP (e.g., MOV AX,[BP + 8] did not change). This is because the value stored in BP has not changed. Although SS:SP is changing, the location pointed to by SS:BP does not. If we do not change BP throughout our program, we are free to use the stack as we wish and still use the offsets developed in the examples coming up.

Functions and Subroutines

High-level languages make the distinction between subroutines and functions, but assembly language does not (it's all procedures).

```
A = FUNC(12,1)    ← A function returns a value.
CALL SUBROUT(A)   ← A subroutine does not.
```

To satisfy your high-level language, you'll have to declare the assembly-language routine as a function or a subroutine. If you don't want to return a value, declare it an external subroutine in the higher level language; if you do want to return a value, declare it as an external function (examples are coming later). Table 10.3 how the higher level languages work:

Table 10.3 Higher Level Language Functions

Language	Returns a Value	Returns No Value
BASIC	Function	Subprogram
FORTRAN	Function	Suroutine
C	Function	Void Function
Pascal	Function	Procedure

Although a subroutine might change the values of the variables passed to it if given their addresses, it doesn't return an immediate value in the way that a function does.

Returning Values Using Functions

If you *do* want to return a value, you will be writing an external function for your language. Returning values in this way is a very important part of interfacing to high-level languages, so let's work through it. The convention (Microsoft, Turbo, etc) is to use these registers to return values from functions in:

Returning	Use
Byte Value	AL
Word Value	AX
Doubleword Value	DX:AX
>4 Bytes	DX:AX = Address

Byte values are simply returned in AL. Word values (like short integers) in AX, and doubleword values in DX:AX (DX = high word, AX = low word). In our examples, we will be dealing with functions that return word values (in AX), or doubleword values (in DX:AX).

Returning Big Values

If you want to return a value (or values, such as an array) longer than four bytes, you must follow a special procedure. First, of course, you must know the format of the data type you are going to work with (array, character string, floating point number, etc). For these details, see the manual of your individual language. Then your assembly-language procedure must pass back the address at which the returned data will be.

Returning Big Values in C

In C, this is easy; you only need to set DX:AX to the address of the data that you want to return (>4 bytes long), and return. If your data is at DS:BX, just set DX to DS and AX to BX, and return. That's it—as long as the data is in the right format, you'll be fine.

Unfortunately, the other three languages that we are dealing with, BASIC, Pascal, and FORTRAN, are more particular. They actually pass you the address at which they expect the data to be returned.

Returning Big Values in BASIC, FORTRAN, and Pascal

When BASIC, Pascal or FORTRAN uses a function that returns a value larger than four bytes, it will automatically push one extra word onto the stack. Normally, the stack would look like this:

3	← BP+8
2	← BP+6
Return Address	← BP+4
	← BP+2
Old BP	← BP

Now, there is one more data item (a word) that is passed to you when a big value (>4 bytes) is expected to be returned by a function. This word is the *offset* address at which the data is to be placed, and will appear on the stack this way:

3	← BP+10
2	← BP+8
Offset	← BP+6

```
┌──────────┐
│ Return   │   ←  BP+4
│ Address  │   ←  BP+2
├──────────┤
│ Old BP   │   ←  BP
└──────────┘
```

The segment address at which you are to return data will be in SS. So, upon return, you will have to take the value at BP+6, the return offset, and place the data you want to return at SS:(return offset). Then, since the language expects the address of the returned data in DX:AX, you must *also* fill DX with the value currently in SS, and fill AX with offset (from BP+6).

Note that this adds two to each of the parameter locations. When preparing the stack to return to the calling program, keep in mind that you will have to pop off this extra parameter, the return offset (i.e., in a RET # statement, as we'll use shortly, add 2 to # to take care of the return offset parameter). Also, since a function only returns one value, a maximum of one address will be pushed this way.

In general, it is not difficult to return values longer than four bytes, but you have to be prepared to use the address that will be pushed in this case.

Returning Data in SUMMER

In our program SUMMER, we want to return a Pascal integer value, so we will use AX. When we left SUMMER, we had loaded the first parameter (that is, a value of 3) into AX and the second parameter (2) into BX. We can just ADD AX,BX like this:

```
SUMMER    PROC    FAR
          PUSH    BP
          MOV     BP,SP

          PUSH    SI
          PUSH    DI
          PUSH    DS
          PUSH    SS

          MOV     AX,[BP+8]
          MOV     BX,[BP+6]

          ADD     AX,BX     ←

          POP     SS
          POP     DS
          POP     DI
          POP     SI
```

Pascal is one of those languages in which we have to make sure that we pop the parameters off the stack (C takes care of this for us). This means that we will have to end SUMMER with a RET # instruction, where # is the number of bytes that we pushed onto the stack before the call to SUMMER was made (in C, we'd just use RET).

In other words, when control returns to the calling program, there should be nothing extra on the stack. Here's how the stack looks when we're ready to return in SUMMER (this is after we've restored SS, DS, DI, and SI):

```
 _____
|       3        |  ← BP+8
|_____|
|       2        |  ← BP+6
|_____|
| Return         |  ← BP+4
| Address        |  ← BP+2
|_____|
| Old BP         |  ← BP
|_____|
```

(The first value that would be popped off is at the bottom, Old BP). A normal FAR RET will pop the two words of return address, but we still have four bytes of parameters to release. So, we will do this: First, restore BP with POP BP, then issue a RET 4 instruction.

RET 4 not only returns us to the calling program, but also pops four additional bytes (two words) off the stack. These words go nowhere—they will not be stored in a register. So this is how we end SUMMER:

```
SUMMER   PROC     FAR
         PUSH     BP
         MOV      BP,SP

         PUSH     SI
         PUSH     DI
         PUSH     DS
         PUSH     SS

         MOV      AX,[BP+8]
         MOV      BX,[BP+6]

         ADD      AX,BX

         POP      SS
         POP      DS
         POP      DI
         POP      SI

         POP      BP        ←
         RET      4         ←
SUMMER   ENDP
```

And now SUMMER is almost ready to be linked into a Pascal program as a function—but not quite.

Perhaps you'll recall that when we linked procedures together earlier in Chapter 7, the segment names became very important. We had to be careful to make sure that code we wanted in the same segment was actually put there—and now we must review such considerations again.

The .CODE, .DATA, and .MODEL Directives

Simplified segment directives

There are standard names used for the data segment, the code segment, and so forth in higher level languages. This means that we'll have to match them in our own procedures before we can link to those languages.

Microsoft has introduced a new feature called *simplified segment directives*. These directives—like .CODE, .DATA, and .STACK—are translated into the standard names for those segments. These directives will make life much easier for us, both in this chapter and in the following two on OS/2, since they will handle this problem automatically.

> If for some reason your language does not use the standard names for its segments, then you will have trouble linking, and must use the correct segment names as listed in the language's manual. (Any language that you can link to will list the correct segment names in its manual.)

The .CODE directive is translated into _TEXT, .DATA is translated as _DATA, and .STACK is translated into STACK. In addition, compilers often store uninitialized data separately since it is more efficient to do so. To accommodate this, there is the .DATA? directive, which is for the uninitialized data—this becomes translated into _BSS (although put into the same group, DGROUP, as _DATA and STACK).

Here's how they work. A normal .ASM file that will be made into an .EXE file may look like this:

```
        DATA_SEG        SEGMENT
                MSG     DB "Here is a message.",0
        DATA_SEG        ENDS

STACK       SEGMENT PARA STACK
    DB      20 DUP("STACK")
STACK       ENDS

        CODE_SEG        SEGMENT
                ASSUME  CS:CODE_SEG,SS:STACK
        PROG_NAME       PROC    FAR
                PUSH    DS
```

```
                        XOR       AX,AX
                        PUSH      AX
                        MOV       AX,DATA_SEG
                        MOV       DS,AX
                        ASSUME       DS:DATA_SEG
                        MOV       AH,OFH
                        INT       10H
                        :
                        :
                        RET
            PROG_NAME         ENDP
            CODE_SEG          ENDS

            END       PROG_NAME
```

And here is the same program using the new directives .DATA, .STACK, and .CODE:

```
            .MODEL SMALL
            .DATA
            MSG       DB "Here is a message.",0

            .STACK 100

            .CODE
            ASSUME    CS:@CODE,SS:STACK
      PROG_NAME         PROC
            PUSH      DS
            XOR       AX,AX
            PUSH      AX
            MOV       AX,DGROUP
            MOV       DS,AX
            ASSUME    DS:DGROUP
            MOV       AH,OFH
            INT       10H
            :
            :

            RET
      PROG_NAME         ENDP

      END       PROG_NAME
```

The whole data segment has become this:

```
.DATA
MSG       DB "Here is a message.",0
```

When assembled, this will act just like our old DATA_SEG declaration, except that the usual internal name (_DATA) will be used instead of DATA_SEG. This makes linking to programs in other languages a breeze, since the segment names are all handled through the simplified directives.

It is also possible to define data segments that will not be combined into DGROUP, the usual data group. To do this, use the

> .FARDATA directive instead (and the actual name of the segment will be FAR_DATA). The directive .FARDATA? can also be used, although we will not use either of these here.

We can add some uninitialized data (i.e. defined with a "?") to our data group this way:

```
          .DATA
          MSG     DB "Here is a message.",0

→         .DATA?
→         PHONE_NUMBER    DB ? DUP(?)

          .CODE
                  :
```

This data, PHONE_NUMBER, may be referred to in just the same way as MSG, since it goes into the same group.

No more ENDS

Note that you do not have to end a simplified segment directive (i.e., like ".DATA ENDS"). The end of the old segment is automatically assumed when a new simplified segment directive is used. Therefore, .DATA? both ends the .DATA directive and starts defining the uninitialized data at the same time.

Using ASSUMEs

We still need, in .EXE files, a way to indicate the name of the data segment or group to use in an ASSUME statement. We used to do it like this:

```
PROG_NAME       PROC        FAR
        PUSH    DS
        XOR     AX,AX
        PUSH    AX
        MOV     AX,DATA_SEG      ←
        MOV     DS,AX
        ASSUME  DS:DATA_SEG      ←
```

What happens with simplified directives is that all data segments (.DATA and .DATA?) are put together into DGROUP, so we can use that for DS:

```
PROG_NAME       PROC
        PUSH    DS
        XOR     AX,AX
        PUSH    AX
        MOV     AX,DGROUP        ←
        MOV     DS,AX
        ASSUME  DS:DGROUP        ←
```

The
@DATA,
@DATA?,
and
@CODE
symbols

If we actually need the name of the real segment itself, that is available too. These symbols are predefined (using EQU) in MASM: @DATA, @DATA?, and @CODE. They translate into the real names for the segments generated by the .DATA, .DATA?, and .CODE directives, respectively. The stack segment is always just called STACK. This means that we can point to the code segment (which is not gathered together into a group like DGROUP as a default, as the data and stack segments are) this way:

```
            CODE
            ASSUME   CS:@CODE,SS:STACK          ←
PROG_NAME            PROC
            PUSH     DS
            XOR      AX,AX
            PUSH     AX
            MOV      AX,DGROUP
            MOV      DS,AX
            ASSUME   DS:DGROUP
```

You may also have noticed that we did not define PROG_NAME as FAR, but just simply as PROG_NAME PROC:

```
            .CODE
            ASSUME   CS:@CODE,SS:STACK
PROG_NAME            PROC    ←
            PUSH     DS
            XOR      AX,AX
            PUSH     AX
            MOV      AX,DGROUP
            MOV      DS,AX
            ASSUME   DS:DGROUP
```

This is because such NEAR and FAR definitions for procedures are taken care of when we specify the *memory model* for our program. This is going to be central to our use of high-level languages.

Memory Models

Defining the memory model (TINY, SMALL, MEDIUM, COMPACT, LARGE or HUGE) has to be done before we use the Microsoft simplified directives. You may have noticed that we did this as the first thing in our sample program above:

```
            .MODEL SMALL      ←
            .DATA
MSG         DB "Here is a message.",0

            .STACK 100

            .CODE
            ASSUME   CS:@CODE,SS:STACK
```

```
PROG_NAME       PROC
        PUSH    DS
        XOR     AX,AX
        PUSH    AX
        MOV     AX,DGROUP
        MOV     DS,AX
        ASSUME  DS:DGROUP
        MOV     AH,0FH
        INT     10H
```

Defining a memory model is crucial, both to use the simplified segment directives and to link to a higher level language. These models set the allowable sizes of the code and data areas. The memory model must match that defined in the higher level language program itself, because calls or data references will have to use one or two word addresses depending on the model used.

Table 10.4 Memory Model Definitions

Model	Means
Tiny	.COM file format
Small	All data fits in one 64K segment, all code fits in one 64K segment. (This means that both data and code can be accessed as near.)
Medium	All data fits in one 64K segment, but code may be greater than 64K.
Compact	Data may be greater than 64K (but no single array may be), code must be less than 64K.
Large	Both data and code may be greater than 64K, but no single array may be.
Huge	Data, Code, and data arrays may be greater than 64K.

Table 10.5 Summary of Memory Models

Model	DATA vs. 64K	CODE vs. 64K	Arrays vs. 64K
Tiny	<	<	< (one common segment)
Small	<	<	<
Medium	<	>	<
Compact	>	<	<
Large	>	>	<
Huge	>	>	>

Using memory models, you can set the size limits of the code and data areas for your program. What model you will need will also depend on the language that you will be using—if you've programmed in higher level languages before, then you probably have already heard about memory models.

For example, some languages do not support memory models below a certain size, and others only support one type. Normally, your compiler will set things up for you to use one or another memory model, which you can select. Usual memory models for each of the languages will be reviewed when we work through examples for each language, which we will do right now.

The BASIC Interface

Procedures called from BASIC should be declared as FAR. Since we are using the .MODEL directive, that is taken care of for us (we don't need to declare procedures NEAR or FAR, and whether the return at the end is near or far will also be adjusted automatically). BASIC uses 64K maximum for data, although code can be longer (in our version of BASIC, QUICKBASIC 4.0), so we will be using .MODEL MEDIUM. If you're in doubt about the model used by your language, check your manual.

Let's say we want a BASIC function that will return the video mode (returned in AL from INT 10H, service 0FH). We might set up a BASIC program like this:

```
10      DEFINT A-Z
20      DECLARE FUNCTION VIDMODE
30      PRINT "The video mode is: ";
40      PRINT VIDMODE    ←
50      END
```

If we had not wanted to return a value, we could have used a subroutine (CALL) instead of a function. Here what happens is this: There are no parameters to push, so when our program starts (after the BP push), this is what the stack looks like:

```
┌───────────┐
│ Return    │   ←  BP+4
│ Address   │   ←  BP+2
├───────────┤
│ Old BP    │   ←  BP
└───────────┘
```

There are no parameters on it. The program will return the video mode as a small integer in BASIC (one word), so it will use AX. This means that we have to zero out AH (which returns the number of screen columns). Here is how our assembly-language program looks:

```
        .MODEL  MEDIUM
        .CODE
                PUBLIC  VIDMODE          ;For BASIC Interface
        VIDMODE PROC
                PUSH    BP
                MOV     BP,SP

                PUSH    SI
                PUSH    DI
                PUSH    DS
                PUSH    SS

→               MOV     AH,0FH
→               INT     10H
→               MOV     AH,0

                POP     SS
                POP     DS
                POP     DI
                POP     SI

                POP     BP
                RET
        VIDMODE ENDP
                END
```

That's all there is to it: Since there were no parameters on the stack, we could simply end the program with a RET. Notice that we had to declare VIDMODE PUBLIC, so that the linker could find it, and that we simply ended with END, not END VIDMODE (since VIDMODE is not the entry point—it is being linked in).

To use this assembly-language routine, just compile the BASIC program, assemble the assembly-language one, and link the two .OBJ files together. The linker will find the definition it needs (VIDMODE) in the VIDMODE.OBJ module, and set things up correctly. Linking to BASIC is that easy.

Passing Parameters in BASIC

If we had parameters to push, it would be a different story. Let's say we wanted to call SUMMER from BASIC. Here is what the BASIC program would look like:

```
10      DEFINT A-Z
20      DECLARE FUNCTION SUMMER(A%,B%)
30      PRINT "3 + 2 = ";
40      PRINT SUMMER(3,2)
50      END
```

Microsoft BASIC conforms to the BASIC calling convention.

Table 10.6 Calling Conventions

Language	Parameters Pushed	Parameters Passed	Return Type
BASIC	In order	As offset addresses	RET #
FORTRAN	In order	As FAR addresses	RET #
C	In REVERSE orde	As values	RET
Pascal	In order	As values	RET #

Parameters must be popped off the stack upon return; they are pushed in the order they appear (here it would be PUSH 3, PUSH 2). Also, in BASIC, parameters are passed as offset addresses (so a subroutine could change them).

Here is what the stack looks like when we start using it in SUMMER:

```
┌──────────────┐
│ Off of 1     │   ←  BP+8
├──────────────┤
│ Off of 2     │   ←  BP+6
├──────────────┤
│ Return       │   ←  BP+4
│ Address      │   ←  BP+2
├──────────────┤
│ Old BP       │   ←  BP
└──────────────┘
```

The return address is always four bytes, no matter what model, since BASIC calls external functions as FAR. Here "Off of 1" is the offset address of the value 3 in memory, "Off of 2" is the address of the value 2, and so on. Since data can take up at most one segment in BASIC, addresses are always passed as only two bytes.

The only unusual thing here is that data is passed as an offset address, and not as an immediate value. This means that we will have to load the data from the passed addresses, then add them (leaving the result in AX) and return:

```
        .MODEL  MEDIUM
        .CODE
                PUBLIC  SUMMER    ;For BASIC Interface
        SUMMER  PROC
                PUSH    BP
                MOV     BP,SP

                PUSH    SI
                PUSH    DI
                PUSH    DS
                PUSH    SS
    →           MOV     BX,[BP+8]
    →           MOV     AX,[BX]
```

```
  →          MOV        BX,[BP+6]
  →          MOV        BX,[BX]

  →          ADD        AX,BX

             POP        SS
             POP        DS
             POP        DI
             POP        SI

             POP        BP
             RET        4

SUMMER       ENDP
             END
```

Notice that we used .MODEL MEDIUM here too, and that at the end we had to pop off the four bytes of passed parameters (two offset addresses at two bytes each) with a RET 4 instruction, which returns and pops four extra bytes off. We return our one-word result, a simple integer, in AX. Now we are able to pass parameters to our BASIC functions. Let's turn to FORTRAN.

The FORTRAN Interface

Fortran is a venerable language, going back many years. Usually, FORTRAN (because of its reputation as a number-cruncher) is compiled as LARGE (if in doubt, check your compiler manual). In Microsoft FORTRAN versions before FORTRAN 4.0, the model used was always LARGE; starting with Version 4.0, Microsoft FORTRAN supports the HUGE and MEDIUM models as well. We will use LARGE.

The FORTRAN INTERFACE instruction

Let's say that we wanted the video state in FORTRAN. We have to set up what is called an *Interface* to VIDMODE. Our program might look like this:

```
INTERFACE TO INTEGER FUNCTION IVID(A)
INTEGER*2 A
END
INTEGER*2 A
A=0
WRITE (*,*) "Video Mode is ",IVID(A)
END
```

Here our interface looks like this:

```
INTERFACE TO INTEGER FUNCTION IVID(A)
INTEGER*2 A
END
```

This indicates to FORTRAN that we are interfacing to a function that will return a value. We have to tell FORTRAN what type of value will be returned, which is why we specify INTEGER (a four-byte integer, the normal INTEGER type in FORTRAN).

In this example, we are beginning our function name—"IVID" (not VIDMODE)—with "I" in deference to FORTRAN's default integer definitions, and passing a parameter to it, even though IVID does not need any parameters. This is because, in FORTRAN, you have to pass at least one parameter to a function to have it called. We will use a dummy parameter named A (defined as a two-byte integer, INTEGER*2, in the INTERFACE statement). We will simply make A zero and pass it to satisfy FORTRAN:

```
      INTERFACE TO INTEGER FUNCTION IVID(A)
      INTEGER*2 A
      END
C
      INTEGER*2 A
→     A=0
      WRITE (*,*) "Video Mode is ",IVID(A)
      END
```

Again, if we were interfacing to a routine that did not return a value, we would call it a subroutine. For example, if we had a subroutine named SORT, the interface could be this:

```
      INTERFACE TO SUBROUTINE SORT(A,B)
      INTEGER*2 A,B
      END
```

Notice that we did not have to indicate the returned data type (like INTEGER) since a subroutine returns no value. All we have to do in IVID is put the video mode into AX and return. Here is our FORTRAN VIDMODE:

```
      .MODEL  LARGE
      .CODE
              PUBLIC IVID       ;For FORTRAN Interface
      IVID PROC
              PUSH    BP
              MOV     BP,SP

              PUSH    SI
              PUSH    DI
              PUSH    DS
              PUSH    SS

→             MOV     AH,0FH
→             INT     10H
→             MOV     AH,0
→             MOV     DX,0
```

```
              POP      SS
              POP      DS
              POP      DI
              POP      SI

              POP      BP
              RET      4
    IVID ENDP
              END
```

IVID is all ready to link into a FORTRAN program. You may have noticed that we ended the program with RET 4. This is to take care of the dummy parameter, A, that was passed to IVID. Let's look at why we have to pop four bytes for just one passed parameter.

Passing Parameters in FORTRAN

The way parameters are passed depends on the memory model used. For LARGE and HUGE models, parameters are passed as two-word addresses (segment and offsets); for MEDIUM models as one-word addresses (offsets alone). Since the FORTRAN program is using the LARGE memory model here, values would be passed as two-word addresses.

The FORTRAN convention (see Table 10.6) specifies that we will have to clear the stack of any parameters upon return. Let's use our example procedure SUMMER, and call it ISUM. ISUM will use two passed values. Here's what the new FORTRAN code will look like, including the new INTERFACE declaration:

```
      INTERFACE TO INTEGER FUNCTION ISUM(A,B)
      INTEGER*2 A,B
      END
C
      INTEGER*2 A,B
      A = 3
      B = 2
      I = ISUM(A,B)
      WRITE (*,*) "3 + 2 = ",I
      END
```

Our new interface looks like this:

```
      INTERFACE TO FUNCTION INTEGER ISUM(A,B)
      INTEGER*2 A,B
      END
```

Here we informed FORTRAN that ISUM will return a four-byte INTEGER value, but that it takes two two-byte integers (INTEGER*2) named A and B as parameters. This is just for convenience in our example program—we can load the two-byte parameters into one register each and add them more easily than the four-byte standard FORTRAN integers.

When we start working our procedure ISUM, FORTRAN will have loaded the stack in compliance with the FORTRAN calling convention.

Table 10.7 Calling Conventions

Language	Parameters Pushed	Parameters Passed	Return Type
BASIC	In order	As offset addresses	RET #
FORTRAN	In order	As FAR addresses	RET #
C	In REVERSE order	As values	RET
Pascal	In order	As values	RET #

In the LARGE model, Microsoft FORTRAN passes parameters as two-word addresses, which we'll have to pick off the stack. The stack will look like this:

```
┌─────────────┐
│ Seg of 2    │  ←  BP+12
│ Off of 2    │  ←  BP+10
├─────────────┤
│ Seg of 1    │  ←  BP+8
│ Off of 1    │  ←  BP+6
├─────────────┤
│ Return      │  ←  BP+4
│ Address     │  ←  BP+2
├─────────────┤
│ Old BP      │  ←  BP
└─────────────┘
```

Where "Seg of 2" is shorthand for segment of parameter 2, "Off of 2" is shorthand for parameter 2's offset, and so on. In order to pass these two values, eight bytes had to be pushed onto the stack, so we'll have to end with RET 8. To get the values of these parameters for ourselves, we'll have to get their segment and offset addresses off the stack. Here is the assembly-language code, ready to be linked in. Notice the model declaration is LARGE, and the number of instructions needed to actually get the values that FORTRAN is passing:

```
.MODEL  LARGE
.CODE
        PUBLIC  ISUM        ;For FORTRAN Interface
ISUM  PROC
        PUSH    BP
        MOV     BP,SP

        PUSH    SI
        PUSH    DI
```

```
              PUSH    DS
              PUSH    SS
       →      MOV     DX,[BP+12]      ;Get segment address
       →      MOV     ES,DX
       →      MOV     BX,[BP+10]      ;Get offset address
       →      MOV     AX,ES:[BX]
       →      MOV     DX,[BP+8]
       →      MOV     ES,DX
       →      MOV     BX,[BP+6]
       →      MOV     BX,ES:[BX]

       →      ADD     AX,BX
       →      MOV     DX,0

              POP     SS
              POP     DS
              POP     DI
              POP     SI

              POP     BP
              RET     8
       ISUM   ENDP
              END
```

And that's it: ISUM is ready to be used with FORTRAN. Notice that since we said that ISUM would return a four-byte value, FORTRAN will read DX:AX after the call. Since the result will fit into AX alone (unless you want to make some provision for overflow into a higher word), we zero DX before returning.

The C Interface

The C calling convention holds for Microsoft C, Quick C, and Turbo C. This convention differs from those used in BASIC, FORTRAN, and Pascal in that the language itself removes passed parameters from the stack after the function call—we will only have to end our programs with RET (as opposed to, say, RET 4).

Language	Parameters Pushed	Parameters Passed	Return Type
BASIC	In order	As offset addresses	RET #
FORTRAN	In order	As FAR addresses	RET #
C	In REVERSE order	As values	RET
Pascal	In order	As values	RET #

C parameters are always passed by value (not as addresses, as is the case with FORTRAN or BASIC), except for arrays, which are passed by reference. This reference will be the address of the first element of the array, and will be either two or four bytes long. For NEAR arrays, it will be two bytes; for FAR arrays it will be four bytes.

As usual, we will let the NEAR or FAR declarations of our procedures be made for us automatically by MASM (which knows what to do depending on the memory model specified).

The C calling convention also differs in that it pushes the values to pass in *reverse* order. We will see this more clearly when we discuss the stack upon entering our assembly-language procedures.

The C Code

Here is the C code that we might use with function VIDMODE:

```
extern int vidmode();
main()
{
        printf("The video mode is: %d\n", vidmode());
}
```

Again, we declared VIDMODE as external with the line "extern int vidmode;" that is, vidmode will return an integer value (one word in C). We will pass no parameters to VIDMODE.

Let's assume that the C program was compiled under the SMALL or COMPACT model (and therefore the call to VIDMODE will be a near call). Here's the way the stack would look when we get into VIDMODE (after the initial PUSH BP):

Return	← BP+2
Old BP	← BP

Since this is a near call, there is only one word (the return offset address) pushed onto the stack by the C call instruction.

C differs once again in the naming of our procedure VIDMODE. Instead of defining a procedure "VIDMODE`, the C naming convention is to use an underscore before the name of the procedure to be linked in like this: "_VIDMODE" (and to also declare it as PUBLIC in the assembly-language program, of course). VIDMODE will return its value in AX; this is how the assembly-language program might look (keep in mind that we have to use "_VIDMODE" and not "VIDMODE"):

```
        .MODEL   SMALL
        .CODE
                 PUBLIC   _VIDMODE            ;For C Interface
        _VIDMODE          PROC
                 PUSH     BP
                 MOV      BP,SP

                 PUSH     SI
                 PUSH     DI
                 PUSH     DS
                 PUSH     SS

→                MOV      AH,0FH
→                INT      10H
→                MOV      AH,0

                 POP      SS
                 POP      DS
                 POP      DI
                 POP      SI

                 POP      BP
                 RET
        _VIDMODE          ENDP
                 END
```

There is nothing special here. The only unusual concerns will appear when we try to pass parameters to a linked function or subroutine.

Passing Parameters to C

As mentioned, C passes parameters as immediate values, except for arrays, and pushes them in reverse order. If we wanted to use our function SUMMER in C, this is the way it might look:

```
extern int SUMMER(int,int);
main()
{
        printf("3 + 2 = %d\n",SUMMER(3,2));
}
```

In the other three languages, the 3 would be pushed (or its address), followed by the 2. However, C pushes parameters in reverse order, so the 2 will be pushed first, followed by the 3. Here is what the stack will look like when we start to use it in SUMMER (note that since we're assuming that the C program was compiled as SMALL or COMPACT, the return address is only one word long):

```
        ┌──────────┐
        │    2     │   ←  BP+6
        ├──────────┤
        │    3     │   ←  BP+4
        ├──────────┤
        │  Return  │   ←  BP+2
        ├──────────┤
        │  Old BP  │   ←  BP
        └──────────┘
```

In the case of LARGE, MEDIUM, or HUGE memory models, the return address will be four bytes long—which means that the locations of all parameters will be shifted up by two bytes:

```
        ┌──────────┐
        │    2     │   ←  BP+8
        ├──────────┤
        │    3     │   ←  BP+6
        ├──────────┤
        │  Return  │   ←  BP+4
        │  Addr    │   ←  BP+2
        ├──────────┤
        │  Old BP  │   ←  BP
        └──────────┘
```

Let's assume the SMALL model for our example. To pick the parameters off the stack, we have to know the order in which they are pushed. Sometimes, of course (as with SUMMER), the order of the parameters will not matter. Here is what SUMMER.ASM would look like:

```
        .MODEL  SMALL
        .CODE
                PUBLIC  _SUMMER         ;For C Interface
_SUMMER PROC
                PUSH    BP
                MOV     BP,SP

                PUSH    SI
                PUSH    DI
                PUSH    DS
                PUSH    SS

  →             MOV     AX,[BP+4]
  →             MOV     BX,[BP+6]

  →             ADD     AX,BX

                POP     SS
                POP     DS
                POP     DI
```

```
                POP     SI

                POP     BP
                RET
     _SUMMER    ENDP
                END
```

Notice that we started the procedure name with an underscore (_SUM-MER), and that we ended with a simple RET, since C will handle the parameters itself. SUMMER is now ready to use with C.

The last language that we will cover is Pascal, which we already have some experience in. Pascal may be the easiest interface to work with that we've come across.

The Pascal Interface

Use the memory model LARGE (i.e., .MODEL LARGE) in Pascal. Here, parameters are passed by value, and we have to clear the stack at the end. In addition, parameters are pushed in the order in which they appear (SUMMER(3,2) would result in 3 being pushed first, followed by 2). The Pascal calling convention is used:

Language	Parameters Pushed	Parameters Passed	Return Type
BASIC	In order	As offset addresses	RET #
FORTRAN	In order	As FAR addresses	RET #
C	In REVERSE order	As values	RET
Pascal	In order	As values	RET #

The Pascal Code

Here's the Pascal code to call VIDMODE:

```
program screener(input, output);
function vidmode(a:integer):integer; extern;
begin
        writeln('The video mode is: ',vidmode(0));
end.
```

Again, we have to pass a dummy parameter to VIDMODE, as we did in FORTRAN. We will just set this value to zero and ignore it. This is what VIDMODE.ASM might look like:

```
        .MODEL  LARGE
        .CODE
                PUBLIC  VIDMODE          ;For Pascal Interface
        VIDMODE PROC
                PUSH    BP
                MOV     BP,SP

                PUSH    SI
                PUSH    DI
                PUSH    DS
                PUSH    SS

→               MOV     AH,0FH
→               INT     10H
→               MOV     AH,

                POP     SS
                POP     DS
                POP     DI
                POP     SI

                POP     BP
                RET     2
        VIDMODE ENDP
                END
```

Notice that we had to end with RET 2; this takes care of the two bytes that we pushed to pass our dummy parameter.

Passing Parameters to Pascal

We used the Pascal version of SUMMER as our first example in this chapter, so we know what SUMMER.ASM will look like already. Here's what a Pascal program that calls SUMMER might look like:

```
program add1(input, output);
function summer(a,b:integer):integer; extern;
var
        a:integer;
        b:integer;

begin
        a := 3;
        b := 2;
        writeln('3 + 2 = ',summer(a,b));
end.
```

The stack as we will work with it will look like this:

```
 _____
|            |
|     3      |   ←  BP+8
|_____|
|            |
|     2      |   ←  BP+6
|_____|
```

```
Return    │ ← BP+4
Address   │ ← BP+2
          │
Old BP    │ ← BP
```

And SUMMER.ASM will look like this (note the addition to our earlier Pascal-compatible SUMMER.ASM of .MODEL LARGE and .CODE):

```
        .MODEL  LARGE
        .CODE
                PUBLIC  SUMMER      ;For Pascal Interface
        SUMMER  PROC
                PUSH    BP
                MOV     BP,SP

                PUSH    SI
                PUSH    DI
                PUSH    DS
                PUSH    SS
→               MOV     AX,[BP+8]
→               MOV     BX,[BP+6]

→               ADD     AX,BX

                POP     SS
                POP     DS
                POP     DI
                POP     SI

                POP     BP
                RET
        SUMMER  ENDP
                END
```

The parameters have been pushed as immediate values, and we know their order from the Pascal calling convention. To reset the stack for return to Pascal, we have to end with RET 4, stripping off the four bytes of parameters that had been pushed.

That's all for Pascal—linking our procedures in is no problem. In fact, since we are dealing with immediate values, it's even easier than most.

High-Level Languages in General

It often pays to abandon high-level languages for assembly language, especially where speed is an asset. Besides speed for such things as indexing, sorting, or math manipulations, assembly language can be used to do things that high-level languages simply cannot (depending on the language, this may include memory manipulation, INT calling, and the like) or are not good at (such as graphics; in assembly language, graphics may be hard to write, but it is fast). If you find yourself frequently using assembly-language routines in your high-level programs, you might want to start putting together a library. Some languages, like FOR-TRAN, will even list assembly-language instructions for its various functions so that you may modify and streamline them.

In general, the interface between high-level languages and assembly language is not a difficult one, although it may prove hard to debug. We'll get a start on that in the next section.

DEBUG

Although we have frequently used DEBUG, we have never done so systematically, and any assembly-language book should devote some time to it. There are other, fancier debuggers than DEBUG; for example, there is Microsoft's Codeview. However, this utility is not available to all readers, and, in the end, would not benefit us much. Codeview's merit is that you can debug programs with all the variable names and comments in place—except in assembly-language .COM files (because there is no header in a .COM file for Codeview to use). Since .COM files predominate in this book, Codeview wouldn't be a very big improvement.

There are only eighteen DEBUG commands, but we should by all means cover them before leaving DOS to enter OS/2. Assembly-language programmers frequently spend a great deal of time with this little program.

Debugging is part of any programmer's life, and (to be true to our philosophy of using examples) we will work through a debugging example right here.

OUTPUT.COM

Our buggy program will be OUTPUT.COM. This program will be of very little utility; it will only tell you if you typed a "switch" after OUTPUT on the command line. If you type something like "OUTPUT /S", OUTPUT will type "Switch Used." If you simply typed OUTPUT, the program will type "No Switch Used."

To check what you have typed on the command line, OUTPUT will look at the command parameter area starting at CS:080H (that is, in the PSP, and before our program, which begins at CS:100H). Here is OUTPUT.ASM. There are five common errors in it (can you spot any?):

```
CODE_SEG        SEGMENT
        ASSUME  CS:CODE_SEG, DS:CODE_SEG
        ORG     100H
ENTRY:  JMP SHORT START
        NO_]MSG DB "No "
        MSG     DB "Switch Used."
START:  LEA     DX,NO_MSG
        MOV     BX,80H
        CMP     BYTE PTR [BX],"/"
        JE      PRINT
        LEA     DX,MSG
PRINT:  MOV     AH,9
        INT     21
        INT     20
CODE_SEG        ENDS
        END     ENTRY
```

OUTPUT.ASM will assemble into OUTPUT.COM, but OUT-PUT.COM will crash your machine. To find out why, let's assume you've created OUTPUT.COM, and now we're going to debug it. When you want to debug a program like OUTPUT.COM, you naturally type:

```
A>DEBUG OUTPUT.COM
```

Passing
parameters
to progams
under
DEBUG

When you want to pass parameters on the command line (like "/S" in "OUTPUT /S"), you use DEBUG like this:

```
A>DEBUG OUTPUT.COM /S
```

Notice that you still specify ".COM" as part of the program's name—otherwise, everything is just like typing "OUTPUT /S".

Our first instruction to DEBUG will be the "R", or Register command, to get our bearings:

```
A>DEBUG OUTPUT.COM /S
-R                       ←
AX=0000  BX=0000  CX=0027  DX=0000  SP=FFFE  BP=0000  SI=0000  DI=0000
DS=0F06  ES=0F06  SS=0F06  CS=0F06  IP=0100    NV UP EI PL NZ NA PO NC
0F06:0100 EB0F           JMP     0111
```

DEBUG lists the first instruction of our program, which is the jump over the data area, JMP SHORT START:

```
CODE_SEG        SEGMENT
        ASSUME  CS:CODE_SEG, DS:CODE_SEG
        ORG     100H
ENTRY:  JMP SHORT START                        ←
       ┌─────────────────────────────────┐
       │ NO_MSG  DB "No "                 │ ← Data Area
       │ MSG     DB "Switch Used."        │
       └─────────────────────────────────┘
START:  LEA     DX,NO_MSG
```

```
            MOV     BX,80H
            CMP     BYTE PTR [BX],"/"
            JE      PRINT
            LEA     DX,MSG
PRINT:      MOV     AH,9
            INT     21
            INT     20
CODE_SEG            ENDS
            END     ENTRY
```

Since we don't want to look at the data area, let's take that jump to the label START (here made into the address 0111H) with the "T", or Trace command:

```
A>DEBUG OUTPUT.COM /S
-R
AX=0000  BX=0000  CX=0027  DX=0000  SP=FFFE  BP=0000  SI=0000 DI=0000
DS=0F06  ES=0F06  SS=0F06  CS=0F06  IP=0100   NV UP EI PL NZ NA PO NC
0F06:0100 EB0F          JMP     0111
-T                              ←
AX=0000  BX=0000  CX=0027  DX=0000  SP=FFFE  BP=0000  SI=0000  DI=0000
DS=0F06  ES=0F06  SS=0F06  CS=0F06  IP=0111   NV UP EI PL NZ NA PO NC
0F06:0111 8D160201      LEA     DX,[0102]                  DS:0102=6F4E
```

This moves us to the LEA instruction:

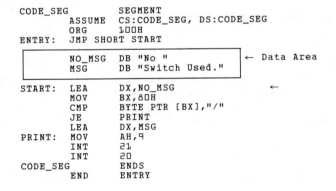

```
CODE_SEG            SEGMENT
            ASSUME  CS:CODE_SEG, DS:CODE_SEG
            ORG     100H
ENTRY:  JMP SHORT START

            NO_MSG  DB "No "              ← Data Area
            MSG     DB "Switch Used."

START:  LEA     DX,NO_MSG                 ←
        MOV     BX,80H
        CMP     BYTE PTR [BX],"/"
        JE      PRINT
        LEA     DX,MSG
PRINT:  MOV     AH,9
        INT     21
        INT     20
CODE_SEG        ENDS
        END     ENTRY
```

If we had wanted to trace through the next five instructions, we could have typed T5. Our Trace command puts us at the beginning of the code proper, so we can unassemble it with "U":

```
A>DEBUG OUTPUT.COM /S
-R
AX=0000  BX=0000  CX=0027  DX=0000  SP=FFFE  BP=0000  SI=0000  DI=0000
DS=0F06  ES=0F06  SS=0F06  CS=0F06  IP=0100   NV UP EI PL NZ NA PO NC
0F06:0100 EB0F          JMP     0111
-T
AX=0000  BX=0000  CX=0027  DX=0000  SP=FFFE  BP=0000  SI=0000  DI=0000
DS=0F06  ES=0F06  SS=0F06  CS=0F06  IP=0111   NV UP EI PL NZ NA PO NC
0F06:0111 8D160201      LEA     DX,[0102]                  DS:0102=6F4E
```

```
-U                        ←
OF06:0111 8D160201    LEA    DX,[0102]
OF06:0115 BB8000      MOV    BX,0080
OF06:0118 803F2F      CMP    BYTE PTR [BX],2F
OF06:011B 7404        JZ     0121
OF06:011D 8D160501    LEA    DX,[0105]
OF06:0121 B409        MOV    AH,09
OF06:0123 CD15        INT    15
OF06:0125 CD14        INT    14
OF06:0127 6F          DB     6F
OF06:0128 6E          DB     6E
OF06:0129 7465        JZ     0190
OF06:012B 6E          DB     6E
OF06:012C 7420        JZ     014E
OF06:012E 6F          DB     6F
OF06:012F 66          DB     66
OF06:0130 206465      AND    [SI+65],AH
```

Taking a look at the program, we expect to see the usual termination, INT 20H, but don't. We see INT 15 followed by INT 14. Taking a hasty look at OUTPUT.ASM, we see that we've used the instructions INT 21 and INT 20, not INT 21H and INT 20H, as we intended (this is a *very* common mistake):

```
CODE_SEG          SEGMENT
         ASSUME   CS:CODE_SEG, DS:CODE_SEG
         ORG      100H
ENTRY:   JMP SHORT START
         NO_MSG   DB "No "
         MSG      DB "Switch Used."
START:   LEA      DX,NO_MSG
         MOV      BX,80H
         CMP      BYTE PTR [BX],"/"
         JE       PRINT
         LEA      DX,MSG
PRINT:   MOV      AH,9
         INT      21         ←
         INT      20         ←
CODE_SEG          ENDS
         END      ENTRY
```

This takes care of two of our errors at once. We change these instructions and reassemble. Regrettably, when we run OUTPUT.COM now, streams of data pour out onto the screen, not at all what we had intended. Once again we use DEBUG.

Following the same steps as above, we can see that our program at least looks good:

```
A>DEBUG OUTPUT.COM /S
-R
AX=0000  BX=0000  CX=0027  DX=0000  SP=FFFE  BP=0000  SI=0000  DI=0000
DS=0F06  ES=0F06  SS=0F06  CS=0F06  IP=0100   NV UP EI PL NZ NA PO NC
OF06:0100 EB0F        JMP    0111
-T
AX=0000  BX=0000  CX=0027  DX=0000  SP=FFFE  BP=0000  SI=0000  DI=0000
DS=0F06  ES=0F06  SS=0F06  CS=0F06  IP=0111   NV UP EI PL NZ NA PO NC
OF06:0111 8D160201    LEA    DX,[0102]                      DS:0102=6F4E
```

```
-U
OF06:0111 8D160201      LEA     DX,[0102]
OF06:0115 BB8000        MOV     BX,0080
OF06:0118 803F2F        CMP     BYTE PTR [BX],2F
OF06:011B 7404          JZ      0121
OF06:011D 8D160501      LEA     DX,[0105]
OF06:0121 B409          MOV     AH,09
OF06:0123 CD21          INT     21          ←
OF06:0125 CD20          INT     20          ←
OF06:0127 3E            DS:
OF06:0128 384100        CMP     [BX+DI+00],AL
OF06:012B 7506          JNZ     0133
OF06:012D 807E8000      CMP     BYTE PTR [BP-80],00
```

Let's try to execute it step by step. The first instruction is LEA DX,[102], or Load an Effective Address into DX. This is the effective address of our label NO_MSG, which DEBUG has turned into an address. DEBUG refers to the memory contents at that address using indirect addressing notation: In this case, the first byte of NO_MSG is transformed into [102]. Since 102H is the address, tracing through this instruction will load 102H into DX:

```
AX=0000  BX=0000  CX=0027  DX=0000  SP=FFFE  BP=0000  SI=0000 DI=0000
DS=OF06  ES=OF06  SS=OF06  CS=OF06  IP=0111     NV UP EI PL NZ NA PO NC
OF06:0111 8D160201      LEA     DX,[0102]                      DS:0102=6F4E
-T                    ←
                                 │
                                 ↓
AX=0000  BX=0000  CX=0027  DX=0102  SP=FFFE  BP=0000  SI=0000  DI=0000
DS=OF06  ES=OF06  SS=OF06  CS=OF06  IP=0115     NV UP EI PL NZ NA PO NC
OF06:0115 BB8000        MOV     BX,0080
-T
```

The next instruction is MOV BX,80H:

```
CODE_SEG          SEGMENT
        ASSUME    CS:CODE_SEG, DS:CODE_SEG
        ORG       100H
ENTRY:  JMP SHORT START

        ┌───────────────────────────────────┐
        │ NO_MSG  DB "No "                   │  ← Data Area
        │ MSG     DB "Switch Used."          │
        └───────────────────────────────────┘

START:  LEA       DX,NO_MSG
        MOV       BX,80H                         ←
        CMP       BYTE PTR [BX],"/"
        JE        PRINT
        LEA       DX,MSG
PRINT:  MOV       AH,9
        INT       21H
        INT       20H
CODE_SEG          ENDS
        END       ENTRY
```

Here we are setting up to point to the command-line parameters passed to us by DOS. If we trace through this instruction, we will load 0080H into BX:

```
AX=0000  BX=0000  CX=0027  DX=0000  SP=FFFE  BP=0000  SI=0000  DI=0000
DS=0F06  ES=0F06  SS=0F06  CS=0F06  IP=0111   NV UP EI PL NZ NA PO NC
0F06:0111 8D160201      LEA     DX,[0102]                    DS:0102=6F4E
-T
AX=0000  BX=0000  CX=0027  DX=0102  SP=FFFE  BP=0000  SI=0000  DI=0000
DS=0F06  ES=0F06  SS=0F06  CS=0F06  IP=0115   NV UP EI PL NZ NA PO NC
0F06:0115 BB8000        MOV     BX,0080
-T    ←

AX=0000  BX=0080  CX=0027  DX=0102  SP=FFFE  BP=0000  SI=0000  DI=0000
DS=0F06  ES=0F06  SS=0F06  CS=0F06  IP=0118   NV UP EI PL NZ NA PO NC
0F06:0118 803F2F        CMP     BYTE PTR [BX],2F             DS:0080=03
-D80
```

Here's where we are in the program:

```
CODE_SEG         SEGMENT
        ASSUME   CS:CODE_SEG, DS:CODE_SEG
        ORG      100H
ENTRY:  JMP SHORT START

        NO_MSG  DB "No "                    ← Data Area
        MSG     DB "Switch Used."

START:  LEA     DX,NO_MSG
        MOV     BX,80H
        CMP     BYTE PTR [BX],"/"            ←
        JE      PRINT
        LEA     DX,MSG
PRINT:  MOV     AH,9
        INT     21H
        INT     20H
CODE_SEG         ENDS
```

We are about to check and see if there was a "/" typed (indicating, for this simple-minded program, that a switch was typed). We can examine what the actual byte that we will check looks like in memory with a memory dump, using the "D" command:

```
AX=0000  BX=0000  CX=0027  DX=0102  SP=FFFE  BP=0000  SI=0000  DI=0000
DS=0F06  ES=0F06  SS=0F06  CS=0F06  IP=0115   NV UP EI PL NZ NA PO NC
0F06:0115 BB8000        MOV     BX,0080
-T

AX=0000  BX=0080  CX=0027  DX=0102  SP=FFFE  BP=0000  SI=0000  DI=0000
DS=0F06  ES=0F06  SS=0F06  CS=0F06  IP=0118   NV UP EI PL NZ NA PO NC
0F06:0118 803F2F        CMP     BYTE PTR [BX],2F             DS:0080=03

-D80  ←
0F06:0080  03 20 2F 53 0D 50 55 54-2E 43 4F 4D 20 2F 53 0D   . /S.PUT.COM /S.
0F06:0090  43 4F 4D 0D 0D 61 73 6D-0D 00 00 00 00 00 00 00   COM..asm........
0F06:00A0  00 00 00 00 00 00 00 00-00 00 00 00 00 00 00 00   ................
```

```
0F06:00B0   00 00 00 00 00 00 00 00-00 00 00 00 00 00 00 00   ................
0F06:00C0   00 00 00 00 00 00 00 00-00 00 00 00 00 00 00 00   ................
0F06:00D0   00 00 00 00 00 00 00 00-00 00 00 00 00 00 00 00   ................
0F06:00E0   00 00 00 00 00 00 00 00-00 00 00 00 00 00 00 00   ................
0F06:00F0   00 00 00 00 00 00 00 00-00 00 00 00 00 00 00 00   ................
```

You can see in this memory dump that the "/S" that we typed is there, followed by the end-of-line character, <cr> = ASCII 13 = 0DH.

> The command-line parameter region has also been used by DEBUG, which is why we see additional characters after what we expect. As long as we use the character count returned to us by DOS or look for the end-of-line character that terminates the command-line parameter string, we will never see what DEBUG has left there.

We notice, however, that [BX] is not pointing to "/", as it should. Instead it is pointing to the value 03. This is the character count—not the beginning of the command-line parameter string.

Although this parameter string is stored *starting* at CS:080H, the first byte in it is the typed character count. For that matter, expecting CS:081H to hold "/" wouldn't work either, since that location holds the ASCII code for the space (ASCII 32 = 20H) that was typed just before "/S". This space is always included in the command-line parameter string:

```
         ↓
OUTPUT /S
```

In fact, we should check for the "/" character starting at CS:082H, not CS:080H, according to our DEBUG memory dump. Here's how we change OUTPUT.ASM to fix the third error:

```
CODE_SEG       SEGMENT
         ASSUME   CS:CODE_SEG, DS:CODE_SEG
         ORG      100H
ENTRY:   JMP SHORT START

         NO_MSG   DB "No "            ← Data Area
         MSG      DB "Switch Used."

START:   LEA      DX,NO_MSG
         MOV      BX,82H              ←Change from 80H to 82H
         CMP      BYTE PTR [BX],"/"
         JE       PRINT
         LEA      DX,MSG
PRINT:   MOV      AH,9
         INT      21H
         INT      20H
CODE_SEG       ENDS
         END      ENTRY
```

Again we assemble and form OUTPUT.COM. And again, the screen fills with characters when we run it. There's still a problem.

Let's take up at the line we just fixed, MOV BX,82H, in DEBUG, and trace through it:

```
AX=0000  BX=0000  CX=0027  DX=0102  SP=FFFE  BP=0000  SI=0000
DI=0000
DS=0F06  ES=0F06  SS=0F06  CS=0F06  IP=0115   NV UP EI PL NZ NA
PO NC
0F06:0115 BB8200          MOV     BX,0082
-T                                        ←
AX=0000  BX=0082  CX=0027  DX=0102  SP=FFFE  BP=0000  SI=0000
DI=0000
DS=0F06  ES=0F06  SS=0F06  CS=0F06  IP=0118   NV UP EI PL NZ NA
PO NC
0F06:0118 803F2F          CMP     BYTE PTR [BX],2F
DS:0082=2F
```

Here we are about to check for "/" again (ASCII 2FH = "/"). To make sure that our "/" is in the right place, we dump memory location CS:0082 with D:

```
AX=0000  BX=0000  CX=0027  DX=0102  SP=FFFE  BP=0000  SI=0000  DI=0000
DS=0F06  ES=0F06  SS=0F06  CS=0F06  IP=0115   NV UP EI PL NZ NA PO NC
0F06:0115 BB8200          MOV     BX,0082
-T
AX=0000  BX=0082  CX=0027  DX=0102  SP=FFFE  BP=0000  SI=0000  DI=0000
DS=0F06  ES=0F06  SS=0F06  CS=0F06  IP=0118   NV UP EI PL NZ NA PO NC
0F06:0118 803F2F          CMP     BYTE PTR [BX],2F             DS:0082=2F
-D82                       ←
0F06:0080       2F 53 0D 50 55 54-2E 43 4F 4D 20 2F 53 0D   /S.PUT.COM /S.
0F06:0090 43 4F 4D 0D 0D 61 73 6D-0D 00 00 00 00 00 00 00   COM..asm........
0F06:00A0 00 00 00 00 00 00 00 00-00 00 00 00 00 00 00 00   ................
0F06:00B0 00 00 00 00 00 00 00 00-00 00 00 00 00 00 00 00   ................
0F06:00C0 00 00 00 00 00 00 00 00-00 00 00 00 00 00 00 00   ................
0F06:00D0 00 00 00 00 00 00 00 00-00 00 00 00 00 00 00 00   ................
0F06:00E0 00 00 00 00 00 00 00 00-00 00 00 00 00 00 00 00   ................
0F06:00F0 00 00 00 00 00 00 00 00-00 00 00 00 00 00 00 00   ................
0F06:0100 EB 0F                                              ..
-T
```

And everything is fine. Now that the program will find "/", we can trace ahead to the point where we print out the message. That is where we will find the INT 21H in our program:

```
CODE_SEG        SEGMENT
        ASSUME  CS:CODE_SEG, DS:CODE_SEG
        ORG     100H
ENTRY:  JMP SHORT START

        NO_MSG  DB "No "                  ← Data Area
        MSG     DB "Switch Used."

START:  LEA     DX,NO_MSG
        MOV     BX,82H
```

```
                CMP     BYTE PTR [BX],"/"   ← We're here now.
                JE      PRINT
                LEA     DX,MSG
        PRINT:  MOV     AH,9
                INT     21H                 ← We want to trace to here.
                INT     20H
        CODE_SEG        ENDS
                END     ENTRY
```

We can trace ahead to this point, watching for the INT 21H instruction:

```
AX=0000  BX=0082  CX=0027  DX=0102  SP=FFFE  BP=0000  SI=0000  DI=0000
DS=0F06  ES=0F06  SS=0F06  CS=0F06  IP=0118   NV UP EI PL NZ NA PO NC
0F06:0118 803F2F       CMP     BYTE PTR [BX],2F              DS:0082=2F
-D82
0F06:0080       2F 53 0D 50 55 54-2E 43 4F 4D 20 2F 53 0D   /S.PUT.COM /S.
0F06:0090    43 4F 4D 0D 0D 61 73 6D-0D 00 00 00 00 00 00 00   COM..asm........
0F06:00A0    00 00 00 00 00 00 00 00-00 00 00 00 00 00 00 00   ................
0F06:00B0    00 00 00 00 00 00 00 00-00 00 00 00 00 00 00 00   ................
0F06:00C0    00 00 00 00 00 00 00 00-00 00 00 00 00 00 00 00   ................
0F06:00D0    00 00 00 00 00 00 00 00-00 00 00 00 00 00 00 00   ................
0F06:00E0    00 00 00 00 00 00 00 00-00 00 00 00 00 00 00 00   ................
0F06:00F0    00 00 00 00 00 00 00 00-00 00 00 00 00 00 00 00   ................
0F06:0100    EB 0F                                            ..
-T        ← Trace through CMP BYTE PTR [BX],"/"
AX=0000  BX=0082  CX=0027  DX=0102  SP=FFFE  BP=0000  SI=0000  DI=0000
DS=0F06  ES=0F06  SS=0F06  CS=0F06  IP=011B   NV UP EI PL ZR NA PE NC
0F06:011B 7404         JZ      0121
-T        ← Trace through JE PRINT
AX=0000  BX=0082  CX=0027  DX=0102  SP=FFFE  BP=0000  SI=0000 DI=0000
DS=0F06  ES=0F06  SS=0F06  CS=0F06  IP=0121   NV UP EI PL ZR NA PE NC
0F06:0121 B409         MOV     AH,09
-T        ← Trace through MOV AH,9


AX=0900  BX=0082  CX=0027  DX=0102  SP=FFFE  BP=0000  SI=0000  DI=0000
DS=0F06  ES=0F06  SS=0F06  CS=0F06  IP=0123   NV UP EI PL ZR NA PE NC
0F06:0123 CD21         INT     21        ← To INT 21H
```

At this point, we are ready to print out the message, which should be,
presumably, that a switch was typed. The address in DX will be where
the message to print is taken from, and we can look at that message with
"D"; in this case, D102:

```
AX=0900  BX=0082  CX=0027  DX=0102  SP=FFFE  BP=0000  SI=0000  DI=0000
DS=0F06  ES=0F06  SS=0F06  CS=0F06  IP=0123   NV UP EI PL ZR NA PE NC
0F06:0123 CD21         INT     21
-D102          ←
0F06:0100       4E 6F 20 53 77 69-74 63 68 20 55 73 65 64   No Switch Used
0F06:0110    2E 8D 16 02 01 BB 82 00-80 3F 2F 74 04 8D 16 05   .........?/t....
0F06:0120    01 B4 09 CD 21 CD 20 3E-38 41 00 75 06 80 7E 80   ....!. >8A.u..~.
0F06:0130    00 75 15 8B 1E 46 43 D1-E3 D1 E3 2B C0 89 87 BE   .u...FC....+....
0F06:0140    3D 89 87 BC 3D E9 64 FF-8D 46 80 50 8D 86 FC FE   =...=.d..F.P....
0F06:0150    50 E8 B2 32 83 C4 04 B8-FF FF 50 B8 05 00 50 8D   P..2......P...P.
0F06:0160    86 FC FE 50 E8 A5 82 83-C4 06 8B 1E 46 43 D1 E3   ...P......FC..
0F06:0170    D1 E3 A1 0E 3C 8B 16 10-3C 89 87 BC 3D 89 97 BE   ....<...<...=...
0F06:0180    3D FF                                             =.
```

Something is still wrong; the message that is about to be typed out is "No Switch Used." At the beginning of the program, DX is loaded with the address of the default message ("No Switch Used."), and it doesn't seem to have been changed.

Looking at our program, we check the area where the address of the correct message should have been loaded (MSG):

```
CODE_SEG        SEGMENT
        ASSUME  CS:CODE_SEG, DS:CODE_SEG
        ORG     100H
ENTRY:  JMP SHORT START

        NO_MSG  DB "No "           ← Data Area
        MSG     DB "Switch Used.'

START:  LEA     DX,NO_MSG
        MOV     BX,82H
        CMP     BYTE PTR [BX],"/"
        JE      PRINT
        LEA     DX,MSG          ←
PRINT:  MOV     AH,9
        INT     21H
        INT     20H
CODE_SEG        ENDS
        END     ENTRY
```

Examine how to get there. Let's assume that [BX], the byte at CS:0082, does equal "/", as it does in our example. First, we compare [BX] with "/":

```
CODE_SEG        SEGMENT
        ASSUME  CS:CODE_SEG, DS:CODE_SEG
        ORG     100H
ENTRY:  JMP SHORT START

        NO_MSG  DB "No "           ← Data Area
        MSG     DB "Switch Used."

START:  LEA     DX,NO_MSG
        MOV     BX,82H
        CMP     BYTE PTR [BX],"/"   ←
        JE      PRINT
        LEA     DX,MSG
PRINT:  MOV     AH,9
        INT     21H
```

Then, if [BX] equals "/", we jump to the label PRINT and print out— without loading DX with the correct address, MSG. In fact, we should only jump to PRINT and print out the default message if [BX] does *not* equal "/", so we can see that we should have used JNE PRINT, not JE PRINT:

```
CODE_SEG          SEGMENT
          ASSUME  CS:CODE_SEG, DS:CODE_SEG
          ORG     100H
ENTRY:    JMP SHORT START

          NO_MSG  DB "No "              ← Data Area
          MSG     DB "Switch Used."

START:    LEA     DX,NO_MSG
          MOV     BX,82H
          CMP     BYTE PTR [BX],"/"
          JNE     PRINT                 ←
          LEA     DX,MSG
PRINT:    MOV     AH,9
          INT     21H
```

This takes care of the fourth error neatly. Now, the correct message ("Switch Used.") appears on the screen. However, we still get the torrent of characters across the screen directly after the message is printed. One more session with DEBUG is needed. Here, though, we will skip over the already-debugged parts, and go directly to the point where the message is printed out.

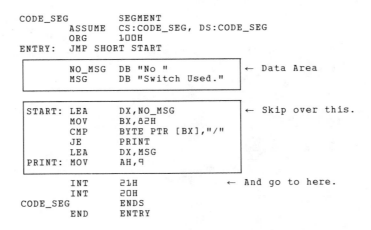

```
CODE_SEG          SEGMENT
          ASSUME  CS:CODE_SEG, DS:CODE_SEG
          ORG     100H
ENTRY:    JMP SHORT START

          NO_MSG  DB "No "              ← Data Area
          MSG     DB "Switch Used."

START:    LEA     DX,NO_MSG             ← Skip over this.
          MOV     BX,82H
          CMP     BYTE PTR [BX],"/"
          JE      PRINT
          LEA     DX,MSG
PRINT:    MOV     AH,9

          INT     21H                   ← And go to here.
          INT     20H
CODE_SEG          ENDS
          END     ENTRY
```

Starting in DEBUG, we can skip over the data by tracing through JMP SHORT START, and then Unassemble the program:

```
A>DEBUG OUTPUT.COM /S
-T

AX=0000  BX=0000  CX=0027  DX=0000  SP=FFFE  BP=0000  SI=0000 DI=0000
DS=0F06  ES=0F06  SS=0F06  CS=0F06  IP=0111   NV UP EI PL NZ NA PO NC
0F06:0111 8D160201       LEA     DX,[0102]
DS:0102=6F4E
```

```
-U
0F06:0111 8D160201      LEA     DX,[0102]
0F06:0115 BB8200        MOV     BX,0082
0F06:0118 803F2F        CMP     BYTE PTR [BX],2F
0F06:011B 7504          JNZ     0121
0F06:011D 8D160501      LEA     DX,[0105]
0F06:0121 B409          MOV     AH,09
0F06:0123 CD21          INT     21            ←
0F06:0125 CD20          INT     20
0F06:0127 3E            DS:
0F06:0128 384100        CMP     [BX+DI+00],AL
0F06:012B 7506          JNZ     0133
0F06:012D 807E8000      CMP     BYTE PTR [BP-80],00
```

We can pick out the instruction that we want to go to as INT 21H, at address 0123H. To execute the program up to this point, all we need to do is type G123 (a simple "G" would have let the program run to the end):

```
-U
0F06:0111 8D160201      LEA     DX,[0102]
0F06:0115 BB8200        MOV     BX,0082
0F06:0118 803F2F        CMP     BYTE PTR [BX],2F
0F06:011B 7504          JNZ     0121
0F06:011D 8D160501      LEA     DX,[0105]
0F06:0121 B409          MOV     AH,09
0F06:0123 CD21          INT     21            ←
0F06:0125 CD20          INT     20
0F06:0127 3E            DS:
0F06:0128 384100        CMP     [BX+DI+00],AL
0F06:012B 7506          JNZ     0133
0F06:012D 807E8000      CMP     BYTE PTR [BP-80],00
-G123                   ←


AX=0900  BX=0082  CX=0027  DX=0105  SP=FFFE  BP=0000  SI=0000 DI=0000
DS=0F06  ES=0F06  SS=0F06  CS=0F06  IP=0123  NV UP EI PL ZR NA PE NC
0F06:0123 CD21          INT     21
```

Here we are, ready to print. The address of the message is 105H, no longer 102H—we are pointing at the right message. On the chance that there may be some error in the message itself, let's dump it and see:

```
-G123

AX=0900  BX=0082  CX=0027  DX=0105  SP=FFFE  BP=0000  SI=0000 DI=0000
DS=0F06  ES=0F06  SS=0F06  CS=0F06  IP=0123  NV UP EI PL ZR NA PE NC
0F06:0123 CD21              INT     21
-D105                   ←
0F06:0100  53 77 69-74 63 68 20 55 73 65 64               Switch Used
0F06:0110  2E 8D 16 02 01 BB 82 00-80 3F 2F 75 04 8D 16 05   .........?/u....
0F06:0120  01 B4 09 CD 21 CD 20 3E-38 41 00 75 06 80 7E 80   ....!. >8A.u..~.
0F06:0130  00 75 15 8B 1E 46 43 D1-E3 D1 E3 2B C0 89 87 BE   .u...FC....+....
0F06:0140  3D 89 87 BC 3D E9 64 FF-8D 46 80 50 8D 86 FC FE   =...=.d..F.P....
0F06:0150  50 E8 B2 32 83 C4 04 B8-FF FF 50 B8 05 00 50 8D   P..2......P...P.
0F06:0160  86 FC FE 50 E8 A5 82 83-C4 06 8B 1E 46 43 D1 E3   ...P........FC..
0F06:0170  D1 E3 A1 0E 3C 8B 16 10-3C 89 87 BC 3D 89 97 BE   ....<...<...=...
0F06:0180  3D FF 36 46 43                                  =.6FC
```

By looking at this memory dump, we can realize that we did not terminate our message with a "/", something required by the string printing service of INT 21H. That was the last bug in OUTPUT. After that, our program works just as expected.

Here's OUTPUT.ASM, all fixed up:

```
CODE_SEG          SEGMENT
          ASSUME  CS:CODE_SEG, DS:CODE_SEG
          ORG     100H
ENTRY:    JMP SHORT START
          NO_MSG  DB "No "
          MSG     DB "Switch Used.$"  ←
START:    LEA     DX,NO_MSG
          MOV     BX,82H
          CMP     BYTE PTR [BX],"/"
          JNE     PRINT
          LEA     DX,MSG
PRINT:    MOV     AH,9
          INT     21H
          INT     20H
CODE_SEG          ENDS
          END     ENTRY
```

While OUTPUT may not be a very productive program, it does at least indicate how a debugging session might work. Typically, there are many steps of debugging and reassembly, with the Trace, Go, and Dump commands all playing a prominent part.

Other DEBUG Commands

We've covered all the DEBUG commands except for these seven: Move, Load, Search, Fill, Compare, Input, and Output. The last two, Input and Output, mimic the I/O bus instructions IN and OUT, which we will not deal with in this book.

Of the remaining five, four (Move, Search, Fill, and Compare) have to do with memory manipulation. There are two ways to specify a certain area of memory in DEBUG, both of which we should cover.

Range or Length

We will use the Search command as an example. Search does just that: It searches. With it you can search for a single byte, or string of bytes (including a character string). Here is an example: We will search the bytes from DS:100 to DS:FFFF for the character "Y":

```
S100 FFFF 'Y'
```

This is an example of specifying a memory *range*—the range from DS:100 to DS:FFFF. We could have searched for bytes by numerical value, like this, which searches for the bytes CDH 20H (machine code for INT 20H):

```
S100 FFFF CD 20
```

Or we could search for a string, like this:

```
S100 FFFF 'Claire'
```

The other way of specifying a memory area to search is with a *length*. Here is an example:

```
S100 L FF00 "Y"
```

DEBUG can take this command all scrunched up as well:

```
S100LFF00 "Y"
```

Here we will search FF00H bytes, starting at DS:0100. For any of these commands—Move, Search, Fill, and Compare—you can specify a length (using L) or a range (specifying beginning and ending points).

The DEBUG Move Command

Move simply moves sections of memory around. For example,

```
M100 102 300
```

will move the bytes DS:100–DS:102 to DS:300–DS:302. You can use a length here as well:

```
M100L3 300
```

and this does the same thing. If you're going to really restructure your programs, however, you're better off reassembling.

The DEBUG Fill Command

This DEBUG command allows you to fill areas of memory with a specified value. This command:

```
F80L3 0
```

fills three bytes starting at DS:0080 with 0. This command, using a range:

```
F80 82 0
```

does the same thing.

The DEBUG Compare Command

If you're trying to compare sections of memory, this command may be for you. Here is the way Compare is used; this example compares the bytes at DS:100 - DS:109 to those at DS:400 - DS:409:

```
C100 109 400
```

Here is the same thing using a range:

```
C100L10 400
```

The DEBUG Load Command

Load is an interesting command that lets you interact directly with the disks. If you've given DEBUG a file name with the N command, you can load that file with a simple L, for load. If we were in DEBUG and wanted to load OUTPUT.COM, this is the way we could do it:

```
A>DEBUG
-NOUTPUT.COM
-L
-
```

You can also load 512 byte sectors directly from the disk. This command:

```
LDS:80 1 5 7
```

will load seven sectors, starting with sector five of disk B: (i.e., disk number 1—drive A is number 0, drive B is number 1, and so forth), and place them in memory starting at DS:0080.

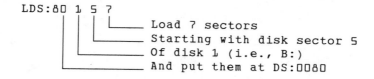

```
LDS:80 1 5 7
              └──────── Load 7 sectors
           └─────────── Starting with disk sector 5
        └────────────── Of disk 1 (i.e., B:)
     └───────────────── And put them at DS:0080
```

All the DEBUG Commands

That completes our review of DEBUG. Just to bring it all together, here is a table with *all* the DEBUG commands, along with examples of their use:

Table 10.9 DEBUG Commands

DEBUG Command		Examples	What it does
A	Assemble	A100	Allows you to type in instructions at CS:100 (DOS 2+ only)
C	Compare	C100 109 400	Compare the bytes at DS:100-109 to DS:400-409
		C100L10 400	Compare 10 bytes from DS:100 to ones at DS:400
D	Dump	DCS:100 110	Dumps bytes CS:100-110 (D alone dumps 128)
		DCS:100	Dumps 128 bytes starting at CS:100
E	Enter	ECS:100 12 10	Enter two bytes 12H and 10H starting at CS:100
		ECS:100	Start entering bytes at CS:100
F	Fill	F80L3 0	Fills three bytes starting at DS:80 with 0
		F80 82 0	Same thing
G	Go	G400	Run program from current location until CS:400
		G400 500	Stops at either CS:400 or CS:500
H	Hex	H E 1	Calculates both E+1 (=0FH) and E (=0DH)
I	Input	I60	Reads a byte from the keyboard port 60H

Table 10.9 DEBUG Commands (*continued*)

DEBUG Command		Examples	What it does
L	Load	L	Loads a file whose name has been set with Name
		LDS:80 1 5 7	Loads seven sectors starting at 5 from B: to DS:80
M	Move	M100 102 300	Moves bytes DS:100*02 to 300-302*
		M100L3 300	Same thing
N	Name	NDORMAT.COM	Names the file
O	Output	OAA 10	10H is output to port AA
Q	Quit	Q	Quit, Exit, Fin, and Stop
R	Register	R	Displays the contents of all registers
		RCX	Displays CX and allows you to modify it
S	Search	S100 FFFF 'Y'	Searches DS:100 to DS:FFFF for "Y"
		S100LFF00 'Y'	Searches FF00 bytes from DS:100 for "Y"
T	Trace	T	Executes the current line
		T5	Executes five lines
U	Unassemble	U100	Unassembles 32 bytes (Default)
		U100 110	Unassembles CS:100 to CS:110
		U100L9	Unassembles nine bytes from CS:100
W	Write	W	Load BX:CX with file size, writes out file
		W80 1 5 7	Writes seven sectors (first is 5) on B: from CS:80

11
Introduction to OS/2

The PS/2

Computer manufacturers have always wondered where to go next with their products. This is always a gamble for them—what if their new machines are rejected by the public? IBM is not immune to it; consider, for example, the PCjr and other fallen stars.

On the other hand, several directions can always be followed with success if you're an established company—more speed and less cost, for example. Also, the PC had some deadly faults—the poor graphics capabilities, for one; relatively slow microprocessors and memory restrictions for two more. So IBM brought out the PS/2.

The PS/2 itself is not such a departure from the PC; it largely follows the rule: more and faster. More disk space, with faster access. More memory to expand into. Faster processors. More keys on the keyboard. Faster clocks.

One significant change was the improved graphics abilities. It had been clear—especially with the success of the Macintosh—that this area had been a disaster before the EGA. Although this doesn't follow the rule of more and faster, it too was a predictable upgrade.

So when the PS/2 appeared, with its 101-key keyboard, large hard drive standard (as well as larger capacity 3.5-inch diskettes), 256-color VGA, and ability to hold megabytes of memory, it was wonderful, but not wholly unexpected.

Micro Follows Mega

Usually, you can know where microcomputers are going simply by looking at mainframe computers. Mainframes represent an established, successful niche of the market. They have taken their present forms over the years—every part of them has proven itself in the marketplace. For example, it was clear even in 1981 that hard disks were on the way, along with bigger memories. The development of the PC has followed this course, within the confines of the microprocessor chips that it has to work with.

This means that Intel determines, to a large extent, where the PC—now PS/2—line will go (in fact, IBM has taken the precaution of acquiring a large chunk of Intel). The IBM microcomputer line is committed to Intel chips. To change now would be almost impossible. If compatibility with earlier versions could not be maintained, IBM would be turning its back on the largest number of software packages ever developed for any computer line.

Multitask-
ing

The Intel chips have not only gotten faster, but they have augmented the instruction set, and allowed for an altogether new ability: *multitasking*.

Of course, multitasking itself is not new. It was put into the Intel chips largely because it also follows the development of mainframe machines, which are multitasking machines. It is inconcievable today to think of a modern mainframe computer that cannot support many users at the same time. Intel decided that it could do no less in the development of its chips; its multitasking follows the development of the big, proven machines.

Single-User Multitasking

On the other hand, what *is* new is the idea of single-user multitasking.

The great majority of IBM microcomputers are single-user machines. Although networks exist, most machines are not connected. Now, although multitasking originated on mainframe computers to handle multiple users, it's being brought to a single-user machine. Single-user multitasking that can run many programs at the same time? This is new, and, to a large extent, it's a risk on IBM's part. And it's the idea behind OS/2.

Why OS/2?

Multitasking is really the only reason behind OS/2. OS/2 may be the result of trying to fit the new Intel chip's multitasking capabilites into a primarily single-user computer. It's true: OS/2 can handle much more memory (up to 16 MB installed) and larger disks, but there is no reason that DOS could not be extended in the same way. DOS currently (Version 4.0) can handle expanded memory to some degree under the Expanded Memory Specification (EMS) standard and disks bigger than 32 MBytes.

DOS 3.3 or 4.0 is the major operating system of PS/2 machines right now, and it looks as though it may be that way for a while. Microsoft is developing new DOS versions, and, it's rumored, has planned DOS versions past 5.0. DOS could certainly be made more friendly, and could perhaps benefit from the use of the mouse, but it can handle the PS/2.

The question "Do we need single-user multitasking?" will be answered as we watch the development of OS/2. Integrated software may be one area in which it could prove itself. It may prove very useful to be able to, say, have your spreadsheet automatically updated when you change entries in your database program. Or, it may turn out that mutitasking will not be used so much to run multiple programs at the same time as in switching back and forth between them, the way the Macintosh's "Finder" does now. We will have to wait and see.

Even so, OS/2 is expensive, memory-intensive, and needs at least 5 MB of disk space. If you want to run OS/2 and DOS, you need 2 MBytes of memory. Running just OS/2 alone needs 1.5 MBytes. Also, of course, you need an 80286 or 80386 microprocessor.

> While OS/2 is up to the capacities of an 80286, it is not yet up to the abilities of the 80386. It runs the 80386 in 80286 mode.

DOS compatibilty mode

From all these requirements, it appears that being able to multitask is not an easy thing to accomplish. In fact, OS/2 brings with it most of the classical parts of a mainframe multitasking operating system, like the use of (we'll examine these soon) hardware "gates," protection "rings," "semaphores" that programs can use to communicate with each other, "pipes," "queues," and other things. Much of OS/2 is devoted to these new, and, to us, perhaps strange things.

OS/2 Is Not so Different

On the other hand, you shouldn't get the idea that programming in OS/2 is so different from what we have been doing; it's not. The writers of OS/2 went to great pains to include DOS compatibility. There is a *DOS compatibility mode* under OS/2, which you can select easily. For most purposes, this puts you back in DOS. Programs that will not run under OS/2 will run here—we'll have to run our macro assembler here. And many programs that will run under OS/2 have been specially designed to run under DOS as well.

Assembly-language instructions like JMP, CMP, JAE, ADD, and so on have not changed. The chips used do not change when we use OS/2; they still use the same instruction set that they always have.

But that's not the only thing. Most of the DOS interrupt services that we have so carefully developed until now in this book are also available in OS/2—under, however, different names.

> If you recall, DOS functions could not be used from a memory-resident program, since DOS is not *re-entrant*. OS/2 *is* re-entrant. You can use any OS/2 function from any program running. This is a tremendous advantage.

Before, under BIOS and DOS, we called these services using the INT instruction in our programs. Now, BIOS and DOS are no longer there. Instead, we will be calling OS/2. In fact, "calling" is the appropriate term for the way we will use OS/2. Under DOS and BIOS, we used system services by loading some registers and using INT. Under OS/2, we will push the values we used to load into registers onto the stack, and then *CALL* OS/2.

Here's an example. Here is how we can print the message "No Worries." under DOS:

```
MESSAGE         DB      "No Worries.$"
     :
     MOV     DX,OFFSET MESSAGE
     MOV     AH,9
     INT     21H
```

We just use service 9 of Interrupt 21H, the major DOS interrupt. We load AH with the number of the service we want, load the data's address into DS:DX, and we're off.

Frequently, this led to some disorganization with the interrupts. As you may recall, some interrupts became huge, like INT 21H, or INT 10H, the BIOS screen interrupt. Another huge interrupt is INT 13H, the disk interrupt. Like most interrupts that have become huge, it did so because more was added to the system. Disks became more and more complex, and INT 13H (originally designed to deal only with floppies) developed not only an immense number of services, but some of the services started developing a number of subservices. Although this sytem still works, it doesn't give the impression of a well thought-out design.

OS/2 is different in this regard. Here you call services by name, not as services under an INT. Here is how we would print out the same message under OS/2:

```
MESSAGE           DB       "No Worries."
MESSAGELENGTH     EQU      $-MESSAGE

        PUSH      DS
        PUSH      OFFSET MESSAGE
        PUSH      MESSAGELENGTH
        PUSH      0                  ;Video handle
        CALL      VioWrtTTY
```

Instead of loading the address into DS:DX, we push DS, then push MESSAGE's offset address. Instead of terminating the string with "$", we explicitly tell OS/2 how long the string to print is by pushing MESSAGELENGTH. Then we push 0 to make sure we use the standard video handle (the "video handle" will always be 0 for us), and CALL a routine named VioWrtTTY.

> Notice how we found the length of MESSAGE in this example: with MESSAGELENGTH EQU $-MESSAGE. Keep in mind that "$" refers to the offset from the beginning of the current segment (here the code segment).

This is how it's done—with a CALL, not an INT. VioWrtTTY is the OS/2 service that prints a character string at the current cursor position. Notice that since it is a call, and the procedure for VioWrtTTY is not present in our program, we will have to declare VioWrtTTY as EXTRN. Somewhere in the program, we will have to have the line: EXTRN VioWrtTTY:FAR.

Frequent use of EXTRN

This is the case for *all* OS/2 services. They will all have to be declared EXTRN, and these references will be picked up at link time. This does not mean that the full code for VioWrtTTY will be linked into your program, as would be normal for linking (that would make all OS/2 programs prohibitively large). Instead, what is linked is a reference to VioWrtTTY, not the whole thing. This is called *dynamic linking*, which we'll see in a moment. When your program is loaded to run, and only then, the rest of VioWrtTTY will be attached.

Understanding OS/2

Despite the similar setup, to understand OS/2, we'll have to become familiar with a new way of looking at the computer, and a new set of concepts (such as the idea of "threads," which is central to OS/2). This will take some examination on our part of just what is going on. To begin understanding OS/2, we'll examine the chip that fathered it, the 80286. We've spent a lot of time discussing the 808X, so it's only fair that we spend some time on its successor.

The 80286

Protected mode

The 80286 chip has two modes of operating: real and protected. The two operating systems for the PS/2 match these modes—DOS (real) and OS/2 (protected).

Real mode is what we have been working in until now. The memory—all 1 MB of it—is available to the user (minus the BIOS 360K at the top, leaving 640K for general use). Here we use segments, and interrupts, and only one program runs at a time.

Protected mode is, as its name suggests, a mode in which multiple programs can run, protected from each other. There are various levels of hierarchy in the computer. And, in protected mode, we no longer use segments, but, rather, segment selectors.

Segment Selectors

Segment selectors look to our programs just like real segment addresses. That is, they are 16-bit numbers that fit into the segment registers. We will work with them here in the same way we used to work with segments.

24-bit addresses

What they really are is a different story. A segment selector points to the segment descriptor table. The segment descriptor pointed to holds the real information about the real segment in memory.

This means that we could have 1343H in the CS register when our program is loaded, and we could think that we are dealing with segment 1343H—that is, 1343:0000 in memory—but we are not. This selector points to an entry in the segment descriptor table, where the real segment address is stored. And this real address does not use the 20 bits we are used to, but 24. This means that we can now address up to 16MB of memory. Quite an improvement.

The reason selectors are useful for multitasking is that OS/2 can move the real segment in memory around wherever it wanted to put it—and the same selector (in a register like CS or DS) would still point to it (although indirectly). If some program finished, segments in memory could be moved around until memory was compacted. Keep in mind that these segments can be of various lengths—they are not necessarily 64K (which is their maximum length).

> A selector is really a memory handle, such as the ones used in the Macintosh. A handle is defined as a pointer to a pointer (if you're ready for that). What makes it useful is that the operating system can change the pointer that points directly to memory, without having to change what the program uses—the pointer to the pointer.

Virtual memory

If the memory is available, OS/2 is a wizard at it; up to 16 MB of it in the machine. And, as if that weren't enough, you can use what is called *virtual memory*. What this means is that if OS/2 runs out of memory in the machine, it will take the least frequently used sections of memory and send them out to the disk. There they will wait until there is either room for them again, or they are specifically referenced by a program then running.

"Swapping" memory out

When a section of memory is sent out to the disk, it is "swapped out." This is a common occurrence in mainframe machines. In the PS/2, however, the disk-acccess time is pretty slow (compared to mainframe hard disks), so it will be noticeable if your program starts to swap out very much. What this means, in practice, is that the 16 MB limit is not truly exceeded by using virtual (disk) memory, but just softened.

In addition to selectors and virtual memory, the 80286 uses almost all the normal tools for multitasking; a complete description of them is beyond this book (a complete description is beyond almost *any* book). But we can mention a few more things that will be important.

Gates

The 80286 uses hardware *gates* in protected mode. When you call a far location, you have to go through a gate before you can access memory in that location. The 80286 maintains a table that tells it whether or not you are qualified to pass through that gate; if not, access is denied. All this is done on a hardware level. This means that each program will stay in its own area of memory, although it can ask for more, or even set up memory to share with other programs.

What is important for us is that if a program attempts to go through an "illegal" gate by making a memory access outside its own memory space, OS/2 terminates the program. A screen will come up, telling you why the program was terminated, and what all the registers were set to. No longer can programs crash the system under OS/2.

Rings

In addition, there are *rings* of protection. Ring 0 is the highest priority ring, and the innermost OS/2 procedures (the OS/2 "kernel") run there. We progress outward to I/O handlers in ring 2, and then to normal application programs, which are always in ring 3, which has the least priority. Depending on which ring your process is in, you will be granted or denied access to certain parts of memory.

**Priority
Levels**

Time-sharing depends on the rings. Inside the same ring, time is allocated equally. However, a program with a lower ring number (and therefore higher priority) will always get time before a program with a higher number (that is, lower priority).

If all this sounds like a hierarchy is being set up in your computer, that's because it is. The 80286 chip enforces rings of priority, isolation of programs, gates for far calls, and other things. No longer is all memory open to you, nor I/O devices, nor the screen buffer (nor interrupts). Although this takes much of the "personal" out of the computer, there are advantages to this scheme too; the primary one is multitasking.

Multitasking Software Concepts

Now that we have seen a little of the chip, we can see that it was built with multitasking in mind. And OS/2 exploits that capability. To make a machine truly multitasking is a demanding problem, and it brings with it new conceptions of how programs will run. Central to multitasking are what OS/2 refers to as "threads."

Threads

A *thread* is an important concept in OS/2: It is what is actively running through programs that are in operation. For example, let's say that you have a notepad popup program under DOS, and are running an editor. The notepad is not running, because it has no *thread*. Under DOS there is only a single thread, and, here, the editor has it. When you pop up the notepad, then it gets the thread.

In OS/2, you can have multiple threads running at once. This is like "voices" in a speaker system. If the speaker has only one voice, like the PC or PS/2 speaker, then even if you emulate a fine instrument, you can only play one at a time. Multiple voices mean that multiple instruments can play at the same time, as in an orchestra. What voices are to a symphony, threads are to OS/2. Saying that OS/2 supports multiple threads means that many programs can be active at once.

I/O Under OS/2

Also, to multitask, the computer can no longer let programs take over I/O devices, as used to happen under DOS. This is one reason why many modem programs or some editors (which write directly to the screen controller chip registers) won't work under OS/2. If you want direct access to an I/O device, instead of using the OS/2 services, you must ask OS/2 for permission.

Communication Between Programs

OS/2 allows programs to pass data and signals back and forth. Although we are not going to dig into those services here (they are far too complicated for this treatment), you can allocate shared segments. This segment can then be reached by multiple programs. In addition, you can ask the system to put aside an open segment that all programs can access.

Sema-
phores

Besides shared segments, there are what are called *semaphores* that are used to communicate between programs. A semaphore is used by two programs as a flag. With it one can tell the other that it is using, for example, a certain part of memory, and that the other should not use it also until the semaphore is *cleared*.

| Semaphores are the basis of multitasking in many ways, and can be read about in any book on operating systems for mainframes. |

Pipes and
queues

Other types of communication can take place through OS/2 constructions like queues and pipes. You are probably familiar with the idea of queues from the PRINT command in DOS. When you queue a number of files to printed, PRINT takes the first one first and starts to print it. The next one in line has to wait (in the queue) until the first one is finished. In the same way, programs in OS/2 can set up queues for use between themselves.

Pipes are a similar idea: Data can be put into a pipe from the output of one program, and read as the input of another. Pipes can accept data from one program at a rate that may be faster than the rate at which the other program can accept it. In this way, they can act as a buffer between programs. Even so, pipes are not inexhaustible. When a pipe fills up, then OS/2 will block the program that fills it until it is at least partially "drained."

With these tools built into it, OS/2 has good support for interprogram (or intraprogram) communication. What we've said here only serves as the briefest of introductions to them; for more details, you should consult an OS/2 book.

Files

The way we handle files is also going to need rethinking under multitasking. We'll discuss this more in the next chapter, when we write an OS/2 assembly-language example that opens, reads, and writes files.

The OS/2 services that will deal with files work in similar ways to their DOS counterparts. The OS/2 services use file handles, just like DOS does (File Control Blocks are not supported any longer). One thing that will be different is the stress put on *how* the files are opened: Do you want to read from the file? Or both read and write? Do you want to deny access to the files by other programs? If so, do you want to deny only programs that will write to the file, or all other programs?

File access

The program that first opens a file can write its own ticket in a number of ways. If it opens the file for both reading and writing, and sets access from other programs to DENY_ALL, then it just about owns the file. On the other hand, a more benign program might open the file for READ_ONLY, and DENY_NONE. Then a second file might open the file for READ_ONLY and yet DENY_WRITE. If a third program tries to open the program for READ_WRITE, it will not be able to, since Program 2 has opened it with a DENY_WRITE. Program 3 is out of luck in this case.

When a file is open, there is a file pointer—actually a *logical file pointer*—that operates just as the file pointer we already know about does. When we read or write, the file pointer is automatically advanced.

Now that we've got a pretty good idea of what multitasking will mean to us, let's jump in and start seeing how to program in OS/2.

Writing an OS/2 Program

Here's where we start to write the code. We can put what we've learned to work. To use OS/2 services instead of the DOS and BIOS ones, we have to know how to reach them.

There are four groups of OS/2 services that we can call from our assembly-language programs—that is, link to—and each of them starts with a particular three-letter combination.

The OS/2 Services

The Vio group of services

Vio means Video Input/Output, and it is the way that you will write to the screen. It replaces BIOS INT 10H (except, notably, in the case of Write and Read dot, since OS/2 does not support graphics in Version 1.0, although a graphics interface is supposed to be in Version 1.1). Examples of the Vio services are VioWrtTTY, VioWrtCharStr, and VioScrollUp. You can get an idea of what they do just from their names.

The Mou group of services

Mou is the prefix for services that deal with the mouse. An example is MouGetPtrPos. This new support for the mouse, and the presence of a mouse port on PS/2s, indicates that IBM anticipates that they might become popular.

The Kbd group of services

Kbd means Keyboard. These services are used for reading what has been typed. Two examples of Kbd services are KbdPeek and KbdCharIn.

The Dos group of services

Dos may be a prefix that you were not expecting. In fact, the commands prefixed with Dos make up most of OS/2. All memory-management services—and this is a big consideration under a multitasking operating system—begin with Dos. The file-management services begin with Dos. In fact, everything that is not I/O-related begins with Dos. Some examples are: DosWrite, DosRead, DosOpen, DosMKDir, and DosGetMachineMode.

> It may be worth noting that IBMBIO and IBMDOS still exist on the disk, just as they do under DOS. IBMBIO is now tiny, and IBMDOS is huge.

In many cases, the use of named procedures makes code easier to read. After all, what is INT 21H service 3FH? It is better to call the similar OS/2 service DosRead.

Higher level languages and OS/2

Also, the calling procedure makes it easier for high-level languages to use OS/2. Under DOS, using assembly-language routines was difficult for users of Pascal, BASIC, or FORTRAN. Now it will be much easier. You used to interact with assembly language from a high-level language by pushing parameters onto the stack, as we've seen. The compiler could sometimes change a call into an INT for you. Now there is no need; you can push parameters onto the stack, and call the routines directly.

As we'll see later, the way OS/2 returns errors is similar to the DOS interrupts too—it uses the AX register. Before, we could check AX for an error code. If AX was zero, this meant there was no error (although some services returned data in AX, or some value that was not zero was returned to indicate no error). Under OS/2, the error code will also be returned in AX, and if it is zero, there was no error. If it was not zero, we will have to track the error down.

When you've filled your program with the Vio, Mou, Dos, and Kbd services, you can link your .OBJ files to OS/2 libraries to make a running .EXE file. As mentioned, this does not link in the routines right there—OS/2 is more canny than that.

Dynamic Linking

This new aspect of OS/2 is called *dynamic linking*. What we have developed so far in this book, OS/2 refers to as *static linking*. In static linking, the .EXE or .COM file is complete. Everything that is necessary to run it is in it. All the code that needs to do the job is there.

Dynamic linking is different. Here is how it works: You run your .ASM file through MASM as you used to do under DOS. In fact, since MASM won't work under OS/2, you'll have to run it under DOS compatibility mode (to put yourself in this mode, just select "DOS Command Prompt" under the "Switch to a running program" part of the OS/2 program selector screen). Then you use the OS/2 linker, LINK (which can also be run under DOS if you wish).

LINK will ask for the name of the .OBJ file, and the names of any libraries you want to give it. One such library—the one we'll use—is called DOSCALLS.LIB. This library (which is supplied on the OS/2 disks) is set up to satisfy references to external calls to the OS/2 services. What usually happens at this point is that the procedure that satisfies the external call in the .ASM file is read in from the library and included in the .EXE file. Here, however, is where the difference comes in.

.DLL files
Instead of procedures, what is in OS/2 .LIB files are the names of *dynamic link library files*, and the locations in those dynamic link library files of the called procedure. The dynamic link library files have the extension .DLL.

Let's take an example. One OS/2 service is named DosOpen, and it is used to open or create files. If we were linking in a call to DosOpen, there would be a reference in DOSCALLS.LIB for DosOpen. It would indicate that DosOpen exists in a .DLL file (actually DOSCALL1.DLL), and give its location there.

When the .EXE file was loaded into memory to run, the loader would see that DosRead is indicated as being found in a .DLL file, and the appropriate .DLL file is read in. The procedure is placed in memory, and its address is placed into the call instruction in the program being loaded.

> If DosRead had already been installed in memory by another pro-
> gram, it is not read in again.

This is what is meant by dynamic linking—the actual linking of the call
to the called procedure is not done until the program is loaded in and run.

OS/2 .EXE File Shell with DosExit

Now we know something about the OS/2 services and how to create an
.EXE file by using LINK under OS/2. We're ready to see what an .EXE
file will look like.

Our OS/2 .EXE file shell isn't so different from what we are used to. In
fact, it's quite similar:

```
        .286C
        .MODEL  SMALL
        .STACK  200H

        .DATA

        .CODE
                EXTRN   DOSEXIT:FAR

ENTRY:  ;Program goes here.

EXIT:   PUSH    1               ;A Normal Exit.
        PUSH    0
        CALL    DOSEXIT

        END     ENTRY
```

At the top, there is a Pseudo-Op ".286C," which begins the .ASM file.
This enables the assembler to assemble instructions for the 80286 and
80287 chips, in lowest priority mode. To assemble instructions that will
need higher authority (and manipulate priveleged tables and registers),
the .286P Pseudo-Op is used. In Versions 5.0 and higher of the macro
assembler, the .286C Pseudo-Op has become simply ".286"; however,
the ".286C" Pseudo-Op is still maintained for compatibility with earlier
assembler versions, and we will use it here so that earlier assemblers may
also be used.

> Although our .EXE file shell doesn't have any PROCs in it, keep in
> mind that if you add one, the main PROC must be declared FAR.

Simplified Segment Directives

Next, notice that we're using the simplified segment directives introduced in Chapter 10 in the discussion of high-level languages:

```
.286C
.MODEL   SMALL       ←
.STACK   200H        ←

.DATA                ←

.CODE                ←
         EXTRN    DOSEXIT:FAR

ENTRY:   ;Program goes here.

EXIT:    PUSH     1              ;A Normal Exit.
         PUSH     0
         CALL     DOSEXIT

         END      ENTRY
```

This is because we have to match segments and groups when we link with DOSCALLS.LIB, and, using the simplified directives, this is all taken care of for us. Unless you match correctly with DOSCALLS, you'll have trouble at link time. With the simplified directives, we won't have to worry about it at all.

Also, we note that we no longer set up the stack at the beginning of the program. With DOS .EXE files, we had to push a two-word address onto the stack so that when the program ended, control would go to DS:0000, where an INT 20H instruction waited. It is not unreasonable to expect that, since there are no longer any interrupts, OS/2 will do things differently.

```
.286C
.MODEL   SMALL
.STACK   200H

.DATA

.CODE
         EXTRN    DOSEXIT:FAR

ENTRY:   ;Program goes here.
                         ← No stack preparation

EXIT:    PUSH     1              ;A Normal Exit.
         PUSH     0
         CALL     DOSEXIT

         END      ENTRY
```

At the end of the program, we use the DosExit call. This is how you end a program under OS/2. To use it, you have to push two words, and then CALL DosExit. The first word pushed is either 0 or 1, and tells DosExit whether or not you want to terminate all "threads." If you recall what a thread means, then you can see what this does—it is possible for a program to have numerous threads executing at the same time. A 0 here means that DosExit should terminate *only* the current thread; a 1 means that *all* threads should be terminated. We will always set this word to 1, since we are not going to deal with multithreaded processes.

The second word pushed is a "termination code," which can be passed back to a program that started the current one. Since we are not going to get that fancy here, we'll always use a "code" of 0:

```
    .286C
    .MODEL   SMALL
    .STACK   200H

    .DATA

    .CODE
         EXTRN    DOSEXIT:FAR

ENTRY:   ;Program goes here.

EXIT:    PUSH     1       ←
         PUSH     0       ←
         CALL     DOSEXIT ←

         END      ENTRY
```

DosExit is also declared as EXTRN FAR in the beginning of the program, as all service calls will have to be from now on.

Stack Preparation Under OS/2

Now that we are familiar with the stack-loading (as opposed to register-loading) calls of OS/2, we have to look at the *type* of things that can be loaded onto the stack. There are three such items:

Type	Explanation
WORD	Just a 16-bit value.
DWORD	A value held in two words, like DX:AX. The high word of a register pair (DX here) is pushed first.
PTR	An address pointer. Here you just push values like DS:BX or ES:DI onto the stack. The *selector* value is pushed first, followed by the offset (like DS and then BX).

Due to the nature of the OS/2 Applications Programming Interface (API), and its heavy reliance on pushing values on the stack, we will become quite familiar with these types.

Defaults when Loading

Loading defaults for CS, SS, DS and AX

When the .EXE file is first loaded, the registers are set to specific values. CS:IP is set to the entry point of the program, as expected. SS:SP is pointed to the top of the stack. DS holds the selector for the data segment. But AX holds something a little new—the selector for the *environment*. This is much like the PSP (Program Segment Prefix) under DOS in that we will be able to find all the characters typed after the program's name on the command line in the environment.

If you are going to use information from the environment, it is usual to move AX into DS (having preserved the data segment's selector, usually in ES). Then DS:0000 is the beginning of the enviroment. At this location, you will find an ASCIIZ string (ASCII terminated with a 0 byte) that gives the current program's full name, including path. For example, if you started a program named GO.EXE in C:\SUB like this:

```
C\SUB>GO
```

then the character appearing at the beginning of the enviroment would be "C:\SUB\GO.EXE",0.

Loading default for BX

The BX register holds the offset, in the environment, of the string of characters typed after the program's name on the command line. If we had typed:

```
C\SUB>GO HI THERE!
```

(and had moved the environment selector into DS), we would find this at DS:BX:

```
" HI THERE!",0
```

Loading defaults for CX and DX

In addition, when the .EXE file is first loaded, DX holds the size of the stack, and CX holds the actual length of the data segment. This information can be useful to the program as it is running.

To produce the .EXE file GO.EXE from the file Go.ASM, we will use MASM under the DOS mode:

```
MASM GO;
```

and then LINK. When we link, we'll have to use OS/2's linker and include the library that will resolve the EXTRN references for us, DOS-CALLS.LIB. Here is the LINK command for GO.OBJ:

```
C>LINK GO          ←Type this
IBM Linker/2  Version 1.00
Copyright (C) IBM Corporation 1987

Copyright (C) Microsoft Corp 1983-1987.  All rights reserved.

Run File [GO.EXE]:
List File [NUL.MAP]:
Libraries [.LIB]: DOSCALLS        ← And this
Definitions File [NUL .DEF]:
```

That's our OS/2 .EXE file shell. It's not much different from its DOS counterpart. In fact, almost everything we examine will have some close DOS or BIOS counterpart, beginning with the first OS/2 programming topic we take up: OS/2 Output.

Because manuals that list the OS/2 services are difficult and expensive to obtain, we'll list many of them here. Of course, we'll include examples of them at work, too (especially in the following Chapter 12, OS/2 in Action), but since we only have two chapters to cover OS/2, we'll emphasize documenting the services.

OS/2 Output (Vio and DosWrite)

The first topic we took up when we started programming in this book was output, and it makes sense to do so again. Although the OS/2 services match BIOS INT 10H, they have a flavor all their own.

Character output is always done in strings in OS/2. If you just want to type out one character, that's a string of length 1. Also, you pass the length of strings to OS/2—you don't terminate them, as you do under DOS (with "$").

You may recall that the BIOS treatment of the cursor when typing out characters was sometimes disappointing because the cursor was not updated. OS/2 is even worse than that (unfortunately) in the majority of its string-printing services. It ignores the cursor altogether—you have to specify a row and column at which printout will start. This awkward method takes some getting used to in your programs.

The DosWrite Service

To use:

```
PUSH    WORD    A file or device handle (=1 to print on screen).
PUSH    PTR     Address of data to be printed.
PUSH    WORD    Number of bytes to print.
PUSH    PTR     Address at which OS/2 is to return the number of bytes
                it actually wrote (more useful for files than
                typing on the screen).
CALL    DOSWRITE
```

Before we get into the Vio services, let's look at DosWrite, similar to the all-purpose DOS INT 21H output service (40H). You simply give DosWrite a handle to write to, the location of the data, and the length of the data, and you're off. This handle could be a handle to a file, which you got when opening or creating a file (we'll cover the OS/2 versions of this in the next chapter), or it could be one of the predefined handles.

In OS/2, the predefined handles are: Standard Input (STDIN = keyboard for all our purposes) = 0; Standard Output (STDOUT = the screen for us) = 1; and Standard Error (STDERR) = 2. These handles are always available (unless you are running under OS/2 detached mode—see the end of this chapter); they do not have to be opened with something like DosOpen, as you have to do for files.

To send output to the screen, we select a handle of 1 (STDOUT). We also have to give DosWrite these things on the stack, in order:

```
WORD    A file or device handle (=1 to print on screen).
PTR     Address of data to be printed
WORD    Number of bytes to print.
PTR     Address at which OS/2 is to return the number of bytes
        it actually wrote (more useful for files than
        typing on the screen).
```

Let's make this clear with an example. Here is a small program, DOS-WRITE.ASM, from beginning to end. All it does is print out our standard message ('No Worries.'):

```
    .286C
 .MODEL  SMALL
 .STACK  200H


 .DATA
MESSAGE         DB      "No Worries."
MESSAGELEN      EQU     $-MESSAGE
NUMBER_BYTES    DW      0

 .CODE
        EXTRN   DOSWRITE:FAR, DOSEXIT:FAR

ENTRY:  PUSH    1
        PUSH    DS
        PUSH    OFFSET  MESSAGE
        PUSH    MESSAGELEN
        PUSH    DS
        PUSH    OFFSET NUMBER_BYTES
        CALL    DOSWRITE

        PUSH    1               ;Exit normally.
        PUSH    0
        CALL    DOSEXIT

        END     ENTRY
```

Since this is our first OS/2 functioning program, let's take a look at it. We simply set up the message in the data segment:

```
.DATA
MESSAGE          DB       "No Worries."    ←
MESSAGELEN       EQU      $-MESSAGE        ←
NUMBER_BYTES     DW       0
```

Note also that since we will require the length of the message, we find it with MESSAGELEN EQU $-MESSAGE, right after the definition of MESSAGE. We've used this method before; this just fills MESSAGELEN with the length of message. Now we add these instructions to the .EXE file shell:

```
.286C
.MODEL   SMALL
.STACK   200H

.DATA
MESSAGE          DB       "No Worries."
MESSAGELEN       EQU      $-MESSAGE
NUMBER_BYTES     DW       0

.CODE
        EXTRN    DOSWRITE:FAR, DOSEXIT:FAR

ENTRY:  PUSH     1                            ←
        PUSH     DS                           ←
        PUSH     OFFSET   MESSAGE             ←
        PUSH     MESSAGELEN                   ←
        PUSH     DS                           ←
        PUSH     OFFSET NUMBER_BYTES          ←
        CALL     DOSWRITE                     ←

        PUSH     1               ;Exit normally.
        PUSH     0
        CALL     DOSEXIT

        END      ENTRY
```

(having carefully declared DosWrite EXTRN). In particular, notice that we are are now pushing immediate values, such as:

```
→       PUSH     1
                 :
        PUSH     OFFSET   MESSAGE
        PUSH     MESSAGELEN
```

This is the first time we have seen this immediate method of pushing values, and it will come in handy with the enormous number of pushes you have to do in the average OS/2 program. Immediate pushing will not work on the 8088 or 8086 chips. To push values there, you must first load them into registers (of course, OS/2 will not work with 8088s or 8086s either).

> In fact, it is common in OS/2 programming to define macros that will do all the pushing for you, and then pass the values to be pushed as parameters. Often, OS/2 programs are simply masses of macros.

In our program, we make the pushes of the video handle (1), the address of MESSAGE, the length of MESSAGE, and the address of the location where OS/2 will return the number of bytes actually typed to the screen.

```
        .286C
        .MODEL  SMALL
        .STACK  200H

        .DATA
MESSAGE             DB      "No Worries."
MESSAGELEN          EQU     $-MESSAGE
NUMBER_BYTES        DW      0

        .CODE
        EXTRN   DOSWRITE:FAR, DOSEXIT:FAR
ENTRY:  PUSH    1                               ←
        PUSH    DS                              ←
        PUSH    OFFSET  MESSAGE                 ←
        PUSH    MESSAGELEN                      ←
        PUSH    DS                              ←
        PUSH    OFFSET NUMBER_BYTES             ←
        CALL    DOSWRITE                        ←
        :
        :
```

and end with DosExit:

```
        .286C
        .MODEL  SMALL
        .STACK  200H

        .DATA
MESSAGE             DB      "No Worries."
MESSAGELEN          EQU     $-MESSAGE
NUMBER_BYTES        DW      0

        .CODE
        EXTRN   DOSWRITE:FAR, DOSEXIT:FAR

ENTRY:  PUSH    1
        PUSH    DS
        PUSH    OFFSET  MESSAGE
        PUSH    MESSAGELEN
        PUSH    DS
        PUSH    OFFSET NUMBER_BYTES
```

```
CALL    DOSWRITE

PUSH    1                    ;Exit normally.
PUSH    0
CALL    DOSEXIT

END     ENTRY
```

Give this little program a try if you want to see our "No Worries." message appear under OS/2. Our first OS/2 program works, and it wasn't so hard to program.

DosWrite types out the bytes that you have selected starting at the current cursor position—as does the next OS/2 service, VioWrtTTY.

VioWrtTTY—TTY Output to Screen (Uses and Updates Cursor)

```
PUSH    PTR      Pointer to the ASCII string to print on the screen.
PUSH    WORD     Length of the string.
PUSH    WORD     The VIO handle (must be 0).
CALL    VIOWRTTTY
```

The first of the Vio services we will work on is VioWrtTTY, which is close to its INT 10H teletype counterpart. Again, you pass the address of the data to be printed, then the number of bytes to print. The Vio handle for the screen, however, is not 1, but 0. We'll see that you have to pass the Vio handle for virtually every Vio service, and it will always be 0. Perhaps in some future version of OS/2, multiple physical screens will be allowed, giving you non-zero Vio handles.

VioWrtTTY types at the cursor location

VioWrtTTY starts printing at the cursor location, unlike all the following Vio services. It treats screen control characters like <cr> (ASCII 13) or <lf> (ASCII 10) as control characters—it does not print them out as funny symbols as some of the BIOS services do. Instead, <cr> will generate a carriage return, <lf> will generate a linefeed, and so forth.

Also, the string to be printed is only ASCII; no screen display attributes are included. You may recall that characters can be typed to the screen and can sometimes be specified as ASCII with a particular attribute under BIOS. This same thing can be done a number of ways under OS/2.

VioWrtCellStr—Write a Cell String

```
PUSH    PTR      Address of cell string (attribute, character,
                 attribute, character...) to be printed.
PUSH    WORD     The number of bytes to be printed.
PUSH    WORD     Screen Row where the string will be printed.
PUSH    WORD     Screen Column where the string will be printed.
PUSH    WORD     Vio Handle (must be 0).
CALL    VIOWRTCELLSTR
```

This is the first of the normal Vio printing services. VioWrtCellStr is an improvement on its BIOS counterpart in that you can specify different attributes for each character to be printed.

> To make the Vio Services that print out at a specifed row, column print out at the cursor position, use the cursor position returned by VioGetCursorPos, covered later.

Character cells

The combination of ASCII character and screen attribute (two bytes) is referred to as a character *cell*. This Vio service will let you print out a whole string of such cells.

The screen attributes that can be used in the Vio services that print attributes work like this:

Figure 11.1 Character Screen Attribute Byte

```
XRGBIRGB
 | |  | |___
 |  |  |    |_____Color of character.
 |  |  |
 |  |  |_____If = 1, makes character intense.
 |  |
 |  |_____Color of background.
 |
 |_____The meaning of "X" is set
                   with VioSetState. If "Blink"
                   is enabled, then X=1 means the
                   character will blink. If
                   "Intensity" is enbled, then X=1
                   means the background will be
                   intense.
```

Examples are 01110100B = 74H, red on a white background, or 00001111 = FH, high intensity white on a black background.

For example, if you wanted to print out four red "A"s (ASCII 41H) on a white background (attribute 74H), followed by three blue "B"s (ASCII 42H) on a white background (attribute 71H), then you could define a *cell string* like this (with attribute first, then ASCII, attribute, ASCII, etc):

```
CELL_STRING     DB 74H, 41H, 74H, 41H, 74H, 41H, 74H, 41H, 74H, 41H
                DB 71H, 42H, 71H, 42H, 71H, 42H, 71H, 42H
```

This service is one where you have to specify the row and column at which your cell string will be printed.

> When you have to specify row and column, remember that (0,0) is the upper-left corner of the screen.

If you want to use a service more like the old BIOS, where you specify what to type and and only one attribute, the next service, VioWrtChar-StrAtt, will let you do so.

VioWrtCharStrAttr—Write Character String with Attribute

```
PUSH    PTR     Address of the character string to print on screen.
PUSH    WORD    The length in bytes of the character string.
PUSH    WORD    Screen Row at which printout will start.
PUSH    WORD    Screen Column at which printout will start.
PUSH    PTR     Address of the attribute byte.
PUSH    WORD    The Vio handle (must be 0).
CALL    VIOWRTCHARSTRATTR
```

This service prints out a character string (specified as a string of ASCII bytes) with a single attribute. It is what you'd expect from seeing the previous services, except that the way you pass the attribute byte to OS/2 seems like a little bit of overkill. Instead of loading the attribute byte into a word (in, say, the lower byte) and pushing that, you pass the *address* (two words) of the attribute byte as stored in memory. Why this is done isn't exactly clear, but that's the way OS/2 expects it.

Let's give VioWrtStrAttr a try ourselves. Let's print out the "No Worries." message with some dramatic attribute—say blue on black, attribute 1. First, we'd start with the .EXE file shell:

```
        .286C
        .MODEL  SMALL
        .STACK  200H

        .DATA

        .CODE
            EXTRN   DosExit:FAR

ENTRY:

            PUSH    1               ;Exit normally.
            PUSH    0
            CALL    DOSEXIT

            END     ENTRY
```

Then we can add the data we'll need—the string itself, the string's length, and the attribute byte (which we'll call ATTRIBYTE):

```
.286C
.MODEL   SMALL
.STACK   200H

.DATA

MESSAGE          DB        "No Worries."                        ←
MESSAGELEN       EQU       $-MESSAGE                            ←
ATTRIBYTE        DB        1          ;Use a blue-on-black attribute. ←

.CODE
        EXTRN    DosExit:FAR

ENTRY:
        PUSH     1                    ;Exit normally.
        PUSH     0
        CALL     DOSEXIT

        END      ENTRY
```

Now we have to set up for VioWrtCharStrAtt. To begin, we have to push a pointer to MESSAGE. Pointers are pushed with the selector register first, so here goes:

```
.286C
.MODEL   SMALL
.STACK   200H

.DATA
MESSAGE          DB        "No Worries."
MESSAGELEN       EQU       $-MESSAGE
ATTRIBYTE        DB        1          ;Use a blue-on-black attribute.

.CODE
        EXTRN    VioWrtCharStrAtt:FAR, DosExit:FAR

ENTRY:  PUSH     DS                   ←
        PUSH     OFFSET  MESSAGE      ←
        PUSH     MESSAGELEN           ←

        PUSH     1                    ;Exit normally.
        PUSH     0
        CALL     DOSEXIT

        END      ENTRY
```

We have followed it with the message's length, as required. Next, we have to select the row and column location of our message on the screen. Let's choose row 10, column 30—near the middle of the screen:

```
.286C
.MODEL   SMALL
.STACK   200H

.DATA
MESSAGE          DB        "No Worries."
MESSAGELEN       EQU       $-MESSAGE
ATTRIBYTE        DB        1          ;Use a blue-on-black attribute.

.CODE
```

```
        EXTRN     VioWrtCharStrAtt:FAR, DosExit:FAR
ENTRY:  PUSH      DS
        PUSH      OFFSET  MESSAGE
        PUSH      MESSAGELEN
        PUSH      10                      ←
        PUSH      30                      ←

        PUSH      1                       ;Exit normally.
        PUSH      0
        CALL      DOSEXIT

        END       ENTRY
```

Finally, we push a pointer to the attribute byte ATTRIBYTE, and the Vio handle (0). Here's the whole program:

```
.286C
.MODEL  SMALL
.STACK  200H

.DATA
MESSAGE        DB        "No Worries."
MESSAGELEN     EQU       $-MESSAGE
ATTRIBYTE      DB        1          ;Use a blue-on-black attribute.

.CODE
        EXTRN     VioWrtCharStrAtt:FAR, DosExit:FAR

ENTRY:  PUSH      DS
        PUSH      OFFSET  MESSAGE
        PUSH      MESSAGELEN
        PUSH      10
        PUSH      30
        PUSH      DS                      ←
        PUSH      OFFSET ATTRIBYTE        ←
        PUSH      0                       ←
        CALL      VioWrtCharStrAtt        ←

        PUSH      1                       ;Exit normally.
        PUSH      0
        CALL      DOSEXIT

        END       ENTRY
```

Another thing you could do under BIOS is to simply print out characters without changing the underlying attributes for those screen positions, and you can do that here too, with VioWrtCharStr.

VioWrtCharStr

```
PUSH      PTR       Address of the character string to print.
PUSH      WORD      Length in bytes of the character string.
PUSH      WORD      Screen Row at which printout will start.
PUSH      WORD      Screen Column at which printout will start.
PUSH      WORD      Vio handle (must be 0).
CALL                VIOWRTCHARSTR
```

VioWrtCharStr prints a string of ASCII characters. When the string is printed on the screen, the attributes for each screen location that were there before are not changed. If VioWrtCharStr is writing over a blue patch, through a red patch, and into a green patch, those are the attributes that will be maintained.

You can use this simple service when you've set up the screen in some way that you want to maintain, instead of having to select some different attribute.

The Cursor

As we've seen, many Vio services act independently of the cursor. If you want to coordinate what you are typing on the screen with the cursor, you'll have to find the cursor position (row, column) and pass it as the row, column at which printout is to begin.

To find the location of the cursor, use VioGetCursorPos.

VioGetCursorPos—Get Cursor Position

```
PUSH    PTR     Address at which OS/2 will return current cursor row.
PUSH    PTR     Address at which OS/2 will return current cursor col.
PUSH    WORD    Vio handle (must be 0)
CALL    VIOGETCURSORPOS
```

This service is pretty self-explanatory. All VioGetCursorPos does is get the cursor's position on the screen.

You may recall that in BIOS this information could be returned in one register (row and column number each taking up one byte). Here, you have to pass an address at which OS/2 will store the row and column numbers.

```
PUSH    PTR     Address at which OS/2 will return current cursor row.
PUSH    PTR     Address at which OS/2 will return current cursor col.
PUSH    WORD    Vio handle (must be 0).
CALL    VIOGETCURSORPOS
```

Other then that, this service is easy to use. The next service is the natural counterpart to this one: VioSetCursorPos.

VioSetCursorPos—Set Cursor Position

```
PUSH    WORD    New Cursor Row Number.
PUSH    WORD    New Cursor Column Number.
PUSH    WORD    Vio handle (must be 0).
CALL    VIOSETCURSORPOS
```

With this service, you can set the cursor position. The parameters you pass are simple: a word that specifies the new cursor row, a word that specifies the new cursor column, and the omnipresent Vio handle (0). To set the cursor to screen position 10,20 (= row,cloumn), do this:

```
PUSH    10
PUSH    20
PUSH    0
CALL    VIOSETCURSORPOS
```

If you have to do a lot of screen work, especially if you are accepting typed input, you'll find this service useful.

Scrolling

In BIOS, there are two ways to scroll (up and down); in OS/2, there are four (up, down, left, and right).

The four services are: VioScrollUp, VioScrollDn, VioScrollLe, and VioScrollRi. You pass the stack parameters to them in the same way

```
PUSH    WORD    Top row of scroll area.
PUSH    WORD    Left column of scroll area.
PUSH    WORD    Bottom row of scroll area.
PUSH    WORD    Right column of scroll area.
PUSH    WORD    Number of rows or columns to scroll (FFFF → Clear
                the scroll area.)
PUSH    PTR     Pointer to a two-byte cell (attribute, cell) that
                will fill the scrolled row or column.
PUSH    WORD    Vio handle (must be 0).
CALL    VIOSCROLLUP/VIOSCROLLDN/VIOSCROLLLE/VIOSCROLLRI
```

With these services, like their BIOS counterparts, you can scroll windows on the screen, or the whole screen. Here, if you indicate that the number of rows or columns that is to be scrolled is FFFFH, the scroll area will be cleared.

Also, you can specify a "fill cell" that will be used to fill the newly blank row or column that has just been scrolled. This way you can make sure that a red window stays red as you are scrolling it, for example.

VioSetMode—Set Video Mode

```
PUSH    PTR     Address of video mode data (see below).
PUSH    WORD    Vio handle (must be 0).
```

Even though OS/2 Version 1.0 is leaving all graphics to Version 1.1, you can still set the screen mode yourself. Table 11.1 presents the allowed screen modes.

Table 11.1 OS/2 Allowed Screen Modes

Type	Colors	Cols	Rows	Res
B&W Text	16	40	25 CGA,EGA,VGA	320x200
			43 EGA,VGA	320x350
			50 VGA	360x400
Text	16	40	25 CGA,EGA,VGA	320x200
			43 EGA,VGA	320x350
			50 VGA	360x400
B&W Text	16	80	25 CGA,EGA,VGA	640x200
			43 EGA,VGA	640x350
			50 VGA	720x400
Text	16	80	25 CGA,EGA,VGA	640x200
			43 EGA,VGA	640x350
			50 VGA	720x400
Graphics	4	-	- CGA,EGA,VGA	320x200
Graphics	2	-	- CGA,EGA,VGA	320x200
Graphics	2	-	- CGA,EGA,VGA	640x200
Mono Text	-	80	25 Mono,EGA,VGA	720x350
Graphics	16	-	- EGA,VGA	320x200
Graphics	4	-	- EGA,VGA	640x200
Graphics	2	-	- EGA,VGA	640x350
Graphics	16	-	- EGA,VGA	640x350
Graphics	2	-	- VGA	640x480
Graphics	16	-	- VGA	640x480
Graphics	256	-	- VGA	320x200

In BIOS, each of these modes has a number associated with it; that is not the case in OS/2. Instead, you explicitly list all the parameters that make up the display mode you want, like number of pixels horizontally and vertically, or number of rows and columns, and so on.

You have to pass VioSetMode the address of a data area that holds this information in memory. That data area is set up like this:

Figure 11.2 VioSetMode/VioGetMode Data Area

```
DW      Length of this data area (including this word).
DB      "Mode Characteristics"
        xxxxxxx0 → Monochrome printer adapter
        xxxxxxx1 → All others
        xxxxxx0x → Text mode
        xxxxxx1x → Graphics mode
        xxxxx0xx → Screen is color (color burst enable)
        xxxxx1xx → Screen is B&W (color burst disable)
DB      Number of colors in this video mode:
        1 → 2 colors (pixels are on or off)
        2 → 4 colors
        4 → 16 colors
DW      Number of text columns.
DW      Number of text rows.
DW      Horizontal resolution in pixels.
DW      Vertical resolution in pixels.
DD      A reserved doubleword. Make these words 0 when you push them.
```

Once you set up the address of this data area on the stack, and push the Vio handle (as usual, 0), you can call VioSetMode.

If the video mode was set correctly, AX will hold 0 on return. If there has been an error, AX will hold 355, which simply means that display does not support the mode requested.

You can also get the current video mode with VioGetMode. This service, which we'll cover next, is much like VioSetMode.

VioGetMode—Get Video Mode

```
PUSH    PTR     Address of video mode data (see VioSetMode).
PUSH    WORD    Vio handle (must be 0).
```

This service will get the current video mode. You first set aside an area in memory that OS/2 will fill, and push its address onto the stack, followed by the Vio handle. Upon return, the data area will be filled out with the values that we already defined in VioSetMode.

VioPopUp

One additional Vio call deserves notice here—and that is VioPopUp.

VioPopUp is not to be used in the way that you might think—it is not used for normal popup utilities. Instead, it is used by programs that are normally cut off from using the screen when they need to grab screen control to report some sort of problem or emergency.

Under OS/2, you can "DETACH" a program, and that program will continue to run. DETACH is a common mainframe command; however, the program can no longer accept input from the keyboard or print out to the screen unless it takes special action—and that action is calling VioPopUp.

You push these parameters for VioPopUp:

```
PUSH    PTR     Address of a one-word option field:
                rrrrrrrr rrrrrrXW  (r = reserved)

                X = 0 → Nontransparent popup (screen cleared).
                  = 1 → Transparent popup.

                W = 0 → Return with error if popup cannot be made.
                  = 1 → Wait for popup.
PUSH    WORD    Vio handle (must be 0).
CALL    VIOPOPUP
```

Selecting a nontransparent popup means that the screen will be cleared before your program starts to type on it. If you are in graphics mode, the screen is reset to text mode. If you ask for a transparent popup, the screen is not reset, and the call will fail if the screen is currently in graphics mode.

The TAKE5 program

Let's write a little program called TAKE5 that you can DETACH, and that will grab the screen and clear it after five minutes are up, with the message: "Time Is Up!" It will wait until you type a key, and then relinquish the screen.

To run TAKE5 after making TAKE5.EXE, just type DETACH TAKE5. In a way, this is like the earlier DOS memory-resident programs, but only slightly. TAKE5 cannot read what is being typed in the main session, it cannot print on the screen (except via VioPopUp), and it is isolated from everyone else. Just how real popup programs develop under OS/2 remains to be seen. You can write what are called "device monitors" that can monitor what is being typed, and so forth, presumably to pick out hot keys and the like. But they are not as flexible as under DOS.

DosSleep   In TAKE5, we'll use a service that will be introduced next chapter called DosSleep. If you pass DosSleep a number of milliseconds as a doubleword like DX:AX (push high word first, then low word), it will suspend the program for that long. Since we want to suspend TAKE5 for five minutes, we need to know how many milliseconds there are in those five minutes. That is 5 (minutes) x 60 (seconds/minute) x 1000 (milliseconds/second) = 300,000 milliseconds. In hex, this is 493E0H. If we put this into the register pair DX:AX, DX would hold 4 and AX would hold 93E0H.

This means that we execute these instructions and then call DosSleep:

```
                              ;493E0H = 300,000 = no. of millisec.s in
5 minutes.
ENTRY:  PUSH    4           ;Push high word             ←
        PUSH    93E0H       ;Push low word              ←
        CALL    DosSleep                                ←
        :
        :
        END     ENTRY
```

After we return, we have to grab the screen with VioPopUp. To do that, we add this code:

```
        .286C
        .MODEL  SMALL
        .STACK  200H

        .DATA

        .CODE
        EXTRN   DOSEXIT:FAR
                        ;493E0H = 300,000 = no. of millisec.s in
                        ;5 minutes.
ENTRY:  PUSH    4           ;Push high word
        PUSH    93E0H       ;Push low word
        CALL    DosSleep

        PUSH    DS                              ←
        PUSH    OFFSET POPUP_OPTIONS            ←
        PUSH    0                               ←
        CALL    VioPopUp                        ←
        :
        :
        END     ENTRY
```

Where POPUP_OPTIONS is defined in the data area to request a non-transparent popup that will wait:

```
        .286C
        .MODEL  SMALL
        .STACK  200H

        .DATA
        POPUP_OPTIONS   DB 1        ←

        .CODE
        EXTRN   DOSEXIT:FAR
                        ;493E0H = 300,000 = no. of millisec.s in
                        ;5 minutes.
ENTRY:  PUSH    4           ;Push high word
        PUSH    93E0H       ;Push low word
```

```
        CALL    DosSleep

        PUSH    DS
        PUSH    OFFSET POPUP_OPTIONS
        PUSH    0
        CALL    VioPopUp
         :
         :
        END     ENTRY
```

After we have control of the screen, we have to print out our message. We can put the message into the data segment like this:

> VioPopUp gives a program control of the screen, keyboard, and mouse.

```
.286C
.MODEL  SMALL
.STACK  200H

.DATA
        MESSAGE DB "Time Is Up!"              ←
        MESSAGELEN EQU $ - MESSAGE            ←
        POPUP_OPTIONS   DB 1

.CODE
        EXTRN   DOSEXIT:FAR
                      ;493E0H = 300,000 = no. of millisec.s in
                      ;5 minutes.
ENTRY:  PUSH    4         ;Push high word
        PUSH    93E0H     ;Push low word
        CALL    DosSleep

        PUSH    DS
        PUSH    OFFSET POPUP_OPTIONS
        PUSH    0
        CALL    VioPopUp
         :
         :
        END     ENTRY
```

And print it out like this:

```
.286C
.MODEL  SMALL
.STACK  200H

.DATA
        MESSAGE DB "Time Is Up!"
        MESSAGELEN EQU $ - MESSAGE
        POPUP_OPTIONS   DB 1

.CODE
        EXTRN   DOSEXIT:FAR
                      ;493E0H = 300,000 = no. of millisec.s in
                      ;5 minutes.
ENTRY:  PUSH    4         ;Push high word
        PUSH    93E0H     ;Push low word
        CALL    DosSleep
```

```
        PUSH    DS
        PUSH    OFFSET POPUP_OPTIONS
        PUSH    0
        CALL    VioPopUp

        PUSH    DS                      ←
        PUSH    OFFSET MESSAGE          ←
        PUSH    MESSAGELEN              ←
        PUSH    0                       ←
        CALL    VioWrtTTY               ←
        :
        :
        END     ENTRY
```

Next we will wait for a key to be struck with the Kbd service KbdCharIn. We will start off the following chapter with these services. Here, we are instructing OS/2 to read a key, and, if no keys are ready, to wait for one:

```
        .286C
        .MODEL  SMALL
        .STACK  200H

        .DATA
        MESSAGE DB "Time Is Up!"
        MESSAGELEN EQU $ - MESSAGE
        POPUP_OPTIONS   DB 1
        CHAR_DATA       DB 0
                SCAN    DB 0
                STATUS  DB 0
                NSHIFT  DB 0
                SHIFT   DW 0
                TSTAMP  DD 0

        .CODE
        EXTRN   DOSEXIT:FAR
                        ;493E0H = 300,000 = no. of millisec.s in
                        ;5 minutes.
ENTRY:  PUSH    4       ;Push high word
        PUSH    93E0H   ;Push low word
        CALL    DosSleep

        PUSH    DS
        PUSH    OFFSET POPUP_OPTIONS
        PUSH    0
        CALL    VioPopUp

        PUSH    DS
        PUSH    OFFSET MESSAGE
        PUSH    MESSAGELEN
        PUSH    0
        CALL    VioWrtTTY

        PUSH    DS                      ←
        PUSH    OFFSET CHAR_DATA        ←
        PUSH    0                       ←
        PUSH    0                       ←
        CALL    KbdCharIn               ←

        :
        :
        END     ENTRY
```

You might note in passing the data area we had to set up for KbdCharIn, just to read in a single key. We'll tackle this in the next chapter. After we receive a key, we just end the popup with VioEndPopUp:

```
        .286C
        .MODEL  SMALL
        .STACK  200H

        .DATA
            MESSAGE DB "Time Is Up!"
            MESSAGELEN EQU $ - MESSAGE
            POPUP_OPTIONS  DB 1
            CHAR_DATA      DB 0
                SCAN       DB 0
                STATUS     DB 0
                NSHIFT     DB 0
                SHIFT      DW 0
                TSTAMP     DD 0

        .CODE
        EXTRN   DOSEXIT:FAR
                        ;493E0H = 300,000 = no. of millisec.s in
                        ;5 minutes.
                        ;493E0H = 300,000 = no. of millisec.s in
                        ;5 minutes.
ENTRY:  PUSH    4        ;Push high word
        PUSH    93E0H    ;Push low word
        CALL    DosSleep

        PUSH    DS
        PUSH    OFFSET POPUP_OPTIONS
        PUSH    0
        CALL    VioPopUp

        PUSH    DS
        PUSH    OFFSET MESSAGE
        PUSH    MESSAGELEN
        PUSH    0
        CALL    VioWrtTTY

        PUSH    DS
        PUSH    OFFSET CHAR_DATA
        PUSH    0
        PUSH    0
        CALL    KbdCharIn

        PUSH    0              ←
        CALL    VioEndPopUp    ←
        :
        :
        END     ENTRY
```

Now we're ready to exit with DosExit. Here's the whole TAKE5.ASM program, including all the EXTRNs:

```
        .286C
        .MODEL  SMALL
        .STACK  200H

        .DATA
            MESSAGE DB "Time Is Up!"
```

```
          MESSAGELEN EQU $ - MESSAGE
          POPUP_OPTIONS   DB 1
          CHAR_DATA       DB 0
                  SCAN    DB 0
                  STATUS  DB 0
                  NSHIFT  DB 0
                  SHIFT   DW 0
                  TSTAMP  DD 0

    .CODE
          EXTRN   DosExit:FAR,DosSleep:FAR,VioPopUp:FAR,
          EXTRN   VioEndPopUp:FAR,VioWrtTTY:FAR,KbdCharIn:FAR

                          ;493E0H = 300,000 = no. of millisec.s in
                          ;5 minutes.
  ENTRY:  PUSH    4       ;Push high word
          PUSH    93E0H   ;Push low word
          CALL    DosSleep

          PUSH    DS
          PUSH    OFFSET POPUP_OPTIONS
          PUSH    0
          CALL    VioPopUp

          PUSH    DS
          PUSH    OFFSET MESSAGE
          PUSH    MESSAGELEN
          PUSH    0
          CALL    VioWrtTTY

          PUSH    DS
          PUSH    OFFSET CHAR_DATA
          PUSH    0
          PUSH    0
          CALL    KbdCharIn

          PUSH    0
          CALL    VioEndPopUp

  EXIT:   PUSH    1                      ;A Normal Exit.
          PUSH    0
          CALL    DosExit

          END     ENTRY
```

Give it a try—just type DETACH TAKE5. Five minutes later, TAKE5 will let you know that the time's up, stopping the program then running. Our first multitasking example!

12

OS/2 in Action

Keyboard Input
The BEEPb Program
Keyboard Buffer Use
File Handling

DosOpen
OS/2 Errors
OS/2 Error Codes
DosClose

The COPIER Program
File Open Modes
OS/2File Pointer
Machine Mode

In the previous chapter, we were introduced to OS/2 and its output services. In this chapter, we'll continue digging into OS/2, looking at its input, file, and other services. Some of these services match what we've come to expect from BIOS and DOS, while others may be completely different. For assembly-language programmers, this means that only very simple .ASM files can be converted quickly from DOS to OS/2. In some cases, programmers have used macros to execute BIOS and DOS services, and sometimes these macros can simply be replaced on a one-for-one basis. But this is rare: OS/2 almost always returns information in a way different from DOS or BIOS. On the other hand, OS/2 often has more to offer, as we'll see in the Keyboard services (Kbd).

Using the Keyboard

The Kbd services can be thought of as a superset of what is offered under DOS and BIOS—that is, they contain all those services and more. Keyboard coverage under OS/2 seems pretty thorough.

Included in the services that we will cover is: reading a single key, two ways of receiving buffered input, reading the keyboard without removing characters from the keyboard buffer, and changing the shift or echo state. All these services begin with the prefix Kbd, except for one, Dos-Read.

The DosRead Service

```
PUSH    WORD    The Kbd handle (STDIN = 0).
PUSH    PTR     Address of the data buffer string will be written to.
PUSH    WORD    Length of the data buffer.
PUSH    PTR     Address of a word that OS/2 will update with the number
                    of bytes read until <cr> was typed.
CALL    DOSREAD
```

DosRead is the counterpart of the all-purpose OS/2 output service, Dos-Write. With DosRead you can read not only from files, but also from devices—like the keyboard.

> You can even use multiple keyboards under OS/2, using the KbdOpen, KbdGetFocus, and KbdClose services.

The device handle for the keyboard we will be using is STDIN = 0. All you have to do is provide DosRead with four quantities: the Kbd handle (0), the address of a data buffer into which OS/2 will write the character string that was typed, the length of that data buffer, and the address of a word that OS/2 will update with the actual number of characters read. If you only want to read one character, set the buffer length to one (or use the service KbdCharIn).

Here is a brief example program to use DosRead to read up to 20 characters from the keyboard and store them in a buffer (named BUFFER):

```
BUFFER_LEN      EQU     20
.286C
.MODEL  SMALL
.STACK  200H

.DATA
        BUFFER  DB BUFFER_LEN DUP(0)
        NUMBER_CHARS    DW      0

.CODE
        EXTRN   DOSEXIT:FAR,DOSREAD:FAR

ENTRY:  PUSH    0           ;STDIN handle.
        PUSH    DS
        PUSH    OFFSET BUFFER
        PUSH    BUFFER_LEN
        PUSH    DS
        PUSH    OFFSET NUMBER_CHARS
        CALL    DOSREAD

EXIT:   PUSH    1                   ;A Normal Exit.
        PUSH    0
        CALL    DOSEXIT

        END     ENTRY
```

> Notice that we defined BUFFER_LEN at the beginning of the program (BUFFER_LEN EQU 20) and then referred to it throughout the code. If we had wanted to modify the buffer length, we would only have to change BUFFER_LEN in one place.

This example is pretty simple. First, we set up the two quantities that we will need in the data segment:

```
BUFFER_LEN        EQU      20
  .286C
  .MODEL   SMALL
  .STACK   200H

  .DATA
        BUFFER  DB BUFFER_LEN DUP(0)     ←
        NUMBER_CHARS    DW       0       ←
```

BUFFER is defined as an area BUFFER_LEN bytes long, and we have set BUFFER_LEN to 20. NUMBER_CHARS is a word that DosRead will update after the call is completed.

When DosRead reads from the keyboard, it places only the ASCII code of the struck keys into the buffer. If your program needs the more specific scan codes or other information, you will have to use KbdCharIn.

Next in the program, we simply put in the call to DosRead:

```
BUFFER_LEN        EQU      20
  .286C
  .MODEL   SMALL
  .STACK   200H

  .DATA
        BUFFER  DB BUFFER_LEN DUP(0)
        NUMBER_CHARS    DW       0

  .CODE
        EXTRN    DOSEXIT:FAR,DOSREAD:FAR

ENTRY:  PUSH     0          ;STDIN handle.    ←
        PUSH     DS                           ←
        PUSH     OFFSET BUFFER                ←
        PUSH     BUFFER_LEN                   ←
        PUSH     DS                           ←
        PUSH     OFFSET NUMBER_CHARS          ←
        CALL     DOSREAD                      ←

EXIT:   PUSH     1                  ;A Normal Exit.
        PUSH     0
        CALL     DOSEXIT

        END      ENTRY
```

Then all we need to do is push the appropriate values onto the stack (recall that selectors are pushed first when you push PTRs) and call DosRead.

There is another way to read in a string of keyboard characters, and that is KbdStringIn, which is similar to DosRead as we have used it.

KbdStringIn—Read a String from the Keyboard

```
PUSH    PTR     The address of the data buffer where the struck key's
                    ASCII codes will be placed.
PUSH    PTR     The address of two words. First word: Input buffer
                    length in bytes. Second word: Number of bytes
                    KbdStringIn placed into the buffer.
PUSH    WORD    When this word = 0 Wait (keep reading until <cr>
                    pressed or buffer is full).
                             = 1 Don't Wait (read what is in the
                                 keyboard buffer and return at once).
PUSH    WORD    Kbd handle (0 for us).
CALL    KBDSTRINGIN
```

| To turn the echoing of characters on and off with Kbd services, use KeySetStatus, examined later. |

Although this is similar to DosRead, the way KbdStringIn expects its data to be pushed differs from DosRead. With KbdStringIn, you can also specify whether or not you want to wait for keys to be struck, or return immediately. Besides other minor things (such as pushing the Kbd handle last instead of first), the only major difference is that KbdStringIn (like all Kbd services) does not allow you to redirect the flow of data, and DosRead does. (In this, they match one major difference between DOS and BIOS—DOS allows redirection; BIOS does not.)

Here is our example program for DosRead converted to using KbdStringIn:

```
BUFFER_LEN        EQU      20
   .286C
   .MODEL   SMALL
   .STACK   200H

   .DATA
          BUFFER   DB BUFFER_LEN DUP(0)
          BUFFER_SIZE       DW      BUFFER_LEN
          NUMBER_CHARS      DW      0

   .CODE
          EXTRN    DOSEXIT:FAR,KBDSTRINGIN:FAR

ENTRY:    PUSH     DS
          PUSH     OFFSET BUFFER
          PUSH     DS
          PUSH     OFFSET BUFFER_SIZE
          PUSH     0       ;Set KbdStringIn up to wait.
          PUSH     0       ;STDIN handle.
```

```
            CALL    KBDSTRINGIN

EXIT:       PUSH    1                   ;A Normal Exit.
            PUSH    0
            CALL    DOSEXIT

            END     ENTRY
```

This program is more or less equivalent to the one using DosRead, except that, of course, we had to make changes in the data segment:

```
BUFFER_LEN       EQU        20
.286C
.MODEL   SMALL
.STACK   200H

.DATA
        BUFFER  DB BUFFER_LEN DUP(0)
        BUFFER_SIZE     DW      BUFFER_LEN          ←
        NUMBER_CHARS    DW      0                   ←

.CODE
        EXTRN   DOSEXIT:FAR,KBDSTRINGIN:FAR
```

and code segment:

```
BUFFER_LEN       EQU        20
.286C
.MODEL   SMALL
.STACK   200H

.DATA
        BUFFER  DB BUFFER_LEN DUP(0)
        BUFFER_SIZE     DW      BUFFER_LEN
        NUMBER_CHARS    DW      0

.CODE
        EXTRN   DOSEXIT:FAR,KBDSTRINGIN:FAR

ENTRY:      PUSH    DS                                  ←
            PUSH    OFFSET BUFFER                       ←
            PUSH    DS                                  ←
            PUSH    OFFSET BUFFER_SIZE                  ←
            PUSH    0       ;Set KbdStringIn up to wait. ←
            PUSH    0       ;STDIN handle.              ←
            CALL    KBDSTRINGIN                         ←

EXIT:       PUSH    1                   ;A Normal Exit.
            PUSH    0
            CALL    DOSEXIT

            END     ENTRY
```

to match the requirements of KbdStringIn.

If neither DosRead nor KbdStringIn contain enough information about the struck characters, then you can use KbdCharIn. This service contains just about everything (and more) that you could want to know about any key that was typed.

KbdCharIn—Read One Key From Keyboard

```
PUSH    PTR     Address of the data field to be filled by OS/2:
                        DB      ASCII character code
                        DB      Scan code
                        DB      Character Status
                        DB      "NLS" Status
                        DW      Shift State
                        DD      Time Stamp
PUSH    WORD    This word = 0 → wait for the character.
                        = 1 → Do NOT wait for the character.
PUSH    WORD    Kbd handle (0 for us).
CALL    KBDCHARIN
```

Here's about a ton of information about a character typed on the keyboard—including the time it was struck.

The Kbd-CharIn data area

In order just to read one character with KbdCharIn, you have to set up a data area (which OS/2 will fill) like this:

```
ASCII_CODE      DB      ?
SCAN_CODE       DB      ?
CHAR_STATUS     DB      ?
NLS_STATUS      DB      ?
SHIFT_STATE     DW      ?
TIME_STAMP      DD      ?
```

Let's go through these items one by one.

ASCII_CODE is clearly just the character's ASCII code—one byte.

SCAN_CODE—for each key on the keyboard (83 for the PC, 101 for the PS/2)—there is an associated scan code. This byte holds the scan code of the key typed. Scan code tables may be found in the OS/2 literature if needed.

Double Byte Character Sets (DBCS)

CHAR_STATUS won't have much meaning for us. KbdCharIn can be used with special country-dependent character sets that can use Double Byte Character Sets (DBCS). This means that for some characters, two bytes will be passed, not just one. The top two bits (bits 7 and 6) of this byte will be set as 11 if this is the only byte in this character, 10 (that is, bit 7 = 1, bit 6 = 0) if this is the first byte of this character, and 01 if this is the last byte.

NLS_STATUS also won't have any meaning for us; this is a reserved byte that is used with country-dependent keyboards.

▌ NLS means National Language Support. ▌

SHIFT_STATE, is, however, useful. This informs you what kinds of keys—shift or control, for example—were pressed when this character was typed. Here are the settings that are used in this word:

Table 12.1 Shift States

Shift State Word	Means
1xxxxxxxxxxxxxxx	SysReq Key down
x1xxxxxxxxxxxxxx	Caps Lock Key Down
xx1xxxxxxxxxxxxx	Num Lock Key Down
xxx1xxxxxxxxxxxx	Scroll Lock Key Down
xxxx1xxxxxxxxxxx	Right Alt Key Down
xxxxx1xxxxxxxxxx	Right Cntrl Key Down
xxxxxx1xxxxxxxxx	Left Alt Key Down
xxxxxxx1xxxxxxxx	Left Cntrl Key Down
xxxxxxxx1xxxxxxx	Insert State On
xxxxxxxxx1xxxxxx	Caps Lock State On
xxxxxxxxxx1xxxxx	Num Lock State On
xxxxxxxxxxx1xxxx	Scroll Lock State On
xxxxxxxxxxxx1xxx	Either Alt Key Down
xxxxxxxxxxxxx1xx	Either Cntrl Key Down
xxxxxxxxxxxxxx1x	Left Shift Key Down
xxxxxxxxxxxxxxx1	Right Shift Key Down

Of course, these values may be combined—more than one setting may apply (more than one bit in the word may be set).

TIME_STAMP is the last item in this data list. This is a 32-bit long (doubleword) quantity that specifies the time (in milliseconds) at which the key was pressed.

After you've pushed the PTR holding the address of the key data field onto the stack, the next word to push specifies the WAIT or NOWAIT options. If this word is 0, KbdCharIn will wait for the key to be pressed; if it is 0, KbdCharIn will *not* wait. Not waiting means that, if no key was ready, KbdCharIn simply returns directly to your program. In this way you can check every now and then to see if the user typed something.

Checking "every now and then" to see whether something happened is referred to as "polling" in a computer. If you can intercept a hardware interrupt, you don't need to poll—hardware interrupts were invented to save time that had been used for polling.

The BEEPb program

Let's make use of KbdCharIn with a small program that accepts characters, and checks for "b." Every time a "b" is typed, the program will beep (using DosBeep).

All we do is set up the data segment with the names of the data words and bytes we've already described:

```
         .286C
         .MODEL   SMALL
         .STACK   200H

         .DATA?            ;Initialized data segment
→        KEY_DATA           LABEL   BYTE
→        ASCII_CODE         DB      ?
→        SCAN_CODE          DB      ?
→        CHAR_STATUS        DB      ?
→        NLS_STATUS         DB      ?
→        SHIFT_STATE        DW      ?
→        TIME_STAMP         DD      ?

         .CODE
                 EXTRN   DOSEXIT:FAR

ENTRY:

EXIT:    PUSH     1                        ;A Normal Exit.
         PUSH     0
         CALL     DOSEXIT

         END      ENTRY
```

Note the use of LABEL in the data segment. Now, we can refer to the first byte of the data area by both names, ASCII_CODE and KEY_DATA. By using one or the other name as appropriate, the code is made more legible.

And then put in this code to use KbdCharIn:

```
         .286C
         .MODEL   SMALL
         .STACK   200H

         .DATA?            ;Initialized data segment
         KEY_DATA           LABEL   BYTE
         ASCII_CODE         DB      ?
         SCAN_CODE          DB      ?
         CHAR_STATUS        DB      ?
         NLS_STATUS         DB      ?
         SHIFT_STATE        DW      ?
         TIME_STAMP         DD      ?

         .CODE
                 EXTRN   DOSEXIT:FAR,KBDCHARIN:FAR,DOSBEEP:FAR

ENTRY:   PUSH     DS                                    ←
         PUSH     OFFSET KEY_DATA                        ←
         PUSH     0         ;Wait for Character          ←
```

```
          PUSH     0        ;Kbd handle                  ←
          CALL     KBDCHARIN                             ←
                   :
                   :
EXIT:     PUSH     1                      ;A Normal Exit.
          PUSH     0
          CALL     DOSEXIT

          END      ENTRY

ENTRY:    PUSH     DS

          PUSH     OFFSET KEY_DATA

          PUSH     0        ;Wait for Character

          PUSH     0        ;Kbd handle

          CALL     KBDCHARIN
```

After KbdCharIn receives a key, we check it (by looking at ASCII_
CODE) to see whether or not it was a "b". If not, we jump back to the
label ENTRY and get the next key. If so, we beep (DosBeep is reviewed
later in this chapter) and exit:

```
.286C
.MODEL  SMALL
.STACK  200H

.DATA?              ;Initialized data segment
          KEY_DATA        LABEL   BYTE
          ASCII_CODE      DB      ?
          SCAN_CODE       DB      ?
          CHAR_STATUS     DB      ?
          NLS_STATUS      DB      ?
          SHIFT_STATE     DW      ?
          TIME_STAMP      DD      ?

.CODE
          EXTRN    DOSEXIT:FAR,KBDCHARIN:FAR,DOSBEEP:FAR

ENTRY:    PUSH     DS
          PUSH     OFFSET KEY_DATA
          PUSH     0        ;Wait for Character
          PUSH     0        ;Kbd handle
          CALL     KBDCHARIN

→         CMP      ASCII_CODE,"b"
→         JNE      ENTRY

→         PUSH     2048     ;Frequency
→         PUSH     40       ;Length of beep
→         CALL     DOSBEEP

EXIT:     PUSH     1                      ;A Normal Exit.
          PUSH     0
          CALL     DOSEXIT

          END      ENTRY
```

And that's all there is to it—our program BEEPb.ASM is done. It will
patiently wait for you to type "b", beep, and then quit.

Your program may only want to *watch* what has been typed. For some reason, you may want to monitor the keyboard input (watching for hot-keys or phrases for example), but not actually remove anything from the keyboard buffer. Under OS/2, this may be done with KbdPeek.

KbdPeek—Examine but Don't Touch Kbd Buffer

```
PUSH    PTR      Address of the data field to be filled by OS/2:
                        DB        ASCII character code
                        DB        Scan code
                        DB        Character Status
                        DB        "NLS" Status
                        DW        Shift State
                        DD        Time Stamp
PUSH    WORD     Kbd handle (0 for us)
CALL    KBDPEEK
```

KbdPeek is the same service, really, as KbdCharIn, except that it does not remove characters from the keyboard buffer, and control returns immediately to the calling program (KbdPeek does not wait for a key to be typed). That's all there is to it.

You set up a data area for KbdPeek, which is the same as that used for KbdCharIn:

```
                        DB        ASCII character code.
                        DB        Scan code.
                        DB        Character Status.
                        DB        "NLS" Status.
                        DW        Shift State.
                        DD        Time Stamp.
```

There are only two more Kbd services that are important enough (or straightforward enough, since we are not going to do things like opening logical keyboards) for us to cover, KbdSetStatus and KbdGetStatus. These are useful because, among other things, they can turn screen echoing of typed keys on or off.

KbdSetStatus and KbdGetStatus

```
PUSH    PTR      Address of the Kbd status data (see below).
PUSH    WORD     Kbd handle (0 for us).
```

To either get or set the keyboard status (which includes things like shift state and others), you have to supply KbdGetStatus or KbdSetStatus with a data area that will receive or specify the keyboard state.

This data area looks like Table 12.2.

Table 12.2 Keyboard Status Data Area

DW	10	← This word holds the length of this data area, which will always be 10 (bytes).
DW	One Word—the enable/disable word set these bits to 1 if:	
	Bits 15-9	(reserved).
	Bit 8	Shift "reporting" should be turned on.
	Bit 7	Set "Turn-around" char length (0→1 byte, 1→ 2 bytes).
	Bit 6	"Turn-around" character will be changed.
	Bit 5	Interim Character Flag to be changed (0 for us).
	Bit 4	Shift state to be changed.
	Bit 3	Turn ASCII mode on.
	Bit 2	Turn Binary mode on.
	Bit 1	Turn Echo on.
	Bit 0	Turn Echo off.
DW	"Turn-around" character	
	Both bytes if bit 7 of the previous word = 1.	
	Low byte if bit 7 of the previous word = 0.	
DW	Interim Character Flag (deals with country-dependent keys)	
DW	Shift State:	

Shift State Word	*Means*
1xxxxxxxxxxxxxxx	SysReq Key down
x1xxxxxxxxxxxxxx	Caps Lock Key Down
xx1xxxxxxxxxxxxx	Num Lock Key Down
xxx1xxxxxxxxxxxx	Scroll Lock Key Down
xxxx1xxxxxxxxxxx	Right Alt Key Down
xxxxx1xxxxxxxxxx	Right Cntrl Key Down
xxxxxx1xxxxxxxxx	Left Alt Key Down
xxxxxxx1xxxxxxxx	Left Cntrl Key Down
xxxxxxxx1xxxxxxx	Insert State On
xxxxxxxxx1xxxxxx	Caps Lock State On
xxxxxxxxxx1xxxxx	Num Lock State On
xxxxxxxxxxx1xxxx	Scroll Lock State On
xxxxxxxxxxxx1xxx	Either Alt Key Down
xxxxxxxxxxxxx1xx	Either Cntrl Key Down
xxxxxxxxxxxxxx1x	Left Shift Key Down
xxxxxxxxxxxxxxx1	Right Shift Key Down

There is a lot of information in this data area; let's take it one word at a time.

The first word in the keyboard status data area is always set to 10 (decimal). This is the length (in bytes) of the keyboard status data area, which is always 10 (for this version of OS/2):

```
DW      10          ← This word holds the length of this data area,
                      which will always be 10 (bytes).
```

The next word allows you to enable or disable certain keyboard states when you use KbdSetStatus. By setting the bits in this word appropriately, you can turn screen echoing of typed characters on or off, toggle the keyboard between ASCII or Binary modes, or change the "turn-around" character:

```
DW      10
DW      One Word_the enable/disable word set these bits to 1 if:
        Bits 15-9 (reserved).
        Bit   8   Shift "reporting" should be turned on.
        Bit   7   Set "Turn-around" char length (0→1 byte, 1→ 2 bytes).
        Bit   6   "Turn-around" character will be changed.
        Bit   5   Interim Character Flag to be changed (0 for us).
        Bit   4   Shift state to be changed.
        Bit   3   Turn ASCII mode on.
        Bit   2   Turn Binary mode on.
        Bit   1   Turn Echo on.
        Bit   0   Turn Echo off.
```

> In Binary mode, the data that comes in from the keyboard is simply treated as raw data—<cr> has no special meaning, and input strings are not terminated when you type <cr> (they will stop accepting data only when the data buffer you specified is full).

The turn-around character

The turn-around character is the character that finishes an input string—usually the carriage return; but we can change that. We can make the turn-around character into whatever character we want, even two characters. To do that, we set bit 7 to 1 for a two-byte turn-around character, and to 0 for a one byte turn-around character. Then, to tell OS/2 that the turn-around character is to be changed, we set bit 6 to 1.

The new turn-around character is stored in the following word—in the low byte if it is one byte long; in both bytes if it is two bytes long:

```
    DW      10
    DW      One Word_the enable/disable word.
→   DW      "Turn-around" character
→               Both bytes if bit 7 of the previous word = 1.
→               Low byte if bit 7 of the previous word = 0.
```

The following word has to do with interim character reporting, which is involved with Double Byte Character Sets used in country-specific keyboard modes, and which we will not cover. This word is the only one that is (slightly) different between KbdSetStatus and KbdGetStatus. For our purposes, the two services use the same Kbd status data area.

```
    DW    10
    DW    One Word_the enable/disable word.
    DW    "Turn-around" character.
→   DW    Interim Character Flag (deals with country-dependent keys).
```

The final word in this status data area is one we have seen before—a Shift State word (see KbdCharIn). Here is where you get the current status of the keyboard returned to you by KbdGetStatus. When using Kbd-SetStatus, you can force a keyboard state using this word, such as turning shift lock on, even though the user has not done so.

Table 12.3 Keyboard Data Area Shift Status

```
      DW    10
      DW    One Word—the enable/disable word.
      DW    "Turn-around" character.
      DW    Interim Character Flag (deals with country-dependent
            keys).
→     DW    Shift State:
```

Shift State Word	Means
1xxxxxxxxxxxxxxx	SysReq Key down
x1xxxxxxxxxxxxxx	Caps Lock Key Down
xx1xxxxxxxxxxxxx	Num Lock Key Down
xxx1xxxxxxxxxxxx	Scroll Lock Key Down
xxxx1xxxxxxxxxxx	Right Alt Key Down
xxxxx1xxxxxxxxxx	Right Cntrl Key Down
xxxxxx1xxxxxxxxx	Left Alt Key Down
xxxxxxx1xxxxxxxx	Left Cntrl Key Down
xxxxxxxx1xxxxxxx	Insert State On
xxxxxxxxx1xxxxxx	Caps Lock State On
xxxxxxxxxx1xxxxx	Num Lock State On
xxxxxxxxxxx1xxxx	Scroll Lock State On
xxxxxxxxxxxx1xxx	Either Alt Key Down
xxxxxxxxxxxxx1xx	Either Cntrl Key Down
xxxxxxxxxxxxxx1x	Left Shift Key Down
xxxxxxxxxxxxxxx1	Right Shift Key Down

The End of Input

That completes our survey of the keyboard services of OS/2. With the exception of some exotic services, we've covered what's available, and, as you can see, there is much to choose from.

Even so, Kbd is a relatively small section of the OS/2 services compared to the next section, Dos. The Dos services are responsible for advanced memory management, session management, file handling, queue and semaphore handling, and many other things. We will largely confine ourselves to what are called the Family API (BIOS and DOS counterpart) services, although not completely. The first set of services to consider are the file-handling services.

File Handling Under OS/2

While file handling is a little more complex under OS/2 simply because it is a multitasking operating system, it is not too much more complex than DOS. This is mainly because the concepts that we are going to use—read-only, file pointers, and so forth—have already been introduced in DOS. With some variation, we'll find ourselves pretty much at home here, and not only in programming, either. OS/2 preserves the file system on disk that DOS uses—the same directory set-up, the use of File Allocation Tables, which thread the disk sectors (into which a file is broken up) together, and so on. We'll start with perhaps the biggest OS/2 file service that we'll cover, DosOpen. The preparation for this service is very taxing, since we have to allow for all the situations that multitasking can permit. Still, to work with files, we *have* to open them, so we'll have to work through this monster OS/2 service.

DosOpen—Opening Files

```
PUSH  PTR    Address of an ASCIIZ filename.
PUSH  PTR    Address of memory word where OS/2 will put file handle.
PUSH  PTR    Address of memory word where OS/2 will put "action code."
                  Action Code = 1 → File existed.
                              = 2 → File was created.
                              = 3 → File was replaced.
PUSH  DWORD  Initial file size for created or replaced files (we
                  will use two words of zeroes).
```

```
PUSH   WORD  File Attribute:
       File Attribute  Means
       --------------  -----
       0               Plain old file.
       1               Read-Only.
       2               Hidden file (hidden from directory searches).
       4               A system file (like IBMDOS.COM).
       8               Used for the volume label of a disk.
       10H             This is the name of a subdirectory.
PUSH   WORD  Open Flag, specifies these options:
             If file does not exist:
                 0000 xxxx → Fail (and return).
                 0001 xxxx → Create it.
             If file does exist:
                 xxxx 0000 → Fail (and return).
                 xxxx 0001 → Open it.
                 xxxx 0010 → Create it (that is, replace it).
PUSH   WORD  Open Mode (= dwfrrrrrisssraaa)
             d = DASD bit. If 1, use whole disk as a file.
                     For normal files, d = 0.
             w = Write-through bit. If 1, do not buffer this
                     data in a disk cache. If 0, disk cache
                     is ok.
             f = Fail Error bit. If 1, report errors with
                     standard OS/2 error codes. If 0, use
                     the system hard error handler.
             r = reserved.
             i = Inheritance bit. If 1, the file handle will
                     be private to this program. If 0, the
                     handle will be inherited by "children"
                     of this program.
             s = Sharing mode.
                         sss = 001 → Deny ALL Requests.
                         sss = 010 → Deny Write Requests.
                         sss = 011 → Deny Read Requests.
                         sss = 100 → Deny NO Requests.
             r = reserved.
             a = Access mode.
                         aa = 00 → Read Only Access.
                         aa = 01 → Write Only Access.
                         aa = 10 → Read/Write Access.
PUSH   DWORD Reserved. Both words must be 0.
CALL   DOSOPEN
```

As you can see, DosOpen is a serious service. Regrettably, we have to wade through all this information before working with files. Let's examine some of these options, argument by argument.

Setting Up the Stack for DosOpen

When we get ready for DosOpen, the first item pushed onto the stack is the address of the ASCIIZ string that holds the filename:

```
  →      PUSH    PTR     Address of an ASCIIZ filename.
```

For example, we could push (selector followed by offset) the address of:

```
FILENAME        DB        "TEST.FIL",0
```

onto the stack like this:

```
PUSH    DS
PUSH    OFFSET FILENAME
```

Filenames are the same as in DOS—eight letters (maximum) for the name, and three letters for the extension. Also, pathnames are as usual.

Following that, we have to push the address at which we want the file handle to be stored:

```
        PUSH    PTR     Address of an ASCIIZ filename.
  →     PUSH    PTR     Address of memory word where OS/2 will put file handle.
```

Since file handles are one word long, that location could be something like this:

```
FILE_HANDLE     DW        ?
```

OS/2 will store the file handle there after it has opened or created the file.

The following item pushed onto the stack is the address at which the "action code" (one word long) that OS/2 returns will be placed:

```
        PUSH    PTR     Address of an ASCIIZ filename.
        PUSH    PTR     Address of memory word where OS/2 will put file handle.
  →     PUSH    PTR     Address of memory word where OS/2 will put "action code".
```

File "action codes"

Following a successful file opening or creation, OS/2 will let you know the action taken (since what you ask it to do may not uniquely specify what it is to do; for example, you may ask it to do different things if the file already existed or did not). The action codes that will be returned are these:

```
        Action Code = 1  →  File existed
                    = 2  →  File was created
                    = 3  →  File was replaced
```

Unless you are creating or replacing (that is, writing over) a file, the next item has no meaning. If, however, you *are* creating or replacing a file, you can specify the file's initial size in this doubleword. We will, when creating files, push two words of zeroes here:

```
    PUSH    PTR     Address of an ASCIIZ filename.
    PUSH    PTR     Address of memory word where OS/2 will put file handle.
    PUSH    PTR     Address of memory word where OS/2 will put "action code."
→   PUSH    DWORD   Initial file size.
```

Following the initial file size doubleword, you ust push the file's attribute if you are creating it or replacing it.

```
    PUSH    PTR     Address of an ASCIIZ filename.
    PUSH    PTR     Address of memory word where OS/2 will put file handle.
    PUSH    PTR     Address of memory word where OS/2 will put "action code".
    PUSH    DWORD   Initial file size.
→   PUSH    WORD    File Attribute.
```

File attributes

Here are the possible file attributes to place in this word:

File Attribute	Means
0	Plain old file
1	Read-Only
2	Hidden file (hidden from directory searches)
4	A system file (like IBMDOS.COM)
8	Used for the volume label of a disk
10H	This is the name of a subdirectory

For most purposes, a file attribute of 0 is used, and that is the attribute that we will use as well.

Next come the opening *options* in the Open Flag.

```
    PUSH    PTR     Address of an ASCIIZ filename.
    PUSH    PTR     Address of memory word where OS/2 will put file handle.
    PUSH    PTR     Address of memory word where OS/2 will put "action code".
    PUSH    DWORD   Initial file size.
    PUSH    WORD    File Attribute.
→   PUSH    WORD    Open Flag.
```

The OS/2 file Open Flag

If the file does not exist, this service can create it (unlike the DOS services, which require a separate service to create files). This word pushed onto the stack specifies what action to take if the file does or does not exist. If the file does not exist, you can either return without creating it, or create it. If the file does exist, then you can return without doing anything, open it, or create it (that is, replace it by opening it up and preparing to write over it). The upper byte of the open flag is 0, and the lower byte will look like this:

```
If file does not exist:
   0000 xxxx → Fail (and return).
   0001 xxxx → Create it.
If file does exist:
   xxxx 0000 → Fail (and return).
   xxxx 0001 → Open it.
   xxxx 0010 → Create it (that is, replace it).
```

The OS/2
file Open
Mode

Finally, after the open flag, the open mode is pushed:

```
    PUSH   PTR     Address of an ASCIIZ filename.
    PUSH   PTR     Address of memory word where OS/2 will put file handle.
    PUSH   PTR     Address of memory word where OS/2 will put "action code".
    PUSH   DWORD   Initial file size.
    PUSH   WORD    File Attribute.
    PUSH   WORD    Open Flag.
  → PUSH   WORD    Open Mode (= dwfrrrrrisssraaa).
```

This is the most important word as far as multitasking is concerned—it specifies how you are going to interact with other programs that request the use of the same file.

The Open Mode word looks like this bit by bit: dwfrrrrrisssraaa, where each letter corresponds to some particular option. Decoding this difficult word will make the differences between opening a file in OS/2 and DOS very clear.

The File Open Mode

Here are the bits in this word:

```
↓
dwfrrrrrisssraaa
```

Direct Disk
Access
(DASD)

The first bit, d, is the DASD bit, which we will set to 0. The DASD bit opens a whole disk as one file. This is called Direct Access.

```
↓
dwfrrrrrisssraaa
0
```

The next bit, w, is the write-through bit. Again, we will not have much use for this bit, and will set it to 0.

```
    ↓
dwfrrrrrisssraaa
 □□
```

If this bit is 1, then writing to the file will not be buffered—all writes will take place as soon as they are requested. This is useful if you expect the power to be shut off on your PS/2, but not so much otherwise, since it makes disk work slower.

Bit f is the fail error bit, which determines how errors will be treated. If you are prepared to treat errors yourself, set this bit to 1 and OS/2 will return standard OS/2 error codes. If this bit is 0, OS/2 will use the system error handler. We'll set this bit to 0 to avoid error handling in our examples.

```
    ↓
dwfrrrrrisssraaa
 □□□
```

The bits marked r are reserved (and we will make them 0).

```
    ↓↓↓↓↓
dwfrrrrrisssraaa
 □□□□□□□
```

Bit i is the inheritance bit. This just indicates whether any "child" processes of the current process will be able to use the same file handle (yes → i = 0; no → i = 1). The term for generating child processes is *spawning*, and since we will not be spawning any secondary processes, this bit will always be 0.

```
         ↓
dwfrrrrrisssraaa
 □□□□□□□□□
```

The next three bits, sss, indicate the sharing mode—the way that other programs can use this file. Here are the available options:

```
sss = 001  →  Deny ALL Requests
sss = 010  →  Deny Write Requests
sss = 011  →  Deny Read Requests
sss = 100  →  Deny NO Requests
```

For example, if we set sss = 001, then we will deny *all* other programs from using this file while we have it open (assuming that no other program has already denied us access before we get a chance to open the file). We'll set these according to our requirements later.

```
            ↓↓↓
dwfrrrrrisssraaa
000000000sss
```

The next bit, r, is reserved (i.e. 0) as well.

```
            ↓
dwfrrrrrisssraaa
000000000sss0
```

The final three bits, aaa, indicate the access mode. This is where we tell OS/2 what we plan on doing with the file. For example: Do we plan to write to the file, or only read from it? Do we plan to both read *and* write? How we set these bits will often determine whether or not we are granted access to a file if another program already has the file open. For example, if we ask for writing access, and another program has already opened the file as DENY_WRITE, then our request will fail. Here are the possible access modes:

```
aaa = 000  →  Read Only Access.
aaa = 001  →  Write Only Access.
aaa = 010  →  Read/Write Access.
```

This is another one that we can't set generally—the way we use these bits will be worked out in our example later.

```
            ↓↓↓
dwfrrrrrisssraaa
000000000sss0aaa
```

With all these options and specifications, we have a lot to choose from before opening a file. The usual default is to allow other programs as much access as is commensurate with what you plan to do.

> Another option will be explored later: file locking. With the Dos-FileLocks service, you can lock specific byte ranges inside a file, and this can sometimes eliminate the need to DENY_WRITE to all other files if you are only interested in a small section of the file.

The DosOpen service continues. The final thing to be pushed for DosOpen is a doubleword of zeroes, and then we can call DosOpen:

```
      PUSH    PTR       Address of an ASCIIZ filename.
      PUSH    PTR       Address of memory word where OS/2 will put file handle.
      PUSH    PTR       Address of memory word where OS/2 will put "action code."
      PUSH    DWORD     Initial file size.
      PUSH    WORD      File Attribute.
      PUSH    WORD      Open Flag.
      PUSH    WORD      Open Mode (= dwfrrrrrisssraaa).
  →   PUSH    DWORD     Reserved. Both words must be 0.
  →   CALL    DOSOPEN
```

These two words are reserved, and are always zero. Now, however, we're all done—we've opened our file.

With all this work setting up to open a file, it may come as a relief to learn that actually reading from it is much easier. This is accomplished with a service that we are already well acquainted with: DosRead. When you give DosRead a predefined handle, such as STDIN (whose default is the keyboard), it can take character input, as we have seen. But the object of DosOpen is to generate a 16-bit file handle by which OS/2 will refer to the file from now on. If that file handle is passed to DosRead, then we can can read as many bytes from the file as we want.

```
DosRead_Read from a File (or Device)

      PUSH    WORD      The file handle.
      PUSH    PTR       Address of the buffer where data will go.
      PUSH    WORD      Length of the input buffer.
      PUSH    PTR       Address of a memory word that OS/2 will update to the
                           number of bytes actually read (and placed into
                           the input buffer).
      CALL    DOSREAD
```

The use of DosRead is simple. All you do is specify needed quantities. For example, you have to push the file handle first, then the address of the buffer where you want the data to be placed. Next, tell OS/2 the length of the input buffer, and, finally, pass it the address of a word in memory that it will update with the number of bytes that it actually read.

▮   OS/2 can read a maximum of 64K bytes at one time (in one read).   ▮

That's all there is to DosRead. It's comparatively simple; we'll put it to work soon.

DosWrite—Write Data to a File

```
PUSH    WORD    Open file handle.
PUSH    PTR     Address of data buffer where data to write is stored.
PUSH    WORD    Length of the data buffer.
PUSH    PTR     Address of a memory word that OS/2 will update with
                    the number of bytes actually written.
CALL    DOSWRITE
```

Here's another service that we've seen before, and that's easy to use. Like DosRead, DosWrite can write to predefined handles as well as to files—it's OS/2's general, all-purpose output service. If you write to handle 1 (STDOUT), then you will be writing to the screen, unless the flow of data has been redirected.

Here all we'll have do is supply our own handle (the file handle provided by DosOpen) the address at which the data may be found, the length of the data (in bytes) to write, and the address of a memory word (like BYTES_WRITTEN DW ?) that OS/2 will fill with the number of bytes actually written.

Logical file pointers

This service, like DosRead, automatically updates the logical file pointer as well. The reason this is referred to as the *logical* file pointer is that other programs can have the file open too, so OS/2 cannot refer to simply *the* file pointer. When we actually use the logical file pointer, it will prove no different to us than before.

Errors

Dealing with file handling is more prone to errors than almost any other operation. For that reason, we'll list a few of the possible error codes that OS/2 returns for common errors, including file handling. On the other hand, we will not list them all, since there are some 486 codes. These codes will be returned in AX—if AX is zero, you may assume that there was no error.

Table 12.4 OS/2 Error Codes

Error Code (in AX)	Means
1	Invalid function code
2	File not found
3	Path not found
4	Too many open files
5	Access denied
6	Invalid handle
7	Memory was corrupted
8	Not enough memory
11	Bad format
12	Invalid access
13	Invalid data
15	Invalid drive
16	Error in the current directory
17	Not the same device
18	No more files
19	Write protect error
20	Bad unit number
21	Drive not ready
22	Bad command
23	CRC (data—usually disk—parity check) error
24	Bad length
25	Seek error
26	Not an OS/2 or DOS disk
27	Sector was not found
28	Out of paper
29	Write fault
30	Read Fault
32	Sharing violation
33	File lock violation
34	Wrong disk
36	Sharing buffer was exceeded
50	Not supported
80	File already exists
82	Cannot make
107	Disk A needs to be changed
108	Drive cannot be accessed (locked)
116	Internal Vio error
120	Internal error
122	Data buffer too small

Table 12.4 OS/2 Error Codes (*continued*)

Error Code (in AX)	Means
142	Specified drive was busy
145	Directory was not empty
150	System trace error
161	Invalid pathname
207	Ring 2 stack is in use
305	Target process is not a descendant
328	Internal system failure
334	Insufficient memory
355	Unsupported video mode
358	Invalid row value
359	Invalid column value
395	Invalid beep frequency
405	The popup was not allocated
406	A popup is already on the screen
430	Illegal function call during popup
483	Error during VioPopUp
486	Reserved Vio parameter is not 0

If you are expecting errors, check for these values—even if you're not expecting errors, it's far better to be prepared than to be out of luck.

DosClose—Close a File

```
PUSH    WORD        The file handle
CALL    DOSCLOSE
```

Here's our easy-to-use file-closing service, DosClose. All you have to do is push the file handle onto the stack and call DosClose—that's it.

Now that we know the full sequence—open (or create) a file, read from a file, write to one, and closes file(s)—let's see them in action, with an example program named COPIER.ASM.

COPIER.ASM

COPIER is a small program that copies files. Unlike our earlier DOS version, this one will copy files of any size. However, since we don't want to get involved in a lot of string manipulation—this example is not about string instructions—we will include the name of the source and target files explicitly in the code, as ASCIIZ strings. If you wish, you can alter the program to read and use the command-line information that may be found in the environment (in which case you may give commands like: "COPIER FILE.TXT FILE.BAK").

First we start with our .EXE file shell:

```
        .286C
        .MODEL   SMALL
        .STACK   200H

        .DATA
→       SOURCE   DB  "FILE.TXT",0
→       TARGET   DB  "FILE.BAK",0

        .CODE
                 EXTRN    DOSEXIT:FAR

ENTRY:
                    :
                    :
EXIT:   PUSH     1                      ;A Normal Exit.
        PUSH     0
        CALL     DOSEXIT

        END      ENTRY
```

We have added the ASCIIZ names of two files, FILE.TXT and FILE.BAK. COPIER's sole purpose is to copy a file named FILE.TXT into a file named FILE.BAK. Assuming you had FILE.TXT on your disk, you can use COPIER to back it up (but that's all it's good for).

Next we have to add DosOpen, which means that we'll have to select from among the various options. In COPIER, we'll have to open FILE.TXT and, if there is some error, we'll just exit (ungraciously). Also, we'll have to create FILE.BAK. As you may recall, we have to pass a wealth of information to DosOpen:

```
PUSH   PTR      Address of an ASCIIZ filename.
PUSH   PTR      Address of memory word where OS/2 will put file handle.
PUSH   PTR      Address of memory word where OS/2 will put "action code."
PUSH   DWORD    Initial file size.
PUSH   WORD     File Attribute.
PUSH   WORD     Open Flag.
PUSH   WORD     Open Mode (= dwfrrrrrrisssraaa).
PUSH   DWORD    Reserved. Both words must be 0.
CALL   DOSOPEN
```

The two words that hold all the options are the open flag and the open mode, and we'll discuss each of them here.

COPIER's Open Flag

The open flag selects DosOpen options depending on whether the file being opened already exists or doesn't. Here are the opening options that are going to be pushed in the "open flag" (these bits make up the lower byte of the word that will be pushed—the top byte is 0):

```
If file does not exist:
   0000 xxxx → Fail (and return).
   0001 xxxx → Create it.
If file does exist:
   xxxx 0000 → Fail (and return).
   xxxx 0001 → Open it.
   xxxx 0010 → Create it (that is, replace it).
```

To open FILE.TXT, we want to make sure that it already exists, and then open it, so we choose an open flag of 0000 0001. The top four bits specify that if the file did not exist, the open attempt is to fail, and the bottom four specify that if the file exists that it should be opened.

To create FILE.BAK, we have a choice: if FILE.BAK already exists, we can either fail or open it for replacement (that is, we will write over it). Let's choose the latter option, as the copy command does. The open flag for the opening of FILE.BAK will be 0001 0010.

COPIER's Open Mode

We also have to select the open mode—what kind of access to give other programs to our files. The open mode word looks like this bit by bit: dwfrrrrrisssraaa, where these will be the important bits (all others we'll set to 0):

```
sss = 001 → Deny ALL Requests.
sss = 010 → Deny Write Requests.
sss = 011 → Deny Read Requests.
sss = 100 → Deny NO Requests.
aaa = 000 → Read Only Access.
aaa = 001 → Write Only Access.
aaa = 010 → Read/Write Access.
```

Since we only want to read from FILE.TXT, sss will be set to 010, deny only write requests, and aaa will be set to 000—read only.

On the other hand, we want to write to FILE.BAK, so we will deny all writing requests (other than ourselves) to FILE.BAK by setting sss = 010 and set aaa to 001 (write only access).

The results of our selections look like this:

```
FILE.TXT open flag: 000000000000001B
         open mode: 00000000001000000B

FILE.BAK open flag: 00000000000010010B
         open mode: 0000000000100001B
```

COPIER's File Handles and Action Codes

Besides selecting options, we have to supply OS/2 with the address of several words for the file handles and action codes.

```
        PUSH    PTR     Address of an ASCIIZ filename.
→       PUSH    PTR     Address of memory word where OS/2 will put file handle.
→       PUSH    PTR     Address of memory word where OS/2 will put "action code."
        PUSH    DWORD   Initial file size.
        PUSH    WORD    File Attribute.
        PUSH    WORD    Open Flag.
        PUSH    WORD    Open Mode (= dwfrrrrrisssraaa).
        PUSH    DWORD   Reserved. Both words must be 0.
        CALL    DOSOPEN
```

Let's add those to our data segment like this:

```
.286C
.MODEL  SMALL
.STACK  200H

.DATA
        SOURCE  DB  "FILE.TXT",0
        TARGET  DB  "FILE.BAK",0
→       HANDLE1 DW      0
→       HANDLE2 DW      0
→       ACTION1 DW      0
→       ACTION2 DW      0

.CODE
        EXTRN   DOSEXIT:FAR

ENTRY:
        :
        :
EXIT:   PUSH    1                   ;A Normal Exit.
        PUSH    0
        CALL    DOSEXIT

        END     ENTRY
```

Now we're practically ready to open the files. We only have to select the file's attributes (we will choose attributes of 0), and an initial file size (a doubleword of zeroes). Here are our open instructions:

```
        .286C
        .MODEL  SMALL
        .STACK  200H

        .DATA
                SOURCE  DB  "FILE.TXT",0
                TARGET  DB  "FILE.BAK",0
                HANDLE1 DW      0
                HANDLE2 DW      0
                ACTION1 DW      0
                ACTION2 DW      0

        .CODE
                EXTRN   DOSEXIT:FAR,DOSOPEN:FAR

ENTRY:          PUSH    DS          ;Selector of filename
     →          PUSH    OFFSET SOURCE   ;Open source first
     →          PUSH    DS          ;Selector of handle
     →          PUSH    OFFSET HANDLE1  ;Offset of handle
     →          PUSH    DS
     →          PUSH    OFFSET ACTION1
     →          PUSH    0           ;High word of initial size
     →          PUSH    0           ;Low word of initial size
     →          PUSH    0           ;File attribute (not used for source)
     →          PUSH    0000000000000001B       ;Open flag
     →          PUSH    0000000000100000B       ;Open mode
     →          PUSH    0
     →          PUSH    0
     →          CALL    DOSOPEN
     →          CMP     AX,0
     →          JNE     EXIT

     →          PUSH    DS          ;Selector of filename
     →          PUSH    OFFSET TARGET   ;Open target next
     →          PUSH    DS          ;Selector of handle
     →          PUSH    OFFSET HANDLE2  ;Offset of handle
     →          PUSH    DS
     →          PUSH    OFFSET ACTION2
     →          PUSH    0           ;High word of initial size
     →          PUSH    0           ;Low word of initial size
     →          PUSH    0           ;File attribute
     →          PUSH    0000000000010010B       ;Open flag
     →          PUSH    0000000000100001B       ;Open mode
     →          PUSH    0
     →          PUSH    0
     →          CALL    DOSOPEN
                :
                :
EXIT:           PUSH    1                       ;A Normal Exit.
                PUSH    0
                CALL    DOSEXIT

                END     ENTRY
```

Note that we exit if the first DosOpen was unsuccessful (AX is not 0), since the source file was not found.

Thirteen pushes for each open call! Still, now we have our files open—we can use the file handles to read and write with. Let's add some data space to our data segment to use as an input and output buffer:

```
        .286C
        .MODEL   SMALL
        .STACK   200H

        .DATA
                SOURCE   DB  "FILE.TXT",0
                TARGET   DB  "FILE.BAK",0
                HANDLE1 DW      0
                HANDLE2 DW      0
                ACTION1 DW      0
                ACTION2 DW      0
    →           BUFFER   DB 60*1024 DUP(0)

         .CODE
                EXTRN    DOSEXIT:FAR,DOSOPEN:FAR

        ENTRY:  PUSH     DS          ;Selector of filename
                PUSH     OFFSET SOURCE   ;Open source first
                PUSH     DS          ;Selector of handle
                :
                :
```

We selected a buffer of 60K, so we can read and write that much at one time. We can add the DosRead instruction fairly easily.

Using DosRead in COPIER

To use DosRead, all we have to provide is the file handle, the address of the buffer, the length of the buffer, and the address of a word to hold the actual byte count read:

```
PUSH    WORD     The file handle
PUSH    PTR      Address of the data buffer
PUSH    WORD     Length of the data buffer
PUSH    PTR      Address of a word that OS/2 will update with the number
                    of bytes read
CALL    DOSREAD
```

We will place the actual byte count in a word named BYTES_READ. For DosWrite, we will need a similar word to hold the count of bytes written, so let's add those two at once to the data segment:

```
        .286C
        .MODEL   SMALL
        .STACK   200H

        .DATA
                SOURCE   DB  "FILE.TXT",0
                TARGET   DB  "FILE.BAK",0
                HANDLE1 DW      0
                HANDLE2 DW      0
                ACTION1 DW      0
                ACTION2 DW      0
    →           BYTES_READ      DW      0
    →           BYTES_WRITTEN   DW      0
                BUFFER   DB 60*1024 DUP(0)
```

```
        .CODE
                EXTRN   DOSEXIT:FAR,DOSOPEN:FAR

        ENTRY:  PUSH    DS          ;Selector of filename
                PUSH    OFFSET SOURCE   ;Open source first
                PUSH    DS          ;Selector of handle
                :
                :
```

We then ask DosRead to read in 60*1024 bytes. Even if the file is much
shorter, there will be no problem, since DosRead will return the number
of bytes actually read in BYTES_READ. Here's how we read from the
input file:

```
        .286C
        .MODEL  SMALL
        .STACK  200H

        .DATA
                SOURCE  DB "FILE.TXT",0
                TARGET  DB "FILE.BAK",0
                HANDLE1 DW      0
                HANDLE2 DW      0
                ACTION1 DW      0
                ACTION2 DW      0
                BYTES_READ      DW      0
                BYTES_WRITTEN   DW      0
                BUFFER  DB 60*1024 DUP(0)

        .CODE
                EXTRN   DOSEXIT:FAR,DOSOPEN:FAR,DOSREAD:FAR

        ENTRY:  PUSH    DS          ;Selector of filename
                PUSH    OFFSET SOURCE   ;Open source first
                PUSH    DS          ;Selector of handle
                PUSH    OFFSET HANDLE1  ;Offset of handle
                PUSH    DS
                PUSH    OFFSET ACTION1
                PUSH    0           ;High word of initial size
                PUSH    0           ;Low word of initial size
                PUSH    0           ;File attribute (not used for source)
                PUSH    0000000000000001B       ;Open flag
                PUSH    0000000001000000B       ;Open mode
                PUSH    0
                PUSH    0
                CALL    DOSOPEN
                CMP     AX,0
                JNE     EXIT

                PUSH    DS          ;Selector of filename
                PUSH    OFFSET TARGET   ;Open target next
                PUSH    DS          ;Selector of handle
                PUSH    OFFSET HANDLE2  ;Offset of handle
                PUSH    DS
                PUSH    OFFSET ACTION2
                PUSH    0           ;High word of initial size
                PUSH    0           ;Low word of initial size
                PUSH    0           ;File attribute
                PUSH    0000000000010010B       ;Open flag
                PUSH    0000000000100001B       ;Open mode
                PUSH    0
                PUSH    0
                CALL    DOSOPEN
```

```
READ_IN:PUSH     HANDLE1                        ←
        PUSH     DS                             ←
        PUSH     OFFSET BUFFER                  ←
        PUSH     60*1024                        ←
        PUSH     DS                             ←
        PUSH     OFFSET BYTES_READ              ←
        CALL     DOSREAD                        ←
        CMP      BYTES_READ,0                   ←
        JE       EXIT                           ←

EXIT:   PUSH     1                    ;A Normal Exit.
        PUSH     0
        CALL     DOSEXIT

        END      ENTRY
```

Notice that the last two lines:

```
READ_IN:PUSH     HANDLE1
        PUSH     DS
        PUSH     OFFSET BUFFER
        PUSH     60*1024
        PUSH     DS
        PUSH     OFFSET BYTES_READ
        CALL     DOSREAD
        CMP      BYTES_READ,0                   ←
        JE       EXIT                           ←
```

will force us to exit if we read no bytes. Tthis means that we can loop until there are no more bytes to read in.

In a minute, we will adjust the exit of the program so that the files are both closed before the program finishes. This means that we will have to provide a normal exit, in addition to the exit taken earlier (when the source file could not be opened). We'll do this as the last step of the program.

Using DosWrite in COPIER

Now we can write the bytes to the output file, FILE.BAK. The number of bytes to write is just the number of bytes that we read—and that's in BYTES_READ. To use DosWrite in writing FILE.BAK, we have to supply it with these things:

```
PUSH     WORD     Open file handle
PUSH     PTR      Address of data buffer where data to write is stored.
PUSH     WORD     Length of the data buffer.
PUSH     PTR      Address of a memory word which OS/2 will update with
                     the number of bytes actually written.
CALL     DOSWRITE
```

In our case, the file handle will be HANDLE2, the address of the buffer will be the address of BUFFER, the number of bytes to write will be in BYTES_READ, and the address of the word that it will update with the

number of bytes written will be the address of BYTES_WRITTEN.
Here's how it looks:

```
        .286C
        .MODEL  SMALL
        .STACK  200H

        .DATA
                SOURCE  DB  "FILE.TXT",0
                TARGET  DB  "FILE.BAK",0
                HANDLE1 DW          0
                HANDLE2 DW          0
                ACTION1 DW          0
                ACTION2 DW          0
                BYTES_READ       DW        0
                BYTES_WRITTEN    DW        0
                BUFFER  DB  60*1024 DUP(0)

        .CODE
                EXTRN   DOSEXIT:FAR,DOSOPEN:FAR,DOSREAD:FAR,DOSWRITE:FAR

ENTRY:  PUSH    DS          ;Selector of filename
        PUSH    OFFSET SOURCE    ;Open source first
        PUSH    DS          ;Selector of handle
        PUSH    OFFSET HANDLE1   ;Offset of handle
        PUSH    DS
        PUSH    OFFSET ACTION1
        PUSH    0           ;High word of initial size
        PUSH    0           ;Low word of initial size
        PUSH    0           ;File attribute (not used for source)
        PUSH    0000000000000001B         ;Open flag
        PUSH    0000000000100000B         ;Open mode
        PUSH    0
        PUSH    0
        CALL    DOSOPEN
        CMP     AX,0
        JNE     EXIT

        PUSH    DS          ;Selector of filename
        PUSH    OFFSET TARGET    ;Open target next
        PUSH    DS          ;Selector of handle
        PUSH    OFFSET HANDLE2   ;Offset of handle
        PUSH    DS
        PUSH    OFFSET ACTION2
        PUSH    0           ;High word of initial size
        PUSH    0           ;Low word of initial size
        PUSH    0           ;File attribute
        PUSH    0000000000010010B         ;Open flag
        PUSH    0000000000100001B         ;Open mode
        PUSH    0
        PUSH    0
        CALL    DOSOPEN

READ_IN:PUSH    HANDLE1
        PUSH    DS
        PUSH    OFFSET BUFFER
        PUSH    60*1024
        PUSH    DS
        PUSH    OFFSET BYTES_READ
        CALL    DOSREAD
        CMP     BYTES_READ,0
        JE      NORMAL_EXIT

WRITE_OUT:
```

```
→       PUSH    HANDLE2
→       PUSH    DS
→       PUSH    OFFSET BUFFER
→       PUSH    BYTES_READ
→       PUSH    DS
→       PUSH    OFFSET BYTES_WRITTEN
→       CALL    DOSWRITE
→       JMP     READ_IN

EXIT:   PUSH    1                       ;A Normal Exit.
        PUSH    0
        CALL    DOSEXIT

        END     ENTRY
```

Notice that as soon as we finish writing, we jump back to the label READ_IN to see if there's any more bytes to get from the file. If not, then we exit. In other words, we can loop over any size file; no longer are we restricting ourselves to 60K or less.

Before exiting, of course, we have to close the files, using DosClose. This is the easiest service to use of the one's we've included so far—we only have to push the file handle. Here, then, is the complete program COPIER.ASM (with, don't forget, all the proper EXTRNs):

```
.286C
.MODEL  SMALL
.STACK  200H

.DATA
        SOURCE  DB  ""FILE.TXT",0
        TARGET  DB  ""FILE.BAK",0
        HANDLE1 DW      0
        HANDLE2 DW      0
        ACTION1 DW      0
        ACTION2 DW      0
        BYTES_READ      DW      0
        BYTES_WRITTEN   DW      0
        BUFFER  DB 60*1024 DUP(0)

.CODE
        EXTRN
DOSEXIT:FAR,DOSOPEN:FAR,DOSREAD:FAR,DOSWRITE:FAR,DOSCLOSE:FAR

ENTRY:  PUSH    DS      ;Selector of filename
        PUSH    OFFSET SOURCE   ;Open source first
        PUSH    DS      ;Selector of handle
        PUSH    OFFSET HANDLE1  ;Offset of handle
        PUSH    DS
        PUSH    OFFSET ACTION1
        PUSH    0       ;High word of initial size
        PUSH    0       ;Low word of initial size
        PUSH    0       ;File attribute (not used for source)
        PUSH    0000000000000001B       ;Open flag
        PUSH    0000000000100000B       ;Open mode
        PUSH    0
        PUSH    0
        CALL    DOSOPEN
        CMP     AX,0
        JNE     EXIT
```

```
                    PUSH    DS         ;Selector of filename
                    PUSH    OFFSET TARGET   ;Open target next
                    PUSH    DS         ;Selector of handle
                    PUSH    OFFSET HANDLE2  ;Offset of handle
                    PUSH    DS
                    PUSH    OFFSET ACTION2
                    PUSH    0          ;High word of initial size
                    PUSH    0          ;Low word of initial size
                    PUSH    0          ;File attribute
                    PUSH    0000000000010010B      ;Open flag
                    PUSH    0000000000100001B      ;Open mode
                    PUSH    0
                    PUSH    0
                    CALL    DOSOPEN

    READ_IN:PUSH    HANDLE1
            PUSH    DS
            PUSH    OFFSET BUFFER
            PUSH    60*1024
            PUSH    DS
            PUSH    OFFSET BYTES_READ
            CALL    DOSREAD
            CMP     BYTES_READ,0
            JE      NORMAL_EXIT

    WRITE_OUT:
            PUSH    HANDLE2
            PUSH    DS
            PUSH    OFFSET BUFFER
            PUSH    BYTES_READ
            PUSH    DS
            PUSH    OFFSET BYTES_WRITTEN
            CALL    DOSWRITE
            JMP     READ_IN

    NORMAL_EXIT:
            PUSH    HANDLE1
            CALL    DOSCLOSE
            PUSH    HANDLE2
            CALL    DOSCLOSE
    EXIT:   PUSH    1                  ;A Normal Exit.
            PUSH    0
            CALL    DOSEXIT

            END     ENTRY
```

The exit at the end can be reached two ways: either the simple exit if the source file was not found (labeled EXIT), or the normal exit (labeled NORMAL_EXIT), which will close both open files. Here is our exit:

```
NORMAL_EXIT:                       ← Close both files before exiting
        PUSH    HANDLE1
        CALL    DOSCLOSE
        PUSH    HANDLE2
        CALL    DOSCLOSE
EXIT:   PUSH    1                  ← Just exit (used if FILE.TXT didn't open)
        PUSH    0
        CALL    DOSEXIT
```

COPIER will jump to NORMAL_EXIT if it has already read in and copied all the bytes of FILE.TXT. The only time it jumps to the label

EXIT is in the beginning of the program, if it couldn't open FILE.TXT properly.

Of course, in a real program, you should let the user know why you are exiting, particularly if it is the result of some error. Now we've gained some expertise in OS/2 file handling. But what if we wanted to not only copy a complete file over, but wanted to work with *records*, as we did in our DOS file handling chapter? There we used a file pointer, and here, we can do the same thing with OS/2's version of it—the logical file pointer.

DosChgFilePtr—Move File Pointer

```
PUSH   WORD    File handle
PUSH   DWORD   Doubleword that indicates how far (in bytes) the
                   file pointer will be moved.
PUSH   WORD    The "method": 0 = Move pointer relative to file start.
                             1 = Move pointer relative to current loc.
                             2 = Move pointer relative to file end.
PUSH   PTR     Address of a double word field in which OS/2 will
                   place the new file pointer.
CALL   DOSCHGFILEPTR
```

Moving the file pointer is a familiar operation. We have to specify a "method" here too—method 0 means that the file pointer will be moved with respect to the beginning of the file, method 1 with respect to the current location in the file, and method 2 with respect to the file end.

Having decided on a method, we fill the DWORD (push high and then low word) value on the stack that will indicate how far to move the pointer. OS/2 will then return, in doubleword memory location, what the new file pointer's location in the file is.

If you want to break your file up into records, you can use DosChgFilePtr to select which record you will read or write next.

DosFileLocks

```
PUSH   WORD    File handle
PUSH   PTR     Address of a pair of doubleword values. If locking a
                   file, these doublewords will be 0. If
                   unlocking a file, the first doubleword
                   contains the offset in the file where unlocking
                   is to start. The second contains
                   the number of bytes to unlock.
PUSH   PTR     Address of a pair of doubleword values. If unlocking a
                   file, these double words will be 0. If
                   locking a file, the first double word
                   contains the offset in the file where locking
                   is to start. The second double word contains
                   the number of bytes to lock.
CALL   DOSFILELOCKS
```

With DosFilelocks, you can lock specific byte ranges inside files that were opened as Deny Read Access or Deny None Access. When a range of bytes is locked, other programs cannot modify them. This is often useful if you want multiple programs to use a file, or want to allow other programs to use the same file you are using, and avoid the time (in disk accessing) that would be taken in continually opening and closing the file.

To lock (or unlock) part of a file, you only have to specify the file handle, and the range to lock or unlock. (the file handle is a word). Then two pointers are pushed onto the stack. Each of these holds the address of a pair of doublewords. One pair is used in locking bytes, and the other in unlocking.

Let's say that you have the pair of double words used in locking at label LOCK_DWORDS, and the pair of double words used in unlocking at label UNLOCK_DWORDS. Here is how to set them if locking or unlocking:

```
        To Lock:

UNLOCK_DWORDS:0000:0000
             0000:0000
LOCK_DWORDS:  xxxx:xxxx  ← Offset in the file to start locking
             yyyy:yyyy  ← Number of bytes to lock

        To Unlock

UNLOCK_DWORDS:xxxx:xxxx  ← Offset in the file to start unlocking
             yyyy:yyyy  ← Number of bytes to unlock
LOCK_DWORDS:  0000:0000
             0000:0000
```

Whether you are locking or unlocking determines which pair of doublewords will be active (non-zero). To specify a byte range in the file, fill the first of the active doublewords with the offset in the file at which to begin, and the second doubleword with the number of bytes to lock or unlock. That's all there is to it.

To use DosFileLocks, all you have to do is this:

```
        PUSH    FILE_HANDLE
        PUSH    DS
        PUSH    OFFSET UNLOCK_DWORDS
        PUSH    DS
        PUSH    OFFSET LOCK_DWORDS
        CALL    DOSFILELOCKS
```

Database programs in particular often use file locking.

Using the OS/2 services, you can also position yourself in different directories.

DosChDir—Change Directory

```
PUSH    PTR       Address of an ASCIIZ pathname string.
PUSH    DWORD     Reserved_must be 0.
CALL    DOSCHDIR
```

You can change the default directory under OS/2 using this service, DosChDir. All you have to do is set up a new pathname as an ASCIIZ string like this:

```
NEW_PATH    DB    "C:\CELLAR:\",0 H
```

push the address of this pathname on the stack, push two words of zeroes, and call DOSCHDIR. Unless there is an error in the pathname, OS/2 will make the new directory the default. You can also change default drives this way. If there is an error in the pathname, you will get one of two errors (returned in AX): 3 means the path was not found, and 16 means that the pathname was invalid.

We will cover only two more Dos services here, DosBeep and Dos-GetMachineMode.

DosBeep—Beeps

```
PUSH    WORD      A frequency in Hertz (from 25 to 32K).
PUSH    WORD      The duration of the beep (in milliseconds).
CALL    DOSBEEP
```

We have seen this service before, but we have never covered it. All DosBeep does is beep. You can select the beep frequency and duration. It might be worth noticing that DETACHed programs, if they cannot gain access to a VioPopUp when there is some emergency, can only communicate to the user via frantic beeps—there is no other method of I/O available to them.

DosGetMachineMode

```
PUSH    PTR       Address of a word in which OS/2 will store:
                          0 → Real Mode
                          1 → Protected Mode

CALL    DOSGETMACHINEMODE
```

This, the last Dos service we will cover, gets the machine mode. It asks for the address of a word, and returns a 0 in that word for real mode operation of the CPU, and 1 if the CPU is operating in protected mode.

So Long to OS/2

That's it for our whirlwind tour of OS/2. The part that we've examined, Family API for the most part, seems not too different in conception from DOS. On the other hand, it has the advantage of being able to run under multitasking. Although it remains to be seen whether OS/2 catches on firmly, there will be at least a number of applications developed that will only be able to run under it. And software developers are just beginning to explore the real possibilities of multitasking for their applications. If the tremendous creative energy that the PC market has shown in the past flowers under OS/2, then we will see a revolution in personal computing.

13

Sample Programs

SCMP the Champ

If you revise files in your PC or PS/2, you may find several different versions of the same file on your disks. And you may not remember which one contains what. In cases like these, you may turn with some hope to the DOS program COMP. There would be nothing better than finding out just how each file differs from the others without having to read them all.

The DOS COMP program

Regrettably, COMP isn't up to the job. Since it compares only files of the same size, it can almost never be used. If you do use it, it will usually quit immediately with the news that the two files are of different sizes.

We already had this interesting information. This failure alone makes COMP practically worthless for comparing text files of any kind. When the files are, by luck, the same size, COMP still is of little use. It will print out byte values in hex, not in ASCII terms, with only up to 10 mismatches.

At best, COMP is a rudimentary comparison program, lacking in all the features that would make it useful. Most large computer operating systems have comparison programs that fill their user's needs much better, and we deserve one as well.

SCMP

What's lacking is a smart compare utility that isn't afraid of different-length files, or of printing text out in English; a program that lets you see immediately what the differences are between files in a way that's easy to understand. In other words, a utility program with real utility.

SCMP is such a program. Even if you have two files that have been worked on separately, SCMP will let you know what's going on. Now you can see just how your second draft is different from the first, or what you did in revising a program that caused the bug.

470

SCMP in Action

What SCMP does is not only find where the files start to differ, but it looks ahead to find where they match again. That is, if you insert some text into a second draft of a file, SCMP will locate the new text (up to a maximum length, beyond which it will not search for further matching text) and print out the correct sections from the two files.

After SCMP has compared your files, it prints out the different sections side by side on the screen for direct comparison. On the left side of the screen, it types out the mismatching section from the first file, and on the right, the comparable section in the second file. This method of side-by-side printing is much better than printing out the different sections in sequence since the differences are much easier to examine when they are side by side. This way, you can glance back and forth to see what's going on immediately. Besides the different parts of the files, SCMP prints out 20 (matching) bytes both before and after the mismatches to establish their context.

Also, SCMP will print out the line number in each file at which the files start to differ. This is especially useful to locate your position in a particular document in case you want to go in and make further changes, or delete the changes that already exist. If the 20 bytes of context on either side of the mismatching text isn't sufficient to let you know where you are, you can always use the line number.

SCMP contains an additional feature. When programmers compare two files, it is often useless to know the line position of mismatches, since what they are comparing doesn't have the usual <cr><lf> at the end of every line. Instead, it is necessary to know the exact position where the files disagree with the byte. For that reason, SCMP also prints out the byte position of the mismatch, in hex.

SCMP will work with files up to 60K long. It is OK to use SCMP on longer files, but it will only read in the first 60K of files longer than that length for comparison. For example, if you had two files, HAMLET.TWO at 37K and OTHELLO.TWO at 79K, SCMP will only compare HAMLET.TWO against the first 60K of OTHELLO.TWO.

Although it is true that SCMP could theoretically read in the rest of longer files in a second read, the logistics of comparing the first and second parts read in from the first file against the first and second parts read in from the other file become rapidly complex. If there is a mismatch that extends across the read-in boundary of one file, for example, SCMP is going to have to be able to do some sophisticated file manipulation, which would probably double the size of an already tight program, without much gain in real utility. If you want to revamp SCMP to work with larger files, you can, but working with more than 60K is beyond the scope of this sample program.

How Different Can the Files Be?

Differences can be up to 2K long.

SCMP can tolerate any difference of up to 2K in length. If the paragraph you've inserted is longer than this, SCMP will consider the two files too different and tell you so. This limit was inserted mostly for reasons of time—it can take almost 10 minutes on a normal PC for SCMP to try all the combinations inside that 2K gap. This is not to say that SCMP is slow—during that time it tries about four million string comparisons. Comparing most files, of course, will take much less time (only about 30 seconds or so). On the PS/2, naturally, this isn't such a problem—you may want to alter SCMP to enlarge this 2K limit.

100 bytes make a match.

To make sure it has a match, SCMP needs to find 100 identical bytes between mismatches. This limit was originally 50 bytes, but that turns out not to be enough for normal use.

Using SCMP

To use SCMP to compare two files, CHAP1.001 and CHAP1.002, just type:

```
SCMP CHAP1.001 CHAP1.002
```

If you forget to type in one or both of the filenames, SCMP will prompt you, as any good program should. Pathnames can be used, like:

```
SCMP C:\ARCHIVES\CHAP1.001 CHAP1.002
```

If you know which file contains the most additions, you can save some time by typing that filename second, since SCMP starts scanning through it first.

Above its listing of the mismatches, SCMP will put the names of the files the text is coming from, so you can keep track of what you see. If the differences begin to scroll off the screen, stop them with ^NumLock (and use any other key to start the display again).

Control Break use

Unfortunately, the 8088 string comparison commands cannot be interrupted by ^Break, so, occasionally, SCMP won't respond when you try to interrupt it. SCMP is not hung, it is just trying to find a match. When SCMP prints out on the screen, it converts noncharacter bytes like carriage returns into blanks; this makes for a smoother display.

SCMP Details

Let's take a look at some of the details of SCMP to help you understand what's going on if you want to work through the listing. The first thing it does is check on the filenames you've given it when you type:

```
SCMP FILE1.TXT FILE2.TXT
```

When you type "FILE1.TXT FILE2.TXT" on the command line, DOS transfers the information to your program. Every program is loaded directly after the Program Segment Prefix, or PSP. The PSP is the 256-byte (100H) long area filled with as many resources as DOS can offer your program. In this case, DOS reads the characters you have typed on the command line following the program's name and places these characters starting at location 81H in the PSP. Location 80H holds the count of characters (including the leading space).

Reading the Filenames

SCMP checks this information at once. It scans down the line of typed-in bytes to see if you've typed anything at all. If not, it knows that it will have to prompt you for the filenames, and does so. If you've typed two filenames, SCMP knows it's reached the end of the first filename when it comes to the space separating them. The program then inserts a zero byte here to make the filename into an ASCIIZ string. When it comes to the end of the second filename, SCMP expects not to find a space, but rather a <cr>, ASCII 13. When it reaches that point, and converts the second name to an ASCIIZ string as well, both filenames are ready to be used. If, on the other hand, you did not include a second filename, SCMP will find the <cr> following the first filename, and will then know that it should prompt you for the second filename.

Opening the Files

After the filenames have been located and converted into ASCIIZ strings, we can open the files. It is at this point that the DOS services enter. As usual, all file handling is done by DOS (unless you are a *very* intrepid programmer). To open the files required, all we must do is point to the location in memory of the corresponding ASCIIZ string, and load this address into the correct registers. Then we call INT 21H, and it takes over. DOS searches the disk for the filename you have specified. If the file is not found, an error is returned and SCMP will let you know what's going on.

If the file is there, it is opened for reading. This means that all the file information is read by DOS into its internal memory and DOS gets ready for some file work. SCMP requests a read of 60K bytes from each of the files.

The 60K (or less) from the first file goes directly after the program SCMP itself in memory (but before the stack SCMP uses at the end of its 64K-long segment). SCMP then takes over the following 64K space in memory for the 60K bytes from the second file and reads them in there. This is a definite advantage of assembly language. If you want 60K bytes somewhere in memory, all you have to do is request them. There is no fooling around with file records, arrays, or anything else. The data is simply there, however much you require.

When the data has all been read in, SCMP closes the files. Now both files are in memory, in the easiest possible format, ready to be compared.

Comparing the Data

SCMP uses the powerful 8088 string commands to do its work. In particular, SCMP uses the REPE CMPSB command: repeat while equal, compare strings byte-by-byte. The SI and DI registers automatically follow our progress through the strings of bytes as we compare them with REPE CMPSB.

Our first task is to compare the two files and see if they match at all. If they do, we need to see how far they match until we come to the first mismatch. It is, of course, the mismatches that we are really interested in.

The variables MATCH1 and MATCH2 hold the locations in files 1 and 2, respectively, where the files are known to *start* matching. The first time through, these variables are loaded with the location of the beginning of the files in memory:

```
MATCH1 →   It was              MATCH2 →   It was
           a dark                         a dark
           and                            and
           stormy                         cool
           night.                         day.
           Heath-                         Heath-
           cliffe                         cliffe
           jumped                         jumped
           astride                        astride
           the                            the
           horse's                        horse's
             :                              :
             :                              :
```

Here we want to find where the files stop matching, so we use REPE CMPSB (to find how many bytes after MATCH1 and MATCH2 match) this way:

```
        GOCMP:   MOV     SI,MATCH1              ;Let's compare!
                 MOV     DI,MATCH2
                 MOV     CX,60*1024            ;Up to 60K for matches.
→       REPE     CMPSB
                 SUB     SI,2                  ;Reposition these.
                 SUB     DI,2
                 :
                 :
                 MOV     LASTMATCH1,SI         ;We will search now for next matches.
                 MOV     LASTMATCH2,DI
```

REPE CMPSB will keep incrementing SI (which points to file 1) and DI (file 2) until the files stop matching, since REPE means repeat while equal. From the final values of SI and DI, we know where the files stopped matching, which was our goal.

The variables LASTMATCH1 and LASTMATCH2 hold the location where the files last matched, and we fill them here:

```
        GOCMP:   MOV     SI,MATCH1              ;Let's compare!
                 MOV     DI,MATCH2
                 MOV     CX,60*1024            ;Up to 60K for matches.
        REPE     CMPSB
                 SUB     SI,2                  ;Reposition these.
                 SUB     DI,2
                 :
                 :
→                MOV     LASTMATCH1,SI         ;We will search now for next matches.
→                MOV     LASTMATCH2,DI
```

We now know how many bytes in the two files matched (could be zero), and where the mismatch started.

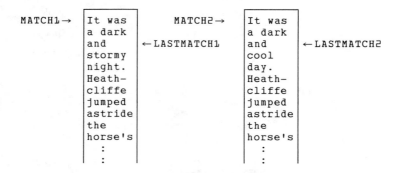

Our next job is to find out where the two files start matching again, if ever.

Finding Matches

This part of the process is the more difficult one. We have to use LASTMATCH1 and LASTMATCH2, the last matches in the files, and find new values for both MATCH1 and MATCH2—the places where the files start matching again. The reason this is more difficult is because SCMP is a smart comparison program. The intervening mismatches need not be the same length; SCMP's job is to find where the files start matching again, despite this fact.

SCMP's algorithm

Here SCMP really goes to work. Starting at the LASTMATCHes, it steadily increments its position in the second file, trying to find matches that correspond to its present position in the first file. After it has gone through 2K of the second file without success, it increments its position in the first file—by a single byte—and tries all over again. Although it sounds like a lot of work, this is exactly the algorithm that a smart comparison program has to pursue to save you the trouble of doing the same thing. Finding the matches again, even though they could be 2K away, is what takes up the time in SCMP.

Here is an outline of the process. Our goal is, starting from LASTMATCH1 in file 1 and LASTMATCH2 in file 2, to find where the files start matching again, MATCH1 and MATCH2:

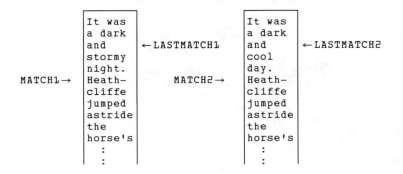

Here is what the code looks like:

```
NOTSAME:
    .....PUSH    LASTMATCH2        ;Set up to search for next match
    :    POP     MATCH2            ; (after intervening mismatch).
    :    MOV     ADD2,0
    :
INNER:..MOV      SI,MATCH1         ;Point to present location.
    : : MOV      DI,MATCH2
    : :
    : : MOV      CX,2048           ;Max of 2K to search/
    : : MOV      DX,CX
REPE: : CMPSB
```

```
   :   : SUB      DX,CX
   :   : CMP      DX,100          ;100 Matching bytes?
   :   : JB       NOTYET          ;No.
   :   : JMP      MATCH           ;Yes. Found a match!
NOTYET: INC      ADD2            ;No match - INC match2 to 2K more or EOF.
   :   : CMP      ADD2,2048
   :   : JAE      INC1
   :   :          :
   :   :          :
GO2:   :.JMP      INNER           ;Loop back to INNER.
   :
INC1:   INC      ADD1            ;No match - INC match2 to 2K more or EOF.
   :    CMP      ADD1,2048
   :    JAE      NOMATCH
   :             :
   :             :
GO1:....JMP      NOTSAME         ;Loop again here over new match-mismatch pair.

NOMATCH:MOV      AL,EOFLAG1      ;At this point no match found, will exit.
        ADD      AL,EOFLAG2      ;Did a file end?
        CMP      AL,0            ;No file ended, files just too different.
        JE       TDIFF
```

There are two loops here. One, the outer loop, loops over the bytes in file 1. The inner loop loops over the bytes in file 2. When the inner loop has looked ahead 2K in file 2 without finding a match to our present location in file 1, we increment our position in file 1. Keep in mind that a match must be at least 100 bytes long for SCMP to consider it real. We begin the loops by loading MATCH1 and MATCH2 from LASTMATCH1 and LASTMATCH2. In our loop, MATCH1 and MATCH2 will hold the present locations in either file; that way, when we exit, MATCH1 and MATCH2 will be set with the positions where the two files start matching again, which is our goal here.

In addition, at the top of the outer loop, we reset MATCH2 to LASTMATCH2 so that we can always search 2K ahead of that position in file 2 as we increment our way through file 1.

```
NOTSAME:
  →.....PUSH     LASTMATCH2      ;Set up to search for next match
  →     POP      MATCH2          ; (after intervening mismatch).
  →     MOV      ADD2,0
        :
INNER:..MOV      SI,MATCH1       ;Point to present location.
  →   : MOV      DI,MATCH2
  →   : :
  →   : MOV      CX,2048         ;Max of 2K to search.
      : : MOV    DX,CX
REPE: : CMPSB
   :  : SUB      DX,CX
```

The memory variables ADD1 (for file 1) and ADD2 (file 2) keep track of just how far we are ahead of LASTMATCH1 and LASTMATCH2. When ADD2 reaches 2K, we haven't found a match in the next 2K of file

2, so we reset ADD2 to zero and increment our position in file 1, and also ADD1.

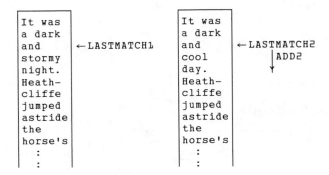

When ADD1 reaches 2K, and we have still not found a match, the files are too different. In other words, we have searched for a match in both file 1 and file 2, and have failed to find one in 2K (in either file). Therefore, we quit, printing a message explaining that the two files are too different.

Since the REPE CMPSB instruction uses CX as an index, we can find how many bytes matched by comparing the final value of CX to its original value (stored in DX). If more that 100 bytes matched, we have found a proper match again, and jump to the location MATCH. If not, we increment our position in file 2, and ADD2 as well to check whether we have gone more than 2K bytes without a match. If we have gone more than 2K in file 2 without a match, we increment our position in file 1 (by jumping to the label INC1 below) and start searching through file 2 again:

```
NOTSAME:
    .....PUSH   LASTMATCH2        ;Set up to search for next match
    :    POP    MATCH2            ; (after intervening mismatch).
    :    MOV    ADD2,0
    :
INNER:..MOV     SI,MATCH1         ;Point to present location.
    : : MOV     DI,MATCH2
    : :
  → : MOV       CX,2048           ;Max of 2K to search/
  → : MOV       DX,CX
REPE: : CMPSB   ←
  → : SUB       DX,CX
  → : CMP       DX,100            ;100 Matching bytes?
  → : JB        NOTYET            ;No.
  → : JMP       MATCH             ;Yes. Found a match!
NOTYET: INC     ADD2        ←     ;No match - INC match2 to 2K more or
EOF.
    : : CMP     ADD2,2048   ←
    : : JAE     INC1        ←
    : :         :
    : :         :
```

This completes the inner loop (labeled INNER). We either exit it because we have found a match, or because we have searched 2048 bytes in file 2 already. Otherwise, we loop by jumping back to INNER and search at a new location in file 2.

If we have to increment our position in file 1, we jump to INC1 and check ADD1 to make sure we haven't gone 2K without a match. If we have, we jump to TDIFF, the "too different" location in the program, which prints out a message saying that the files are too different, and quits.

If we haven't gone for 2K yet in both files, we jump back to the top of the outer loop (labeled NOTSAME), reset ADD2 and MATCH2, and start scanning through file 2 to find a match to our new location in file 1:

```
NOTSAME:
     .....PUSH    LASTMATCH2          ;Set up to search for next match
     :    POP     MATCH2              ; (after intervening mismatch).
     :    MOV     ADD2,0
     :
INNER:..MOV       SI,MATCH1           ;Point to present location.
     : : MOV      DI,MATCH2
     : :
     : : MOV      CX,2048             ;Max of 2K to search/
     : : MOV      DX,CX
REPE: : CMPSB
     : : SUB      DX,CX
     : : CMP      DX,100              ;100 Matching bytes?
     : : JB       NOTYET              ;No.
     : : JMP      MATCH               ;Yes. Found a match!
NOTYET: INC       ADD2                ;No match - INC match2 to 2K more or EOF.
     : : CMP      ADD2,2048
     : : JAE      INC1
     : : :        :
     : : :        :
GO2: :.JMP        INNER               ;Loop back to INNER.
     :
INC1:  INC        ADD1        ←       ;No match - INC match2 to 2K more or EOF.
  →    CMP        ADD1,2048
  →    JAE        NOMATCH
     :            :
     :            :
GO1:....JMP       NOTSAME     ←       ;Loop again here over new match-mismatch pair.

NOMATCH:MOV       AL,EOFLAG1          ;At this point no match found, will exit.
       ADD        AL,EOFLAG2          ;Did a file end?
       CMP        AL,0                ;No file ended, files just too different.
       JE         TDIFF
```

If we end up at the location NOMATCH, there have been no matches found. Before jumping to TDIFF and assuming the files are too different, we first check if one or the other file ended (using EOFLAG1 and EOFLAG2, which are set in the inner and outer loops). If either file ended, that is handled differently from files that are considered too different. In this case, we print out the files from where they last matched to where one file ends.

Now that We Have a Match

Now we have the two positions we need for each file, LASTMATCH and MATCH. The LASTMATCHes record the locations at which the files last matched, and the MATCHes are the positions where they start to match again. In other words, the mismatch we've been looking for extends from LASTMATCH1 to MATCH1 in file 1 and LASTMATCH2 to MATCH2 in file 2.

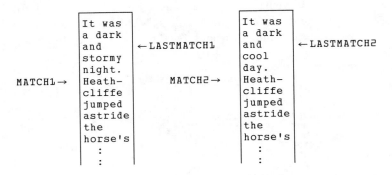

Note that LASTMATCH and MATCH may be at the same position in one of the files if additional material has only been added to the other file.

Printing Out the Mismatch

To report this mismatch, all we must do is print out the mismatch and 20 bytes around it on either side to establish context. This is a little more difficult than it sounds because, naturally, we want to make sure our 20 bytes of context do not extend beyond or before the file in memory, and because of the special format we will use in printing out.

SCMP prints out mismatches side by side for ready comparison. If we come across any screen-control characters (such as tabs, carriage returns, or line feeds), we will convert them into spaces to make reading the two parts of the screens easier.

Essentially, the printing out process (done by the subroutine TYPEOUT in SCMP) locates positions 20 bytes before LASTMATCH1 and LASTMATCH2 and 20 bytes after MATCH1 and MATCH2, and prints the intervening bytes out.

This is accomplished by writing over a blank 80-byte space in memory first with bytes from file 1 and, for the second half, with bytes from the second file. This line, once assembled, is simply printed out with DOS' line printing service, service 9.

Printing out
the
filename

SCMP takes care of several more things. In addition to simply typing out the mismatches, it would be helpful to print out the filename corresponding to each half of the screen. For that reason, SCMP prints out a header preceding the mismatch typeout that gives the names of the two files being compared. It is, of course, easy to get these filenames because we had to have them in order to open the files in the first place. All we need to do is load the filenames into this header from the ASCIIZ strings in which they are stored.

Besides the filename, it would also be useful to know where in each file we are. Its easy enough to get the byte number showing our location in either file, because that's just LASTMATCH. SCMP converts LASTMATCH into hexadecimal and prints it out in the header underneath the filename.

For those who are not adept at reading hex, SCMP also prints out the line number. This is done differently from how you may expect. To know the line number, you have to count the number of <cr><lf>s from the beginning of the file. But SCMP uses REPE CMPSB to find matches in the files; this instruction can't also be used to find <cr><lf> pairs at the same time. In addition, if we loop repeatedly over bytes in file 2, it will be difficult to keep track of <cr><lf> pairs correctly. To do the job properly, in less time than other methods, SCMP simply counts the number of <cr><lf>s from the beginning of the file to LASTMATCH every time it prints out a mismatch. In this way you're sure of getting an accurate count.

Give SCMP a try. Once you've used it a number of times, you may want to add it to your arsenal of utilities. Here's the whole listing:

Listing 13.1 SCMP.ASM

```
CODE_SEG        SEGMENT
        ASSUME  CS:CODE_SEG
        ORG     100H
HERE:   JMP     THERE
        NOTSEEN DB      'File Not Found' ;Disk error messages.
        CRLF    DB      13,10,'$'
        ERR:    DB      'Disk Error$'
        PROMPT1 DB      13,10,'Name of first file? $'   ;In case you did not
        PROMPT2 DB      13,10,'Name of second file? $' ; specify these.
        SAME_MSG        DB 'Files are identical.',13,10,'$'
        TDIFF_MSG       DB 'No match in 2K - files are too different.',13,10,'$'
        TSHORT_MSG      DB 'File is too short to find match.',13,10,'$'
        HEAD1   DB      26 dup(32)      ;Header with filenames.
        SPACES2 DB      13 dup(32),179
        HEAD2   DB      26 DUP(32)
        SPACES4 DB      13 DUP(32),13,10,'$'
        SECTION_HEAD    DB 3 DUP(205),'Line ',
        LINE1   DB      10 DUP(205),'Byte '
        BYTE1   DB      15 DUP(205),216, 3 DUP(205),'Line ',
        LINE2   DB      10 DUP(205),'Byte '
        BYTE2   DB      15 DUP(205),13,10,'$' ;Divider.
        NOLFS1  DW      0
```

Listing 13.1 SCMP.ASM *(continued)*

```
                NOLFS2          DW      0
                PART_1  DB      39 DUP(32),179              ;One line of the display.
                PART_2  DB      39 DUP(32),13,10,'$'
                NAME2   DB      50,0,48 DUP(0)  ;Second filename if typed in.
                NUMREAD1        DW      ?       ;Number of bytes read in from file 1.
                NUMREAD2        DW      ?       ;Number of bytes read in from file 2.
                FILEONE DW      82H             ;Address of 1st File name
                ENDONE  DW      0
                FILETWO DW      0               ;Address of 2nd File name
                ENDTWO  DW      0
                FILEND1 DW      0               ;End of read-in files in memory
                FILEND2 DW      0               ;End of read-in files in memory
                HANDLE1 DW      0       ;File handles of source and target files.
                HANDLE2 DW      0
                ADD1    DW      0       ;Keeps track of how many bytes we have
                ADD2    DW      0       ; compared - up to 2K.
                BX1     DW      0       ;Stores BX locations for typeout.
                BX2     DW      0
                EOFLAG1 DB      0       ;End of file flag for files 1 and 2.
                EOFLAG2 DB      0
                MISMATCHFLAG    DB      0       ;Has there been a mismatch?
                MATCH1  DW      0               ;Place where next match found.
                MATCH2  DW      0
                LASTMATCH1      DW      0       ;Place where last match was found.
                LASTMATCH2      DW      0
                NUMPRINT        DW      0       ;Number of bytes to be printed.
                CORR1   DW      0       ;Corrects against trying to print out before
                CORR2   DW      0       ; file begins in memory.
                LINESTYPED      DB      0       ;Number of lines typed on screen.
                PAGEPROMPT DB   21 DUP(220),' Type any character for next screen.
                                DB 22 DUP(220),'$'
                FILE2FOUND      DB      0

THERE           PROC    NEAR                       ;Our procedure
FILES:          MOV     BX,80H          ;Were any filenames at all typed?
                CMP     BYTE PTR [BX],0
                JNE     YESNAME         ;Yes, check for second name.
                LEA     DX,PROMPT1      ;No, get both filenames.
                MOV     AH,9
                INT     21H
                MOV     SI,OFFSET FILEONE
                MOV     BX,80H
                CALL    GETNAME
                MOV     SI,OFFSET FILETWO
                MOV     BX,ENDONE
                INC     BX
                CALL    GETNAME
                JMP     READY


YESNAME:MOV     BX,81H                          ;Make the filenames into ASCIIZ
CHKSPC: CMP     BYTE PTR [BX+1],' '
                JA      UP                      ;Kill leading spaces.
                INC     FILEONE
                INC     BX
                JMP     SHORT   CHKSPC
UP:             INC     BX                      ;Scan type-in for space, <cr>
                CMP     BYTE PTR [BX],' '       ;Space?
                JNE     NOSPACE
                CMP     FILE2FOUND,0
                JE      SPACE1
                JMP     SHORT   ENDF2
SPACE1: MOV     BYTE PTR [BX],0         ;Put the Z in ASCIIZ
                MOV     FILETWO,BX
                INC     FILETWO                 ;Store filename starting location
                MOV     FILE2FOUND,1
NOSPACE:CMP     BYTE PTR [BX],13        ;If not a space, a <cr>?
                JNE     UP
ENDF2:  MOV     BYTE PTR [BX],0         ;If yes, replace with a 0
```

Listing 13.1 SCMP.ASM *(continued)*

```
        CMP     FILETWO,0
        JNZ     READY
        LEA     DX,PROMPT2      ;No second filename if we are here.
        MOV     AH,9            ;Get second filename.
        INT     21H
        MOV     FILETWO,OFFSET NAME2+2  ;Put name in NAME2.
        MOV     AH,0AH          ;Use buffered input.
        LEA     DX,NAME2
        INT     21H
        MOV     BX,FILETWO      ;Make the filenames into ASCIIZ
UP2:    INC     BX              ;Scan type-in for space, <cr>
        CMP     BYTE PTR [BX],13 ;Carriage return?
        JNE     UP2             ;No, keep going.
        MOV     BYTE PTR [BX],0 ;Yes, put the Z in ASCIIZ

READY:  LEA     DX,CRLF         ;Send <cr> <lf> so screen looks good.
        MOV     AH,9
        INT     21H
        MOV     AX,3D00H        ;Open the source file.
        MOV     DX,FILEONE      ;Point to its name.
        INT     21H
        JNC     OKFILE1         ;Carry Flag → some problem, assume
        LEA     DX,NOTSEEN      ;  file doesn't exist, say so.
        MOV     AH,9
        INT     21H
        JMP     OUT             ;Exit
OKFILE1:MOV     HANDLE1,AX      ;Save source file's handle in HANDLE1.
        MOV     AX,3D00H        ;Open the source file.
        MOV     DX,FILETWO      ;Point to its name.
        INT     21H
        JNC     OKFILE2         ;Carry Flag → some problem, assume
        LEA     DX,NOTSEEN      ;  file doesn't exist, say so.
        MOV     AH,9
        INT     21H
        JMP     OUT             ;Exit
OKFILE2:MOV     HANDLE2,AX      ;Save source file's handle in HANDLE1.

        LEA     DI,THEBOTTOM    ;Fill file 1 space with 1s.
        MOV     CX,30*1024      ;60k BYTES.
        MOV     AX,0101h
REP     STOSW

        MOV     BX,HANDLE1
        MOV     CX,60*1024      ;Ask for 60K bytes to be read from file
        LEA     DX,THEBOTTOM    ;And put at end of program
        MOV     AH,3FH          ;Read
        INT     21H
        MOV     NUMREAD1,AX
        ADD     AX,OFFSET THEBOTTOM ;Actually read AX bytes
        MOV     FILEND1,AX
        DEC     FILEND1         ;Find how far the file extends in mem.
;Now read file 2 in.
        MOV     BX,HANDLE2
        MOV     CX,60*1024      ;Ask for 60K bytes to be read from file
        MOV     AX,ES
        ADD     AX,1000H
        MOV     ES,AX           ;Point to next segment.
        MOV     dx,0
        MOV     AH,3FH          ;Read
        PUSH    DS
        PUSH    ES
        POP     DS
        PUSH    AX
        PUSH    CX
        MOV     DI,0            ;Fill file 2 space with 2s.
        MOV     CX,30*1024      ;60k bytes.
        MOV     AX,0202h
REP     STOSW
```

Listing 13.1 SCMP.ASM *(continued)*

```
            POP     CX
            POP     AX

            INT     21H                       ;Store number of bytes read from file.
            POP     DS
            MOV     NUMREAD2,AX
            MOV     FILEND2,AX
            DEC     FILEND2                    ;Find how far the file extends in mem.
            JMP     BEGIN1

ERROR:      LEA     DX,ERR                    ;Was there a problem?
            MOV     AH,9
            INT     21H
            JMP     OUT

BEGIN1:     LEA     DX,THEBOTTOM              ;Set up for comparison.
            MOV     MATCH1,DX                 ;Start matches out at beginnings
            MOV     MATCH2,0                  ; of files.

GOCMP:      MOV     SI,MATCH1                 ;Let's compare!
            MOV     DI,MATCH2
            MOV     CX,60*1024                ;Up to 60K for matches.
REPE        CMPSB
            SUB     SI,2                      ;Reposition these.
            SUB     DI,2

            MOV     MATCH1,SI                 ;And store location of new matches.
            MOV     MATCH2,DI
            MOV     ADD1,0
            MOV     LASTMATCH1,SI             ;We will search now for next matches.
            MOV     LASTMATCH2,DI
            MOV     AX,NUMREAD2
            CMP     AX,NUMREAD1               ;Are files the same?
            JNE     LENCHK
            CMP     SI,FILEND1                ;Reach end of file, and files
            JNE     LENCHK                    ; same size, without a
            CMP     MISMATCHFLAG,0            ; mismatch?
            JNE     LENCHK
            LEA     DX,SAME_MSG               ;Yes, files are same, say so and
            MOV     AH,9                      ; quit.
            INT     21H
            JMP     OUT
LENCHK:     MOV     CX,NUMREAD1          ;Files too short?
            CMP     CX,100               ;Need at least 100 bytes.
            JB      TSHORT
            MOV     CX,NUMREAD2
            CMP     CX,100
            JA      NOTSAME              ;Files ok but not identical.
TSHORT:     LEA     DX,TSHORT_MSG        ;At least one file is too short.
            MOV     AH,9                 ;Say so and leave.
            INT     21H
            JMP     OUT

NOTSAME:    PUSH    LASTMATCH2           ;Set up to search for next match
            POP     MATCH2               ; (after intervening mismatch).
            MOV     ADD2,0

INNER:      MOV     SI,MATCH1            ;Point to present location.
            MOV     DI,MATCH2
            MOV     CX,2048              ;Max of 2K to search/
            MOV     DX,CX
REPE        CMPSB
            SUB     DX,CX
            CMP     DX,100               ;100 Matching bytes?
            JB      NOTYET               ;No.
            JMP     MATCH                ;Yes. Found a match!
NOTYET:     INC     ADD2                 ;No match - INC match2 to 2K more or EOF.
            CMP     ADD2,2048
```

Listing 13.1 SCMP.ASM *(continued)*

```
        JAE     INC1

        MOV     AX,LASTMATCH2   ;Reached the end of the file?
        ADD     AX,ADD2
        MOV     MATCH2,AX
        CMP     AX,FILEND2
        JBE     GO2
        MOV     EOFLAG2,1

        MOV     ADD2,2048       ;If yes, add 2048 to end this loop.
        MOV     AX,FILEND2
        MOV     MATCH2,AX

GO2:    JMP     INNER           ;Loop back to INNER.

INC1:   INC     ADD1            ;No match - INC match2 to 2K more or EOF.
        CMP     ADD1,2048
        JAE     NOMATCH

        MOV     AX,LASTMATCH1   ;Did file 1 end?
        ADD     AX,ADD1
        MOV     MATCH1,AX
        CMP     AX,FILEND1
        JBE     GO1
        MOV     EOFLAG1,1

        MOV     ADD1,2048       ;Yes, set ADD1 accordingly.
        MOV     AX,FILEND1
        MOV     MATCH1,AX

GO1:    JMP     NOTSAME         ;Loop again here over new match-mismatch pair.
NOMATCH:MOV     AL,EOFLAG1      ;At this point no match found, will exit.
        ADD     AL,EOFLAG2      ;Did a file end?
        CMP     AL,0            ;No file ended, files just too different.
        JE      TDIFF

                                ;One or both files ended.
TYP:    MOV     AX,FILEND1              ;Do the appropriate thing.
        CMP     AX,LASTMATCH1
        JNE     REST
        MOV     AX,FILEND2
        CMP     AX,LASTMATCH2
        JNE     REST
        JMP     OUT

REST:   MOV     AX,FILEND1              ;Print out rest of file that did not
        MOV     MATCH1,AX              ; end (up to 2K).
        MOV     AX,FILEND2
        MOV     MATCH2,AX
        CALL    TYPEOUT
        CMP     MISMATCHFLAG,0         ;Put closing dividing line on screen?
        JNE     NOLAST
        MOV     CX,39
        MOV     DL,196
        MOV     AH,2                   ;This part does
T3:     INT     21H                    ; line graphics on the screen
        LOOP    T3                     ; to make the display pretty.
        MOV     DL,193
        INT     21H
        MOV     CX,39
        MOV     DL,196
T4:     INT     21H
        LOOP    T4

NOLAST: JMP     OUT
TDIFF:  LEA     DX,TDIFF_MSG           ;Files are too different -- 2K without
        MOV     AH,9                   ; a match. Quit.
        INT     21H
        JMP     OUT
```

Listing 13.1 SCMP.ASM *(continued)*

```
MATCH:                              ;This is where we come after finding a match,
          MOV    MISMATCHFLAG,1     ; and, therefore, an intervening mismatch.
          CALL   TYPEOUT            ;Type out from lastmatches to matches.
          JMP    GOCMP              ;And go back for more.

CLOSE:    MOV    BX,HANDLE1         ;Here we close both files.
          MOV    AH,3EH             ;Use Service 3EH.
          INT    21H
          MOV    BX,HANDLE2
          MOV    AH,3EH
          INT    21H
OUT:      CMP    MISMATCHFLAG,0     ;The grand exit.
          JE     INT20H             ;Should we put a line on the screen
          MOV    CX,39              ; to complete the display?
          MOV    DL,196
          MOV    AH,2
T1:       INT    21H                ;Line graphics.
          LOOP   T1
          MOV    DL,193
          INT    21H
          MOV    CX,39
          MOV    DL,196
T2:       INT    21H
          LOOP   T2
INT20H:   INT    20H                ;Thaaaaaaat's all folks.
THERE     ENDP

TYPEOUT   PROC   NEAR       ;This types out from lastmatches to matches, plus
          PUSH   AX         ; 20 bytes either side.
          PUSH   BX
          PUSH   CX
          PUSH   DX
          PUSH   DI
          PUSH   SI         ;Save everything important.

          PUSH   AX         ;Now for some line graphics.
          PUSH   BX
          PUSH   CX         ;This part puts out the lines
          PUSH   SI         ; of the header.
          CALL   PAGECHECK
          MOV    CX,39
          MOV    DL,196
          MOV    AH,2
A1:       INT    21H
          LOOP   A1
          MOV    DL,197
          INT    21H
          MOV    CX,39
          MOV    DL,196
A2:       INT    21H
          LOOP   A2
          MOV    DL,13
          INT    21H
          MOV    DL,10
          INT    21H
          MOV    BX,FILEONE        ;Here we are looking at the name of file 1.
          LEA    SI,HEAD1
          MOV    CX,50             ;Allow up to 50 characters.
L11:      MOV    AL,[BX]           ;Get character.
          CMP    AL,0              ;Is it the end of the ASCIIZ name?
          JE     Z1
          CMP    AL,'\'            ;Capitalize if needed.
          JLE    M1
          SUB    AL,'a'-'A'
M1:       MOV    [SI],AL           ;Store in the line to be printed out.
          INC    SI                ;And point to the next character.
          INC    BX
          LOOP   L11               ;Go back for more.
```

Listing 13.1 SCMP.ASM *(continued)*

```
Z1:        MOV       BX,FILETWO          ;Now do the same for file 2.
           LEA       SI,HEAD2
           MOV       CX,50               ;Put it in the line to be printed out.
L12:       MOV       AL,[BX]
           CMP       AL,0
           JE        Z2
           CMP       AL,'\'
           JLE       M2
           SUB       AL,'a'-'A'
M2:        MOV       [SI],AL             ;Point to next character.
           INC       SI
           INC       BX
           LOOP      L12
Z2:        MOV       AH,9                ;Print out the heading line with
           LEA       DX,HEAD1            ; DOS Service 9.
           CALL      PAGECHECK
           INT       21H
           POP       SI                  ;Restore registers.
           POP       CX
           POP       BX
           POP       AX

;LASTMATCH1 goes to BYTE1, LASTMATCH2 to BYTE2.

           LEA       SI,BYTE1
           MOV       DX,LASTMATCH1
           SUB       DX,OFFSET THEBOTTOM
           INC       DX
           MOV       CX,0
ALOOP:     CMP       DX,0                              ;Find and load byte location in files.
           JE        ADONE
           MOV       AX,DX
           AND       AX,0FH
           CMP       AX,10
           JL        AADD
           SUB       AX,10
           ADD       AX,'A'-'0'
AADD:      ADD       AX,'0'
           INC       CX
           PUSH      AX
           PUSH      CX
           MOV       CX,4                ;This comes out in hex.
           SHR       DX,CL
           POP       CX
           JMP       SHORT   ALOOP
ADONE:     POP       AX
           MOV       [SI],AL
           INC       SI
           LOOP      ADONE
           MOV       BYTE PTR [SI],'H'

           LEA       SI,BYTE2            ;Now for the second file.
           MOV       DX,LASTMATCH2
           INC       DX
           MOV       CX,0
BLOOP:     CMP       DX,0                ;Repeat above procedure.
           JE        BDONE
           MOV       AX,DX
           AND       AX,0FH
           CMP       AX,10
           JL        BADD
           SUB       AX,10
           ADD       AX,'A'-'0'
BADD:      ADD       AX,'0'
           INC       CX
           PUSH      AX
           PUSH      CX
           MOV       CX,4
```

Listing 13.1 SCMP.ASM *(continued)*

```
        SHR     DX,CL
        POP     CX
        JMP     SHORT    BLOOP
BDONE:  POP     AX
        MOV     [SI],AL              ;Also comes out in hex.
        INC     SI
        LOOP    BDONE
        MOV     BYTE PTR [SI],'H'

        PUSH    DS                   ;Find linenumbers for both files.
        PUSH    ES
        PUSH    DI
        PUSH    SI

        MOV     NOLFS1,1             ;Number of line feeds seen.
        MOV     NOLFS2,1

        MOV     DI,0
        MOV     CX,LASTMATCH2
REP2:   MOV     AL,10
REPNE   SCASB                        ;Set NOLFS2
        JCXZ    NOMOLF2
        INC     NOLFS2
        JMP     SHORT    REP2

NOMOLF2:MOV     DI,OFFSET THEBOTTOM
        MOV     CX,LASTMATCH1
        SUB     CX,DI
        PUSH    DS
        POP     ES
REP1:   MOV     AL,10
REPNE   SCASB                        ;Set NOFLS1
        JCXZ    NOMOLF1
        INC     NOLFS1
        JMP     SHORT    REP1

NOMOLF1:POP     SI
        POP     DI
        POP     ES
        POP     DS

        LEA     SI,LINE1             ;Put into header.
        MOV     DX,NOLFS1
        MOV     CX,0
CLOOP:
        CMP     DX,0
        JE      CDONE
        MOV     AX,DX
        MOV     BX,10
        MOV     DX,0
        DIV     BX
        ADD     DX,'0'               ;Find linenumber for file 1.
        INC     CX
        PUSH    DX
        MOV     DX,AX

        JMP     SHORT    CLOOP
CDONE:  POP     AX
        MOV     [SI],AL
        INC     SI
        LOOP    CDONE

        LEA     SI,LINE2
        MOV     DX,NOLFS2
        MOV     CX,0
DLOOP:
        CMP     DX,0
        JE      DDONE
```

Listing 13.1 SCMP.ASM *(continued)*

```
          MOV       AX,DX
          MOV       BX,10
          MOV       DX,0
          DIV       BX                      ;Find line number for file 2.

          ADD       DX,'0'
          INC       CX
          PUSH      DX
          MOV       DX,AX

          JMP       SHORT     DLOOP
DDONE:    POP       AX
          MOV       [SI],AL
          INC       SI
          LOOP      DDONE

          LEA       DX,SECTION_HEAD         ;Print out line divider for this
          MOV       AH,9                    ; mismatch.
          CALL      PAGECHECK
          INT       21H

          MOV       CORR1,0         ;CORRs used if we try to print out
          MOV       CORR2,0         ; before the file starts in memory.
          MOV       BX,LASTMATCH1
          SUB       BX,20                   ;Set CORRs (to be used later to
          CMP       BX,OFFSET THEBOTTOM     ; adjust loop indices).
          JA        NOTBEF1
          SUB       BX,OFFSET THEBOTTOM
          MOV       CORR1,BX
          MOV       BX,OFFSET THEBOTTOM
NOTBEF1:  MOV       BX1,BX
          MOV       BX,LASTMATCH2
          SUB       BX,20                   ;Now for CORR2.
          CMP       BX,0FFE0H
          JB        NOTBEF2
          MOV       CORR2,BX
          MOV       BX,0
NOTBEF2:  MOV       BX2,BX

          LEA       SI,PART_1       ;Loop over bytes to print.
          MOV       CX,MATCH1
          SUB       CX,LASTMATCH1
          ADD       CX,40           ;Set everything up here.
          ADD       CX,CORR1
          MOV       NUMPRINT,CX     ;This is to find NUMPRINT, the number
          MOV       AX,MATCH2       ; of bytes to print.
          SUB       AX,LASTMATCH2   ;NUMPRINT is the bigger of the number of
          ADD       AX,40           ; bytes that need to be printed from each file.
          ADD       CX,CORR2
          CMP       CX,AX
          JA        LOOPER
          MOV       NUMPRINT,AX     ;Store NUMPRINT.

LOOPER:   CMP       NUMPRINT,2*1024         ;Max to print -- do not print more than
          JBE       OKP                     ; 2K.
          MOV       NUMPRINT,2*1024

OKP:      MOV       AX,0            ;Loop over all bytes to print.

TRANS1:   PUSH      CX              ;Start off with all spaces in the line
          MOV       CX,39           ; to be printed.
          MOV       AL,' '
          LEA       DI,PART_1       ;Here we fill PART_1.
          PUSH      ES
          PUSH      DS
          POP       ES
REP       STOSB                     ;With REP STOSB.
          POP       ES
```

Listing 13.1 SCMP.ASM *(continued)*

```
         POP    CX

         MOV    AX,0
         MOV    BX,BX1
         LEA    SI,PART_1
PR1:     MOV    DL,[BX]              ;Print from file 1.
         INC    BX                   ;Get one character.
         CMP    DL,' '               ;Is it ok?
         JAE    P1
         MOV    DL,249               ;No, make it a space.
P1:      CMP    DL,'$'
         JNE    P11
         MOV    DL,249
P11:     MOV    CX,MATCH1
         ADD    CX,20                ;Are we past end?
         CMP    BX,CX
         JA     P391
         MOV    [SI],DL              ;No, everything ok, print this char.
         INC    AX                   ;And point to next one.
         INC    SI

         CMP    BX,FILEND1           ;Do not print out past end of file.
         JA     P391

         CMP    AX,39                ;Done 39 chars without passing MATCH+20?
         JB     PR1
P391:    MOV    BX1,BX               ;Get BX back.

         MOV    BX,LASTMATCH2
         SUB    BX,20
         LEA    SI,PART_2            ;Set up to do part 2 -- that is, print
         MOV    CX,MATCH2            ; from file 2.
         SUB    CX,LASTMATCH2
         ADD    CX,40
         ADD    CX,CORR2
         MOV    AX,0

TRANS2:  PUSH   CX                   ;Fill up part_2 with blanks
         MOV    CX,39
         MOV    AL,' '
         LEA    DI,PART_2
         PUSH   ES
         PUSH   DS
         POP    ES
REP      STOSB                       ;Using REP STOSB.
         POP    ES
         POP    CX

         MOV    AX,0
         MOV    BX,BX2               ;Get the correct beginning place.
         LEA    SI,PART_2
PR2:     MOV    DL,ES:[BX]           ;Print from file 2.
         INC    BX
         CMP    DL,' '               ;Is the character ok?
         JAE    P2
         MOV    DL,249               ;No, make it a space.
P2:      CMP    DL,'$'
         JNE    P3
         MOV    DL,249
P3:      MOV    CX,MATCH2
         ADD    CX,20                ;Are we 20 chars past MATCH?
         CMP    BX,CX
         JA     P392
         MOV    [SI],DL              ;Everything ok -- put char in line to be
         INC    AX                   ; printed.
         INC    SI

         CMP    BX,FILEND2                    ;Do not print out past end of file.
```

Listing 13.1 SCMP.ASM *(continued)*

```
        JA      P392

        CMP     AX,39           ;Done 39 characters without going 20 past
        JB      PR2             ; MATCH?
P392:   MOV     BX2,BX

        LEA     DX,PART_1       ;Print one line.
        MOV     AH,9
        CALL    PAGECHECK
        INT     21H

        SUB     NUMPRINT,39     ;More lines to print?
        CMP     NUMPRINT,0      ;Check by subtracting the number printed,
        JL      POPS            ;39, from NUMPRINT. If more, go
        JMP     LOOPER          ;back and do them too.

POPS:   POP     SI              ;Restore all.
        POP     DI
        POP     DX
        POP     CX
        POP     BX
        POP     AX
        RET
TYPEOUT ENDP


PAGECHECK       PROC    NEAR
        INC     LINESTYPED
        CMP     LINESTYPED,23
        JL      OUTP
        PUSH    AX
        PUSH    DX
        MOV     LINESTYPED,0
        LEA     DX,PAGEPROMPT
        MOV     AH,9
        INT     21H
        MOV     AH,7
        INT     21H
        POP     DX
        POP     AX
OUTP:   RET
PAGECHECK       ENDP


GETNAME         PROC    NEAR
        ;Reads in filename to loc. [BX]. Loads name markers from [SI].
        PUSH    AX
        PUSH    BX
        PUSH    DX
        PUSH    SI
        PUSH    BX      ;Load DS:DX for function call.
        POP     DX
        MOV     [BX],40 ;Allow Max 40 chars for filename.
        MOV     [SI],BX ;Load FILEONE or FILETWO
        ADD     WORD PTR [SI],2
        MOV     AH,0AH
        INT     21H
        ADD     BL,[BX+1]
        MOV     BYTE PTR [BX],0
        MOV     [SI+2],BX               ;Set end of filename mark.
        POP     SI
        POP     DX
        POP     BX
        POP     AX
        RET
GETNAME ENDP


THEBOTTOM:                              ;Read-in file starts here.
        CODE_SEG        ENDS
        END     HERE            ;So long
```

The LOG Program

Log Your PC Sessions

There are many times when it's desirable to keep track of what you're doing. That is, it would frequently be useful to send output to *both* screen and file. In other words, to log your computer sessions.

For example, you may want to record the errors from some program to present to the manufacturer. Or you may want to record what you do for tax purposes. Or you may be writing a training manual and need examples of how things work; there are any number of reasons and, until now, few solutions. LOG is one solution. LOG will let you interact with your PC or PS/2 freely, and record what happens on the screen (both your input and the program's output).

Like commercial loggers for the big computers, however, LOG is not meant to be used with programs like word processors that send the cursor all over the page. If you change a line in the middle of the screen, just recording the changed line would make little sense. And recording the entire screen for an added comma would make as little sense. Instead, LOG is designed for use with programs that send output to the screen normally, without screen manipulation (although clearing the screen is fine). For example, LOG is perfect to use in a debugging session, or when you want to record errors in compiling and linking, with calculator programs, or for use with anything DOS does (directory searches, deleting files, protecting files, setting the time, printing a file, etc.), and so forth.

Using LOG

To use LOG, just type "LOG" at DOS level. The program will attach itself in memory and start logging. To terminate logging, type "LOG" to DOS again, and it will write a file named LOG01.TXT in the directory you're in. LOG01.TXT contains the complete log of the session. The next time (type "LOG" again to start logging once more), LOG will produce LOG02.TXT, and so on up to LOG99.TXT. Keep in mind that every time you load LOG it starts out with LOG01.TXT, to avoid filling the disk with log files.

Disk use   LOG differs intentionally from redirection in that it uses a buffer in memory to store screen data, rather than holding a file open on disk. This was done so that you could change diskettes without problem, as is not the case when using redirection. LOG's buffer in memory is 30K long, and is long enough to hold about 80 screens worth of material.

How LOG Works

Let's go through some of the details of LOG to get you started on the actual listing.

When LOG is first loaded, it notices what kind of screen you're using. Different types of screens hold their data in different areas of memory. After it's installed, LOG watches the screen carefully. For example, when the cursor is moved down a line, that is a signal that the previous line is now complete. LOG stores the completed line (after removing the trailing blanks that fill it out on the screen) and updates its row position.

If there is a request to scroll the screen, LOG will intercept it and record the line before it scrolls up. Similarly, if a program clears the screen, LOG moves its position up to the top row, and is ready to record again. Since LOG watches the screen directly, it can record whatever appears there, whether a program is using DOS or BIOS to put it there, or whether the program put it directly into the screen buffer. Redirection, on the other hand, frequently works only if programs use DOS exclusively for output.

Using COM-MAND. COM

Once you've stored your session on the PC and wish to dump it, all you have to do is to type "LOG" to DOS. To start logging again, type the same thing. To be able to do this, LOG watches what you type to COMMAND.COM by intercepting COMMAND.COM's type-in buffer in memory, and using a type-in buffer of its own. If you type "LOG", the logger toggles a flag, turning itself on or off, and removes the command before DOS sees it. All other commands are passed on without change. In this way, once it's loaded, LOG seems to become a DOS command like any other. Once you've loaded LOG for the first time, you can type "LOG" at DOS level anytime, without needing to have the program itself in the default directory.

LOG is a good program that provides quite a change from redirection. Now, you can see what's going on *and* record it. LOG is your invisible stenographer, ever attentive, ever available. If you want to show someone else what's been happening on your computer, such a program can be invaluable. Here's the (lengthy) listing:

Listing 13.2 LOG.ASM

```
BUFFLEN EQU    30*1024          ;Length of screen data buffer.

INTERRUPTS     SEGMENT AT 0H
        ORG    10H*4            ;This is to use INT 10
VID_INT        LABEL  WORD      ; which is the VIDEO interrupt
        ORG    1CH*4            ;This is to use INT 1C
TIMER_INT      LABEL  WORD      ; which is the timer interrupt
        ORG    21H*4            ;holds the address of its service routine
```

Listing 13.2 LOG.ASM *(continued)*

```
DOS_INT         LABEL   WORD
INTERRUPTS      ENDS

SCREEN   SEGMENT AT 0B000H           ;A dummy segment to use as the
SCREEN   ENDS                        ;Extra Segment

CODE_SEG        SEGMENT
        ASSUME  CS:CODE_SEG
        ORG     100H                 ;ORG = 100H to make this into a
                                     ; ''.COM'' file
FIRST:  JMP     LOAD_LOGGER

        OLD_TIME_INT    DW      2 DUP(?) ;The address INT 1C uses normally
        INT21   LABEL   DWORD   ;For the call to INT 21H
        OLD_DOS_INT     DW 2 DUP(?)
        INT10   LABEL   DWORD           ;For the call to INT 10H.
        OLD_VID_INT     DW 2 DUP(?)
        SCREEN_SEG_OFFSET       DW      0       ;0 for mono, 8000H for cga.
        COUNT10         DW      0       ;Used to update clock every 500 counts
        SCURS           DW      0       ;Location of the cursor on the screen
        VIDEO_PORT      DW      ?       ;Video status port - check for scanning
        DISPLAY         DW      5 DUP (073AH)   ; Initial value for the clock
        LINE    DB      80 DUP(?)       ;Holds the line taken from screen.
        LINEND  DB      2 DUP(?)
        LOGON   DB      0FFH    ;Logging flag
        NEWLINE DW      0       ;Position where new line will go in buff.
        OLDLINE DW      0       ;Position of oldline in buff.
        ROWTOGET        DW  0   ;For getline
        LINELEN DW      0       ;Returned by getline
        LASTROWNUM DW   0       ;Last stored row number
        CURSOR  DB      0       ;Row position of cursor.
        FILENAME        DB      'LOG'           ;Store logged data in this file.
        FILENUMBER1     DB      '0'
        FILENUMBER2     DB      '1.TXT',0
        OLD_DS  DW      ?       ;Old address of DOS read-in buffer.
        OLD_DX  DW      ?
        FIRST_FLAG      DB 1    ;Used by DOS_Watch.
        COMMAND_ADDR    DW ?    ;Used by DOS_Watch.
        KEY1    DB      'LOG',0DH       ;Toggles prog on and off.
        KEY2    DB      'log',0DH
        KEY3    DB      'Log',0DH
        FILE_DONE   DB  'Logging Terminated, file created.',13,10,'$'
        LOGON_MSG DB    'Logging started, type LOG to end.'
        CR      DB      13,10,'$'
        BUFEND  DW      0       ;End of buffer.

LOGGER  PROC    NEAR    ;The timer interrupt will now come here.

        PUSH    AX                      ;Save the used registers for good form
        PUSH    BX
        PUSH    CX
        PUSH    DI
        PUSH    SI
        PUSH    DS
        PUSH    ES

        PUSHF                           ;First, call old time interrupt
        CALL    DWORD PTR OLD_TIME_INT

        ASSUME  DS:CODE_SEG
        PUSH    CS
        POP     DS

        MOV     CX,COUNT10              ;Prepare to test if we should
        INC     CX                      ; check the screen.
        MOV     COUNT10,CX              ;Store incremented or zeroed value
        CMP     CX,10                   ;10 timer counts
        JAE     GOLOG
```

Listing 13.2 LOG.ASM *(continued)*

```
SOLONG: JMP      OUT
GOLOG:  MOV      COUNT10,0                  ;Reset Count10
        CMP      LOGON,0                    ;Logging on?
        JNE      GETCURS
        JMP      OUT
GETCURS:MOV      AH,3                       ;Get cursor position on screen.
        MOV      BH,0
        INT      10H
        MOV      CURSOR,DH
                                   ;CHECK IF WE'RE ON A NEW LINE
        CMP      DH,0               ;On top line, not complete yet.
        JNE      NOT0
        JMP      OUT
NOT0:   CMP      DH,1     ;CLS, etc leaves cursor on line 1, not 0.
        JNE      DECDH
        MOV      LASTROWNUM,0    ;If screen was cleared, go to top.
        JMP      OUT
DECDH:  DEC      DH               ;Point to last complete line.
        CMP      DH,BYTE PTR LASTROWNUM
        JNE      CHANGED
        JMP      OUT                        ;If no line change, jmp out.
CHANGED:CMP      LASTROWNUM,24    ;Let VID_WATCH handle scrolls.
        JGE      OUT
        CMP      DH,BYTE PTR LASTROWNUM
        JB       LESS
INCL:   INC      LASTROWNUM                 ;Get screen lines, LASTROWNUM to
        PUSH     LASTROWNUM                 ; CURSOR-1.
        POP      ROWTOGET
        CALL     GETLINE          ;Get line from screen
        CALL     LOADLINE         ;Put into buff.
        MOV      DH,CURSOR        ;Check if we are done.
        DEC      DH
        MOV      DL,BYTE PTR LASTROWNUM
        CMP      DH,DL
        JBE      SOLONG                   ;Yes.
        JMP      SHORT   INCL             ;No, get another line.

LESS:   MOV      LASTROWNUM,0
OUT:    POP      ES               ;Having done Pushes, here are the Pops
        POP      DS
        POP      SI
        POP      DI
        POP      CX
        POP      BX
        POP      AX

        IRET                             ;An interrupt needs an IRET

LOGGER  ENDP

VID_WATCH      PROC   FAR
        PUSH     ES                         ;Save all used registers.
        PUSH     DS
        PUSH     BP         ;This program stores lines when screen scrolls.
        PUSH     AX
        PUSH     BX
        PUSH     CX
        PUSH     DX
        CLI
        CMP      AH,06            ;Is this the INT 10H Service we want to
        JE       GO2             ; intercept?
        JMP      OUT3                       ;No.
GO2:    CMP      DH,24            ;Yes -- bottom of screen?
        JNE      OUT3
        ASSUME   DS:CODE_SEG      ;Set up DS.
        PUSH     CS
        POP      DS
        CMP      LOGON,0                    ;Are we logging?
```

Listing 13.2 LOG.ASM *(continued)*

```
          JE        OUT3                    ;No.
          MOV       ROWTOGET,24             ;Yes, store bottom line before it
          CALL      GETLINE                 ; scrolls up.
          CALL      LOADLINE
          MOV       LASTROWNUM,24
OUT3:     STI
          POP       DX
          POP       CX                      ;The POPs for the case where we don't
          POP       BX                      ; handle Service 0AH.
          POP       AX
          POP       BP
          POP       DS
          POP       ES
          ASSUME    DS:NOTHING
          JMP       INT10                   ;Let INT 21H take over.
VID_WATCH           ENDP

LOADLINE            PROC    NEAR            ;Loads line from line to buff.
                                            ; UPDATES OLDLINE NEWLINE
          PUSH      CX
          PUSH      DI
          PUSH      SI
          PUSH      DS
          PUSH      ES
          MOV       CX,LINELEN              ;Get ready to transfer LINELEN bytes.
          PUSH      CS
          POP       DS
          PUSH      CS
          POP       ES
          MOV       DI,NEWLINE              ;Move line from NEWLINE into BUFF.
          CMP       DI,BUFEND               ;Do not write past end of buffer.
          JA        POPSA
          LEA       SI,LINE
REP       MOVSB                             ;Move the line.
          DEC       NEWLINE                 ;Set up for next line to be moved in.
          MOV       CX,NEWLINE
          MOV       OLDLINE,CX
          MOV       CX,LINELEN
          ADD       NEWLINE,CX
POPSA:    POP       ES                      ;Restore registers.
          POP       DS
          POP       SI
          POP       DI
          POP       CX
          RET
LOADLINE            ENDP

GETLINE PROC        NEAR                    ;Gets line from screen into line, adds crlf
                                            ;UPDATES LINE, LINELEN (INCLUDES CRLF).
          PUSH      AX                      ;Save the used registers for good form
          PUSH      BX
          PUSH      CX
          PUSH      DI
          PUSH      SI
          PUSH      DS
          PUSH      ES

          ASSUME    DS:CODE_SEG
          PUSH      CS
          POP       DS
          ASSUME    ES:SCREEN               ;Set up screen as the Extra Segment
          MOV       CX,SCREEN
          MOV       ES,CX

          LEA       SI,LINE
          PUSH      ROWTOGET
          POP       AX
          MOV       CX,160                  ;160 bytes per row on screen
```

Listing 13.2 LOG.ASM *(continued)*

```
        MUL     CX              ;AX now has dist. into screen buffer.
        MOV     BX,AX
        ADD     BX,SCREEN_SEG_OFFSET
        MOV     CX,80
        MOV     DX,VIDEO_PORT           ;This is the screen status port

        CLI
SCAN_LOW:                       ;Start waiting for a new horizontal scan -
        IN      AL,DX           ;Make sure the video controller scan status
        TEST    AL,1            ; is low
        JNZ     SCAN_LOW
        MOV     AH,ES:[BX]      ;Move byte to be written to the screen into AH

SCAN_HIGH:                      ;After port has gone low, it must go high
        IN      AL,DX           ; before it is safe to write directly to
        TEST    AL,1            ; the screen buffer in memory
        JZ      SCAN_HIGH

        MOV     DS:[SI],AH      ;Do the move to the screen, one byte at a time
        ADD     BX,2
        INC     SI
        LOOP    SCAN_LOW        ;Go back for next byte
        STI

        STD
        ASSUME  ES:CODE_SEG     ;Now kill trailing blanks.
        PUSH    CS
        POP     ES
        LEA     DI,LINEND       ;Find where blanks stop.
        DEC     DI
        MOV     CX,80
        MOV     AL,' '
REPE    SCASB
        ADD     DI,2    ;Point to end of line
        MOV     BYTE PTR ES:[DI],13     ;Put in <cr><lf>.
        INC     DI
        MOV     BYTE PTR ES:[DI],10
        ADD     CX,4            ;Now set up LINELEN for LOADLINE.
        MOV     LINELEN,CX
        CLD

        POP     ES              ;Restore registers.
        POP     DS
        POP     SI
        POP     DI
        POP     CX
        POP     BX
        POP     AX
        RET

GETLINE ENDP

DOS_WATCH       PROC    FAR             ;The DOS interrupt will now come here.
        PUSH    ES                      ;Save all used registers.
        PUSH    DS
        PUSH    BP
        PUSH    AX
        PUSH    BX
        PUSH    CX
        CMP     AH,0AH                  ;Is this the DOS Service we want to
        JE      GO                      ; intercept?
        JMP     OUT2                    ;No.
GO:
        MOV     BX,DX                   ;Yes. Get length of original buffer.
        MOV     CL,BYTE PTR DS:[BX]
        PUSH    DS                      ;Save DS:DX, address of original buffer.
        ASSUME  DS:CODE_SEG
        PUSH    CS                      ;Make DS=CS to use local labels.
```

Listing 13.2 LOG.ASM *(continued)*

```
            POP     DS
            POP     OLD_DS
            PUSH    DX
            POP     OLD_DX
            MOV     BX,80H                  ;We will use DS:80H for our buffer.
            MOV     BYTE PTR DS:[BX],CL     ;Store legal length from original buff.
            MOV     BP,SP                   ;Prepare to get IP of return address.
            CMP     FIRST_FLAG,1            ;First time through?
            JNE     NOT_FIRST               ;No -- check if COMMAND.COM is calling.
            MOV     BX,SS:[BP+4]            ;Yes, LOG.COM must have just ended,
            MOV     COMMAND_ADDR,BX         ; so we are at monitor level -- get
            MOV     FIRST_FLAG,0            ; calling addr in COMMAND.COM from stack

            JMP     OUT2
NOT_FIRST:                                  ;Not the first time through, check COMMAND addr.
            MOV     BX,SS:[BP+4]            ;Get ret addr from stack.
            CMP     BX,COMMAND_ADDR         ;Compare to what we know is COMMAND.COM
            JE      INTERCEPT               ;If not equal, not at monitor level.
            JMP     OUT2                    ;If not equal, not at monitor level.
INTERCEPT:                                  ;We are at monitor level, check for keys being typed.
            MOV     DX,80H                  ;Get typein to OUR buffer instead of COMMAND's.
            MOV     AH,0AH                  ;Use Service 0AH.
            PUSHF                           ;CALL INT 21 (we would intercept and INT 21 instruction)
            CALL    INT21
            PUSHF                           ;Save flags.
            CLD                             ;Set upward flag for string commands.
            PUSH    CS                      ;Set ES to CODE_SEG.
            POP     ES

            LEA     DI,KEY1                 ;Start by checking for KEY1.
            MOV     BP,DI                   ;BP will hold address of current KEY.
            MOV     AX,3    ;Loop over 3 keys.
CMPLOOP:    MOV     SI,82H                  ;Point to the read-in string.
            MOV     BX,81H                  ;Get its length.
            XOR     CX,CX                   ;Use CX as counter for REPE.
            MOV     CL,BYTE PTR [BX]
            CMP     CL,0                    ;If nothing typed, skip the checking.
            JG      CHECK1
            JMP     NOMATCH
CHECK1:     CMP     CL,3                    ;If more than 4 characters typed, skip also.
            JLE     DOCMP
            JMP     NOMATCH
DOCMP:
REPE        CMPSB                           ;Compare type-in to key.
            JNZ     NEXT                    ;If zero flag not set, last char didn't match.
            JCXZ    MAYBE                   ;All chars matched. Was it the right length?
            JMP     SHORT NEXT
MAYBE:      CMP     BYTE PTR [DI],0DH ;If next char in key is <cr>, end of key, so
            JE      FOUND                   ;typed-in string was the right length.

NEXT:       ADD     BP,4                    ;Point to next key.
            MOV     DI,BP                   ;Fill DI, which changes in REPE CMPSB, from BP.
            DEC     AX                      ;BP, unlike DI, will always hold key addr.
            JNZ     CMPLOOP                 ;If AX is 0, have checked all keys.
            JMP     NOMATCH
;SEND <CR> AND WRITE FILE - 40 BYTES, THEN <CR><LF> AT A TIME.
FOUND:      NOT     LOGON   ;LOG was typed -- toggle LOGON.
            CMP     LOGON,0
            JNE     STARTLOG                ;Logging on or off?

            MOV     AH,9
            LEA     DX,CR                   ;First send a <CR><LF> to monitor.
            PUSHF
            CALL    INT21
                                            ;Logging off here.
            LEA     BP,CR                   ;Open filename to store.
            MOV     AH,3CH
            LEA     DX,FILENAME             ;Create file if necessary.
```

Listing 13.2 LOG.ASM *(continued)*

```
          MOV      CX,0
          PUSHF
          CALL     INT21

          MOV      BX,AX    ;Get file handle in BX.
          LEA      DX,BUFF
          MOV      CX,NEWLINE
          SUB      CX,DX    ;Get number of bytes to write in CX.
          MOV      AH,40H   ;Write to the file.
          PUSHF
          CALL     INT21

          MOV      AH,3EH          ;Close file.
          PUSHF
          CALL     INT21           ;And let people know we are done.
          MOV      AH,9
          LEA      DX,FILE_DONE
          PUSHF
          CALL     INT21
                                   ;Prepare for next time.
          INC      FILENUMBER2
          CMP      FILENUMBER2,'9' ;Change filename.
          JLE      NUMOK
          MOV      FILENUMBER2,'0' ;If last digit > 9, increment first digit.
          INC      FILENUMBER1
NUMOK:    MOV      LASTROWNUM,0    ;Start from top of screen.
          LEA      AX,BUFF         ;Reuse same space, BUFF.
          MOV      OLDLINE,AX
          MOV      NEWLINE,AX
          POPF
          JMP      SHORT   SENDCR  ;Send a <cr>, not LOG, to DOS.
STARTLOG:
          LEA      BP,CR           ;Here logging is on.
          MOV      AH,9
          LEA      DX,CR           ;First send a <CR><LF> to monitor.
          PUSHF
          CALL     INT21
          LEA      DX,LOGON_MSG
          MOV      AH,9            ;Let people know we are logging.
          PUSHF
          CALL     INT21
          POPF
          JMP      SHORT   SENDCR  ;Send a <cr>, not LOG, to DOS.

NOMATCH:MOV        BP,82H          ;No match, point to typed in command.
          POPF
SENDCR:   PUSH     OLD_DS          ;Now use MOVSB to move command to COMMAND buffer
          POP      ES
          MOV      DI,OLD_DX       ;Get DX of DS:DX.
          ADD      DI,2            ;Point to where type-in is to go.
          MOV      SI,BP
          MOV      AL,0            ;AL will hold char count.
FILL:     MOVSB                    ;Move char to COMMAND.
          CMP      BYTE PTR [SI-1],0DH  ;Reached the command's end?
          JE       FINFIL          ;Yes.
          INC      AL              ;No, inc char count.
          JMP      FILL            ;Loop again.
FINFIL:   MOV      DI,OLD_DX       ;Done will string move.
          INC      DI              ;Give COMMAND char count in its buffer.
          MOV      BYTE PTR ES:[DI],AL
          POP      CX              ;The POPs.
          POP      BX
          POP      AX
          POP      BP
          POP      DS
          POP      ES
          IRET                     ;Finish with IRET.
OUT2:     POP      CX              ;The POPs for the case where we don't
```

Listing 13.2 LOG.ASM *(continued)*

```
            POP     BX                      ; handle Service 0AH.
            POP     AX
            POP     BP
            POP     DS
            POP     ES
            ASSUME  DS:NOTHING
            JMP     INT21                   ;Let INT 21H take over.
DOS_WATCH   ENDP

BUFF    LABEL BYTE

LOAD_LOGGER     PROC    NEAR    ;This procedure intializes everything

        ASSUME  DS:CODE_SEG

        LEA     AX,BUFF         ;Set up buffer at end.
        MOV     OLDLINE,AX
        MOV     NEWLINE,AX

        MOV     DX,OFFSET LOAD_LOGGER   ;Set up BUFLEN to make sure we
        ADD     DX,BUFFLEN              ;do not overwrite it.
        SUB     DX,90
        MOV     BUFEND,DX

        LEA     DX,LOGON_MSG            ;Let people know we are logging.
        MOV     AH,9
        INT     21H

        ASSUME  DS:INTERRUPTS   ;The data segment will be the Interrupt area
        MOV     AX,INTERRUPTS
        MOV     DS,AX
        CLI

        MOV     AX,TIMER_INT            ;Get the old interrupt service routine
        MOV     OLD_TIME_INT,AX         ; address and put it into our location
        MOV     AX,TIMER_INT[2]         ;OLD_TIME_INT so we can still call it.
        MOV     OLD_TIME_INT[2],AX

        MOV     TIMER_INT,OFFSET LOGGER ;Now load the address of our clock
        MOV     TIMER_INT[2],CS         ;routine into TIMER_INT so the timer

        MOV     AX,DOS_INT              ;Get the old interrupt service routine
        MOV     OLD_DOS_INT,AX          ;address and put it into our location
        MOV     AX,DOS_INT[2]           ;OLD_DOS_INT so we can call it.
        MOV     OLD_DOS_INT[2],AX

        MOV     DOS_INT,OFFSET DOS_WATCH   ;Now load the address of DOS_Watch
        MOV     DOS_INT[2],CS              ;routine into the interrupt vector.

        MOV     AX,VID_INT             ;Get the old interrupt service routine
        MOV     OLD_VID_INT,AX         ;address and put it into our location
        MOV     AX,VID_INT[2]          ;OLD_VID_INT so we can call it.
        MOV     OLD_VID_INT[2],AX

        MOV     VID_INT,OFFSET VID_WATCH   ;Now load the address of VID_Watch
        MOV     VID_INT[2],CS              ;routine into the interrupt vector.
                                          ; interrupt will call LOGGER
        MOV     AH,15                  ;Ask for service 15 of INT 10H
        INT     10H                    ;This tells us how display is set up
        SUB     AH,40                  ;Move to twenty places before edge
        SHL     AH,1                   ;Mult by two (char & attribute bytes)
        MOV     VIDEO_PORT,03BAH       ;Assume this is a monochrome display
        TEST    AL,4                   ;Is it?
        JNZ     EXIT                   ;Yes - jump out
        MOV     SCREEN_SEG_OFFSET,8000H ;No - set up for graphics display
        MOV     VIDEO_PORT,03DAH
EXIT:   MOV     DX,OFFSET LOAD_LOGGER  ;Set up everything but LOAD_LOGGER to
```

Listing 13.2 LOG.ASM *(continued)*

```
          ADD     DX,BUFFLEN                ;stay and attach itself to DOS
          INT     27H
LOAD_LOGGER       ENDP

     CODE_SEG     ENDS

     END     FIRST   ;END "FIRST" so 8088 will go to FIRST first.
```

The CRUNCH Program

Freeze-Dry Your Files

For many PC users there seems to be a number of items the PC or PS/2 never has enough of—memory, speed, and, of course, disk space. The number of times you have probably been faced with that blankly neutral message, "Insufficient disk space," is certainly large, but it probably still provokes annoyance. There are few things more irritating than having your PC or PS/2, normally the most reliable of friends, reject the last five pages of text you've feverishly typed in.

Naturally, you can purchase more disk space. And yet, the amount of room demanded never seems to match the amount available. To stem this tide, we might take a look at just what it is you've been storing.

As often as not, the large programs you've acquired at great expense are not tightly written. They usually contain data areas that lie fallow on the disk, doing nothing more than taking up space. Practically every program needs a data area of some sort, and, unless the programmer was especially careful, your favorite .EXE file may contain thousands and thousands of zeroes. Even IBM programs, normally among the most efficiently coded, are not immune to this problem. The Macro assembler alone contains about 3K of repeated bytes in data areas.

Spreadsheet files can be even more of a problem. As soon as you dimension a spreadsheet, the program often reserves space for all possible entries that will fit in that space. You may be astonished to find your checkbook entries for the month taking up 36K. Again, most of the space is unused, filled with zeroes or some repeated marker, waiting for eventual use.

A programmer once remarked that he'd like to freeze-dry some of his programs and store them somewhere safe until they were really needed. With the utility we're going to develop here, you can do just that.

CRUNCH

CRUNCH reads in files in great, 62K gulps, and searches through them for repeated 16-bit words. Using the string commands, it can speed through this process as only assembly language can. If it finds even six consecutive words that are the same, CRUNCH can start saving you disk space. And, with a length of 780 bytes for CRUNCH.COM, this is one program that can pay for itself quickly.

CRUNCH uses a "tag."

CRUNCH counts the number of matching words, and writes a three-word "tag" in the output file, followed by the number of repetitions and the word that was repeated. In this way, thousands of bytes can be condensed into just five words. When it is time to expand the file again, CRUNCH can find these tags and reconstruct the data areas without fault.

Using CRUNCH

To crunch a file named HUGE.EXE into LITTLE.CRN, just type:

```
CRUNCH HUGE.EXE LITTLE.CRN
```

CRUNCH will ask whether you wish to expand or compact HUGE.EXE, and you type "C" for Compact (the other option is "E" for Expand). HUGE.EXE is read into memory, and CRUNCH goes to work on it, producing LITTLE.CRN. To reproduce HUGE.EXE again, you can type:

```
CRUNCH LITTLE.CRN HUGE.EXE
```

and type "E" for Expand when CRUNCH asks you. If you forget which file goes first, or what to type to compact a file, just type "CRUNCH" and it will prompt you for the correct answers.

A Few Notes on CRUNCH

It is worth noticing that this is one of the programs in which assembly language excels. To read in the source file, all the assembly-language programmer needs to do is ask for a specific number of bytes from a certain file.

The data in memory is in as simple a form to use as the applications programmer could wish. It is not in an array, nor is it in unwieldy character strings. It is simply there, at the memory location you've selected. CRUNCH uses the string instructions to advantage. We can scan through immense numbers of words quickly, or compare strings just as fast to find embedded tags.

Once we've done our work, we don't even face the unpleasant task of working with files on the lowest level; we simply inform DOS how many bytes we want to have written out to a particular file, and it does the work for us.

Here, we use DOS services 3CH–40H to create, open, close, read from, and write to files. To find repeating words, we can use the string instruction REPE SCASW; which means, Repeat while equal, Scan the string (for a particular word). The 8088 will scan up to 64K words this way in one single command. To find tags, we can compare strings using a similar command, REPE CMPSW, which can match strings up to 64K words long. CRUNCH uses all the power of assembly language to work as fast as it can—and it just might save you some disk space.

Here's CRUNCH's whole listing:

Listing 13.3 CRUNCH.ASM

```
CODE_SEG        SEGMENT
        ASSUME  CS:CODE_SEG
        ORG     100H
HERE:   JMP     THERE
        CRLF    DB      13,10,'$'              ;Messages follow.
        PROMPT  DB      13,10,'Compact (C) or Expand (E)? $'
        NOTSEEN DB      13,10,'File Not Found$' ;Disk error messages.
        FULL:   DB      13,10,'Disk Full$'
        PROMPT1 DB      13,10,'Name of source file? $'  ;In case you did not
        PROMPT2 DB      13,10,'Name of file to be created? $' ; specify
                                              ; these.
        NAME2   DB      13,0,12 DUP(0) ;Second filename if typed in.
        TAG     DB      'SDH',92H,57H,30H         ;Identifier that precedes
        REPNUM  DW      ?       ; number of words that follow and
        REPWORD DW      ?       ; what word it is.
        NUMREAD DW      ?       ;Number of bytes read in from source file.
        FILETWO DW      0              ;Address of 2nd File name
        FILEND  DW      0              ;End of read-in files in memory
        HANDLE1 DW      0       ;File handles of source and target files.
        HANDLE2 DW      0
        CURLOC  DW      0       ;Current location in file section in memory.
        STARTWRITE      DW      0    ;Last point we wrote from in file
                                     ; section.
        COREFLAG        DB      0    ;The Compact or Expand flag
THERE:  PROC    NEAR                         ;Our procedure
FILES:  MOV     BX,80H          ;Were any filenames at all typed?
        CMP     BYTE PTR [BX],0
        JNE     YESNAME         ;Yes, check for second name.
        LEA     DX,PROMPT1      ;No, get first filename.
        MOV     AH,9
        INT     21H
        MOV     AH,0AH
        MOV     DX,80H
        MOV     BYTE PTR [BX],13            ;Filename max of 12 charS (plus
                                 ; <CR>).
```

Listing 13.3 CRUNCH.ASM *(continued)*

```
            INT      21H
YESNAME:MOV      BX,81H                        ;Make the filenames into ASCIIZ
UP:     INC      BX                            ;Scan type-in for space, <cr>
        CMP      BYTE PTR [BX],' '             ;Space?
        JNE      NOSPACE
        MOV      BYTE PTR [BX],0               ;Put the Z in ASCIIZ
        MOV      FILETWO,BX
        INC      FILETWO                       ;Store filename starting location
NOSPACE:CMP      BYTE PTR [BX],13              ;If not a space, a <cr>?
        JNE      UP
        MOV      BYTE PTR [BX],0               ;If yes, replace with a 0
        CMP      FILETWO,0
        JNZ      ASK
        LEA      DX,PROMPT2          ;No second filename if we are here.
        MOV      AH,9                          ;Get second filename.
        INT      21H
        MOV      FILETWO,OFFSET NAME2+2  ;Put name in NAME2.
        MOV      AH,0AH                        ;Use buffered input.
        LEA      DX,NAME2
        INT      21H
        MOV      BX,FILETWO                    ;Make the filenames into ASCIIZ
UP2:    INC      BX                            ;Scan type-in for space, <cr>
        CMP      BYTE PTR [BX],13              ;Carriage return?
        JNE      UP2                           ;No, keep going.
        MOV      BYTE PTR [BX],0               ;Yes, put the Z in ASCIIZ
ASK:    LEA      DX,PROMPT           ;Are we going to compact or expand?
        MOV      AH,9                ;Load prompt and ask.
        INT      21H
        MOV      AH,1
        INT      21H                 ;Response - C or E - will come in AL.
        CMP      AL,'a'              ;Capitalize if needed.
        JL       CORE
        SUB      AL,'a'-'A'
CORE:   CMP      AL,'C'              ;Set C or E flag (COREFLAG).
        JNE      MAYBEE
        MOV      COREFLAG,AL
        JMP      SHORT READY         ;We are going to compact -- go ahead.
MAYBEE: CMP      AL,'E'              ;Are we going to expand?
        JNE      ASK                 ;Response invalid -- try again.
        MOV      COREFLAG,AL         ;Set COREFLAG to E.
READY:  LEA      DX,CRLF             ;Send <cr> <lf> so screen looks good.
        MOV      AH,9
        INT      21H
        MOV      AX,3D00H                      ;Open the source file.
        MOV      DX,82H                        ;Point to its name.
        INT      21H
        JNC      OKFILE1                       ;Carry Flag --> some problem, assume
        LEA      DX,NOTSEEN                    ;  file doesn't exist, say so.
        MOV      AH,9
        INT      21H
        JMP      OUT                           ;Exit
OKFILE1:MOV      HANDLE1,AX                    ;Save source file's handle in
                                              ;  HANDLE1.
        MOV      AH,3CH                        ;Create target file.
        MOV      CX,0                          ;Use attribute 0.
        MOV      DX,FILETWO
        INT      21H                           ;Create the file
        MOV      HANDLE2,AX
        JNC      TOPPER                        ;If error, exit.
        JMP      ERROR
```

Listing 13.3 CRUNCH.ASM *(continued)*

```
TOPPER:  MOV      BX,HANDLE1
         MOV      CX,62*1024          ;Ask for 62K bytes to be read from
                                      ; file
         LEA      DX,THEBOTTOM        ;And put at end of program
         MOV      AH,3FH              ;Read
         INT      21H
         MOV      NUMREAD,AX
         ADD      AX,OFFSET THEBOTTOM ;Actually read AX bytes
         MOV      FILEND,AX
         DEC      FILEND              ;Find how far the file
                                      ; extends in mem.
         LEA      SI,THEBOTTOM        ;File starts at THEBOTTOM.
         MOV      CURLOC,SI           ;CURLOC is current location in file
         MOV      STARTWRITE,SI       ; in memory. STARTWRITE is where to
                                      ; start writing from.
CURLOOP:MOV       AX,CURLOC
         CMP      AX,FILEND           ;Past end of file section in memory?
         JB       FILLSI              ;No, set up SI.
         JMP      DONE        ;Yes, write out last stuff from startwrite.
FILLSI:  MOV      SI,CURLOC           ;SI points to our place in file
                                      ; section.
         MOV      DI,SI               ;DI also.

CONDNSE:CMP       COREFLAG,'C'        ;HERE WE CRUNCH!
         JE       OKCON
         JMP      EXPAND              ;Otherwise we expand.
OKCON:   MOV      CX,FILEND
         SUB      CX,DI               ;Get the number of bytes to end of file
                                      ; section.
         PUSH     CX
         MOV      AX,[DI]             ;Get ready to look for repeats.
         ADD      DI,2                ;Point to next word.
REPE     SCASW                        ;And scan.
         POP      DX
         SUB      DX,CX               ;How many repeats? >=1.
         MOV      REPNUM,DX           ;Store number of reps.
         CMP      REPNUM,5            ;Store tag if more than 5 word reps.
         JLE      INCCUR       ;Not enough repeats of this word, on to
                                      ; next.

         MOV      REPWORD,AX          ;Found enough repeats, store REPWORD
         MOV      DX,STARTWRITE       ;Write out STARTWRITE to CURLOC.
         MOV      BX,HANDLE2          ; in file 2.
         MOV      AH,40H              ;Use Service 40H.
         MOV      CX,CURLOC           ;Find number of bytes to write.
         SUB      CX,DX
         MOV      DI,CX               ;Save to check after write.
         INT      21H                 ;Write it out.
         CMP      DI,AX               ;If error, (returned)AX .NE. (orig.)DI
         JE       CONT
         JMP      ERROR
CONT:    MOV      DX,CURLOC           ;Reset STARTWRITE for next time.
         ADD      DX,REPNUM           ;Convert to bytes for address!
         ADD      DX,REPNUM           ; that is, add REPNUM twice.
         MOV      STARTWRITE,DX

         LEA      DX,TAG              ;Now write out tag.
         MOV      CX,10               ;Tag is 5 words long.
         MOV      BX,HANDLE2          ;Get file 2.
         MOV      AH,40H              ;Again use Service 40H.
```

Listing 13.3 CRUNCH.ASM *(continued)*

```
          MOV      DI,CX
          INT      21H                      ;Write it out
          CMP      DI,AX                    ;If error, (returned)AX .NE.
                                            ; (orig.)CX

          JE       INCCUR
          JMP      ERROR

INCCUR:   MOV      AX,REPNUM                ;Set new CURLOC past (possibly) repeated
                                            ; words.
          ADD      CURLOC,AX                ;Add REPNUM in twice.
          ADD      CURLOC,AX                ;Again, convert to bytes for address!
          JMP      CURLOOP                  ;Search for more.

EXPAND:                                     ;HERE WE EXPAND!
          MOV      CX,3                     ;Search for 3 word taghead.
          LEA      DI,TAG
REPE      CMPSW
          JNZ      NOFIND                   ;If found, Zerflag set, CX=0.
          JCXZ     FOUNDTAG
NOFIND:   INC      CURLOC                   ;Not found, check starting at next word.
          JMP      CURLOOP
FOUNDTAG:                                   ;Found tag! Write STARTWRITE to CURLOC and expand
                                            ; tag.
          MOV      DX,STARTWRITE            ;Write out STARTWRITE to CURLOC.
          MOV      BX,HANDLE2
          MOV      AH,40H
          MOV      CX,CURLOC                ;File size to write
          SUB      CX,DX
          MOV      DI,CX
          INT      21H                      ;Write it out
          CMP      DI,AX                    ;If error, (returned)AX .NE.
                                            ; (orig.)DI

          JE       CON2
          JMP      ERROR
CON2:     MOV      SI,CURLOC                ;No error. Get REPNUM and REPWORD.
          MOV      CX,[SI+6]                ;Get REPNUM from tag.
          MOV      REPNUM,CX
          MOV      AX,[SI+8]                ;Get REPWORD from tag.
          MOV      REPWORD,AX

ELOOP:    LEA      DX,REPWORD               ;Expand tag here.
          MOV      BX,HANDLE2               ;Put expansion in file 2.
          MOV      CX,2                     ;Write one word at a time (DOS buffers it).
          MOV      AH,40H
          INT      21H
          CMP      AX,2                     ;Did two bytes get written?
          JE       DECNUM                   ;Ok then!
          JMP      ERROR                    ;Uh oh.
DECNUM:   DEC      REPNUM                   ;Loop over REPNUM.
          JNZ      ELOOP

          ADD      CURLOC,10                ;Jump past tag in file section.
          PUSH     CURLOC
          POP      STARTWRITE               ;Get ready for write next time.

          MOV      AX,FILEND                ;Do not write out tail end if file
          CMP      STARTWRITE,AX            ; ended in repeated words.
          JAE      CHECKFORMORE

          JMP      CURLOOP                  ;Go back for more of 1st file section.
```

Listing 13.3 CRUNCH.ASM *(continued)*

```
DONE:      MOV     BX,HANDLE2      ;Write out remainder (tail end) of file here.
           MOV     AH,40H
           MOV     DX,STARTWRITE
           MOV     CX,FILEND              ;File size to write
           CMP     DX,CX
           JA      CHECKFORMORE
           SUB     CX,DX
           INC     CX
           INT     21H                    ;Write it out
           CMP     AX,CX                  ;If error, (returned)AX .NE.
                                          ; (orig.)CX
           JE      CHECKFORMORE
ERROR:     LEA     DX,FULL                ;Assume disk is full, say
                                          ; so, leave
           MOV     AH,9
           INT     21H
           JMP     OUT

CHECKFORMORE:                             ;Now loop over another file section if
                                          ; needed.
           MOV     AX,NUMREAD     ;Did we read in 62K before?
           CMP     AX,62*1024
           JNE     CLOSE          ;If no, assume file is done.
           JMP     TOPPER         ;Get next section to read in.
CLOSE:     MOV     BX,HANDLE1     ;Here we close both files.
           MOV     AH,3EH         ;Use Service 3EH.
           INT     21H
           MOV     BX,HANDLE2
           MOV     AH,3EH
           INT     21H
OUT:       INT     20H
THERE      ENDP
THEBOTTOM:                                ;Read-in file starts here.
           CODE_SEG        ENDS
           END     HERE
```

So Long to the Sample Programs

That's it for the sample programs. If you don't want to type them in yourself (and avoid hours slaving away over a hot keyboard), you can send away for the diskette that accompanies this book. Even if you don't want to actually use these programs, you might still spend a little time working through the listings to get a little more programming practice in. When learning to program, nothing works better than doing it or seeing it done.

Appendix
BIOS and DOS Reference

This appendix is intended for use as a reference. We will work through all the interrupts that are available, from 0 to FFH, reviewing the ones that are useful.

Bios Interrupts

Interrupt 0—Divide By 0

This is the first of the BIOS interrupts—BIOS uses interrupts 0 to 1FH, and DOS continues from 20H upward. Interrupt 0 is the divide by zero routine; if a divide by zero occurs, then this interrupt is called. It prints out its message, "Divide Overflow," and usually stops program execution.

Interrupt 1—Single Step

No one, except a debugger, uses this interrupt. It is used to single step through code, with a call to this interrupt between executed instructions.

Interrupt 2—Non-Maskable Interrupt (NMI)

This is a hardware interrupt. This interrupt cannot be blocked off by using STI and CLI; it always gets executed when called.

Interrupt 3—Breakpoint

This is another debugger interrupt. DEBUG uses this interrupt with the Go command. If you want to execute all the code up to a particular address and then stop, DEBUG will insert an INT 3 into the code at that point and then give control to the program. When the INT 3 is reached, DEBUG can take control again.

Interrupt 4—Overflow

This is similar to INT 0. If there is an overflow condition, this interrupt is called. Usually, though, no action is called for, and BIOS simply returns.

Interrupt 5—Print Screen

This interrupt was chosen by BIOS to print the screen out. If you use the PrtSc key on the keyboard, this is the interrupt that gets called. Needless to say, your program can also issue an INT 5 by just including that instruction in the program. There are no arguments to be passed.

Interrupts 6 and 7—Reserved

Interrupt 8—Time of Day

This is another hardware interrupt. This interrupt is called to update the internal time of day (stored in the BIOS data area) 18.2 times a second. If the date needs to be changed, this interrupt will handle that, too.

This interrupt calls INT 1CH as well. If you want to intercept the timer and do something 18.2 times a second, it is recommended you intercept INT 1CH instead of this one.

Interrupt 9—Keyboard

This hardware interrupt may be intercepted by memory-resident programs.

Interrupt 0AH—Reserved

Interrupts 0BH-0FH

These interrupts point to the BIOS routine D_EOI, which is BIOS' End of Interrupt routine. All this routine does is reset the interrupt handler at port 20H and return.

INT 10H Service 0—Set Screen Mode

Input

AH = 0
AL = Mode

Mode (in AL)	Display Lines	Number of Colors	Adapters	Maximum Pages
0	40x25	B&W text	CGA, EGA, VGA	8
1	40x25	Color text	CGA, EGA, VGA	8
2	80x25	B&W text	CGA, EGA, VGA	4 (CGA) 8 (EGA, VGA)
3	80x25	Color text	CGA, EGA, VGA	4 (CGA) 8 (EGA, VGA)
4	320x200	4	CGA, EGA, VGA	1
5	320x200	B&W	CGA, EGA, VGA	1
6	640x200	2 (on or off)	CGA, EGA, VGA	1
7	80x25	Monochrome	MDA, EGA, VGA	1 (MDA) 8 (EGA, VGA)
8	160x200	16	PCjr	1
9	320x200	16	PCjr	1
A	640x200	1	PCjr	1
B	Reserved for future use.			
C	Reserved for future use.			
D	320x200	16	EGA, VGA	8
E	640x200	16	EGA, VGA	4
F	640x350	monochrome	EGA, VGA	2
10H	640x350	16	EGA, VGA	2
11H	640x480	2	VGA	1
12H	640x480	16	VGA	1
13H	320x200	256	VGA	1

INT 10H Service 1—Set Cursor Type

Input	Output
AH = 1	New cursor
CH = cursor start line	
CL = cursor end line	

INT 10H Service 2—Set Cursor Position

Input	Output
DH,DL = row, column	Cursor position changed
BH = page number	
AH = 2	

Note: DH,DL = 0,0 = Upper Left

INT 10H Service 3—Find Cursor Position

Input   *Output*

BH = page number   DH,DL = row, column of cursor
AH = 3   CH,CL = cursor mode currently set

INT 10H Service 4—Read Light Pen Position

Input   *Output*

AH = 4   AH = 0→light pen switch not down
                                    AL = 1→DH,DL = row, column of light pen position
                                         CH raster line (vertical) 0–199
                                         BX pixel column (horizontal) 0–319,639

INT 10H Service 5—Set Active Display Page

Input   *Output*

AL = 0–7 (screen modes 0,1)   Active page changed
      0–3 (screen modes 2,3)
AH = 5

Note: Different pages available in alphanumeric modes only (graphics adapters).

INT 10H Service 6—Scroll Active Page Up

Input

AL = #lines blanked at bottom (0→blank whole area)
CH,CL = upper left row,column of area to scroll
DH,DL = lower right row,column of area to scroll
BH = attribute used on blank line
AH = 6

INT 10H Service 7—Scroll Active Page Down

Input

AL = #lines blanked at bottom (0→blank whole area)
CH,CL = upper left row,column of area to scroll
DH,DL = lower right row,column of area to scroll
BH = attribute used on blank line
AH = 7

INT 10H Service 8—Read Attribute and Character at Cursor Position

Input

BH = page number
AH = 8

Output

AL = character read (ASCII)
AH = attribute of character (alphanumerics only)

INT 10H Service 9—Write Attribute and Character at Cursor Position

Input

BH = page number
BL→alpha modes = attribute
    graphics modes = color
CX = count of characters to write
AL = IBM ASCII code
AH = 9

Output

Character written on screen at cursor position

INT 10H Service A—Write Character ONLY at Cursor Position

Input

BH = page number
CX = count of characters to write
AL = IBM ASCII code
AH = 0AH

Output

Character written on screen at cursor position

INT 10H Service B—Set Color Palette

Input

BH = palette color ID
BL   BH = 0→BL = background color
       BH = 1→BL = palette number
            (0 = green/red/yellow)
            (1 = cyan/magenta/white)
AH = 11

INT 10H Service C—Write Dot

Input

DX = row number(0–199)   [0,0] is upper left
CX = column number(0–319,639)
AL = color value (0–3)
AH = 12

Note: If bit 7 of AL is 1, the color value is XORed with the current value of the dot.

INT 10H Service D—Read Dot

Input   *Output*

DX = row number(0–199)   AL = color value (0–3)
CX = column number(0–319,639)
AH = 13

[0,0] is upper left.

Note: If bit 7 of AL is 1, the color value is XORed with the current value of the dot.

INT 10H Service E—Teletype Write to Active Page

Input

AL = IBM ASCII code
BL = Foreground color (graphics mode)
AH = 14

INT 10H Service FH—Return Video State

Input   *Output*

AH = 15   AH = number of alphanumeric columns on screen
            AL = current mode (see INT 10H Service 0)
            BH = active display page

INT 10H Service 10H— Set Palette Registers

Default Palette Colors (0–15) on EGA

Color Value	Color	rgbRGB
0	Black	000000
1	Blue	000001
2	Green	000010
3	Cyan	000011
4	Red	000100
5	Magenta	000101
6	Brown	010100
7	White	000111
8	Dark Gray	111000
9	Light Blue	111001
10	Light Green	111010
11	Light Cyan	111011
12	Light Red	111100
13	Light Magenta	111101
14	Yellow	111110
15	Intense White	111111

INT 10H Service 10H Function 0—Set Individual Palette Register

Input

AH = 10H
AL = 0
BL = palette register to set (0–15)
BH = value to set (0–63)

INT 10H Service 10H Function 1—Set Overscan (Border) Register

Input

AH = 10H
BH = value to set (0–63)

INT 10H Service 10H Function 2—Set All Palette Registers

Input

AH = 10H
AL = 2
ES:BX = address of a 17-byte table holding color selections (0–63)
       Bytes 0–15   hold color selections for palette registers 0–15
        Byte 16   holds the new overscan (border) color

INT 10H Service 10H Function 7—Read Individual Palette Register

Input   *Output*

AH = 10H   BH = register setting
AL = 7
BL = register to read (color value)

INT 10H Service 10H Function 8—Read Overscan (Border) Register

Input   *Output*

AH = 10H   BH = overscan setting
AL = 8

INT 10H Service 10H Function 10H—Set DAC Register

Input

AH = 10H
AL = 10H
BX = register to set (0–255)
CH = green intensity
CL = blue intensity
DH = red intensity

INT 10H Service 10H Function 12H—Set DAC Registers

Input

AH = 10H
AL = 12H
BX = first register to set (0–255)
CX = number of registers to set (1–256)
ES:DX = address of a table of color intensities. Three bytes are used for each DAC register (use only lower 6 bits of each byte). Table is set up: red, green, blue, red, green, blue. . .

INT 10H Service 10H Function 13H—Select Color Page Mode

Input

AH = 10H
AL = 13H
BL = 0 select color paging mode
        BH = 0 Selects 4 DAC register pages of 64 registers each.
        BH = 1 Selects 16 DAC register pages of 16 registers each.
BL = 1 Select Active Color Page
    For use with 4 page mode:
        BH = 0 Selects the first block of 64 DAC registers.
        BH = 1 Selects the second block of 64 DAC registers.
        BH = 2 Selects the third block of 64 DAC registers.
        BH = 3 Selects the fourth block of 64 DAC registers.
    For use with 16 page setting:
        BH = 0 Selects the first block of 16 DAC registers.
        BH = 1 Selects the second block of 16 DAC registers.
        BH = 2 Selects the 15th block of 16 DAC registers.
        BH = 3 Selects the 16th block of 16 DAC registers.

INT 10H Service 11H—Character Generator

INT 10H Service 12H—Alternate Select

Input

AH = 12H
BL = 30H
AL = 0→200 screen scan lines
   = 1→350 screen scan lines
   = 2→400 screen scan lines

INT 11H—Equipment Determination

Output

Bits of AX
15,14 = number of printers
13 not used
12 game adapter attached
11,10,9 number of RS232 cards installed
8 unused
7,6 number of diskette drives
    $(00 \rightarrow 1; 01 \rightarrow 2; 10 \rightarrow 3; 11 \rightarrow 4$ If Bit $0 = 1)$
5,4 video mode
    (00 Unused, 01 = 40x25 Color Card
    10 = 80x25 Color Card, 11 = 80x25 Monochrome)
3,2 motherboard RAM
    (00 = 16K,01 = 32K,10 = 48K,11 = 64K)
1 not used
0 = 1 if there are diskette drives attached

INT 12H—Determine Memory Size

Output

AX = number of contiguous 1K memory blocks

INT 13H Service 0—Reset Disk

Input   *Output*

AH = 0   No Carry→AH = 0, success
           Carry→AH = error code (see Service 1).

Note: hard disk systems: DL = 80H→reset diskette(s)
                         DL = 81H→reset hard disk

INT 13H Service 1—Read Status of Last Operation

Input   *Output*

AH = 1   Disk error codes:
           AL = 00   no error
           AL = 01   bad command passed to controller
           AL = 02   address mark not found
           AL = 03   diskette is write protected
           AL = 04   sector not found
           AL = 05   reset failed
           AL = 07   drive parameters wrong
           AL = 09   DMA across segment end
           AL = 0BH   bad track flag seen
           AL = 10H   bad error check seen
           AL = 11H   data is error corrected
           AL = 20H   controller failure
           AL = 40H   seek operation has failed
           AL = 80H   no response from disk
           AL = 0BBH undefined error
           AL = 0FFH sense operation failed

Note: DL = Drive number; set bit 7 to 1 for hard disks.
Note: For hard disks, Drive number in DL can range from 80H to 87H.

INT 13H Service 2—Read Sectors into Memory

Input
AH = 2

Output
No Carry →AL = number sectors read (diskette)

Input
DL = drive number

Output
Carry →AH = disk error code. (see Service 1)

Input
DH = head number
CH = cylinder or track (floppies) number
CL = bits 7,6 high 2 bits of 10-bit cylinder number
CL = sector number (bits 0–5)
AL = number of sectors to read (floppies 1–8
                                   hard disks 1–80H
                                   hard disks read/write long 1–79H)
ES:BX = address of buffer for reads and writes

Note: DL = Drive number; set bit 7 to 1 for hard disks.
Note: For hard disks, Drive number in DL can range from 80H to 87H.

INT 13H Service 3—Write Sectors to Disk

Input
AH = 3

Output
No Carry →AL = number sectors written (diskette)

Input
DL = drive number

Output
Carry →AH = disk error code. (see Service 1)

Input
DH = head number
CH = cylinder or track (floppies) number
CL = bits 7,6 high 2 bits of 10-bit cylinder number
CL = sector number (bits 0–5)
AL = number of sectors to write (floppies 1–8
                           hard disks 1–80H
                           hard disks read/write long 1–79H)
ES:BX = address of buffer for reads and writes

Note: DL = Drive number; set bit 7 to 1 for hard disks.
Note: For hard disks, Drive number in DL can range from 80H to 87H.

INT 13H Service 4—Verify Sectors

Input
AH = 4

Output
No Carry →AH = 0, success

Input
DL = drive number

Output
Carry →AH = disk error code. (see Service 1)

Input
DH = head number
CH = cylinder or track (floppies) number
CL = bits 7,6 high 2 bits of 10-bit cylinder number
CL = sector number (bits 0–5)
AL = number of sectors (floppies 1–8
                          Hard Disks 1-80H
                          Hard Disks Read/Write Long 1-79H)

Note: DL = Drive number; set bit 7 to 1 for hard disks.
Note: For hard disks, Drive number in DL can range from 80H to 87H.

INT 13H Service 8—Return Drive Parameters

This service works *only* on hard disks and PS/2s.

Input
AH = 8
Output
DL = number of drives attached to controller

Input
DL = drive number (0 based)
Output
DH = maximum value for head number
CH = maximum cylinder value
CL = bits 7,6 high 2 bits of 10-bit cylinder number
CL = maximum value for sector number (bits 0–5)
BL (for PS/2 diskettes only)
   = 1→360K drive
   = 2→1.2 Mbyte drive
   = 3→720K drive
   = 4→1.44 Mbyte drive

Note: DL = Drive number; set bit 7 to 1 for hard disks.
Note: For hard disks, Drive number in DL can range from 80H to 87H.

INT 13H Services 0AH and 0BH—Reserved

INT 13H Service 0CH—Seek

This service works *only* on hard disks.

Input
AH = 0CH
Output
No Carry →AH = 0, success

Input
DH = head number
Output
Carry →AH = disk error code. (see Service 1)

Input
DL = drive number (80H-87H allowed)
CH = cylinder number
CL = sector number; bits 7,6 of CL = high 2 bits of 10-bit cylinder number

Note: DL = Drive number; set bit 7 to 1 for hard disks
Note: For hard disks, Drive number in DL can range from 80H to 87H.

INT 13H Service 0DH—Alternate Disk Reset

INT 13H Services 0EH and 0FH—Reserved

INT 13H Service 10H—Test Drive Ready

INT 13H Service 11H—Recalibrate Hard Drive

This service works *only* on hard disks.

Input
AH = 11H (read)
Output
No Carry→AH = 0, success
Carry→AH = disk error code (dee Service 1)

Input
DL = drive number (80H–87H allowed)

Note: DL = Drive number; set bit 7 to 1 for hard disks.
Note: For hard disks, Drive number in DL can range from 80H to 87H.

INT 13H—Diagnostic Services

These services work *only* on hard disks.

Input
AH = 12H (RAM diagnostic)
Output
No Carry→AH = 0, success

Input
AH = 13H (drive diagnostic)
Output
Carry→AH = disk error code (see Service 1)

Input
AH = 14H (controller diagnostic)
DL = drive number (80H-87H allowed)

Note: DL = Drive number; set bit 7 to 1 for hard disks
Note: For hard disks, Drive number in DL can range from 80H to 87H

INT 13H Service 19H—Park Heads PS/2 Only

Input (PS/2)   *Output*

DL = Drive Number   Carry = 1→error, AH = error code
                              = 0→success

Note: DL = Drive number; set bit 7 to 1 for hard disks
Note: For hard disks, Drive number in DL can range from 80H to 87H

INT 14H, AH = 0—Initialize RS232 Port

Input   *Output*

AH = 0
Bits of AL:
0,1   Word length 01→7 bits, 11→8 bits
2   Stop bits 0→1, 1→2 stop bits
3,4   Parity 00→none, 01→odd, 11→even
5,6,7   Baud rate 000→110
                           001→150
                           010→300
                           011→600
                           100→1200
                           101→2400
                           110→4800
                           111→9600

INT 14H, AH = 1—Send Character Through Serial Port

Input
AH = 1
Output
If bit 7 of AH is set, failure

Input
AL = character to send
Output
If bit 7 is not set, bits 0–6 hold status (see INT 14H, AH = 3)

INT 14H, AH = 2 Receive Character from Serial Port

Input
AH = 2

Output
AL = character received
AH = 0, success
  Otherwise, AH holds an error code (see INT 14H, AH = 3)

INT 14H, AH = 3—Return Serial Port's Status

Input   *Output*

AH = 3   AH bits set:
              7→time out
              6→shift register empty
              5→holding register empty
              4→break detected
              3→framing error
              2→parity error
              1→overrun error
              0→data ready
              AL bits set:
              7→received line signal detect
              6→ring indicator
              5→data set ready
              4→clear to send
              3→delta receive line signal detect
              2→trailing Edge Ring Detector
              1→delta Data Set Ready
              0→delta Clear to Send

INT 15H, Cassette I/O

Input
AH = 0→turn cassette motor on
AH = 1→turn cassette motor off
AH = 2→read one or more 256 byte blocks. Store data at ES:BX. CX = Count of Bytes to read.

Output
DX = number of bytes actually read
Carry flag set if error
If Carry, AH = 01→CRC error
        = 02→Data transitions lost
        = 04→no data found

Input
AH = 3→write one or more 256 byte blocks from ES:BX. Count of bytes to write in CX.

Note: In recent BIOS versions, new items have been added to this interrupt, such as joystick support, the ability to switch processor mode (protected or not), mouse support, and some BIOS parameters.

INT 16H, Service 0—Read Key from Keyboard

Input   *Output*

AH = 0   AH = scan code AL = ASCII code

INT 16H, Service 1—Check if Key Ready to be Read

Input   *Output*

AH = 1   Zero flag = 1→buffer empty
              Zero flag = 0→AH = scan code
                          AL = ASCII code

INT 16H, Service 2—Find Keyboard Status

Input   *Output*

AH = 2   AL = keyboard status byte

INT 17H Service 0—Print character in AL

Input   *Output*

AH = 0   AH = 1→printer time out
AL = character to be printed
DX = printer number (0,1,2)

INT 17H Service 1—Initialize Printer Port

Input   *Output*

AH = 1   AH = printer status:
DX = printer number (0,1,2)   Bits set of AH:
                                7→printer not busy
                                6→acknowledge
                                5→out of paper
                                4→selected
                                3→I/O error
                                2→unused
                                1→also unused
                                0→time out

INT 17H Service 2—Read Printer Status into AH

Input   *Output*

AH = 2   AH set to status byte as in INT 17H, AH = 1
DX = printer number (0,1,2)

INT—18H Resident BASIC

This interrupt starts up ROM resident BASIC in the PC.

INT 19H—Bootstrap

This interrupt boots the machine (try it with DEBUG).

INT 1AH Service 0—Read Time of Day

Input   *Output*

AH = 0   CX = high word of timer count
             DX = low word of timer count
             AL = 0 If timer has not passed 24 hours since last read

Note: Timer count increments by 65536 in one hour.

INT 1AH Service 1—Set Time of Day

Input

AH = 1
CX = high word of timer count
DX = low word of timer count

Note: Timer count increments by 65,536 in one hour

INT 1BH—Keyboard Break Address

INT 1CH—Timer Tick Interrupt

INT 1DH—Video Parameter Tables

INT 1EH—Diskette Parameters

INT 1FH—Graphics Character Definitions

DOS Interrupts

INT 20H—Terminate

Programs are usually ended with an INT 20H.

Interrupt 21H

Interrupt 21H is the DOS service interrupt. To call one of these services, load AH with the service number, and the other registers as shown.

INT 21H Service 0—Program Terminate

Input

AH = 0

INT 21H Service 1—Keyboard Input

Input   *Output*

AH = 1   AL = ASCII code of struck key
             Does echo on screen
Checks for ^C or ^Break

INT 21H Service 2—Character Output on Screen

Input

DL = IBM ASCII character
AH = 2

INT 21H Service 3—Standard Auxiliary Device Input

Input   *Output*

AH = 3   Character in AL

INT 21H Service 4—Standard Auxiliary Device Output

Input

AH = 4
DL = character to output

INT 21H Service 5—Printer Output

Input

AH = 5
DL = character to output

INT 21H Service 6—Console I/O

Input		*Output*
AH = 6		
DL = FF	→	AL holds character if one ready
DL < FF	→	Type ASCII code in DL out
		Does *not* Echo on screen

Does *not* check for ^C or ^Break

INT 21H Service 7—Console Input Without Echo

Input	*Output*
AH = 7	AL = ASCII code of struck key
	No Echo on screen

Does *not* Check for ^C or ^Break

INT 21H Service 8—Console Input w/o Echo with ^C Check

Input	*Output*
AH = 8	AL = ASCII code of struck key
	Does *not* Echo the typed key

Checks for ^C or ^Break

DOS INT 21H Service 9—String Print

Input

DS:DX point to a string that ends in "$".
AH = 9

INT 21H Service A—String Input

Input

AH = 0AH
[DS:DX] = length of buffer

Output

Buffer at DS:DX filled
Echo the typed keys

Checks for ∧C or ∧Break

INT 21H Service 0BH—Check Input Status

Input

AH = 0BH

Output

AL = FF→character ready
AL = 00→nothing to read in

∧Break is checked for

INT 21H Service 0CH—Clear Keyboard Buffer and Invoke Service

Input

AH = 0CH
AL = keyboard function #

Output

Standard output from the selected service

∧Break is checked for

INT 21H Service 0DH—Disk Reset

Input

AH = 0DH

INT 21H Service 0EH—Select Disk

Input

AH = 0EH
DL = drive number
        (DL = 0→A
         DL = 1→B
         and so on)

INT 21H Service 0FH—Open Pre-Existing File

Input   *Output*

DS:DX points to an FCB   AL = 0→success
AH = 0FH   AL = FF→failure

INT 21H Service 10H—Close File

Input   *Output*

DS:DX points to an FCB   AL = 0→success
AH = 10H   AL = FF→failure

INT 21H Service 11H—Search for First Matching File

Input   *Output*

DS:DX points to an unopened FCB   AL = FF→Failure
AH = 11H   AL = 0→Success
                                              DTA holds FCB for match

Note: DTA is at CS:0080 in .COM files on startup

INT 21H Service 12H—Search for Next Matching File

Input   *Output*

DS:DX points to an unopened FCB   AL = FF→failure
AH = 12H   AL = 0→success
                                              DTA holds FCB for match

Note: Use this after Service 11H.

INT 21H Service 13H—Delete Files

Input   *Output*

DS:DX points to an unopened FCB   AL = FF→failure
AH = 13H   AL = 0→success

INT 21H Service 14H—Sequential Read

Input

DS:DX points to an opened FCB
AH = 14H
Current block and record set in FCB

Output

Requested record put in DTA
AL = 0 success
    1 end of file, no data in record
    2 DTA segment too small for record
    3 end of file; record padded with 0

Record address incremented.

INT 21H Service 15H—Sequential Write

Input

DS:DX points to an opened FCB
AH = 15H
Current block & record set in FCB

Output

One record read from DTA and written
AL = 0 success
    1 disk full
    2 DTA segment too small for record

Record address incremented.

INT 21H Service 16H—Create File

Input

DS:DX points to an unopened FCB
AH = 16H

Output

AL = 0 success
   = FF directory full

INT 21H Service 17H—Rename File

Input

DS:DX points to a MODIFIED FCB
AH = 17H

Output

AL = 0 success
   = FF failure

Note: Modified FCB→Second file name starts six bytes after the end of the first file name, at DS:DX + 11H.

INT 21H Service 18H—Internal to DOS

INT 21H Service 19H—Find Current Disk

Input   *Output*

AH = 19H   AL = current disk (0 = A, 1 = B, and so on)

INT 21H Service 1AH—Set the DTA Location

Input   Output

DS:DX points to new DTA address   None
AH = 1AH

Note: DTA = Disk Transfer Address, the data area used with FCB services.
Note: Default DTA is 128 bytes long, starting at CS:0080 in the PSP.

INT 21H Service 1BH—FAT Information for Default Drive

Input   Output

AH = 1BH   DS:BX points to the "FAT Byte"
               DX = number of clusters
               AL = number of sectors/cluster
               CX = size of a sector (512 bytes)

Note: Files are stored in clusters—the smallest allocatable unit on a disk.

INT 21H Service 1CH—FAT Information for Specified Drive

Input   Output

AH = 1CH   DS:BX points to the "FAT byte"
DL = drive number (0 = Default 1 = A...) DX = number of clusters
                                         AL = number of sectors/cluster
                                         CX = size of a sector (512)

Note: Files are stored in clusters—the smallest allocatable unit on a disk.

INT 21H Services 1DH–20H—Internal to DOS

INT 21H Service 21H—Random Read

Input
DS:DX points to an opened FCB
Set FCB's random record field at DS:DX + 33 and DS:DX + 35
AH = 21H

Output
AL = 00 success
   = 01 end of file, no more data
   = 02 not enough space in DTA segment
   = 03 end of file, partial record padded with 0s

INT 21H Service 22H—Random Write

Input
DS:DX points to an opened FCB
Set FCB's random record field at DS:DX + 33 and DS:DX + 35
AH = 21H

Output
AL = 00 success
    = 01 disk is full
    = 02 not enough space in DTA segment

INT 21H Service 23H—File Size

Input
DS:DX points to an unopened FCB
AH = 23H

Output
AL = 00 success
    = FF no file found that matched FCB
Random record field set to file length in records, rounded up

INT 21H Service 24H—Set Random Record Field

Input
DS:DX points to an opened FCB
AH = 24H

Output
Random record field set to match current record and current block

INT 21H Service 25H—Set Interrupt Vector

Input
AH = 25H
AL = interrupt number
DS:DX = new address

Note: This service can help you intercept an interrupt vector.

INT 21H Service 26H—Create a New Program Segment (PSP)

INT 21H Service 27H—Random Block Read

Input
DS:DX points to an opened FCB
Set FCB's random record field at DS:DX + 33 and DS:DX + 35
AH = 27H

Output
AL = 00 success
    = 01 end of file, no more data
    = 02 not enough space in DTA segment
    = 03 end of file, partial record padded with 0s
CX = Number of records read
Random record fields set to access next record

Note: The data buffer used in FCB services is the DTA, or Disk Transfer Area.

INT 21H Service 28H—Random Block Write

Input
DS:DX points to an opened FCB
Set FCB's random record field at DS:DX + 33 and DS:DX + 35
CX = number of records to write
AH = 28H

Output
AL = 00 success
    = 01 disk is full
    = 02 not enough space in DTA segment
Random record fields set to access next record

Note: CX = 0→file set to the size indicated by the Random Record field.
Note: The data buffer used in FCB services is the DTA, or Disk Transfer Area.

INT 21H Service 29H—Parse Filename

Input
DS:SI = command line to parse
ES:DI = address to put FCB at
AL = Bit 0 = 1→leading separators are scanned off command line
Bit 1 = 1→drive ID in final FCB will be changed *only* if a drive was specified
Bit 2 = 1→Filename in FCB changed *only* if command line includes filename
Bit 3 = 1→Filename extension in FCB will be changed *only* if command line contains a filename extension
AH = 29H

Output
DS:SI = 1st character after filename
ES:DI = valid FCB

Note: If the command line does not contain a valid filename, ES:[DI + 1] will be a blank.

INT 21H Service 2AH—Get Date

Input	*Output*
AH = 2AH	CX = year - 1980
	DH = month (1 = January, etc.)
	DL = day of the month

INT 21H Service 2BH—Set Date

Input	*Output*
CX = year - 1980	AL = 0 success
DH = month (1 = January, etc.)	AL = FF date not valid
DL = day of the month.	
AH = 2BH	

INT 21H Service 2CH—Get Time

Input	*Output*
AH = 2CH	CH = Hours (0–23)
	CL = minutes (0–59)
	DH = seconds (0–59)
	DL = hundredths of seconds (0–99)

INT 21H Service 2DH—Set Time

Input

AH = 2DH
CH = hours (0–23)
CL = minutes (0–59)
DH = seconds (0–59)
DL = hundreds of seconds (0–99)

Output

AL = 0 success
AL = FF time is invalid

INT 21H Service 2EH—Set or Reset Verify Switch

Input

AH = 2EH
DL = 0
AL = 1→turn verify on
 = 0→turn verify off

INT 21H Service 2FH—Get Current DTA

Input

AH = 2FH

Output

ES:BX = current DTA address

Note: The data buffer used in FCB services is the DTA, or Disk Transfer Area.

INT 21H Service 30H—Get DOS Version Number

Input

AH = 30H

Output

AL = major version number (3 in DOS 3.10)
AH = minor version number (10 in DOS 3.10)
BX = 0
CX = 0

Note: If AL returns 0, you are working with a version of DOS before 2.0.

INT 21H Service 31H—Terminate Process and Keep Resident

Input

AH = 31H
AL = binary exit code
DX = size of memory request in paragraphs

Note: Exit code can be read by a parent program with Service 4DH. It can also be
tested by ERRORLEVEL commands in batch files.

INT 21H Service 32H—Internal to DOS

INT 21H Service 33H—Control-Break Check

Input	*Output*
AH = 33H	
AL = 0→ check state of ∧Break Checking	DL = 0→Off.
	DL = 1→On.
= 1→ set the state of ∧Break Checking	
(DL = 0→turn it off	
DL = 1→turn it on)	

INT 21H Service 34H—Internal to DOS

INT 21H Service 35H—Get Interrupt Vector

Input	*Output*
AH = 35H	ES:BX = interrupt's vector
AL = interrupt number	

INT 21H Service 36H—Get Free Disk Space

Input	*Output*
AH = 36H	AX = 0FFFH→drive number invalid
DL = drive number (0 = Default	AX = number of sectors/cluster
1 = A...)	BX = number of available clusters
	CX = size of a sector (512)
	DX = number of clusters

Note: Files are stored in clusters—the smallest allocatable unit on a disk.

INT 21H Service 37H—Internal to DOS

INT 21H Service 38H—Returns Country Dependent Information

Input   *Output*

AH = 38H   Filled in 32-byte block (see below)
DS:DX = address of 32-byte block
AL = 0

The 32-byte block looks like this:

2 bytes DATE/TIME format
1 byte of currency symbol (ASCII)
1 byte set to 0
1 byte thousands separator (ASCII)
1 byte set to 0
1 byte decimal separator (ASCII)
1 byte set to 0
24 bytes used internally

The DATE/TIME format has these values:

0 = USA (H:M:S M/D/Y)
1 = EUROPE (H:M:S D/M/Y)
2 = JAPAN (H:M:S D:M:Y)

Note: In DOS 3 + you can set, as well as read, these values.

INT 21H Service 39H—Create a Subdirectory

Input
AH = 39H
DS:DX point to ASCIIZ string with directory name
Output
No Carry→success
Carry→AH has error value
       AH = 3 path not found
       AH = 5 access denied

INT 21H Service 3AH—Delete a Subdirectory

Input
AH = 3AH
Output
No Carry→success

Input
DS:DX point to ASCIIZ string with directory name
Output
Carry→AH has error value
       AH = 3 path not found
       AH = 5 access denied or subdirectory not empty

INT 21H Service 3BH—Change Current Directory

Input
AH = 3BH
DS:DX point to ASCIIZ string with directory name

Output
No Carry→success
Carry→AH has error value
       AH = 3 path not found

INT 21H Service 3CH—Create a File

Input
DS:DX points to ASCIIZ filename
CX = attribute of file
AH = 3CH

Output
No Carry→AX = file handle
Carry→AL = 3 path not found
       = 4 too many files open
       = 5 directory full, or previous read-only file exists

INT 21H Service 3DH—Open a File

Input	*Output*
DS:DX points to ASCIIZ filename	No Carry→AX = file handle
AL = Access Code.	Carry→AL = error code (check error table)
AH = 3DH	

Access Codes: AL = 0   File opened for reading
                  AL = 1   File opened for writing
                  AL = 2   File opened for reading and writing

Access Code DOS 3 + : isssraaa
    i = 1→file is not to be inherited by child processes
    i = 0→file handle will be inherited
    sss = 000→compatibility mode
    sss = 001→deny all
    sss = 010→deny write
    sss = 011→deny read
    sss = 100→deny none
    r = reserved
    aaa = 000→read access
    aaa = 001→write access
    aaa = 010→read/write access

INT 21H Service 3EH—Close a File Handle

Input

BX holds a valid file handle
AH = 3EH

Output

Carry→AL = 6→invalid handle

INT 21H Service 3FH—Read from File or Device

Input

DS:DX = data buffer address
CX = number of bytes to read
BX = file handle
AH = 3FH

Output

No Carry→AX = number of bytes read
Carry→AL = 5   access denied
        AL = 6   invalid handle

INT 21H Service 40H—Write to File or Device

Input

DS:DX = data buffer address
CX = number of bytes to write
BX = file handle
AH = 40H

Output

No Carry→AX = number of bytes written
Carry→AL = 5   access denied
        AL = 6   invalid handle

Note: Full disk is *not* considered an error: check the number of bytes you want to write (CX) against the number actually written (returned in AX). If they do not match, the disk is probably full.

INT 21H Service 41H—Delete a File

Input

DS:DX = ASCIIZ filename
AH = 41H

Output

No Carry→success
Carry→AL = 2   file not found
       AL = 5   access denied

Note: No wildcards allowed in filename.

INT 21H Service 42H—Move Read/Write Pointer

Input

Output

BX = file handle
CX:DX = desired offset
AL = method value
AH = 42H ↓
Method values (AL):

No Carry →DX:AX = new location of pointer
Carry →AL = 1 illegal function number
   AL = 6 invalid handle

   AL = 0   read/write pointer moved to CX:DX from the start of the file
   AL = 1   pointer incremented CX:DX bytes
   AL = 2   pointer moved to end-of-file plus offset (CX:DX).

INT 21H Service 43H—Change File's Attribute

Input

Output

DS:DX = ASCIIZ filestring
AL = 1→File attribute changed
   CX holds new attribute
AL = 0→File's current attribute
   returned in CX
AH = 43H

No Carry →success
Carry →AL = 2 file not found
   AL = 3 path not found
   AL = 5 access denied
If AL was 0, CX returns the attribute

INT 21H Service 44H—I/O Control

INT 21H Service 45H—Duplicate a File Handle

Input

Output

BX = file handle to duplicate
AH = 45H

No Carry →AX = new, duplicated handle
Carry →AL = 4 too many files open
   AL = 6 invalid handle

INT 21H Service 46H—Force Duplication of a File Handle

Input

Output

BX = file handle to duplicate
CX = second file handle
AH = 46H

No Carry →handles refer to same "stream"
Carry →AL = 6 invalid handle

INT 21H Service 47H—Get Current Directory on Specified Drive

Input

AH = 47H
DS:SI point to 64-byte buffer
DL = drive number

Output

No Carry →success, ASCIIZ at DS:SI
Carry →AH = 15 invalid drive specified

Note: Drive letter is *not* included in returned ASCIIZ string.

INT 21H Service 48H—Allocate Memory

Input
AH = 48H
BX = number of paragraphs requested

Output
No Carry →AX:0000 memory block address
      Carry →AL = 7 memory control blocks destroyed
      AL = 8 insufficient memory, BX contains maximum allowable request

INT 21H Service 49H—Free Allocated Memory

Input
AH = 49H
ES = segment of block being freed

Output
No Carry →success
Carry →AL = 7 memory control blocks destroyed
     = 9 incorrect memory block address

INT 21H Service 4AH— SETBLOCK

Input
AH = 4AH
ES = segment of block to modify
BX = requested size in paragraphs

Output
No Carry →success
Carry →AL = 7 memory control blocks destroyed
     = 8 insufficient memory; BX holds maximum possible request
     = 9 invalid memory block address

INT 21H Service 4BH—Load or Execute a program—EXEC

Input

AH = 4BH
DS:DX = ASCIIZ string with drive, pathname, filename.
ES:BX = parameter block address (see below)
AL = 0→load and execute the program
       3→load but create no PSP, don't run (overlay)

Parameter Block for AL = 0:

    Segment address of environment to pass (Word)
    Address of command to put at PSP + 80H (DWord)
    Address of default FCB to put at PSP + 5CH (DWord)
    Address of 2nd default FCB to put at PSP + 6CH (DWord)

Parameter Block for AL = 3:

    Segment address to load file at (Word)
    Relocation factor for image (Word)

Output

No Carry →success
Carry:
      AL = 1 invalid function number
          2 file not found on disk
          5 access denied
          8 insufficient memory for requested operation
          10 invalid environment
          11 invalid format

INT 21H Service 4CH—Exit

Input

AH = 4CH
AL = binary return code

Note: This service can end a program.

INT 21H Service 4DH—Get Return Code of Subprocess

Input   *Output*

AH = 4DH   AL = binary return code from subprocess
              AH = 0 if subprocess ended normally
                   1 if subprocess ended with a ^Break
                   2 if it ended with a critical device error
                   3 if it ended with Service 31H

INT 21H Service 4EH—Find First Matching File

Input
DS:DX→ASCIIZ filestring
CX = attribute to match
AH = 4EH

Output
Carry→AL = 2 no match found
       AL = 18 no more files
No Carry→DTA filled as follows:
        21 bytes reserved.
        1 byte found attribute
        2 bytes file's time
        2 bytes file's date
        2 bytes low word of size
        2 bytes high word of size
        13 bytes name and extension of found file in ASCIIZ form (no pathname)

Note: The data buffer used in FCB services is the DTA, or Disk Transfer Area. See
       earlier services.

INT 21H Service 4FH—Find Next Matching File

Input
Use Service 4EH *before* 4FH
AH = 4FH

Output
Carry→AL = 18 no more files
No Carry→DTA filled as follows:
        21 bytes reserved
        1 byte found attribute
        2 bytes file's time
        2 bytes file's date
        2 bytes low word of size
        2 bytes high word of size
        13 bytes name and extension of found file in ASCIIZ form (*no* pathname)

Note: The data buffer used in FCB services is the DTA, or Disk Transfer Area. See ear-
       lier services.

INT 21H Services 50H–53H—Internal to DOS

INT 21H Service 54H—Get Verify State

Input

AH = 54H

Output

AL = 0→verify is OFF
1→verify is ON

INT 21H Service 55H—Internal to DOS

INT 21H Service 56H—Rename File

Input
DS:DX = ASCIIZ filestring to be renamed
ES:DI = ASCIIZ file string that holds the new name
AH = 56H

Output
No Carry →success
Carry→AL = 3 path not found
   AL = 5 access denied
   AL = 17 not same device

Note: File *cannot* be renamed to another drive.

INT 21H Service 57H—Get or Set a File's Date & Time

Input

BX = File handle
AL = 0→get date & time . . . .

AL = 1→set time to CX . . . .
   set date to DX

Output

No carry:
CX returns time
DX returns date

File's date and time set

Carry→AL = 1 invalid function number
   6 invalid handle

The time and date of a file are stored like this:

$$\text{Time} = 2048 \times \text{Hours} + 32 \times \text{Minutes} + \text{Seconds}/2$$

$$\text{Date} = 512 \times (\text{Year} - 1980) + 32 \times \text{Month} + \text{Day}$$

INT 21H Service 58H—Internal to DOS

INT 21H Service 59H—Get Extended Error DOS 3+

Input	*Output*
AH = 59H	AX = extended error
BX = 0	BH = error class
	BL = suggested action
	CH = locus

Note: This error-handling service is very lengthy, and involves the many DOS 3+ extended errors.

INT 21H Service 5AH—Create Unique File DOS 3+

Input
AH = 5AH
DS:DX = address of an ASCIIZ path (ending with "\")
CX = file's attribute

Output
AX = error if carry is set
DS:DX = ASCIIZ path and filename

INT 21H Service 5BH—Create a New File DOS 3+

Input
AH = 5BH
DS:DX = address of an ASCIIZ path (ending with "\")
CX = file's attribute

Output
AX = Error if carry is set
   = Handle if Carry is not set

INT 21H Service 5CH—Lock and Unlock Access to a File DOS 3+

Input	*Output*
AH = 5CH	If Carry = 1, AX = error
AL = 0→lock byte range	
1→Unlock byte range	
BX = file handle	
CX = byte range start (high word)	
DX = byte range start (low word)	
SI = Number bytes to (un)lock (high word)	
DI = Number bytes to (un)lock (low word)	

INT 21H Service 5E00H—Get Machine Name DOS 3+

Input

AX = 5E00H
DS:DX = buffer for computer name
CL = NETBIOS number
AX = error if carry set

Output

DS:DX = ASCIIZ computer name
CH = 0→name not defined

INT 21H Service 5E02—Set Printer Setup DOS 3+

Input

AX = 5E02H
BX = redirection list index
CX = length of setup string
DS:DI = pointer to printer setup buffer

Output

AX = error if carry is set

INT 21H Service 5E03—Get Printer Setup DOS 3+

Input
AX = 5E03H
BX = redirection list index
ES:DI = pointer to printer setup buffer

Output
AX = error if carry is set
CX = length of data returned
ES:DI = filled with printer setup string

INT 21H Service 5F03—Redirect Device DOS 3+

Input
AX = 5F03H
BL = device type
        = 3→printer device
        = 4→file device
CX = value to save for caller
DS:SI = source ASCIIZ device name
ES:DI = destination ASCIIZ network path with password

Output
AX = error if carry is set

INT 21H Service 5F04H—Cancel Redirection DOS 3+

Input   *Output*

AX = 5F04H   AX = error if carry is set
DS:SI = ASCIIZ device name or path

INT 21H Service 62H—Get Program Segment Prefix DOS 3+

Input   *Output*

AX = 62H   BX = segment of currently executing program

INT 21H Service 67H—Set Handle Count DOS 3.30

Input
AX = 67H
BX = Number of allowed open handles (up to 255)
Output
AX = error if carry is set

INT 21H Service 68H—Commit File (Write Buffers) DOS 3.30

Input   *Output*

AX = 68H   BX = File Handle

Note: 68H is the last of the DOS 3.3 INT 21H services.

INT 22H—Terminate Address

INT 23H—Control Break Exit Address

INT 24H—Critical Error Handler

AH filled this way:

0   Diskette is write protected
1   Unknown unit
2   The requested drive is not ready
3   Unknown command
4   Cyclic redundancy check error in the data

5   Bad request structure length
6   Seek error
7   Media type unknown
8   Sector not found
9   The printer is out of paper
A   Write fault
B   Read fault
C   General failure

If you just execute an IRET, DOS will take an action based on the contents of AL. If AL = 0, the error will be ignored. If AL = 1, the operation will be retried. If AL = 2, the program will be terminated through INT 23H.

INT 25H—Absolute Disk Read

Input

AL = drive number
CX = number of sectors to read
DX = first logical sector
DS:BX = buffer address

Output

No Carry → success
Carry → AH = 80H Disk didn't respond
AH = 40H seek failed
AH = 20H controller failure
AH = 10H bad CRC error check
AH = 08   DMA overrun
AH = 04   sector not found
AH = 03   write protect error
AH = 02   address mark missing
AH = 00   error unknown

Note: Flags left on stack after this INT call because information is returned in current flags. After you check the flags that were returned, make sure you do a POPF. Also, this INT destroys the contents of *all* registers.

INT 26H—Absolute Disk Write

Input

AL = Drive Number
CX = number of sectors to write
DX = first logical sector
DS:BX = buffer address

Output

No Carry→success
Carry→AH = 80H disk didn't respond.
AH = 40H seek failed
AH = 20H controller failure
AH = 10H bad CRC error check
AH = 08   DMA overrun
AH = 04   sector not found
AH = 03   write protect error
AH = 02   address mark missing
AH = 00   error unknown

Note: Flags left on stack after this INT call because information is returned
in current flags. After you check the flags that were returned, make
sure you do a POPF. Also, this INT destroys the contents of *all*
registers.

INT 27H—Terminate and Stay Resident

Input

DS:DX = point directly after end of code that is to stay resident

INTs 28H-2EH Internal to DOS

INT 2FH Multiplex Interrupt

INT 30H-3FH DOS Reserved

INT 40H-5FH Reserved

INT 60H-67H Reserved for User Software

INTs 68H-7FH Not Used

INTs 80H-85H Reserved by BASIC

INTs 86H-F0H Used by BASIC Interpreter

INTs F1H-FFH Not Used

Index

About the Author

Steven Holzner earned his BS degree at MIT and a Ph.D at Cornell, where he was a lecturer in physics. He has travelled to over 30 countries, lived for a year each in Hong Kong and Hawaii, and spends summers in Austria. Steven now resides in Southern California, next to the beach.